PROJECT MANAGEMENT
A SYSTEMS APPROACH TO PLANNING, SCHEDULING AND CONTROLLING

PROJECT MANAGEMENT
A SYSTEMS APPROACH TO PLANNING, SCHEDULING AND CONTROLLING

Third Edition

HAROLD KERZNER, Ph.D.

Division of Business Administration
Baldwin-Wallace College
Berea, Ohio

VNR VAN NOSTRAND REINHOLD
——————————— *New York*

Library of Congress Catalog Card Number 88-25137
ISBN 0-442-20751-4

Printed in the United States of America

Van Nostrand Reinhold
115 Fifth Avenue
New York, New York 10003

Van Nostrand Reinhold International Company Limited
11 New Fetter Lane
London EC4P 4EE, England

Van Nostrand Reinhold
480 La Trobe Street
Melbourne, Victoria 3000, Australia

Nelson Canada
1120 Birchmount Road
Scarborough, Ontario M1K 5G4, Canada

15   14   13   12   11   10   9   8   7   6   5   4   3

Library of Congress Cataloging-in-Publication Data

Kerzner, Harold.
    Project management : a systems approach to planning, scheduling,
and controlling / Harold Kerzner.—3rd ed.
        p. cm.
    Bibliography: p.
    Includes index.
    ISBN 0-442-20751-4
    1. Industrial project management.   I. Title.
HD69.P75K47 1989
658.4′04—dc19   88-25137

to
DR. HERMAN KRIER
my Friend and Guru,
who taught me well the
meaning of the word "persistence"

Preface

With the approach of the 1990s, the growth and acceptance of project management is continuing at a phenomenal pace. Almost all colleges and universities are offering project management courses, and numerous masters and even doctoral programs in project management should be evident in the near future.

This book is addressed not only to those undergraduate and graduate students who wish to understand and improve upon their project management skills, but also to those functional managers and upper-level executives who must provide continuous support to all projects. During the past several years, management's knowledge and understanding of project management has matured to the point where almost every company and industry is using project management in one form or another. These companies have come to the realization that project management and productivity are related. Project management coursework is now consuming more and more of training budgets than ever before.

General reference is provided in the text to engineers. However, the reader should not consider project management as strictly engineering-related. The engineering examples are the result of the fact that project management first appeared in the engineering disciplines, and we should be willing to learn from their mistakes, regardless of the industry that we are in.

The textbook is designed for undergraduate and graduate level courses in both business and engineering. The structure of the text is based upon the author's belief that project management is much more behavioral than quantitative. The first five chapters are part of the basic core of knowledge needed to understand project management. Chapters 6 through 8 deal with the support functions of time management, conflicts, and other special topics. Chapters 9 and 10 describe executive involvement and the critical success factors for predicting project success. It may seem strange that ten chapters on organizational behavior and structuring are needed prior to the "hard-core" chapters of planning, scheduling, and controlling. These first ten chapters are framework chapters needed to develop the cultural environment for all projects and systems. These chapters are necessary for the reader to understand the difficulties in achieving cross-functional cooperation on projects and why the people involved, all of whom may have different backgrounds, cannot simply be forged into a cohesive work-unit without any friction. Chapters 11 through 15 are the quantitative chapters on planning, scheduling, and cost control. Chapter 16 deals with tradeoffs on time, cost, and performance. Chapters 17 through 20 cover the more advanced topics in project management, as well as future trends. The text contains forty-two case studies, two multiple-choice exams, and more than 330 discussion questions. An instructor's manual is available to college/university adopters by writing to the author on university letterhead.

The problems and case studies at the end of each chapter cover a variety of industries. Almost all of the case studies are real-world situations taken from the author's consulting practice. Feedback from colleagues that are using the text has provided me with fruitful criticism, most of which has been incorporated into the third edition.

To Dynamic Graphics, Inc., I express my sincere gratitude for permission to use many of their cartoons throughout the text. Unless otherwise indicated, all cartoon artwork is provided by Dynamic Graphics, Inc., 6707 N. Sheridan Road, Peoria, IL, 61614. The artwork is copyrighted. Any reproduction is strictly prohibited without the permission of Dynamic Graphics, Inc.

Valuable criticism was made by many colleagues. In particular, I am indebted to those industrial/government training managers, such as Gay Puckett, Judy Douglas, John Battle, and Jim Weaver, whose dedication and commitment to quality project management education and training have led to valuable changes in this edition.

To Dr. Mark Collier, Vice President for Academic Affairs, I again express my deepest appreciation and respect for his never-ending support and encouragement toward conducting meaningful research for this text. Finally, the future of project management rests with those college and university faculty members who have the foresight to plan for the future by keeping in touch with the realities of the public and industrial environments and strive to develop new project management coursework at the undergraduate and graduate levels. To the Business Division administrators, Professor Ron Ehresman, Professor Gary Packwood, Professor Ed Monsour, and Dr. Earl Peck, I give my everlasting thanks for their support and encouragement for project management.

Harold Kerzner
Baldwin-Wallace College

Contents

PROJECT MANAGEMENT
A SYSTEMS APPROACH
TO PLANNING,
SCHEDULING
AND CONTROLLING

1
Overview

1.0 INTRODUCTION

Executives will be facing increasingly complex challenges during the next decade. These challenges will be the result of high escalation factors for salaries and raw materials, increased union demands, pressure from stockholders, and the possibility of long-term, high inflation accompanied by a mild recession and a lack of borrowing power with financial institutions. These environmental conditions have existed before, but not to the degree that they do today.

In the past, executives have attempted to ease the impact of these environmental conditions by embarking on massive cost-reduction programs. The usual results of these programs have been early retirement, layoffs, and a reduction in manpower through attrition. As jobs become vacant, executives pressure line managers to accomplish the same amount of work with fewer resources, either by improving efficiency or by upgrading performance requirements to a higher position on the learning curve. Because people costs are more inflationary than the cost of equipment or facilities, executives are funding more and more capital equipment projects in an attempt to increase or improve productivity without increasing labor.

Unfortunately, the modern executive is somewhat limited in how far he can go to reduce manpower without running a high risk to corporate profitability. Capital equipment projects are not always the answer. Thus, executives have been forced to look elsewhere for the solutions to their problems.

Almost all of today's executives are in agreement that the solution to the majority of corporate problems involves obtaining better control and use of existing corporate resources. Emphasis is being placed on looking internally rather than externally for the solution to these problems. As part of the attempt to achieve an internal solution, executives are taking a hard look at the ways corporate activities are being managed. Project management is one of the techniques now under consideration.

The project management approach is relatively modern. It is characterized by new methods of restructuring management and adapting special management techniques, with the purpose of obtaining better control and use of existing resources. Twenty years ago project management was confined to the

Department of Defense contractors and construction companies. Today, the concept behind project management is being applied in such diverse industries and organizations as defense, construction, pharmaceuticals, chemicals, banking, hospitals, accounting, advertising, law, state and local governments, and the United Nations.

The rapid rate of change in both technology and the marketplace has created enormous strains upon existing organizational forms. The traditional structure is highly bureaucratic, and experience has shown that it cannot respond rapidly enough to a changing environment. Thus, the traditional structure must be replaced by project management, or other temporary management structures that are highly organic and can respond very rapidly as situations develop inside and outside the company.

Project management has long been discussed by corporate executives and academics as one of several workable possibilities for organizational forms of the future that could integrate complex efforts and reduce bureaucracy. The acceptance of project management has not been easy, however. Many executives are not willing to accept change and are inflexible when it comes to adapting to a different environment. The project management approach requires a departure from the traditional business organizational form which is basically vertical and which emphasizes a strong superior–subordinate relationship.

1.1 UNDERSTANDING PROJECT MANAGEMENT

In order to understand project management, one must begin with the definition of a project. A project can be considered to be any series of activities and tasks that:

- Have a specific objective to be completed within certain specifications
- Have defined start and end dates
- Have funding limits (if applicable)
- Consume resources (i.e., money, people, equipment)

Project management, on the other hand, involves project planning and project monitoring and includes such items as:

- Project planning
  - Definition of work requirements
  - Definition of quantity of work
  - Definition of resources needed
- Project monitoring
  - Tracking progress
  - Comparing actual to predicted

- Analyzing impact
- Making adjustments

Successful project management can then be defined as having achieved the project objectives:

- Within time
- Within cost
- At the desired performance/technology level
- While utilizing the assigned resources effectively and efficiently

The potential benefits from project management are:

- Identification of function responsibilities to ensure that all activities are accounted for, regardless of personnel turnover
- Minimizing the need for continuous reporting
- Identification of time limits for scheduling
- Identification of a methodology for tradeoff analysis
- Measurement of accomplishment against plans
- Early identification of problems so that corrective action may follow
- Improved estimating capability for future planning
- Knowing when objectives cannot be met or will be exceeded

Unfortunately, the benefits cannot be achieved without overcoming obstacles such as:

- Project complexity
- Customer's special requirements
- Organizational restructuring
- Project risks
- Changes in technology
- Forward planning and pricing

Project management can mean different things to different people. Quite often, people misunderstand the concept because they have ongoing projects within their company and feel that they are using project management to control these activities. In such a case, the following might be considered an appropriate definition:

Project management is the art of creating the illusion that any outcome is the result of a series of predetermined, deliberate acts when, in fact, it was dumb luck.

Although this might be the way that some companies are running their projects, this is not project management. Project management is designed to make better use of existing resources by getting work to flow horizontally as well as vertically within the company. This approach does not really destroy the vertical, bureaucratic flow of work but simply requires that line organizations talk to one another horizontally so work will be accomplished more smoothly throughout the organization. The vertical flow of work is still the responsibility of the line managers. The horizontal flow of work is the responsibility of the project managers, and their primary effort is to communicate and coordinate activities horizontally between the line organizations.

Figure 1–1 shows how many companies are structured. There are always "class or prestige" gaps between various levels of management. There are also functional gaps between working units of the organization. If we superimpose the management gaps on top of the functional gaps, we find that companies are made up of small operational islands that refuse to communicate with one another for fear that giving up information may strengthen their opponents. The project manager's responsibility is to get these islands to communicate cross-functionally toward common goals and objectives.

The following would be an overview definition of project management:

> Project management is the planning, organizing, directing, and controlling of company resources for a relatively short-term objective that has been established to complete specific goals and objectives. Furthermore, project management utilizes the systems approach to management by having functional personnel (the vertical hierarchy) assigned to a specific project (the horizontal hierarchy).

The above definition requires further comment. Classical management is usually considered to have five functions or principles:

- Planning
- Organizing
- Staffing
- Controlling
- Directing

You will notice that, in the above definition, the staffing function has been omitted. This was intentional because the project manager does not staff the project. Staffing is a line responsibility. The project manager has the right to request specific resources, but the final decision of what resources will be committed rests with the line managers.

We should also comment on what is meant by a "relatively" short-term pro-

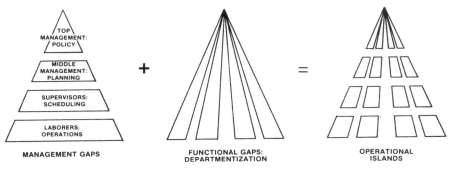

Figure 1-1. Why are systems necessary?

ject. Not all industries have the same definition for a short-term project. In engineering, the project might be for six months or two years; in construction, three to five years; in nuclear components, ten years; and in insurance, two weeks. Long-term projects, which consume resources full-time, are usually set up as a separate division (if large enough) or simply as a line organization.

Figure 1-2 is a pictorial representation of project management. The objective of the figure is to show that project management is designed to manage or control company resources on a given activity, within time, within cost, and within performance. Time, cost, and performance are the constraints on the

Figure 1-2. Overview of project management.

project. If the project is to be accomplished for an outside customer, then the project has a fourth constraint: good customer relations. The reader should immediately realize that it is possible to manage a project internally within time, cost, and performance and then alienate the customer to such a degree that no further business will be forthcoming. Executives often select project managers based upon who the customer is and what kind of customer relations will be necessary.

1.2 DEFINING PROJECT SUCCESS

In the previous section, we defined project success as the completion of an activity within the constraints of time, cost, and performance. This was the definition that has pertained for the past 20 years or so. Today, the definition of project success has been modified to include completion:

- within the allocated time period
- within the budgeted cost
- at the proper performance or specification level
- and acceptance by the customer/user
- with minimum or mutually agreed upon scope changes
- without disturbing the main work flow of the organization
- without changing the corporate culture

The last three elements require further explanation. Very few projects are completed within the original scope of the project. Scope changes are inevitable and have the potential to destroy not only the morale on a project, but the entire project itself. Scope changes *must* be held to a minimum and those that are required *must* be approved by both the project manager and the customer/user.

Project managers must be willing to manage (and make concessions/tradeoffs, if necessary) such that the company's main work flow is not altered. Most project managers view themselves as self-employed entrepreneurs after project go-ahead, and would like to divorce their project from the operations of the parent organization. This is not always possible. The project manager must be willing to manage within the guidelines, policies, procedures, rules, and directives of the parent organization.

All corporations have corporate cultures, and even though each project may be inherently different, the project manager should not expect his assigned personnel to deviate from cultural norms. If the company has a cultural standard of openness and honesty when dealing with customers, then this cultural value should remain in place for all projects, regardless of who the customer/user is or how strong the project manager's desire for success is.

As a final note, it should be understood that simply because a project is a success, the company does *not* have to be successful as a whole in their project management endeavors. Excellence in project management is defined as a continuous stream of successfully managed projects. Any project can be driven to success through formal authority and strong executive meddling. But, in order for a continuous stream of successful projects to occur, there must exist a strong corporate commitment to project management, and this commitment *must be visible*.

1.3 THE PROJECT MANAGER—LINE MANAGER INTERFACE

We have stated that the project manager must control company resources within time, cost, and performance. Most companies have six resources:

- Money
- Manpower
- Equipment
- Facilities
- Materials
- Information/technology

Actually, the project manager does *not* control any of these resources directly, except perhaps money (i.e., the project budget).[1] Resources are controlled by the line managers, functional managers, or, as they are often called, resources managers. The project managers must, therefore, negotiate with the line managers for all project resources. When we say that a project manager controls project resources, we really mean that he controls those resources (which are temporarily loaned to him) *through the line managers.*

It should become obvious at this point that successful project managment is strongly dependent upon:

- A good daily working relationship between the project manager and those line managers who directly assign resources to projects
- The ability of functional employees to report vertically to their line manager at the same time that they report horizontally to one or more project managers

These two items become critical. In the first item, functional employees who are assigned to a project manager still take technical direction from their line

---

1. Here we are assuming that the line manager and project manager are not the same individual.

managers. Second, employees who report to multiple managers will always favor the manager who controls their purse strings. Thus, most project managers appear to always be at the mercy of the line managers.

Classical management has often been defined as a process in which the manager does not necessarily perform things for himself, but accomplishes objectives through others in a group situation. This basic definition also applies to the project manager. In addition, a project manager must help himself. There is nobody else to help him.

If we take a close look at project management, we will see that the project manager actually works for the line managers, not vice versa. Many executives do not realize this. They have a tendency to put a halo around the head of the project manager and give him a bonus at project termination, when, in fact, the credit should really go to the line managers, who are continually pressured to make better use of their resources. The project manager is simply the agent through whom this is accomplished. So, why do some companies glorify the project management position?

To illustrate the role of the project manager, consider the time, cost, and performance constraints in Figure 1–2. Many functional managers, if left alone, would recognize only the performance constraint: "Just give me another $50,000 and two more months, and I'll give you the ideal technology."

The project manager, as part of these communicating, coordinating, and integrating responsibilities, reminds the line managers that there are also time and cost constraints on the project. This is the starting point for better resource control.

Project managers depend on line managers. When the project manager gets in trouble, the only place he can go is to the line manager because additional resources are almost always required to alleviate the problems. When a line manager gets in trouble, he usually goes first to the project manager and requests either additional funding or some type of authorization.

To illustrate this working relationship between the project and line manager, consider the following situation:

Project Manager (addressing the line manager): "I have a serious problem. I'm looking at a $50,000 cost overrun on my project and I need your help. I'd like you to do the same amount of work that you are currently scheduled for but in 3,000 less man-hours. Since your organization is burdened at $20/hour, this would more than compensate for the cost overrun."

Line Manager: "Even if I could, why should I? You know that good line managers can always make work expand to meet budget. I'll look over my manpower curves and let you know tomorrow."

The following day . . .

Line Manager: "I've looked over my manpower curves and I have enough work to keep my people employed. I'll give you back the 3,000 hours you need but remember, *you owe me one!*"

Several months later . . .

Line Manager: "I've just seen the planning for your new project that's supposed to start two months from now. You'll need two people from my department. There are two employees that I'd like to use on your project. Unfortunately, these two people are available now. If I don't pick these people up on your charge number right now, some other project might pick them up in the interim period, and they won't be available when your project starts."

Project Manager: "What you're saying is that you want me to let you sandbag against one of my charge numbers, knowing that I really don't need them."

Line Manager: "That's right. I'll try to find other jobs (and charge numbers) for them to work on temporarily so that your project won't be completely burdened. Remember, you owe me one."

Project Manager: "O.K. I know that I owe you one, so I'll do this for you. Does this make us even?"

Line Manager: "Not at all! But you're going in the right direction."

When the project management/line management relationship begins to deteriorate, the project almost always suffers. Executives must promote a good working relationship between line and project management. One of the most common ways of destroying this relationship is by asking, "Who contributes to profits—the line or project manager?" Project managers feel that they control all project profits because they control the budget. The line managers, on the other hand, argue that they must staff with appropriately budgeted-for personnel, supply the resources at the desired time, and supervise the actual performance. Actually, both the vertical and horizontal lines contribute to profits. These types of conflicts can destroy the entire project management structure.

The previous examples should indicate that project management is more behavioral than quantitative. Effective project management requires an understanding of:

- Quantitative tools and techniques
- Organizational structures
- Organizational behavior

Most people understand the quantitative tools for planning, scheduling, and controlling work. It is imperative that project managers understand totally the operations of each line organization. In addition, the project manager must understand his own job description, especially where his authority begins and ends. During an in-house seminar on engineering project management, the author asked one of the project engineers to provide a description of his job as a project engineer. During the discussion that followed, several project managers, and line managers, said that there was a great deal of overlapping between their job descriptions and that of the project engineer.

Organizational behavior is important because the functional employees at the interface position find themselves reporting to more than one boss—a line manager and one project manager for each project they are assigned to. Executives must provide proper training so functional employees can report effectively to multiple managers.

1.4   DEFINING THE PROJECT MANAGER'S ROLE

The project manager is responsible for coordinating and integrating activities across multiple, functional lines. In order to do this, the project manager needs strong communicative and interpersonal skills, must become familiar with the operations of each line organization, and should have a general knowledge of the technology (unless he is managing R&D activities, in which case a command of technology is more important than a general understanding).

An executive with a computer manufacturer stated that his company was looking externally for project managers. When asked if the executive expected candidates to have a command of computer technology, the executive remarked: "You give me an individual who has good communicative skills and interpersonal skills, and I'll give him a job. I can teach people the technology and give them technical experts to assist them in decision making. But I cannot teach somebody how to work with people."

The project manager's job is not an easy one. Managers may have increasing responsibility, but very little authority. This lack of authority can force them to "negotiate" with upper-level management as well as functional management for control of company resources, as shown in Figure 1–3. They may often be treated as outsiders by the formal organization. Yet, even with these problems and roadblocks, they have managed to survive. J. Robert Fluor has described the new responsibilities of project managers at Fluor Corporation:[2]

Project management continues to become more challenging and we think this trend will continue. This means we have to pay special attention to the development of pro-

---

2. J. Robert Fluor, "Development of Project Managers," keynote address to the Project Management Institute, Ninth International Seminar Symposium, Chicago, Illinois, October 24, 1977.

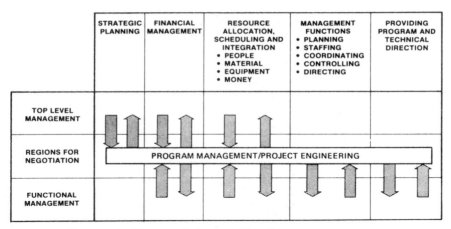

STRATEGIC PLANNING	FINANCIAL MANAGEMENT	RESOURCE ALLOCATION, SCHEDULING AND INTEGRATION • PEOPLE • MATERIAL • EQUIPMENT • MONEY	MANAGEMENT FUNCTIONS • PLANNING • STAFFING • COORDINATING • CONTROLLING • DIRECTING	PROVIDING PROGRAM AND TECHNICAL DIRECTION
TOP LEVEL MANAGEMENT				
REGIONS FOR NEGOTIATION	PROGRAM MANAGEMENT/PROJECT ENGINEERING			
FUNCTIONAL MANAGEMENT				

Figure 1-3. The negotiation activities of systems management.

ject managers who are capable of coping with jobs that range from small to mega projects and with life spans of several months to ten years. At Fluor, a project manager must not only be able to manage the engineering, procurement and construction aspects of a project, he or she must also be able to manage aspects relating to finance, cost engineering, schedule, environmental considerations, regulatory agency requirements, inflation and cost escalations, labor problems, public and client relations, employee relations and changing laws. That's primarily on the domestic side. On international projects, the list of additional functions and considerations adds totally different complications.

In the project environment, everything seems to revolve about the project manager. Although the project organization is a specialized, task-oriented entity, it cannot exist apart from the traditional structure of the organization. The project manager, therefore, must walk the fence between the two organizations. The term interface management is often used for this role, which can be described as:[3]

● Managing human interrelationships in the project organization
● Maintaining the balance between technical and managerial project functions
● Coping with risk associated with project management
● Surviving organizational restraints

3. David L. Wilemon and John P. Cicero, "The Project Manager—Anomalies and Ambiguities," *Academy of Management Journal,* September 1970.

Organizational restraints have a tendency to develop into organizational conflict, often requiring that top management take an active role in conflict resolution by:

- Setting a selection criterion for projects
- Establishing priorities among projects

To be effective as a project manager, an individual must have management as well as technical skills. Unfortuately, businessmen sometimes find it difficult at times to think as businessmen. Executives have found that it is usually easier to train engineers rather than businessmen to fill project management positions.

Because the engineers often consider their careers limited in the functional disciplines, they look toward project management and project engineering as career path opportunities. But becoming a manager entails learning about psychology, human behavior, organizational behavior, interpersonal relations, and communications. MBA programs have come to the rescue of individuals desiring the background to be effective project managers.

The average age of project managers in industry is between thirty and forty. There are three reasons for this:

- An individual often makes his most profitable contribution to society between thirty and forty. If individuals do not begin climbing the corporate ladder by the time they are forty, they may be severely limited in career growth.
- When is an individual most concerned about money? (All the time is not an acceptable answer!) It is not between the ages of twenty and thirty because to a person coming right out of college, any money looks good. It is not between the ages of forty and fifty because, by that time, individuals are fairly set in their ways and living styles. But between the ages of thirty and forty, the individual is thinking about financial security, the future, a new home, travel, and educating his children!
- The younger individual in most cases is willing to take more risks than the older individual in order to meet the project objective. Furthermore, the younger individual is often willing to work long hours including overtime and weekends.

One final comment should be made concerning the young project manager's desire to take risks. Frequently the young risk taker does not fully understand the extent of the risk being taken, because of a lack of experience or a lack of objectivity when implementing one's creative ideas. Although this is a problem, it has a positive aspect if it reflects youth's positive attitude and aggressiveness;

an almost innocent view that "it won't or can't happen to me." Far less positive is the rationale upon which risk decisions are frequently made by the younger person. When a risk is taken primarily to further an individual's career, rather than for the betterment of the project (or business); where the risk taker seeks immediate recognition, if successful, and is willing to look for a new job if the risk becomes a reality; the risk decision-making process becomes flawed and poor decisions can result.

Actually, the age of the project manager varies from industry to industry. Data processing project managers are usually younger than the average because current knowledge of computer technology is a necessity. R&D project managers may span the entire range because of technology requirements. Manufacturing and construction project managers are often older because their experience is important.

In the past, executives motivated and retained qualified personnel primarily with financial incentives. Today other ways are being used. Some people are more title-oriented than money-oriented. For example, a change in title sometimes motivates people to stay with a company simply because they want to put the new title on their resume at a later date.

Another method, and by far the best, is work challenge. Perhaps the lowest turnover rates of any professions in the world are in project management and project engineering. In a project environment, the project managers and project engineers get to see their project through from "birth to death." Being able to see the fruits of one's efforts is highly rewarding. A senior project manager in a construction company commented on why he never accepted a vice-presidency that had been offered to him: "I can take my children and grandchildren into ten countries in the world and show them facilities which I have built as the project manager. What do I show my kids as an executive? The size of my office? My bank account? A stockholder's report?"

Work challenge and other nonmonetary rewards are becoming increasingly important today so that people are refusing to leave project management positions.

The project manager is actually a general manager and gets to know the total operation of the company. In fact, project managers get to know more about the total operation of a company than most executives know. That is why project management is often used as a training ground to prepare future general managers who will be capable of filling top management positions. This is not a bad idea, provided that executives know the general management aspect is the result of experience in integrating work horizontally. Placing an individual into project management for the sole purpose of training a future general manager is not recommended unless the company is willing to risk the failure of the project to provide such training.

1.5 DEFINING THE FUNCTIONAL MANAGER'S ROLE

Assuming that the project and functional managers are not the same person, we can identify a specific role for the functional manager. There are two elements to his role:

- The functional manager has the responsibility to define *how* the task will be done and *where* the task will be done (i.e., the technical criteria).
- The functional manager has the responsibility to provide sufficient resources to accomplish the objective with the project's constraints (i.e., *who* will get the job done).

In other words, once the project manager identifies the requirements for the project (i.e., what work has to be done and the constraints), it becomes the line manager's responsibility to identify the technical criteria. Except perhaps in R&D efforts, the line manager should be the recognized technical expert. If the line manager believes that certain technical portions of the project manager's requirements are unsound, then the line manager has the right, by virtue of his expertise, to take exception and plead his case to a higher authority.

In Section 1.1 we stated that all resources (including personnel) are controlled by the line manager. The project manager has the right to request specific staff, but the final appointments rest with the line managers. Project managers view line managers as rather shady characters (see Figure 1–4) who never keep their promises. In a project environment, the line managers are under tremendous pressure to live up to their commitments. Unfortunately, project managers do not realize the line manager's problems. The line manager has to cope with:

- Unlimited work requests (especially during competitive bidding)
- Predetermined deadlines
- All requests having a high priority
- Limited number of resources
- Limited availability of resources
- Unscheduled changes in the project plan
- Unpredicted lack of progress
- Unplanned absence of resources
- Unplanned breakdown of resources
- Unplanned loss of resources
- Unplanned turnover of personnel

Only in a very few industries will the line manager be able to identify to the project manager in advance exactly what resources will be available when the project is scheduled to begin. Actually, it is not important for the project manager to have the best available resources. Functional managers should not commit to certain people's availability. Rather, the functional manager should commit to achieving his portion of the objective within time, cost, and performance even if he has to use average or below-average personnel. If the project manager is unhappy with the assigned functional resources, then the project manager should closely track that portion of the project. Only if and when the project manager is convinced by the evidence that the assigned resources are unacceptable, should he then confront the line manager and demand better resources.

Just the fact that a project manager is assigned does not alleviate the line manager of his functional responsibility to perform. If a functional manager assigns resources such that the constraints are not met, then *both* the project and functional manager will be blamed. One company is even considering evaluating line managers for merit increases and promotion based upon how often they have lived up to their commitments to the project managers. Therefore, it is extremely valuable to everyone concerned to have all project commitments *made visible to all.*

Project management is not designed to be a unity of command methodology. It is designed to have shared authority and responsibility between the project

Figure 1–4. Do functional managers live up to commitments?

Table 1–1. Dual Responsibility.

	RESPONSIBILITY	
TOPIC	PROJECT MANAGER	LINE MANAGER
Rewards	Give recommendation: Informal	Provide rewards: Formal
Direction	Milestone (summary)	Detailed
Evaluation	Summary	Detailed
Measurement	Summary	Detailed
Control	Summary	Detailed

and line managers. The project managers plan, monitor, and control the project, whereas the functional managers are responsible for performing the work. Table 1–1 below shows this shared responsibility.

The one exception to Table 1–1 occurs when the project and line manager are the same person. This situation happens more often than not and creates a conflict of interest situation. If a line manager has to assign resources to six projects, one of which is under his direct control, he might save the best resources for his project. In this case, his project will be a success at the expense of all of the other projects.

1.6 DEFINING THE EXECUTIVE'S ROLE

In a project environment there are new expectations of and for the executives, as well as a new interfacing role.[4] Executives are expected to interface a project as follows:

- In project planning and objective-setting
- In conflict resolution
- In priority-setting
- As project sponsor[5]

Executives are expected to interface with projects very closely at project initiation and planning, but to remain at a distance during execution unless needed for priority-setting and conflict resolution. One reason why executives "meddle" during project execution is that they are not getting accurate infor-

---

4. The expectations will be discussed later in Section 9.3.
5. The role of the project sponsor will be discussed in Section 10.1.

mation from the project manager as to project status. If project managers provide executives with meaningful status reports, then the so-called meddling may be reduced or even eliminated.

1.7 WORKING WITH EXECUTIVES

Success in project management is like a three-legged stool. The first leg is the project manager, the second leg is the line manager, and the third leg is senior management. If any of the three legs fail, then even delicate balancing may not prevent the stool from toppling down.

The critical mode in project management is the project manager-line manager interface. At this interface, the project and line manager must view each other as equals and be willing to share authority, responsibility, and accountability. In excellently managed companies, project managers do not negotiate for resources but simply ask for the line manager's commitment to executing his portion of the work within time, cost, and performance. Therefore, in excellent companies, it should not matter who the line manager assigns as long as the line manager lives up to his commitments.

Since the project and line managers are "equals," senior management involvement is necessary to provide advice and guidance to the project manager, as well as to provide encouragement to the line managers to keep their promises. When the executive acts in this capacity, he or she assumes the role of a project sponsor, as shown in Figure 1–5.[6] The exact person appointed as the project sponsor is based upon the dollar value of the project, the priority of the project, and who the customer is.

The ultimate objective of the project sponsor is to provide behind-the-scenes assistance to project personnel for projects both "internal" to the company, as well as "external," as shown in Figure 1–5. Projects can still be successful without this commitment and support, as long as all work flows smoothly. But in time of crisis, having a "big brother" available as a possible sounding board will surely help.

When an executive is required to act as a project sponsor, then the executive has the responsibility to make effective and timely project decisions. To accomplish this, the executive needs timely, accurate, and complete data for such decisions. The project manager must be made to realize that keeping management informed serves this purpose, and the all-too-common practice of "stonewalling" will prevent an executive from making effective decisions related to the project.

---

6. Section 10.1 describes the role of the project sponsor in more depth.

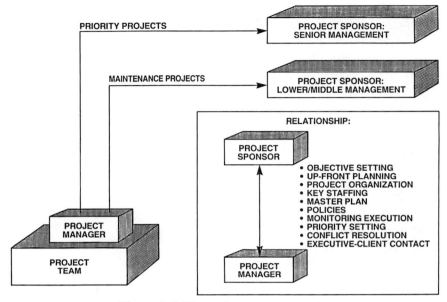

Figure 1–5 The project sponsor interface.

1.8 THE PROJECT MANAGER AS THE PLANNING AGENT

The major responsibility of the project manager is planning. If project planning is performed correctly, then it is conceivable that the project manager will work himself out of a job because the project can run itself. This rarely happens, however. Few projects are ever completed without some conflict or tradeoffs for the project manager to resolve.

In most cases, the project manager provides overall or summary definitions of the work to be accomplished, but the line managers (the true experts) do the detailed planning. Although project managers cannot control or assign line resources, they must make sure that the resources are adequate and scheduled to satisfy the needs of the project, not vice versa. As the architect of the project plan, the project manager must provide:

- Complete task definitions
- Resource requirement definitions
- Major timetable milestones
- Definition of end-item quality and reliability requirements
- The basis for performance measurement

These factors, if properly established, result in:

- Assurance that functional units will understand their total responsibility toward achieving project needs.
- Assurance that problems resulting from scheduling and allocation of critical resources are known beforehand.
- Early identification of problems that may jeopardize successful project completion so that effective corrective action and replanning can be taken to prevent or resolve the problems.

Project managers are responsible for project administration and, therefore, must have the right to establish their own policies, procedures, rules, guidelines, and directives—provided these policies, guidelines, and so on, conform to overall company policy. Companies with mature project management structures usually have rather loose company guidelines so that project managers have some degree of flexibility in how to control their projects. However, there are certain administrative requirements project managers cannot establish. As an example, the project manager cannot make any promises to a functional employee concerning:

- Promotion
- Grade
- Salary
- Bonus
- Overtime
- Responsibility
- Future work assignments

These seven items can be administered by line managers only, but the project manager can have indirect involvement by telling the line manager how well an employee is doing (and putting it in writing), requesting overtime because the project budget will permit it, and offering individuals the opportunity to perform work above their current pay grade. Such work above pay grade can cause severe managerial headaches, however, if coordination with the line manager does not take place because the individual will expect immediate rewards if he performs well.

The establishment of project administrative requirements is part of project planning. Executives must either work with the project managers at project initiation or act as resource persons. Improper project administrative planning can create a situation that requires:

- A continuous revision and/or establishment of company and/or project policies, procedures, and directives

- A continuous shifting in organizational responsibility and possible unnecessary restructuring
- A need for staff to acquire new knowledge and skills

If these situations occur simultaneously on several projects, there can be confusion throughout the organization.

1.9 PROJECT CHAMPIONS

Corporations encourage employees to think up new ideas which, if approved by the corporation, will generate monetary and nonmonetary rewards for the idea generator. One such reward is to identify the individual as a "project champion." Unfortunately, all too often the project champion becomes the project manager and, although the idea was technically sound, the project fails.

Table 1–2 provides a comparison between project managers and project champions. The conclusion to be drawn from Table 1–2 is that the project champions may become so attached to the technical side of the project that they become derelict in their administrative responsibilities. Perhaps, therefore, the project champion might function best as a project engineer rather than the project manager.

This comparison does not mean that technically oriented project managers/champions will fail. Rather, it implies that the selection of the "proper" project manager should be based upon *all* facets of the project.

Table 1–2. **Project Managers Versus Project Champions.**

PROJECT MANAGERS	PROJECT CHAMPIONS
• Prefer to work in groups	• Prefer working individually
• Committed to his managerial and technical responsibilities	• Committed to technology
• Committed to the corporation	• Committed to the profession
• Seek to achieve the objective	• Seek to exceed the objective
• Are willing to take risks	• Are unwilling to take risks; try to test everything
• Seek what is possible	• Seek perfection
• Think in terms of short time spans	• Think in terms of long time spans
• Manage people	• Manage things
• Are committed to and pursue material values	• Are committed to and pursue intellectual values

1.10 THE DOWN SIDE RISK OF PROJECT MANAGEMENT

Project management is much too often recognized only as a high-salaried, highly challenging position where the project manager receives excellent training in general management.

For projects that are done for external sources, the project manager is first viewed as starting out with a pot of gold (see Figure 1–6) and then as having to manage the project so that sufficient profits will be made for the stockholders (see Figure 1–7). If the project manager performs well, then the expected result is as shown in Figure 1–8.

For projects external to the company, the project manager's responsibility is shown in Figure 1–7. Unfortunately, in going from Figure 1–6 to Figure 1–7, the project manager may experience a change in health (as shown in Figure 1–9), especially if he falls in love with his project.

There are severe down side risks that are not always evident. Some project management positions may require not only a sixty-hour work week, but also extensive time away from home. (See Figures 1–10 through 1–13.) When a

Figure 1–6. Project initiation and funding.

project manager begins to fall in love more with the job than with his family, the result is usually lack of friends, a poor home life, and possibly divorce. During the birth of the missile and space programs, companies estimated that the divorce rate among project managers and project engineers was probably twice the national average. Accepting a project management assignment is not always compatible with raising a young family. The following have been found to be characteristics of the workaholic project manager:

- Every Friday he thinks that there are only two more working days until Monday.
- At 5:00 P.M. he considers the working day only half over.
- He has no time to rest or relax.
- He always takes home work from the office.
- He takes work with him on vacations.

1.11 THE GROWTH OF PROJECT MANAGEMENT

The growth of project management has come about more through necessity than through desire. Its slow growth can be attributed mainly to lack of accep-

Figure 1–7. Booking profits for the stockholders.

Figure 1–8. Successful project completion.

tance of the new management techniques necessary for its successful implementation. An inherent fear of the unknown acted as a deterrent for those managers wishing to change over.

Between the middle and late 1960s, more and more executives began searching for new management techniques and organizational structures that could be quickly adapted to a changing environment. The table below and Figure 1–14 identify two major variables that executives consider with regard to organizational restructuring:

AT PROJECT TERMINATION

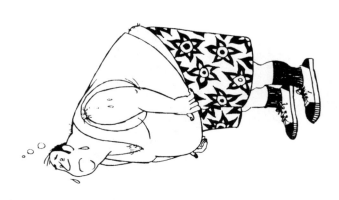

AT PROJECT INITIATION

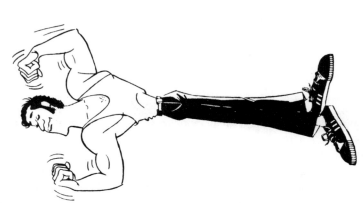

Figure 1–9. Project manager's health.

Figure 1–10. Effective project management: no pressure.

Figure 1–11. Effective project management: good home life.

Figure 1–12. Effective project management: meet new people.

Figure 1–13. Effective project management: limited travel.

TYPE OF INDUSTRY	TASKS	ENVIRONMENT
A	Simple	Dynamic
B	Simple	Static
C	Complex	Dynamic
D	Complex	Static

Almost all type C and most type D industries have project-management-related structures. The key variable appears to be task complexity. Companies that have complex tasks and that also operate in a dynamic environment find project management mandatory. Such industries would include aerospace, defense, construction, high-technology engineering, computers, and electronic instrumentation.

Other than aerospace, defense, and construction, the majority of the companies in the 1960s maintained an informal method for managing projects. In

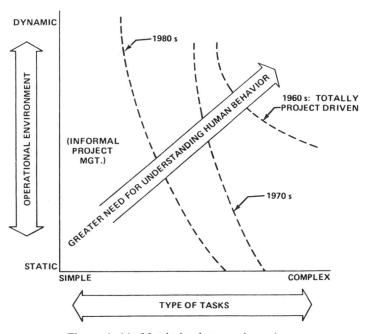

Figure 1-14. Matrix implementation scheme.

informal project management, just as the words imply, the projects were handled on an informal basis where the authority of the project manager was minimized. Most projects were handled by functional managers and stayed in one or two functional lines, and formal communications were either unnecessary or handled informally because of the good working relationships between line managers. Many organizations today, such as low technology manufacturing, have line managers who have been working side by side for ten or more years. In such situations, informal project management may be effective on capital equipment or facility development projects.

By 1970 and again during the early 1980s, more and more companies departed from informal project management and restructured to formalize the project management process, mainly because the size and complexity of their activities had grown to a point that they were unmanageable within the current structure. Figure 1–15 shows what happened to one such construction company. The following five questions normally give some insight as to whether or not formal project management is necessary:

- Are the jobs complex?
- Are there dynamic environmental considerations?
- Are the constraints tight?
- Are there several activities to be integrated?
- Are there several functional boundaries to be crossed?

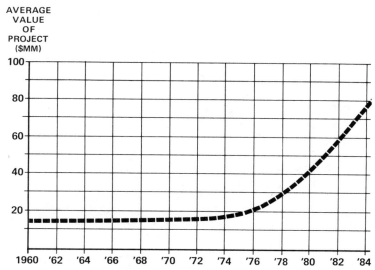

Figure 1–15. Average project size capability for a construction company, 1960–84.

If any of these questions is answered yes, then some form of formalized project management may be necessary. It is possible for formalized project management to exist in only one functional department or division, such as for R&D or perhaps just for certain types of projects. Some companies have successfully implemented both formal and informal project management concurrently, but these companies are few and far between. Today we realize that the last two questions may be the most important.

The moral here is that not all industries need project management, and executives must determine whether there is an actual need before making a commitment. Several industries with simple tasks, whether in a static or a dynamic environment, do not need project management. Manufacturing industries with slowly changing technology do not need project management, unless of course they have a requirement for several special projects, as capital equipment activities, that could interrupt the normal flow of work in the routine manufacturing operations.

The slow growth rate and acceptance of project management were related to the fact that the limitations of project management were readily apparent, yet the advantages were not completely recognizable. Project management requires organizational restructuring. The question, of course, is "How much restructuring?" Executives have avoided the subject of project management for fear that "revolutionary" changes must be made in the organization. As will be seen later, in Chapter 3, project management can be achieved with little departure from the existing traditional structure.

Project management restructuring permitted companies to:

- Accomplish tasks that could not be effectively handled by the traditional structure
- Accomplish one-time activities with minimum disruption of routine business

The second item implies that project management is a "temporary" management structure and, therefore, causes minimum organizational disruption. The major problems identified by those managers who endeavored to adapt to the new system all revolved about conflicts in authority and resources.

Three major problems were identified by Killian:[7]

- Project priorities and competition for talent may interrupt the stability of the organization and interfere with its long-range interests by upsetting the normal business of the functional organization.

---

7. William P. Killian, "Project Management—Future Organizational Concepts," *Marquette Business Review*, Vol. 2, 1971, pp. 90–107.

- Long-range planning may suffer as the company gets more involved in meeting schedules and fulfilling the requirements of temporary projects.
- Shifting people from project to project may disrupt the training of new employees and specialists. This may hinder their growth and development within their fields of specialization.

Another major concern was the fact that project management required upper-level managers to relinquish some of their authority through delegation to the middle managers. In several situations, middle managers soon occupied the power positions, even more so than upper-level managers.

Despite these limitations, there were several driving forces behind the project management approach. According to John Kenneth Galbraith, these forces stem from "the imperatives of technology." The six imperatives are the following:[8]

- The time span between project initiation and completion appears to be increasing.
- The capital committed to the project prior to the use of the end item appears to be increasing.
- As technology increases, the commitment of time and money appears to become inflexible.
- Technology requires more and more specialized manpower.
- The inevitable counterpart of specialization is organization.
- The above five "imperatives" identify the necessity for more effective planning, scheduling, and control.

As the driving forces overtook the restraining forces, project management began to mature. Executives began to realize that the approach was in the best interest of the company. Project management, if properly implemented, can make it easier for executives to overcome such internal and external obstacles as:

- Unstable economy
- Shortages
- Soaring costs
- Increased complexity
- Heightened competition
- Technological changes

---

8. From *The New Industrial State* by John Kenneth Galbraith. Copyright© 1967, 1971, 1978, by John Kenneth Galbraith (3rd edition). Reprinted by permission of Houghton Mifflin Company.

- Societal concerns
- Consumerism
- Ecology
- Quality of work

Project management may not eliminate these problems, but may make it easier for the company to adapt to a changing environment.

If these obstacles are not controlled, the results can be:

- Decreased profits
- Increased manpower needs
- Cost overruns, schedule delays, and penalty payments occurring earlier and earlier
- An inability to cope with new technology
- R&D results too late to benefit existing product lines
- New products introduced into the marketplace too late
- Temptation to make hasty decisions that prove to be costly
- Management insisting on earlier and greater return on investment
- Greater difficulty in establishing on-target objectives in real time
- Problems in relating cost to technical performance and scheduling during the execution of the project

Project management became a necessity for many companies. They began to expand into multiple product lines, many of which were often dissimilar, and organizational complexities grew almost without bound. This growth can be attributed to:

- Technology increasing at an astounding rate
- More money invested in R&D
- More information available
- Shortening of project life cycles

To satisfy the requirements imposed by the above four factors, management was "forced" into organizational restructuring; the traditional organizational form which had survived for so many decades was found to be inadequate for integrating activities across functional "empires."

By 1970, the environment began to change rapidly. Companies such as aerospace, defense, and construction pioneered in implementing project management, and other industries soon followed, some with great reluctance. NASA and the Department of Defense "forced" subcontractors into accepting project management. The 1970s also brought much more published data on project management. As an example:[9]

- Project teams and task forces will become more common in tackling complexity. There will be more of what some people call temporary management systems as project management systems where the men who are needed to contribute to the solution meet, make their contribution, and perhaps never become a permanent member of any fixed or permanent management group.

The definition simply states that the purpose of project management is to put together the best possible team to achieve the objective, and, at termination, the team is disbanded. Nowhere in the definition do we see the authority of the project manager or his rank, title, or salary.

Because current organizational structures are unable to accommodate the wide variety of interrelated tasks necessary for successful project completion, the need for project management has become apparent. It is usually first identified by those lower-level and middle managers who find it impossible to control their resources effectively for the diverse activities within their line organization. Quite often middle managers feel the impact of a changing environment more than upper-level executives.

Once the need for change is identified, middle management must convince upper-level management that such a change is actually warranted. If top-level executives cannot recognize the problems with resource control, then project management will not be adopted, at least formally. Informal acceptance, however, is another story.

In 1978, the author received a request from an automobile equipment manufacturer who was considering formal project management. The author was permitted to speak with several middle managers. The following comments were made:

- "Here at ABC Company (a division of XYZ Corporation), we have informal project management. By this, I mean that work flows the same as it would in formal project management except that the authority, responsibility, and accountability are implied rather than rigidly defined. We have been very successful with this structure, especially when you consider that the components we sell cost 30 percent more than our competitors, and that our growth rate has been in excess of 12 percent each year for the past six years. The secret of our success has been our quality and our ability to meet schedule dates."

---

9. Reprinted from the October 17, 1970 issue of *Business Week* by special permission, © 1970 by McGraw Hill, Inc., New York, New York 10020. All rights reserved.

- "Our informal structure works well because our department managers do not hide problems. They aren't afraid to go into another department manager's office and talk about the problems they're having controlling resources. Our success is based upon the fact that all of our department managers do this. What's going to happen if we hire just one or two people who won't go along with this approach? Will we be forced to go to formalized project management?"
- "This division is a steppingstone to greatness in our corporation. It seems that all of the middle managers who come to this division get promoted either within the division, to higher management positions in other divisions, or to a higher position at corporate headquarters."

At this point, the author conducted two three-day seminars on engineering project management for seventy-five of the lower-, middle-, and upper-level managers. The seminar participants were asked whether or not they wanted to adopt formal project management. The following concerns were raised by the participants:

- "Will I have more or less power and/or authority?"
- "How will my salary be affected?"
- "Why should I permit a project manager to share the resources in my empire?"
- "Will I get top management visibility?"

Even with these concerns, the majority of the attendees felt that formalized project management would alleviate a lot of their present problems.

Although the middle levels of the organization, where resources are actually controlled on a day-to-day basis, felt positive about project management, convincing the top levels of management was another story. If you were the chief executive officer of this division, earning a salary in six figures, and looking at a growth rate of 12 percent per year for the last five years, would you "rock the boat" simply because your middle managers want project management?

This example highlights three major points:

- The final decision for the implementation of project management does (and will always) rest with executive management.
- Executives must be willing to listen when middle management identifies a crisis in controlling resources. This is where the need for project management should first appear.
- Executives are paid to look out for the long-range interest of the corporation and should not be swayed by near-term growth rate or profitability.

Today, ABC Company is still doing business the way it was done in the past—with informal project management. The company is a classic example of how informal project management can be made to work successfully. The author agrees with the company executives that, in this case, formal project management is not necessary.

William C. Goggin, board chairman and chief executive officer of Dow Corning, describes a situation in his corporation that was quite different from the one at ABC:[10]

Although Dow Corning was a healthy corporation in 1967, it showed difficulties that troubled many of us in top management. These symptoms were, and still are, common ones in U.S. business and have been described countless times in reports, audits, articles and speeches. Our symptoms took such forms as:

- Executives did not have adequate financial information and control of their operations. Marketing managers, for example, did not know how much it cost to produce a product. Prices and margins were set by division managers.
- Cumbersome communications channels existed between key functions, especially manufacturing and marketing.
- In the face of stiffening competition, the corporation remained too internalized in its thinking and organizational structure. It was insufficiently oriented to the outside world.
- Lack of communications between divisions not only created the antithesis of a corporate team effort but also was wasteful of a precious resource—people.
- Long-range corporate planning was sporadic and superficial; this was leading to overstaffing, duplicated effort and inefficiency.

Once the need for project management has been defined, the next logical question is, "How long a conversion period will be necessary before a company can operate in a project management environment?" To answer this question we must first look at Figure 1–16. Technology, as expected, has the fastest rate of change, and the overall environment of a business must adapt to rapidly changing technology.

In an ideal situation, the organizational structure of a company would immediately adapt to the changing environment. In a real situation, this will not be a smooth transition but more like the erratic line shown in Figure 1–16. This erratic line is a trademark or characteristic of the traditional structure. Project management structures, however, can, and often do, adapt to a rapidly changing environment with a relatively smooth transition.

---

10. William C. Goggin, "How the Multidimensional Structure Works at Dow Corning," *Harvard Business Review*, January–February 1974, p. 54. Copyright © 1973 by the President and Fellows of Harvard College; All rights reserved.

RATE OF CHANGE →

COMPANY BUSINESS SYSTEMS

TECHNOLOGY

(EACH SLICE REPRESENTS AN
UPDATED SYSTEM)

ENVIRONMENT

ORGANIZATION

PEOPLE

BUSINESS
GOALS AND
OBJECTIVES

TIME (YEARS) →

Figure 1–16. Systems in a changing environment.

Even though an executive can change the organizational structure with the stroke of a pen, people are responsible for its implementation. However, it can be seen in Figure 1–16 that people have the slowest rate of change. Edicts, documents signed by executives, and training programs will not convince employees that a new organizational form will work. Employees will be convinced only after they see the new system in action, and this takes time.

As a ground rule, it often takes two to three years to convert from a traditional structure to a project management structure. The major reason for this is that in a traditional structure the line employee has one and only one boss; in a project management structure the employee reports vertically to his line manager and horizontally to every project manager on whose activities he is assigned, either temporarily or full-time. This situation often leads to a cultural shock condition. Employees will perform in a new system because they are directed to do so but will not have confidence in it or become dedicated until after they have been involved in several different projects and believe that they can effectively report to more than one boss.

When an employee is told that he will be working horizontally as well as vertically, his first concern is his take-home pay. Employees always question whether or not they can be evaluated fairly if they report to several managers during the same time period. One of the major reasons why project management fails is that top-level executives neglect to consider that any organizational change must be explained in terms of the wage and salary administration program.[11] This must occur *before* change is made. If change comes first, and employees are not convinced that they can be evaluated correctly, they may very likely try to sabotage the whole effort. From then on, it will probably be a difficult, if not impossible, task to rectify the situation. However, once the organizational employees accept project management and the procedure of reporting in two directions, the company can effectively and efficiently convert from one project management organizational form to another. After all, weren't most of us educated throughout our childhood on how to report to two bosses—a mother and a father?

Not all companies need two to three years to convert to project management. The ABC Company described earlier would probably have very little trouble in converting because informal project management is well accepted. In the early 1960s, TRW was forced to convert to a project management structure almost overnight. The company was highly successful in this, mainly because of the loyalty and dedication of the employees. The TRW employees were willing to give the system a chance. Any organizational structure, no matter how bad, will work if the employees are willing to make it work. Yet other companies can spend three to five years trying to implement change and drastically fail. The literature describes many cases where project management has failed because:

- There was no need for project management.
- Employees were not informed about how project management should work.
- Executives did not select the appropriate projects or project managers for the first few projects.
- There was no attempt to explain the effect of the project management organizational form on the wage and salary administration program.
- Employees were not convinced that executives were in total support of the change.

Some companies (and executives) are forced into project management before they realize what has happened, and if recognition at the top levels of management does not occur soon afterward, chaos seems inevitable. As an example, consider a highly traditional company that purchased a computer a few years ago. The company has five divisions: engineering, finance, manufacturing, marketing, and personnel. Not knowing where to put the computer, the

---

11. The mechanisms for employee evaluation in a project environment will be discussed further in Section 8.1.

chief executive officer created an electronic data processing (EDP) department and placed it under finance and accounting. The executive's rationale was that since the purpose for buying the computer was to eliminate repetitive tasks and the majority of these were in accounting and finance, that was where EDP belonged. The vice president for accounting and finance might not be qualified to manage the EDP department, but that seemed beside the point.

The EDP department has a staff of scientific and business computer programmers and systems analysts. The scientific programmers spend almost all of their time working in the engineering division writing engineering programs; they must learn engineering in order to do this. In this company, the engineer does not consider himself to be a computer programmer, but does the computer programmer consider himself to be an engineer?

The company's policy is that merit and cost-of-living increases are given out in July of each year. This year the average salary increase will be 7 percent. However, the president wants the increase given according to merit, and not as a flat rate across the board. After long hours of deliberation, it was decided that engineering, manufacturing, and marketing would receive 8 percent raises, and finance and personnel 5.5 percent.

After announcement of the salary increases, the scientific programmers began to complain because they felt they were doing engineering-type work and should therefore be paid according to the engineering pay scale. Management tried to resolve this problem by giving each division its own computer and personnel. However, this resulted in duplication of effort and inefficient use of personnel.

With the rapid advancements in computer technology of recent years, management realized the need for timely access to information for executive decision making. In a rather bold move, executives created a new division called management information systems (MIS). The MIS division now has full control of all computer operations and gives the EDP personnel the opportunity to show that they actually contribute to corporate profits.

Elevating the computer to the top levels of the organization was a significant step toward project management. Unfortunately, many executives did not fully realize what had happened. Because of the need for a rapid information retrieval system that can integrate data from a variety of line organizations, the MIS personnel soon found that they were working horizontally, not vertically. Today, MIS packages cut across every division of the company. Thus, the project management concept for handling a horizontal flow of work emerged.

With the emergence of data processing project management, executives were forced to find immediate answers to such questions as:

- Can we have project management strictly for data processing projects?
- Should the project manager be the programmer or the user?

- How much authority should be delegated to the project manager, and will this delegated authority cause a shift in the organizational equilibrium?

The answers to these questions have not been and still are not easy to solve. Today, IBM provides its customers with the opportunity to hire IBM as the in-house data processing project management team. This partially eliminates the necessity for establishing internal project management relationships that could easily become permanent.

In TRW Nelson Division,[12] data processing project management began with MIS personnel acting as the project leaders. However, after two years, the company felt that the people best qualified to be the project leaders were the technical experts (i.e., users). Therefore, the MIS personnel now act as team members and resource personnel rather than as the project managers.

There are many different types of projects. Each of these projects can have its own organizational form and can operate concurrently with other active projects. This diversity of projects has contributed to the implementation of full project management in several industries.

J. Robert Fluor, chairman, chief executive officer, and president of the Fluor Corporation, commented on twenty years of operations in a project environment:[13]

The need for flexibility has become apparent since no two projects are ever alike from a project management point of view. There are always differences in technology; in the geographical locations; in the client approach; in the contract terms and conditions; in the schedule; in the financial approach to the project; and in a broad range of international factors, all of which require a different and flexible approach to managing each project. We found the task force concept, with maximum authority and accountability resting with the project manager, to be the most effective means of realizing project objectives. And while basic project management principles do exist at Fluor, there is no single standard project organization or project procedure yet devised that can be rigidly applied to more than one project.

Today, our company and others and their projects managers are being challenged as never before to achieve what earlier would have been classified as "unachievable" project objectives. Major projects often involve the resources of a large number of organizations located on different continents. The efforts of each must be directed and coordinated toward a common set of project objectives of quality performance, cost and time of completion as well as many other considerations.

As project management developed, some essential factors in its successful implementation were recognized. The major factor was the role of the project

---

12. The TRW Nelson Division case study appears at the end of Chapter 1.
13. J. Robert Fluor, "Development of Project Managers," keynote address to the Project Management Institute, Ninth International Seminar Symposium, Chicago, Illinois, October 24, 1977.

manager, which became the focal point of integrative responsibility. This need for integrative responsibility was first identified in research and development activities:[14]

Recently, R&D technology has broken down the boundaries that used to exist between industries. Once-stable markets and distribution channels are now in a state of flux. The industrial environment is turbulent and increasingly hard to predict. Many complex facts about markets, production methods, costs and scientific potentials are related to investment decisions.

All of these factors have combined to produce a king-size managerial headache. There are just too many crucial decisions to have them all processed and resolved through regular line hierarchy at the top of the organization. They must be integrated in some other way.

Providing the project manager with integrative responsibility resulted in:

- Total accountability assumed by a single person
- Project rather than functional dedication
- A requirement for coordination across functional interfaces
- Proper utilization of integrated planning and control

Without project management, these four elements have to be accomplished by executives, and it is very questionable whether these activities should be part of an executive's job description. An executive in a Fortune 500 corporation stated that he was spending seventy hours a week acting as an executive and as a project manager, and he did not feel that he was performing either job to the best of his abilities. During a presentation to the CEO staff, the executive stated what he expected of the organization after project management implementation:

- Push decision-making down in the organization
- Eliminate the need for committee solutions
- Trust the decision of peers

Those executives who chose to accept project management soon found the advantages of the new technique:

- Easy adaptation to an ever-changing environment
- Ability to handle a multidisciplinary activity within a specified period of time

---

14. Paul R. Lawrence and Jay W. Lorsch, "New Management Job: The Integrator," *Harvard Business Review*, November–December 1967, p. 142. Copyright © 1967 by the President and Fellows of Harvard College; All rights reserved.

- Horizontal as well as vertical work flow
- Better orientation toward customer problems
- Easier identification of activity responsibilities
- A multidisciplinary decision-making process
- Innovation in organizational design

1.12 PROJECT-DRIVEN VS. NON-PROJECT-DRIVEN ORGANIZATIONS

On the micro level, virtually all organizations are either marketing-, engineering-, or manufacturing-driven. But on the macro level, the organizations are either project- or non-project-driven. In a project-driven organization, such as construction or aerospace, all work is characterized through projects, with each project as a separate cost center having its own profit and loss statement. The total profit to the corporation is simply the summation of the profits on all projects. In a project-driven organization, everything centers around the projects.

In the non-project-driven organization, such as low-technology manufacturing, profit and loss are measured on vertical or functional lines. In this type of organization, projects exist merely to support the product lines or functional lines. Priority resources are assigned to the revenue-producing functional line activities rather than the projects.

Project management in a non-project-driven organization is generally more difficult for these reasons:

- Projects may be few and far between.
- Not all projects have the same project management requirements, and therefore they cannot be managed identically. This difficulty results from poor understanding of project management and a reluctance of companies to invest in proper training.
- Executives do not have sufficient time to manage projects themselves, yet refuse to delegate authority.
- Projects tend to be delayed because approvals most often follow the vertical chain of command. As a result, project work stays too long in functional departments.
- Because project staffing is on a "local" basis, only a portion of the organization understands project management and sees the system in action.
- There exists heavy dependence upon subcontractors and outside agencies for project management expertise.

Non-project-driven organizations may also have a steady stream of projects, all of which are usually designed to enhance the manufacturing operations. Some projects may be customer-requested, such as:

- The introduction of statistical dimensioning concepts to improve process control
- The introduction of process changes to enhance the final product
- The introduction of process change concepts to enhance product reliability

If these changes are not identified as specific projects, the result can be:

- Poorly defined responsibility areas within the organization
- Poor communications, both internal and external to the organization
- Slow implementation
- A lack of a cost tracking system for implementation
- Poorly defined performance criteria

Figure 1–17 shows the tip-of-the-iceberg syndrome, which can occur in all types of organizations but is most common for non-project-driven organizations. On the surface, all we see is a lack of authority for the project manager. But beneath the surface we see the causes; there is excessive executive meddling due to lack of understanding of project management, which, in turn, resulted from an inability to recognize the need for proper training.

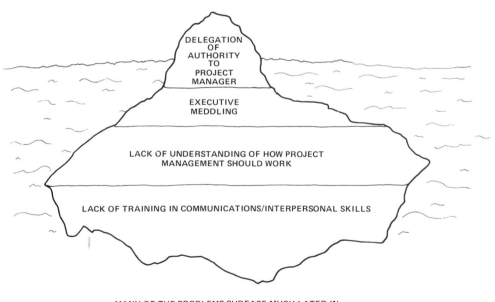

Figure 1–17. The tip-of-the iceberg syndrome for matrix implementation.

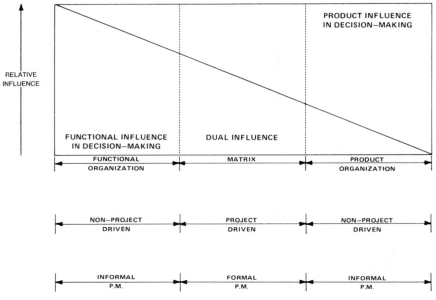

Figure 1–18. Decision-making influence.

In the previous section we stated that project management could be handled on either a formal or an informal basis. As can be seen from Figure 1–18, informal project management most often appears in non-project-driven organizations. It is doubtful that informal project management would work in a project-driven organization where the project manager has profit and loss responsibility.

1.13 MARKETING IN THE PROJECT-DRIVEN ORGANIZATION[15]

To the realistic manager, winning new contracts is the lifeblood of any project-oriented business. The practices of the project-oriented company are, however, substantially different from traditional product businesses and require highly specialized and disciplined team efforts among marketing, technical, and operating personnel, plus significant customer involvement. Projects are different from products in many respects, especially marketing. Marketing projects

---

15. Adapted from H. Kerzner and H. J. Thamhain, *Project Management For the Small and Medium-Sized Business* (New York: Van Nostrand Reinhold, 1983), pp. 195–197.

require the ability to identify, pursue, and capture one-of-a-kind business opportunities, and are characterized by:

- *A systematic effort.* A systematic approach is usually required to develop a new program lead into an actual contract. The project acquisition effort is often highly integrated with ongoing programs and involves key personnel from both the potential customer and the performing organization.
- *Custom design.* While traditional businesses provide standard products and services for a variety of applications and customers, projects are custom-designed items to fit specific requirements of a single customer community.
- *Project life cycle.* Project-oriented businesses have a well-defined beginning and end and are not self-perpetuating. Business must be generated on a project-by-project basis rather than by creating demand for a standard product or service.
- *Marketing phase.* Long lead times often exist between the project definition, start-up, and completion phases of a project.
- *Risks.* There are risks present, especially in the research, design, and production of programs. The program manager not only has to integrate the multidisciplinary tasks and project elements within budget and schedule constraints, but also has to manage inventions and technology while working with a wide variety of technically-oriented prima donnas.
- *The technical capability to perform.* Technical ability is critical to the successful pursuit and acquisition of a new project.

In spite of the risks and problems, profits on projects are usually very low in comparison with commercial business practices. One may wonder why companies pursue project businesses. Clearly, there are many reasons why projects are good business:

- Although immediate profits (as a percentage of sales) are usually small, the return on capital investment is often very attractive. Progress payment practices keep inventories and receivables to a minimum and enable companies to undertake projects many times larger in value than the assets of the total company.
- Once a contract has been secured and is being managed properly, the project may be of relatively low financial risk to the company. The company has little additional selling expenditure and has a predictable market over the life cycle of the project.
- Project business must be viewed from a broader perspective than motivation for immediate profits. Projects provide an opportunity to develop

the company's technical capabilities and build an experience base for future business growth.

● Winning one large project often provides attractive growth potential, such as: (1) growth with the project via additions and changes; (2) follow-on work; (3) spare parts, maintenance, and training; and (4) being able to compete effectively in the next project phase, such as nurturing a study program into a development and finally a production contract.

Customers come in various forms and sizes. For small and medium-size businesses, particularly, it seems to be a true challenge to compete for contracts from large industrial or governmental organizations. Although the contract to a firm may be relatively small, it is often subcontracted via a larger organization. Selling to such a diversified heterogeneous customer is a true marketing challenge that requires a highly sophisticated and disciplined approach.

The first step in a new business development effort is to define the market to be pursued. The market segment for a new program opportunity is normally in an area of relevant past experience, technical capability, and customer involvement. Good marketeers in the program business have to think as product line managers. They have to understand all dimensions of the business and be able to define and pursue market objectives that are consistent with the capabilities of their organizations.

Program businesses operate in an opportunity-driven market. It is a common mistake, however, to believe that these markets are unpredictable and unmanageable. Market planning and strategizing is important. New project opportunities develop over periods of time, sometimes years for larger projects. These developments must be properly tracked and cultivated to form the bases for management actions such as (1) bid decisions, (2) resource commitment, (3) technical readiness, and (4) effective customer liaison. This strategy of winning new business is supported by systematic, disciplined approaches, which are illustrated in Figure 1–19.

1.14 CLASSIFICATION OF PROJECTS

The principles of project management can be applied to any type of project and to any industry. However, the relative degree of importance of these principles can vary from project to project and industry to industry. Table 1.3 shows a brief comparison of certain industries/projects.

For those industries that are project-driven, such as aerospace and large construction, the high dollar value of the projects mandates a much more rigorous project management approach. For non-project-driven industries, projects may be managed more informally than formally, especially if no immediate profit is involved.

Table 1-3. Classification of Projects/Characteristics.

	TYPE OF PROJECT/INDUSTRY					
	IN-HOUSE R&D	SMALL CONSTRUCTION	LARGE CONSTRUCTION	AEROSPACE/ DEFENSE	MIS	ENGINEERING
Need for Interpersonal Skills	Low	Low	High	High	High	Low
Importance of Organizational Structure	Low	Low	Low	Low	High	Low
Time Management Difficulties	Low	Low	High	High	High	Low
Number of Meetings	Excessive	Low	Excessive	Excessive	High	Medium
Project Manager's Supervisor	Middle Management	Top Management	Top Management	Top Management	Middle Management	Middle Management
Project Sponsor Present	Yes	No	Yes	Yes	No	No
Conflict Intensity	Low	Low	High	High	High	Low
Cost Control Level	Low	Low	High	High	Low	Low
Level of Planning/Scheduling	Milestones only	Milestones only	Detailed plan	Detailed plan	Milestones only	Milestones only

1.15 LOCATION OF THE PROJECT MANAGER

The success or failure of project management could easily depend upon the location of the project manager within the organization. Two questions must be answered:

- What salary should the project manager earn?
- To whom should the project manager report?

Figure 1–20 shows a typical organizational hierarchy where the numbers represent pay grades. Ideally, the project manager should be the same pay grade as the individuals with whom he must negotiate on a daily basis. Using this criterion, and assuming that the project manager interfaces at the department manager level, then the project manager should earn a salary between grades 20 and 25. An environment where the project manager earns substantially more or less money than the line manager will usually create conflict.

The ultimate reporting location of the project manager (and perhaps his salary) is heavily dependent upon whether the organization is project- or non-project-driven, and whether or not the project manager is responsible for profit or loss. In addition, Martin has shown other good reasons for having project managers report either high or low:[16]

Projects should be located wherever in the organization they can function most effectively. Several reasons for having the project manager report directly to a high level in the organization may be mentioned:

- The project manager is charged with getting results from the coordinated efforts of many functions. He should, therefore, report to the man who directs all those functions.
- The project manager must have adequate organizational status to do his job effectively.
- To get adequate and timely assistance in solving problems that inevitably appear in any important project, the project manager needs direct and specific access to an upper echelon of management.
- The customer, particularly in a competitive environment, will be favorably impressed if his project manager reports to a high organizational echelon.

Good reasons may also exist for having the project manager report to a lower echelon:

- It is organizationally and operationally inefficient to have too many projects, especially small ones, diverting senior executives from more vital concerns.

---

16. Charles Martin, *Project Management: How to Make it Work* (New York: AMACOM, a division of American Management Associations, 1976), p. 80.

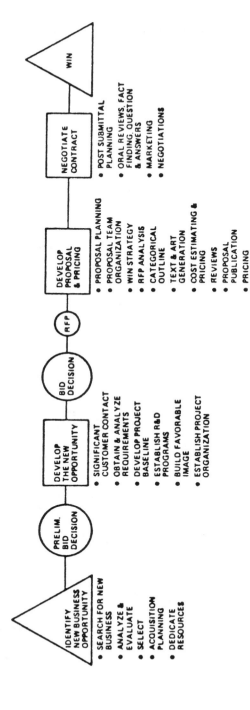

Figure 1-19. The phases of winning new contracts in project-oriented businesses.

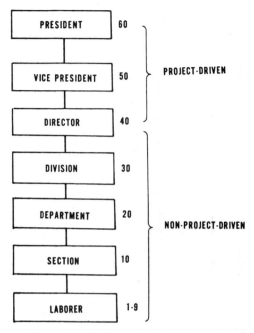

Figure 1–20. Organizational hierarchy.

- Although giving a small project a high place in the organization may create the illusion of executive attention, its real result is to foster executive neglect of the project.
- Placing a junior project manager too high in the organization will alienate senior functional executives on whom he must rely for support.

Project managers can end up reporting both high and low in an organization during the life cycle of the project. During the planning phase of the project, the project manager may report high, whereas during implementation, he may report low. Likewise, the positioning of the project manager may be dependent upon the risk of the project, the size of the project, or the customer.

Finally, it should be noted that even if the project manager reports low, he should still have the right to interface with top executives during project planning although there may be two or more reporting levels between the project manager and the executives. At the opposite end of the spectrum, the project manager should have the right to go directly into the depths of the organization instead of having to follow the chain of command downward, especially during planning. As an example, see Figure 1–21. The project manager had two weeks to plan and price out a small project. Most of the work was to be accomplished within one section. The project manager was told that all requests for work, even estimating, had to follow the chain of command from the executive down through the section supervisor. By the time the request was received by the section supervisor, twelve of the fourteen days were gone, and only an order-of-magnitude estimate was possible. The lesson to be learned here is:

> The chain of command should be used for approving projects, not planning them.

Forcing the project manager to use the chain of command (in either direction) for project planning can result in a great deal of unproductive time and idle time costing.

1.16 DIFFERING VIEWS OF PROJECT MANAGEMENT

Many companies, especially those with project-driven organizations, have differing views of project management. Some people view project management as an excellent means toward achieving objectives, while others view it as a threat. In project-driven organizations, there are three career paths that lead to executive management:

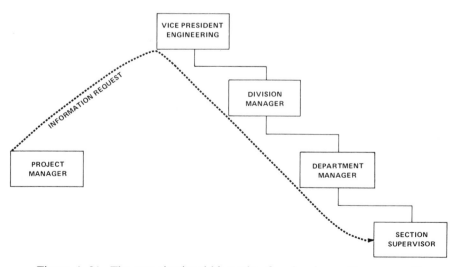

Figure 1–21. The organizational hierarchy: for planning and/or approval?

- Through project management
- Through project engineering
- Through line management

In project-driven organizations, the fast-track position is in project management, whereas in a non-project-driven organization, it would be line management. Even though line managers support the project management approach, at the same time they resent the project manager because his promotions and top-level visibility are greater. In one construction company, a department manager was told that he had no chance for promotion above his present department manager position unless he went into project management or project engineering. As the vice president for engineering stated, "In order to get promoted higher up, you must go into project management or project engineering so as to get to know the operation of the total company." A second construction company requires that individuals aspiring to become even a department manager first spend a "tour of duty" as an assistant project manager or project engineer.

Executives may also dislike project managers because more authority and control must be delegated. However, once executives realize that it is a necessary methodology to do business, project management becomes important as shown in the following letter:[17]

In order to sense and react quickly and to insure rapid decision-making, lines of communication should be the shortest possible between all levels of the organization. People with the most knowledge must be available at the source of the problem, and they must have decision-making authority and responsibility. Meaningful data must be available on a timely basis and the organization must be structured to produce this environment.

In the aerospace industry, it is a serious weakness to be tied to fixed organization charts, plans, and procedures. With regard to organization, we successfully married the project concept of management with a central function concept. What we came up with is an organization within an organization—one to ramrod the day-to-day problems; the other to provide support for existing projects and to anticipate the requirements for future projects.

The project system is essential in getting complicated jobs done well and on time, but it solves only part of the management problem. When you have your nose to the project grindstone, you are often not in a position to see much beyond that project. This

---

17. Letter from J. Donald Rath, vice-president of Martin-Marietta Corporation, Denver Division, to J. E. Webb, of NASA, October 18, 1963.

is where the central functional organization comes in. My experience has been that you need this central organization to give you depth, flexibility, and perspective. Together, the two parts permit you to see both the woods and the trees.

Initiative is essential at all levels of the organization. We try to press the level of decision to the lowest possible rung of the managerial ladder. This type of decision-making provides motivation and permits recognition for the individual and the group at all levels. It stimulates action and breeds dedication.

With this kind of encouragement, the organization can become a live thing—sensitive to problems and able to move in on them with much more speed and understanding than would be normally expected in a large operation. In this way, we can regroup or reorganize easily as situations dictate and can quickly focus on a "crisis." In this industry a company must always be able to reorient itself to meet new objectives. In a more staid, old-line organization, frequent reorientation usually accompanied by a corresponding shift of people's activities, could be most upsetting. However, in the aerospace industry, we must be prepared for change. The entire picture is one of change.

PROBLEMS

1-1 In the project environment the cause and effect relationships are almost always readily apparent. Good project management will examine the effect in order to better understand the cause and possibly prevent it from occurring again. Below are causes and effects. For each one of the effects, select the possible cause or causes that may have existed to create this situation:

Effects

1. Late completion of activities
2. Cost overruns
3. Substandard performance
4. High turnover in project staff
5. High turnover in functional staff
6. Two functional departments performing the same activities on one project

Causes

a. Top management not recognizing this activity as a project
b. Too many projects going on at one time
c. Impossible schedule commitments
d. No functional input into the planning phase
e. No one person responsible for the total project
f. Poor control of design changes
g. Poor control of customer changes
h. Poor understanding of the project manager's job
i. Wrong person assigned as project manager

    j. No integrated planning and control
    k. Company resources are overcommitted
    l. Unrealistic planning and scheduling
    m. No project cost accounting ability
    n. Conflicting project priorities
    o. Poorly organized project office

(This problem has been adapted from Russell D. Archibald, *Managing High-Technology Programs and Projects,* New York: John Wiley, 1976, p. 10.)

1–2 Because of the individuality of people, there always exists differing views of what management is all about. Below are lists of possible perspectives and a selected group of organizational members. For each individual select the possible ways that this individual might view project management:

Individuals

1. Upper-level managers
2. Project managers
3. Functional managers
4. Project team members
5. Scientists and consultants

Perspectives

a. A threat to established authority
b. A source for future general managers
c. A cause of unwanted change in ongoing procedures
d. A means to an end
e. A significant market for their services
f. A place to build an empire
g. A necessary evil to traditional management
h. An opportunity for growth and advancement
i. A better way to motivate people toward an objective
j. A source of frustration in authority
k. A way of introducing controlled changes
l. An area of research
m. A vehicle for introducing creativity
n. A means of coordinating functional units
o. A means of deep satisfaction
p. A way of life

1–3 Consider an organization that is composed of upper-level, middle- and lower-level managers, and laborers. Which of the groups should have first insight that an organizational restructuring may be necessary?

1–4 How would you defend the statement that a project manager must help himself?

1-5 Will project management work in all companies? If not, identify those companies in which project management may not be applicable and defend your answers.

1-6 In a project organization, do you think that there might be a conflict in opinions over whether the project managers or functional managers contribute to profits?

1-7 What attributes should a project manager have? Can an individual be trained to become a project manager? If a company were changing over to a project management structure, would it be better to promote and train from within or hire from the outside?

1-8 Do you think that functional managers would make good project managers?

1-9 What types of projects might be more appropriate for functional management rather than project management, and vice versa?

1-10 Do you think that there would be a shift in the relative degree of importance of the following terms in a project management environment as opposed to a traditional management environment?

    a. Time management
    b. Communications
    c. Motivation

1-11 Classical management has often been defined as a process in which the manager does not necessarily perform things for himself, but accomplishes objectives through others in a group situation. Does this definition also apply to project management?

1-12 Which of the following are basic characteristics of project management?

    a. Customer problem orientation
    b. Responsibility identification
    c. Systems approach to decision making
    d. Adaptation to a changing environment
    e. Multidisciplinary activity in a finite time duration
    f. Horizontal and vertical organizational relationships

1-13 Project managers are usually dedicated and committed to the project. Who should be "looking over the shoulder" of the project manager to make sure that the work and requests are also in the best interest of the company? Does your answer depend upon the priority of the project?

1-14 Is project management designed to transfer power from the line managers to the project manager?

1-15 Explain how career paths and career growth can differ between project-driven and non-project-driven organizations. In each organization, is the career path fastest in project management, project engineering, or line management?

1-16 Explain how the following statement can have a bearing upon who is ultimately selected as part of the project team:

"There comes a time in the life cycle of all projects when one must shoot the design engineers and begin production."

1–17 How do you handle a situation where the project manager has become a generalist, but still thinks that he is an expert?

CASE STUDY: JACKSON INDUSTRIES

"I wish the hell that they had never invented computers," remarked Tom Ford, president of Jackson Industries. "This damn computer has been nothing but a thorn in our side for the past ten years. We're gonna resolve this problem now. I'm through watching our people fight with one another. We must find a solution to this problem."

In 1966, Jackson Industries decided to rent an IBM-360 computer, primarily to handle the large, repetitive tasks found in the accounting and finance functions of the organization. It was only fitting, therefore, that control of the computer came under the director of finance, Al Moody. For two years, operations went smoothly. In 1968, the computer department was reorganized in three sections; scientific computer programming, business computer programming, and systems programming. The reorganization was necessary because the computer department had grown into the fifth largest department, employing some thirty people, and was experiencing some severe problems working with other departments.

After the reorganization, Ralph Gregg, the computer department manager, made the following remarks in a memo distributed to all personnel:

The Computer Department has found it increasingly difficult to work with engineering and operations functional departments which continue to permit their personnel to write and document their own computer programs. In order to maintain some degree of consistency, the Computer Department will now assume the responsibility for writing all computer programs. All requests should be directed to the department manager. My people are under explicit instructions that they are to provide absolutely no assistance to any functional personnel attempting to write their own programs without authorization from me. Company directives in this regard will be forthcoming.

The memo caused concern among the functional departments. If engineering wanted a computer program written, they would now have to submit a formal request and then have the person requesting the program spend a great deal of time explaining the problem to the scientific programmer assigned to this effort. The department managers were reluctant to have their people "waste time" in training the scientific programmers to be engineers. The computer department manager countered this argument by stating that once the programmer was fully familiar with the engineering problem, then the engineer's time could be spent more fruitfully on other activities until the computer program was ready for implementation.

This same problem generated more concern by department managers when they were involved in computer projects that required integration among several departments. Although Jackson Industries operated on a traditional structure, the new directive implied that the computer department would be responsible for managing all projects involving computer programming even if they crossed into other departments. Many people looked upon this as a "baby" project management structure within the traditional organization.

In June 1977, Al Moody and Ralph Gregg met to discuss the deterioration of working relationships between the computer department and other organizations.

Al Moody: "I'm getting complaints from the engineering and operations departments that they can't get any priorities established on the work to be done in your group. What can we do about it?"

Ralph Gregg: "I set the priorities as I see fit, for what's best for the company. Those guys in the engineering and operations have absolutely no idea how long it takes to write, debug, and document a computer program. Then they keep feeding me this crap about how their projects will slip if this computer program isn't ready on time. I've told them what problems I have, and yet they still refuse to let me participate in the planning phase of their activities."

Al Moody: "Well, you may have a valid gripe there. I'm more concerned about this closed shop you've developed for your department. You've built a little empire down there and it looks like your people are unionized where the rest of us are not. Furthermore, I've noticed that your people have their own informal organization and tend to avoid socializing with the other employees. We're supposed to be one big, happy family, you know. Can't you do something about that?"

Ralph Gregg: "The problem belongs to you and Tom Ford. For the last three years, the average salary increase for the entire company has been 7.5 percent and our department has averaged a mere 5 percent because you people upstairs do not feel as though we contribute anything to company profits. My scientific programmers feel that they're doing engineering work and that they're making the same contribution to profits as is the engineer. Therefore, they should be on the engineering pay structure and receive an 8 percent salary increase."

Al Moody: "You could have given your scientific programmers more money. You had a budget for salary increases, the same as everyone else."

Ralph Gregg: "Sure I did. But my budget was less than everyone else's. I could have given the scientific people 7 percent and everyone else 3 percent. That would be an easy way to tell people that we think they should look for another job. My people do good work and do, in fact, contribute to profits. If Tom Ford doesn't change his impression of us, then I expect to lose some of my key people. Maybe you should tell him that."

Al Moody: "Between you and me, all of your comments are correct. I agree with your concerns. But my hands are tied, as you know.

"We are contemplating the installation of a management information system for all departments and, especially, for executive decision making. Tom is contemplating creating a new position, Director of Information Services. This would move the computer out of a department under finance and up to the directorate level. I'm sure this would have an impact on yearly salary increases for your people.

"The problem that we're facing involves the managing of projects under the new directorate. It looks like we'll have to create a project management organization just for this new directorate. Tom likes the traditional structure and wants to leave all other directorates intact. We know that this new directorate will have to integrate the new computer projects across multiple departments and divisions. Once we solve the organizational structure problem, we'll begin looking at implementation. Got any good ideas about the organizational structure?"

Ralph Gregg: "You bet I do. Make me director and I'll see that the work gets done."

CASE STUDY: TRW NELSON MIS AND MATERIALS MANAGEMENT SYSTEMS UPGRADE: A PROJECT MANAGEMENT APPROACH[18]

Company Background

TRW Inc. was formed in 1957 by the merger of Thompson Products, Inc., a manufacturer of automobile and aircraft parts, and Ramo-Wooldridge Corporation, a leader in advance planning for ballistic weapons systems and space technology. Today, the Cleveland-based, worldwide corporation has three major industry segments described generally as follows:

- Car and Truck includes a broad range of chassis, engine, and other components as original equipment and replacement parts for passenger cars, trucks, farm machinery, and other off-highway vehicles.
- Electronics and Space Systems includes four classes of products and services: electronic components; electronic systems, equipment, and services; computer-based and analytical services; and spacecraft design and manufacture.
- Industrial and Energy includes lines of basic industrial components such as fasteners, tools and bearings; energy-related products, such as pumps and valves, and aircraft products consisting primarily of jet engine components.

Industrial and Replacement (I & R) is an operating segment of TRW consisting of the Marlin-Rockwell Division, the Energy Products Group, Aftermarket Operations, the United Greenfield Divisions, and the United-Carr Divisions. TRW Nelson is a unit of United-Carr, manufacturing stud welding fasteners, stud welding systems, and cold formed parts.

In 1975, management laid out new direction for TRW which Chairman, Ruben F. Mettler (then president) stated would represent " . . . an even stronger commitment to quality of earnings and quality and strength of our balance sheet.

"Let me start with debt leverage. We have felt for years that we should manage the company to maintain an A rating on our debt securities. That has led us to operate

---

with an approximate 40/60 debt/equity ratio as an upper limit on our leverage. We decided, for reasons that I'll describe later, that we want to reduce that leverage. We're moving towards a 30/70 target. We want to move beyond the A rating and towards the AA category.

"We're placing an added emphasis on return on assets employed. Our average return on assets employed has been roughly 10 percent during the past five years. Our new target is 15 percent. A combination of a 15 percent return on assets employed, and 30/70 leverage would result in a return on equity of 20 percent as compared with an average of about 14 percent in recent years. This higher return on equity is a key element of the new direction."[19]

A. William Reynolds, executive vice-president of I & R, defined the new direction for his units by noting that the debt/equity and ROAE goals required the I & R group, which accounted for 25 percent of TRW assets at that time, to improve its working capital ratio.

"To improve working capital ratios, we simply must improve our systems of control, especially in the areas of inventory and receivables management." Mr. Reynolds went on to point out that in most units of I & R, excellent customer service is the key element, the critical factor of competitive success. He also pointed out that ROAE levels of 15 percent are found only in larger, *leadership* companies. Again, he emphasized that excellence in customer service is obtained only with excellent systems of control.

A number of specific financial and operating goals evolved from this "new direction." In total, these became known as the "1980 Goals" stressing MIS and Materials Management Systems with the objectives of commonality and excellence. In order to define excellence and assure movement toward common systems, Mr. Reynolds decided to draw on internal expertise. MIS and Materials Management advisory boards were formed from representatives of key units. These ongoing committees were charged with providing definition and guidance, and examining the Materials and MIS plans of each unit to assure conformance and progress toward the stated goals.

Project Management Background

The problems facing Nelson management were twofold. First, the TRW top management commitment to commonality and excellence of systems was unmistakable and Nelson was determined to be supportive. On the other hand, the concurrent drive for quality of earnings and return on assets employed meant that every expense, every job description, and every outlay was under careful scrutiny. The systems upgrade would, therefore, be accomplished without the addition of staff or consultive help.

Second, although Nelson management was receptive to the guidance coming from the divisional MIS and Materials Management Committees, it was also concerned about maintaining the company's own priorities. Management felt it was entirely consistent to be fully supportive of corporate goals and, at the same time, approach the

---

19. From an address to institutional investors in Chicago in December 1975, as quoted in the 1975 annual report.

various tasks in the sequence that would allow Nelson the earliest payoffs in terms of better expense and asset management.

The approach to this problem of overhauling systems with the personnel available, personnel already fully committed to their functional duties, did not evolve overnight. However, project management, in the context of drawing on resources across the entire organization, was considered from the very start. This approach, which is highly structured and predominant in the construction and aerospace industries (TRW Systems, formerly Ramo Wooldridge Corp., was a pioneer in project or program management) had been used less formally on occasion at Nelson, usually in the form of "Task Forces."

In 1970–71, such a transorganization team approach had been used on two occasions when unusually large contracts for Nelson equipment had been received from automotive customers. Similarly, in 1972, the project management approach had been applied to plan and coordinate the move of production facilities into a newly constructed plant. Likewise, an ad hoc group was set up in 1973 to investigate and recommend an approach to the company's long-range MIS hardware and staff needs.

Additionally, Nelson had, for a number of years, used product managers in its marketing effort. These managers would take charge of a product judged promising and coordinate its development across the functional areas of the company, including market research, production planning, production and sales.

The Evolution of an Approach

In 1975, TRW Nelson was in an unusually good position to address the challenges of MIS Systems upgrade. An experienced MIS manager had been hired two years earlier, and in early 1974 had supervised the transition from one generation of data processing equipment to the next. The balance of 1974 was spent updating existing applications, improving operating procedures, and extending know-how. By mid-1975, the company was prepared with both human and hardware resources to support a first-class MIS program.

At this point, an MIS steering committee was formed at the suggestion of the I & E MIS advisory board. Consisting of the MIS Manager; the Materials Manager; the Controller; the Manager, Manufacturing; and the Manager, Design Engineering, the committee was charged with screening proposed MIS projects and requests for MIS services. The committee assigned priorities to projects based on payoffs claimed weighed against resource expenditure. Appeal was available through the Vice President for Administration, and ultimately the Vice President and General Manager.

1975—The projects undertaken for the balance of 1975 were "upgrade" in nature, understandably finance and accounting oriented, and designed for eventual conversion to CRT input and inquiry:

Order Entry and Billing
Accounts Payable
Accounts Receivable
Etc.

Also conspicuous about these projects was the fact that they were led by MIS people.

1976—As 1976 unfolded, three facts became apparent:

1. "Management support" was evident by the sheer weight of commitment from divisional general managers on down, but as far as budget or direction was concerned, TRW Nelson would have to find the time, people, and expertise from their existing organization.
2. Project selection and prioritization was a complicated task and critical to success.
3. How to approach, budget, and execute any given project (even what that project would eventually entail) could not always be readily determined.
4. User-leadership would be required for nonfinancial projects.

A typical 1976 project, however, was still outlined by the MIS manager and with the exception of the MRP and Order Entry projects, was still assigned to the MIS manager or an MIS programmer-analyst for leadership. 1976 projects included:

Production Reporting (for factory incentive)
Materials-Inventory Control (redesign of inventory reporting system)
Materials-Inventory Control (MRP Phase I)
Accounting (consolidation of financial reporting)
Materials-Customer Service (customer order entry and inquiry—CRT)
Credit Department (tie-in, TRW National Credit Service)
Accounting (accounts payable to on-line—CRT)
Accounting (payroll system update)
Materials-Inventory Control (surplus and obsolescence reporting)

1977—By August, 1976, when 1977 plans were being finalized, another milestone had been reached. In addition to a MIS Steering Committee and better defined and structured projects, *user project leadership had become established at TRW Nelson.* Dependence was still heavy on the MIS manager for project structuring, but enthusiastic leadership was being received from the various functional departments. As an example, 1977 major projects and their leaders were as follows:

Project	*Project Leader*
Automated Purchasing System	Purchasing Manager
Capital Assets Perpetual Inventory	Production Engineer
MRP Phase II ('76 carryover)	Materials Manager
Elyria Plant On-Line CRT	Materials Manager
On Line Costing	Manager, Cost Department
Mechanization, Personnel Records	Supervisor, Personnel
On-Line Order Entry ('76 carryover)	Manager, Customer Service

Each of the above project leaders had served on previous committees and was an experienced manager. Also, each was in a position to benefit significantly from the successful integration of his project. For these reasons, the transition from MIS to functional leaders was not as difficult as had been envisioned.

The System Today

The following are projects completed in 1977:

Scheduled Projects Completed
  Capital Assets
  On-Line Order Entry
  Elyria On-Line
  Fastener Product Analysis
  Purchasing (Phase I and II)
  Material Requirements Planning—Phase II
  Labor and Production Reporting Revision—Phase I

Nonscheduled Projects Completed
  Warehouse Effectiveness Report
  Standard Routing Revision (Fasteners)
  Surplus Sales Incentive Program
  West Coast Inventory Revision
  Bills of Material On-Line Inquiry
  Production Value Added Revision

The high degree of successful completion can be attributed, at least in part, to the project management approach as it has informally developed at TRW Nelson.

Table 1–4 is a list of 1978 planned projects. A total degree of user involvement has evolved. Project identification and leadership has been entirely lifted from the MIS department (except where appropriate) and placed in the department where payoff is expected.

Figure 1–22 is a display of the project matrix, the overlay of '78 projects on the

Table 1–4. TRW Nelson: 1978 Projects.

SCHEDULED PROJECTS	PROJECT LEADER
A–100 Purchasing (Phase III)	Purchasing Manager
A–102 M.R.P. (Phase III)	Supervisor, P & IC Equipment Products
A–103 Mechanization, Personnel	Supervisor, Personnel
A–107 Extend MIS Standards Worldwide	MIS Manager
A–108 Extend Material Management Standards Worldwide	Materials Manager
A–111 Warehouse Data Collection	Warehouse Coordinator/Customer Service Manager
A–112 On-Line Costing	Supervisor, Cost Department
A–114 Automated Financial Modeling	Controller
A–115 Labor and Production Reporting	Manufacturing Manager
A–117 Expanded Financial Reporting	Supervisor, Cost Department
A–119 Automated Production Order Entry	Supervisor, P & IC Fastener Products

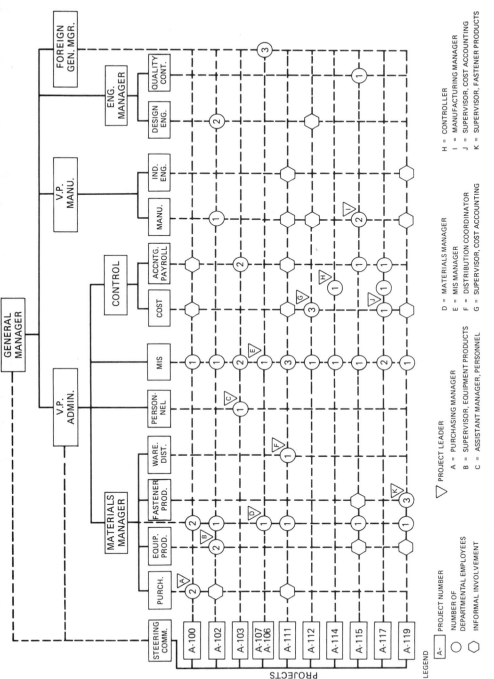

Figure 1-22. Project leadership structure.

LEGEND

A- PROJECT NUMBER

○ NUMBER OF DEPARTMENTAL EMPLOYEES

⬡ INFORMAL INVOLVEMENT

▽ PROJECT LEADER

A = PURCHASING MANAGER
B = SUPERVISOR, EQUIPMENT PRODUCTS
C = ASSISTANT MANAGER, PERSONNEL

D = MATERIALS MANAGER
E = MIS MANAGER
F = DISTRIBUTION COORDINATOR
G = SUPERVISOR, COST ACCOUNTING

H = CONTROLLER
I = MANUFACTURING MANAGER
J = SUPERVISOR, COST ACCOUNTING
K = SUPERVISOR, FASTENER PRODUCTS

61

Table 1–5.   TRW Nelson: 1979–1980 Projects.

A–109   *New Surplus and Obsolete Inventory Reporting System*

An asset control project intended to replace an existing involved manual routine with an automated system. This system will allow immediate action decisions, reduce inventories, and facilitate the profitable disposal of surplus and obsolete items.

A–110   *Capacity Planning and Machine Center Loading*

This project will be a follow-up of MRP (A-102), labor reporting (A-115), and equipment routings (to be assigned) and will close the loop of manufacturing reporting and control systems. The system will provide further improvement of facilities and labor resource utilization.

A–118   *Equipment Routing Revisions*

The entire line of equipment and accessories will be revised to conform with the present method utilized in the stud area. This will provide actual reporting of production on a daily basis and the performance to standard reports necessary.

A–111   *Expansion of Warehouse Data Collection*

This project will be a continuation of the original project and will expand to include production reporting and purchasing information as required.

A–107   *Extension of MIS Standards to Profit Centers Outside USA*

This project will be a continuous one of vitalizing proven systems installed at Lorain at other locations outside of the USA. This will be accomplished by the cross-training of personnel at each location.

TRW Nelson functional organization. It should be noted that the entire functional organization is not represented—only that portion involved in active projects.

Table 1–5 is a listing of projects planned for 1979 and beyond. These future projects will take on greater definition as the 1978 projects evolve. Also, comparing the 1978 and 1979 lists will reveal the transitory quality of the matrix. Table 1–5 is a "snapshot" of the interrelationships as they will exist going into 1978. Almost immediately this picture will begin to alter as projects and project phases are completed until an entirely new matrix develops for 1979—and so on.

Project Management

Obviously, the development of a project approach was not without problems. At first, some people were uncomfortable operating outside of their functional areas with traditional lines of authority and responsibility. Others had difficulty working in groups. Slowly, however, the approach became accepted and then benefits began to accrue:

1. The general level of MIS awareness and expertise has been improved throughout the organization. Increased awareness is the foremost benefit of all—the key to

success for the whole system. Instead of being handed a system and admonished to make it work, employees are sharing in the design, implementation and debugging of *their own* systems.

2. New systems are more readily accepted. People tend to be more receptive to change when they participate in it.

3. Membership on project teams and the inherent forced transorganizational relationships have gone far to reduce departmental provincialism. Informal lines of communication have been established and a higher degree of interdepartmental understanding achieved.

4. Project management is an excellent supplemental management training ground. For example, project A-119 (Figure 1–22 and Table 1–5) was assigned to a new production and inventory control supervisor. The objective of the project was an idea for a quick data processing payoff that he sold to the MIS steering committee. His project background was membership on the On-Line Order Entry project completed in 1977. He is charged now with full project responsibility including design, planning, scheduling, obtaining and motivating human resources, debugging, and implementation. His instructions are to proceed entirely on his own, report regularly, and ask for help when obstacles become insurmountable.

5. The project management approach offers opportunities. For the leader, there is the opportunity to spread his wings and get the feel of management beyond his functional responsibilities. For all project members, there are the opportunities for learning and individual visibility that would not be available otherwise.

6. Finally, the project-matrix approach has allowed TRW Nelson to deal with an immense task—the parameters of which are constantly changing—with a conventionally structured organization and without the expense and sometimes questionable results obtained from consultants.

2
Systems Theory and Concepts

2.0 INTRODUCTION

Organizational theory and management philosophies have undergone a dramatic change in recent years with the emergence of the systems approach to management. Because project management is an outgrowth of systems management, it is only fitting that the underlying principles of general systems theory be described. Simply stated, general systems theory can be classified as a management approach that attempts to integrate and unify scientific information across many fields of knowledge. Systems theory attempts to solve problems by looking at the total picture rather than through an analysis of the individual components.

General systems theory has been in existence for more than three decades. Darwin defined his "whole" as being a system of nature. Keynes defined his "whole" as being the entire economic system. Both Darwin and Keynes conceptualized their systems as being as large in size as one could imagine, provided that the individual components could still be identified and integrated into a systematic whole. Unfortunately, as is often the case with new theory development, the practitioners require years of study and analysis before implementation is deemed feasible and finally accepted as a way of life.

2.1 GENERAL SYSTEMS THEORY GROWTH

In 1951, Ludwig von Bertalanffy, a biologist, described so-called open systems using anatomy nomenclature. The human body, muscles, skeleton, circulatory system, and so on, were all described as subsystems of the total system (the human being). Dr. von Bertalanffy's contribution was important in that he identified how specialists in each subsystem could be integrated so as to get a better understanding of the interrelationships, thereby contributing to the overall knowledge of the operations of the system. Thus, the foundation was laid for the evolution and outgrowth of project management.

In 1956, Kenneth Boulding identified the communications problems that can occur during systems integration. Professor Boulding was concerned with the fact that subsystem specialists (i.e., physicists, economists, chemists, sociologists, etc.) have their own languages. He advocated that, in order for successful integration to take place, all subsystem specialists must speak a common language, such as mathematics.

Professor Boulding further postulated that all areas of scientific interest can be categorized according to their level of development.[1] The universe, for example, can be viewed as a hierarchy of system levels where all things exist at some level within the structure. Boulding's classification model looks like this:

1. The first level is that of static structure. It might be called the level of frameworks; for example, the anatomy of the universe.
2. The next level is that of the simple dynamic system with predetermined, necessary motions. This might be called the level of clockworks.
3. The third level is the control mechanism, or cybernetic system, which might be nicknamed the level of the thermostat. The system is self-regulating in maintaining equilibrium.
4. The fourth level is that of the "open system" or self-maintaining structure. This is the level at which life begins to differentiate from not-life; it might be called the cell.
5. The next level might be called the genetic-societal level; it is typified by the plant, and it dominates the empirical world of the botanist.
6. The animal system level is characterized by mobility, teleological behavior, and self-awareness.
7. The next level is the "human" level, that is, of the individual human being considered as a system with self-awareness and the ability to utilize language and symbolism.
8. The social system or systems of human organization constitute the next level with the consideration of the content and meaning of messages, the nature and dimensions of value systems, the transcription of images into historical record, the symbolizations of art, music, and poetry, and the complex gamut of human emotion.
9. Transcendental systems complete the classification of levels. These are the ultimates and absolutes and the inescapables and unknowables, and they also exhibit systematic structure and relationship.

Although these nine levels appear somewhat vague, they can be categorized. The first three levels can be classified as the mechanical or physical sciences and provide knowledge for the physical sciences, astronomy, physics, and

---

1. Kenneth E. Boulding, "General Systems Theory: The Skeleton of Science," *Management Science,* Vol. 2, No. 3, April 1956, pp. 197–208.

chemistry. The next three levels describe the biological sciences and deal with such subjects as biology, zoology, and botany. The last three levels describe the arts and (social) sciences and consider such disciplines as the social sciences, arts and sciences, religion, and humanities.

It is interesting to note that both Dr. von Bertalanffy and Professor Boulding talk about "disciplines, specialties, and functions." The important usage of these disciplines, specialties, and functions is that they must be able to integrate and interrelate all of the activities so that the proper contribution will be made to each higher level in the hierarchy of systems.

2.2 SYSTEMS THEORY AND BUSINESS[2]

It wasn't until the early sixties that practitioners were able to translate the general systems theories of Professor Boulding and Dr. von Bertalanffy into a meaningful business theory that could be applied to business world problem-solving. In a textbook entitled *The Theory and Management of Systems,* Richard Johnson, Fremont Kast, and James Rosenzweig related the corporate enterprise structure in this nation to an open-ended cell:[3]

An organism is an open system which maintains a constant state while matter and energy which enter it keep changing (so-called dynamic equilibrium). The organism is influenced by, and influences, its environment. Such a description of a system adequately fits the typical business organization. The business organization is a man-made system which has a dynamic interplay with its environment—customers, competitors, labor organizations, suppliers, government and many other agencies. Furthermore, the business organization is a system of interrelated parts working in conjunction with each other in order to accomplish a number of goals, both those of the organization and those of individual participants.

These authors went on to relate how the description of business, as a smoothly running machine, coincided with Boulding's second level of classification—that of clockwork systems. Comparison of a business organization to a human body followed, with skeletal and muscle systems representing the operating line elements and the circulatory system as a necessary staff function. The nervous system stood for the communication system. The brain symbolized top-level

---

2. A majority of the information in this section has been extracted from Col. Alvin Kayloe, "Resource Allocation and Control of the Weapon System Acquisition Process," Ph.D. thesis, University of Colorado, 1969. Reprinted by permission of Col. Alvin Kayloe.
3. R. A. Johnson, F. E. Kast, and J. A. Rosenzweig, *The Theory and Management of Systems,* 2nd edition (New York: McGraw-Hill, 1967).

management or the executive committee. This last description laid the framework for an analysis of an organization as a group of interrelated functions operating toward a common goal.

Almost at once, businessmen and organization theorists began to review the basic idea of applying system theory to business. There was universal acceptance of the Johnson, Kast, and Rosenzweig theory. Franklin Moore summed up the general feeling by stating that the flow of resources is the basic force that identifies the dynamic nature of a system.[4]

This implies the creation of a management technique that is able to cut across many organizational disciplines—such as finance, manufacturing, engineering, marketing, and so on—while still carrying out the functions of management. This technique has come to be called systems management, project management, or matrix management (the terms are used interchangeably).

2.3 DEVELOPMENT OF THE BUSINESS SYSTEM

Modern practitioners of systems management have attempted to redefine the hierarchy of systems first proposed by Boulding so as to obtain a more definitive picture of the business system. A representative grouping of system levels is shown in Figure 2–1. The outermost level represents the upper-level systems, which include the universe, solar system, earth, and homocentric systems. (Some authors prefer to define these as separate levels. Because the attempt here is to accentuate the business system, these levels have been combined.) The second level is the environmental level and includes those effects that may result from economic, social, political, legal, and technological conditions. The interface between the first two levels therefore identifies the way that man interacts with the environment.

The third level is the business firm system. Present-day theoreticians are focusing ever increasing attention on the business system by defining the purpose of the business system as:

- The development of relationships and channels between organizational resources
- So that information can be obtained
- Which will assist in the decision-making process
- Which is a necessary link in order that company goals and objectives can be achieved

---

4. Franklin G. Moore, ed., *A Management Sourcebook* (New York: Harper and Row, 1964), p. 104.

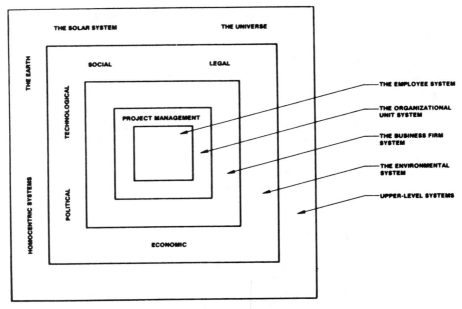

Figure 2-1. The hierarchy of systems.

A variety of business systems and subsystems can exist within the organization. A representative list of such systems could include:

- Organizations systems
- Information systems
  - Informal information systems
  - Formal information systems
  - Management information systems
  - Operating information systems
  - Decision-making information systems
- Financial information systems
- Marketing information systems
- Inventory control systems
- Personnel information systems
- Production/operations information systems

Most business firm systems include such functions as resource control, decision making, and production. The relationships between these functions are shown in Figure 2-2, in which the business firm is represented as a dynamic systems model. For every decision that management makes, actions and strategies are developed to achieve the most effective utilization of the resources of money, equipment, facilities, technology, manpower, and materials. The output from resource control, together with the management policies developed during decision making, provides input to the production function. The output from the production function can be a product, services, or some other form of end-item.

The rate of output of the end-item provides information that is used as feedback for additional management decision-making by comparing the end-item rate of output with environmental and competitive information. This comparison occurs at the interface between the environmental systems level and the business firm level.

The fourth level in the hierarchy of systems is the organizational unit system. This level defines the organizational structure by which management controls the business firm system. It is at this level that project management has an impact upon the organizational unit system. Of course, project management is just one form of organizational structure that can be used at this level.

The fifth and innermost level is the employee system level. It is at this level that the greatest interaction takes place. The interface between the fourth and fifth levels defines the employer–employee relationships that must exist within the business firm. In later chapters we will describe the conflicts and problems that can occur at this interface.

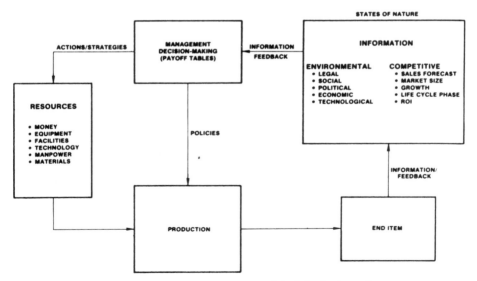

Figure 2–2. A dynamic systems model of the business firm.

Modern business systems are not without their problems, the biggest one being the necessity to respond to a rapidly changing environment. Unfortunately, the response is relatively slow, as was shown in Figure 1–15. Technology and the environment change much faster than the organization can adapt, and as expected, the people subsystem requires additional time to adapt.

The growth of the business system concept was a necessity for companies to compete and survive in the business world. As more and more companies began to expand into multiple product lines, many of which were dissimilar, organizational complexities grew almost without bound. The reasons for this can be attributed to:

- Technology increasing at an astounding rate (especially EDP)
- More and more money invested in R&D
- More and more information available because of rapid feedback of information
- Shortening of project life cycles inducing more and more changes
- Development of decision-making tools as operations research and management science

In order to satisfy the requirements imposed by the above factors, management was "forced" into organizational restructuring; the traditional organizational form which had survived for many decades was now found to be inadequate to integrate activities across functional boundaries.

The introduction of new systems within an organization can create severe adaptability problems. Most individuals, even at top levels of management, are generally reluctant to incorporate new systems and risk "rocking the boat." Adaptation to a new system is often a slow and tedious process. Individual needs must be considered in new system development and incorporation. This includes project management as well.

2.4 MODELING THE BUSINESS SYSTEM

As business system concepts began to grow and mature, more and more emphasis was placed upon development of systems models that could accurately exhibit the actual behavior of the components and demonstrate the ways in which they interrelate to the total picture. Listed below are various groups of systems models:

- Communications
  - Oral
  - Written
- Schematic models

- Static models (set of relationships fixed in time)
  - Bar (Gantt) charts
  - Arrow diagrams
- Flow rate models (flow of relationships)
  - PERT/time
  - PERT/cost
  - Precedence networks
  - CPM
  - Decision trees
- Dynamic models (transformation of relationships)
- Iconic models
- Analog models
- Symbolic (mathematical) models
  - Deterministic
  - Probabilistic
- Conceptual models

Communications models imply, or often assert in words, that certain results will be achieved from specific managerial actions. Unfortunately, such communications models are seldom used for such large, complex relationships as might exist in a business system. In attempting to describe realistic conditions, such models tend to become long and unreadable.

Schematic models are used most frequently and are subdivided into static, flow rate, and dynamic models. Static models define sets of relationships that are fixed in time. They are almost always described by some form of chart showing the start and end date for some activity. Flow rate models identify the flow of relationships of activities shown on the static model charts; flow rate models show the start and end dates of activities just as the static models did, but also show the interrelationships between these activities. Static and flow rate models are the types most often used in project management and will be described in depth in later chapters.

Dynamic models are the third classification of schematic models and identify the transformation of relationships rather than activities. These models are most effective in describing total systems, as was shown in Figure 2–2. Dynamic models tend to become "black boxes" in which an input is somehow manipulated by a processor so as to obtain an output. A feedback loop between the output and input provides data for corrective action to be taken in order to achieve the desired output. In Figure 2–2, resources would be the input, policies and production would be the processor, and the end-item would be the output.

Iconic, analog, symbolic, and conceptual models are also sometimes used to describe systems. Iconic models are either scaled-up or scaled-down replicas of

72 PROJECT MANAGEMENT

an actual system. Operational trainers, such as those used for pilot training, would be an example. Analog models are a means of representing physical properties of the system by other physical properties. For example, the gas gauge in an automobile represents the gasoline level in a fuel tank. Symbolic models attempt to represent the properties and relationships of the system elements through symbolic or mathematical expressions and equations.

Many operations research models are also symbolic models. Consider a model describing the amount of inventory that should be maintained. If the inventory demand is unknown, then probability theory must be used, and the symbolic model can then be defined as a probabilistic model (based upon probability theory), in which case the final result can be a hit-or-miss condition. If the demand and other variables are known with certainty, then the predictions should be exact, and the opportunity for chance should be minimal. Under such conditions we redefine the symbolic model as a deterministic model.

Conceptual models are nonmathematical models that attempt to describe a concept or theory that could simply be a figment of the individual's imagination. Conceptual models are most often used in such hard research sciences as physics, chemistry, and engineering.

2.5 SYSTEMS, PROGRAMS, AND PROJECTS: A DEFINITION

In the preceding sections the word "systems" has been used rather loosely. The exact definition of a system depends upon the users, environment, and ultimate goal. Modern business practitioners define a system as:

> A group of elements, either human or nonhuman, that is organized and arranged in such a way that the elements can act as a whole toward achieving some common goal, objective, or end.

Systems are collections of interacting subsystems that either span or interconnect all schools of management. Systems, if properly organized, can provide a synergistic output.

Systems are characterized by their boundaries or interface conditions. For example, referring back to Figure 2–1, if the business firm system were completely isolated from the environmental system, then a closed system would exist, in which case management would have complete control over all system components. If the business system does in fact react with the environment, then the system is referred to as open. All social systems, for example, are categorized as open systems. Open systems must have permeable boundaries.

If a system is significantly dependent upon other systems for its survival, then the system can be further defined as an extended system. Not all open systems are extended systems. Extended systems are ever changing ones and can impose great hardships upon individuals who desire to work in a regimented atmosphere. Flippo and Munsinger provide further definitions for extended systems:[5]

The concept of extended systems must also include significant others in the environment who have control over resources required by the system, and who consume its outputs. Not only is there dependency and consequent significant interface with labor unions, but the extended system must also include suppliers of materials, financial institutions, government, consumer pressure groups, educational institutions, and customers. In large systems, specialized personnel are often hired to function in the boundary-spanning positions working toward a better matching of the interfaces.

Military and government organizations were the first to attempt to define clearly the boundaries of systems, programs, and projects. Below are two such definitions for systems:

- Air Force
  - A composite of equipment, skills, and techniques capable of performing and/or supporting an operational role. A complete system includes related facilities, equipment, material services, and personnel required for its operation to the degree that it can be considered as a self-sufficient unit in its intended operational and/or support environment.
- NASA
  - One of the principal functioning entities comprising the project hardware within a project or program. The meaning may vary to suit a particular project or program area. Ordinarily a "system" is the first major subdivision of project work;(spacecraft systems, launch vehicle systems).

Systems tend to imply an infinite lifetime, but with constant upgrading.

Programs can be construed as the necessary first-level elements of a system. Two representative definitions of programs are given below:

- Air Force
  - The integrated, time-phased tasks necessary to accomplish a particular purpose.
- NASA
  - A relative series of undertakings which continue over a period of time (normally years) and which are designed to accomplish a broad, sci-

---

5. E. B. Flippo and G. M. Munsinger, *Management,* 3rd edition (Boston: Allyn and Bacon, 1976), p. 9.

entific or technical goal in the NASA long-range plan; (lunar and planetary exploration, manned spacecraft systems.)

Programs can be regarded as subsystems. However, programs are generally defined as time-phased efforts, whereas systems exist on a continuous basis.

Projects are also time-phased efforts (much shorter than programs) and are the first level of breakdown of a program. A typical definition would be:

- NASA/Air Force
  - A project is within a program as an undertaking with a scheduled beginning and end, and which normally involves some primary purpose.

As shown in Table 2–1, the government sector tends to run efforts as programs, headed by a program manager. The majority of the industrial sector, on the other hand, prefers to describe efforts as projects, headed by a project manager. Whether we call our undertaking project management or program management is inconsequential because the same policies, procedures, and guidelines that regulate programs most often apply to projects also. For the remainder of this text, programs and projects will be discussed interchangeably. However, the reader should be aware that projects are normally the first-level subdivision of a program. This breakdown will be discussed in Chapter 11.

Once a group of tasks is selected and considered to be a project, the next step is to define the kinds of project units. There are four categories of projects:

- Individual projects: These are short-duration projects normally assigned to a single individual who may be acting as both a project manager and a functional manager.
- Staff projects: These are projects that can be accomplished by one organizational unit, say a department. A staff or task force is developed from each section involved. This works best if only one functional unit is involved.
- Special projects: Very often special projects occur that require certain pri-

Table 2–1. Definition Summary.

LEVEL	SECTOR	TITLE
System*	—	—
Program	Government	Program managers
Project	Industry	Project managers

*Definitions, as used here, do not include in-house industrial systems such as management information systems or shop floor control systems.

mary functions and/or authority to be assigned temporarily to other individuals or units. This works best for short-duration projects. Long-term projects can lead to severe conflicts under this arrangement.

- Matrix or aggregate projects: These require input from a large number of functional units and usually control vast resources.

Each of these categories of projects can require different responsibilities, job descriptions, policies, and procedures.

Project management may now be defined as the process of achieving project objectives through the traditional organizational structure and over the specialties of the individuals concerned. Project management is applicable for any ad hoc (unique, one-time, one-of-a-kind) undertaking concerned with a specific end objective. In order to complete a task, a project manager must:

- Set objectives
- Establish plans
- Organize resources
- Staff
- Set up controls
- Issue directives
- Motivate personnel
- Apply innovation for alternative actions
- Remain flexible

The type of project will often dictate which of these functions a project manager will be required to perform.

2.6 PRODUCT VS. PROJECT MANAGEMENT: A DEFINITION

For all practical purposes, there is no basic difference between program management and project management. But what about product management? Project management and product management are similar, with one major exception: the project manager focuses on the end date of his project, whereas the product manager is not willing to admit that his product line will ever end. The product manager wants his product to be as long-lived and profitable as possible. Even when the demand for the product diminishes, the product manager will always look for spin-offs to keep his product alive.

Figure 2–3 shows the relationship between project and product management. When the project is in the R&D phase, a project manager is involved. Once the product is developed and introduced into the marketplace, control is taken over by the product manager. In some situations, the project manager can become the product manager. Both product and project management can, and do, exist concurrently within companies.

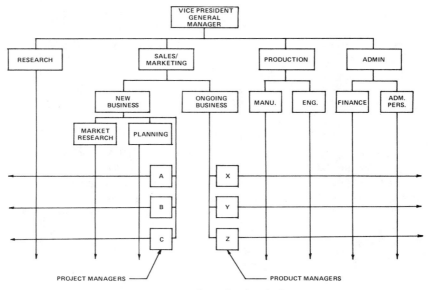

Figure 2–3. Organizational chart.

Figure 2–3 shows that product management can operate horizontally as well as vertically. When a product is shown horizontally on the organizational chart, the implication is that the product line is not big enough to control its own resources full-time and therefore shares key functional resources similarly to project management. If the product line were large enough to control its own resources full-time, it would be shown as a separate division or a vertical line on the organization chart.

Also shown in Figure 2–3 is the remarkable fact that the project manager (or project engineer) is reporting to a marketing-type person. Should executives permit project managers and project engineers to report to a marketing-type individual even if the project entails a great amount of engineering? Many executives today would attest that the answer is "yes." The reason for this is that technically oriented project leaders get too involved with the technical details of the project and lose insight into when and how to "kill" a project. Remember, most technical leaders have been trained in an academic rather than a business environment. Their commitment to success often does not take into account such important parameters as return on investment, profitability, competition, and marketability.

To alleviate these problems, project managers and project engineers, especially on R&D-type projects, are now reporting to marketing so that marketing input will be included in all R&D decisions. Many executives have been forced into this position because of the high costs incurred during R&D, especially since, in case of a severe need to reduce costs, the R&D organization is usually the first to feel the pinch. Executives must exercise caution with regard to this structure in which both product and project managers report to the marketing function. The marketing executive could become the focal point of the entire organization, with the capability of building a very large empire.

2.7 PROJECT LIFE CYCLES

Every program, project, or product has certain phases of development. A clear understanding of these phases permits managers and executives to better control total corporate resources in the achievement of desired goals. The phases of development are known as life-cycle phases. However, the breakdown and terminology of these phases differ, depending upon whether we are discussing products or projects.

During the past few years, there has been at least partial agreement about the life-cycle phases of a product. They include:

- Research and development
- Market introduction
- Growth
- Maturity
- Deterioration
- Death

Today, there is no agreement among industries, or even companies within the same industry, about the life-cycle phases of a project. This is understandable because of the complex nature and diversity of projects.

The theoretical definitions of the life-cycle phases of a system, as defined by Cleland and King, can be applied to a project.[6] These phases include:

- Conceptual
- Definition
- Production
- Operational
- Divestment

The first phase, the conceptual phase, includes the preliminary evaluation of an idea. Table 2–2 defines the efforts attributed to this phase. Most important

---

6. D. I. Cleland and W. R. King, *Systems Analysis and Project Management* (New York: McGraw-Hill, 1975), pp. 187–190.

Table 2-2. Conceptual Phase.

- Determine existing needs or potential deficiencies of existing systems
- Establish system concepts which provide initial strategic guidance to overcome existing or potential deficiencies
- Determine initial technical, environmental and economic feasibility and practicability of the system
- Examine alternative ways of accomplishing the system objectives
- Provide initial answers to the questions
  - What will the system cost?
  - When will the system be available?
  - What will the system do?
  - How will the system be integrated into existing systems?
- Identify the human and nonhuman resources required to support the system
- Select initial system designs which will satisfy the system objectives
- Determine initial system interfaces
- Establish a system organization

From *Systems Analysis and Project Management* by David I. Cleland and William Richard King. Copyright © 1968, 1975 by McGraw-Hill, Inc. Used with permission of McGraw-Hill Book Company. p. 187.

in this phase is a preliminary analysis of risk and the resulting impact on the time, cost, and performance requirements, together with the potential impact on company resources. The conceptual phase also includes a "first cut" at the feasibility of the effort.

The second phase is the definition phase, and, as shown in Table 2-3, it is mainly a refinement of the elements described under the conceptual phase. The definition phase requires a firm identification of the resources to be required together with the establishment of realistic time, cost, and performance param-

Table 2-3. Definition Phase.

- Firm identification of the human and nonhuman resources required
- Preparation of the final system performance requirements
- Preparation of the detailed plans required to support the system
- Determination of realistic cost, schedule and performance requirements
- Identification of those areas of the system where high risk and uncertainty exist, and delineation of plans for further exploration of these areas
- Definition of intersystem and intrasystem interfaces
- Determination of necessary support subsystems
- Identification and initial preparation of the documents required to support the system, such as policies, procedures, job descriptions, budget and funding papers, letters, memoranda, etc.

From *Systems Analysis and Project Management* by David I. Cleland and William Richard King. Copyright © 1968, 1975 by McGraw-Hill, Inc. Used with permission of McGraw-Hill Book Company. p. 188.

eters. This phase also includes the initial preparation of all documentation necessary to support the system. For a project based upon competitive bidding, the conceptual phase would include the decision of whether or not to bid, and the definition phase would include the development of the total bid package (i.e., time, schedule, cost, and performance).

Analyzing system costs during the conceptual and definition phases is not an easy task because of the amount of estimating involved. As shown in Figure 2–4, most project or system costs can be broken down into operating (recurring) and implementation (nonrecurring) categories. The implementation costs include one-time expenses such as construction of a new facility, purchasing computer hardware, or detailed planning. Operating costs, on the other hand, include recurring expenses such as manpower. The operating costs may be reduced as shown in Figure 2–4 if personnel perform at a higher position on the learning curve. The identification of a learning curve position is vitally important during the definition phase when firm cost positions must be established. Of course, it is not always possible to know what individuals will be available or how soon they can perform at a higher learning curve position.

Once the approximate total cost of the project is determined, a cost–benefit analysis should be conducted similar to Figure 2–5 to determine if the estimated value of the information obtained from the system exceeds the cost of obtaining the information. This analysis is often included as part of a feasibility study. There are several situations, such as in competitive bidding, where the

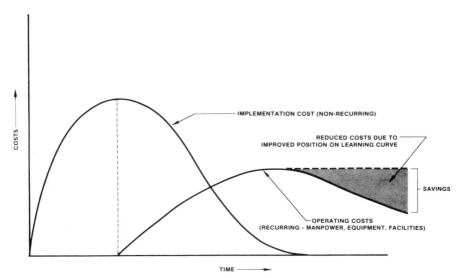

Figure 2–4. System costs.

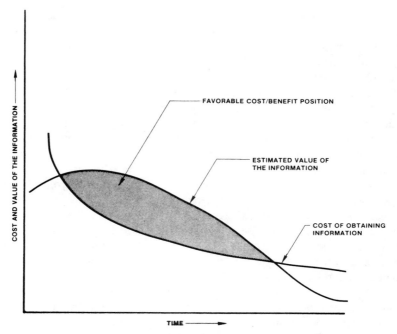

Figure 2–5. Cost/benefit analysis.

feasibility study is actually the conceptual and definition phases. Because of the costs that can be incurred during these two phases, top-management approval is almost always necessary before the initiation of such a feasibility study.

The third phase is the production (or acquisition) phase and includes such items as those listed in Table 2–4. This phase is predominantly a testing and final standardization effort so that operations can begin. Almost all documentation must be completed in this phase.

The fourth phase is the operational phase and, as shown in Table 2–5, integrates the project's product or services into the existing organization. If the project were developed for establishment of a marketable product, then this phase could include the product life-cycle phases of market introduction, growth, maturity, and a portion of deterioration.

The final phase, as shown in Table 2–6, is divestment and includes the reallocation of resources. The question to be answered is, "Where should the resources be reassigned?" Consider a company that sells products on the open consumer market. As one product begins the deterioration and death phases of its life cycle (i.e. the divestment phase of a system), then new products or proj-

Table 2–4. Production Phase.

- Updating of detailed plans conceived and defined during the preceding phases
- Identification and management of the resources required to facilitate the production processes such as inventory, supplies, labor, funds, etc.
- Verification of system production specifications
- Beginning of production, construction, and installation
- Final preparation and dissemination of policy and procedural documents
- Performance of final testing to determine adequacy of the system to do the things it is intended to do
- Development of technical manuals and affiliated documentation describing how the system is intended to operate
- Development of plans to support the system during its operational phase

From *Systems Analysis and Project Management* by David I. Cleland and William Richard King. Copyright © 1968, 1975 by McGraw-Hill, Inc. Used with permission of McGraw-Hill Book Company. p. 188.

Table 2-5. Operational Phase.

- Use of the system results by the intended user or customer
- Actual integration of the project's product or service into existing organizational systems
- Evaluation of the technical, social, and economic sufficiency of the project to meet actual operating conditions
- Provision of feedback to organizational planners concerned with developing new projects and systems
- Evaluation of the adequacy of supporting systems

From *Systems Analysis and Project Management* by David I. Cleland and William Richard King. Copyright © 1968, 1975 by McGraw-Hill, Inc. Used with permission of McGraw-Hill Book Company. p. 189.

Table 2-6. Divestment Phase.

- System phasedown
- Development of plans transferring responsibility to supporting organizations
- Divestment or transfer of resources to other systems
- Development of "lessons learned from system" for inclusion in qualitative-quantitative data base to include:
  - Assessment of image by the customer
  - Major problems encountered and their solution
  - Technological advances
  - Advancements in knowledge relative to department strategic objectives
  - New or improved management techniques
  - Recommendations for future research and development
  - Recommendations for the management of future programs, including interfaces with with associate contractors
  - Other major lessons learned during the course of the system

From *Systems Analysis and Project Management* by David I. Cleland and William Richard King. Copyright © 1968, 1975 by McGraw-Hill, Inc. Used with permission of McGraw-Hill Book Company. p. 190.

ects must be established. Such a company would, therefore, require a continuous stream of projects as a necessity for survival, as shown in Figure 2–6. As projects A and B begin their decline, new efforts (project C) must be developed for resource reallocation. In the ideal situation these new projects will be established at such a rate that total revenue will increase and company growth will be clearly visible.

The divestment phase evaluates the efforts on the total system and serves as input to the conceptual phases for new projects and systems. This final phase also has an impact on other ongoing projects with regard to priority identification.

Thus far no attempt has been made to identify the size of a project or system. Large projects generally require full-time staffs, whereas small projects, although they undergo the same system life-cycle phases, may require only part-time people. This implies that an individual can be responsible for multiple projects, possibly with each project existing in a different life-cycle phase. The following questions must be considered in multi-project management:

- Are the project objectives the same?
  - For the good of the project?

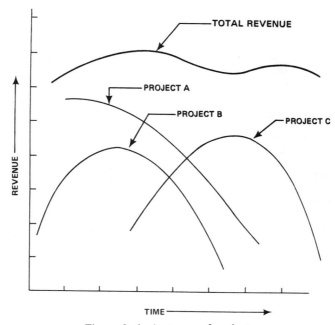

Figure 2–6. A stream of projects.

- For the good of the company?
- Is there a distinction between large and small projects?
- How do we handle conflicting priorities?
  - Critical vs. critical projects
  - Critical vs. noncritical projects
  - Noncritical vs. noncritical projects

Later chapters will discuss methods of resolving conflicts and establishing priorities.

The phases of a project and those of a product are compared in Figure 2–7. Notice that the life-cycle phases of a product generally do not overlap, whereas the phases of a project can and often do overlap.

Table 2–7 identifies the various life-cycle phases that are commonly used. Even in mature project management industries such as construction, one could survey ten different construction companies and find ten different definitions for the life cycle phases.

The life cycle phases for computer programming, as listed in Table 2–7, are also shown in Figure 2–8 to illustrate how manpower resources can build up and decline during a project. In Figure 2–8, PMO is the present method of operations, and PMO′ will be the "new" present method of operations after conversion. This life cycle would probably be representative of a twelve-month activity. Most executives prefer short data processing life cycles because computer technology changes at a very rapid rate. An executive of a major utility commented that his company was having trouble determining how to terminate a computer programming project to improve customer service because by the time a package is ready for full implementation, an updated version appears on the scene. Should the original project be canceled and a new project begun? The solution appears to lie in establishing short data processing project life-cycle phases, perhaps through segmented implementation. In any case, we can conclude that:

- Top management is responsible for the periodic review of major projects. This should be accomplished, at a minimum, at the completion of each life-cycle phase.

More and more companies are preparing procedural manuals for project management and for structuring work using life-cycle phases. There are several reasons for this trend:

- Clear delineation of the work to be accomplished in each phase may be possible.

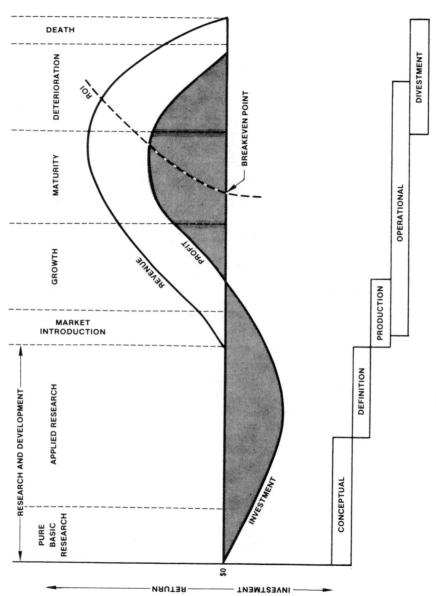

Figure 2–7. System/product life cycles.

Table 2-7. Life Cycle Phase Definitions.

ENGINEERING	MANUFACTURING	COMPUTER PROGRAMMING	CONSTRUCTION
• Startup	• Formation	• Conceptual	• Planning, data
• Definition	• Buildup	• Planning	gathering and
• Main	• Production	• Definition and design	procedures
• Termination	• Phase-out	• Implementation	• Studies and basic
	• Final audit	• Conversion	engineering
			• Major review
			• Detail engineering
			• Detail engineering/
			construction
			overlap
			• Construction
			• Testing and
			commissioning

- Pricing and estimating may be easier if well-structured work definitions exist.
- There exist key decision points at the end of each life cycle phase so that incremental funding is possible.

As a final note, the reader should be aware that not all projects can be simply transposed into life-cycle phases (e.g., R&D). In such a case it might be possible (even in the same company) for different life-cycle-phase definitions to

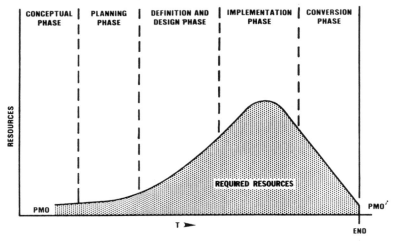

Figure 2-8. Definition of a project life cycle.

exist because of schedule length, complexity, or just the difficulty of managing them.

2.8 SYSTEMS THINKING

Ultimately, all decisions and policies are made on the basis of judgments; there is not any other way, and there never will be. In the end, analysis is but an aid to the judgment and intuition of the decision-maker.

The systems approach may be defined as a logical and disciplined process of problem solving. The word process indicates an active ongoing system that is fed by input from its parts.

Systems approach definitions should be considered. The systems approach:

- Forces review of the interrelationship of the various subsystems.
- Is a dynamic process that integrates all activities into a meaningful total system.
- Systematically assembles and matches the parts of the system into a unified whole.
- Seeks an optimal solution or strategy in solving a problem.

The systems approach to problem solving has phases of development similar to the life-cycle phases shown in Figure 2–7. These phases are defined as follows:

- *Translation:* Terminology, problem objective, and criteria and constraints are defined and accepted by all participants.
- *Analysis:* All possible approaches to or alternatives to the solution of the problem are stated.
- *Trade-off:* Selection criteria and constraints are applied to the alternatives to meet the objective.
- *Synthesis:* The best solution in reaching the objective of the system is the result of the combination of analysis and trade-off phases.

Other terms essential to the systems approach are as follows:

- *Objective:* The function of the system or the strategy that must be achieved.
- *Requirement:* A partial need to satisfy the objective.
- *Alternative:* One of the selected ways to implement and satisfy a requirement.
- *Selection criteria:* Performance factors used in evaluating the alternatives to select a preferable alternative.

- *Constraint:* An absolute factor—which describes conditions that the alternatives *must* meet.

A common error by potential decision-makers (those dissatisfied individuals with authority to act) who base their thinking solely on subjective experience, judgment, and intuition is that they fail to recognize the existence of alternatives. Subjective thinking is inhibited or affected by personal bias resulting from conditions within the brain and sense organs.

Objective thinking, on the other hand, is a fundamental characteristic of the systems approach and is exhibited or characterized by emphasis upon the tendency to view events, phenomena, and ideas as external and apart from self-consciousness. Objective thinking is unprejudiced and exists independent of the mind.

The systems analysis process, as shown in Figure 2–9, begins with systematic examination and comparison of those alternative actions that are related to the accomplishment of the desired objective. The alternatives are then compared on the basis of the resource cost and the associated benefits. The inputs from the constraints and limitations identify the explicit consideration of the uncertainty variables. The loop is then completed using feedback in order to determine how compatible each alternative is with the objectives of the organization.

The above analysis can be arranged in steps:

- Input data to mental process.
- Analyze data.
- Predict outcomes.
- Evaluate outcomes and compare alternatives.
- Choose the best alternative.
- Take action.
- Measure results and compare them with predictions.

The systems approach to thinking is most effective if individuals can be trained to be ready with alternative actions that directly tie in with the prediction of outcomes. The basic tool is the outcome array, which represents the matrix of all possible circumstances. This outcome array can be developed only if the decision-maker thinks in terms of the wide scope of possible outcomes. Outcome descriptions force the decision-maker to spell out clearly just what he is trying to achieve (i.e., his objectives).

Systems thinking is vital for the success of a project. Project management systems urgently need new ways of strategically viewing, questioning, and analyzing project needs for alternative nontechnical as well as technical solutions. The ability to analyze the total project, rather than the individual parts, is the first prerequisite for successful project management.

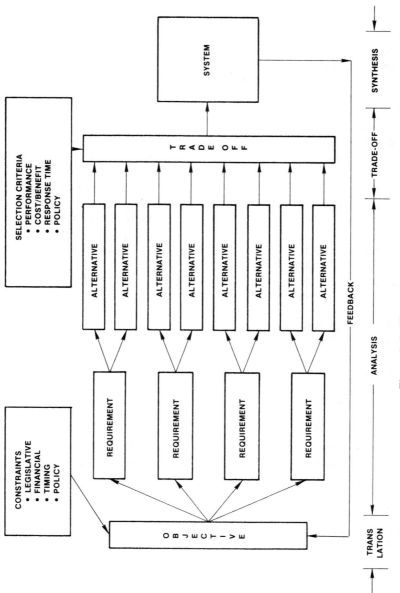

Figure 2–9. The systems approach.

PROBLEMS

2–1 Can the organizational chart of a company be considered as a systems model? If so, what kind of systems model?

2–2 Do you think that someone could be a good systems manager but a poor project manager? What about the reverse situation? State any assumptions that you may have to make.

2–3 Can we consider R&D as a system? If so, under what circumstances?

2–4 For each of the following projects, state whether we are discussing an open, closed, or extended system:

   a. A high-technology project
   b. New product R&D
   c. An on-line computer system for a bank
   d. Construction of a chemical plant
   e. Developing an in-house cost accounting reporting system

2–5 Can an entire organization be considered as a model? If so, what type?

2–6 Systems can be defined as a combination or interrelationship of subsystems. Does a project have subsystems?

2–7 If a system can, in fact, be broken down into subsystems, what problems can occur during integration?

2–8 How could suboptimization occur during systems thinking and analysis?

2–9 Would a cost–benefit analysis be easier or harder to perform in a traditional or project management organizational structure?

2–10 What impact could the product life cycle have upon the selection of the project organizational structure?

2–11 In the development of a system, what criteria should be used to determine where one phase begins, when another phase ends, and where overlap can occur?

2–12 Consider the following expression: "Damn the torpedoes: full-speed ahead." Is it possible that this military philosophy can be applied to project management and lead to project success?

2–13 A typical construction project has the following seven phases. Compare these phases to those defined by Cleland and King.

   Phase I—Planning, data gathering, and procedures
   Phase II—Studies and basic engineering
   Phase III—Major review
   Phase IV—Detail engineering
   Phase V—Detail engineering/construction overlap
   Phase VI—Construction
   Phase VII—Testing and commissioning

2-14 Consider a project that has life-cycle phases as defined by Cleland and King in Tables 2–2 through 2–6. State whether each of these phases would be of a short or long duration for:

   a. A computer project
   b. R&D
   c. New product introduction
   d. A home construction project
   e. Construction of a nuclear power plant

2-15 Considering the Cleland and King definition of the various life-cycles phases of a project, plot resources required as a function of time and identify each life-cycle phase in your figure.

CASE STUDY: L. P. MANNING CORPORATION

In March 1977, the Marketing Division of the L. P. Manning Corporation performed a national survey to test the public's reaction to a new type of toaster. Manning had achieved success in the past and established themselves as a leader in the home appliance industry.

Although the new toaster was just an idea, the public responded favorably. In April of the same year, the vice presidents for planning, marketing, engineering, and manufacturing all met to formulate plans for the development and ultimately the production of the new toaster. Marketing asserted that the manufacturing cost must remain below $30 per unit or else Manning Corporation would not be competitive. Based upon the specifications drawn up in the meeting, manufacturing assured marketing that this cost could be met.

The engineering division was given six months to develop the product. Manning's executives were eager to introduce the product for the Christmas rush. This might give them an early foothold on a strong market share.

During the R&D phase, marketing continually "pestered" engineering with new designs and changes in specifications such that the new product would be easier to market. The ultimate result was a one-month slip in the schedule.

Pushing the schedule to the right greatly displeased manufacturing personnel. According to the vice-president for manufacturing, speaking to the marketing manager: "I've just received the final specifications and designs from engineering. This is not what we had agreed upon last March. These changes will cause us to lose at least one additional month to change our manufacturing planning. And because we're already one month behind, I don't see any way that we could reschedule our Christmas production facilities to accommodate this new product. Our established lines must come first. Furthermore, our estimating department says that these changes will increase the cost of the product by at least 25 to 35 percent. And, of course, we must include the quality control section which has some question as to whether or not we can actually live with these specifications. Why don't we just cancel this project or at least postpone it until next year?"

CASE STUDY: PROJECT FIRECRACKER

"Don, project management is the only way to handle this type of project. With forty million dollars at stake we can't afford not to use this approach."

"Listen, Jeff, your problem is you take seminars given by these ivory tower professors and you think you're an expert. I've been in this business for forty years and I know how to handle this job—and it isn't through project management."

History and Background

Jeff Pankoff, a registered professional engineer, came to work for National Corporation after receiving a mechanical engineering degree. After he arrived at National he was assigned to the engineering department. Soon thereafter, Jeff realized that he needed to know more about statistics, and he enrolled in the graduate school of a local university. When he was near completion of his masters of science, National transferred Jeff to one of its subsidiaries in Ireland to set up an engineering department. After a successful three years, Jeff returned to National's home office and was promoted to chief engineer. Jeff's department increased to eighty engineers and technicians. Spending a considerable time in administration, Jeff decided an MBA would be useful, so he enrolled in a program at a nearby university. At the time when this project began, Jeff was near the end of the MBA program.

National Corporation, a large international corporation with annual sales of about $600 million, employs 8,000 people worldwide and is a specialty machine, component, and tool producer catering to the automotive and aircraft manufacturers. The company is over a hundred years old and has a successful and profitable record.

National is organized in divisions according to machine, component, and tool production facilities. Each division is operated as a profit center. (See Exhibit 2–1.) Jeff was assigned to the Tool Division.

National's Tool Division produces a broad line of regular tools as well as specials. Specials amounted to only about 10 percent of the regular business, but over the last five years had increased from 5 percent to the current 10 percent. Only specials that were similar to the regular tools were accepted as orders.

National sells all its products through about 3,000 industrial distributors located throughout the United States. In addition, National employs 200 sales representatives who work with the various distributors to provide product seminars.

The traditional approach to project assignments is used. The engineering department, headed by Jeff, is basically responsible for the purchase of capital equipment and the selection of production methods used in the manufacture of the product. Project assignments to evaluate and purchase a new machine tool or to determine the production routing for a new product are assigned to the engineering department. Jeff assigns the project to the appropriate section, and under the direction of a project engineer, the project is completed.

The project engineer works with all the departments reporting to the vice president, including production, personnel, plant engineering, product design (the project engineer's link to sales), and time study. As an example of the working relationship, the

Exhibit 2-1.

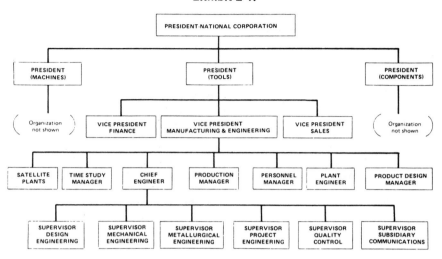

project engineer selects the location of the new machine and devises instructions for its operation with production. With personnel the engineer establishes the job description for the new job as well as for the selection of people to work on the new machine. The project engineer works with plant engineering on the moving of the machine to the proper location and instructs plant engineering on the installation and services required (air, water, electricity, gas, etc.). It is very important that the project engineer work very closely with the product design department, which develops the design of the product to be sold. Many times the product designed is too ambitious an undertaking or cannot be economically produced. Interaction between departments is essential in working out such problems.

After the new machine is installed, an operator is selected and the machine is ready for production. Time study, with the project engineer's help, then establishes the incentive system for the job.

Often a customer requests certain tolerances that cannot be adhered to by manufacturing. In such a case, the project engineer contacts the product design department, which contacts the sales department, which in turn contacts the customer. The communication process is then reversed, and the project engineer gets an answer. Based upon the number of questions, the total process may take four to five weeks.

As the company is set up, the engineering department has no authority over time study, production, product design, etc. The only way that the project engineer can get these departments to make commitments is through persuasion or through the chief engineer, who could go to the vice president of manufacturing and engineering. If the engineer is convincing, the vice president will dictate to the appropriate manager what must be done.

Salaries in all departments of the company are a closely guarded secret. Only the vicepresident, the appropriate department manager, and the individual know the exact salary. Don Wolinski, the vice-president of manufacturing and engineering, pointed out that this approach was the "professional way" and an essential aspect of smooth business operations.

The Ill-Fated Project

Jeff Pankoff, the chief engineer for National, flew to Southern California to one of National's (tool) plants. Ben Ehlke, manager of the Southern California plant (SCP), wanted to purchase a computer numerical controlled (CNC) machining center for $250,000. When the request came to Jeff for approval, he had many questions and wanted some face-to-face communication.

The Southern California plant supplied the aircraft industry, and one airplane company provided 90 percent of SCP's sales. Jeff was mainly concerned about the sales projections used by Ehlke in the justification of the machining center. Ehkle pointed out that this was based on what the airplane company had told him they expected to buy over the next five years. Since this estimate was crucial to the justification, Jeff suggested that a meeting be arranged with the appropriate people at the airplane company to explore these projections. Since the local National sales representative was ill, the distributor salesman, Jack White, accompanied Jeff and Ben. While at the airplane company (APC), the chief tool buyer of APC, Tom Kelly, was informed that Jeff was there. Jeff received a message from the receptionist that Tom Kelly wanted to see Jeff before he left the building. After the sales projections were reviewed and Jeff was convinced that they were as accurate and as reliable as they possibly could be, he asked the receptionist to set up an appointment with Tom Kelly.

When Jeff walked into Kelly's office the fireworks began. He was greeted with, "What's wrong with National? They refused to quote on this special part. We sent them a print and asked National for their price and delivery, indicating it could turn into a sizable order. They turned me down flat saying that they were not tooled up for this business. Now I know that National is tops in the field and that National can provide this part. What's wrong with your sales department?"

All this came as a complete surprise to Jeff. The distributor salesman knew about it but never thought to mention it to him. Jeff looked at the part print and asked, "What kind of business are you talking about?" Kelly said, without batting an eye, "Forty million dollars per year."

Jeff realized that National had the expertise to produce the part and would require only one added machine (a special press costing $20,000) to have the total manufacturing capability. Jeff also realized he was in an awkward situation. The National sales representative was not there, and he certainly could not speak for sales. However, a $40 million order could not be passed over lightly. Kelly indicated that he would like to see National get 90 percent of the order if they would only quote on the job. Jeff told Kelly that he would take the information back and discuss it with the vice presidents of sales, manufacturing, and engineering and that most likely the sales vice president would contact him next.

On the return flight, Jeff reviewed in his mind his meeting with Kelly. Why did Bob Jones, National's sales vice president, refuse to quote? Did he know about the possible

$40 million order? Although Jeff wasn't in sales, he decided that he would do whatever possible to land this order for National. That evening Jack White called from California. Jack said he had talked to Kelly after Jeff left and told Kelly that if anybody could make this project work, it would be Jeff Pankoff. Jeff suggested that Jack White call Bob Jones with future reports concerning this project.

The next morning, before Jeff had a chance to review his mail, Bob Jones came storming into his office. "Who do you think you are committing National to accept an order on your own without even a sales representative present? You know that all communication with a customer is through sales."

Jeff replied, "Let me explain what happened."

After Jeff's explanation, Jones said, "Jeff, I hear what you're saying, but no matter what the circumstances, all communications with any customer must go through proper channels."

Following the meeting with Jones, Jeff went to see Wolinski, his boss. He filled Wolinski in on what had happened. Then he said, "Don, I've given this project considerable thought. Jones is agreeable to quoting this job. However, if we follow our normal channels, we will experience too many time delays and problems. Through the various stages of this project, the customer will have many questions and changes and will require continuous updating. Our current system will not allow this to happen. It will take work from all departments to implement this project, and unless all departments work under the same priority system, we won't have a chance. What we need, Don, is project management. Without this approach where one man heads the project with authority from the top, we just can't make it work."

Wolinski looked out the window and said, "We have been successful for many years using our conventional approach to project work. I grant you that we have not had an order of this magnitude to worry about, but I see no reason why we should change even if the order were for 100 million dollars."

"Don, project management is the only way to handle this type of project. With forty million dollars at stake we can't afford not to use this approach."

"Listen Jeff, your problem is you take seminars given by these ivory tower professors and you think you're an expert. I've been in this business for forty years and I know how to handle this job—and it isn't through project management. I'll call a meeting of all concerned department managers so we can get started on quoting this job."

That afternoon, Jeff and the other five department managers were summoned to a meeting in Wolinski's office. Wolinski summarized the situation and informed the assembled group that Jeff would be responsible for the determination of the methods of manufacture and the associated manufacturing costs that would be used in the quotation. The method of manufacture, of course, would be based upon the design of the part provided by product design. Wolinski appointed Jeff and Waldo Novak, manager of product design, as co-heads of the project. He further advised that the normal channels of communication with sales through the product design manager would continue as usual on this project.

The project began. Jeff spent considerable time requesting clarification of the drawings submitted by the customer. All these communications went through Waldo. Before the manufacturing routing could be established for quotation purposes, questions concerning the drawing had to be answered. The customer was getting anxious to receive the quotation because their management had to select a supplier within eight weeks. One week was already lost owing to communication delay. Wolinski decided that to speed up the quoting process he would send Jeff and Waldo along with Jones, the sales vice president, to see the customer. This meeting at APC helped clarify many questions. After Jeff returned, he began laying out the alternative routing for the parts. He assigned two of his most creative technicians and an engineer to run isolated tests on the various methods of manufacturing. From the results he would then finalize the routing that would be used for quoting. Two weeks of the eight were gone, but Jeff was generally pleased until the phone rang. It was Waldo.

"Say Jeff, I think if we change the design on the back side of the part, it will add to its strength. In fact, I've assigned one of my men to review this and make this change, and it looks good."

While this conversation was going on, Wolinski popped into Jeff's office and said that sales had promised that National would ship APC a test order of 100 pieces in two weeks. Jeff was irate. Product design was changing the product. Sales was promising delivery of a test order that no one could even describe yet.

Needless to say, the next few days were long and difficult. It took three days for Jeff and Waldo to resolve the design routing problem. Wolinski stayed in the background and would not make any position statement except he wanted everything "yesterday." By the end of the third week the design problem was resolved, and the quotation was prepared and sent out to the customer. The quotation was acceptable to APC pending the performance of the 100 test parts.

At the start of the fourth week, Jeff, with the routing in hand, went to Charlie Henry, the production manager, and said he needed 100 parts by Friday. Charlie looked at the routing and said, "The best I can do is a two-week delivery."

After discussing the subject for an hour, the two men agreed to see Wolinski. Wolinski said he'd check with sales and attempt to get an extension of one week. Sales asked the distributor salesman to request an extension. Jack White was sure it would be okay so he replied to Bob Jones without checking that the added week was in fact acceptable.

The 100 pieces went out in three weeks rather than two. That meant the project was at the end of the sixth week and only two remained. Inspection received the test pieces on Monday of the seventh week and immediately reported them not to be in specification. Kelly was upset. He was counting heavily on National to provide these parts. Kelly had received four other quotations and test orders from National's competitors. The prices were similar, and the test parts were to specification. However, National's parts, although out of specification, looked better than their competitors'. Kelly reminded Jones that the customer now had only nine days left before the contract would be let. That meant the 100 test parts had to be made in nine days. Jones immediately called Wolinski who agreed to talk to his people to try to accomplish this.

The tools were shipped in eleven days, two days after the customer had awarded orders to three of National's competitors. Kelly was disappointed in National's performance but told Jones that National would be considered for next year's contract, at least a part of it.

Jeff, hearing from Waldo that National lost the order, returned to his office, shut the door and thought of the hours, nearly round the clock, that were spent on this job. Hours were wasted because of poor communications, nonuniform priorities, and the fact that there was no project manager. "I wonder if Wolinski learned his lesson; probably not. This one cost the company at least six million dollars in profits, all because project management was not used." Jeff concluded that his work was really cut out for him. He decided that he must convince Wolinski and others of the advantages of using project management. Although Wolinski had attended a one-day seminar on project management two years ago, Jeff decided that one of his objectives during the coming year would be to get Wolinski to the point where he would, on his own, suggest becoming more knowledgeable concerning project management. Jeff's thought was that if the company was to continue to be profitable it must use project management.

The phone rang, it was Wolinski. He said, "Jeff, do you have a moment to come down to my office? I'd like to talk about the possibility of using, on a trial basis, this project management concept you mentioned to me a few months ago."

3
Organizational Structures

3.0 INTRODUCTION

During the past ten years there has been a so-called hidden revolution in the introduction and development of new organizational structures. Management has come to realize that organizations must be dynamic in nature; that is, they must be capable of rapid restructuring should environmental conditions so dictate. These environmental factors evolved from the increasing competitiveness of the market, changes in technology, and a requirement for better control of resources for multiproduct firms. Wallace identifies four major factors that caused the onset of the organizational revolution:[1]

- The technology revolution (complexity and variety of products, new materials and processes, and the effects of massive research)
- Competition and the profit squeeze (saturated markets, inflation of wage and material costs, and production efficiency)
- The high cost of marketing
- The unpredictability of consumer demands (due to high income, wide range of choices available, and shifting tastes)

Much has been written about how to identify and interpret those signs that indicate that a new organizational form may be necessary. According to Grinnel and Apple, there are five general indications that the traditional structure may not be adequate for managing projects:[2]

- Management is satisfied with its technical skills, but projects are not meeting time, cost, and other project requirements.
- There is a high commitment to getting project work done, but great fluctuations in how well performance specifications are met.

---

1. W. L. Wallace, "The Winchester-Western Division Concept of Product Planning" (New Haven: Olin Mathieson Corporation, January 1963), pp. 2–3.
2. S. K. Grinnell and H. P. Apple, "When Two Bosses are Better Than One," *Machine Design,* January 1975, pp. 84–87.

- Highly talented specialists involved in the project feel exploited and misused.
- Particular technical groups or individuals constantly blame each other for failure to meet specifications or delivery dates.
- Projects are on time and to specifications, but groups and individuals aren't satisfied with the achievement.

Unfortunately many companies do not realize the necessity for organizational change until it is too late. Management continually looks externally (i.e., to the environment) for solutions to problems rather than internally. A typical example would be that new product costs are continually rising while the product life cycle may be decreasing. Should emphasis be placed on lowering costs or developing new products?

If we assume that an organizational system is composed of both human and nonhuman resources, then we must analyze the sociotechnical subsystem whenever organizational changes are being considered. The social system is represented by the organization's personnel and their group behavior. The technical system includes the technology, materials, and machines necessary to perform the required tasks.

Behavioralists contend that there is no one best structure to meet the challenges of tomorrow's organizations. The structure used, however, must be one that optimizes company performance by achieving a balance between the social and the technical requirements. According to Sadler:[3]

Since the relative influence of these (sociotechnical) factors change from situation to situation, there can be no such thing as an ideal structure making for effectiveness in organizations of all kinds, or even appropriate to a single type of organization at different stages in its development.

There are often real and important conflicts between the type of organizational structure called for if the tasks are to be achieved with minimum cost, and the structure that will be required if human beings are to have their needs satisfied. Considerable management judgment is called for when decisions are made as to the allocation of work activities to individuals and groups. High standardization of performance, high manpower utilization and other economic advantages associated with a high level of specialization and routinization of work have to be balanced against the possible effects of extreme specialization in lowering employee attitudes and motivation.

Organizations can be defined as groups of people who must coordinate their activities in order to meet organizational objectives. The coordination function

---

3. Philip Sadler, "Designing an Organizational Structure," *Management International Review,* Vol. 11, No. 6, 1971, pp. 19–33.

requires strong communications and a clear understanding of the relationships and interdependencies among people. Organizational structures are dictated by such factors as technology and its rate of change, complexity, resource availability, products and/or services, competition, and decision-making requirements. The reader must keep in mind that *there is no such thing as a good or bad organizational structure; there are only appropriate or inappropriate ones.*

Even the simplest type of organizational change can induce major conflicts. The creation of a new position, the need for better planning, the lengthening or shortening of the span of control, the need for additional technology (knowledge), and centralization or decentralization can result in major changes in the sociotechnical subsystem. Argyris has defined five conditions that form the basis for organizational change requirements:[4]

These requirements . . . depend upon (1) continuous and open access between individuals and groups, (2) free, reliable communication, where (3) independence is the foundation for individual and departmental cohesiveness and (4) trust, risk-taking and helping each other is prevalent so that (5) conflict is identified and managed in such a way that the destructive win-lose stances with their accompanying polarization of views are minimized. . . . Unfortunately these conditions are difficult to create. . . . There is a tendency toward conformity, mistrust and lack of risk-taking among the peers that results in focusing upon individual survival, requiring the seeking out of the scarce rewards, identifying one's self with a successful venture (be a hero) and being careful to avoid being blamed for or identified with a failure, thereby becoming a "bum." All these adaptive behaviors tend to induce low interpersonal competence and can lead the organization, over the long-run, to become rigid, sticky, and less innovative, resulting in less than effective decisions with even less internal commitment to the decision on the part of those involved.

Today, organizational restructuring is a compromise between the traditional (classical) and the behavioral schools of thought; management must consider the needs of the individuals as well as the needs of the company. After all, is the organization structured to manage people or to manage work?

There are a wide variety of organizational forms for restructuring management. The exact method depends upon the people in the organization, the company's product lines, and management's philosophy. A poorly restructured organization can sever communication channels that may have taken months or years to cultivate; cause a restructuring of the informal organization, thus creating new power, status, and political positions; and eliminate job satisfaction and motivational factors to such a degree that complete discontent is the result.

---

4. Chris Argyris, "Today's Problems with Tomorrow's Organizations," *The Journal of Management Studies,* February 1967, pp. 31–55.

Sadler defines three tasks that must be considered because of the varied nature of organizations: control, integration, and external relations.[5] If the company's position is very sensitive to the environment, then management may be most concerned with the control task. For an organization with multiple products, each requiring a high degree of engineering and technology, the integration task can become primary. Finally, for situations with strong labor unions and repetitive tasks, external relations can predominate, especially in strong technological and scientific environments where strict government regulations must be adhered to.

In the sections that follow, a variety of organizational forms will be presented. Obviously, it is an impossible task to describe all possible organizational structures. Each of the organizational forms included is used to describe how the project management organization evolved from the classical theories of management. For each organizational form, advantages and disadvantages are listed in terms of both technology and social systems. Sadler has prepared a six-question checklist that explores a company's tasks, social climate, and relationship to the environment:[6]

- To what extent does the task of organization call for close control if it is to be performed efficiently?
- What are the needs and attitudes of the people performing the tasks? What are the likely effects of control mechanisms on their motivation and performance?
- What are the natural social groupings with which people identify themselves? To what extent are satisfying social relationships important in relation to motivation and performance?
- What aspect of the organization's activities needs to be closely integrated if the overall task is to be achieved?
- What organizational measures can be developed which will provide an appropriate measure of control and integration of work activities, while at the same time meeting the needs of people and providing adequate motivation?
- What environmental changes are likely to affect the future trend of company operations? What organizational measures can be taken to insure that the enterprise responds to these effectively?

The answers to these questions are not easy. For the most part, they are a matter of the judgment exercised by organizational and behavioral managers.

---

5. Philip Sadler, "Designing an Organizational Structure," *Management International Review*, Vol. 11, No. 6, 1971, pp. 19–33.
6. Ibid.

3.1 ORGANIZATIONAL WORK FLOW

Organizations are continually restructured to meet the demands imposed by the environment. Restructuring can produce a major change in the role of individuals in both the formal and the informal organization. Many researchers believe that the greatest usefulness of behavioralists lies in their ability to help the informal organization adapt to changes and resolve the resulting conflicts. Unfortunately, behavioralists cannot be totally effective unless they have an input into the formal organization as well. Conflicts arise out of changes in the formal structure. Whatever organizational form is finally selected, formal channels must be developed so that each individual has a clear description of the authority, responsibility, and accountability necessary for the flow of work to proceed.

In the discussion of organizational structures, the following definitions will be used:

- Authority is the power granted to individuals (possibly by their position) so that they can make final decisions for others to follow.
- Responsibility is the obligation incurred by individuals in their roles in the formal organization in order to effectively perform assignments.
- Accountability is the state of being totally answerable for the satisfactory completion of a specific assignment.

Authority and responsibility can be delegated (downward) to lower levels in the organization whereas accountability usually rests with the individual. Accountability is the summation of authority and responsibility. Yet, many executives refuse to delegate and argue that an individual can have total accountability just through responsibility.

Even with these clearly definable divisions of authority, responsibility, and accountability, establishing good interface relationships between the project and functional managers can take a great deal of time, especially during the conversion from a traditional to a project organizational form. Trust is the key to success here; it can overcome any problems in authority, responsibility, or accountability. When trust exists, the normal progression in the growth of the project–functional interface bond is as follows:

- Even though a problem exists, both the project and functional managers deny that any problem exists.
- When the problem finally surfaces, each manager blames the other.
- As trust develops, both managers readily admit responsibility for several of the problems.

- The project and functional managers meet face-to-face to work out the problem.
- The project and functional managers begin to formally and informally anticipate the problems that can occur.

For each of the organizational structures described in the following sections, advantages and disadvantages are listed. Many of the disadvantages stem from possible conflicts arising from problems in authority, responsibility, and accountability. The reader should identify these conflicts as such.

3.2 TRADITIONAL (CLASSICAL) ORGANIZATION

For more than two centuries, the traditional management structure has survived with organizational forms such as those depicted in Figure 3–1.[7] However, recent business developments, such as the rapid rate of change in technology and position in the marketplace, as well as increased stockholder demands, have created strains on the existing organizational forms. Fifty years ago companies could survive with only one or perhaps two product lines. The classical management organization, as shown in Figure 3–2, was found to be satisfactory for control, and conflicts were at a minimum.[8]

However, with the passing of time, companies found that survival depended upon multiple product lines (i.e., diversification) and vigorous integration of technology into the existing organization. As organizations grew and matured, managers found that company activities were not being integrated effectively, and that new conflicts were arising in the well-established formal and informal channels. Managers began searching for more innovative organization forms that would alleviate the integration and conflict problems.

Before a valid comparison can be made with the newer forms, the advantages and disadvantages of the traditional structure must be shown. Table 3–1 lists the advantages of the traditional organization. As seen in Figure 3–2, the general manager has beneath him all of the functional entities necessary to either perform R&D or develop and manufacture a product. All activities are performed within the functional groups and are headed by a department (or, in some cases, a division) head. Each department maintains a strong concentration of technical expertise. Since all of the project must flow through the functional departments, each project can benefit from the most advanced tech-

---

7. Figure 3–1 is designed to bring humor to the subject of organizational structures and is not intended to offend any specific nationality or group of people.
8. Many authors refer to classical organizations as pure functional organizations. This can be seen from Figure 3–2. Also note that the department level is below the division level. In some organizations these titles are reversed.

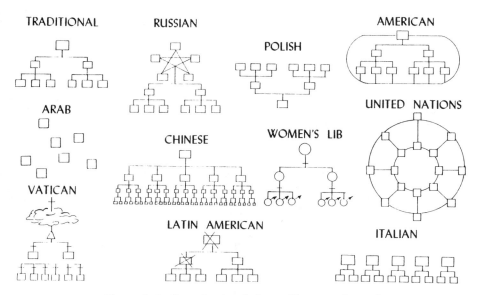

Figure 3–1. Organizational charts. (Source unknown)

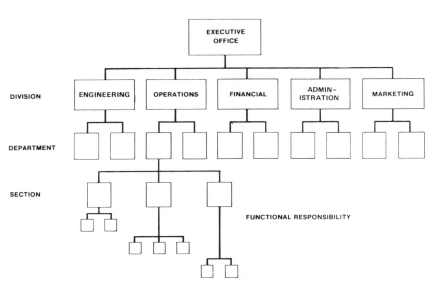

Figure 3–2. The traditional management structure.

Table 3-1. Advantages of the Classical Traditional Organization.

- Easier budgeting and cost control are possible.
- Better technical control is possible.
  - Specialists can be grouped to share knowledge and responsibility.
  - Personnel can be used on many different projects.
  - All projects will benefit from the most advanced technology (better utilization of scarce personnel).
- It provides flexibility in the use of manpower.
- It provides a broad manpower base to work with.
- It provides continuity in the functional disciplines; policies, procedures, and lines of responsibility are easily defined and understandable.
- It readily admits mass production activities within established specifications.
- It provides good control over personnel, since each employee has one and only one person to report to.
- Communication channels are vertical and well established.
- Quick reaction capability exists, but may be dependent upon the priorities of the functional managers.

nology, thus making this organizational form well suited to mass production. Functional managers can hire a wide variety of specialists and provide them with easily definable paths for career progression.

The functional managers maintain absolute control over the budget. They establish their own budgets, upon approval from above, and specify requirements for additional personnel. Because the functional manager has manpower flexibility and a broad base from which to work, most projects are normally completed within cost.

Both the formal and informal organizations are well established, and levels of authority and responsibility are clearly defined. Because each person reports to only one individual, communication channels are well structured. If a structure has this many advantages, then why are we looking for other structures?

For each advantage, there is almost always a corresponding disadvantage. Table 3-2 lists the disadvantages of the traditional structure. The majority of these disadvantages are related to the fact that there is no strong central authority or individual responsible for the total project. As a result, integration of activities that cross functional lines becomes a difficult chore, and top-level executives must get involved with the daily routine. Conflicts occur as each functional group struggles for power. The strongest functional group dominates the decision-making process. Functional managers tend to favor what is best for their functional groups rather than what is best for the project. Many times, ideas will remain functionally oriented with very little regard for ongoing projects. In addition, the decision-making process is slow and tedious.

Because there exists no customer focal point, all communications must be

Table 3–2. Disadvantages of the Traditional / Classical Organization

- No one individual is directly responsible for the total project (i.e., no formal authority; committee solutions).
- It does not provide the project-oriented emphasis necessary to accomplish the project tasks.
- Coordination becomes complex, and additional lead time is required for approval of decisions.
- Decisions normally favor the strongest functional groups.
- There is no customer focal point.
- Response to customer needs is slow.
- There is difficulty in pinpointing responsibility; this is the result of little or no direct project reporting, very little project-oriented planning, and no project authority.
- Motivation and innovation are decreased.
- Ideas tend to be functionally oriented with little regard for ongoing projects.

channeled through upper-level management. Upper-level managers then act in a customer-relations capacity and refer all complex problems down through the vertical chain of command to the functional managers. The response to the customer's needs therefore becomes a slow and aggravating process because the information must be filtered through several layers of management. If problem solving and coordination are required to cross functional lines, then additional lead time is required for the approval of decisions. All trade-off analyses must be accomplished through committees chaired by upper-level management.

Projects have a tendency to fall behind schedule in the classical organizational structure. Completing all projects and tasks on time, with a high degree of quality and efficient use of available resources, is all but impossible without continuous involvement of top-level management. Incredibly large lead times are required. Functional managers attend to those tasks that provide better benefits to themselves and their subordinates first. Priorities may be dictated by requirements of the informal as well as formal departmental structure.

With the growth of project management in the late 1960s, executives began to realize that many of the problems that had surfaced to the executive levels of management were the result of weaknesses in the traditional structure. William Goggin identified the problems that faced Dow Corning:[9]

Although Dow Corning was a healthy corporation in 1967, it showed difficulties that troubled many of us in top management. These symptoms were, and still are, common

---

9. William C. Goggin, "How the Multidimensional Structure Works at Dow Corning," *Harvard Business Review,* January–February 1974, p. 54. Copyright © 1973 by the President and Fellows of Harvard College; All rights reserved.

ones in U.S. business and have been described countless times in reports, audits, articles and speeches. Our symptoms took such form as:

- Executives did not have adequate financial information and control of their operations. Marketing managers, for example, did not know how much it cost to produce a product. Prices and margins were set by division managers.
- Cumbersome communications channels existed between key functions, especially manufacturing and marketing.
- In the face of stiffening competition, the corporation remained too internalized in its thinking and organizational structure. It was insufficiently oriented to the outside world.
- Lack of communications between divisions not only created the antithesis of a corporate team effort but also was wasteful of a precious resource—people.
- Long-range corporate planning was sporadic and superficial; this was leading to over-staffing, duplicated effort and inefficiency.

Executive analysis of the traditional structure identified by Carlisle, are:[10]

- Functional organizations tend to emphasize the separate functional elements at the expense of the whole organization.
- Under functional departmentation there is no group that effectively integrates the various functions of an organization and monitors them from the "big picture standpoint."
- Functional organizations do not tend to develop "general managers."
- Functional organizations emphasize functional relationships based on the vertical organizational hierarchy.
- Functional organizations tend to fragment other management processes.
- Functional organizations develop a strong resistance to change.
- Functional segregation through the formal organization process encourages conflict among the various functions.
- The emphasis on the various operating functions focuses attention on the internal aspects and relations of the company to the detriment of its external relations.
- Functional organizations tend to be closed systems.

3.3 DEVELOPING WORK INTEGRATION POSITIONS

As companies grew in size, more and more emphasis was placed upon multiple ongoing programs with high-technology requirements. Organizational pitfalls soon appeared, especially in the integration of the flow of work. As management discovered that the critical point in any program is the interface between functional units, the new theories of "interface management" developed.

---

10. Howard M. Carlisle, "Are Functional Organizations Becoming Obsolete?" *Management Review,* January 1969, pp. 4–6; By permission of American Management Associations.

Because of the interfacing problems, management began searching for innovative methods to coordinate the flow of work between functional units without modification to the existing organizational structure. This coordination was achieved through several integrating mechanisms:[11]

- Rules and procedures
- Planning processes
- Hierarchical referral
- Direct contact

By specifying and documenting management policies and procedures, management attempted to eliminate conflicts between functional departments. Management felt that, even though many of the projects were different, the actions required by the functional personnel were repetitive and predictable. The behavior of the individuals should therefore be easily integrated into the flow of work with minimum communication necessary between individuals or functional groups.

Another means of reducing conflicts and minimizing the need for communication was detailed planning. Functional representation would be present at all planning, scheduling, and budget meetings. This method worked best for nonrepetitive tasks and projects.

In the traditional organization, one of the most important responsibilities of upper-level management was the resolution of conflicts through "hierarchical referral." The continuous conflicts and struggle for power between the functional units consistently required that upper-level personnel resolve those problems resulting from situations that were either nonroutine or unpredictable and for which no policies or procedures existed.

The fourth method is direct contact and interactions by the functional managers. The rules and procedures, as well as the planning process method, were designed to minimize ongoing communications between functional groups. The quantity of conflicts that executives had to resolve forced key personnel to spend a great percentage of their time as arbitrators, rather than as managers. To alleviate problems of hierarchical referral, upper-level management requested that all conflicts be resolved at the lowest possible levels. This required that functional managers meet face-to-face to resolve conflicts.

In many organizations, these new methods proved ineffective, primarily because there still existed a need for a focal point for the project to ensure that all activities would be properly integrated.

---

11. Jay R. Galbraith, "Matrix Organization Designs," *Business Horizons,* February 1971, pp. 29–40. Galbraith defines a fifth mechanism, liaison departments, which will be discussed later in this section.

When the need for project managers was acknowledged, the next logical question was that of where in the organization to place them. Executives preferred to keep project managers as low as possible in the organization. After all, if they reported to someone high up, they would have to be paid more and would pose a continuous threat to management.

The first attempt to resolve this problem was to develop project leaders or coordinators within each functional department, as shown in Figure 3–3. Section-level personnel were temporarily assigned as project leaders and would return to their former positions at project termination. This is why the term "project leader" is used rather than "project manager," as the word "manager" implies a permanent relationship. This arrangement proved effective for coordinating and integrating work within one department, provided that the correct project leader was selected. Some employees considered this position as an increase in power and status, and conflicts occurred about whether assignments should be based upon experience, seniority, or capability. Some employees wanted the title merely so they could use it on their resumes. Furthermore, the project leaders had almost no authority, and section-level managers refused to take directions from them. Many section managers were afraid that if they did

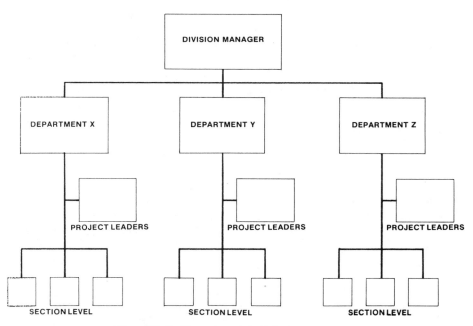

Figure 3–3. Departmental project management.

take direction, they were admitting that the project leaders were next in line for the department manager's position.

When the activities required efforts that crossed more than one functional boundary, say two or more sections or departments, conflicts arose. The project leader in one department did not have the authority to coordinate activities in any other department. Furthermore, the creation of this new position caused internal conflicts within each department. As a result, many employees refused to become dedicated to project management and were anxious to return to their "secure" jobs. Quite often, especially when cross-functional integration was required, the division manager was forced to act as the project manager. If the employee enjoyed the assignment of project leader, he would try to "stretch out" the project as long as possible.

Even though we have criticized this organizational form, it does not mean that it cannot work. Any organizational form (yes, any form) will work if the employees want it to work. As an example, a computer manufacturer has a midwestern division with three departments within it, as in Figure 3–3, and approximately fourteen people per department. When a project comes in, the division manager determines which department will handle most of the work. Let us say that the work load is 60 percent department X, 30 percent Y, and 10 percent department Z. Since most of the effort is in department X, the project leader is selected from that department. When the project leader goes into the other two departments to get resources, he will almost always get the resources he wants. There are two reasons why this organizational form works in this case:

- The other department managers know that they may have to supply the project leader on the next activity.
- There are only three functional boundaries or departments involved (i.e., a small organization).

This structure works best in small organizations where minimal cross-communication is necessary.

The next step in the evolution of project management was the task force concept. The rationale behind the task force concept was that integration could be achieved if each functional unit placed a representative on the task force. The group could then jointly solve problems as they occurred, provided that budget limitations were still adhered to. Theoretically, decisions could now be made at the lowest possible levels, thus expediting information and reducing, or even eliminating, delay time.

The task force was composed of both part-time and full-time personnel from each department involved. Daily meetings were held to review activities and discuss potential problems. Functional managers soon found that their task force employees were spending more time in unproductive meetings than in performing functional activities. In addition, the nature of the task force position caused many individuals to shift membership within the informal organization. Many functional managers then placed nonqualified and inexperienced individuals on task forces. The result was that the group soon became ineffective because they either did not have the information necessary to make the decisions, or lacked the authority (delegated by the functional managers) to allocate resources and assign work.

Development of the task force concept was a giant step toward conflict resolution: work was being accomplished on time, schedules were being maintained, and costs were usually within budget. But integration and coordination were still problems because there were no specified authority relationships or individuals to oversee the entire project through completion. Many attempts were made to overcome this by placing various people in charge of the task force: functional managers, division heads, and even upper-level management had opportunities to direct task forces. However, without formal project authority relationships, task force members maintained loyalty to their functional organizations, and when conflicts came about between the project and functional organization, the project always suffered.

Although the task force concept was a step in the right direction, the disadvantages strongly outweighed the advantages. A strength of the approach was that it could be established very rapidly and with very little paperwork. Integration, however, was complicated; work flow was difficult to control; and functional support was difficult to obtain because it was almost always strictly controlled by the functional manager. In addition, task forces were found to be grossly ineffective on long-range projects.

The next step in the evolution of work integration was the establishment of liaison departments, particularly in engineering divisions that perform multiple projects involving a high level of technology (see Figure 3–4). The purpose of the liaison department was to handle transactions between functional units within the (engineering) division. The liaison personnel received their authority through the division head. The liaison department actually did not resolve conflicts. However, their prime function was to assure that all departments work toward the same requirements and goals. Liaison departments are still in existence in many large companies and typically handle engineering changes and design problems.

Unfortunately, the liaison department is simply a scale-up of the project coordinator within the department. The authority given to the liaison department extends only to the outer boundaries of the division. If a conflict came about between the manufacturing and engineering divisions, for example, hierarchical referral would still be needed for resolution. Today, liaison departments are synonymous with project engineering and systems engineering

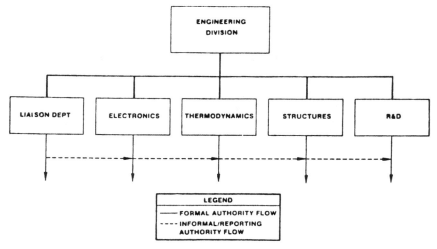

Figure 3–4. Engineering division with liaison department.

departments, and the individuals in these departments have the authority to span the entire organization.

3.4 LINE-STAFF ORGANIZATION

It soon became obvious that control of a project must be given to personnel whose first loyalty is directed toward the completion of the project. For this purpose, the project management position must be separated from any controlling influence of the functional managers. Figure 3–5 shows a typical line-staff organization.

Two possible situations can exist with this form of line-staff project control. In the first situation, the project manager serves only as the focal point for activity control, that is, a center for information. The prime responsibility of the project manager is to keep the division manager informed of the status of the project and to "harass" or attempt to "influence" managers into completing activities on time. Referring to such early project managers, Galbraith stated, "Since these men had no formal authority, they had to resort to their technical competence and their interpersonal skills in order to be effective."[12]

The project manager in the first situation maintained monitoring authority

---

12. Jay R. Galbraith, "Matrix Organization Designs," *Business Horizons,* February 1971, pp. 29–40.

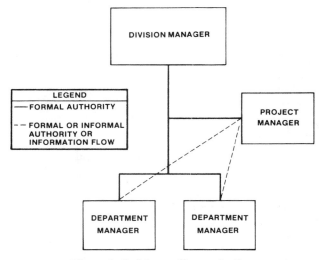

Figure 3–5. Line-staff organization.

only, despite the fact that both he and the functional manager reported to the same individual. Both work assignments and merit reviews were made by the functional managers. Department managers refused to take direction from the project managers because to do so would seem an admission that the project manager was next in line to be the division manager.

The amount of authority given to the project manager posed serious problems. Almost all upper-level and division managers were from the classical management schools and therefore maintained serious reservations about how much authority to relinquish. Many of these managers considered it a demotion if they had to give up any of their long-established powers.

In the second situation, the project manager is given more authority; using the authority vested in him by the division manager, he can assign work to individuals in the functional organizations. The functional manager, however, still maintains the authority to perform merit reviews, but cannot enforce both professional and organizational standards in the completion of an activity. The individual performing the work is now caught in a web of authority relationships, and additional conflicts develop because functional managers are forced to share their authority with the project manager.

Although this second situation did occur during the early stages of matrix project management, it did not last because:

- Upper-level management was not ready to cope with the problems arising from shared authority.

- Upper-level management was reluctant to relinquish any of its power and authority to project managers.
- Line-staff project managers who reported to a division head did not have any authority or control over those portions of a project in other divisions; that is, the project manager in the engineering division could not direct activities in the manufacturing division.

3.5 PURE PRODUCT ORGANIZATION

The pure project organization, as shown in Figure 3–6, develops as a division within a division. As long as there exists a continuous flow of projects, work is stable and conflicts are at a minimum. The major advantage of this organizational flow is that one individual, the program manager, maintains complete line authority over the entire project. Not only does he assign work, but he also conducts merit reviews. Because each individual reports to only one person, strong communication channels develop that result in a very rapid reaction time.

In pure product organizations, long lead times became a thing of the past. Trade-off studies could be conducted as fast as time would permit without the need to look at the impact on other projects (unless, of course, identical facil-

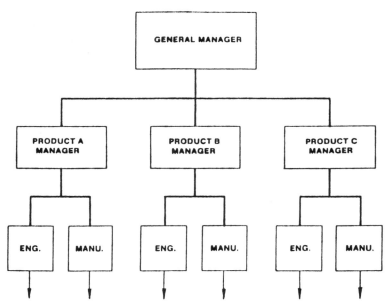

Figure 3–6. Pure product structure.

ities or equipment were required). Functional managers were able to maintain qualified staffs for new product development without sharing personnel with other programs and projects.

The responsibilities attributed to the project manager were entirely new. First of all, his authority was now granted by the vice president and general manager. The program manager handled all conflicts, both those within his organization and those involving other projects. Interface management was conducted at the program manager level. Upper-level management was now able to spend more time on executive decision-making rather than conflict arbitration.

The major disadvantage with the pure project form is the cost of maintaining the organization. There is no chance for sharing an individual with another project in order to reduce costs. Personnel are usually attached to these projects long after they are needed because once an employee is given up, the project manager might never be able to get him back. Motivating personnel becomes a problem. At project completion, functional personnel do not "have a home" to return to. Many organizations place these individuals into an overhead labor pool from which selection can be made during new project development. People still in the labor pool for a certain period of time may be laid off indefinitely. As each project comes to a close, people become uneasy and often strive to prove their worth to the company by overachieving, a condition that is only temporary. It is very difficult for management to convince key functional personnel that they do, in fact, have career opportunities in this type of organization.

In pure functional (traditional) structures, technologies are well developed, but project schedules often fall behind. In the pure project structure, the fast reaction time keeps activities on schedule, but technology suffers because without strong functional groups, which maintain interactive technical communcation, the company's outlook for meeting the competition may be severely hampered. The engineering department for one project might not communicate with its counterpart on other projects, and duplication of efforts can easily occur.

The last major disadvantage of this organizational form lies in the control of facilities and equipment. The most frequent conflict is that which occurs when two projects require use of the same piece of equipment or facilities at the same time. Hierarchical referral is required to alleviate this problem. Upper-level management can assign priorities to these projects. This is normally accomplished by defining certain projects as strategic, tactical, or operational—the same definitions usually given to plans.

Table 3–3 summarizes the advantages of this organizational form, and Table 3–4 lists the disadvantages.

Table 3–3. Advantages of the Product Organizational Form.

- It provides complete line authority over the project (i.e., strong control through a single project authority).
- The project participants work directly for the project manager. Unprofitable product lines are easily identified and can be eliminated.
- There are strong communications channels.
- Staffs can maintain expertise on a given project without sharing key personnel.
- Very rapid reaction time is provided.
- Personnel demonstrate loyalty to the project; better morale with product identification.
- A focal point develops for out-of-company customer relations.
- There is flexibility in determining time (schedule), cost, and performance trade-offs.
- Interface management becomes easier as unit size is decreased.
- Upper-level management maintains more free time for executive decision-making.

Table 3–4. Disadvantages of the Product Organizational Form.

- Cost of maintaining this form in a multiproduct company would be prohibitive due to duplication of effort,,facilities, and personnel; inefficient usage.
- There exists a tendency to retain personnel on a project long after they are needed. Upper-level management must balance workloads as projects start up and are phased out.
- Technology suffers because, without strong functional groups, outlook of the future to improve company's capabilities for new programs would be hampered (i.e., no perpetuation of technology).
- Control of functional (i.e., organizational) specialists requires top-level coordination.
- There is a lack of opportunities for technical interchange between projects.
- There is a lack of career continuity and opportunities for project personnel.

3.6 MATRIX ORGANIZATIONAL FORM

The matrix organizational form is an attempt to combine the advantages of the pure functional structure and the product organizational structure. This form is ideally suited for companies, such as construction, that are "project-driven." Figure 3–7 shows a typical matrix structure. Each project manager reports directly to the vice president and general manager. Since each project represents a potential profit center, the power and authority used by the project manager come directly from the general manager. The project manager has total responsibility and accountability for project success. The functional departments, on the other hand, have functional responsibility to maintain technical excellence on the project. Each functional unit is headed by a department manager whose prime responsibility is to ensure that a unified technical base is maintained and that all available information can be exchanged for each project. Department managers must also keep their people aware of the latest technical accomplishments in the industry.

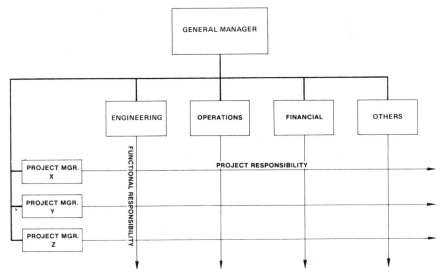

Figure 3–7. Pure matrix structure.

Project management is a "coordinative" function, whereas matrix management is a collaborative function division of project management. In the coordinative or project organization, work is generally assigned to specific people or units who "do their own thing." In the collaborative or matrix organization, information sharing may be mandatory, and several people may be required for the same piece of work. In a project organization, authority for decision-making and direction rests with the project leader, whereas in a matrix it rests with the team.

Certain ground rules exist for matrix development:

- Participants must spend full time on the project; this ensures a degree of loyalty.
- Horizontal as well as vertical channels must exist for making commitments.
- There must be quick and effective methods for conflict resolution.
- There must be good communication channels and free access between managers.
- All managers must have an input into the planning process.
- Both horizontally and vertically oriented managers must be willing to negotiate for resources.
- The horizontal line must be permitted to operate as a separate entity except for administrative purposes.

These ground rules simply state some of the ideal conditions that matrix structures should possess. Each ground rule brings with it advantages and
disadvantages.

Before describing the advantages and disadvantages of this structure, the
organization concepts must be introduced. The basis for the matrix approach
is an attempt to create synergism through shared responsibility between project
and functional management. Yet this is easier said than done. *No working environment is the same, and, therefore, no two companies will have the same
matrix design.* The following questions must be answered before successful
operation of a matrix structure can be achieved;

- If each functional unit is responsible for one aspect of a project, and other
  parts are conducted elsewhere (possibly subcontracted to other companies), how can a synergistic environment be created?
- Who decides which element of a project is most important?
- How can a functional unit (operating in a vertical structure) answer questions and achieve project goals and objectives that are compatible with
  other projects?

The answers to these questions depend upon mutual understanding between
the project and functional managers. Since both individuals maintain some
degree of authority, responsibility, and accountability on each project, they
must continuously negotiate. Unfortunately, the program manager might only
consider what is best for his project (disregarding all others), whereas, the
functional manager might consider his organization more important than each
project.

In Chapter 1 we stated that project management is more behavioral than
quantitative and that interpersonal skills and communicative skills are
extremely important attributes of the project manager. Figure 3–8 shows why
these skills are so important in matrix management. (The source for Figure 3–
8 is unknown.)

In the matrix:

- There should be no disruption due to dual accountability.
- A difference in judgment should not delay work in progress.

In order to get the job done, project managers sometimes need adequate
organizational status and authority. A corporate executive contends that
the organization chart shown in Figure 3–7 can be modified to show that the
project managers have adequate organizational authority by placing the
department manager boxes at the tip of the functional arrowheads. The executive further contends that, with this approach, the project managers appear

Figure 3–8. Matrix humor. (Source unknown)

to be higher in the organization than their departmental counterparts but are actually equal in status. Executives who prefer this method must exercise due caution because the line and project managers may not feel that there still exists an equality in the balance of power.

Problem solving in this type of environment is a fragmented and diffused process. The project manager acts as a unifying agent for project control of resources and technology. He must maintain open channels of communication between himself and functional units as well as between functional units themselves to prevent suboptimization of individual projects. The problems of routine administration can and do become a cost-effective requirement.

In many situations, functional managers have the power and means of making a project manager look good, provided that they can be motivated enough to think in terms of what is best for the project. Unfortunately, this is not always accomplished. As stated by Mantell:[13]

There exists an inevitable tendency for heirarchically arrayed units to seek solutions and to identify problems in terms of scope of duties of particular units rather than looking beyond them. This phenomenon exists without regard for the competence of the executive concerned. It comes about because of authority delegation and functionalism.

Such "tunnel vision" can exist at all levels of management.

The project environment and functional environment cannot be separated; they must interact. The location of the project and functional unit interface is the focal point for all activities.

The functional manager controls departmental resources (i.e., people). This poses a problem because, although the project manager maintains the maximum control (through the line managers) over all resources including cost and personnel, the functional manager must provide staff for the project's requirements. It is therefore inevitable that conflicts occur between functional and project managers;

These conflicts revolve about items such as project priority, manpower costs, and the assignment of functional personnel to the project manager. Each project manager will, of course, want the best functional operators assigned to his program. In addition to these problems, the accountability for profit and loss is much more difficult in a matrix organization than in a project organization. Project managers have a tendency to blame overruns on functional managers, stating that the cost of the function was excessive. Whereas functional managers have a tendency to blame excessive costs on project managers with the argument that there were too many changes, more work required than defined initially and other such arguments.[14]

The individual placed at the interface position has two bosses: he must take direction from both the project manager and the functional manager. The

13. Leroy H. Mantell, "The Systems Approach and Good Management," *Business Horizons,* October 1972, p. 50.
14. William P. Killian, "Project Management—Future Organizational Concepts," *Marquette Business Review,* Vol. 2, 1971, pp. 90–107.

merit review and hiring and firing responsibilities still rest with the department manager. Merit reviews are normally made by the functional manager after discussions with the program manager. The functional manager may not have the time necessary to measure the progress of this individual continuously. He must rely upon the word of the program manager for merit review and promotion. The interface members generally give loyalty to the person signing their merit review. This poses a problem, especially if conflicting orders are given by the functional and project managers. The simplest solution is for the individual at the interface to ask the functional and project managers to communicate with each other to resolve the problem. This type of situation poses a problem for project managers:

- How does a project manager motivate an individual working on a project (either part-time or full-time) so that his loyalties are with the project?
- How does a project manager convince an individual to perform work according to project direction and specifications when these requests may be in conflict with department policy, especially if the individual feels that his functional boss may not regard him with much favor?

There are many advantages to matrix structures, as shown in Table 3–5. Functional units exist primarily as support for a project. Because of this, key

Table 3–5. Advantages of a Pure Matrix Organizational Form.

- The project manager maintains maximum project control (through the line managers) over all resources, including cost and personnel.
- Policies and procedures can be set up independently for each project, provided that they do not contradict company policies and procedures.
- The project manager has the authority to commit company resources, provided that scheduling does not cause conflicts with other projects.
- Rapid responses are possible to changes, conflict resolution, and project needs (as technology or schedule).
- The functional organizations exist primarily as support for the project.
- Each person has a "home" after project completion. People are susceptible to motivation and end-item identification. Each person can be shown a career path.
- Because key people can be shared, the program cost is minimized. People can work on a variety of problems; that is, better people control is possible.
- A strong technical base can be developed, and much more time can be devoted to complex problem solving. Knowledge is available for all projects on an equal basis.
- Conflicts are minimal, and those requiring hierarchical referrals are more easily resolved.
- There is a better balance between time, cost, and performance.
- Rapid development of specialists and generalists occurs.
- Authority and responsibility are shared.
- Stress is distributed among the team (and the functional managers).

people can be shared and costs can be minimized. People can be assigned to a variety of challenging problems. Each person, therefore, has a "home" after project completion. Each person can be shown a career path in the company. People in these organizations are especially responsive to motivation and end-item identification. Functional managers find it easy to develop and maintain a strong technical base and can, therefore, spend more time on complex problem-solving. Knowledge can be shared for all projects.

The matrix structure can provide a rapid response to changes, conflicts, and other project needs. Conflicts are normally minimal, but those requiring resolution are easily resolved using hierarchical referral.

This rapid response is a result of the project manager's authority to commit company resources, provided that scheduling conflicts with other projects can be eliminated. Furthermore, the project manager has the authority independently to establish his own project policies and procedures, provided that they do not conflict with company policies. This can do away with much red tape and permit a better balance between time, cost, and performance.

The matrix structure provides us with the best of two worlds: the traditional structure and the matrix structure. The advantages of the matrix structure eliminate almost all of the disadvantages of the traditional structure. The word "matrix" often brings fear to the hearts of executives because it implies radical change, or at least they think that it does. If we take a close look at Figure 3–7, we can see that the traditional structure is still there. The matrix is simply horizontal lines superimposed over the traditional structure. The horizontal lines will come and go as projects start up and terminate, but the traditional structure will remain forever.

Matrix structures are not without their disadvantages, as shown in Table 3 –6. The first three elements in Table 3–6 are due to the horizontal and vertical work flow requirements of a matrix. Actually the flow may even be multidimensional if the project manager has to report to customers, corporate or other personnel in addition to his superior and the functional line managers.

Most companies believe that if they have enough resources to staff all of the projects that come along, then the company is "overstaffed." As a result of this philosophy, priorities may change continuously, perhaps even daily. Management goals for a project may be drastically different from the project's goals, especially if executive involvement is lacking during the definition of project's requirements in the planning phase. In a matrix, conflicts and their resolution may be a continuous process, especially if priorities change continuously. Regardless of how mature an organization becomes, there will always exist difficulty in monitoring and control because of the complex, multidirectional work flow. Another disadvantage of the matrix organization is that more administrative personnel are needed to develop policies and procedures, and therefore both direct and indirect administrative costs will increase. In addi-

Table 3–6. Disadvantages of a Pure Matrix Organizational Form.

- Multidimensional information flow.
- Multidimensional work flow.
- Dual reporting.
- Continuously changing priorities.
- Management goals different from project goals.
- Potential for continuous conflict and conflict resolution.
- Difficulty in monitoring and control.
- Company-wide, the organizational structure is not cost-effective because more people than necessary are required, primarily administrative.
- Each project organization operates independently. Care must be taken that duplication of efforts does not occur.
- More effort and time are needed initially to define policies and procedures, compared to traditional form.
- Functional managers may be biased according to their own set of priorities.
- Balance of power between functional and project organizations must be watched.
- Balance of time, cost, and performance must be monitored.
- Although rapid response time is possible for individual problem resolution, the reaction time can become quite slow.
- Employees and managers are more susceptible to role ambiguity than in traditional form.
- Conflicts and their resolution may be a continuous process (possibly requiring support of an organizational development specialist).
- People do not feel that they have any control over their own destiny when continuously reporting to multiple managers.

tion, it is impossible to manage projects with a matrix if there are steep horizontal or vertical pyramids for supervision and reporting because each manager in the pyramid will want to reduce the authority of the managers operating within the matrix. Each project organization operates independently. This poses a problem in that duplication of effort can easily occur; for example, two projects might be developing the same cost accounting procedure, or functional personnel may be doing similar R&D efforts on different projects. Both vertical and horizontal communication is a must in a project matrix organization.

Functional managers are human and, therefore, may be biased according to their own set of priorities. Project managers, however, must realize that their project is not the only one, and that a proper balance is needed; this includes a balance of power between functional and project units as well as a proper balance between time, cost, and performance.

One of the advantages of the matrix is a rapid response time for problem resolution. This rapid response generally applies to slow-moving projects where problems occur within each functional unit. On fast-moving projects, the reaction time can become quite slow, especially if the problem spans more than one functional unit. This slow reaction time exists because the functional employees assigned to the project do not have the authority to make decisions, allocate functional resources, or change schedules. Only the line managers have this authority. Therefore, in times of crisis, functional managers must be actively brought into the "big picture" and invited to team meetings.

Middleton has listed four additional undesirable results that can develop from the use of matrix organizations and can affect company capabilities:[15]

- Project priorities and competition for talent may interrupt the stability of the organization and interfere with its long-range interests by upsetting the traditional business of functional organizations.
- Long-range plans may suffer as the company gets more involved in meeting schedules and fulfilling the requirements of temporary projects.
- Shifting people from project to project may disrupt the training of employees and specialists, thereby hindering the growth and development within their fields of specialization.
- Lessons learned on one project may not be communicated to other projects.

In addition to the above-mentioned disadvantages, Davis and Lawrence have identified nine matrix pathologies:[16]

- Power struggles: The horizontal vs. vertical hierarchy.
- Anarchy: Formation of organizational islands during periods of stress.
- Groupitis: Confusing the matrix as being synonymous with group decision-making.
- Collapse during economic crunch: Flourishing during periods of growth and collapsing during lean times.
- Excessive overhead: How much matrix supervision is actually necessary?
- Decision strangulation: Too many people involved in decision-making.
- Sinking: Pushing the matrix down into the depths of the organization.
- Layering: A matrix within a matrix.
- Navel gazing: Becoming overly involved in the internal relationships of the organization.

The matrix structure therefore becomes a compromise in an attempt to obtain the best of two worlds. In pure product management, technology suffered because there did not exist any single group for planning and integration. In the pure functional organization, time and schedule are sacrificed. Matrix project management is an attempt to obtain maximum technology and performance in a cost-effective manner and within time and schedule constraints.

---

15. C. J. Middleton, "How to Set Up a Project Organization," *Harvard Business Review,* March–April 1967. Copyright © 1967 by the President and Fellows of Harvard College; All rights reserved.
16. Adapted from Stanley M. Davis and Paul R. Lawrence, *Matrix,* © 1977, Addison-Wesley Publishing Co., Reading, Massachusetts, pp. 129–144. Reprinted with permission.

We should note that with proper executive-level planning and control, all of the disadvantages can be eliminated. This is the only organizational form where such control is possible. However, care must be taken with regard to the first disadvantage listed in Table 3–6. There is a natural tendency when going to a matrix to create more positions in executive management than are actually necessary in order to get better control, and this will drive up the overhead rates. This may be true in some companies, but there is a point where the matrix will become mature and fewer people will be required at the top levels of management. When executives wish to reduce cost, they normally begin at the top by combining positions when slots become vacant. This is a natural fallout of having mature project and line managers with less top-level interference.

Previously we identified the necessity for the project manager to be able to establish his own policies, procedures, rules, and guidelines. Obviously, with personnel reporting in two directions and to multiple managers, conflicts over administration can easily occur. According to Shannon:[17]

When operating under a matrix management approach, it is obviously extremely important that the authority and responsibility of each manager be clearly defined, understood and accepted by both functional and program people. These relationships need to be spelled out in writing. It is essential that in the various operating policies, the specific authority of the program direction, and the authority of the functional executive be defined in terms of operational direction.

Most practitioners consider the matrix to be a two-dimensional system where each project represents a potential profit center and each functional department represents a cost center. (This interpretation can also create conflict because functional departments may feel that they no longer have an input into corporate profits.) For large corporations with multiple divisions, the matrix is no longer two-dimensional, but multidimensional.

William C. Goggin has described geographical area and space and time as the third and fourth dimensions of the Dow Corning Matrix:[18]

Geographical areas . . . business development varied widely from area to area, and the profit-center and cost-center dimensions could not be carried out everywhere in the

---

17. Robert Shannon, "Matrix Management Structures," *Industrial Engineering,* March 1972, pp. 27–28. Published and copyright 1972 by the American Institute of Industrial Engineers, Inc., Norcross, Georgia 30092.
18. William C. Goggin, "How the Multidimensional Structure Works at Dow Corning," *Harvard Business Review,* January–February 1974, pp. 56–57. Copyright © 1973 by the President and Fellows of Harvard College; All rights reserved.

same manner. . . . Dow Corning area organizations are patterned after our major U.S. organizations. Although somewhat autonomous in their operation, they subscribe to the overall corporate objectives, operating guidelines, and planning criteria. During the annual planning cycle, for example, there is a mutual exchange of sales, expense, and profit projections between the functional and business managers headquartered in the United States and the area managers around the world.

Space and time. . . . A fourth dimension of the organization denotes fluidity and movement through time. . . . The multidimensional organization is far from rigid; it is constantly changing. Unlike centralized or decentralized systems that are too often rooted deep in the past, the multidimensional organization is geared toward the future: Long-term planning is an inherent part of its operation.

Goggin then went on to describe the advantages that Dow Corning expected to gain from the multidimensional organization:

- Higher profit generation even in an industry (silicones) price-squeezed by competition. (Much of our favorable profit picture seems due to a better overall understanding and practice of expense controls through the company.)
- Increased competitive ability based on technological innovation and product quality without a sacrifice in profitability.
- Sound, fast decision making at all levels in the organization, facilitated by stratified but open channels of communications, and by a totally participative working environment.
- A healthy and effective balance of authority among the businesses, functions, and areas.
- Progress in developing short- and long-range planning with the support of all employees.
- Resource allocations that are proportional to expected results.
- More stimulating and effective on-the-job training.
- Accountability that is more closely related to responsibility and authority.
- Results that are visible and measurable.
- More top-management time for long-range planning and less need to become involved in day-to-day operations.

Obviously, the matrix structure is the most complex of all organizational forms. Careful consideration must be given as to where and how the matrix organization fits into the total organization. Grinnell and Apple define four stiuations where it is most practical to consider a matrix:[19]

- When complex, short-run products are the organization's primary output.
- When a complicated design calls for both innovation and timely completion.

---

19. S. K. Grinnell, and H. P. Apple, "When Two Bosses are Better Than One," *Machine Design,* January 1975, pp. 84–87.

- When several kinds of sophisticated skills are needed in designing, building, and testing the products—skills then need constant updating and development.
- When a rapidly changing marketplace calls for significant changes in products, perhaps between the time they are conceived and delivered.

Matrix implementation requires:

- Training in matrix operations
- Training in how to maintain open communications
- Training in problem-solving
- Compatible reward systems
- Role definitions

An excellent report on when the matrix will and will not work was made by Wintermantel:[20]

- Situational factors conducive to successful matrix applications:
  - Similar products produced in common plants but serving quite different markets.
  - Different products produced in different plants but serving the same market or customer and utilizing a common distribution channel.
  - Short-cycle contract businesses where each contract is specifically defined and essentially unrelated to other contracts.
  - Complex, rapidly changing business environment which requires close multi-functional integration of expertise in response to change.
  - Intensive customer focus businesses where customer responsiveness and solution of customer problems is considered critical (and where the assigned matrix manager represents a focal point within the component for the customer).
  - A large number of products/projects/programs which are scattered over many points on the maturity curve and where limited resources must be selectively allocated to provide maximum leverage.
  - Strong requirement for getting into and out of businesses on a timely and low cost basis. May involve fast buildup and short lead times. Frequent situations where you may want to test entrance into a business arena without massive commitment of resources and with ease of exit assured.
  - High technology businesses where scarce state-of-the-art technical talent must be spread over many projects in the proposal/advanced design stage, but where less experienced or highly talented personnel are adequate for detailed design and follow-on work.

---

20. Richard E. Wintermantel, "Application of the Matrix Organization Mode in Industry," *Proceedings of the Eleventh Project Management Institute Seminar Symposium,* 1979, pp. 493–497. Original data source is *General Electric Organization Planning Bulletin,* No. 6, November 3, 1976.

- Situations where products are unique and discrete but where technology, facilities or processes have high commonality, are interchangeable or are interdependent.
- Situational factors tending toward nonviable matrix applications:
  - Single product line or similar products produced in common plants and serving the same market.
  - Multiple products produced in several dedicated plants serving different customers and/or utilizing different distribution channels.
  - Stable business environment where changes tend to be glacial and relatively predictable.
  - Long, high volume runs of a limited number of products utilizing mature technology and processes.
  - Little commonality or interdependence in facilities, technology or processes.
  - Situations where only one profit center can be defined and/or small businesses where critical mass considerations are unimportant.
  - Businesses following a harvest strategy wherein market share is being consciously relinquished in order to maintain high prices and generate maximum positive cash flow.
  - Businesses following a heavy cost take-out strategy where achieving minimum costs is critical.
  - Businesses where there is unusual need for rapid decisions, frequently on a sole-source basis, and wherein time is not usually available for integration, negotiation and exploration of a range of action alternatives.
  - Heavy geographic dispersion wherein time/distance factors make close interpersonal integration on a face-to-face recurrent basis quite difficult.

3.7 MODIFICATION OF MATRIX STRUCTURES

The matrix can take many forms, but there are basically three common varieties. Each type represents a different degree of authority attributed to the program manager and indirectly identifies the relative size of the company. As an example, in the matrix of Figure 3–7 all program managers report directly to the general manager. This type of arrangement works best for small companies that have a minimum number of projects and assumes that the general manager has sufficient time to coordinate activities between his project managers. In this type of arrangement, all conflicts between projects are hierarchically referred to the general manager for resolution.

As companies grew in size and the number of projects, the general manager found it increasingly difficult to act as the focal point for all projects. A new position was created, that of director of programs or manager of programs or projects. This is shown in Figure 3–9. The director of programs was responsible for all program management. This freed the general manager from the daily routine of having to monitor all programs himself.

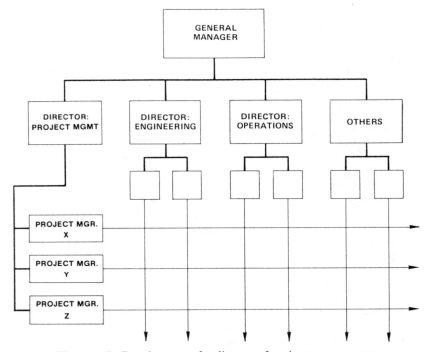

Figure 3–9. Development of a director of project management.

Beck has elaborated on the basic role of this new position, the manager of project managers (M.P.M.):[21]

One difference in the roles of the M.P.M. and the project manager is that the M.P.M. must place a great deal more emphasis on the overview of a project than on the nuts and bolts, tools, networks and the details of managing the project. The M.P.M. must see how the project fits into the overall organizational plan and how projects interrelate. His perspective is a little different from the project manager who is looking at the project on its own merits rather than how it fits into the overall organization.

The M.P.M. is a project manager, a people manager, a change manager and a systems manager. In general, one role cannot be considered more important than the other. The M.P.M. has responsibilities for managing the projects, directing and leading people and the project management effort, and planning for change in the orga-

---

21. Dale R. Beck, "The Role of the Manager of Project Managers," *Proceedings of the Ninth Annual International Seminar/Symposium on Project Management,* October 24–26, 1977, Chicago, Illinois, pp. 139–141.

nization. The Manager of Project Managers is a liaison between the Project Management Department and upper management as well as functional department management and acts as a systems manager when serving as a liaison.

Executives contend that an effective span of control is five to seven people. Does this apply to the director of project management as well? Consider a company that has fifteen projects going on at once. There are three projects over $5 million, seven are between $1 and $3 million, and five projects are under $700,000. Each project has a full-time project manager. Can all fifteen project managers report to the same person? The company solved this problem by creating a deputy director of project management. All projects over $1 million reported to the director, and all projects under $1 million went to the deputy director. The director's rationale soon fell by the wayside when he found that the more severe problems that were occupying his time were occurring on the smaller-dollar-volume projects, where flexibility in time, cost, and performance was nonexistent and trade-offs were almost impossible. If the project manager is actually a general manager, then the director of project management should be able to supervise effectively more than seven project managers. The desired span of control, of course, will vary from company to company and must take into account:

- The demands imposed on the organization by task complexity
- Available technology
- The external environment
- The needs of the organizational membership
- The types of customers and/or products

These variables influence the internal functioning of the company. Executives must realize that there is no one best way to organize under all conditions. This includes span of control.

As companies expand, it is inevitable that new and more complex conflicts arise. The control of the engineering functions poses such a problem:

- Should the project manager have ultimate responsibility for the engineering functions of a project, or should there be a deputy project manager who reports to the director of engineering and controls all technical activity?

Although there are pros and cons for both arrangements, the problem resolved itself in the company mentioned above when projects grew so large that the project manager became unable to handle both the project management and project engineering functions. Then, as shown in Figure 3–10, a chief

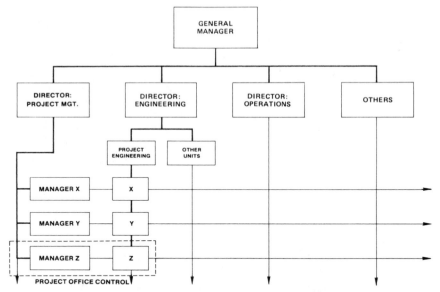

Figure 3–10. Placing project engineering in the project office.

project engineer was assigned to each project as deputy project manager, but remained functionally assigned to the director of engineering. The project manager was now responsible for time and cost considerations, whereas the project engineer was concerned with technical performance. The project engineer can be either "solid" vertically and "dotted" horizontally, or vice versa. There are also situations where the project engineer may be "solid" in both directions. The decision usually rests with the director of engineering. Of course, in a project where the project engineer would be needed on a part-time basis only, he would be solid vertically and dotted horizontally.

Engineering directors usually demand that the project engineer be solid vertically in order to give technical direction. As one director of engineering stated, "Only engineers that report to me will have the authority to give technical direction to other engineers. After all, how else can I be responsible for the technical integrity of the product when direction comes from outside my organization?"

This subdivision of functions is necessary in order to control large projects adequately. However, for small projects, say $100,000 or less, it is quite common on R&D projects for an engineer to serve as the project manager as well as the project engineer. Here, the project manager must have technical expertise, not merely understanding. Furthermore, this individual can still be

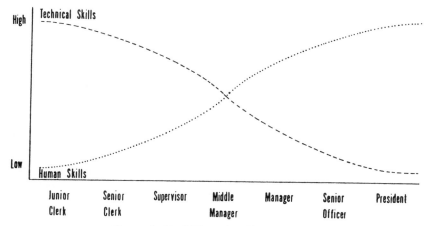

Figure 3–11. Philosophy of management.

attached to a functional engineering support unit other than project engineering. As an example, a mechanical engineering department receives a government contract for $75,000 to perform tests on a new material. The proposal is written by an engineer attached to the department. When the contract is awarded, this individual, although not in the project engineering department, can fulfill the role of project manager and project engineer while still reporting to the manager of the mechanical engineering department. This arrangement works best (and is cost-effective) for short-duration projects that cross a minimum number of functional units.

Finally, we must discuss the characteristics of a project engineer. In Figure 3–11, most people would place the project manager to the right of center with stronger human skills than technical skills, and the project engineer to the left of center with stronger technical skills than human skills. The question, of course, is, "How far from the center point will the project manager and project engineer be?" Today, many companies are merging project management and project engineering into one position. This can be seen on p. 126. Both the project manager and project engineer have similar functions above the dotted line but are different below the line.[22] The main reason for separating project management from project engineering is so that the project engineer will remain "solid" to the director of engineering in order to have the full authority to give technical direction to engineering.

---

22. Procurement, reliability, and maintainability may fall under the responsibility of the project engineer in some companies.

Project Management	*Project Engineering*
• Total project planning	• Total project planning
• Cost control	• Cost control
• Schedule control	• Schedule control
• System specifications	• System specifications
• Logistics support	• Logistics support

• Contract control	• Configuration control
• Report preparation and distribution	• Fabrication, testing and production technical leadership support
• Procurement	
• Identification of reliability and maintainability requirements	
• Staffing	
• Priority scheduling	
• Management information systems	

3.8 MATRIX LAYERING

Matrix layering can be defined as the creation of one matrix within a second matrix. For example, a company can have a total company matrix, and each division or department (i.e., project engineering) can have its own internalized matrix. In the situation of a matrix within a matrix, all matrices are formal rather than informal operations.

Matrix layering can also be a mix of formal and informal organizations. The formal matrix exists for work flow, but there can also exist an informal matrix for information flow. There are also authority matrices, leadership matrices, reporting matrices, and informal technical direction matrices. Figures 3–12 and 3–13 identify the design matrix and construction matrix that can exist within the total company matrix.[23]

Another example of layering would be the multidimensional matrix, shown in Figure 3–14, where each slice represents either time, distance, or geographic area. For example, a New York bank utilizes a multinational matrix to control operations in foreign countries. In this case, each foreign country would represent a different slice of the total matrix.

---

23. Marc S. Caspe, "An Overview of Project Management and Project Management Services," *Proceedings of the Ninth Annual Seminar Symposium on Project Management,* 1979, pp. 8–9.

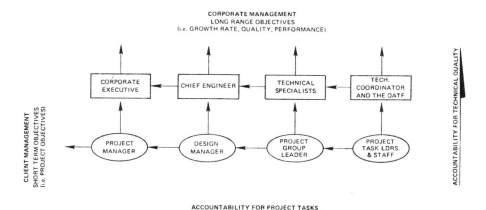

Figure 3-12. The design organization matrix.

3.9 SELECTING THE ORGANIZATIONAL FORM

Project management has matured as an outgrowth of the need to develop and produce complex and/or large projects in the shortest possible time, within anticipated cost, and with required reliability and performance, and (when applicable) to realize a profit. Granted that modern organizations have become so complex that traditional organizational structures and relationships no longer allow for effective management, how can executives determine which organizational form is best, especially since some projects last for only a few weeks or months while others may take years?

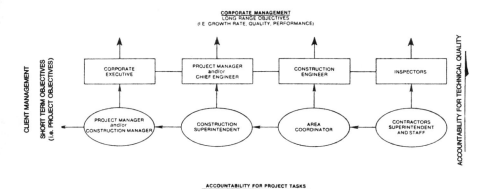

Figure 3-13. The construction organization matrix.

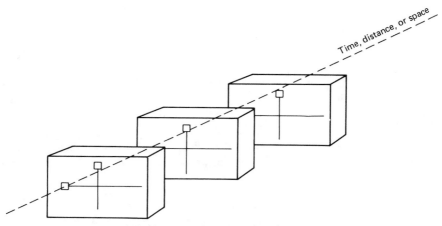

Figure 3–14. The multidimensional matrix.

To answer such a question, we must first determine whether or not the necessary characteristics exist to warrant a project management organizational form. Generally speaking, the project management approach can be effectively applied to a one-time undertaking that is:[24]

- Definable in terms of a specific goal
- Infrequent, unique, or unfamiliar to the present organization
- Complex with respect to interdependence of detailed tasks
- Critical to the company

Once a group of tasks is selected and considered to be a project, the next step is to define the kinds of projects, described in Section 2.5. These include individual, staff, special, and matrix or aggregate projects.

Unfortunately, many companies do not have a clear definition of what a project is. As a result, large project teams are often constructed for small projects when they could be handled more quickly and effectively by some other structural form. All structural forms have their advantages and disadvantages, but the project management approach, even with its disadvantages, appears to be the best possible alternative.

The basic factors that influence the selection of a project organizational form are:

- Project size
- Project length

---

24. John M. Stewart, "Making Project Management Work," *Business Horizons*, Fall 1965, p.54.

- Experience with project management organization
- Philosophy and visibility of upper-level management
- Project location
- Available resources
- Unique aspects of the project

This last item requires further comment. Project management (especially with a matrix) usually works best for the control of human resources and thus may be more applicable to labor-intensive projects rather than capital-intensive projects. Labor-intensive organizations have formal project management, whereas capital-intensive organizations may use informal project management. Figure 3–15 shows how matrix management was implemented by an electric equipment manufacturer. The company decided to use fragmented matrix management for facility development projects. After observing the success of the fragmented matrix, the executives expanded matrix operations to include interim and ongoing capital equipment projects. The first three levels were easy to implement. The fourth level, ongoing business, was more difficult to convert to a matrix because of functional management resistance and the fear of losing authority.

Four fundamental parameters must be analyzed when considering implementation of a project organizational form:

- Integrating devices
- Authority structure
- Influence distribution
- Information system

Project management is a means of integrating all company efforts, especially research and development, by selecting an appropriate organizational form.

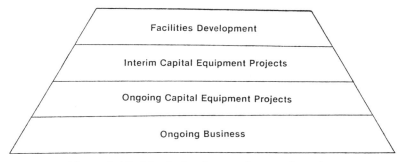

Figure 3–15. Matrix development in manufacturing.

Two questions arise when we think of designing the organization to facilitate the work of the integrators:[25]

- Is it better to establish a formal integration department, or simply to set up integrating positions independent of one another?
- If individual integrating positions are set up, how should they be related to the larger structure?

Informal integration works best if, and only if, effective collaboration can be achieved between conflicting units. Without any clearly defined authority, the role of the integrator is simply to act as an exchange medium across the interface of two functional units. As the size of the organization increases, formal integration positions must exist, especially in situations where intense conflict can occur (e.g., research and development).

Not all organizations need a pure matrix structure to achieve this integration. Many problems can be solved simply through the scalar chain of command, depending upon the size of the organization and the nature of the project. The organization needed to achieve project control can vary in size from one person to several thousand people. The organizational structure needed for effective project control is governed by the desires of top management and project circumstances.

Unfortunately, integration and specialization appear to be diametrically opposed. As described by Davis:[26]

When organization is considered synonymous with structure, the dual needs of specialization and coordination are seen as inversely related, as opposite ends of a single variable, as the horns of a dilemma. Most managers speak of this dilemma in terms of the centralization–decentralization variable. Formulated in this manner, greater specialization leads to more difficulty in coordinating the differentiated units. This is why the (de)centralization pendulum is always swinging, and no ideal point can be found at which it can come to rest.

The division of labor in a heirarchical pyramid means that specialization must be defined either by function, by product, or by area. Firms must select one of these dimensions as primary and then subdivide the other two into subordinate units further down the pyramid. The appropriate choice for primary, secondary and tertiary dimensions is based largely upon the strategic needs of the enterprise.

Top management must decide upon the authority structure that will control the integration mechanism. The authority structure can range from pure functional authority (traditional management), to product authority (product man-

---

25. William P. Killian, "Project Management—Future Organizational Concepts," *Marquette Business Review,* Vol 2, 1971, pp. 90–107.
26. Stanley M. Davis, "Two Models of Organization: Unity of Command Versus Balance of Power," *Sloan Management Review,* Fall 1974, p. 30. Reprinted by permission of the publisher. Copyright © 1974 by the Sloan Management Review Association. All rights reserved.

agement), and finally to dual authority (matrix management). This range is shown in Figure 3–16. From a management point of view, organizational forms are often selected based upon how much authority top management wishes to delegate or surrender.

Integration of activities across functional boundaries can also be accomplished by influence. Influence includes such factors as participation in budget planning and approval, design changes, location and size of offices, salaries, and so on. Influence can also cut administrative red tape and develop a much more unified informal organization.

Information systems also play an important role. Previously we stated that one of the advantages of several project management structures is the ability to make both rapid and timely decisions with almost immediate response to environmental changes. Information systems are designed to get the right information to the right person at the right time in a cost-effective manner. Organizational functions must facilitate the flow of information through the management network.

Galbraith has described additional factors that can influence organizational selection. These factors are:[27]

- Diversity of product lines
- Rate of change of the product lines

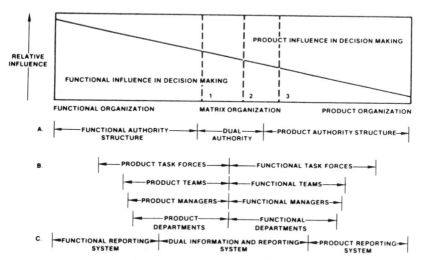

Figure 3–16. The range of alternatives. (Source: Jay R. Galbraith, "Matrix Organization Designs," *Business Horizons,* February 1971, p. 37.)

---

27. Jay R. Galbraith, "Matrix Organization Designs," *Business Horizons,* February 1971, pp. 29–40.

- Interdependencies among subunits
- Level of technology
- Presence of economies of scale
- Organizational size

A diversity of product lines requires both top-level and functional managers to maintain knowledge in all areas. Diversity makes it more difficult for managers to make realistic estimates concerning resource allocations and the control of time, cost, schedules, and technology. The systems approach to management requires sufficient information and alternatives to be available so that effective trade-offs can be established. For diversity in a high-technology environment, the organizational choice might, in fact, be a trade-off between the flow of work and the flow of information. Diversity tends toward strong product authority and control.

Many functional organizations consider themselves as companies within a company and pride themselves on their independence. This attitude poses a severe problem in trying to develop a synergistic atmosphere. Successful project management requires that functional units recognize the interdependence that must exist in order for technology to be shared and schedule dates to be met. Interdependency is also required in order to develop strong communication channels as well as coordination.

The use of new technologies poses a serious problem in that technical expertise must be established in all specialties, including engineering, production, material control, and safety. Maintaining technical expertise works best in strong functional disciplines, provided the information is not purchased outside the organization. The main problem, however, is that of how to communicate this expertise across functional lines. Independent R&D units can be established as opposed to integrating R&D into each functional department's routine efforts. Organizational control requirements are much more difficult in high-technology industries with ongoing research and development than with pure production groups.

Economies of scale and size can also affect organizational selection. The economies of scale are most often controlled by the amount of physical resources that a company has available. For example, a company with limited facilities and resources might find it impossible to compete with other companies on production or competitive bidding for larger dollar-volume products. Such a company must rely heavily on maintaining multiple projects (or products), each of low cost or volume, whereas a larger organization may need only three or four projects large enough to sustain the organization. The larger the economies of scale, the more the organization tends to favor pure functional management.

The size of the organization is important in that it can limit the amount of technical expertise in the economies of scale. While size may have little effect on the organizational structure, it does have a severe impact on the economies of scale. Small companies, for example, cannot maintain large specialist staffs and, therefore, incur a larger cost for lost specialization and lost economies of scale.

The four factors described above for organizational form selections together with the six alternatives of Galbraith can be regarded as universal in nature. Beyond these universal factors, we must look at the company in terms of its product, business base, and personnel. Goodman has defined a set of subfactors related to R&D groups:[28]

- Clear location of responsibility
- Ease and accuracy of communication
- Effective cost control
- Ability to provide good technical supervision
- Flexibility of staffing
- Importance to the company
- Quick reaction capability to sudden changes in the project
- Complexity of the project
- Size of the project with relation to other work in-house
- Form desired by customer
- Ability to provide a clear path for individual promotion

Goodman asked various managers to select from the above list and rank the factors from most important to least important in terms of how they would be considered in designing an organization. Both general management and project management personnel were queried. With one exception—the flexibility of staffing—the response from both groups correlated to a coefficient of 0.811. Clear location of responsibility was seen as the most important factor, and a path for promotion the least important.

Middleton conducted a mail survey to aerospace firms in an attempt to determine how well the companies using project management met their objectives. Forty-seven responses were received. Tables 3–7 and 3–8 identify the rusults. Middleton stated, "In evaluating the results of the survey, it appears that a company taking the project organization approach can be reasonably certain that it will improve controls and customer (out-of-company) relations, but internal operations will be more complex."[29]

---

28. Richard A. Goodman, "Organizational Preference in Research and Development," *Human Relations*, Vol. 3, No. 4, 1970, pp. 279–298.
29. C. J. Middleton, "How to Set Up a Project Organization," *Harvard Business Reivew*, March–April 1967, pp. 73–82. Copyright © 1967 by the President and Fellows of Harvard College; All rights reserved.

Table 3–7. Major Company Advantages of Project Management.

ADVANTAGES	PERCENT OF RESPONDENTS
• Better control of projects	92%
• Better customer relations	80%
• Shorter product development time	40%
• Lower program costs	30%
• Improved quality and reliability	26%
• Higher profit margins	24%
• Better control over program security	13%

OTHER BENEFITS

- Better project visibility and focus on results
- Improved coordination among company divisions doing work on the project
- Higher morale and better mission orientation for employees working on the project.
- Accelerated development of managers due to breadth of project responsibilities

(Source: C. J. Middleton, "How to Set Up a Project Organization," *Harvard Business Review*, March–April 1967, pp. 73–82).

The way in which companies operate their project organization is bound to affect the organization, both during the operation of the project and after the project has been completed and personnel have been disbanded. The overall effects on the company must be looked at from a personnel and cost control standpoint. This will be accomplished, in depth, in later chapters. Although project management is growing, the creation of a project organization does not necessarily ensure that an assigned objective will be accomplished successfully. Furthermore, weaknesses can develop in the areas of maintaining capability and structural changes.

Table 3–8. Major Company Disadvantages of Project Management.

DISADVANTAGES	PERCENT OF RESPONDENTS
• More complex internal operations	51%
• Inconsistency in application of company policy	32%
• Lower utilization of personnel	13%
• Higher program costs	13%
• More difficult to manage	13%
• Lower profit margins	2%

OTHER DISADVANTAGES

- Tendency for functional groups to neglect their job and let the project organization do everything
- Too much shifting of personnel from project to project
- Duplication of functional skills in project organization

(Source: C. J. Middleton, "How to Set Up a Project Organization," *Harvard Business Review*, March–April 1967, pp. 73–82).

Project management structures have been known to go out of control:[30]

When a matrix appears to be going out of control, executives revert back to classical management. This results in:
- Reduced authority for the project manager
- All project decision-making performed at executive levels
- Increase in executive meddling in projects
- Creation of endless manuals for job descriptions

This can sometimes be prevented by frequently asking for authority/responsibility clarification and by the use of linear responsibility charts.

An almost predictable result of using the project management approach is the increase in management positions. Killian describes the results of two surveys:[31]

One comapny compared its organization and management structure as it existed before it began forming project units with the structure that existed afterward. The number of departments had increased from 65 to 106, while total employment remained practically the same. The number of employees for every supervisor had dropped from 13.4 to 12.8. The company concluded that a major cause of this change was the project groups [see footnote 29 for reference article].

Another company uncovered proof of its conclusion when it counted the number of second-level and higher management positions. It found that it had 11 more vice presidents and directors, 35 more managers, and 56 more second-level supervisors. Although the company attributed part of this growth to an upgrading of titles, the effect of the project organization was the creation of 60 more management positions.

Although the project organization is a specialized, task-oriented entity, it seldom, if ever, exists apart from the traditional structure of the organization.[32] All project management structures overlap the traditional structure. Furthermore, companies can have more than one project organizational form in existence at one time. A major steel product, for example, has a matrix structure for R&D and a product structure elsewhere.

Accepting a project management structure is a giant step from which there may be no return. The company may have to create more management positions without changing the total employment levels. In addition, incorporation of a project organization is almost always accompanied by the upgrading of

30. Adapted from L. E. Greiner, and V. E. Schein, "The Paradox of Managing a Project-Oriented Matrix: Establishing Coherence within Chaos," *Sloan Management Review,* Winter 1981, p. 17, by permission of the publisher. Copyright © 1981 by the Sloan Management Review Association. All rights reserved.
31. William P. Killian, "Project Management—Future Organizational Concepts," *Marquette Business Review,* Vol. 2, 1971, pp. 90–107.
32. Allen R. Janger, "Anatomy of the Project Organization," *Business Management Record,* November 1963, pp. 12–18.

jobs. In any event, management must realize that whichever project management structure is selected, a dynamic state of equilibrium will be necessary.

3.10 STRUCTURING THE SMALL COMPANY

Small and medium-size companies generally prefer to have the project manager report fairly high up in the chain of command, even though the project manager may be working on a relatively low-priority project. Project managers are usually viewed as less of a threat in small organizations than in the larger ones, thus creating less of a problem if they report high up.

Organizing the small company for projects involves two major questions:

- Where should the project manager be placed within the organization?
- Are the majority of the projects internal or external to the organization?

These two questions are implicitly related. For either large, complex projects or those involving outside customers, project managers generally report to a high level in the organization. For small or internal projects, the project manager reports to a middle or lower-level manager.

Small and medium-size companies have been very successful in managing internal projects using departmental project management (see Figure 3-3), especially when only a few functional groups must interface with one another. Quite often, line managers are permitted to wear multiple hats and also act as project managers, thereby reducing the need for hiring additional project managers.

Customers external to the organization are usually favorably impressed if a small company identifies a project manager who is dedicated and committed to their project, even if only on a part-time basis. Thus outside customers, particularly through a competitive bidding environment, respond favorably toward a matrix structure, even if the matrix structure is simply eyewash for the customer. For example, consider the matrix structure shown in Figure 3-17. Both large and small companies that operate on a matrix usually develop a separate organizational chart for each customer. Figure 3-17 represents the organizational chart that would be presented to Alpha Company. The Alpha Company project would be identified with bold lines and would be placed immediately below the vicepresident, regardless of the priority of the project. After all, if you were the Alpha Company customer, would you want your project to appear at the bottom of the list?

Figure 3–17 also identifies two other key points that are important to small companies. First, only the name of the Alpha Company project manager, Bob Ray, need be identified. The reason for this is that Bob Ray may also be the project manager for one or more of the other projects, and it is usually not a

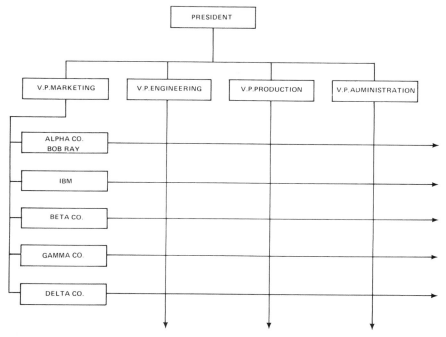

Figure 3–17. Matrix for a small company.

good practice to let the customer know that Bob Ray will have split loyalties among several projects. Actually, the organization chart shown in Figure 3–17 is for a machine tool company employing 280 people, with five major and thirty minor projects. The company has only two full-time project managers. Bob Ray manages the projects for Alpha, Gamma, and Delta Companies; the Beta Company project has the second full-time project manager; and the IBM project is being managed personally by the vicepresident of engineering, who happens to be wearing two hats.

The second key point is that small companies generally should not identify the names of functional employees because:

- The functional employees are probably part-time.
- It is usually best in small companies for all communications to be transmitted through the project manager.

Another example of how a simple matrix structure can be used to impress the customers is shown in Figure 3–18. The company identified here actually contains only thirty-eight employees. Very small companies normally assign

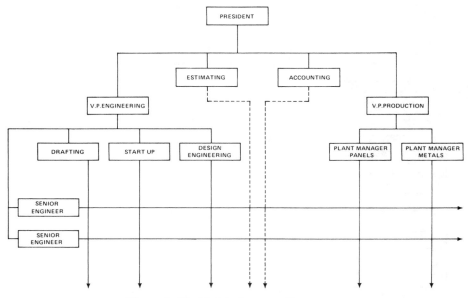

Figure 3–18. Matrix for a small company.

the estimating department to report directly to the president, as shown in Figure 3–18. In addition, the senior engineers, who appear to be acting in the role of project managers, may simply be the department managers for drafting, startup, and/or design engineering. Yet, from an outside customer's perspective, the company has a dedicated and committed project manager for the project.

3.11 TRANSITIONAL MANAGEMENT[33]

Organizational redesign is occurring at a rapid rate because of shorter product life cycles, rapidly changing environments, accelerated development of sophisticated information systems, and increased marketplace competitiveness. Because of these factors, more and more companies are considering project management organizations as a solution.

The obvious question is, "Why have some companies been able to implement this change in a short period of time while other companies require years?" The

---

33. Adapted from Harold Kerzner and David I. Cleland, "Transitional Management: The Key to Successful Implementation of Project Management," Proceedings of the 1984 Project Management Institute Seminar/Symposium on Project Management, Oct. 8–10, 1984, pp. 181–194.

answer is that successful implementation requires good transitional management.

Transitional management is the art and science of managing the conversion period from one organizational design to another. Transitional management necessitates an understanding of the new goals, objectives, roles, expectations, and fears that people consider.

- Senior management: maintain or increase current power and authority and delegate as little as possible.
- Line management: Minimize the project manager's involvement and impact on the functional empire.
- Project managers: accept and adapt to the newer responsibilities with minimum disruption to the organization.
- Employees: receive additional monetary and nonmonetary rewards, be evaluated correctly, and obtain more visibility with management.

Some people fear change, while others look at it as a chance to demonstrate their creativity. It is the responsibility of the transitional managers to remove personnel fears and stimulate creativity and the desire to achieve in line with corporate objectives.

A survey was conducted of executives, managers, and employees in 38 companies which had implemented matrix management. Almost all executives felt that the greatest success can be achieved through proper training and education, both during and after transition. In addition to training, executives stated that the following 15 challenges must be accounted for during transition:

- Transfer of power: Some line managers will find it extremely difficult to accept someone else managing their projects, whereas some project managers will find it difficult to give orders to workers who belong to someone else.
- Trust: The secret to a successful transition without formal executive authority will be trust between line managers, between project managers, and between project and line managers. It takes time for trust to develop. Senior management should encourage it throughout the transition life cycle.
- Policies and Procedures: The establishment of well-accepted policies and procedures is a slow and tedious process. Trying to establish rigid policies and procedures at project initiation will lead to difficulties.
- Hierarchical consideration: During transition, every attempt should be made to minimize hierarchical considerations which could affect successful organizational maturity.
- Priority scheduling: Priorities should be established only when needed, not on a continual basis. If priority shifting is continuous, confusion and disenchantment will occur.

- Personnel problems: During transition there will be personnel problems, as moving to new locations, status changes, and new informal organizations. These problems should be addressed on a continuous basis.
- Communications: During transition, new channels of communications should be built but not at the expense of destroying old ones. Transition phases should show employees that communication can be multidirectional; i.e., a project manager talking directly to functional employees.
- Project manager acceptance: Resistance to the project manager position can be controlled through proper training. People tend to resist what they do not understand.
- Competition: Although some competition is healthy within an organization, it can be detrimental during transition. Competition should not be encouraged at the expense of the total organization.
- Tools: It is common practice for each line organization to establish their own tools and techniques. During transition, no attempt should be made to force the line organizations to depart from their current practice. Rather, it is better for the project managers to develop tools and techniques which can be integrated with those in the functional groups.
- Contradicting demands: During transition and after maturity, contradicting demands will exist as a way of life. When they first occur during transition, they should be handled in a "working atmosphere" rather than a crisis mode.
- Reporting: If any type of standardization is to be developed, it should be for project status reporting and should be the same, regardless of the size of the project.
- Teamwork: Systematic planning with strong functional input will produce teamwork. Using planning groups during transition will not obtain the necessary functional and project commitments.
- Theory X–Theory Y: During transition, functional employees may soon find themselves managed under either Theory X or Theory Y approaches. People must realize (through training) that this is a way of life in project management, especially during crises.
- Overmanagement costs: A mistake often made by executives is that projects can be managed with less resources. This usually leads to disaster because undermanagement costs may be an order of magnitude greater than overmanagement costs.

Transition to a project-driven matrix organization is not easy. Several caveats are in order for managers and professionals contemplating such a move:

- Proper planning and organization of the transition on a life-cycle basis will facilitate a successful change.

- Training of the executives, line managers, and employees in project management knowledge, skills, and attitudes is critical to a successful transition and probably will shorten the transition time.
- Employee involvement and acceptance may be the single most important function during transition.
- The strongest driving force toward success during transition is a demonstration of commitment to and involvement in project management by senior executives.
- Organizational behavior becomes important during transition.
- It is extremely important that commitments made by senior executives prior to transition be preserved both during and following transition.
- Major concessions by senior management will come slowly.
- Schedule or performance compromises are not acceptable during transition; cost overruns may be acceptable.
- Conflict intensity among participants increases during transitions.
- If project managers are willing to manage with only implied authority during transition, then the total transition time may be drastically reduced.
- It is not clear how long transition will take.

Transition from a classical or product organization to a project-driven organization is not easy. With proper understanding, training, demonstrated commitment, and patience, transition will have a good chance for success.

PROBLEMS

3-1 Much has been written about how to identify and interpret signs that indicate that a new organizational form is needed. Grinnell and Apple have identified five signs in addition to those previously described in Section 3.6:[34]

- Management is satisfied with its technical skills, but projects are not meeting time, cost, and other project requirements.
- There is a high commitment to getting project work done, but great fluctuation in how well performance specifications are met.
- Highly talented specialists involved in the project feel exploited and misused.
- Particular technical groups or individuals constantly blame each other for failure to meet specifications or delivery dates.
- Projects are on time and to specification, but groups and individuals aren't satisfied with the achievement.

Grinnell and Apple state that there is a good chance that a matrix structure will eliminate or alleviate these problems. Do you agree or disagree? Does your answer depend upon the type of project? Give examples or counter-examples to defend your answers.

---

34. See note 19 above.

3–2 One of the most difficult problems facing management is that of how to minimize the transition time between changeover from a purely traditional organizational form to a project organizational form. Managing the changeover is difficult in that management must consistently "provide individual training on teamwork and group problem solving; also, provide the project and functional groups with assignments to help build teamwork."[35]

TRW Systems Group tried to make almost an instantaneous conversion from a traditional to a matrix organizational form. Managing the conversion was accomplished through T-groups and special study sessions. Describe the problems associated with new organizational form conversion. Which project form should be easiest to adopt to? State how long a period you might need for conversion from a traditional structure to a product structure, matrix structure, and task force structure. (Note: the TRW Systems Group Studies can be found in cases 9-476-117, 9-413-066, and 9-413-069 distributed by the Intercollegiate Case Clearing House. See Bibliography.)

3–3 Do you think that personnel working in a project organizational structure should undergo "therapy" sessions or seminars on a regular basis so as to better understand their working environment? If yes, how frequently? Does the frequency depend upon the project organizational form selected, or should they all be treated equally?

3–4 Which organizational form would be best for the following corporate strategies?[36]

    a. Developing, manufacturing, and marketing many diverse but interrelated technological products and materials.
    b. Having market interests that span virtually every major industry.
    c. Becoming multinational with a rapidly expanding global business.
    d. Working in a business environment of rapid and drastic change, together with strong competition.

3–5 Robert E. Shannon ("Matrix Management Structures," *Industrial Engineering,* March 1972, pp. 27–29. Published and copyright 1972 by the American Institute of Industrial Engineers Inc., Norcross, GA 30092) made the following remarks:

When operating under a matrix management approach, it is obviously extremely important that the responsibility and authority of each manager be clearly defined, understood, and accepted by both functional and program people. These relationships need to be spelled out in writing. It is essential that in the various operating policies, the specific authority of the program manager be clearly defined in terms of program direction, and that the authority of the functional executive be defined in terms of operational direction.

Do you think that documenting relationships are necessary in order to operate effectively in any project organizational structure? How would you relate Shannon's remarks to a statement made in the previous chapter that each project can set up its

---

35. See note 19 above.
36. See note 18 above.

own policies, procedures, rules, and directives as long as they conform to company guidelines?

3-6 In general, how could each of the following parameters influence your choice for an organizational structure? Explain your answers in as much depth as possible.

 a. The project cost
 b. The project schedule
 c. The project duration
 d. The technology requirements
 e. The geographical locations
 f. The required working relationships with the customer

3-7 In general, what are the overall advantages and disadvantages of superimposing one organizational form over another?

3-8 In deciding to go to a new organizational form, what impact should the capabilities of the following groups have upon your decision?

 a. Top management
 b. Middle management
 c. Lower-level management

3-9 Should a company be willing to accept a project that requires immediate organizational restructuring? If so, what factors should you consider?

3-10 Figure 2-7 identifies the different life cycles of programs, projects, systems, and products. For each of the life cycles' phases, select a project organizational form that you feel would work best. Defend your answer with examples, advantages, and disadvantages.

3-11 A major steel producer in the United States uses a matrix structure for R&D. Once the product is developed, the product organizational structure is used. Are there any advantages to this setup?

3-12 A major American manufacturer of automobile parts has a division that has successfully existed for the past ten years with multiple products, a highly sophisticated R&D section, and a pure traditional structure. The growth rate for the past five years has been 12 percent. Almost all middle and upper-level managers who have worked in this division have received promotions and transfers to either another division or corporate headquarters. According to "the book," this division has all the prerequisites signifying that they should have a project organizational form of some sort, and yet they are extremely successful without it. Just from the amount of information presented, how can you account for their continued success? What do you think would be the major obstacles in convincing the personnel that a new organizational form would be better? Do you think that continued success can be achieved under the present structure?

3-13 Several authors contend that technology suffers in a pure product organizational form because there is no one group responsible for long-range planning, whereas the pure functional organization tends to sacrifice time and schedule. Do you agree or disagree with this statement? Defend your choice with examples.

3-14 Below are three statements that are often used to describe the environment of a matrix. Do you agree or disagree? Defend your answer.

  a. Project management in a matrix allows for fuller utilization of personnel.
  b. The project manager and functional manager must agree on priorities.
  c. Decision making in a matrix requires continuous trade-offs on time, cost, technical risk and uncertainty.

3-15 Assume that you have to select a project organizational form for a small company. For each form described in this chapter, discuss the applicability and state the advantages and disadvantages as they apply to this small company. (You may find it necessary to first determine the business base of the small company.)

3-16 How would each person identified below respond to the question, "How many bosses do you have?"

  a. Project manager
  b. Functional team member
  c. Functional manager
(Repeat for each organizational form discussed in Chapter 3.)

3-17 If a project were large enough to contain its own resources, would a matrix organizational form be acceptable?

3-18 One of the most common reasons for not wanting to adopt a matrix is the excessive administrative costs and accompanying overhead rates. Would you expect the overhead rates to decrease as the matrix matures? (Disregard other factors which can influence the overhead rates, such as business base, growth rate, etc.)

3-19 Which type of organizational structure is best for R&D personnel to keep in touch with other researchers?

3-20 Which type of organizational form fosters teamwork in the best manner?

3-21 Canadian bankers have been using the matrix organizational structure to create "banking general managers" for all levels of a bank. Does the matrix structure readily admit itself to a banking environment in order to create future managers? Can we consider a branch manager as a matrix project manager?

3-22 A major utility company in Cleveland has what is commonly called "fragmented" project management where each department maintains project managers through staff positions. The project managers occasionally have to integrate activities that involve departments other than their own. Each project normally requires involvement of several people. The company also has product managers operating out of a rather crude project (product) organizational structure. Recently, the product managers and project managers were competing for resources within the same departments.

To complicate matters further, management has put a freeze on hiring. Last week top management identified 120 different projects that could be undertaken. Unfortunately, under the current structure there are not enough staff project managers available to handle these projects. Also, management would like to make better use of the scarce functional resources.

Staff personnel contend that the solution to the above problems is the establishment of a project management division under which there will be a project management department and a product management department. The staff people feel that under this arrangement better utilization of line personnel will be made, and that each project can be run with fewer staff people, thus providing the opportunity for more projects. Do you agree or disagree, and what problems do you foresee?

3–23 Some organizational structures are considered to be "project-driven." Define what is meant by "project-driven." Which organizational forms described in this chapter would fall under your definition?

3–24 Are there any advantages to having a single project engineer as opposed to having a committee of key functional employees who report to the director of engineering?

3–25 The major difficulty in the selection of a project organization form involves placement of the project manager. In the evolutionary process, the project manager started out reporting to a department head and ultimately ended up reporting to a senior executive. In general, what were the major reasons for having the project manager report higher and higher in the organizational structure?

3–26 Ralph is a department manager who is quite concerned about the performance of the people beneath him. After several months of analysis, Ralph has won the acceptance of his superiors for setting up a project management structure in his department. Out of the twenty-three departments in the company, his will be the only one with formalized project management. Can this situation be successful even though several projects require interfacing with other departments?

3–27 A large electronics corporation has a multimillion dollar project in which 90 percent of the work stays within one division. The division manager wants to be the project manager. Should this be allowed even though there exists a project management division?

3–28 The internal functioning of an organization must consider:

- The demands imposed on the organization by task complexity
- Available technology
- The external environment
- The needs of the organizational membership

Considering these facts, should an organization search for the one best way to organize under all condition? Should managers examine the functioning of an organization relative to its needs, or vice versa?

3–29 Project managers, in order to get the job accomplished, need adequate organizational status and authority. One corporate executive contends that the organizational chart, such as that in Figure 3–7, can be modified to show that the project managers have adequate authority by placing the department managers in boxes at the tip of the functional responsibility arrowheads. The executive further contends that, with this approach, the project managers appear to be higher in the organization than their departmental counterparts but are actually equal in status. Do you agree or disagree with the executive's idea? Will there be a proper balance of power between project and department managers with this organizational structure?

3-30 Defend or attack the following two statements concerning the operation of a matrix:

- There should be no disruption due to dual accountability.
- A difference in judgment should not delay work in progress.

3-31 A company has fifteen projects going on at once. Three projects are over $5 million, seven projects are between $1 million and $3 million, and five projects are between $500,000 and $700,000. Each project has a full-time project manager. Just based upon this information, which organizational form would be best? Can all the project managers report to the same person?

3-32 A major insurance company is considering the implementation of project management. The majority of the projects in the company are two weeks in duration, with very few existing beyond one month. Can project management work here?

3-33 The definition of project management in Section 1.8 identifies project teams and task forces. How would you distinguish between a project team and a task force, and what industries and/or projects would be applicable to each?

3-34 Can informal project management work in a structured environment at the same time as formal project management and share the same resources?

3-35 Several people believe that the matrix structure can be multidimensional (as shown in Figure 3-14). Explain the usefulness of such a structure.

3-36 Many companies have informal project management where work flows horizontally, but in an informal manner. What are the characteristics of informal project management? Which types of companies can operate effectively with informal project management?

3-37 Some companies have tried to develop a matrix within a matrix. Is it possible to have a matrix for formal project control and an internal authority matrix, communication matrix, responsibility matrix, or a combination of several of these?

3-38 Is it possible for a matrix to get out of control because of too many small projects, each competing for the same shared resources? If so, how many projects are too many? How can management control the number of projects? Does your answer depend upon whether the organization is project-driven or non-project-driven?

3-39 A government subcontractor operates with a pure specialized product management organizational structure and has four product lines. All employees are required to have a top secret security clearance. The subcontractor's plant is structured such that each of the four product lines occupies a secured area in the building. Employees wear security badges that give them access to the different areas. Most of the employees are authorized to have access only to their area. Only the executives have access to all four areas. For security reasons, functional employees are not permitted to discuss the product lines with each other.

Many of the projects performed in each of the product lines are identical, and severe duplication of efforts exist. Management is interested in converting over to a matrix structure to minimize the duplication of effort. What problems must be overcome before and during matrix implementation?

3–40 A company has decided to go to full project management utilizing a matrix structure. Can the implementation be done in stages? Can the matrix be partially implemented, say in one portion of the organization, and then gradually expanded across the rest of the company?

3–41 A company has two major divisions, both housed under the same roof. One division is the aerospace group, where all activities are performed within a formal matrix. The second division is the industrial group, which operates with pure product management, except for the MIS department, which has an informal matrix. If both divisions have to share common corporate resources, what problems can occur?

3–42 Several Fortune 100 corporations have a corporate engineering group that assumes the responsibility of the project management/project engineering function for all major capital projects in all divisions worldwide. Explain how the corporate engineering function should work, as well as its advantages and disadvantages.

CASE STUDY: JONES AND SHEPHARD ACCOUNTANTS, INC.

By 1970, Jones and Shephard Accountants, Inc. (J&S) was ranked eighteenth in size by the American Association of Accountants. In order to compete wih the larger firms, J&S formed an Information Services Division designed primarily for studies and analyses. By 1975, the Information Services Division (ISD) had fifteen employees.

In 1977, the ISD purchased three minicomputers. With this increased capacity, J&S expanded its services to help satisfy the needs of outside customers. By September 1978, the internal and external work loads had increased to a point where the ISD now employed over fifty people.

The director of the division was very disappointed in the way that activities were being handled. There was no single person assigned to push through a project, and outside customers did not know who to call to get answers regarding project status. The director found that most of his time was being spent on day-to-day activities such as conflict resolution instead of strategic planning and policy formulation.

The biggest problems facing the director were the two continuous internal projects (called Project X and Project Y, for simplicity) which required month-end data collation and reporting. The director felt that these two projects were important enough to require a full-time project manager on each effort.

In October 1978, corporate announced that the ISD director would be reassigned on February 1, 1979, and that the announcement of his replacement would not be made until the middle of January. The same week that the announcement was made,

Exhibit 3-1. ISD Organizational Chart.

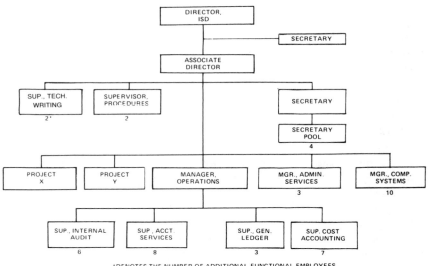

*DENOTES THE NUMBER OF ADDITIONAL FUNCTIONAL EMPLOYEES

two individuals were hired from outside the company to take charge of Project X and Project Y. Exhibit 3–1 shows the organizational structure of the ISD.

Within the next thirty days, rumors spread throughout the organization about who would become the new director. Most people felt that the position would be filled from within the division and that the most likely candidates would be the two new project managers. In addition, the associate director was due to retire in December, thus creating two openings.

On January 3, 1979 a confidential meeting was held between the ISD director and the systems manager.

ISD Director: "Corporate has approved my request to promote you to division director. Unfortunately, your job will not be an easy one. You're going to have to restructure the organization somehow so that our employees will not have as many conflicts as they are now faced with. My secretary is typing up a confidential memo for you explaining my observations on the problems within our division.

"Remember, your promotion should be held in the strictest of confidence until the final announcement later this month. I'm telling you this now so that you can begin planning the restructuring. My memo should help you." (See Exhibit 3–2 for the memo.)

The systems manager read the memo and, after due consideration, decided that some form of matrix would be best. To help him structure the organization properly, an outside consultant was hired to help identify the potential problems with changing over to a matrix. The following problem areas were identified by the consultant:

1. The operations manager controls more than 50 percent of the people resources. You might want to break up his empire. This will have to be done very carefully.
2. The secretary pool is placed too high in the organization.

EXHIBIT 3-2
CONFIDENTIAL MEMO

From: ISD Director
To: Systems Manager
Date: January 3, 1979

Congratulations on your promotion to division director. I sincerely hope that your tenure will be productive both personally and for corporate. I have prepared a short list of the major obstacles that you will have to consider when you take over the controls.

1. Both Project X and Project Y managers are highly competent individuals. In the last four or five days, however, they have appeared to create more conflicts for us than we had previously. This could be my fault for not delegating them sufficient authority, or could be a result of the fact that several of our people consider these two individuals as prime candidates for my position. In addition, the operations manager does not like other managers coming into his "empire" and giving direction.
2. I'm not sure that we even need an associate director. That decision will be up to you.
3. Corporate has been very displeased with our inability to work with outside customers. You must consider this problem with any organizational structure you choose.
4. The corporate strategic plan for our division contains an increased emphasis on special, internal MIS projects. Corporate wants to limit our external activities for a while until we get our internal affairs in order.
5. I made the mistake of changing our organizational structure on a day-to-day basis. Perhaps it would have been better to design a structure that could satisfy advanced needs, especially one that we can grow into.

---

3. The supervisors who now report to the associate director will have to be reassigned lower in the organization if the associate director's position is abolished.
4. One of the major problem areas will be trying to convince corporate management that their change will be beneficial. You'll have to convince them that this change can be accomplished without having to increase division manpower.

5. You might wish to set up a separate department or a separate project for customer relations.
6. Introducing your employees to the matrix will be a problem. Each employee will look at the change differently. Most people have the tendency of looking first at the shift in the balance of power—have I gained or have I lost power and status?

The systems manager evaluated the consultant's comments and then prepared a list of questions to ask the consultant at their next meeting:

1. What should the new organizational structure look like? Where should I put each person, specifically the managers?
2. When should I announce the new organizational change? Should it be at the same time as my appointment or at a later date?
3. Should I invite any of my people to provide input to the organizational restructuring? Can this be used as a technique to ease power plays?
4. Should I provide inside or outside seminars to train my people for the new organizational structure? How soon should they be held?

CASE STUDY: FARGO FOODS*

Fargo foods is a $2 billion a year international food manufacturer with canning facilities in 22 countries. Fargo products include meats, poultry, fish, vegetables, vitamins, and cat and dog foods. Fargo Foods has enjoyed a 12.5 percent growth rate each of the past eight years primarily due to the low overhead rates in the foreign companies.

During the past five years, Fargo had spent a large portion of retained earnings on capital equipment projects in order to increase productivity without increasing labor. An average of three new production plants have been constructed in each of the last five years. In addition, almost every plant has undergone major modifications each year in order to increase productivity.

In 1975, the president of Fargo Foods implemented formal project management for all construction projects using a matrix. By 1979, it became obvious that the matrix was not operating effectively or efficiently. In December 1979, the author consulted for Fargo Foods by interviewing several of the key managers and a multitude of functional personnel. Below are the several key questions and responses addressed to Fargo Foods:

Q. Give me an example of one of your projects.

A. "The project begins with an idea. The idea can originate anywhere in the company. The planning group picks up the idea and determines the feasibility. The planning group then works "informally" with the various line organizations to determine rough estimates for time and cost. The results are then fed back to the planning group and to the top management planning and steering committees. If top management decides to undertake the project, then top management selects the project manager and we're off and running."

---

*Disguised case.

Q. Do you have any problems with this arrangement?

A. "You bet! Our executives have the tendency of equating rough estimates as detailed budgets and rough schedules as detailed schedules. Then, they want to know why the line managers won't commit their best resources. We almost always end up with cost overruns and schedule slippages. To make matters even worse, the project managers do not appear to be dedicated to the projects. I really can't blame them. After all, they're not involved in planning the project, laying out the schedule, and establishing the budget. I don't see how any project manager can become dedicated to a plan in which the project manager has no input and may not even know the assumptions or considerations that were included. Recently, some of our more experienced project managers have taken a stand on this and are virtually refusing to accept a project assignment unless they can do their own detailed planning at the beginning of the project in order to verify the constraints established by the planning group. If the project managers come up with different costs and schedules (and you know that they will), the planning group feels that they have just gotten slapped in the face. If the costs and schedules are the same, then the planning group runs upstairs to top management asserting that the project managers are wasting money by continuously wanting to replan."

Q. Do you feel that replanning is necessary?

A. "Definitely! The planning group begins their planning with a very crude statement of work, expecting our line managers (the true experts) to read in between the lines and fill in the details. The project managers develop a detailed statement of work and a work breakdown structure, thus minimizing the chance that anything would fall through the crack. Another reason for replanning is that the ground rules have changed between the time that the project was originally adopted by the planning group and the time that the project begins implementation. Another possibility, of course, is that technology may have changed or people can be smarter now and can perform at a higher position on the learning curve."

Q. Do you have any problems with executive meddling?

A. "Not during the project, but initially. Sometimes executives want to keep the end date fixed but take their time in approving the project. As a result, the project manager may find himself a month or two behind scheduling before he even begins the project. The second problem is when the executive decides to arbitrarily change the end date milestone but keep the front end milestone fixed. On one of our projects it was necessary to complete the project in half the time. Our line managers worked like dogs to get the job done. On the next project, the same thing happened, and, once again, the line managers came to the rescue. Now, management feels that line managers cannot make good estimates and that they (the executives) can arbitrarily change the milestones on any project. I wish that they would realize what they're doing to us. When we put forth all of our efforts on one project, then all of the other projects suffer. I don't think our executives realize this."

Q. Do you have any problems selecting good project managers and project engineers?

A. "We made a terrible mistake several years by selecting our best technical experts as the project managers. Today, our project managers are doers, not managers. The project managers do not appear to have any confidence in our line people and often try to do all of the work themselves. Functional employees are taking technical direction from the project managers and project engineers instead of the line managers. I've heard one functional employee say, 'Here come those project managers again to beat me up. Why can't they leave me alone and let me do my job?' Our line employees now feel that this is the way that project management is supposed to work. Somehow, I don't think so."

Q. Do you have any problems with the line manager/project manager interface?

A. "Our project managers are technical experts and therefore feel qualified to do all of the engineering estimates without consulting with the line managers. Sometimes this occurs because not enough time or money is allocated for proper estimating. This is understandable. But when the project managers have enough time and money and refuse to get off their ivory towers and talk to the line managers, then the line managers will always find fault with the project manager's estimate even if it is correct. Sometimes I just can't feel any sympathy for the project managers. There is one special case that I should mention. Many of our project managers do the estimating themselves but have courtesy enough to ask the line manager for his blessing. I've seen line managers who were so loaded with work that they look the estimate over for two seconds and say, 'It looks fine to me. Let's do it.' Then when the cost overrun appears, the project manager gets blamed."

Q. Where are your project engineers located in the organization?

A. "We're having trouble deciding that. Our project engineers are primarily responsible for coordinating the design efforts (i.e., electrical, civil, HVAC, etc. . . .). The design manager wants these people reporting to him if they are responsible for coordinating efforts in his shop. The design manager wants control of these people even if they have their name changed to assistant project managers. The project managers, on the other hand, want the project engineers to report to them with the argument that they must be dedicated to the project and must be willing to complete the effort within time, cost, and performance. Furthermore, the project managers argue that project engineers will be more likely to get the job done within the constraints if they are not under the pressure of being evaluated by the design manager. If I were the design manager, I would be a little reluctant to let someone from outside of my shop integrate activities that utilize the resources under my control. But I guess this gets back to interpersonal skills and the attitudes of the people. I do not want to see a 'brick wall' set up between project management and design."

Q. I understand that you've created a new estimating group. Why was that done?

A. "In the past we have had several different types of estimates such as first guess, detailed, 10 percent complete, etc. . . . Our project managers are usually the first people at the job site and give a shoot-from-the-hip estimate. Our line managers do estimating as do some of our executives and functional employees. Because we're in a relatively slow changing environment, we should have well-established standards, and the estimating department can maintain uniformity in our estimating policies. Since most of our work is approved based upon first-guess estimates, the question is, 'Who should give the first-guess estimate? Should it be the estimator who does not understand the processes but knows the estimating criteria, or the project engineer who understands the processes but does not know the estimates, or the project manager who is an expert in project management? Right now, we are not sure where to place the estimating group. The vicepresident of engineering has three operating groups beneath him; project management, design and procurement. We're contemplating putting estimating under procurement, but I'm not sure how this will work."

Q. How can we resolve these problems that you've mentioned?

A. "I wish I knew!"

CASE STUDY: QUASAR COMMUNICATIONS, INC.

Quasar Communications, Inc. (QCI) is a thirty-year-old, $50 million division of Communication Systems International, the world's largest communications company. QCI employs about 340 people, of which more than 200 are engineers. Ever since the company was founded thirty years ago, engineers have held every major position within the company, including president and vicepresident. The vicepresident for accounting and finance, for example, has an electrical engineering degree from Purdue and a master's degree in business administration from Harvard.

QCI, up until 1976, was a traditional organization where everything flowed up and down. In 1976, QCI hired a major consulting company to come in and train *all* of their personnel in project management. Because of the reluctance of the line managers to accept formalized project management, QCI adopted an informal, fragmented project management structure where the project managers had lots of responsibility but very little authority. The line managers were still running the show.

In 1979, QCI had grown to a point where the majority of their business base revolved around twelve large customers and thirty to forty small customers. The time had come to create a separate line organization for project managers, where each individual could be shown a career path in the company and the company could benefit by creating a body of planners and managers dedicated to the completion of a project. The project management group was headed up by a vice president and included the following full-time personnel:

- Four individuals to handle the twelve large customers
- Five individuals for the thirty to forty small customers

- Three individuals for R&D projects
- One individual for capital equipment projects

The nine customer project managers were expected to be able to handle two to three projects at one time if necessary. Because the customer requests did not usually come in at the same time, it was anticipated that each project manager would handle only one project at a time. The R&D and capital equipment project managers were expected to handle several projects at once.

In addition to the above personnel, the company also maintained a staff of four product managers who controlled the profitable off-the-shelf product lines. The product managers reported to the vice president of marketing and sales.

In October 1979, the vice president for project management decided to take a more active role in the problems that project managers were having and held counseling sessions for each project manager. The following major problem areas were discovered:

R&D Project Management

P.M.: "My biggest problem is working with these diverse groups that aren't sure what they want. My job is to develop new products that can be introduced into the market place. I have to work with engineering, marketing, product management, manufacturing, quality assurance, finance, and accounting. Everyone wants a detailed schedule and product cost breakdown. How can I do that when we aren't even sure what the end item will look like or what materials are needed? Last month I prepared a detailed schedule for the development of a new product, assuming that everything would go according to the plan. I work with the R&D engineering group to establish what we considered to be a realistic milestone. Marketing pushed the milestone to the left because they wanted the product to be introduced into the market place earlier. Manufacturing then pushed the milestone to the right, claiming that they would need more time to verify the engineering specifications. Finance and accounting then pushed the milestone to the left asserting that management wanted a quicker return on investment. Now, how can I make all of the groups happy?"

V.P.: "Whom do you have the biggest problems with?"

P.M.: "That's easy; marketing! Every week marketing gets a copy of the project status report and decides whether or not to cancel the project. Several times marketing has canceled projects without even discussing it with me, and I'm supposed to be the project leader."

V.P.: "Marketing is in the best position to cancel the project because they have the inside information on the profitability, risk, return on investment, and competitive environment."

P.M.: "The situation that we're in now makes it impossible for the project manager to be dedicated to a project where he does not have all of the information at hand. Perhaps we should either have the R&D project managers report to someone in marketing or have the marketing group provide additional information to the project managers."

Small Customer Project Management

P.M.: "I find it virtually impossible to be dedicated to and effectively manage three projects that have priorities that are not reasonably close. My low-priority customer always suffers. And even if I try to give all of my customers equal status, I do not know how to organize myself and have effective time management on several projects."

P.M.: "Why is it that the big projects carry all of the weight and the smaller ones suffer?"

P.M.: "Several of my projects are so small that they stay in one functional department. When that happens, the line manager feels that he is the true project manager operating in a vertical environment. On one of my projects I found that a line manager had promised the customer that additional tests would be run. This additional testing was not priced out as part of the original statement of work. On another project the line manager made certain remarks about the technical requirements of the project. The customer assumed that the line managers's remarks reflected company policy. Our line managers don't realize that only the project manager can make commitments (on resources) to the customer as well as company policy. I know this can happen on large projects as well, but it is more pronounced on small projects."

Large Customer Project Management

P.M.: "Those of us who manage the large projects are also marketing personnel, and occasionally, we are the ones who bring in the work. Yet, everyone appears to be our superior. Marketing always looks down upon us, and when we bring in a large contract, marketing just looks down upon us as if we're riding their coat tails or as if we were just lucky. The engineering group outranks us because all managers and executives are promoted from there. Those guys never live up to commitments. Last month I sent an inflammatory memo to a line manager because of his poor response to my requests. Now, I get no support at all from him. This doesn't happen all of the time, but when it does, it's frustrating."

P.M.: "On large projects, how do we, the project managers, know when the project is in trouble? How do we decide when the project will fail? Some of our large projects are total disasters and should fail, but management comes to the rescue and pulls the best resources off of the good projects to cure the ailing projects. We then end up with six marginal projects and one partial catastrophe as opposed to six excellent projects and one failure. Why don't we just let the bad projects fail?"

V.P.: "We have to keep up our image for our customers. In most other companies, performance is sacrificed in order to meet time and cost. Here at QCI, with our professional integrity at stake, our engineers are willing to sacrifice time and cost in order to meet specifications. Several of our customers come to us because of this. Last year we had a project where, at the scheduled project termination date, engineering was able to satisfy only 75 percent of the customer's performance specifications. The project manager showed the results to the customer, and the customer decided to change his specification requirements to agree with the product that we designed. Our engineering people thought that this was a 'slap in the face' and refused to sign off the engineering drawings. The problem went all the way up to the president for resolution. The final result was that the customer would give us an additional few months if we would spend our own money to try to meet the original specification. It cost us a bundle, but we did it because our integrity and professional reputation was at stake."

Capital Equipment Project Management

P.M.:   "My biggest complaint is with this new priority scheduling computer package we're supposedly considering to install. The way I understand it, the computer program will establish priorities for *all* of the projects in-house, based upon the feasibility study, cost benefit analysis, and return on investment. Somehow I feel as though my projects will always be the lowest priority, and I'll never be able to get sufficient functional resources."

P.M.:   "Every time I lay out a reasonable schedule for one of our capital equipment projects, a problem occurs in the manufacturing area and the functional employees are always pulled off of my project to assist manufacturing. And now I have to explain to everyone why I'm behind schedule. Why am I always the one to suffer?

The vice president carefully weighed the remarks of his project managers. Now came the difficult part. What, if anything, could the vice president do to amend the situation given the current organizational environment?"

4
Organizing and Staffing the Project Office and Team

4.0 INTRODUCTION

Successful project management, regardless of the organizational structure, is only as good as the individuals and leaders who are managing the key functions. Project management is not a one-person operation; it requires a group of individuals dedicated to the achievement of a specific goal. Project management includes:

- A project manager
- An assistant project manager
- A project (home) office
- A project team

Generally, project office personnel are assigned full-time to the project and work out of the project office, whereas the project team members work out of the functional units and may spend only a small percentage of their time on the project. Normally, project office personnel report directly to the project manager, but they may still be solid to their line function just for administrative control. A project office usually is not required on small projects, and sometimes the project can be accomplished by just one person who may fill all of the project office positions.

Before the staffing function begins, five basic questions are usually considered:

- What are the requirements for an individual to become a successful project manager?
- Who should be a member of the project team?
- Who should be a member of the project office?
- What problems can occur during recruiting activities?
- What can happen downstream to cause the loss of key team members?

On the surface, these questions may not seem especially complex. But when we apply them to a project environment (which is by definition a "temporary" situation) where a constant stream of projects is necessary for corporate growth, the staffing problems become overly complex, especially if the organization is understaffed. Conflicts and priority-setting become a way of life during the staffing functions.

4.1 THE STAFFING ENVIRONMENT

For a full understanding of the problems that occur during staffing, we must first investigate the characteristics of project management, including the project environment, the project management process, and the project manager.

Two major kinds of problems are related to the project environment: personnel performance problems and personnel policy problems. Personnel performance is difficult for many individuals in the project environment because it represents a change in the way of doing business. Individuals, regardless of how competent they are, find it difficult to adapt continuously to a changing situation in which they report to multiple managers. As a result, some people have come to resent change. Most individuals prefer a stable situation, and projects, by definition, are temporary assignments. On the other hand, many individuals thrive on temporary assignments because it gives them a "chance for glory." These individuals are usually highly creative and enjoy challenging work. The challenge is more important than the cost of failure.

Unfortunately, in some situations the line employees might consider the chance for glory more important than the project. For example, an employee pays no attention to the instructions of the project manager and performs the task his own way. When the project manager asks why, the employee asks, "Well, isn't my way better?" In this situation, the employee wants only to be recognized as an achiever and really does not care if the project is a success or failure. If the project fails, the employee still has a functional home to return to. Even the instructions of the line manager can be ignored if the individual wants that "one chance for glory" where he will be identified as an achiever with good ideas.

The second major performance problem lies in the project/functional interface where an individual suddenly finds himself reporting to two bosses, the functional manager and the project manager. If the functional manager and the project manager are in total agreement about the work to be accomplished, then performance at the interface may not be hampered. But if conflicting directions are received, then the individual at the interface, regardless of his capabilities and experience, may let his performance suffer because of his compromising position. In this case, the employee will "bend" in the direction of the manager who controls his purse strings.

Personnel policy problems can create havoc in an organization, especially if the "grass is greener" in a project environment than in the functional environment. Functional organizations are normally governed by unit manning documents that specify grade and salary for the employees. Project offices, on the other hand, have no such regulations because, by definition, projects are different from each other and, therefore, require different structures. It is a fact, however, that opportunities for advancement are greater in the project office than in the functional organization. The functional organization may be regulated by a unit manning document regardless of how well employees perform, whereas the project office promotes according to achievement. The difficulty here rests in the fact that one can distinguish between grade 7, 8, 9, 10, and 11 employees, in a line organization, whereas for a project manager the distinction might appear only in the size of the project or the amount of responsibility. Bonuses for outstanding performance are easier to obtain in the project office than in the line organization; but, although bonuses may create the illusion of stimulating competition, the real result is creation of conflict and jealousy between the horizontal and vertical elements.

Many of the characteristics of the project management process have already been discussed. Project management is organized:

- To achieve a single set of objectives.
- Through a single project of a finite lifetime.
- To operate as a separate company entity except for administrative purposes.

Because each project is different, the project management process allows each project to have its own policies, procedures, rules, and standards, provided they fall within broad company guidelines. Each project must be recognized as a project by top management so that the project manager has the delegated authority necessary to enforce the policies, procedures, rules, and standards.

Project management is successful only if the project manager and his team are totally dedicated to the successful completion of the project. This requires each team member of the project team and office to have a good understanding of the fundamental project requirements, which include:

- Customer liaison
- Project direction
- Project planning
- Project control
- Project evaluation
- Project reporting

Every member of the project office (and sometimes the project team) must have the ability to satisfy these requirements. Since these requirements cannot generally be fulfilled by single individuals, members of the project office, as well as functional representatives, must work together as a team. This teamwork concept is vital to the success of a project.

Ultimately, the person with the greatest influence during the staffing phase is the project manager. The personnel attributes and abilities of project managers will either attract or deter highly desirable individuals. A project manager must like trouble. He or she must be capable of evaluating risk and uncertainty. Other basic characteristics include:

- Honesty and integrity
- Understanding of personnel problems
- Understanding of project technology
- Business management competence
  - Management principles
  - Communications
- Alertness and quickness
- Versatility
- Energy and toughness
- Decision-making ability

The project manager must exhibit honesty and integrity with his subordinates as well as line personnel thus fostering an atmosphere of trust, as shown in Figure 4–1. He or she should not make unfulfilled or often impossible promises such as immediate promotions for everyone if a follow-on contract is received. Honesty, integrity, and an understanding of personnel problems can often eliminate any problems or conflicts that detract from the creation of a truly dedicated environment. Most project managers have "open door" policies for project as well as line personnel. On temporarily assigned activities, such as a project, managers cannot wait for personnel to iron out their own problems for fear that time, cost, and performance requirements will not be satisfied. As an example, a line employee is having problems at home, and it is beginning to affect his performance on the project. The project manager talks to his line manager and is greeted with the statement, "Just give him a little time, and he'll work out the problem himself." In this situation, the line manager may not recognize the time constraint on the project.

Project managers should have both business management and technical expertise. They must understand the fundamental principles of management, especially those involving the rapid development of temporary communication channels. Project managers must understand the technical implications of a

Figure 4–1. Deal from the top of the deck.

problem, since they are ultimately responsible for all decision-making. They may have a staff of professionals to assist them. However, many good technically oriented managers have failed because they have become too involved with the technical side of the project rather than the management side. There are several strong arguments for having a project manager who has more than just an understanding of the technology. Technical expertise is ideal, but it is not always possible because the individual tends to become a generalist, and a general understanding without business management sense can become a major problem, as illustrated in the following example. A young woman with a computer manufacturer was responsible for managing all projects involving a specific product line. Marketing came to her stating that they had found a customer for the product line, but major modifications had to be made. Since she only had an understanding of technology, she met with the true experts, the line managers, who informed her that the modifications were impossible. She had the authority to spend up to $1 million to make the modifications, but if the line managers were correct, the $1 million would be wasted. She called a meeting between engineering and marketing, but each held their ground and no final decision was reached. She ultimately called a meeting between line managers and the vice president for engineering. The line managers held their ground with the vice president, and the project was eventually rejected.

Because a project has a relatively short time duration, decision-making must be rapid and effective. Managers must be alert and quick in their ability to perceive "red flags" that can eventually lead to serious problems. They must demonstrate their versatility and toughness in order to keep subordinates dedicated to goal accomplishment. Executives must realize that the project manager's objectives during staffing are to:

- Acquire the best available assets and try to improve them.
- Provide a good working environment for all personnel.
- Make sure that all resources are applied effectively and efficiently so that all constraints are met, if possible.

4.2 SELECTING THE PROJECT MANAGER: AN EXECUTIVE DECISION

Probably the most difficult decision facing upper-level management is the selection of the project managers. Some managers work best on long-duration projects where decision-making can be slow; others may thrive on short-duration projects that can result in a constant-pressure environment. Upper-level management must know the capabilities and shortcomings of their project managers. A director was asked whom he would choose for a key project manager position—an individual who had been a project manager on previous programs in which there were severe problems and cost overruns, or a new aggressive individual who might have the capability to be a good project manager but had never had the opportunity. The director responded that he would go with the seasoned veteran assuming that the previous mistakes would not be made again. The argument here is that the project manager must learn from his own mistakes so they will not be made again. The new individual is apt to make the same mistakes the veteran made. However, executives cannot always go with the seasoned veterans without creating frustrating career path opportunities for the younger personnel. Stewart has commented on this type of situation:[1]

Though the project manager's previous experience is apt to have been confined to a single functional area of business, he must be able to function on the project as a kind of general manager in miniature. He must not only keep track of what is happening but also play the crucial role of advocate for the project. Even for a seasoned manager, this task is not likely to be easy. Hence, it is important to assign an individual whose administrative abilities and skills in personal relations have been convincingly demonstrated under fire.

---

1. John M. Stewart, "Making Project Management Work," *Business Horizons*, Fall 1965, p. 63.

Charles Martin has commented on the fact that project manager selection is a general management responsibility:[2]

- A project manager is given license to cut across several organizational lines. His activities, therefore, take on a flavor of general management, and must be done well.
- Project management will not succeed without good project managers. Thus, if general management sees fit to establish a project, it should certainly see fit to select a good man as its leader.
- A project manager is far more likely to accomplish desired goals if it is obvious that general management has selected and appointed him.

The selection process for project managers is not an easy one. Five basic questions must be considered:

- What are the internal and external sources?
- How do we select?
- How do we provide career development in project management?
- How can we develop project management skills?
- How do we evaluate project management performance?

Project management cannot succeed unless a good project manager is at the controls. The selection process is an upper-level management responsibility because the project manager is delegated the authority of the general manager to cut across organizational lines in order to accomplish the desired objectives successfully. It is far more likely that project managers will succeed if it is obvious to the subordinates that the general manager has appointed them. Usually, a brief memo to the line managers will suffice. The major responsibilities of the project manager include:

- To produce the end item with the available resources and within the constraints of time, cost, and performance/technology.
- To meet contractual profit objectives.
- To make all required decisions whether they be for alternatives or termination.
- To act as the customer (external) and upper-level and functional management (internal) communications focal point.
- To "negotiate" with all functional disciplines for accomplishment of the necessary work packages within time, cost, and performance/technology.
- To resolve all conflicts, if possible.

---

2. Charles C. Martin, *Project Management: How to Make it Work* (AMACOM, 1976), p. 234.

If these responsibilities were applied to the total organization, they might reflect the job description of the general manager. This analogy between project and general managers is one of the reasons why future general managers are asked to perform functions that are implied, rather than spelled out in the job description. As an example, you are the project manager on a high-technology project. As the project winds down, an executive asks you to write a paper so that he can present it at a technical meeting in Tokyo. His name will appear first on the paper. Should this be a part of your job? As this author sees it, you really don't have much of a choice.

In order for project managers to fulfill their responsibilities successfully, they are constantly required to demonstrate their skills in interface, resource, and planning and control management. These implicit responsibilities are shown below:

- Interface Management
  - Product interfaces
    - Performance of parts or subsections
    - Physical connection of parts or subsections
  - Project interfaces
  - Customer
  - Management (functional and upper-level)
  - Change of responsibilities
  - Information flow
  - Material interfaces (inventory control)
- Resource Management
  - Time (schedule)
  - Manpower
  - Money
  - Facilities
  - Equipment
  - Material
  - Information/technology
- Planning and Control Management
  - Increased equipment utilization
  - Increased performance efficiency
  - Reduced risks
  - Identification of alternatives to problems
  - Identification of alternative resolutions to conflicts

Consider the following advertisement for a facilities planning and development project manager (adapted from *The New York Times*, January 2, 1972):

"Personable, well-educated, literate individual with college degree in Engineering to work for a small firm. Long hours, no fringe benefits, no security, little chance for advancement are among the inducements offered. Job requires wide knowledge and experience in manufacturing, materials, construction techniques, economics, management and mathematics. Competence in the use of the spoken and written English is required. Must be willing to suffer personal indignities from clients, professional derision from peers in the more conventional jobs, and slanderous insults from colleagues.

Job involves frequent extended trips to inaccessible locations throughout the world, manual labor and extreme frustration from the lack of data on which to base decisions.

Applicant must be willing to risk personal and professional future on decisions based upon inadequate information and complete lack of control over acceptance of recommendations by clients. Responsibilities for the work are unclear and little or no guidance is offered. Authority commensurate with responsibility is not provided either by the firm or its clients.

Applicant should send resume, list of publications, references and other supporting documentation to . . . ."

Fortunately, these types of job descriptions are very rare today as maturity in project management continues.

Finding the man or woman with the right qualifications is not any easy task because the selection of project managers is based more on personal characteristics than on the job description. In Section 4.1 a brief outline of desired characteristics was presented. Russell Archibald defines a broader range of desired personal characteristics:[3]

- Flexibility and adaptability
- Preference for significant initiative and leadership
- Aggressiveness, confidence, persuasiveness, verbal fluency
- Ambition, activity, forcefulness
- Effectiveness as a communicator and integrator
- Broad scope of personal interests
- Poise, enthusiasm, imagination, spontaneity
- Able to balance technical solutions with time, cost, and human factors
- Well organized and disciplined
- A generalist rather than a specialist
- Able and willing to devote most of his time to planning and controlling
- Able to identify problems
- Willing to make decisions
- Able to maintain a proper balance in the use of time

---

3. Russell D. Archibald, *Managing High-Technology Programs and Projects* (New York: Wiley, 1976), p. 55.

Figure 4–2 is a humorous summation of these elements.

This ideal project manager would probably have doctorates in engineering, business, and psychology, and experience with ten different companies in a variety of project office positions, and would be about twenty-five years old. Good project managers in industry today would probably be lucky to have 70 to 80 percent of these characteristics. The best project managers are willing and able to identify their own shortcomings and know when to ask for help. Project managers who believe that they can do it all themselves may end up as shown in Figure 4–3.

Figures 4–4 and 4–5 show the basic knowledge and responsibilities that construction project managers should possess. It is understandable that the apprenticeship program for training construction project managers could easily be ten years.[4,5]

The difficulty in staffing, especially for project managers or assistant project managers, is in determining what questions to ask during an interview to see if an individual has the necessary or desired characteristics. There are numerous situations in which individuals are qualified to be promoted vertically but not horizontally. An individual with poor communication skills and interpersonal skills can be promoted to a line management slot because of his technical expertise, but this same individual is not qualified for project management promotion.

Most executives have found that the best way to interview is by reading each element of the job description to the potential candidate. Many individuals want a career path in project management but are totally unaware of what the project manager's duties are.

So far we have discussed the personal characteristics of the project manager. There are also job-related questions to consider, such as:

- Are feasibility and economic analyses necessary?
- Is complex technical expertise required? If so, is it within the individual's capabilities?
- If the individual is lacking expertise, will there be sufficient back-up strength in the line organizations?
- Is this the company's or the individual's first exposure to this type of project and/or client? If so, what are the risks to be considered?
- What is the priority for this project, and what are the risks?

---

4. Source for Figure 4–4: V. E. Cole, W. B. Ball, and D. S. Barrie, "Managing the Project," *Proceedings of the Ninth International Seminar/Symposium on Project Management,* The Project Management Institute, 1977, p. 57.
5. Source for Figure 4–5: L. J. Weber, W. Riethmeier, A. F. Westergard, and K. O. Hartley, "The Project Sponsor's View," *Proceedings of the Ninth International Seminar/Symposium on Project Management,* The Project Management Institute, 1977, p. 76.

Figure 4–2. Keep your nose to the grindstone.

Figure 4–3. Let the experts do it.

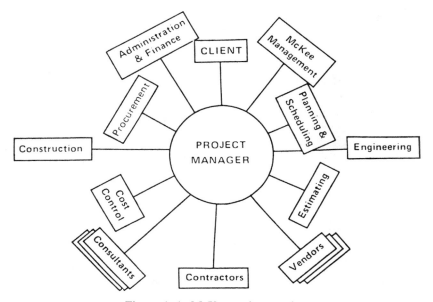

Figure 4–4. McKee project services.

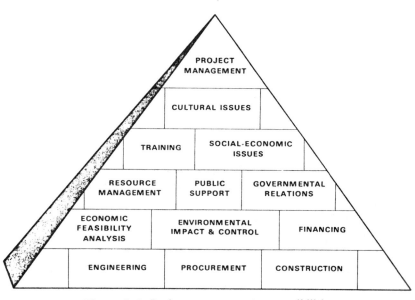

Figure 4–5. Project management responsibilities.

- With whom must the project manager interface, both inside and outside the organization?

Most good project managers generally know how to perform feasibility studies and cost/benefit analyses. Sometimes this capability can create organizational conflict. A major utility company begins each computer project with a feasibility study in which a cost/benefit analysis is performed. The project managers, all of whom report to a project management division, perform the study themselves without any direct functional support. The functional managers argue that the results are grossly inaccurate because the functional experts are not involved. The project manager, on the other hand, argues that they never have sufficient time or money to perform a complete analysis. This type of conflict requires executive attention. Some companies resolve this by having a special group simply to perform these types of analyses.

Most companies would prefer to find project managers from within. Unfortunately, this is easier said than done. The following remarks by Robert Fluor illustrate this point:[6]

On-the-job training is probably the most important aspect in the development of a project manager. This includes assignments to progressively more responsible positions in engineering and construction management and project management. It also includes rotational assignments in several engineering department disciplines, in construction, procurement, cost and scheduling, contract administration, and others. . . . We find there are great advantages to developing our project managers from within the company. There are good reasons for this:

- They know the corporate organization, policies, procedures, and the key people. This allows them to give us quality performance quicker.
- They have an established performance record which allows us to place them at the maximum level of responsibility and authority.
- Clients prefer a proven track record within the project manager's present organization.

There are also good reasons for recruiting from outside the company. A new project manager hired from the outside would be less likely to have strong informal ties to any one line organization and thus could show impartiality on the project. Some companies further require that the individual spend an apprenticeship period of twelve to eighteen months in a line organization to find out how the company functions, to become acquainted with some of the people, and to understand the company's policies and procedures.

One of the most important but often least understood characteristics of good

---

6. J. Robert Fluor, "Development of Project Managers—Twenty Years' Study at Fluor," Keynote address to Project Management Institute Ninth International Seminar/Symposium, Chicago, Illinois, October 24, 1977.

project managers is their ability to understand and know both themselves and their employees in terms of strengths and weaknesses. They must understand human behavior. Each manager must understand that in order for employees to perform efficiently:

- They must know what they are supposed to do, preferably in terms of an end product.
- They must have a clear understanding of authority and its limits.
- They must know what their relationship with other people is.
- They should know what constitutes a job well done in terms of specific results.
- They should know where and when they are falling short.
- They must be made aware of what can and should be done to correct unsatisfactory results.
- They must feel that their superior has an interest in them as individuals.
- They must feel that their superior believes in them and is anxious for their success and progress.

4.3 SKILL REQUIREMENTS FOR PROGRAM MANAGERS[7]

Programs are often complex and multifaceted. Managing these programs represents a challenge requiring skills in team building, leadership, conflict resolution, technical expertise, planning, organization, entrepreneurship, administration, management support, and the allocation of resources. This section examines these skills relative to program management effectiveness. A key factor to good program performance is the program manager's ability to integrate personnel from many disciplines into an effective work team.

To get results, the program manager must relate to (1) the people to be managed, (2) the task to be done, (3) the tools available, (4) the organizational structure, and (5) the organizational environment, including the customer community.

All work factors are interrelated and operate under the limited control of the program manager. With an understanding of the interaction of corporate organization and behavior elements, the manager can build an environment conducive to the working team's needs. The internal and external forces that impinge on the organization of the project must be reconciled to mutual goals. Thus the program manager must be both socially and technically aware to understand how the organization functions and how these functions will affect the program organization of the particular job to be done. In addition, the program manager must understand the culture and value system of the organi-

7. Adapted from Harold Kerzner and Hans J. Thamhain, *Project Management for the Small and Medium-Size Business* (New York: Van Nostrand Reinhold, 1983), pp. 263–272.

zation he is working with. Research and experience show that effective program management performance is directly related to the level of proficiency at which these skills are mastered.

Ten specific skills are identified (in no particular order) and discussed in this section:

- Team building
- Leadership
- Conflict resolution
- Technical expertise
- Planning
- Organization
- Entrepreneurship
- Administration
- Management support
- Resource allocation

It is important that the personal management traits underlying these skills operate to form a homogeneous management style. The right mixture of skill levels depends on the project task, the techniques employed, the people assigned, and the organizational structure. To be effective, program managers must consider all facets of getting the job done. Their management style must facilitate the integration of multidisciplinary program resources for synergistic operation. The days of the manager who gets by with technical expertise alone or pure administrative skills are gone.

Team Building Skills

Building the program team is one of the prime responsibilities of the program manager. Team building involves a whole spectrum of management skills required to identify, commit, and integrate the various task groups from the traditional functional organization into a single program management system.

To be effective, the program manager must provide an atmosphere conducive to teamwork. He must nurture a climate with the following characteristics:

- Team members committed to the program
- Good interpersonnel relations and team spirit
- The necessary expertise and resources
- Clearly defined goals and program objectives
- Involved and supportive top management
- Good program leadership
- Open communication among team members and support organizations

- A low degree of detrimental interpersonal and intergroup conflict

Three major considerations are involved in all of the above factors aimed toward integration of people from many disciplines into an effective team: (1) effective communications, (2) sincere interest in the professional growth of team members, and (3) commitment to the project.

Leadership Skills

An absolutely essential prerequisite for program success is the program manager's ability to lead the team within a relatively unstructured environment. It involves dealing effectively with managers and supporting personnel across functional lines with little or no formal authority. It also involves information processing skills, the ability to collect and filter relevant data valid for decision-making in a dynamic environment. It involves the ability to integrate individual demands, requirements, and limitations into decisions that benefit overall project performance. It further involves the program manager's ability to resolve intergroup conflicts, an important factor in overall program performance.

Perhaps more than in any other position below the general manager's level, quality leadership depends heavily on the program manager's personal experience and credibility within the organization. An effective management style might be characterized this way:

- Clear project leadership and direction
- Assistance in problem solving
- Facilitating the integration of new members into the team
- Ability to handle interpersonnel conflict
- Facilitating group decisions
- Capability to plan and elicit commitments
- Ability to communicate clearly
- Presentation of the team to higher management
- Ability to balance technical solutions against economic and human factors

The personal traits desirable and supportive of the above skills are:

- Project management experience
- Flexibility and change-orientation
- Innovative thinking
- Initiative and enthusiasm
- Charisma and persuasiveness
- Organization and discipline

Conflict Resolution Skills

Conflict is fundamental to complex task management. It is often determined by the interplay of the program organization and the larger host organization and its multifunctional components. Understanding the determinants of conflicts is important to the program manager's ability to deal with conflicts effectively. When conflict becomes dysfunctional, it often results in poor program decision-making, lengthy delays over issues, and a disruption of the team's efforts, all negative influences to program performance. However, conflict can be beneficial when it produces involvement and new information and enhances the competitive spirit.

A number of suggestions have been derived from various research studies aimed at increasing the program manager's ability to resolve conflict and thus improve the overall program performance. Program managers must:

- Understand interaction of the organizational and behavioral elements in order to build an environment conducive to their team's motivational needs. This will enhance active participation and minimize unproductive conflict.
- Communicate effectively with all organizational levels regarding both project objectives and decisions. Regularly scheduled status review meetings can be an important communication vehicle.
- Recognize the determinants of conflict and their timing in the project life cycle. Effective project planning, contingency planning, securing of commitments, and involving top management can help to avoid or minimize many conflicts before they impede project performance.

The value of the conflict produced depends upon the ability of the program manager to promote beneficial conflict while minimizing its potential hazardous consequences. The accomplished manager needs a "sixth sense" to indicate when conflict is desirable, what kind of conflict will be useful, and how much conflict is optimal for a given situation. In the final analysis, he has the sole responsibility for his program and how conflict will contribute to its success or failure.

Technical Skills

The program manager rarely has all the technical, administrative, and marketing expertise needed to direct the program single-handedly. Nor is it necessary or desirable. It is essential, however, for the program manager to understand the technology, the markets, and the environment of the business to participate effectively in the search for integrated solutions and technological innovations. More important, without this understanding the integrated consequences of local decisions on the total program, the potential growth ramifications, and relationships to other business opportunities cannot be foreseen by the manager. Further technical expertise is necessary to evaluate technical concepts and solutions, to communicate effectively in technical terms with the project team, and to assess risks and make trade-offs between cost, schedule, and technical issues. This is why in complex problem-solving situations so many project managers must have an engineering background.

Taken together, technical expertise is important to the successful management of engineering projects. It is composed of an understanding of the:

- Technology involved
- Engineering tools and techniques employed
- Specific markets, their customers, and requirements
- Product applications
- Technological trends and evolutions
- Relationship among supporting technologies
- People who are part of the technical community

The technical expertise required for effective management of engineering programs is normally developed through progressive growth in engineering or supportive project assignments in a specific technology area. Frequently, the project begins with an exploratory phase leading into a proposal. This is normally an excellent testing ground for the future program manager. It also allows top management to judge the new candidate's capacity for managing the technological innovations and integration of solutions needed for success.

Planning Skills

Planning skills are helpful for any undertaking; they are absolutely essential, however, for the successful management of large complex programs. The project plan is the road map that defines how to get from the start to the final results.

Program planning is an ongoing activity at all organizational levels. However, the preparation of a project summary plan, prior to project start, is the responsibility of the program manager. Effective project planning requires particular skills far beyond writing a document with schedules and budgets. It requires communication and information processing skills to define the actual resource requirements and administrative support necessary. It requires the ability to negotiate the necessary resources and commitments from key personnel in various support organizations with little or no formal authority, including the definition of measurable milestones.

Effective planning requires skills in the areas of:

- Information processing
- Communication
- Resource negotiations
- Securing commitments
- Incremental and modular planning
- Assuring measurable milestones
- Facilitating top management involvement

In addition, the program manager must assure that the plan remains a viable document. Changes in project scope and depth are inevitable. The plan should reflect necessary changes through formal revisions and should be the guiding document throughout the life cycle of the program. Nothing is more useless than an obsolete or irrelevant plan.

Finally, program managers need to be aware that planning can be overdone. If not controlled, planning can become an end in itself and a poor substitute for innovative work. Individuals retreat to the utopia of no responsibility where innovative actions cannot be taken "because it is not in the plan." It is the responsibility of the program manager to build flexibility into the plan and police it against such misuse.

Organizational Skills

The program manager must be a social architect, that is, must understand how the organization works and how to work with the organization. Organizational skills are particularly important during project formation and startup when the program manager establishes the program organization by integrating people from many different disciplines into an effective work team. It requires far more than simply constructing a project organization chart. At a minimum, it requires defining the reporting relationships, responsibilities, lines of control, and information needs. Supporting skills in the area of planning, communication, and conflict resolution are particularly helpful. A good program plan and a task matrix are useful organizational tools. In addition, the organizational effort is facilitated by clearly defined program objectives, open communication channels, good program leadership, and senior management support.

Entrepreneurial Skills

The program manager also needs a general management perspective. For example, economic considerations are one important area that normally affects the organization's financial performance. However, objectives often are much broader than profits. Customer satisfaction, future growth, cultivation of related market activities, and minimum organizational disruptions of other programs might be equally important goals. The effective program manager is concerned with all these issues.

Entrepreneurial skills are developed through actual experience. However, formal MBA-type training, special seminars, and cross-functional training programs can help to develop the entrepreneurial skills needed by program managers.

Administrative Skills

Administrative skills are essential. The program manager must be experienced in planning, staffing, budgeting, scheduling, and other control techniques. In dealing with technical personnel, the problem is seldom to make people understand administrative techniques such as budgeting and scheduling, but to impress upon them that costs and schedules are just as important as elegant technical solutions.

Particularly on larger programs, managers rarely have all the administrative skills required. While it is important that the program managers understand the company's operating procedures and available tools, it is often necessary for the program manager to free himself from administrative details regardless of his ability to handle them. He has to delegate considerable administrative tasks to support groups or hire a project administrator.

Some helpful tools for the manager in the administration of his program include: (1) the meeting, (2) the report, (3) the review, and (4) budget and schedule controls. Program managers must be thoroughly familiar with these available tools and know how to use them effectively.

Management Support Building Skills

The program manager is surrounded by a myriad of organizations that either support him or control his activities. An understanding of these interfaces is important to program managers as it enhances their ability to build favorable relationships with senior management. Management support is often an absolute necessity for dealing effectively with interface groups. Project organizations are shared-power systems with personnel of many diverse interests and "ways of doing things." These power systems have a tendency toward imbalance. Only a strong leader backed by senior management can prevent the development of unfavorable biases.

Four key variables influence the project manager's ability to create favorable relationships with senior management: (1) his ongoing credibility, (2) the visibility of his program, (3) the priority of his program relative to other organizational undertakings, and (4) his own accessibility. All these factors are interrelated and can be developed by the individual manager. Furthermore, senior management can aid such development significantly.

Resource Allocation Skills

A program organization has many bosses. Functional lines often shield support organizations from direct financial control by the project office. Once a task has been authorized, it is often impossible to control the personnel assignments, priorities, and indirect manpower costs. In addition, profit accountability is difficult owing to the interdependencies of various support departments and the often changing work scope and contents.

Effective and detailed program planning may facilitate commitment and reinforce control. Part of the plan is the "Statement of Work," which establishes a basis for resource allocation. It is also important to work out specific agreements with all key contributors and their superiors on the tasks to be performed and the associated budgets and schedules. Measurable milestones are not only important for hardware components, but also for the "invisible" program components such as systems and software tasks. Ideally, these commitments on specs, schedules, and budgets should be established through involvement by key personnel in the early phases of project formation such as the proposal phase. This is the time when requirements are still flexible, and trade-offs among performance, schedule, and budget parameters are possible. Further, this is normally the time when the competitive spirit among potential contributors is highest, often leading to a more cohesive and challenging work plan.

4.4 SPECIAL CASES IN PROJECT MANAGER SELECTION

Thus far we have assumed that the project is large enough for a full-time project manager to be appointed. This is not always the case. There are four major problem areas in staffing projects:

- Part-time vs. full-time assignments
- Several projects assigned to one project manager
- Projects assigned to functional managers
- The project manager role retained by the general manager

The first problem is generally related to the size of the project. If the project is small (in time duration or cost), a part-time project manager may be selected. Many executives have fallen into the trap of letting line personnel act as part-time project managers while still performing line functions. If the employee has a conflict between what is best for the project and what is best for his line organization, the project will suffer. It is only natural that the employee will favor the place the salary increases come from.

It is a common practice for one project manager to control several projects, especially if they are either related or similar. Problems come about when the projects have drastically different priorities. The low-priority efforts will be neglected.

If the project is a high-technology effort that requires specialization and can be performed by one department, then it is not unusual for the line manager to take on a dual role and act as project manager as well. This can be difficult to do, especially if the project manager is required to establish the priorities for the work under his supervision. The line manager may keep the best resources for the project, regardless of the priority. Then that project will be a success at the expense of every other project he must supply resources to.

Probably the worst situation is that in which an executive fills the role of project manager for a particular effort. The executive may not have the time necessary for total dedication to the achievement of the project. He cannot make effective decisions as a project manager while still discharging normal duties. Additionally, the executive may hoard the best resources for his project.

4.5 SELECTING THE WRONG PROJECT MANAGER

Even though executives know the personal characteristics and traits that project managers should possess, and even though job descriptions are often clearly defined, management may still select the wrong person. Below are several common criteria by which the wrong person may be selected.

Maturity

Some executives consider gray hair and baldness to be a sure indication of maturity, but this is not the type of maturity needed for project management. Maturity in project management generally comes from exposure to several types of projects in a variety of project office positions. In aerospace and defense, it is possible for a project manager to manage the same type of project for ten years or more. When placed on a new project, the individual may try to force personnel and project requirements to adhere to the same policies and procedures that existed on the ten-year project. The project manager may know only one way of managing projects. Perhaps, in this case, the individual would best function as an assistant project manager on a new project.

Hard-nosed Tactics

Applying hard-nosed tactics to subordinates can be very demoralizing. Project managers must give people sufficient freedom to get the job done, without providing continuous supervision and direction. A line employee who is given "freedom" by his line manager but suddenly finds himself closely supervised by the project manager will be a very unhappy individual. Employees must be trained to understand that supervised pressure will occur in time of crisis. If the project manager provides continuous supervised pressure, then he may find it difficult to obtain a qualified staff for the next project.

Maturity in project management means maturity in dealing with people. Line managers, because of their ability to control an employee's salary, need only one leadership style and can force the employees to adapt. The project manager on the other hand, cannot control salaries and must have a wide variety of leadership styles. The project manager must adapt a leadership style to the project employees, whereas the reverse is true in the line organization.

Availability

Executives should not assign individuals as project managers simply because of availability. People have a tendency to cringe when you suggest that project managers be switched halfway through a project. For example, Manager X is halfway through his project. Manager Y is waiting for an assignment. A new project comes up, and the executive switches Managers X and Y. There are several reasons for this. The most important phase of a project is planning, and, if it is accomplished correctly, the project could conceivably run itself. Therefore, Manager Y should be able to handle Manager X's project.

There are several other reasons why this switch may be necessary. The new project may have a higher priority and require a more experienced manager. Second, not all project managers are equal, especially when it comes to planning. When an executive finds a project manager who demonstrates extraordinary talents at planning, there is a natural tendency for the executive to want this project manager to plan all projects. An experienced project manager once commented to the author, "Once, just once, I'd like to be able to finish a project." There are other reasons for having someone take over a project in midstream. The director of project management calls you into his office and tells you that one of your fellow project managers has had a heart attack midway through the project. You will be taking over his project, which is well behind schedule and overrunning costs. The director of project management then "orders" you to complete the project within time and cost. How do you propose to do it? Perhaps the only viable solution to this problem is to step into a phone booth and begin taking off your clothes in order to expose the big "S" on your chest.

Technical Expertise

Executives quite often promote technical line managers without realizing the consequences. Technical specialists may not be able to divorce themselves from the technical side of the house and become project managers rather than project doers. There are also strong reasons to promote technical specialists to project managers. These people often:

- Have better relationships with fellow researchers
- Can prevent duplication of effort
- Can foster teamwork
- Have progressed up through the technical ranks
- Are knowledgeable in many technical fields
- Understand the meaning of profitability and general management philosophy
- Are interested in training and teaching
- Understand how to work with perfectionists

As described by Taylor and Watling:[8]

It is often the case, therefore, that the Project Manager is more noted for his management technique expertise, his ability to "get on with people" than for his sheer technical prowess. However, it can be dangerous to minimize this latter talent when choosing Project Managers dependent upon project type and size. The Project Manager should preferably be an expert either in the field of the project task or a subject allied to it.

Promoting an employee to project management because of his technical expertise may be acceptable if, and only if, the project requires this expertise and technical direction as in R&D efforts. For projects in which a "generalist" is acceptable as a project manager, there may be a great danger in assigning highly technical personnel. According to Wileman and Cicero:[9]

- The greater the project manager's technical expertise, the higher the propensity that he will overly involve himself in the technical details of the project.

---

8. W. J. Taylor and T. F. Watling, *Successful Project Management* (London: Business Books Limited, 1972), p. 32.
9. D. L. Wileman and J. P. Cicero, "The Project Manager—Anomalies and Ambiguities," *Academy of Management Journal,* Vol. 13, 1970, pp. 269–282.

- The greater the project manager's difficulty in delegating technical task responsibilities, the more likely it is that he will overinvolve himself in the technical details of the project. (Depending upon his expertise to do so.)
- The greater the project manager's interest in the technical details of the project, the more likely it is that he will defend the project manager's role as one of a technical specialist.
- The lower the project manager's technical expertise, the more likely it is that he will overstress the non-technical project functions (administrative functions).

If an expert is selected, then the individual must learn how to use people effectively. As an example, in 1972 a company (with $100 million in sales today) implemented project management with the adoption of a matrix. The decision was made that the best technical experts would staff the project management slots. The technical experts then began usurping the authority of the line managers by giving continuous technical direction to the line people. Unfortunately, management felt that this was the way the system should operate. When an employee was assigned to a project, the employee knew that the project manager would not stand behind him unless he followed the project manager's directions. Today management is trying to clear up the problem of who are the true technical experts—the project managers or the line managers.

Customer Orientation

Executives quite often place individuals as project managers simply to satisfy a customer request. Being able to communicate with the customer does not guarantee project success, however. If the choice of project manager is simply a concession to the customer, then the executive must insist upon providing a strong supporting team. This is often an unavoidable situation and must be lived with.

New Exposure

Executives run the risk of project failure if an individual is appointed project manager simply to gain exposure to project management. An executive of a utility company wanted to rotate his line personnel into project management for twelve to eighteen months and then return them to the line organization where they would be more well-rounded individuals and better understand the working relationship between project management and line management. There are two major problems with this. First, the individual may become technically obsolete after eighteen months in project management. Second, and more important, individuals who get a taste of project management will generally not want to return to the line organization.

Company Exposure

The mere fact that individuals have worked in a variety of divisions does not guarantee that they will make good project managers. Their working in a variety of divisions may indicate that they couldn't hold any one job. In that case, they have reached their true level of incompetency, and putting them into project management will only maximize the damage they can do to the company. Some executives contend that the best way to train a project manager is by rotation through the various functional disciplines for two weeks to a month in each organization. Other executives maintain that this is useless because the individual cannot learn anything in so short a period of time.

Tables 4–1 and 4–2 identify current thinking on methods for training project managers.[10]

Finally, there are three special points to consider:

- Individuals should not be promoted to project management simply because they are at the top of their pay grade.
- Project managers should be promoted and paid based upon performance, not upon the number of people supervised.
- It is not necessary for the project manager to be the highest ranking or salaried individual on the project team with the rationale that sufficient "clout" is needed.

4.6 DUTIES AND JOB DESCRIPTIONS

Since projects, environments, and organizations differ from company to company as well as project to project, it is not unusual for companies to struggle to provide reasonable job descriptions of the project manager and associated personnel. Below is a simple list identifying the duties of a project manager in the construction industry:[11]

- Planning
- Become completely familiar with all contract documents
- Develop the basic plan for executing and controlling the project
- Direct the preparation of project procedures
- Direct the preparation of the project budget
- Direct the preparation of the project schedule
- Direct the preparation of basic project design criteria and general specifications

---

10. Adapted from Harold Kerzner and Hans J. Thamhain, *Project Management for the Small and Medium-Sized Business* (New York: Van Nostrand Reinhold, 1983), pp. 334–341.
11. Source unknown.

Table 4-1. Methods and Techniques for Developing Project Managers.

I. Experiencial training/on-the-job
   Working with experienced professional leader
   Working with project team member
   Assigning a variety of project management responsibilities, consecutively
   Job rotation
   Formal on-the-job training
   Supporting multifunctional activities
   Customer liaison activities
II. Conceptional training/schooling
   Courses, seminars, workshops
   Simulations, games, cases
   Group exercises
   Hands-on exercises in using project manegement techniques
   Professional meetings
   Conventions, symposia
   Readings, books, trade journals, professional magazines
III. Organizational development
   Formally established and recognized project management function
   Proper project organization
   Project support systems
   Project charter
   Project management directives, policies and procedures

Table 4-2. How to Train Project Managers.

COMPANY MANAGEMENT SAY PROJECT MANAGERS CAN BE TRAINED
IN A COMBINATION OF WAYS:

Experiencial learning, on-the-job	60%
Formal education and special courses	20%
Professional activities, seminars	10%
Readings	10%

- Direct the preparation of the plan for organizing, executing, and controlling field construction activities
- Review plans and procedures periodically and institute changes if necessary
- Organizing
  - Develop organization chart for project
  - Review project position descriptions, outlining duties, responsibilities, and restrictions for key project supervisors
  - Participate in the selection of key project supervisors
  - Develop project manpower requirements
  - Continually review project organization and recommend changes in organizational structure and personnel, if necessary

- Directing
  - Direct all work on the project that is required to meet contract obligations
  - Develop and maintain a system for decision-making within the project team whereby decisions are made at the proper level
  - Promote the growth of key project supervisors
  - Establish objectives for project manager and performance goals for key project supervisors
  - Foster and develop a spirit of project team effort
  - Assist in resolution of differences or problems between departments or groups on assigned projects
  - Anticipate and avoid or minimize potential problems by maintaining current knowledge of overall project status
  - Develop clear written strategy guidelines for all major problems with clear definitions of responsibilities and restraints
- Controlling
  - Monitor project activities for compliance with company purpose and philosophy and general corporate policies
  - Interpret, communicate, and require compliance with the contract, the approved plan, project procedures, and directives of the client
  - Maintain personal control of adherence to contract warranty and guarantee provisions
  - Closely monitor project activities for conformity to contract scope provisions. Establish change notice procedure to evaluate and communicate scope changes
  - See that the plans for controlling and reporting on costs, schedule, and quality are effectively utilized
  - Maintain effective communications with the client and all groups performing project work

A more detailed job description of a construction project manager (for a utility company) appears below:

DUTIES:
Under minimum supervision establishes the priorities for and directs the efforts of personnel (including their consultants or contractors) involved or to be involved on project controlled tasks to provide required achievement of an integrated approved set of technical, manpower, cost and schedule requirements.

1. Directs the development of initial and revised detailed task descriptions and forecasts of their associated technical, manpower, cost and schedule requirements for tasks assigned to the Division.

2. Directs the regular integration of initial and revised task forecasts into Divisional technical, manpower, cost and schedule reports and initiates the approval cycle for the reports.

3. Reviews conflicting inter- and extra-divisional task recommendations or actions that may occur from initial task description and forecast development until final task completion and directs uniform methods for their resolution.

4. Evaluates available and planned additions to Division manpower resources, including their tasks applications, against integrated technical and manpower reports and initiates actions to assure that Division manpower resources needs are met by the most economical mix of available qualified consultant and contractor personnel.

5. Evaluates Divisional cost and schedule reports in light of new tasks and changes in existing tasks and initiates actions to assure that increases or decreases in task cost and schedule are acceptable and are appropriately approved.

6. Prioritizes, adjusts and directs the efforts of Division personnel (including their consultants and contractors) resource allocations as necessary to both assure the scheduled achievement of state and federal regulatory commitments and maintain Divisional adherence to integrated manpower, cost and schedule reports.

7. Regularly reports the results of Divisional manpower, cost and schedule evaluations to higher management.

8. Regularly directs the development and issue of individual task and integrated Project programs reports.

9. Recommends new or revised Division strategies, goals and objectives in light of anticipated long-term manpower and budget needs.

10. Directly supervises project personnel in the regular preparation and issue of individual task descriptions and their associated forecasts, integrated Division manpower, cost and schedule reports and both task and Project progress reports.

11. Establishes basic organizational and personnel qualification requirements for Division (including their consultants or contractors) performance on tasks.

12. Establishes the requirements for, directs the development of and approves control programs to standardize methods used for controlling similar types of activities in the Project and in other Division Departments.

13. Establishes the requirements for, directs the development of and approves administrative and technical training programs for Divisional personnel.

14. Approves recommendations for the placement of services or material purchase orders by Division personnel and assures that the cost and schedule data associated with such orders is consistent with approved integrated cost and schedule reports.

15. Promotes harmonious relations among Division organizations involved with Project tasks.

16. Exercises other duties related to Divisional project controls as assigned by the project manager.

QUALIFICATIONS:

1. A Bachelor of Science Degree in Engineering or a Business Degree with a minor in Engineering or Science from an accredited four (4) year college or university.
2. a) (For Engineering Graduate) Ten (10) or more years of Engineering and Construction experience including a minimum of five (5) years of supervisory experience and two (2) years of management and electric utility experience.

   b) (For Business Graduate) Ten (10) or more years of management experience including a minimum of five (5) years of supervisory experience in an engineering and construction related management area and two (2) years of experience as the manager or assistant manager of major engineering and construction related projects and two (2) recent years of electric utility experience.
3. Working knowledge of state and federal regulations and requirements which apply to major design and construction projects such as fossil and nuclear power stations.
4. Demonstrated ability to develop high level management control programs.
5. Experience related to computer processing of cost and schedule information.
6. Registered Professional Engineer and membership in appropriate management and technical societies is desirable (but not necessary).
7.* At least four (4) years of experience as a staff management member in an operating nuclear power station or in an engineering support on- or off-site capacity.
8.* Detailed knowledge of federal licensing requirement for nuclear power stations.
9.* Reasonably effective public speaker.

Because of the potential overlapping nature of job descriptions in a project management environment, some companies try to define responsibilities for each project management position, as shown in Table 4–3.[12]

Occasionally, an attempt is made to create specialized definitions for the project manager. As described by Shah:[13]

Like a physician, a project manager must be an expert diagnostician; he must guard his project from infection, detect symptoms, diagnose causes and prescribe cures for a multitude of afflictions.

*Qualifications 7 through 9 apply only for Nuclear Project Directors.

12. Harold Kerzner and Hans J. Thamhain, *Project Management for the Small and Medium-Sized Business* (New York: Van Nostrand Reinhold, 1983), p. 292.
13. Ramesh P. Shah, "Cross Your Bridges Before You Come to Them," *Management Review,* December 1971, p. 21.

Table 4–3. Project Management Positions and Responsibilities.

PROJECT MANAGEMENT POSITION	TYPICAL RESPONSIBILITY	SKILL REQUIREMENTS
● Project Administrator ● Project Coordinator ● Technical Assistant	Coordinating and integrating of subsystem tasks. Assisting in determining technical and manpower requirements, schedules, and budgets. Measuring and analyzing project performance regarding technical progress, schedules, and budgets.	● Planning ● Coordinating ● Analyzing ● Understanding the organization
● Task Manager ● Project Engineer ● Assistant Project Manager	Same as above, but stronger role in establishing and maintaining project requirements. Conducting trade-offs. Directing the technical implementation according to established schedules and budgets.	● Technical expertise ● Assessing trade-offs ● Managing task implementation ● Leading task specialists
● Project Manager ● Program Manager	Same as above, but stronger role in project planning and controlling. Coordinating and negotiating requirements between sponsor and performing organizations. Bid proposal development and pricing. Establishing project organization and staffing. Overall leadership toward implementing project plan. Project profit. New business development.	● Overall program leadership ● Team building ● Resolving conflict ● Managing multidisciplinary tasks ● Planning and allocating resources ● Interfacing with customers/sponsors
● Executive Program Manager	Title reserved for very large programs relative to host organization. Responsibilities same as above. Focus is on directing overall program toward desired business results. Customer liaison. Profit performance. New business development. Organizational development.	● Business leadership ● Managing overall program businesses ● Building program organizations ● Developing personnel ● Developing new business
● Director of Programs ● V.P. Program Development	Responsible for managing multiprogram businesses via various project organizations, each led by a project manager. Focus is on business planning and development; profit performance; technology development, establishing policies and procedures; program management guidelines; personnel development; organizational development.	● Leadership ● Strategic planning ● Directing and managing program businesses ● Building organizations ● Selecting and developing key personnel ● Identifying and developing new business

4.7   THE ORGANIZATIONAL STAFFING PROCESS

Staffing the project organization can become a long and tedious effort, especially on large and complex engineering projects. Three major questions must be answered:

- What people resources are required?
- Where will the people come from?
- What type of project organizational structure will be best?

To determine the people resources required, the types of individuals (possibly job descriptions) must be decided upon, as well as how many individuals from each job category are necessary and when these individuals will be needed.

Consider the following situation: as a project manager, you have an activity that requires three separate tasks, all performed within the same line organization. The line manager promises you the best available resources right now for the first task but cannot make any commitments beyond that. The line manager may have only below-average workers available for the second and third tasks. However, the line manager is willing to make a deal with you. He can give you an employee who can do the work but will only give an average performance. If you accept the average employee, the line manager will guarantee that the employee will be available to you for all three tasks. How important is continuity to you? There is no clearly definable answer to this question. Some people will always want the best resources and are willing to fight for them, whereas others prefer continuity and dislike seeing new people coming and going. The author prefers continuity, provided that the assigned employee has the ability to do the up-front planning needed during the first task. The danger in selecting the best employee is that a higher-priority project may come along, and you will lose the employee; or if the employee is an exceptional worker, he may simply be promoted off your project.

Sometimes, a project manager may have to make concessions to get the right people. For example, during the seventh, eighth, and ninth months of your project you need two individuals with special qualifications. The functional manager says that they will be available two months earlier, and that if you don't pick them up then, there will be no guarantee of their availability during the seventh month. Obviously, the line manager is pressuring you, and you may have to give in. There is also the situation in which the line manager says that he'll have to borrow people from another department in order to fulfill his commitments for your project. You may have to live with this situation, but be very careful—these employees will be working at a low level on the learning curve, and overtime will not necessarily resolve the problem. You must expect mistakes here.

Line managers often place new employees on projects so they can be upgraded. Project managers often resent this and immediately go to top management for help. If a line manager says that he can do the work with lower-level people, then the project manager must believe the line manager. After all, the line manager, not the assigned employees, made the commitment to do the work, and it is the line manager's neck that is stuck out.

Mutual trust between project and line managers is crucial, especially during staffing sessions. Once a project manager has developed a good working relationship with employees, the project manager would like to keep those individuals assigned to his activities. There is nothing wrong with a project manager requesting the same administrative and/or technical staff as before. Line managers realize this and usually agree to it.

There must also be mutual trust between the project managers themselves. Project managers must work as a total team, recognize each other's needs, and be willing to make decisions that are in the best interest of the company.

Once the resources are defined, the next question must be whether staffing will be from within the existing organization or from outside sources, such as new hires or consultants. Outside consultants are advisable if, and only if, internal manpower resources are being fully utilized on other programs, or if the company does not possess the required project skills. The answer to this question will indicate which organizational form is best for achievement of the objectives. The form might be a matrix, product, or staff project management structure.

Not all companies permit a variety of project organizational forms to exist within the main company structure. Those that do, however, consider the basic questions of classical management before making a decision. These include:

- How is labor specialized?
- What should the span of management be?
  - How much planning is required?
  - Are authority relationships delegated and understood?
  - Are there established performance standards?
  - What is the rate of change of the job requirements?
- Should we have a horizontal or vertical organization?
  - What are the economics?
  - What are the morale implications?
- Do we need a unity-of-command position?

As in any organization, the subordinates can make the superior look good in the performance of his duties. Unfortunately, the project environment is symbolized by temporary assignments in which the main effort put forth by the project manager is to motivate his (temporary) subordinates toward project dedication and to make them fully understand that:

- Teamwork is vital for success.
- Esprit de corps contributes to success.
- Conflicts can occur beween project and functional tiers.
- Communication is essential for success.
- Conflicting orders may be given by the:
  - Project manager
  - Functional manager
  - Upper-level manager
- Unsuccessful performance may result in transfer or dismissal from the project as well as disciplinary action.

Earlier we stated that a project operates as a separate entity but remains attached to the company through company administration policies and procedures. Although project managers can establish their own policies, procedures, and rules, the criteria for promotion must be based upon company standards. Therefore, we can ask:

- What commitments can a project manager make to his prospective subordinates?
- What promises can a project manager make regarding an individual's assignment after termination?

The first question involves salary, grade, responsibility, evaluation for promotion, bonuses, and overtime pay. There are many documented cases of project managers promising subordinates "the world" as a means of motivating them, when in fact the managers knew that these promises could not be kept.

The second question deals with the equity principle of job reassignment. According to Martin:[14]

After reassignment at the end of his tour on a project, a person should have the same prospects for the future that he would have had if he had performed equally well (or badly) in a normal assignment not connected with the project during the same period.

After unkept promises on previous projects, a project manager will find it very difficult to get top-quality personnel to volunteer for another project. Even if top management orders key individuals to be assigned to his project, they will always be skeptical about any promises that he may make.

Selecting the project manager is only one-third of the staffing problem. The next step, selecting the project office personnel and team members, often can be a time-consuming chore. The project office consists of personnel who are

---

14. Charles C. Martin, *Project Management: How to Make it Work* (New York: AMACOM, A Division of American Management Associations, 1976), p. 41.

usually assigned as full-time members of the project. In selecting the project office staff, the project manager first must evaluate all potential candidates, whether or not they are assigned to another project. This evaluation process should include active project team members, functional team members available for promotion or transfer, and outside applicants.

Upon completion of the evaluation process, the project manager meets with upper-level management. This coordination is required to assure that:

- All assignments fall within current policies on rank, salary, and promotion.
- The individuals selected can work well with both the project manager (formal reporting) and upper-level management (informal reporting).
- The individuals selected have good working relationships with the functional personnel.

Good project office personnel cannot be trained overnight. Good training is usually identified as experience with several types of projects. Project managers do not "train" project office members, primarily because time constraints do not often permit this luxury. Project office personnel must be self-disciplined, especially during the first few assignments.

The third and final step in the staffing of the project office is a meeting between the project manager, upper-level management, and the project manager on whose project the requested individuals are currently assigned. Project managers are very reluctant to give up qualified personnel to the staff of other project offices, but, unfortunately, this procedure is a way of life in a project environment. Upper-level management attends these meetings to show all negotiating parties that top management is concerned with maintaining the best possible mix of individuals from available resources and to help resolve staffing conflicts. Staffing from within is a negotiation process in which upper-level management establishes the ground rules and priorities.

The selected individuals are then notified of the anticipated change and asked their opinions. If individuals have strong resentment to being transferred or reassigned, alternate personnel may be selected because projects cannot operate effectively under discontented managers. Upper-level managers, however, have the authority to direct changes regardless of the desires of the individuals concerned.

Figure 4–6 shows the major concern that project managers have in employee selection. In order to avoid the loss of key people, project managers should seek employees who have the necessary (not superior) skills and use these resources *only* when needed. Hoarding good talent unnecessarily creates organizational conflict.

Figure 4–7 shows the typical staffing pattern as a function of time. There is a manpower buildup in the early phases and a manpower decline in the later stages. This means that the project manager should bring people on board as *needed* and release them as *early* as possible.

There are several psychological approaches that the project manager can use during the recruitment and staffing process. Consider the following:

- Line managers often receive no visibility or credit for a job well done. Be willing to introduce line managers to the customer.
- Be sure to show people how they can benefit by working for you or on your project.
- Any promises made during recruitment should be documented. The functional organization will remember them long after your project terminates.
- As strange as it may seem, the project manager should encourage conflicts to take place during recruiting and staffing. These conflicts should be brought to the surface and resolved. It is better for these conflicts to be resolved during the initial planning stages than to have major confrontations later.

Figure 4–6. What happens to your project if you lose a key employee?

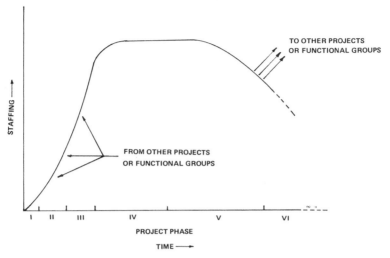

Figure 4–7. Staffing pattern vs. time.

Most companies have both formal and informal guidelines for the recruiting and assigning of project personnel. Below are examples of such guidelines as defined by Charles Martin:[15]

- Unless some other condition is paramount, project recruiting policies should be as similar as possible to those normally used in the organization for assigning people to new jobs.
- Everyone should be given the same briefing about the project, its benefits, and any special policies related to it. For a sensitive project, this rule can be modified to permit different amounts of information to be given to different managerial levels, but at least everyone in the same general classification should get the same briefing. It should be complete and accurate.
- Any commitments made to members of the team about treatment at the end of the project should be approved in advance by general management. No other commitments should be made.
- Every individual selected for a project should be told why he or she was chosen.
- A similar degree of freedom should be granted all people, or at least all those within a given job category, in the matter of accepting or declining a project assignment.

15. Charles C. Martin, *Project Management: How to Make it Work* (New York: AMACOM, A Division of American Management Associations, 1976), p. 241.

This last one is a major consideration in the recruiting process: How much discretion is to be given to the employee concerning the proposed assignment? Several degrees of permissiveness appear possible:

- The project is explained and the individual is asked to join and given complete freedom to decline, no questions asked.
- The individual is told he will be assigned to the project. However, he is invited to bring forward any reservations he may have about joining. Any sensible reason he offers will excuse him from the assignment.
- The individual is told he is assigned to the project. Only a significant personal or career preference is accepted as a reason for excusing him from joining the project.
- The individual is assigned to the project as he would be to any other work assignment. Only an emergency can excuse him from serving on the project team.

The recruitment process is not without difficulties. What is unfortunate is that problems of recruiting and retaining good personnel are more difficult in a project organizational structure than in one that is purely traditional. Clayton Reeser identifies nine potential problems related to personnel that can exist in project organizations:[16]

- Personnel connected with project forms of organization suffer more anxieties about possible loss of employment than members of functional organizations.
- Individuals temporarily assigned to matrix organizations are more frustrated by authority ambiguity than permanent members of functional organizations.
- Personnel connected with project forms of organization that are nearing their phase-out are more frustrated by what they perceive to be "make work" assignments than members of functional organizations.
- Personnel connected with project forms of organization feel more frustrated because of lack of formal procedures and role definitions than members of functional organizations.
- Personnel connected with project forms of organization worry more about being set back in their careers than members of functional organizations.
- Personnel connected with project forms of organization feel less loyal to their organization than members of functional organizations.
- Personnel connected with project forms of organization have more anxieties in feeling that there is no one concerned about their personal development than members of functional organizations.
- Permanent members of project forms of organization are more frustrated by multiple levels of management than members of functional organizations.

---

16. Clayton Reeser, "Some Potential Human Problems of the Project Form of Organization," *Academy of Management Journal*, Vol. XII, 1969, pp. 462–466.

- Frustrations caused by conflict are perceived more seriously by personnel connected with project forms of organization than members of functional organizations.

Grinnell and Apple have identified four additional major problems associated with staffing:[17]

- People trained in single line-of-command organizations find it hard to serve more than one boss.
- People may give lip service to teamwork, but not really know how to develop and maintain a good working team.
- Project and functional managers sometimes tend to compete rather than cooperate with each other.
- Individuals must learn to do more "managing" of themselves.

Thus far we have discussed staffing the project. Unfortunately, there are also situations in which employees must be terminated from the project because of:

- Nonacceptance of rules, policies, and procedures
- Nonacceptance of established formal authority
- Professionalism being more important to them than company loyalty
- Their stressing technical competency at the expense of the budget and schedule
- Incompetency

There are three possible solutions for working with incompetent personnel. First, the project manager can provide an on-the-spot appraisal of the employee. This includes identification of weaknesses, corrective action to be taken, and threat of punishment if the situation continues. The second solution for incompetency is reassignment of the employee to less critical activities. This solution is usually not preferred by project managers. The third solution, and the most frequent one, is the removal of the employee.

Project managers have the right to get people removed from their projects, especially for incompetence. However, although project managers can get project office people (who report to the project manager) removed directly, the removal of a line employee is an indirect process and must be accomplished through the line manager. The removal of the line employee should be made to look like a transfer; otherwise the project manager will be branded as an individual who gets people fired from his projects.

---

17. S. K. Grinnell and H. P. Apple, "When Two Bosses Are Better than One," *Machine Design,* January 1975, pp. 84–87.

Executives must be ready to cope with the staffing problems that can occur in a project environment. C. Ray Gullett has summarized these major problems:[18]

- Staffing levels are more variable in a project environment.
- Performance evaluation is more complex and more subject to error in a matrix form of organization.
- Wage and salary grades are more difficult to maintain under a matrix form of organization. Job descriptions are often of less value.
- Training and development are more complex and at the same time more necessary under a project form of organization.
- Morale problems are potentially greater in a matrix organization.

4.8 THE PROJECT OFFICE

The project team is a combination of the project office and functional employees as shown in Figure 4–8. Although the figure identifies the project office personnel as assistant project managers, some employees may not have any such title. The advantage of such a title is that it entitles the employee to speak directly to the customer. For example, the project engineer might also be called the assistant project manager for engineering. The title is important because when the assistant project manager speaks to the customer, he represents the company, whereas the functional employee represents himself.

The project office is an organization developed to support the project manager in carrying out his duties. Project office personnel must have the same dedication toward the project as the project manager and must have good working relationships with both the project and functional managers. The responsibilities of the project office include:

- Acting as the focal point of information for both in-house control and customer reporting.
- Controlling time, cost, and performance to adhere to contractual requirements.
- Ensuring that all work required is documented and distributed to all key personnel.
- Ensuring that all work performed is both authorized and funded by contractual documentation.

---

18. C. Ray Gullett, "Personnel Management in the Project Environment," *Personnel Administration/Public Personnel Review,* November–December 1972, pp. 17–22.

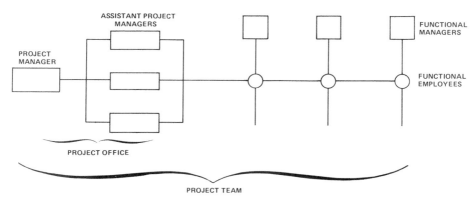

Figure 4–8. Project organization.

The major responsibility of the project manager and the project office personnel is the integration of work across the functional lines of the organization. Functional units, such as engineering, R&D, and manufacturing, together with extra-company subcontractors, must work toward the same specifications, designs, and even objectives. The lack of proper integration of these functional units is the most common cause of project failure. The team members must be dedicated to all activities required for project success, not just their own functional responsibilities. The problems resulting from lack of integration can best be solved by full-time membership and participation of project office personnel. Not all team members are part of the project office. Functional representatives, performing at the interface position, also act as integrators but at a closer position to where the work is finally accomplished (i.e., the line organization).

One of the biggest challenges facing project managers is determining the size of the project office. The optimal size is determined by a trade-off between the maximum number of members necessary to assure compliance with requirements and the minimum number for keeping the total administrative costs under control. Membership is determined by factors such as project size, internal support requirements, type of project (i.e., R&D, qualification, production), level of technical competency required, and customer support requirements. Membership size is also influenced by how strategic management views the project to be. There is a tendency to enlarge project offices if the project is considered strategic, especially if follow-on work is possible.

On large projects, and even on some smaller efforts, it is often impossible to achieve project success without permanently assigned personnel. The four major activities of the project office, shown below, indicate the need for using full-time people:

- Integration of activities
- In-house and out-of-house communication
- Scheduling with risk and uncertainty
- Effective control

These four activities require continuous monitoring by trained project personnel. The training of good project office members may take weeks or even months, and can extend beyond the time allocated for a project. Because key personnel are always in demand, project managers should ask themselves and upper-level management one pivotal question when attempting to staff the project office:

> Are there any projects downstream that might cause me to lose key members of my team?

If the anwer to this question is yes, then it might benefit the project to have the second- or third-choice person selected for the position or even to staff the position on a part-time basis. Another alternative, of course, would be to assign the key members to activities that are not so important and that can be readily performed by replacement personnel. This, however, is impractical because such personnel will not be employed efficiently.

Program managers would like nothing better than to have all of their key personnel assigned full-time for the duration of the program. Unfortunately, this is undesirable, if not impossible, for many projects because:[19]

- Skills required by the project vary considerably as the project matures through each of its life-cycle phases.
- Building up large permanently assigned project offices for each project inevitably causes duplication of certain skills (often those in short supply), carrying of people who are not needed on a full-time basis or for a long period, and personnel difficulties in reassignment.
- The project manager may be diverted from his primary task and become the project engineer, for example, in addition to his duties of supervision, administration, and dealing with the personnel problems of a large office rather than concentrating on managing all aspects of the project itself.
- Professionally trained people often prefer to work within a group devoted to their professional area, with permanent management having qualifications in the same field, rather than becoming isolated from their specialty peers by being assigned to a project staff.

19. Russell D. Archibald, *Managing High-Technology Programs and Projects* (New York: Wiley, 1976), p. 82.

- Projects are subject to sudden shifts in priority or even to cancellation, and full-time members of a project office are thus exposed to potentially serious threats to their job security; this often causes a reluctance on the part of some people to accept a project assignment.

All of these factors favor keeping the full-time project office as small as possible and dependent upon established functional departments and specialized staffs to the greatest extent possible for performance of the various tasks necessary to complete the project. The approach places great emphasis on the planning and control procedures used on the project. On the other hand, there are valid reasons for assigning particular people of various specialties to the project office. These specialties usually include:

- Systems analysis and engineering (or equivalent technical discipline) and product quality and configuration control, if the product requires such an effort
- Project planning, scheduling, control, and administrative support

Many times a project office is staffed by promotion of functional specialists. Unless careful examination of individual qualifications is made, disaster can easily result. This situation is quite common to engineering firms with a high percentage of technical employees.

In professional firms, personnel are generally promoted to management on the basis of their professional or technical competence rather than their managerial ability. While this practice may be unavoidable, it does tend to promote men with insufficient knowledge of management techniques and creates a frustrating environment for the professional down the line.[20]

With regard to the training needed by technicians who aspire to high positions in a world of increasing professionalism in management, more than half of the technically trained executives studied . . . wished that they had had "more training in the business skills traditionally associated with the management function." In fact, 75 percent admitted that there were gaps in their nontechnical education. . . . Essentially, the engineer whose stock in trade has always been "hard skills" will need to recognize the value of such "soft skills" as psychology, sociology, and so forth, and to make serious and sustained efforts to apply them to his current job.[21]

There is an unfortunate tendency today for executives to create an environment where line employees feel that the "grass is greener" in project manage-

---

20. William P. Killian, "Project Management—Future Organizational Concept," *Marquette Business Review,* 1971, pp. 90–107.
21. Richard A. Koplow, "From Engineer to Manager—And Back Again," *IEEE Transactions on Engineering Management,* Vol. EM-14, No. 2, June 1967, pp. 88–92.

ment and project engineering than in the line organization. How should an executive handle a situation where line specialists continually apply for transfer to project management? The solution being incorporated today is the development of a dual ladder system, as shown in Figure 4–9, with a pay scale called "consultant." This particular company created the consultant position because:

- There were several technical specialists who were worth more money to the company but who refused to accept a management position to get it.
- Technical specialists could not be paid more money than line managers.

Promoting technical specialists to a management slot simply to give them more money can:

- Create a poor line manager
- Turn a specialist into a generalist
- Leave a large technical gap in the line organization

Line managers often argue that they cannot perform their managerial duties and control these "prima donnas" who earn more money and have a higher pay grade than the line managers. That is faulty reasoning. Every time the consultants do something well, it reflects upon the entire line organization, not merely upon themselves.

The concept of having functional employees with a higher pay grade than the line manager can also be applied to the horizontal project. It is possible for a junior project manager suddenly to find that the line managers have a higher pay grade than the project manager. It is also possible for assistant project managers (as project engineers) to have a higher pay grade than the project manager. Project management is designed to put together the best mix of people to achieve the objective. If this best mix requires that a grade 7 report to a grade 9 (on a "temporary" project), then so be it. Executives should not let salaries, and pay grades, stand in the way of constructing a good project organization.

Another major concern is the relationship that exists between project office personnel and functional managers. In many organizations, membership in the project office is considered to be more important than in the functional department. Functional members have a tendency to resent an individual who has just been promoted out of a functional department and into project management. Killian has described ways of resolving potential conflicts:[22]

---

22. William P. Killian, "Project Management—Future Organizational Concept," *Marquette Business Review*, 1971, pp. 90–107.

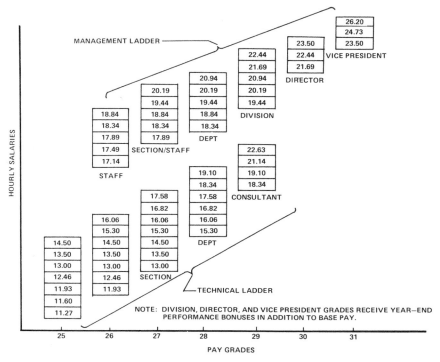

Figure 4–9. Exempt, upper-level pay structure.

It must be kept in mind that veteran functional managers cannot be expected to accept direction readily from some lesser executive who is suddenly labelled a Project Manager. Management can avoid this problem by:

- Selecting a man who already has a high position of responsibility or placing him high enough in the organization.
- Assigning him a title as important-sounding as those of functional managers.
- Supporting him in his dealings with functional managers.

If the Project Manager is expected to exercise project control over the functional departments, then he must report to the same level as the departments, or higher.

Executives can severely hinder project managers by limiting their authority to select and organize (when necessary) a project office and team. According to Cleland:[23]

---

23. David I. Cleland, "Why Project Management," *Business Horizons,* Winter 1964, p. 85.

His [project manager's] staff should be qualified to provide personal administrative and technical support. He should have sufficient authority to increase or decrease his staff as necessary throughout the life of the project. The authorization should include selective augmentation for varying periods of time from the supporting functional areas.

Sometimes, a situation occurs in the project office in which the assistant project manager does not fully understand the intentions of the project manager. For example, an assistant project manager became convinced that the project manager was making decisions that were not in the best interest of the project. Unfortunately, what is in the best interest of the company may not be in the best interest of the project. The cause of this problem was a communication breakdown in the project office.

Many executives have a misconception concerning the makeup and usefulness of the project office. People who work in the project office should be individuals whose first concern is project management, not the enhancement of their technical expertise. It is almost impossible for individuals to perform for any extended period of time in the project office without becoming cross-trained in a second or third project office function. For example, the project manager for cost could acquire enough expertise eventually to act as the assistant to the assistant project manager for procurement. This technique of project office cross-training is an excellent mechanism for creating good project managers.

People who are placed in the project office should be individuals who are interested in making a career out of project management. These dedicated individuals must realize that there may not be bigger and better projects for them to manage downstream, and they may have to take a step backward and manage a smaller project or simply be assistant project managers. It is not uncommon for an individual to rotate back and forth between project management and assistant project management.

We have mentioned two important facts concerning the project management staffing process:

- The individual who aspires to become a project manager must be willing to give up technical expertise and become a generalist.
- Individuals can be qualified to be promoted vertically but not horizontally.

Let us elaborate on these two points. Once an employee has demonstrated the necessary attributes to be a good project manager, there are three ways the individual can become a project manager or part of the project office. The executive can:

- Promote the individual in salary and grade and transfer him into project management.
- Laterally transfer the individual into project management without any salary or grade increase. If, after three to six months, the employee demonstrates that he can perform, he will receive an appropriate salary and grade increase.
- Give the employee a small salary increase without any grade increase or a grade increase without any salary increase, with the stipulation that additional awards will be forthcoming after the observation period, assuming that the employee can handle the position.

Many executives believe in the philosophy that once an individual enters the world of project management, there are only two places to go: up in the organization or out the door. If an individual is given a promotion and pay increase and is placed in project management and fails, his salary may not be compatible with that of his previous line organization, and now there is no place for him to go. Most executives, and employees, prefer the second method because it actually provides some protection for the employee. Of course, the employee might not want to return having been branded a failure in project management.

Many companies don't realize until it is too late that promotions to project management may be based upon a different set of criteria from promotions to line management. Promotions on the horizontal line are strongly based upon communicative skills, whereas line management promotions are based upon technical skills. An employee was interviewed for promotion to a project management position. The following two questions were asked by the executive:

- Can you write, and I really mean it, can you write?
- Are you willing to give up your car pool?

Almost every corporation has line managers who are extremely poor communicators but were promoted to their positions to reward them for technical excellence.

4.9 THE FUNCTIONAL TEAM

The project team consists of the project manager, the project office (whose members may or may not report directly to the project manager), and the functional or interface members (who must report horizontally as well as vertically for information flow). Functional team members are often shown on organizational charts as project office team members. This is normally done to satisfy customer requirements.

Upper-level management can have an input into the selection process for functional team members just as with project office membership. However, executives should not take an active role unless the project and functional managers cannot come to an agreement. If executives continually step in and tell line managers how to staff a project, then the line managers will feel that the executives are usurping the line managers' authority, and, of course, the project will suffer. Functional management must be represented at all staffing meetings. Functional staffing is directly dependent upon project requirements and, therefore, must include function management because:

- Functional managers generally have more expertise and can identify high-risk areas.
- Functional managers must develop a positive attitude toward project success. This is best achieved by inviting their participation in the early activities of the planning phase.

Functional team members are not always full-time. They can be full-time or part-time for either the duration of the project or only specific phases.

The selection process for both the functional team member and the project office must include evaluation of any special requirements. The most common special requirements develop from:

- Changes in technical specifications
- Special customer requests
- Organizational restructuring because of deviations from existing policies
- Compatability with the customer's project office

Each of these factors has a direct impact on whether an individual should be assigned to the project office or the functional interface.

A typical project office may include between ten and thirty members, whereas the total project team may be in excess of a hundred people. Large staffs inherently create additional work and increase communication channel noise to such a degree that information reporting may become a slow process. Large staffs also create difficult problems with regard to customer relations.

For large projects, it is desirable to have a full-time functional representative from each major division or department assigned permanently to the project, and perhaps even to the project office. Such representation might include:

- Program management
- Project engineering
- Engineering operations
- Manufacturing operations
- Procurement

- Quality control
- Cost accounting
- Publications
- Marketing
- Sales

Both the project manager and team members must understand fully the responsibilities and functions of each other team member so that total integration can be achieved as rapidly and effectively as possible. On high-technology programs the chief project engineer assumes the role of deputy project manager. Project managers must understand the problems that the line managers have when selecting and assigning the project staff. Line managers try to staff with people who understand the need for teamwork. Unfortunately, these people may simply be the average or below-average employees because the senior people may consider themselves to be gods and may not have any respect for other disciplines. As an example, a department manager hired a fifty-four-year old engineer who had two master's degrees in engineering disciplines. For the past thirty years, the new employee was a true loner, never having worked in a project management organization. How should the department manager handle this situation?

First, the department manager gave the individual an overload of work so that he would ask for help. Instead, the individual worked overtime and did a good job. Next, the manager put the individual in charge of a line project and assigned two people to report to him. These two people were idle most of the time because the individual was still doing all the work himself (and quite well). The department manager did not want to lose this employee. Today, the employee is assigned only those tasks that he can do himself.

When employees are attached to a project, the project manager must identify the "star" employees. These are the employees who are vital for the success of the project and who can either make or break the project manager. Most of the time, star employees are found in the line organization, not the project office.

As a final point, we should discuss the responsibilities that the project manager can assign to an employee. Project managers can assign line employees added responsibilities within the scope of the project. If the added responsibilities can result in upgrading, then the project manager should consult with the line manager before such situations are initiated. Quite often, line managers (or even personnel representatives) send "check" people into the projects to verify that employees are performing at their proper pay grade. This is very important when working with blue-collar workers who, by union contractual agreements, must be paid at the grade level at which they are performing.

Also, project managers must be willing to surrender resources when they are no longer required. If the project manager constantly cries wolf in a situation where a problem really does not exist or is not as severe as the project manager makes it out to be, the line manager will simply pull away the resources (this is the line manager's right), and a deteriorating working relationship will result.

4.10 THE PROJECT ORGANIZATIONAL CHART

One of the first requirements of the project startup phase is to develop the organizational chart for the project and determine its relationship to the parent organizational structure. Figure 4–10 shows, in abbreviated form, the six major programs at Dalton Corporation. Our concern is with the Midas Program. Although the Midas Program may have the lowest priority of the six programs, it is placed at the top, and in boldface, to give the impression that it is the top priority. This type of representation usually makes the client or customer feel that his program is important to the contractor.

The employees shown in Figure 4–10 may be part-time or full-time, depending upon the project's requirements. Perturbations on Figure 4–10 might include one employee's name identified on two or more vertical positions (i.e., the project engineer on two projects) or the same name in two horizontal boxes (i.e., for a small project, the same person could be the project manager and project engineer). Remember, this type of chart is for the customer's benefit and may not show the true "dotted/solid" reporting relationships in the company.

The next step is to show the program office structure, as illustrated in Figure 4–11. Note that the chief of operations and the chief engineer have dual reporting responsibility; they report directly to the program manager and indirectly to the directors. Again, this may be just for the customer's benefit with the real reporting structure being reversed. Beneath the chief engineer, there are three positions. Although these positions appear as solid lines, they might actually be dotted lines. For example, Ed White might be working only part-time on the Midas project but is still shown on the chart as a permanent program office member. Jean Flood, under contracts, might be spending only ten hours per week on the Midas Program.

If the function of two positions on the organizational chart takes place at different times, then both positions may be shown as manned by the same person. For example, Ed White may have his name under both engineering design and engineering testing if the two activities are far enough apart that he can perform them independently.

The people shown in the project office organizational chart, whether full-

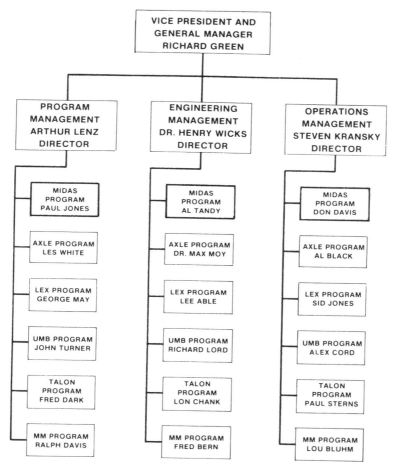

Figure 4–10. Dalton Corporation.

time or part-time, may not be physically sitting in the project office. For full-time, long-term assignments, as in construction projects, the employees may be physically sitting side by side (see Figure 4–12), whereas for part-time assignments, it may be imperative for them to sit in their functional group.[24] Remember, these types of charts may simply be eyewash for the customer.

---

24. Source for Figure 4–12 is F. A. Hollenbach and D. P. Schultz, "The Organization and Controls of Project Management," *Proceedings of the Ninth Annual Seminar/Symposium on Project Management*, 1977.

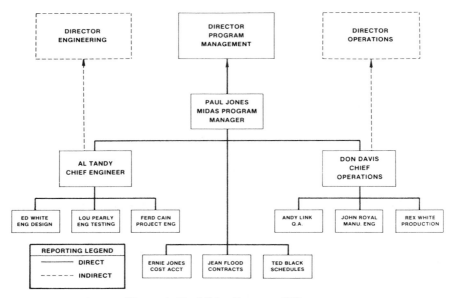

Figure 4–11. Midas Program Office.

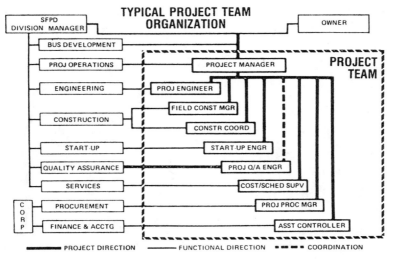

Figure 4–12. Typical project team organization.

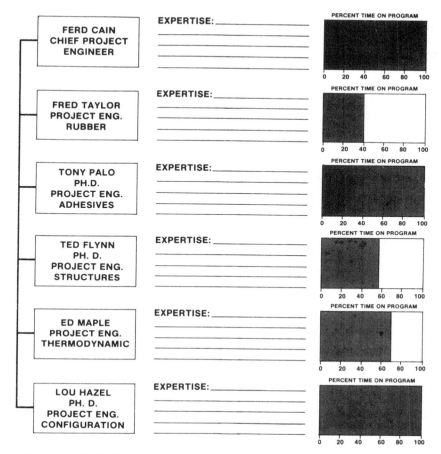

Figure 4–13. Project engineering department manning for Midas Program.

Most customers realize that the top-quality personnel may be shared with other programs and projects. Project manning charts, such as the one shown in Figure 4–13, can be used for this purpose. These manning charts are also helpful in preparing the management volume of proposals to show the customer that key personnel will be readily available on his project.

4.11 SPECIAL PROBLEMS

There are always special problems that influence the organizational staffing process. For example, the department shown in Figure 4–14 has a departmental matrix. All activities stay within the department. Project X and Project Y are managed by line employees who have been temporarily assigned to the projects, whereas Project Z is headed by supervisor B. The department's activities involve high-technology engineering as well as R&D.

The biggest problem facing the department managers is that of training their new employees. The training process requires nine to twelve months. The employees become familiar with the functioning of all three sections, and only after training is an employee assigned to one of the sections. Line managers claim that they do not have sufficient time to supervise training. As a result, the department manager in the example found staff person C to be the most competent person to supervise training. A special departmental training project was set up, as shown in Figure 4–14.

At the end of six months, all new employees were up for their first performance evaluation. The staff person signed the evaluation forms. Within forty-eight hours, the personnel department began screaming that only managers could sign evaluation forms, and since the staff person was not a manager,

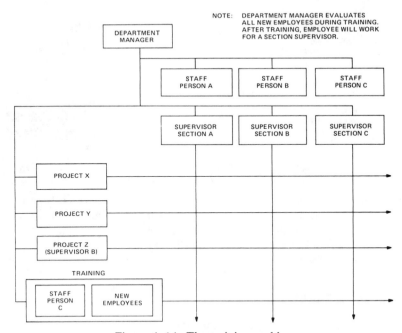

Figure 4–14. The training problem.

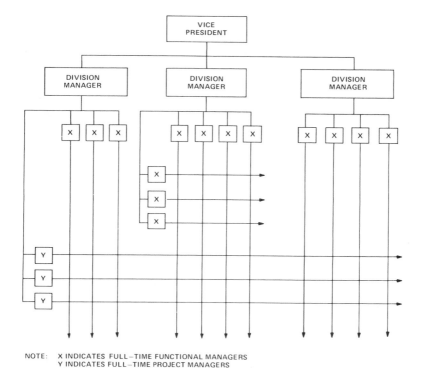

NOTE: X INDICATES FULL–TIME FUNCTIONAL MANAGERS
       Y INDICATES FULL–TIME PROJECT MANAGERS

Figure 4–15. Utility service organization.

personnel could not accept the evaluations. There were now four options available to the department manager:

- Request that the personnel department be disbanded.
- Request personnel to change their procedures.
- Speed up training and, before six months were up, assign the employees to one of the sections.
- Continue as before, but with the department manager to sign the evaluation forms after staff person C filled them out.

The first two choices were found to be impossible, and the third was impractical. The company is now using the fourth approach.

Figure 4–15 shows a utility company that has three full-time project managers controlling three projects, all of which cut across the central division.

Unfortunately, the three full-time project managers cannot get sufficient resources from the central division because the line managers are also acting as divisional project managers and saving the best resources for their own projects, regardless of the priority.

The obvious solution to the problem is that the central division line managers not be permitted to wear two hats. Instead, one full-time project manager can be added to the left division to manage all three central division projects. It is usually best for all project managers to report to the same division for priority-setting and conflict resolution.

Line managers have a tendency to feel demoted when they are suddenly told that they can no longer wear two hats. For example, Mr. Adams is a department manager with thirty years of experience in a company. For the last several years, he has worn two hats and acted as both project manager and functional manager on a variety of projects. He is regarded as an expert in his field. The company decided to incorporate formal project management and established a project management department. Mr. Bell, a thirty-year-old employee with three years of experience with the company, was assigned as the project manager. In order to staff his project, Bell asked Adams for Mr. Cane (Bell's friend) to be assigned to the project as the functional representative. Cane has been with the company for two years. Adams agreed to the request and informed Cane of his new assignment, closing with the remarks, "This project is yours all the way. I don't want to have anything to do with it. I'll be busy with paperwork as a result of the new organizational structure. Just send me a memo once in a while telling me what's happening."

During the project kickoff meeting, it became obvious to everyone that the only person with the necessary expertise was Adams. Without his support, the time duration of the project could be expected to double.

The real problem here was that Adams wanted to feel important and needed, and was hoping that the project manager would come to him asking for his assistance. The project manager correctly analyzed the situation but refused to ask for the line manager's help. Instead, the project manager asked an executive to step in and force the line manager to help. The line manager gave his help, but with great reluctance. Today, the line manager provides poor support to the projects that come across his line organization.

PROBLEMS

4-1 From S. K. Grinnell and H. P. Apple ("When Two Bosses are Better Than One," *Machine Design*, January 1975, pp. 84–87):

The authors identify four major problems associated with staffing. Discuss each problem and identify the type of individual most likely to be involved (i.e., engineer, contract administrator, cost accountant, etc.) and in which organizational form this problem would be most apt to occur:

- People trained in single-line-of-command organizations find it hard to serve more than one boss.
- People may give lip service to teamwork, but not really know how to develop and maintain a good working team.
- Project and functional managers sometimes tend to compete rather than cooperate with each other.
- Individuals must learn to do more "managing" of themselves.

4-2 David Cleland ("Why Project Management?" *Business Horizons,* Winter 1964, p. 85) made the following remarks:

His (Project manager's) staff should be qualified to provide personal administrative and technical support. He should have sufficient authority to increase or decrease his staff as necessary throughout the life of the project. This authorization should include selective augmentation for varying periods of time from the supporting functional agencies.

Do you agree or disagree with these statements? Should the type of project or type of organization play a dominant role in your answer?

4-3 The contractor's project office is often structured to be compatible with the customer's project office, sometimes on a one-to-one basis. Some customers view the contractor's project organization merely as an extension of their own company. Below are three statements concerning this relationship. Are these statements true or false? Defend your answers.

- There must exist mutual trust between the customer and contractor together with a close day-to-day working relationship.
- The project manager and the customer must agree on the hierarchy of decision that each must make, either independently or jointly. (Which decisions can each make independently or jointly?)
- Both the customer and contractor's project personnel must be willing to make decisions as fast as possible.

4-4 C. Ray Gullet ("Personnel Management in the Project Organization," *Personnel Administration/Public Personnel Review,* November–December 1972, pp. 17–22) has identified five personnel problems. How would you, as a project manager, cope with each problem?

- Staffing levels are more variable in a project environment.
- Performance evaluation is more complex and more subject to error in a matrix form of organization.
- Wage and salary grades are more difficult to maintain under a matrix form of organization. Job descriptions are often of less value.
- Training and development are more complex and at the same time more necessary under a project form of organization.
- Morale problems are potentially greater in a matrix organization.

4-5 Ramesh P. Shah ("Project Management: Cross Your Bridges Before You Come to Them," *Management Review,* December 1971, pp. 21–27) states, "Like a physician, a project manager must be an expert diagnostician; he must guard his project from infection, detect symptoms, diagnose causes and prescribe cures for a multitude of afflictions." What is intended by the words "infection, symptoms, diagnose causes, and affliction?"

4-6 Paul is a project manager for an effort that requires twelve months. During the seventh, eighth, and ninth months he needs two individuals with special qualifications. The functional manager has promised that these individuals will be available two months before they are needed. If Paul does not assign them to his project at that time, they will be assigned elsewhere and he will have to do with whomever will be available later. What should Paul do? Do you have to make any assumptions in order to defend your answer?

4-7 Some of the strongest reasons for promoting functional engineers to project engineers are:

- Better relationships with fellow researchers
- Better prevention of duplication of effort
- Better fostering of teamwork

These reasons are usually applied to R&D situations. Could they also be applied to product life-cycle phases other than R&D?

4-8 The following have been given as qualifications for a successful advanced-technology project manager:

- Career has progressed up through the technical ranks
- Knowledgeable in many engineering fields
- Understands general management philosophy and the meaning of profitability
- Interested in training and teaching his superiors
- Understands how to work with perfectionists

Can these same qualifications be modified for non-R&D project management? If so, how?

4-9 W. J. Taylor and T. F. Watling (*Successful Project Management,* London: Business Books, 1972, p. 32) state:

It is often the case, therefore, that the Project Manager is more noted for his management technique expertise, his ability to "get things done" and his ability to "get on with people" than for his sheer technical prowess. However, it can be dangerous to minimize this latter talent when choosing Project Managers dependent upon project type and size. The Project Manager should preferably be an expert either in the field of the project task or a subject allied to it.

How dangerous can it be if this latter talent is minimized? Will it be dangerous under all circumstances?

4-10 Frank Boone is the most knowledgeable piping engineer in the company. For five years, the company has turned down his application for transfer to project engineering and project management stating that he is too valuable to the company in his current position. If you were a project manager, would you want this individual as part of your functional team? How should an organization cope with this situation?

4-11 Tom Weeks is manager of the insulation group. During a recent group meeting, Tom commented, "The company is in trouble. As you know, we're bidding on three programs right now. If we win just one of them, we can probably maintain our current work level. If, by some slim chance, we were to win all three, you'll all be managers tomorrow." The company won all three programs, but the insulation group did not hire anyone, and there were no promotions. What would you, as a project manager on one of the new projects, expect your working relations to be with the insulation group?

4-12 You are a project engineer on a high-technology program. As the project begins to wind down, your boss asks you to write a paper so that he can present it at a technical meeting. His name goes first on the paper. Should this be part of your job? How do you feel about this situation?

4-13 Research has indicated that the matrix structure is often confusing because it requires multiple roles for people, with resulting confusion about these roles (Keith Davis, *Human Relations at Work,* New York: McGraw-Hill, 1967, pp. 296–297). Unfortunately, not all program managers, project managers, and project engineers possess the necessary skills to operate in this environment. Stuckenbruck has stated, "The path to success is strewn with the bodies of project managers who were originally functional line managers and then went into project management" (Linn Stuckenbruck, "The Effective Project Manager," *Project Management Quarterly,* Vol. VII, No. 1, March 1976, pp. 26–27).

What do you feel is the major cause for this downfall of the functional manager?

4-14 For each of the organizational forms shown below, who determines what resources are needed, when they are needed and how they will be employed? Who has the authority and responsibility to mobilize these resources?

a. Traditional organization
b. Matrix organization
c. Product line organization
d. Line/staff project organization

4-15 Do you agree or disagree that project organizational forms encourage peer-to-peer communications and dynamic problem-solving?

4-16 The XYZ Company operates on a traditional structure. The company has just received a contract to develop a new product line for a special group of customers. The company has decided to pull out selected personnel from the functional departments and set up a single product organizational structure to operate in parallel with the functional departments.

a. Set up the organizational chart.
b. Do you think this setup can work? Does your answer depend upon how many years this situation must exist?

4–17 You are the project engineer on a program similar to one that you directed previously. Should you attempt to obtain the same administrative and/or technical staff that you had before?

4–18 A person assigned to your project is performing unsatisfactorily. What should you do? Will it make a difference if he is in the project office or a functional employee?

4–19 You have been assigned to the project office as an assistant project engineer. You are to report to the chief project engineer who reports formally to the project manager and informally to the vice president of engineering. You have never worked with this chief project engineer before. During the execution of the project, it becomes obvious to you that the chief project engineer is making decisions that do not appear to be in the best interest of the project. What should you do about this?

4–20 Should individuals be promoted to project management because they are at the top of their functional pay grade?

4–21 Should one functional department be permitted to "borrow" (on a temporary basis) people from another functional department in order to fulfill project manning requirements? Should this be permitted if overtime is involved?

4–22 Should a project manager be paid for performance or for the number of people he supervises?

4–23 Should a project manager try to upgrade his personnel?

4–24 Why should a functional manager assign his best people to you on a long-term project?

4–25 A coal company has adopted the philosophy that the project manager for new mine startup projects will be the individual who will eventually become the mine superintendent. The coal company believes that this type of "ownership" philosophy is good. Do you agree?

4–26 Can a project manager be considered as a "hired gun?"

4–27 Manufacturing organizations are using project management/project engineering strictly to give new employees exposure to total company operations. After working on one or two projects, each approximately one to two years in duration, the employee is transferred to line management for his career path and opportunities for advancement. Can a situation such as this, where there is no career path in either project management or project engineering, work successfully? Could there be any detrimental effects on the projects?

4–28 Can a project manager create dedication and a true winning spirit and still be hated by all?

4–29 Can anyone be trained to be a project manager?

4–30 A power and light company has part-time project management in which an individual acts as both a project manager and a functional employee at the same time. The utility company claims that this process prevents an employee from becoming "technically obsolete," and that when the employee returns to full-time functional duties, he or she is a more well-rounded individual. Do you agree or disagree? What are the arrangement's advantages and disadvantages?

4-31 Some industries consider the major criterion for promotion and advancement to be gray hair and/or baldness. Is this type of maturity advantageous?

4-32 In Figure 4-11 we showed that Al Tandy and Don Davis (as well as other project office personnel) reported on a solid line to the project manager and on a dotted line functionally. Could this situation be reversed, with the project office personnel reporting dotted to the project manager and solid functionally?

4-33 Most organizations have "star" people who are usually identified as those individuals who are the key to success. How does a project manager identify these people? Can they be in the project office, or must they be functional employees or managers?

4-34 Considering your own industry, what job-related or employee-related factors would you wish to know before selecting someone to be a project manager or a project engineer on an effort valued at:

   a. $30,000?
   b. $300,000?
   c. $3,000,000?
   d. $30,000,000?

4-35 One of the major controversies in project management occurs over whether or not the project manager needs a command of technology in order to be effective. Consider the following situation:

You are the project manager on a research and development project. Marketing informs you that they have found a customer for your product and that you must make major modifications to satisfy the customer's requirements. The engineering functional managers tell you that these modifications are impossible. Can a project manager without a command of technology make a viable decision as to whether to risk additional funds and support marketing, or should he believe the functional managers and tell marketing that the modifications are impossible? How can a project manager, either with or without a command of technology, tell whether the functional managers are giving him an optimistic or a pessimistic opinion?

4-36 As a functional employee, you demonstrate that you have exceptionally good writing skills. You are then promoted to the position of special staff assistant to the division manager and told that you are to assume full responsibility for all proposal work that must flow through your division. How do you feel about this? Is it a promotion? Where can you go from here?

4-37 Government policy-makers contend that only high-ranking individuals (high GS grades) can be project managers because a good project manager needs sufficient "clout" to make the project go. In government, the project manager is generally the highest grade on the project team. How can problems of pay grade be overcome? Is the government's policy effective?

4-38 A major utility company is worried about the project manager's upgrading functional employees. On an eight-month project that employs four hundred full-time project employees, the department managers have set up "check" people whose responsibility is to see that functional employees do not have unauthorized (i.e., not approved by the functional manager) work assignments above their current grade level. Can this system work? What if the work is at a position below their grade level?

4-39 A major utility company begins each computer project with a feasibility study in which a cost/benefit analysis is performed. The project managers, all of whom report to a project management division, perform the feasibility study themselves without any functional support. The functional personnel argue that the feasibility study is inaccurate because the functional "experts" are not involved. The project managers, on the other hand, stipulate that they never have sufficient time or money to involve the functional personnel. Can this situation be resolved?

4-40 How would you go about training individuals within your company or industry to be good project managers? What assumptions are you making?

4-41 Should project teams be allowed to evolve by themselves?

4-42 At what point or phase in the life cycle of a project should a project manager be appointed?

4-43 Top management generally has two schools of thought concerning project management. One school states that the project manager should be used as a means for coordinating activities that cut across several functional departments. The second school states that the project management position should be used as a means of creating future general managers. Which school of thought is correct?

4-44 Some executives feel that personnel working in a project office should be cross-trained in several assistant project management functions. What do you think about this?

4-45 A company has a policy that employees wishing to be project managers must first spend one to one and a half years in the functional employee side of the house so that they can get to know the employees and company policy. What do you think about this?

4-46 Your project has grown to a point where there now exist openings for three full-time assistant project managers. Unfortunately, there are no experienced assistant project managers available. You are told by upper-level management that you will fill these three positions by promotions from within. Where in the organization should you look? During an interview, what questions should you ask potential candidates? Is it possible that you could find candidates who are qualified to be promoted vertically but not horizontally?

4-47 A functional employee has demonstrated the necessary attributes of a potentially successful project manager. Top management can:

- Promote the individual in salary and grade and transfer him into project management.

- Laterally transfer the employee into project management without any salary or grade increase. If, after three to six months, the employee demonstrates that he can perform, he will receive an appropriate salary and grade increase.
- Give the employee either a grade increase without any salary increase, or a small salary increase without any grade increase, under the stipulation that additional awards will be given at the end of the observation period, assuming that the employee can handle the position.

If you were in top management, which method would you prefer? If you dislike the above three choices, develop your own alternative. What are the advantages and disadvantages of each choice? For each choice, discuss the ramifications if the employee cannot handle the project management position.

CASE STUDY: GOVERNMENT PROJECT MANAGEMENT

A major government agency is organized to monitor government subcontractors as shown in Exhibit 4–1. Below are the vital characteristics of certain project office team members:

Project Manager: Directs all project activities and acts as the information focal point for the subcontractor.

Assistant Project Manager: Acts as chairman of the steering committee and interfaces with both in-house functional group and contractor.

Department Managers: Act as members of the steering committee for any projects that utilize their resources. These slots on the steering committee must be filled by the department managers themselves, not by functional employees.

Exhibit 4-1.

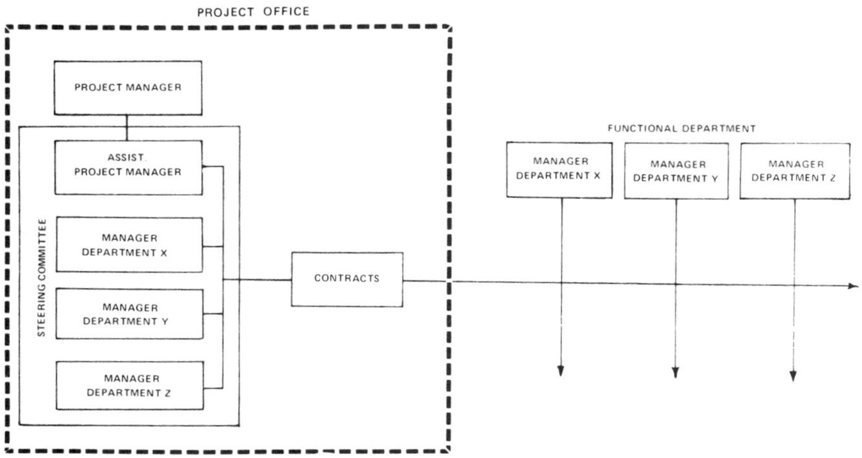

Contracts Officer: Authorizes all work directed by the project office to in-house functional groups and to the customer, and ensures that all work requested is authorized by the contract. The contracts officer acts as the focal point for all contractor cost and contractual information.

1. Explain how this structure should work.
2. Explain how this structure actually works.
3. Can the project manager be a military type who is reassigned after a given tour of duty?
4. What are the advantages and disadvantages of this structure?
5. Could this be used in industry?

CASE STUDY: FALLS ENGINEERING

Falls Engineering is a $250-million chemical and material operation employing 900 people and located in New York. The plant has two distinct manufacturing product lines: industrial chemicals and computer materials. Both divisions are controlled by one plant manager, but direction, strategic planning, and priorities are established by corporate vice presidents in Chicago. Each division has its own corporate vice president, list of projects, list of priorities, and manpower control. The chemical division has been at this location for the past twenty years. The materials division is, you might say, the tenant in the landlord–tenant relationship with the materials division manager reporting dotted to the plant manager and solid to the corporate vice president. (See Exhibit 4–2.)

The chemical division employed 3,000 people in 1968. By 1973, there were only 600 employees. In 1974, the materials division was formed and located on the chemical division site with a landlord–tenant relationship. The materials division has grown from $50 million in 1975 to $120 million in 1979. Today, the materials division employs 350 people.

The chemical division has a much larger construction and facilities group compared to the materials division. However, for capital equipment projects, the materials group has to "rent" resources from the chemical group in order to get the projects accomplished. All projects are geared toward manufacturing because this is where the profits are.

All projects originate in construction or engineering but usually are designed to support production. The engineering and construction departments have projects that span the entire organization directed by a project coordinator. The project coordinator is a line employee who is temporarily assigned to coordinate a project in his line organization in addition to performing his line responsibilities. Assignments are made by the division managers (who report to the plant manager) and are based upon technical expertise. The coordinators have monitoring authority only and are not noted for being good planners or negotiators. The coordinators report to their respective line managers.

Basically, a project can start in either division with the project coordinators. The coordinators draw up a large scope of work and submit it to the project engineering group who arrange for design contractors, depending upon the size of the project. Pro-

Exhibit 4-2. Falls Engineering Organizational Chart.

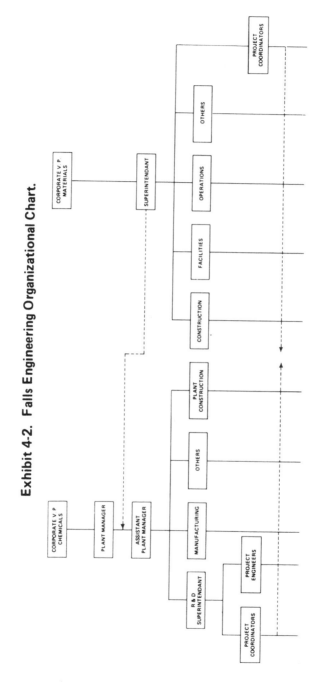

ject engineering places it upon their design schedule according to priority and produces prints and specifications, and receives quotes. A construction cost estimate is then produced following 60–75 percent design completion. The estimate and project papers are prepared, and the project is circulated through the plant and in Chicago for approval and authorization. Following authorization, the design is completed, and materials are ordered. Following design, the project is transferred to either of two plant construction groups for construction. The project coordinators then arrange for the work to be accomplished in their areas with minimum interference from manufacturing forces. In all cases, the coordinators act as project managers and must take the usual constraints of time, money, and performance into account.

Falls Engineering has 300 projects listed for completion between 1980 and 1982. In the last two years, less than 10 percent of the projects were completed within time, cost, and performance constraints. Line managers find it increasingly difficult to make resource commitments because crises always seem to develop, including a number of fires.

Profits are made in manufacturing, and everyone knows it. Whenever a manufacturing crisis occurs, line managers pull resources off the projects, and, of course, the projects suffer. Project coordinators are trying, but with very little success, to put some slack onto the schedules to allow for contingencies.

The breakdown of the 300 plant projects is shown below:

Number of Projects	$ Range
120	less than $50,000
80	$50,000–200,000
70	$250,000–750,000
20	$1–3 million
10	$4–8 million

Corporate realized the necessity for changing the organizational structure. A meeting was set up between the plant manager, plant executives, and corporate executives to resolve these problems once and for all. The plant manager decided to survey his employees concerning their feelings about the present organizational structure. Below are their comments:

- "The projects we have the most trouble with are the small ones under $200,000. Can we use informal project management for the small ones and formal project management on the large ones?"
- "Why do we persist in using computer programming to control our resources? These sophisticated packages are useless because they do not account for firefighting."
- "Project coordinators need access to various levels of management, in both divisions."
- "Our line managers do not realize the necessity for effective planning of resources. Resources are assigned based upon emotions and not need."
- "Sometimes a line manager gives a commitment but the project coordinator cannot force him to keep it."

- "Line managers always find fault with project coordinators who try to develop detailed schedules themselves."
- "If we continuously have to 'crash' project time, doesn't that indicate poor planning?"
- "We need a career path in project coordination so that we can develop a body of good planners, communicators, and integrators."
- "I've seen project coordinators who have no interest in the job, cannot work with diverse functional disciplines, and cannot communicate. Yet, someone assigned them as a project coordinator."
- "Any organizational system we come up with has to be better than the one we have now."
- "Somebody has to have total accountability. Our people are working on projects and, at the same time, do not know the project status, the current cost, the risks, and the end date."
- "One of these days I'm going to kill an executive while he's meddling in my project."
- "Recently, management made changes requiring more paperwork for the project coordinators. How many hours a week do they expect me to work?"
- "I've yet to see any documentation describing the job description of the project coordinator."
- "I have absolutely no knowledge about who is assigned as the project coordinator until work has to be coordinated in my group. Somehow, I'm not sure that this is the way the system should work."
- "I know that we line managers are supposed to be flexible, but changing the priorities every week isn't exactly my idea of fun."
- "If the projects start out with poor planning, then management does not have the right to expect the line managers always to come to the rescue."
- "Why is it the line managers always get blamed for schedule delays, even if it's the result of poor planning up front?"
- "If management doesn't want to hire additional resources, then why should the line managers be made to suffer? Perhaps, we should cut out some of these useless projects. Sometimes I think management dreams up some of these projects simply to spend the allocated funds."
- "I have yet to see a project I felt had a realistic deadline."

After preparing alternatives and recommendations, as plant manager, try to do some role playing by putting yourself in the shoes of the corporate executives. Would you as a corporate executive approve the recommendation? Where does profitability, sales, return on investment, and so on enter in your decision?

CASE STUDY: WHITE MANUFACTURING

In 1975, White Manufacturing realized the necessity for project management in the manufacturing group. A three-man project management staff was formed. Although the staff was shown on the organizational chart as reporting to the manufacturing operations manager, they actually worked for the vice president and had sufficient authority to integrate work across all departments and divisions. As in the past, the vice-president's position was filled by the manufacturing operations manager. Manufacturing operations was directed by the former manufacturing manager who came from manufacturing engineering. See Exhibit 4–3.

In 1978, the manufacturing manager created a matrix in the manufacturing department with the manufacturing engineers acting as departmental project managers. This benefited both the manufacturing manager and the group project managers since all information could be obtained from one source. Work was flowing very smoothly.

In January 1979, the manufacturing manager resigned his position effective March, and the manufacturing engineering manager began packing his bags ready to move up to the vacated position. In February, the vice president announced that the position would be filled from outside. He said also that there would be an organizational restructuring and that the three project managers would now be staff to the manufacturing manager. When the three project managers confronted the manufacturing operations manager, he said, "We've hired the new man in at a very high salary. In order to justify this salary, we have to give him more responsibility."

On March 1, 1979, the new manager took over and immediately made the following declarations:

1. The project managers will never go "upstairs" without first going through him.
2. The departmental matrix will be dissolved and he (the department manager) will handle all of the integration.

How do you account for the actions of the new department manager? What would you do if you were one of the project managers?

CASE STUDY: MARTIG CONSTRUCTION COMPANY

Martig Construction was a family-owned mechanical subcontractor business that had grown from $5 million in 1976 to $25 million in 1978. Although the gross profit had

Exhibit 4-3. White Manufacturing Organizational Structure.

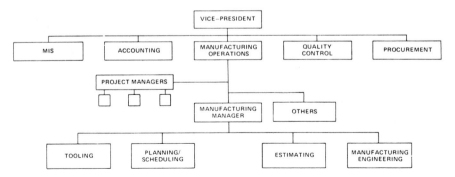

increased sharply, the profit as a percentage of sales declined drastically. The question was, "Why the decline?" The following observations were made:

1. Since Martig senior died in July of 1978, Martig junior has tried unsuccessfully to convince the family to let him sell the business. Martig junior, as company president, has taken an average of eight days of vacation per month for the past year. Although the project managers are supposed to report to Martig, they appear to be calling their own shots and are in a continuous struggle for power.
2. The estimating department consists of one man, John, who estimates all jobs. Martig wins one job in seven. Once a job is won, a project manager is selected and is told that he must perform the job within the proposal estimates. Project managers are not involved in proposal estimates. They are required, however, to provide feedback to the estimator so that standards can be updated. This very seldom happens because of the struggle for power. The project managers are afraid that the estimator might be next in line for executive promotion since he is a good friend of Martig.
3. The procurement function reports to Martig. Once the items are ordered, the project manager assumes procurement responsibility. Several times in the past, the project manager has been forced to spend hour after hour trying to overcome shortages or simply to track down raw materials. Most project managers estimate that approximately 35 percent of their time involves procurement.
4. Site superintendents believe they are the true project managers, or at least at the same level. The superintendents are very unhappy about not being involved in the procurement function and, therefore, look for ways to annoy the project managers. It appears that the more time the project manager spends at the site, the longer the work takes; the feedback of information to the home office is also distorted.

CASE STUDY: THE CARLSON PROJECT

"I sympathize with your problems, Frank," stated Joe McGee, Manager of Project Managers. "You know as well as I do that I'm supposed to resolve conflicts and coordinate efforts among all projects. Staffing problems are your responsibility."

Frank: "Royce Williams has a résumé that would choke a horse. I don't understand why he performs with a lazy, I-don't-care attitude. He has fifteen years of experience in a project organizational structure, with ten of those years being in project offices. He knows the work that has to be done."

McGee: "I don't think that it has anything to do with you personally. This happens to some of our best workers sooner or later. You can't expect guys to give 120 percent all of the time. Royce is at the top of his pay grade, and being an exempt employee, he doesn't get paid for overtime. He'll snap out of it sooner or later."

Frank: "I have deadlines to meet on the Carlson Project. Fortunately, the Carlson Project is big enough that I can maintain a full-time project office staff of eight employees, not counting myself.

"I like to have all project office employees assigned full-time and qualified in two or three project office areas. It's a good thing that I have someone else checked out in Royce's area. But I just can't keep asking this other guy to do his own work and that of Royce's. This poor guy has been working sixty to seventy hours a week and Royce has been doing only forty. That seems unfair to me."

McGee: "Look Frank, I have the authority to fire him, but I'm not going to. It doesn't look good if we fire somebody because they won't work free overtime. Last year we had a case similar to this, where an employee refused to work on Monday and Wednesday evenings because it interfered with his MBA classes. Everyone knew he was going to resign the instant he finished his degree, and yet there was nothing that I could do."

Frank: "There must be other alternatives for Royce Williams. I've talked to him as well as to other project office members. Royce's attitude doesn't appear to be demoralizing the other members, but it easily could in a short period of time."

McGee: "We can reassign him to another project, as soon as one comes along. I'm not going to put him on my overhead budget. Your project can support him for the time being. You know, Frank, the grapevine will know the reason for his transfer. This might affect your ability to get qualified people to volunteer to work with you on future projects. Give Royce a little more time and see if you can work it out with him. What about this guy, Harlan Green, from one of the functional groups?"

Frank: "Two months ago, we hired Gus Johnson, a man with ten years of experience. For the first two weeks that he was assigned to my project, he worked like hell and got the work done ahead of schedule. His work was flawless. That was the main reason why I wanted him. I know him personally, and he's one great worker.

"During weeks three and four, his work slowed down considerably. I chatted with him and he said that Harlan Green refused to work with him if he kept up that pace."

McGee: "Did you ask him why?"

Frank: "Yes. First of all, you should know that for safety reasons, all men in that department must work in two- or three-men crews. Therefore, Gus was not allowed to work alone. Harlan did not want to change the standards of performance for fear that some of the other employees would be laid off.

"By the end of the first week, nobody in the department would talk to Gus. As a matter of fact, they wouldn't even sit with him in the cafeteria. So, Gus had to either conform to the group or remain an outcast. I feel partially responsible for what has happened, since I'm the one who brought him here.

"I know this has happened before, in the same department. I haven't had a chance to talk to the department manager as yet. I have an appointment to see him next week."

McGee: "There are solutions to the problem, simple ones at that. But, again, it's not my responsibility. You can work it out with the department manager."

"Yeah," thought Frank. "But what if we can't agree?"

5
Management Functions

5.0 INTRODUCTION

As we have stated, the project manager measures his success by how well he can negotiate with both upper-level and functional management for the resources necessary to achieve the project objective. Moreover, the project manager may have a great deal of delegated authority but very little power. Hence, the managerial skills he requires for successful performance may be drastically different from those of his functional management counterparts.

The difficult aspect of the project management environment is that the individuals at the project–functional interface must report to two bosses. Functional managers and project managers, by virtue of their different authority levels and responsibilities, treat their people in different fashions depending upon their "management school" philosophies. There are generally five management schools, as described below:

- *The classical/traditional school:* Management is the process of getting things done (i.e., possibly achieving objectives) by working both with and through people operating in organized groups. Emphasis is placed upon the end item or objective, with little regard for the people involved.
- *The empirical school:* Managerial capabilities can be developed by studying the experiences of other managers, whether or not the situations are similar.
- *The behavioral school:* Two classrooms are considered within this school. First we have the human relations classroom in which we emphasize the interpersonal relationship between individuals and their work. The second classroom includes the social system of the individual. Management is considered to be a system of cultural relationships involving social change.
- *The decision theory school:* Management is a rational approach to decision making using a system of mathematical models and processes, such as operations research and management science.
- *The management systems school:* Management is the development of a systems model, characterized by input, processing, and output, and directly identifies the flow of resources (money, equipment, facilities, per-

sonnel, information, and material) necessary to obtain some objective by either maximizing or minimizing some objective function. The management systems school also includes contingency theory, which stresses that each situation is unique and must be optimized separately within the constraints of the system.

In a project environment, functional managers are generally practitioners of the first three schools of management, whereas project managers utilize the last two. This imposes hardships on both the project managers and functional representatives. The project manager must motivate functional representatives toward project dedication on the horizontal line using management system theory and quantitative tools, often with little regard for the employee. After all, the employee might be assigned for a very short-term effort, whereas the end item is the most important objective. The functional manager, however, expresses more concern for the individual needs of the employee using the traditional or behavioral schools of management.

Modern practitioners still tend to identify management responsibilities and skills in terms of the principles and functions developed in the early management schools, namely:

- Planning
- Organizing
- Staffing
- Controlling
- Directing

Although these management functions have generally been applied to traditional management structures, they have recently been redefined for temporary management positions. Their fundamental meanings remain the same, but the applications are different.

5.1 CONTROLLING

Controlling is a three-step process of measuring progress toward an objective, evaluating what remains to be done, and taking the necessary corrective action to achieve or exceed the objectives. These three steps, measuring, evaluating, and correcting, are defined as follows:

- *Measuring:* determining through formal and informal reports the degree to which progress toward objectives is being made.
- *Evaluating:* determining cause of and possible ways to act upon significant deviations from planned performance.

- *Correcting:* taking control action to correct an unfavorable trend or to take advantage of an unusually favorable trend.

The project manager is responsible for ensuring the accomplishment of group and organizational goals and objectives. To effect this, he must have a thorough knowledge of standards and cost control policies and procedures so that a comparison is possible between operating results and preestablished standards. The project manager must then take the necessary corrective actions. Later chapters will provide a more in-depth analysis of control, especially the cost control function.

In Chapter 1, we stated that project managers must understand organizational behavior in order to be effective and must have strong interpersonal skills. This is especially important during the controlling function. As stated by Doering:[1]

The team leader's role is crucial. He is directly involved and must know the individual team member well, not only in terms of their technical capabilities but also in terms of how they function when addressing a problem as part of a group. The technical competence of a potential team member can usually be determined from information about previous assignments, but it is not so easy to predict and control the individual's interaction within and with a new group, since it is related to the psychological and social behavior of each of the other members of the group as a whole. What the leader needs is a tool to measure and characterize the individual members so that he can predict their interactions and structure his task team accordingly.

5.2 DIRECTING

Directing is the implementing and carrying out (through others) of those approved plans that are necessary to achieve or exceed objectives. Directing involves such steps as:

- *Staffing:* seeing that a qualified person is selected for each position.
- *Training:* teaching individuals and groups how to fulfill their duties and resonsibilities.
- *Supervising:* giving others day-to-day instruction, guidance, and discipline as required so that they can fulfill their duties and responsibilities.
- *Delegating:* assigning work, responsibility, and authority so others can make maximum utilization of their abilities.

---

1. Robert D. Doering, "An Approach Toward Improving the Creative Output of Scientific Task Teams," *IEEE Transactions on Engineering Management,* February 1973, pp. 29–31.

- *Motivating:* encouraging others to perform by fulfilling or appealing to their needs.
- *Counseling:* holding private discussions with another about how he might do better work, solve a personal problem, or realize his ambitions.
- *Coordinating:* seeing that activities are carried out in relation to their importance and with a minimum of conflict.

Directing subordinates is not an easy task because of both the short time duration of the project and the fact that the employees might still be assigned to a functional manager while temporarily assigned to your effort. The luxury of getting to "know" one's subordinates may not be possible in a project environment.

Project managers must be decisive and move forward rapidly whenever directives are necessary. It is better to decide an issue and be 10 percent wrong than it is to wait for the last 10 percent of a problem's input and cause a schedule delay and improper use of resources. Directives are most effective when the KISS (keep it simple, stupid) rule is applied. Directives should be written with one simple and clear objective so that subordinates can work effectively and get things done right the first time. Orders must be issued in a manner that expects immediate compliance. Whether people will or will not obey an order depends mainly on the amount of respect they have for you. Therefore, never issue an order that you cannot enforce. Oral orders and directives should be disguised as suggestions or requests. The requestor should ask the receiver to repeat the oral orders so that there is no misunderstanding.

Project managers must understand human behavior, perhaps more so than functional managers. The reason for this is that project managers must continually motivate people toward successful accomplishment of project objectives. Motivation cannot be accomplished without at least a fundamental knowledge of human behavior.

Douglas McGregor advocated that most workers can be catagorized into one of two groups.[2] The first group, often referred to as Theory X, assumes that the average worker is inherently lazy and requires supervision. Theory X further assumes that:

- The average worker dislikes work and avoids work whenever possible.
- To induce adequate effort, the supervisor must threaten punishment and exercise careful supervision.
- The average worker avoids increased responsibility and seeks to be directed.

---

2. Douglas McGregor, *The Human Side of Enterprise* (New York: McGraw-Hill, 1960), pp. 33–34.

The manager who accepts Theory X normally exercises authoritarian-type control over workers and allows little participation during decision making. Theory X employees generally favor lack of responsibility, especially in decision making.

According to Theory Y, employees are willing to get the job done without constant supervision. Theory Y further assumes that:

- The average worker wants to be active and finds the physical and mental effort on the job satisfying.
- Greatest results come from willing participation which will tend to produce self-direction toward goals without coercion and control.
- The average worker seeks opportunity for personal improvement and self-respect.

The manager who accepts Theory Y normally advocates participation and a management–employee relationship. However, in working with professionals, especially engineers, special care must be exercised because these individuals often pride themselves on their ability to find a better way to achieve the end result regardless of cost. The risk of this happening rises with the numbers of professional degrees that one possesses. The problem with this is that it is the responsibility of the functional manager to determine "how" the job will be done once the project manager states "what" must be done. Project management has the right to insist that an individual who is given free rein to accomplish an objective will also fully understand the necessity of time, cost, and performance constraints. This situation holds true for several engineering disciplines in which engineers consistently strive to exhibit their individuality by seeking new and revolutionary solutions to problems for which well-established solutions already exist. Under these conditions, project managers must become authoritarian leaders and treat Theory Y employees as though they are Theory X. Employees must be trained in how to report to two bosses at the same time. This problem occurs when the employee's line manager treats him as though he is a Theory Y employee, but the project manager treats him as if he is Theory X. Employees must realize that this situation will occur.

Many psychologists have established the existence of a prioritized hierarchy of needs that motivate individuals toward satisfactory performance. Maslow was the first to identify these needs.[3] The first level is that of the basic or physiological needs, namely, food, water, clothing, shelter, sleep, and sexual satisfaction. Simply speaking, man's primal desire to satisfy these basic needs motivates him to do a good job. However, once a need becomes satisfied, man is no

---

3. Abraham Maslow, *Motivation and Personality* (New York: Harper and Brothers, 1954).

longer motivated unless there is a lower-level need that motivates him further. Fulfilled needs are not motivators.

After an employee has fulfilled his physiological needs, he turns to the next lower need, safety. Safety needs include economic security and protection from harm, disease, and violence. Safety needs must be considered on projects that may include handling of dangerous materials or anything else that could produce bodily harm. Safety can also include security. It is important that project managers realize this because these managers may find that as a project nears termination, functional employees are more interested in finding a new role for themselves than in giving their best to the current situation.

The next level contains the social needs, including love, belonging, togetherness, approval, and group membership. At this level, the informal organization plays a dominant role. Many people refuse promotions to project management (as project managers, project office personnel, or functional representatives) because they fear that they will lose their "membership" in the informal organization. This problem can occur even on short-duration projects. In a project environment, project managers generally do not belong to any informal organization and, therefore, tend to look outside the organization to fulfill this need. Project managers consider authority and funding to be very important in gaining project support. Functional personnel, however, prefer friendship and work assignments. In other words, the project manager can use the project itself as a means of helping fulfill the third level for the line employees (i.e., team spirit).

The two lowest needs are esteem and self-actualization. The esteem need includes self-eseem (self-respect), reputation, the esteem of others, recognition, and self-confidence. Highly technical professionals are often not happy unless esteem needs are fulfilled. For example, many engineers strive to publish and invent as a means of satisfying these needs. These individuals often refuse promotions to project management because they believe that they cannot satisfy esteem needs in this position. Being called a project manager does not carry as much importance as being considered an expert in one's field by one's peers. The lowest need is self-actualization and includes doing what one can do best, desiring to utilize one's potential, full realization of one's potential, constant self-development, and a desire to be truly creative. Many good project managers find this level to be the most important and consider each new project as a challenge by which they can achieve self-actualization.

Project managers must motivate temporarily assigned individuals by appealing to their desires to fulfill the lowest two levels. Of course, the motivation process should not be developed by making promises that the project manager knows cannot be met. Project managers must motivate by providing:

- A feeling of pride or satisfaction for one's ego
- Security of opportunity

- Security of approval
- Security of advancement, if possible
- Security of promotion, if possible
- Security of recognition
- A means for doing a better job, not a means to keep a job

Understanding professional needs is an important factor in helping people realize their true potential. Such needs include:

- Interesting and challenging work
- Professionally stimulating work environment
- Professional growth
- Overall leadership (ability to lead)
- Tangible rewards
- Technical expertise (within the team)
- Management assistance in problem solving
- Clearly defined objectives
- Proper management control
- Job security
- Senior management support
- Good interpersonal relations
- Proper planning
- Clear role definition
- Open communications
- A minimum of changes

Motivating employees so that they feel secure on the job is not easy, especially since a project has a finite lifetime. Specific methods for producing security in a project environment include:

- Letting the people know why they are where they are
- Making the individuals feel that they belong where they are
- Placing individuals in positions for which they are properly trained
- Letting the employees know how their efforts fit into the big picture

Since project managers cannot motivate by promising material gains, they must appeal to each person's pride. The guidelines for proper motivation are:

- Adopt a positive attitude
- Do not criticize management
- Do not make promises that cannot be kept
- Circulate customer reports
- Give each person the attention he requires

There are several ways of motivating project personnel. Some effective ways include:

- Giving assignments that provide challenges
- Clearly defining performance expectations
- Giving proper criticism as well as credit
- Giving honest appraisals
- Providing a good working atmosphere
- Developing a team attitude
- Providing a proper direction (even if Theory Y)

5.3 PROJECT AUTHORITY

Project management structures create a web of relationships that can cause chaos in the delegation of authority and the internal authority structure. Four questions must be considered in describing project authority:

- What is project authority?
- What is power, and how is it achieved?
- How much project authority should be granted to the project manager?
- Who settles project authority interface problems?

One form of the project manager's authority can be defined as the legal or rightful power to command, act, or direct the activities of others. The breakdown of the project managers authority is shown in Figure 5–1. Authority can be delegated from one's superiors. Power, on the other hand, is granted to an individual by his subordinates and is a measure of their respect for him. A manager's authority is a combination of his power and influence such that subordinates, peers, and associates willingly accept his judgment.

In the traditional structure, the power spectrum is realized through the hierarchy, whereas in the project strucure, power comes from credibility, expertise, or being a sound decision-maker.

Authority is the key to the project management process. The project manager must manage across functional and organizational lines by bringing together activities required to accomplish the objectives of a specific project. Project authority provides the way of thinking required to unify all organizational activities toward accomplishment of the project regardless of where they are located. The project manager who fails to build and maintain his alliances will soon find opposition or indifference to his project requirements.

The amount of authority granted to the project manager varies according to project size, management philosophy, and management interpretation of potential conflicts with functional managers. There do exist, however, certain

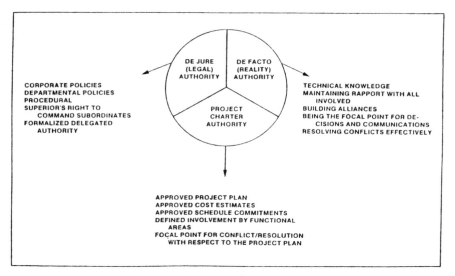

CORPORATE POLICIES
DEPARTMENTAL POLICIES
PROCEDURAL
SUPERIOR'S RIGHT TO
    COMMAND SUBORDINATES
FORMALIZED DELEGATED
    AUTHORITY

DE JURE (LEGAL) AUTHORITY
DE FACTO (REALITY) AUTHORITY
PROJECT CHARTER AUTHORITY

TECHNICAL KNOWLEDGE
MAINTAINING RAPPORT WITH ALL
    INVOLVED
BUILDING ALLIANCES
BEING THE FOCAL POINT FOR DE-
    CISIONS AND COMMUNICATIONS
RESOLVING CONFLICTS EFFECTIVELY

APPROVED PROJECT PLAN
APPROVED COST ESTIMATES
APPROVED SCHEDULE COMMITMENTS
DEFINED INVOLVEMENT BY FUNCTIONAL
    AREAS
FOCAL POINT FOR CONFLICT/RESOLUTION
    WITH RESPECT TO THE PROJECT PLAN

Figure 5–1. Project authority breakdown. Source: Bill Eglinton, "Matrix Project Management Myths and Realities," *Proceedings of the PMI Seminar/Symposium on Project Management,* Toronto, Ontario, Canada, p. IV-G.33.

fundamental elements over which the project manager must have authority in order to maintain effective control. According to Steiner and Ryan:[4]

The project manager should have broad authority over all elements of the project. His authority should be sufficient to permit him to engage all necessary managerial and technical actions required to complete the project successfully. He should have appropriate authority in design and in making technical decisions in development. He should be able to control funds, schedule and quality of product. If subcontractors are used, he should have maximum authority in their selection.

Generally speaking, a project manager should have more authority than his responsibility calls for, the exact amount of authority usually depending upon the amount of risk that the project manager must take. The greater the risk, the greater the amount of authority. A good project manager knows where his authority ends and does not hold an employee responsible for duties that he (the project manager) does not have the authority to enforce. Some projects

---

4. George A. Steiner and William G. Ryan, *Industrial Project Management* (New York: Macmillan, Copyright © 1968 by theTrustees of Columbia University in the City of New York), p. 24.

are directed by project managers who have only monitoring authority. These project managers are referred to as influence project managers.

Failure to establish authority relationships can result in:

- Poor communication channels
- Misleading information
- Antagonism, especially from the informal organization
- Poor working relationships with superiors, subordinates, peers, and associates
- Surprises for the customer

The following are the most common sources of power and authority problems in a project environment:

- Poorly documented or no formal authority
- Power and authority perceived incorrectly
- Dual accountability of personnel
- Two bosses (who often disagree)
- The project organization encouraging individualism
- Subordinate relations stronger than peer or superior relationships
- Shifting of personnel loyalties from vertical to horizontal lines
- Group decision-making based upon the strongest group
- Ability to influence or administer rewards and punishment
- Sharing resources among several projects

The project management organizational structure is an arena of continuous conflict and negotiation. Although there are many clearly defined authority boundaries between functional and project management responsibilities, the fact that each project can be inherently different from all others almost always creates new areas where authority negotiations are necessary.

The project manager does not have unilateral authority in the project effort. He frequently negotiates with the functional manager. The project manager has the authority to determine the "when" and "what" of the project activities, whereas the functional manager has the authority to determine "how the support will be given." The project manager accomplishes his objectives by working with personnel who are largely professional. For professional personnel, project leadership must include explaining the rationale of the effort as well as the more obvious functions of planning organizing, directing, and controlling.

Certain ground rules exist for authority control through negotiations:

- Negotiations should take place at the lowest level of interaction.
- Definition of the problem must be the first priority:

- The issue
- The impact
- The alternative
- The recommendations
- Higher-level authority should be used if, and only if, agreement cannot be reached.

The critical stage of any project is planning. This includes more than just planning the activities to be accomplished; it also includes the planning and establishment of the authority relationships that must exist for the duration of the project. Because the project management environment is an ever changing one, each project establishes its own policies and procedures, a situation that can ultimately result in a variety of authority relationships. It is therefore possible for functional personnel to have different responsibilities on different projects, even if the tasks are the same.

During the planning phase the project team develops a responsibility matrix that contain such elements as:

- General management responsibility
- Operations management responsibility
- Specialized responsibility
- Must be consulted
- May be consulted
- Must be notified
- Must approve

The responsibility matrix is often referred to as a linear responsibility chart (LRC). Linear responsibility charts identify the participants, and to what degree an activity will be performed or a decision will be made. The LRC attempts to clarify the authority relationships that can exist when functional units share common work. As described by Cleland and King:[5]

The need for a device to clarify the authority relationships is evident from the relative unity of the traditional pyramidal chart, which (1) is merely a simple portrayal of the overall functional and authority models and (2) must be combined with detailed position descriptions and organizational manuals to delineate authority relationships and work performance duties.

---

5. From *Systems Analysis and Project Management* by David I. Cleland and William Richard King, p. 271. Copyright © 1968, 1975 McGraw-Hill Inc. Used with permission of McGraw-Hill Book Company.

Figure 5–2 shows a typical linear responsibility chart. The rows, which indicate the activities, responsibilities, or functions required, can be all of the tasks in the work breakdown structure. The columns identify either positions, titles, or the people themselves. If the chart will be given to an outside customer, then only the titles should appear, or the customer will call the employees directly without going through the project manager. The symbols indicate the degrees of authority or responsibility existing between the rows and columns.

Another example of an LRC is shown in Figure 5–3. In this case, the LRC is used to describe how internal and external communications should take place. This type of chart can be used to eliminate communications conflicts. Consider a customer who is unhappy about having all of his information filtered through the project manager and requests that his line people be permitted to talk to your line people on a one-on-one basis. You may have no choice

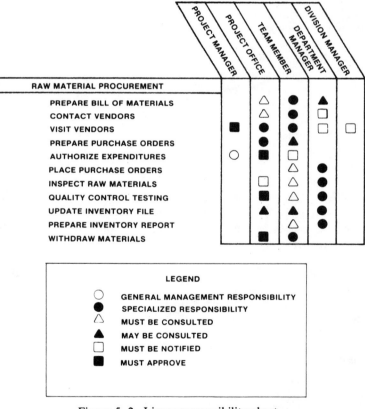

Figure 5–2. Linear responsibility chart.

INITIATED FROM	REPORTED TO													
	INTERNAL							EXTERNAL (CUSTOMER)**						
	PROJECT MANAGER	PROJECT OFFICE	TEAM MEMBER	DEPARTMENT MANAGERS	FUNCTIONAL EMPLOYEES	DIVISION MANAGER	EXECUTIVE MANAGEMENT	PROJECT MANAGER	PROJECT OFFICE	TEAM MEMBER	DEPARTMENT MANAGER	FUNCTIONAL EMPLOYEES	DIVISION MANAGER	EXECUTIVE MANAGER
PROJECT MANAGER	▨	O	◆	△	▲	▲	◆	O	O	■	■	■	■	△
PROJECT OFFICE	O	▨	O	O	▲	▲	▲	O	O	△	△	■	■	△
TEAM MEMBER	◆	O	▨	◆	◷	■	■	■	■	▲	▲	▲	■	■
DEPARTMENT MANAGER	▲	△	O	▨	O	◆	■	△	△	△	△	△	■	■
FUNCTIONAL EMPLOYEES	▲	▲	O	O	▨	■	■	▲	▲	▲	▲	▲	■	■
DIVISION MANAGERS	△	▲	▲	▲	▲	▨	△	■	■	■	■	■	△	△
EXECUTIVE MANAGEMENT	△	▲	▲	▲	▲	▲	▨	△	△	▲	▲	■	△	△

*CAN VARY FROM TASK TO TASK AND CAN BE WRITTEN OR ORAL
**DOES NOT INCLUDE REGULARLY SCHEDULED INTERCHANGE MEETINGS

LEGEND

O	DAILY
◆	WEEKLY
◷	MONTHLY
▲	AS NEEDED
△	INFORMAL
■	NEVER

Figure 5-3. Communications responsibility matrix.*

but to permit this, but you should make sure that the customer understands that:

- Functional employees cannot make commitments for additional work or resources.
- Functional employees give their own opinion and not that of the company. Company policy comes through the project office.

Linear responsibility charts can be used to alleviate some of these problems.

Figures 5-4 and 5-5 are examples of modified LRCs. Figure 5-4 is used to show the distribution of data items, and Figure 5-5 identifies the skills distribution in the project office.

The responsibility matrix attempts to answer such questions as: "Who has signature authority? Who must be notified? Who can make the decision?" The questions can only be answered by clear definitions of authority, responsibility, and accountability:

- Authority is the right of an individual to make the necessary decisions required to achieve his objectives or responsibilities.

DATA ITEM DISTRIBUTION MATRIX		PROJECT MANAGER	PROJECT OFFICE	TEAM MEMBER	LINE MANAGER	EXECUTIVE MANAGEMENT	CUSTOMER AND CONTRACTOR'S PERSONNEL
DATA ITEM	REPORT DESCRIPTION						
1	MONTHLY COST SUMMARIES	X	X			X	
2	MILESTONE REPORTS	X	X	X	X	X	
3	MANPOWER CURVES	X	X		X		
4	INVENTORY UTILIZATION	X	X				
5	PRESSURE TEST REPORT	X	X		X		
6	HUMIDITY TESTS	X	X		X		
7	HOTLINE REPORTS	X	X	X	X	X	
8	SCHEDULING SUMMARIES	X	X	X	X		

Figure 5-4. Data distribution matrix.

- Responsibility is the assignment for completion of a specific event or activity.
- Accountability is the acceptance for success or failure.

The linear responsibility chart, although a valuable tool for management, does have a weakness in that it does not describe how people interact within the program. The LRC must be considered with the organization for a full understanding of how interactions between individuals and organizations take place. As described by Karger and Murdick, the LRC has merit:[6]

Obviously the chart has weaknesses, of which one of the larger ones is that it is a mechanical aid. Just because it says that something is a fact does not make it true. It is very difficult to discover, except generally, exactly what occurs in a company—and with whom. The chart tries to express in specific terms relationships that cannot always be delineated so clearly; moreover, the degree to which it can be done depends

6. D. W. Karger and R. G. Murdick, *Managing Engineering and Research,* (New York: Industrial Press, 1963), p. 89.

FUNCTIONAL AREAS OF EXPERTISE \ PROJECT TEAM	ABLE, J.	BAKER, P.	COOK, D.	DIRK, L.	EASLEY, P.	FRANKLIN, W.	GREEN, C.	HENRY, L.	IMHOFF, R.	JULES, C.	KLEIN, W.	LEDGER, D.	MAYER, O.	NEWTON, A.	OLIVER, G.	PRATT, L.
ADMINISTRATIVE MANAGEMENT		a				a		a			a	a			a	
COST CONTROL		b	b		b	b	b				b	b		b	b	
ECONOMIC ANALYSIS	c			c				c	c				c			c
ENERGY SYSTEMS		d	d		d		d			d			d		d	d
ENVIRONMENTAL IMPACT ASSESSMENT	e	e	e						e		e		e			
INDUSTRIAL ENGINEERING	f				f					f						
INSTRUMENTATION	g			g		g					g				g	
PIPING AND DESIGN LAYOUT	h		h		h	h				h			h			
PLANNING AND SCHEDULING		i		i	i			i				i		i		i
PROJECT MANAGEMENT	j			j		j					j				j	
PROJECT REPORTING		k	k		k			k	k			k		k		k
QUALITY CONTROL		l	l			l	l	l	l							
SITE EVALUATION		m				m			m	m				m		
SPECIFICATION PREPARATION			n	n			n				n		n			n
SYSTEMS DESIGN		o	o		o		o	o		o		o			o	

Figure 5-5. Personnel skills matrix.

on the specific situation. This is the difference between the formal and informal organizations mentioned. Despite this, the Linear Responsibility Chart is one of the best devices for organization analysis known to the authors.

Linear responsibility charts can result from customer-imposed requirements above and beyond normal operations. For example, the customer may require as part of its quality control that a specific engineer supervise and approve all testing of a certain item or that another individual approve all data released to the customer over and above program office approval. Customer requirements similar to those identified above necessitate LRCs and can cause disruptions and conflicts within an organization.

Several key factors affect the delegation of authority and responsibility, both from upper-level management to project management and from project management to functional management. These key factors include:

- The maturity of the project management function
- The size, nature, and business base of the company
- The size and nature of the project
- The life cycle of the project
- The capabilities of management at all levels

Once agreement has been reached as to the project manager's authority and responsibility, the results must be documented to clearly delineate his role in regard to:

- His focal position
- Conflict between the project manager and functional managers
- Influence to cut across functional and organizational lines
- Participation in major management and technical decisions
- Collaboration in staffing the project
- Control over allocation and expenditure of funds
- Selection of subcontractors
- Rights in resolving conflicts
- Voice in maintaining integrity of the project team
- Establishment of project plans
- Providing a cost-effective information system for control
- Providing leadership in preparing operational requirements
- Maintaining prime customer liaison and contact
- Promoting technological and managerial improvements
- Establishment of project organization for the duration
- Cutting red tape

Documenting the project manager's authority is necessary because:

- All interfacing must be kept as simple as possible.
- The project manager must have the authority to "force" functional managers to depart from existing standards and possibly incur risk.
- The project manager must gain authority over those elements of a program that are not under his control. This is normally achieved by earning the respect of the individuals concerned.
- The project manager should not attempt to fully describe the exact authority and responsibilities of his project office personnel or team members. Instead, he should encourage problem-solving rather than role definition.

5.4 INTERPERSONAL INFLUENCES

There exist a variety of relationships (although they are not always clearly definable) between power and authority. These relationships are usually measured by "relative" decision power as a function of the authority structure, and are strongly dependent upon the project organizational form.

Consider the following statements made by project managers:

- "I've had good working relations with Department X. They like me and I like them. I can usually push through anything ahead of schedule."
- "I know it's contrary to department policy, but the test must be conducted according to these criteria or else the results will be meaningless" (remark made to a team member by a research scientist who was temporarily promoted to project management for an advanced state-of-the-art effort).

These two statements reflect the way two project managers get the job done.

Project managers are generally known for having a lot of delegated authority but very little formal power. They must, therefore, get jobs done through the use of interpersonal influences. There are five such interpersonal influences:

- *Formal authority:* the ability to gain support because project personnel perceive the project manager as being officially empowered to issue orders.
- *Reward power:* the ability to gain support because project personnel perceive the project manager as capable of directly or indirectly dispensing valued organizational rewards (i.e., salary, promotion, bonus, future work assignments).
- *Penalty power:* the ability to gain support because the project personnel perceive the project manager as capable of directly or indirectly dispen-

sing penalties that they wish to avoid. Penalty power usually derives from the same source as reward power, with one being a necessary condition for the other.

- *Expert power:* the ability to gain support because personnel perceive the project manager as possessing special knowledge or expertise (which functional personnel consider as important).
- *Referent power:* the ability to gain support because project personnel feel personally attracted to the project manager or his project.

The following six situations are examples of referent power (the first two are also reward power):

- The employee might be able to get personal favors from the project manager.
- The employee feels that the project manager is a winner and the rewards will be passed down to the employee.
- The employee and the project manager have strong ties, such as the same foursome for golf.
- The employee likes the project manager's manner of treating people.
- The employee wants identification with a specific product or product line.
- The employee has personal problems and believes that he can get empathy or understanding from the project manager.

Figure 5–6 shows how project managers perceive their influence style.[7]

Like relative power, interpersonal influences can be identified with various project organizational forms as to their relative value. This is shown in Figure 5–7.

For any temporary management structure to be effective, there must exist a rational balance of power between functional and project management. Unfortunately, a balance of equal power is often impossible to obtain because each project is inherently different from others, and the project managers possess different leadership abilities. Organizations, nevertheless, must attempt to obtain such a balance so that trade-offs can be effectively accomplished according to the merit of the individuals and not as a result of some established power structure.

Achievement of this balance is a never-ending challenge for management. If time and cost constraints on a project cannot be met, the project influence in decision-making increases, as can be seen in Figure 5–7. If the technology or

---

7. Source: *Seminar in Project Management Workbook,* © 1979 by Hans J. Thamhain. Reproduced by permission.

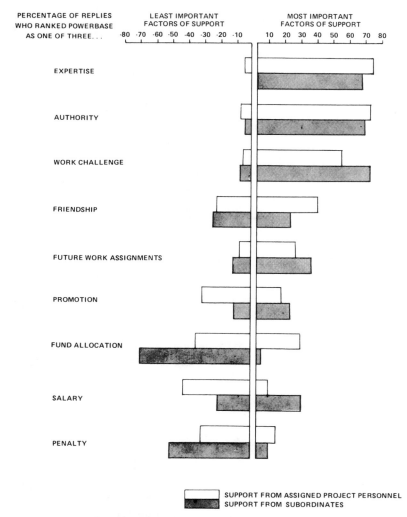

Figure 5–6. Significance of factors in support to project management.

performance constraints need reappraisal, then the functional influence in decision-making will dominate.

Regardless of how much authority and power a project manager develops over the course of the project, the ultimate factor in his ability to get the job done is usually his leadership style. Project managers, because of the inherent authority gaps that develop at the project–functional interface, must rely heav-

The Range of Alternatives

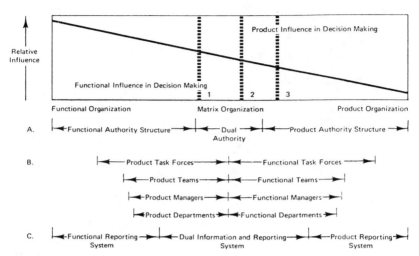

Figure 5–7. The range of alternatives. (Source: Jay R. Galbraith, "Matrix Organization Designs," *Business Horizons,* February 1971, p. 37.)

ily upon supplementary techniques for getting the job done. These supplementary techniques include factors that directly affect the leadership style, and include such things as developing bonds of trust, friendship, and respect with the functional workers. Of course, the relative importance of these techniques can vary depending upon the size and scope of the project.

5.5 BARRIERS TO PROJECT TEAM DEVELOPMENT

Most people within project-driven and non-project-driven organizations have differing views of project management.[8] Table 5–1 compares the project and functional viewpoints of project management. These differing views can create severe barriers to successful project management operations.

Perhaps the most common barriers occur as a result of the need to delegate. The following results, identified by MacKenzie, apply to project management:[9]

- Barriers in the delegator
  - Preference for operating

---

8. Original source is David I. Cleland, "Project Management," *Systems, Organizations, Analyses, Management: A Book of Readings,* David I. Cleland and William R. King, editors (New York: McGraw-Hill Inc., 1969), pp. 281–290.
9. R. Alec MacKenzie, *The Time Trap* (New York: McGraw-Hill, 1972), p. 135.

Table 5–1.   Comparison of the Functional and the Project Viewpoints.*

PHENOMENA	PROJECT VIEWPOINT	FUNCTIONAL VIEWPOINT
Line–staff organizational dichotomy	Vestiges of the hierarchical model remain: the line functions are placed in a support position. A web of authority and responsibility exists.	Line functions have direct responsibility for accomplishing the objectives; line commands, and staff advises.
Scalar principle	Elements of the vertical chain exist, but prime emphasis is placed on horizontal and diagonal work flow. Important business is conducted as the legitimacy of the task requires.	The chain of authority relationships is from superior to subordinate throughout the organization. Central, crucial, and important business is conducted up and down the vertical hierarchy.
Superior– subordinate relationship	Peer-to-peer, manager-to-technical expert, associate-to-associate, etc., relationships are used to conduct much of the salient business.	This is the most important relationship; if kept healthy, success will follow. All important business is conducted through a pyramiding structure of superiors and subordinates
Organizational objectives	Management of a project becomes a joint venture of many relatively independent organizations. Thus, the objective becomes multilateral.	Organizational objectives are sought by the parent unit (an assembly of suborganizations) working within its environment. The objective is unilateral.
Unity of direction	The project manager manages across functional and organizational lines to accomplish a common interorganizational objective.	The general manager acts as the one head for a group of activities having the same plan.
Parity of authority and responsibility	Considerable opportunity exists for the project manager's responsibility to exceed his authority. Support people are often responsible to other managers (functional) for pay, performance reports, promotions, etc.	Consistent with functional management; the integrity of the superior–subordinate relationship is maintained through functional authority and advisory staff services.
Time duration	The project (and hence the organization) is finite in duration.	Tends to perpetuate itself to provide continuing facilitative support.

*Source: David I. Cleland, "Project Management," in David I. Cleland and William R. King, eds., *Systems, Organizations, Analysis, Management: A Book of Readings* (New York: McGraw-Hill, Inc., 1969), pp. 281–290.

- Demand that everyone "know all the details"
- "I can do it better myself" fallacy
- Lack of experience in the job or in delegating
- Insecurity
- Fear of being disliked
- Refusal to allow mistakes
- Lack of confidence in subordinates
- Perfectionism, leading to overcontrol
- Lack of organizational skill in balancing workloads
- Failure to delegate authority commensurate with responsibility
- Uncertainty over tasks and inability to explain
- Disinclination to develop subordinates
- Failure to establish effective controls and to follow up
- Barriers in the delegatee
  - Lack of experience
  - Lack of competence
  - Avoidance of responsibility
  - Overdependence on the boss
  - Disorganization
  - Overload of work
  - Immersion in trivia
- Barriers in the situation
  - One-man-show policy
  - No toleration of mistakes
  - Criticality of decisions
  - Urgency, leaving no time to explain (crisis management)
  - Confusion in responsibilities and authority
  - Understaffing

The understanding of barriers to project team building can help in developing an environment conducive to effective team work. The following barriers to team building were identified and analyzed in a field study by Thamhain and Wilemon.[10] They are typical for many project environments:

Differing Outlooks, Priorities, and Interests. A major barrier exists when team members have professional objectives and interests that are different from the project objectives. These problems are compounded when the team relies on support organizations that have different interests and priorities.

---

10. For detailed discussion see H. J. Thamhain and D. L. Wilemon, "Team Building in Project Management," *Proceedings of the Annual Symposium of the Project Management Institute,* October 1979.

Role Conflicts. Team development efforts are thwarted when role conflicts exist among the team members, such as ambiguity over who does what within the project team and in external support groups.

Project Objectives/Outcomes Not Clear. Unclear project objectives frequently lead to conflict, ambiguities, and power struggles. It becomes difficult, if not impossible, to define roles and responsibilities clearly.

Dynamic Project Environments. Many projects operate in a continual state of change. For example, senior management may keep changing the project scope, objectives, and resource base. In other situations, regulatory changes or client demands can drastically affect the internal operations of a project team.

Competition Over Team Leadership. Project leaders frequently indicated that this barrier most likely occurs in the early phases of a project or if the project runs into severe problems. Obviously, such cases of leadership challenge can result in barriers to team building. Frequently, these challenges are covert challenges to the project leader's ability.

Lack of Team Definition and Structure. Many senior managers complain that teamwork is severely impaired because it lacks clearly defined task responsibilities and reporting structures. We find this situation is most prevalent in dynamic organizationally unstructured work environments such as computer systems and R&D projects. A common pattern is that a support department is charged with a task but no one leader is clearly delegated the responsibility. As a consequence, some personnel are working on the project but not entirely clear on the extent of their responsibilities. In other cases, problems result when a project is supported by several departments without interdisciplinary coordination.

Team Personnel Selection. This barrier develops when personnel feel unfairly treated or threatened during the staffing of a project. In some cases, project personnel are assigned to a team by functional managers, and the project manager has little or no input into the selection process. This can impede team development efforts, especially when the project leader is given available personnel vs. the best, hand-picked team members. The assignment of "available personnel" can result in several problems (e.g., low motivation levels, discontent, and uncommitted team members). We've found, as a rule, that the more power the project leader has over the selection of his/her team members, and the more negotiated agreement there is over the assigned task, the more likely it is that team-building efforts will be fruitful.

Credibility of Project Leader. Team-building efforts are hampered when the project leader suffers from poor credibility within the team or from other managers. In such cases, team members are often reluctant to make a commitment to the project or the leader. Credibility problems may come from poor managerial skills, poor technical judgments, or lack of experience relevant to the project.

Lack of Team Member Commitment. Lack of commitment can have several sources; for example: the team members having professional interests elsewhere; the feeling of insecurity that is associated with projects; the unclear nature of the rewards that may be forthcoming upon successful completion; and intense interpersonal conflicts within the team.

Lack of team member commitment may result from suspicious attitudes existing between the project leader and a functional support manager, or between two team members from two warring functional departments. Finally, low commitment levels are likely to occur when a "star" on a team "demands" too much effort from other team members or too much attention from the team leader. One team leader put it this way: "A lot of teams have their prima donnas and you learn to live and function with them. They can be critical to overall project success. But some stars can be so demanding on everyone that they'll kill the team's motivation."

Communication Problems. Not surprisingly, poor communication is a major enemy to effective team development. Poor communication exists on four major levels: problems of communication among team members, between the project leader and the team members, between the project team and top management, and between the project leaders and the client. Often the problem is caused by team members simply not keeping others informed on key project developments. Yet the "whys" of poor communications patterns are far more difficult to determine. The problem can result from low motivation levels, poor morale, or carelessness. It was also discovered that poor communication patterns between the team and support groups result in severe team-building problems, as does poor communication with the client. Poor communication practices often lead to unclear objectives and poor project control, coordination, and work flow.

Lack of Senior Management Support. Project leaders often indicate that senior management support and commitment is unclear and subject to waxing and waning over the project life cycle. This behavior can result in an uneasy feeling among team members and lead to low levels of enthusiasm and project commitment. Two other common problems are that senior management often does not help set the right environment for the project team at the outset, nor do they give the team timely feedback on their performance and activities during the life of the project.

Project managers who are successfully performing their role not only recognize these barriers but also know when in the project life cycle they are most likely to occur. Moreover, these managers take preventive actions and usually foster a work environment that is conducive to effective teamwork. The effective team builder is usually a social architect who understands the interaction of organizational and behavior variables and can foster a climate of active participation and minimal conflict. This requires carefully developed skills in leadership, administration, organization, and technical expertise on the project. However, besides the delicately balanced management skills, the project manager's sensitivity to the basic issues underlying each barrier can help to increase success in developing an effective project team. Specific suggestions for team building are advanced in Table 5–2.

Table 5–2. Barriers to Effective Team Building and Suggested Handling Approaches.

BARRIER	SUGGESTIONS FOR EFFECTIVELY MANAGING BARRIERS (HOW TO MINIMIZE OR ELIMINATE BARRIERS)
Differing Outlooks, Priorities, Interests, and Judgments of Team Members	Make effort early in the project life cycle to discover these conflicting differences. Fully explain the scope of the project and the rewards which may be forthcoming upon successful project completion. Sell "team" concept and explain responsibilities. Try to blend individual interests with the overall project objectives.
Role Conflicts	As early in a project as feasible, ask team members where they see themselves fitting into the project. Determine how the overall project can best be divided into subsystems and subtasks (e.g., the work breakdown structure). Assign/negotiate roles. Conduct regular status review meetings to keep team informed on progress and watch for unanticipated role conflicts over the project's life.
Project Objectives/Outcomes Not Clear	Assure that all parties understand the overall and interdisciplinary project objectives. Clear and frequent communication with senior management and the client becomes critically important. Status review meetings can be used for feedback. Finally, a proper team name can help to reinforce the project objectives.
Dynamic Project Environments	The major challenge is to stabilize external influences. First, key project personnel must work out an agreement on the principal project direction and "sell" this direction to the total team. Also educate senior management and the customer on the detrimental consequences of unwarranted change. It is critically important to forecast the "environment" within which the project will be developed. Develop contingency plans.

Table 5-2. Barriers to Effective Team Building and Suggested Handling Approaches. (Continued)

BARRIER	SUGGESTIONS FOR EFFECTIVELY MANAGING BARRIERS (HOW TO MINIMIZE OR ELIMINATE BARRIERS)
Competition Over Team Leadership	Senior management must help establish the project manager's leadership role. On the other hand, the project manager needs to fulfill the leadership expectations of team members. Clear role and responsibility definition often minimizes competition over leadership.
Lack of Team Definition and Structure	Project leaders need to sell the team concept to senior management as well as to their team members. Regular meetings with the team will reinforce the team notion as will clearly defined tasks, roles and responsibilities. Also, visibility in memos and other forms of written media as well as senior management and client participation can unify the team.
Project Personnel Selection	Attempt to negotiate the project assignments with potential team members. Clearly discuss with potential team members the importance of the project, their role in it, what rewards might result upon completion, and the general "rules-of-the road" of project management. Finally, if team members remain uninterested in the project, then replacement should be considered.
Credibility of Project Leader	Credibility of the project leader among team members is crucial. It grows with the image of a sound decision maker in both general management and relevant technical expertise. Credibility can be enhanced by the project leaders' relationship to other key managers who support the team's efforts.
Lack of Team Member Commitment	Try to determine lack of team member commitment early in the life of his project and attempt to change possible negative views toward the project. Often, insecurity is a major reason for the lack of commitment; try to determine why insecurity exists, then work on reducing the team members' fears. Conflicts with other team members may be another reason for lack of commitment. It is important for the project leader to intervene and mediate the conflict quickly. Finally, if a team member's professional interests lie elsewhere, the project leader should examine ways to satisfy part of the team member's interests or consider replacement.

Table 5-2. Barriers to Effective Team Building and Suggested Handling Approaches. (*Continued*)

BARRIER	SUGGESTIONS FOR EFFECTIVELY MANAGING BARRIERS (HOW TO MINIMIZE OR ELIMINATE BARRIERS)
Communication Problems	The project leader should devote considerable time communicating with individual team members about their needs and concerns. In addition, the leader should provide a vehicle for timely sessions to encourage communications among the individual team contributors. Tools for enhancing communications are status meetings, reviews, schedules, reporting system, and colocation. Similarly, the project leader should establish regular and thorough communications with the client and senior management. Emphasis is placed on written and oral communications with key issues and agreements in writing.
Lack of Senior Management Support	Senior management support is an absolute necessity for dealing effectively with interface groups and proper resource commitment. Therefore, a major goal for project leaders is to maintain the continued interest and commitment of senior management in their projects. We suggest that senior management become an integral part of project reviews. Equally important, it is critical for senior management to provide the proper environment for the project to function effectively. Here the project leader needs to tell management at the onset of the program what resources are needed. The project manager's relationship with senior management and ability to develop senior management support is critically affected by his own credibility and the visibility and priority of his project.

5.6 SUGGESTIONS FOR HANDLING THE NEWLY FORMED TEAM[11]

A major problem faced by many project leaders is managing the anxiety that usually develops when a new team is formed. The anxiety experienced by team members is normal and predictable. It is a barrier, however, to getting the team quickly focused on the task. In other words, if team members are suffering from anxiety, their attention consciously or subconsciously will be focused on resolution of their own anxieties rather than the needs of the project.

---

11. Adapted from Harold Kerzner and Hans J. Thamhain, *Project Management for the Small and Medium-Size Business,* (New York: Van Nostrand Reinhold, 1983), pp. 310–312.

This anxiety may come from several sources. For example, if the team members have never worked with the project leader, they may be concerned about his leadership style and its effect on them. In a different vein, some team members may be concerned about the nature of the project and whether it will match their professional interests and capabilities. Other team members may be concerned about whether the project will help or hinder their career aspirations. Further, team members can be highly anxious about life-style/work-style disruptions that the project may bring. As one project manager remarked, "Moving a team member's desk from one side of the room to the other can sometimes be just about as traumatic as moving someone from Chicago to Manila." As the quote suggests, seemingly minor changes can cause unanticipated anxiety among team members.

Another common concern among newly formed teams is whether or not there will be an equitable distribution of the work load among team members and whether each member is capable of pulling his/her own weight. In some newly formed teams, members not only might have to do their own work, but they also must train other team members. Within reason this is bearable, necessary, and often expected. However, when it becomes excessive, anxiety increases, and morale can fall.

Certain steps taken early in the life of a team can be effective in terms of handling the above problems. First, we recommend that the project leader at the start of the project talk with each team member on a one-to-one basis about the following:

1. What the objectives are for the project.
2. Who will be involved and why.
3. The importance of the project to the overall organization or work unit.
4. Why the team member was selected and assigned to the project. What role he/she will perform.
5. What rewards might be forthcoming if the project is successfully completed.
6. What problems and constraints are likely to be encountered.
7. The rules-of-the-road that will be followed in managing the project (e.g., regular status review meetings).
8. What suggestions the team member has for achieving success.
9. What the professional interests of the team member are.
10. What challenge the project will present to individual members and the entire team.
11. Why the team concept is so important to project management success and how it should work.

A frank, open discussion of the above questions with each team member is likely to reduce his/her initial anxiety. Consequently, the team member is likely to be more attentive to the needs of the project. Of course, the opposite reaction is possible, too. A frank discussion, for example, may actually increase a team member's anxiety level. Often, however, the source of the anxiety can be identified and dealt with in a timely manner.

Dealing with these anxieties and helping team members feel that they are an integral part of the team can yield rich dividends. First, as noted in Figure 5–8, the more effective the project leader is in developing a feeling of team membership, the higher the quality of the information that is likely to be contributed by team members. Team members will openly share their ideas and approaches. By contrast, when a team member does not feel part of the team and does not trust others in team deliberations, information will not be shared willingly or openly. One project leader emphasized this point:

There's nothing worse than being on a team when no one trusts anyone else. . . . Such situations lead to gamesmanship and a lot of watching what you say because you don't want your own words to bounce back in your face. . . .

Second, the greater the feeling of team membership and the better the information exchange among team members, the more likely it is that the team will be able to develop effective decision-making processes. The reason is that the team members feel committed to the project, and they feel free to share their information and develop effective problem-solving approaches. Third, the team is likely to develop more effective project control procedures. Project control

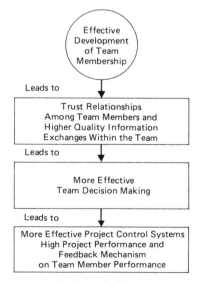

Figure 5–8. Team building outcomes.

procedures can be divided into two basic types. The first type is the quantitative control procedures traditionally used to monitor project performance (PERT/CPM, networking, work breakdown structures, etc.). The second is represented by the willingness and ability of project team members to give feedback to each other regarding performance. Again, trust among the project team members makes the feedback process easier and more effective. Without a high level of trust, project personnel are often reluctant to give constructive feedback to fellow team members.

5.7 TEAM BUILDING AS AN ONGOING PROCESS[12]

While proper attention to team building is critical during early phases of a project, it is a never ending process. The project manager is continually monitoring team functioning and performance to see what corrective action may be needed to prevent or correct various team problems. Several barometers provide good clues of potential team dysfunctioning. First, noticeable changes in performance levels for the team and/or for individual team members should always be investigated. Such changes can be symptomatic of more serious problems (e.g., conflict, lack of work integration, communication problems, and unclear objectives). Second, the project leader and team members must be aware of the changing energy levels of team members. These changes, too, may signal more serious problems or that the team is tired and stressed. Sometimes changing the work pace, taking time off, or selling short-term targets can serve as a means to reenergize team members. More serious cases, however, can call for more drastic action (e.g., reappraising project objectives and/or the means to achieve them). Third, verbal and nonverbal clues from team members may be a source of information on team functioning. It is important to hear the needs and concerns of team members (verbal clues) and to observe how they act in carrying out their responsibilities (nonverbal clues). Finally, detrimental behavior of one team member toward another can be a signal that a problem within the team warrants attention.

We highly recommend that project leaders hold regular meetings to evaluate overall team performance and deal with team functioning problems. The focus of these meetings can be directed toward "what we are doing well as a team" and "what areas need our team's attention." This approach often brings positive surprises in that the total team is informed of progress in diverse project areas (e.g., a breakthrough in technology development, a subsystem schedule met ahead of the original target, or a positive change in the client's behavior toward the project). After the positive issues have been discussed, attention should be devoted to areas needing team attention. The purpose of this part of

---

12. Ibid, pp. 312–314

the review session is to focus on actual or potential problem areas. The meeting leader should ask each team member for his observations on these issues. Then, an open discussion should be held to ascertain how significant the problems really are. Assumptions should, of course, be separated from the facts of each situation. Next, assignments should be agreed upon on for best handling of these problems. Finally, a plan for problem followup should be developed. The process should result in better overall performance and promote a feeling of team participation and high morale.

Over the life of a project, the problems encountered by the project team are likely to change, and as old problems are identified and solved, new ones will emerge.

In summary, effective team building is a critical determinant of project success. While the process of team building can entail frustrations and energy on the part of all concerned, the rewards can be great.

Social scientists generally agree that there are several indicators of effective and ineffective teams. At any point in the life of a team, the project manager should be aware of certain effectiveness/ineffectiveness indicators, which are summarized in Table 5–3.

In the next decade, we anticipate important developments in team building. As shown in Figure 5–8, these developments will lead to higher performance

Table 5–3. Project Team Characteristics: Effective vs. Ineffective.

THE EFFECTIVE TEAM'S LIKELY CHARACTERISTICS	THE INEFFECTIVE TEAM'S LIKELY CHARACTERISTICS
• High performance and task efficiency	• Low performance
• Innovative/creative behavior	
• Commitment	• Low commitment to project objectives
• Professional objectives of team members coincide with project requirements	
• Team members highly interdependent, interface effectively	• Unclear project objectives and fluid commitment levels from key participants
• Capacity for conflict resolution, but conflict encouraged when it can lead to beneficial results	• Unproductive gamesmanship, manipulation of others, hidden feelings, conflict avoidance at all costs
• Effective communication	• Confusion, conflict, inefficiency
• High trust levels	• Subtle sabotage, fear, disinterest, or footdragging
• Results orientation	
• Interest in membership	• Cliques, collusion, isolation of members
• High energy levels and enthusiasm	• Lethargy/unresponsiveness
• High morale	
• Change orientation	

levels, increased morale, and a pervasive commitment to final results that can withstand almost any kind of adversity.

5.8 LEADERSHIP IN A PROJECT ENVIRONMENT

Leadership can be defined as a style of behavior designed to integrate both the organizational requirements and one's personal interests into the pursuit of some objective. All managers have some sort of leadership responsibility. If time permits, successful leadership techniques and practices can be developed.

Leadership is composed of several complex elements, the three most common being:

- The person leading
- The people being led
- The situation (i.e., the project environment)

Project managers are often selected or not selected because of their leadership styles. The most common reason for not selecting an individual is his inability to balance the technical and managerial project functions. Wilemon and Cicero have defined four characteristics of this type of situation:[13]

- The greater the project manager's technical expertise, the higher his propensity to overinvolve himself in the technical details of the project.
- The greater the project manager's difficulty in delegating technical task responsibilities, the more likely it is that he will overinvolve himself in the technical details of the project (depending upon his ability to do so).
- The greater the project manager's interest in the technical details of the project, the more likely it is that he will defend the project manager's role as one of a technical specialist.
- The lower the project manager's technical expertise, the more likely it is that he will overstress the nontechnical project functions (administrative functions).

There have been several surveys to determine what leadership techniques are best. The following are the results of a survey by Richard Hodgetts:[14]

- Human Relations–oriented leadership techniques
  - "The project manager must make all the team members feel that their efforts are important and have a direct effect on the outcome of the program."

---

13. D. L. Wilemon and John P. Cicero, "The Project Manager: Anomalies and Ambiguities," *Academy of Management Journal,* Vol. 13, pp. 269–282, 1970.
14. Richard M. Hodgetts, "Leadership Techniques in Project Organizations," *Academy of Management Journal,* Vol. 11, pp. 211–219, 1968.

- "The project manager must educate the team concerning what is to be done and how important its role is."
- "Provide credit to project participants."
- "Project members must be given recognition and prestige of appointment."
- "Make the team members feel and believe that they play a vital part in the success (or failure) of the team."
- "By working extremely close with my team I believe that one can win a project loyalty while to a large extent minimizing the frequency of authority-gap problems."
- "I believe that a great motivation can be created just by knowing the people in a personal sense. I know many of the line people better than their own supervisor does. In addition, I try to make them understand that they are an indispenable part of the team."
- "I would consider the most important technique in overcoming the authority-gap to be understanding as much as possible the needs of the individuals with whom you are dealing and over whom you have no direct authority."
- Formal Authority–oriented leadership techniques
  - "Point out how great the loss will be if cooperation is not forthcoming."
  - "Put all authority in functional statements."
  - "Apply pressure beginning with a tactful approach and minimum application warranted by the situation and then increasing it."
  - "Threaten to precipitate high-level intervention and do it if necessary."
  - "Convince the members that what is good for the company is good for them."
  - "Place authority on full-time assigned people in the operating division to get the necessary work done."
  - "Maintain control over expenditures."
  - "Utilize implicit threat of going to general management for resolution."
  - "It is most important that the team members recognize that the project manager has the charter to direct the project."

5.9 LIFE-CYCLE LEADERSHIP

Perhaps the best model for analyzing leadership in a project management environment was developed by Hersey and Blanchard.[14A] The model, as shown in Figure 5–9, is the life-cycle theory of leadership. Hersey and Blanchard contend that leadership styles must change according to the maturity of the employees, with maturity defined as job-related experience, willingness to

---

14A. Paul Hersey and Kenneth Blanchard, *Management of Organizational Behavior* (Englewood Cliffs, N.J.: Prentice-Hall, 1979), p. 165.

accept job responsibility, and desire to achieve. This definition of maturity is somewhat different from other behavioral management definitions, which define maturity as age or emotional stability.

As shown in Figure 5–9, the subordinates enter the organization in Quadrant D, which is high task and low relationships behavior. In this quadrant, the leadership style is almost pure task-oriented behavior and is an autocratic approach, where the leader's main concern is the accomplishment of the objective, often with very little concern for the employees or their feelings. The leader is very forceful and relies heavily upon his own abilities and judgment. Other people's opinions may be of no concern. Hersey and Blanchard assume that, in the initial stage, there is anxiety, tension, and confusion among new employees, so that relationship behavior is inappropriate.

In Quadrant C, employees begin to understand their tasks and the leader tries to develop stong behavioral relationships. The development of trust and understanding between the leader and subordinates becomes a driving force for the strong behavioral relationships. However, although the leader begins utilizing behavioral relationships, there still exists a strong need for high task behavior as well, since The employees may not have achieved the level of competency to assume full responsibility.

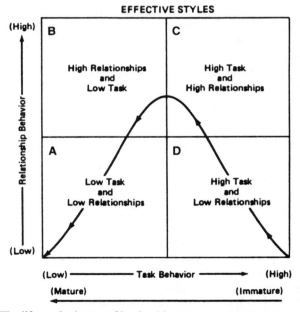

Figure 5–9. The life-cycle theory of leadership. (*Source:* Adapted from Paul Hersey and Kenneth H. Blanchard, *Management of Organizational Behavior,* 3rd ed., p. 165. Copyright © 1979. Used by permission of Prentice-Hall, Inc.)

Quadrant B is often regarded as pure relationship behavior, where the leader is perhaps more interested in gaining the respect of the employees than in achieving the objectives. Referent power becomes extremely important. This behavior can be characterized by delegation of authority and responsibility (often excessive), participative management, and group decision making. Hersey and Blanchard believe that, in this phase, the employees no longer need directives and are knowledgeable enough about the job and self-motivated to the extent that they are willing to assume more responsibility for the task. Therefore, the leader can try to straighten his relationships with subordinates.

In Quadrant A, the employees are experienced in the job and confident about their own abilities, and are trusted to handle the work themselves. The leader demonstrates low task and low relationship behavior as the employees mature.

This type of life cycle approach to leadership is extremely important to project managers, because it implies that effective leadership must be dynamic and flexible rather than static and rigid. (See Figure 5–10). Effective leaders are neither pure task or relationship behavioralists, but maintain a balance between them. However, in time of crisis, a leader may be required to demonstrate a pure behavioral style or a pure task style.

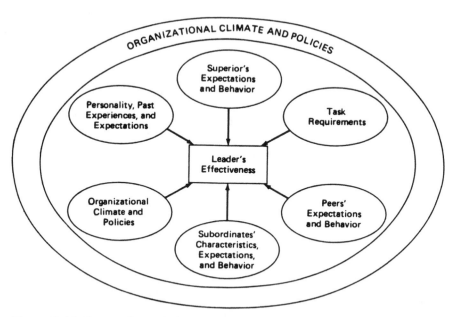

Figure 5–10. Personality and situational factors that influence effective leadership. *Source:* James A. F. Stoner, *Management,* 2nd Edition, Prentice-Hall Inc., Englewood Cliffs, N.J. Used by permission.

The project management environment is highly situational, and each employee may have to be treated differently. In a situational environment, the four quadrants in Figure 5–9 can be described as:

Quadrant A: Delegating
Quadrant B: Participating
Quadrant C: Selling
Quadrant D: Telling

In pure project management, the situation is even more complex. Line managers have *sufficient time* to develop a meaningful relationship with subordinates to the point that they get to know each other quite well. The line manager can then "train" his subordinates to adapt to the the line manager's leadership style.

Project managers, on the other hand, are under a severe time constraint and may have to develop a different leadership style for each team member. To illustrate this graphically, the quadrants in Figure 5–9 should be three-dimensional, with the third axis being the life-cycle phase of the project. In other words, the leadership style is dependent not only upon the situation, but upon the life-cycle phase of the project.

5.10 ORGANIZATIONAL IMPACT

In most companies, whether or not project-oriented, the impact of management emphasis upon the organization is well known. In the project environment there also exists a definite impact due to leadership emphasis. The leadership emphasis is best seen by employee contributions, organizational order, employee performance, and the project manager's performance:

- Contributions from people
  - A good project manager encourages actve cooperation and responsible participation. The result is that both good and bad information is contributed freely.
    - A poor project manager maintains an atmosphere of passive resistance with only responsive participation. This results in information being withheld.
- Organizational order
  - A good project manager develops policy and encourages acceptance. A low price is paid for contributions.
  - A poor project manager goes beyond policies and attempts to develop procedures and measurements. A high price is normally paid for contributions.

- Employee performance
  - A good project manager keeps people informed and satisfied (if possible) by aligning motives with objectives. Positive thinking and cooperation are encouraged. A good project manager is willing to give more responsibility to those willing to accept it.
  - A poor project manager keeps people uninformed, frustrated, defensive, and negative. Motives are aligned with incentives rather than objectives. The poor project manager develops a "stay out of trouble" atmosphere.
- Performance of the project manager
  - A good project manager assumes that employee misunderstandings can and will occur, and therefore blames himself. A good project manager constantly attempts to improve and be more communicative. He relies heavily on moral persuasion.
  - A poor project manager assumes that employees are unwilling to cooperate and therefore blames subordinates. The poor project manager demands more through authoritarian attitudes and relies heavily on material incentives.

Management emphasis also impacts the organization. The following four categories show this management emphasis resulting for both good and poor project management:

- Management problem-solving
  - A good project manager performs his own problem-solving at the level for which he is responsible through delegation of problem-solving responsibilities.
  - A poor project manager will do subordinate problem-solving in known areas. For areas that he does not know, he requires that his approval be given prior to idea implementation.
- Organizational order
  - A good project manager develops, maintains, and uses a single integrated management system in which authority and responsibility are delegated to the subordinates. In addition, he knows that occasional slippages and overruns will occur, and simply tries to minimize their effect.
  - A poor project manager delegates as little authority and responsibility as possible, and runs the risk of continual slippages and overruns. A poor project manager maintains two management information systems: one informal system for himself and one formal (eyewash) system simply to impress his superiors.

- Performance of people
  - A good project manager finds that subordinates willingly accept responsibility, are decisive in attitude toward the project, and are satisfied.
  - A poor project manager finds that his subordinates are reluctant to accept responsibility, are indecisive in their actions, and seem frustrated.
- Performance of the project manager
  - A good project manager assumes that his key people can "run the show." He exhibits confidence in those individuals working in areas in which he has no expertise, and exhibits patience with people working in areas where he has a familiarity. A good project manager is never too busy to help his people solve personal or professional problems.
  - A poor project manager considers himself indispensable, is overcautious with work performed in unfamiliar areas, and becomes overly interested in work he knows. A poor project manager is always tied up in meetings.

5.11 EMPLOYEE/MANAGER PROBLEMS

The two major problem areas in the project environment are the "who has what authority and responsibility" question, and the resulting conflicts associated with the individual at the project/functional interface. Almost all project problems in some way or another involve these two major areas. Other problem areas found in the project environment include:

- The pyramidal structure
- Superior–subordinate relationships
- Departmentation
- Scalar chain of command
- Organizational chain of command
- Power and authority
- Planning goals and objectives
- Decision-making
- Reward and punishment
- Span of control

The two most common employee problems involve the assignment and resulting evaluation processes. Personnel assignments were discussed in Chapter 4. In summary:

- People should be assigned to tasks commensurate with their skills.
- Whenever possible, the same person should be assigned to related tasks.
- The most critical tasks should be assigned to the most responsible people.

The evaluation process in a project environment is difficult for an employee at the functional/project interface, especially if hostilities develop between the functional and project managers. In this situation, the interfacing employee almost aways suffers owing to a poor rating by either the project manager or his supervisor. Unless the employee continually keeps his superior abreast of his performance and achievements, the supervisor must rely solely upon the input received from project office personnel. This can result in a performance evaluation process that is subject to error.

Three additional questions must be answered with regard to employee evaluation:

- Of what value are job descriptions?
- How do we maintain wage and salary grades?
- Who provides training and development, especially under conditions where variable manloading can exist?

If each project is, in fact, different from all others, then it becomes almost an impossible task to develop accurate job descriptions. In many cases, wage and salary grades are functions of a unit manning document which specifies the number, type, and grade of all employees required on a given project. Although this might be a necessity in order to control costs, it also is difficult to achieve because variable manloading changes project priorities. Variable manloading creates several difficulties for project managers, especially if new employees are included. Project managers like to have seasoned veterans assigned to their activities because there generally does not exist sufficient time for proper and close supervision of the training and development of new employees. Functional managers, however, contend that the training has to be accomplished on someone's project, and sooner or later all project managers must come to this realization.

On the manager level, the two most common problems involve personal values and conflicts. Personal values are often attributed to the "changing of the guard." New managers have a different sense of values from that of the older, more experienced managers. Miner identifies some of these personal values attributed to new managers:[15]

- Less trust, especially of people in positions of authority.
- Increased feelings of being controlled by external forces and events, and thus belief that they cannot control their own destinies. This is a kind of change that makes for less initiation of one's own activities and a greater

15. John B. Miner, "The OD-Management Development Conflict," *Business Horizons,* December 1973, p. 32.

likelihood of responding in terms of external pressures. There is a sense of powerlessness, although not necessarily a decreased desire for power.

- Less authoritarian and more negative attitudes toward persons holding positions of power.
- More independence, often to the point of rebelliousness and defiance.
- More freedom, less control in expressing feelings, impulses, and emotions.
- Greater inclination to live in the present and to let the future take care of itself.
- More self-indulgence.
- Moral values that are relative to the situation, less absolute, and less tied to formal religion.
- A strong and increasing identification with their peer and age groups, with the youth culture.
- Greater social concern and greater desire to help the less fortunate.
- More negative attitude toward business,the management role in particular. A professional position is clearly preferred to managing.
- A desire to contribute less to an employing organization and to receive more from the organization.

Previously, we defined one of the attributes of a project manager as liking risks. Unfortunately, the amount of risk that today's managers are willing to accept varies not only with their personal values but alo with the impact of current economic conditions and top management philosophies. If top management views a specific project as vital for the growth of the company, then the project manager may be directed to assume virtually no risks during the execution of the project. In this case the project manager may attempt to pass all responsibility to higher or lower management claiming that "his hands are tied." Wilemon and Cicero identify problems with risk identification:[16]

- The project manager's anxiety over project risk varies in relation to his willingness to accept final responsibility for the technical success of his project. Some project managers may be willing to accept full responsibility for the success or failure of their projects. Others, by contrast, may be more willing to share responsibility and risk with their superiors.
- The greater the length of stay in project management, the greater the tendency for project managers to remain in administrative positions within an organization.
- The degree of anxiety over professional obsolescence varies with the length of time the project manager spends in project management positions.

---

16. D. L. Wilemon, and John P. Cicero, "The Project Manager: Anomalies and Ambiguities," *Academy of Management Journal,* Vol.13, 1970, pp. 269–282.

The amount of risk that managers will accept also varies with age and experience. Older, more experienced managers tend to take few risks, whereas the younger, more aggressive managers may adopt a risk-lover policy in hopes of achieving a name for themselves.

Conflicts exist at the project/functional interface regardless of how hard we attempt to structure the work. Authority and responsibility relationships can vary from project to project. In general, however, there does exist a relatively definable boundary between the project and functional manager. According to Cleland and King, this interface can be defined by the following relationships:[17]

- Project manager
  - *What* is to be done?
  - *When* will the task be done?
  - *Why* will the task be done?
  - *How much* money is available to do the task?
  - *How well* has the total project been done?
- Functional manager
  - *Who* will do the task?
  - *Where* will the task be done?
  - *How* will the task be done?
  - *How well* has the functional input been integrated into the project?

Another difficulty arises from the way the functional manager views the project. Many functional managers consider the project as simply a means toward an end and therefore identify problems and seek solutions in terms of their immediate duties and responsibilities rather than looking beyond them. This problem also exists at the horizontal hierarchy level. The problem comes about as a result of authority and responsibility relationships, and may not have anything at all to do with the competence of the individuals concerned. This situation breeds conflicts which can also have an impact on he amount of risk that a manager wishes to accept. William Killian defined this inevitable conflict between the functional and project manager:[18]

The conflicts revolve about items such as project priority, manpower costs, and the assignment of functional personnel to the project manager. Each project manager will, of course, want the best functional operators assigned to his project. In addition to

---

17. From *Systems Analysis and Project Management* by David I. Cleland and William Richard King, p. 237. copyright © 1968, 1975 by McGraw-Hill, Inc. Used with permission of McGraw-Hill Book Company.
18. William P. Killian, "Project Management—Future Organizational Concepts," *Marquette Business Review*, Vol. 2, 1971, pp. 90–107.

these problems, the accountability for profit and loss is much more difficult in a matrix organization than in a project organization. Project managers have a tendency to blame overruns on functional managers, stating that the cost of the function was excessive. Whereas functional managers have a tendency to blame excessive costs on project managers with the argument that there were too many changes, more work required than defined initially, and other such arguments.

Another major trouble area is in problem reporting and resolution. Major conflicts can arise during problem resolution sessions, not only for the above-mentioned reasons, but also because the time constraints imposed on the project often prevent both parties from taking a logical approach. Project managers tend to want to make immediate decisions, after which the functional manager asserts that his way is "the only way" the problem can be resolved. One of the major causes for prolonged problem-solving is a lack of pertinent information. In order to ease potential conflicts, all pertinent information should be made available to all parties concerned as early as possible. The following information should be reported by the project manager:[19]

- The problem
- The cause
- The expected impact on schedule, budget, profit, or other pertinent area
- The action taken or recommended and the results expected of that action
- What top management can do to help

5.12 MANAGEMENT PITFALLS

The project environment offers numerous opportunities for project managers and team members to get into trouble. These activities that readily create problems are referred to as management pitfalls. Lack of planning, for example, can be considered a management pitfall. Other common types of management pitfalls are:

- Lack of self-control (knowing oneself)
- Activity traps
- Managing vs. doing
- People vs. task skills
- Ineffective communications
- Time management
- Management bottlenecks

---

19. Russell D. Archibald, *Managing High-Technology Programs and Projects* (New York: Wiley, 1976), p. 230.

Knowing oneself, especially one's capabilities, strengths, and weaknesses, is the first step toward successful project management. Too often, managers will assume that they are jacks-of-all-trades and indispensable to the organization. The ultimate result is that such managers tend to "bite off more than they can chew," and then find that insufficient time exists for training additional personnel. (This, of course, assumes that the project budget provided sufficient funding for additional positions that were never utilized.)

The following lines illustrate self-concept:

> The "me" I think I am
> The "me" I wish I were
> The "me" I really am
> The "me" I try to project
> The "me" others perceive
> The "me" I used to be
> The "me" others try to make me.
> *Author Unknown*

> *Four Men*
> It chanced upon a winter's night
> Safe sheltered from the weather.
> The board was spread for only one,
> Yet four men dined together.
> There sat the man I meant to be
> In glory, spurred and booted.
> And close beside him, to the right
> The man I am reputed.
> The man I think myself to be
> His seat was occupying
> Hard by the man I really am
> To hold his own was trying.
> And all beneath one roof we met
> Yet none called his fellow brother
> No sign of recognition passed
> They knew not one another.
> *Author Unknown*

Activity traps result when the means become the end, rather than the means to achieve the end. The most common activity traps are team meetings and customer technical interchange meetings. Another common activity trap is the development of special schedules and charts that cannot be used for customer reporting but are used to inform upper-level management of project status.

Managers must always evaluate whether or not the time spent to develop these charts is worth the effort. Sign-off documents, such as manufacturing plans, provide yet another activity trap by requiring that the project manager and/or several key project team members sign off all documentation. Proper project planning and the delegation of authority and responsibility can reduce this activity trap.

We previously defined one of the characteristics of poor leadership as the inability to obtain a balance between management functions and technical functions. This can easily develop into an activity trap where the individual becomes a doer rather than a manager. Unfortunately, there often exists a very fine line between managing and doing. As an example, consider a project manager who was asked by one of his technical people to make a telephone call to assist him in solving a problem. Simply making the phone call is doing work that should be done by the project team members or even the functional manager. However, if the person being called requires that someone in absolute authority be included in the conversation, then this can be considered managing instead of doing.

There are several other cases where one must become a doer in order to be an effective manager and command the loyalty and respect of subordinates. Assume a special situation where you must schedule subordinates to work overtime, say on special holidays or even weekends. By showing up at the plant during these times, just to make a brief appearance before the people in question, you can create a better working atmosphere and understanding with the subordinates.

Another major pitfall is the decision to utilize either people skills or task skills. Is it better to utilize subordinates with whom you can obtain a good working relationship or to employ highly skilled people simply to get the job done? Obviously, the project manager would like nothing better than to have the best of both worlds. Unfortunately, this is not always possible. Consider the following situations:

- There exists a task that will take three weeks to complete. John has worked for you before, but not on such a task as this. John, however, understands how to work with you. Paul is very competent but likes to work alone. He can get the job done within constraints. Should you employ people or task skills? (Would your answer change if the task were three months instead of three weeks?)
- There exist three tasks, each one requiring two months of work. Richard has the necessary people skills to handle all three tasks, but he will not be able to do so as efficiently as a technical specialist. The alternate choice is to utilize three technical specialists.

In both situations there should be more information made available to assist in the final decision. However, based upon the amount of information given, the author prefers task skills so as not to hinder the time or performance constraints on the project. Generally speaking, for long-duration projects that require constant communications with the customer, it might be better to have permanently assigned employees who can perform a variety of tasks. Customers dislike seeing a steady stream of new faces.

Highly technical industries are modifying the marketing function because of this distinction between people and task skills. In the past, people skills were considered to be of extreme importance in marketing technology. Today the trend is toward giving more importance to the task skill. The result has been that the project manager and project engineer must undertake marketing efforts in addition to their everyday duties. The marketing function has, therefore moved down to middle management.

It is often said that a good project manager must be willing to work sixty to eighty hours a week to get the job done. This might be true if continually fighting fires or if budgeting constraints prevent employing additional staff. The major reason, however, is the result of ineffective time management. Prime examples might include the continuous flow of paperwork, unnecessary meetings, unnecessary phone calls, and acting as a tour guide for visitors. Improper time management becomes an activity trap where the project manager becomes controlled by the job rather than controlling the job himself. The final result is that the project manager must work long and arduous hours in order to find time for creative thinking.

To be effective, the project manager must estabish time management rules and then ask himelf four questions:

- Rules for time management
  - Conduct a time analysis (time log)
  - Plan solid blocks for important things
  - Classify your activities
  - Establish priorities
  - Establish opportunity cost on activities
  - Train your system (boss, subordinate, peers)
  - Practice delegation
  - Practice calculated neglect
  - Practice management by exception
  - Focus on opportunities—not on problems
- Questions
  - What am I doing that I don't have to be doing at all?
  - What am I doing that can be done better by someone else?

- What am I doing that could be done sufficiently well by someone else?
- Am I establishing the right priorities for my activities?

This type of time management analysis can greatly reduce such proverbial "time robbers" as:

- Incomplete work
- A job poorly done (must be done over)
- Delayed decisions
- Poor communications channels
- Uncontrolled telephone calls
- Casual visitors
- Waiting for people
- Failure to delegate
- Poor retrieval system

5.13 COMMUNICATIONS

Proper communications are vital to the success of the project. Communications are the process by which information is exchanged. Communications can be:

- Written formal
- Written informal
- Oral formal
- Oral informal

Noise tends to distort or destroy the information within the message. Noise results from our own personality screens which dictate the way we present the message, and perception screens which may cause us to "perceive" what we thought was said. Noise therefore can cause ambiguity:

- Ambiguity causes us to hear what we want to hear.
- Ambiguity causes us to hear what the group wants.
- Ambiguity causes us to relate to past experiences without being discriminatory.

The communications process is more than simply conveying a message; it is also a source for control. Proper communications let the employees in on the act because employees need to know and understand. Communication must convey both information and motivation. The problem, therefore, is how to communicate. Below are six simple steps:

- Think through what you wish to accomplish.
- Determine the way you will communicate.
- Appeal to the interest of those affected.
- Give playback on ways others communicate to you.
- Get playback on what you communicate.
- Test effectiveness through reliance on others to carry out your instructions.

Knowing how to communicate does not guarantee that a clear message will be generated. There are techniques that can be used to improve communications. These techniques include:

- Obtaining feedback, possibly in more than one form
- Establishing multiple communications channels
- Using face-to-face communications if possible
- Determining how sensitive the receiver is to your communications
- Being aware of symbolic meanings such as expressions on people's faces
- Communicating at the proper time
- Reinforcing words with actions
- Using a simple language
- Using redundancy (i.e., saying it two different ways) whenever possible

Techniques can vary from project to project. For example, on one project the customer may require that all test data be made available, in writing, as soon as testing occurs and possibly before your own people have had a chance to examine the results. This type of clear and open communication cannot exist indefinitely because the customer might form his own opinion of the data before hearing the project office position. Similarly, project managers should not expect functional managers to provide them with immediate raw test data until functional analysis is conducted.

With every effort to communicate there are always barriers. The barriers include:

- Receiver hearing what he wants to hear. This results from people doing the same job so long that they no longer listen.
- Sender and receiver having different perceptions. This is vitally important in interpreting contractual requirements, statements of work, and proposal information requests.
- Receiver evaluating the source before accepting the communications.
- Receiver ignoring conflicting information and doing as he pleases.
- Words meaning different things to different people.

- Communicators ignoring nonverbal cues.
- Receiver being emotionally upset.

The scalar chain of command can also beome a barrier with regard to in-house communications. The project manager must have the authority to go to the general manager or counterpart to communicate effectively Without direct upward communication, it is possible that filters can develop such that the final message gets distorted.

Three important conclusions can be drawn about communications techniques and barriers:

- Don't assume that the message you sent will be received in the form you sent it.
- The swiftest and most effective communications take place among people with common points of view. The manager who fosters a good relationship with his associates will have little difficulty in communicating with them.
- Communications must be established early in the project.

Communication problems in project management require the answering of the following three questions:

- What are the channels of communication?
- What information is really important?
- Will I be punished for bringing forth bad news?

In a project environment, communications are often filtered. There are several reasons for the filtering of upward communications:

- Unpleasantness for the sender
- Receiver cannot obtain inormation from any other source
- To embarrass a superior
- Lack of mobility or status for the sender
- Insecurity
- Mistrust

Information filtering can occur through:

- Methods
- Blocking
- Withholding
- Partial transmittal

Communication is also listening. Good project managers must be willing to listen to their employees, both professionally and personally. The advantages of listening properly are that:

- Subordinates know you are sincerely interested.
- You obtain feedback.
- Employee acceptance is fostered.

The successful manager must be willing to listen to an individual's story from beginning to end, without interruptions. The manager must be willing to see the problem through the eyes of the subordinate. Finally, before making a decision, the manager should ask the subordinate for his solutions to the problem.

Project managers should ask themselves four questions:

- Do I make it easy for employees to talk to me?
- Am I sympathetic to their problems?
- Do I attempt to improve human relations?
- Do I make an extra effort to remember names and faces?

Team meetings are suposedly meetings of the mind where information giving, receiving, and listening take place. Team meetings must be effective, or else they become time management pitfalls. It is the responsibility of the project manager to ensure that meetings are valuable and necessary for the exchange of information. The following are general guides for conducting a more effective meeting:

- Start on time. If you wait for people, you reward tardy behavior.
- Develop agenda "objectives." Generate a list and proceed; avoid getting hung up on the order of topics.
- Conduct one piece of business at a time.
- Allow each member to contribute in his own way. Support, challenge, and counter; view differences as helpful; dig for reasons or views.
- Silence does not always mean agreement. Seek opinions: "What's your opinion on this, Peggy?"
- Be ready to confront the verbal member: "Okay, we've heard from Mike on this matter; now how about some other views?"
- Test for readiness to make a decision.
- Make the decision.
- Test for commitment to the decision.
- Assign roles and responsibilities (only after decision-making).

- Agree on follow-up or accountability dates.
- Indicate the next step for this group.
- Set the time and place for the next meeting.
- End on time.
- Was the meeting necessary?

Team meetings quite often provide individuals with means of exhibiting suppressed ideas. The following three humorous quotations identify these:

- "In any given meeting, when all is said and done, 90 percent will be said—10 percent will be done."—Orben's *Current Comedy*
- "A committee meeting provides a great chance for some people who like to hear their own voices talk and talk, while others draw crocodiles or a lady's legs. It also prevents the men who can think and make quick decisions from doing so."—Lin Yutang, *The Pleasures of a Nonconformist (World)*
- "Having served on various committees, I have drawn up a list of rules: Never arrive on time or you will be stamped a beginner. Don't say anything until the meeting is half over; this stamps you as being wise. Be as vague as possible; this prevents irritating the others. When in doubt, suggest that a subcommittee be appointed. Be the first to move for adjournment; this will make you popular—it's what everyone is waiting for."—Harry Chapman, quoted in *Think*

Many times, company policies and procedures can be established for the development of communications channels for project personnel. Table 5–4 illustrates such communications guidelines.

5.14 PROJECT REVIEW MEETINGS

Project review meetings are necessary to convince key personnel that orderly progress is being made on a project. There are three types of review meetings:

- Project team review meetings
- Executive management review meetings
- Customer project review meetings

Most projects have weekly, bimonthly, or monthly meetings in order to keep the project manager and his team informed about the project's status. These meetings are flexible and should be called only if positive benefits will result. Team meetings should not be called just for the sake of having meetings. Having both too many or too few meetings can prove detrimental.

Executive management has the right to require monthly status review meetings. However, if the project manager believes that other meeting dates are better (because they occur at a point where progress can be identified), then he should request changes in date from top management.

Customer review meetings are often the most critical and most inflexibly scheduled. Every attempt must be made to adhere to the requirements for such meetings. Project managers often overlook the fact that their project is simply one of several interrelated projects for the customer. Project managers must allow time to prepare handouts and literature well in advance of the meeting. This preparation and/or travel time must be accounted for in the budget.

5.15. PROJECT MANAGEMENT BOTTLENECKS

Poor communications can easily produce communications bottlenecks. These bottlenecks can occur in both the parent and client organizations. The most common bottleneck occurs when all communications between the customer and the parent organization must flow through the project office. There are two major disadvantages to this type of arrangement. First, requiring that all information pass through the project office may be a necessity but develops slow reaction times. Second, regardless of the qualifications of the project office members, the client always fears that the information he receives will be "filtered" prior to disclosure.

Customers not only like first-hand information, but also prefer that their technical specialists be able to communicate directly with the parent organization's technical specialists. Many project managers dislike this arrangement, for they fear that the technical specialists may say or do something contrary to project strategy or thinking. These fears can be allayed by telling the customer that this situation will be permitted if, and only if, the customer realizes that the remarks made by the technical specialists do not, in any way, shape, or form, reflect the position of the project office or company. Furthermore, only the project office can authorize commitment of resources or the providing of information for a customer request. This will alleviate the necessity for having a project representative present during all discussions, but will require that records be provided to the project office of all communications with the customer.

For long-duration projects the customer may require that the contractor have an established customer representative office in the contractor's facilities. The idea behind this is sound in that all information to the customer must flow through the customer's project office at the contractor's facility. This creates a problem in that it attempts to sever direct communications channels between the customer and contractor project managers. The result is that in many situations, the establishment of a local project office is merely an eyewash situation to satisfy contractual requirements, whereas actual communications go

Table 5-4. Communications Policy.

PROGRAM MANAGER	FUNCTIONAL MANAGER	RELATIONSHIP
Communications The program manager utilizes existing authorized communications media to the maximum extent rather than create new ones.	*Communications*	*Communications* Communications up, down, and laterally are essential elements to the success of programs in multi-program organization, and to the morale and motivation of supporting functional organizations. In principle, communication from the program manager should be channeled through the program team member to functional managers.
Approves program plans, subdivided work description, and/or work authorizations, and schedules defining specific program requirements.	Assures his organization's compliance with all such program direction received.	Program definition must be within the scope of the contract as expressed in the program plan and work breakdown structure.

Signs correspondence that provides program direction to functional organizations. Signs correspondence addressed to the customer that pertains to the program except that which has been expressly assigned by the general manager, the function organizations, or higher management in accordance with division policy.

Assures his organization's compliance with all such program direction received. Functional manager provides the program manager with copies of all "Program" correspondence released by his organization that may affect program performance. Ensures that the program manager is aware of correspondence with unusual content, on an exception basis, through the cognizant program team member or directly if such action is warranted by the gravity of the situation.

In the program manager's absence, the signature authority is transferred upward to his reporting superior unless an acting program manager has been designated. Signature authority for correspondence will be consistent with established division policy.

Reports program results and accomplishments to the customer and to the general manager, keeping them informed of significant problems and events.

Participates in program reviews, being aware of and prepared in matters related to his functional specialty. Keeps his line or staff management and cognizant program team member informed of significant problems and events relating to any program in which his personnel are involved.

Status reporting is the responsibility of functional specialists. The program manager utilizes the specialist organizations. The specialists retain their own channels to the general manager but must keep the program manager informed.

from customer to contractor as though the local project office did not exist. This creates an antagonistic local customer project office.

The last bottleneck to be discussed occurs when the customer's project manager considers himself to be in a higher position than the contractor's project manager and, therefore, seeks some higher authority to which to communicate. As an example, the customer has a $130 million program and subcontract $5 million out to you. Even though you are the project manager and report to either the vice president and general manager or the director of program management, the customer's project manager may wish to communicate directly with the vice president or one of the directors. Project managers who seek status can often jeopardize the success of the project by creating rigid communications channels.

Figure 5–11 identifies why communications bottlenecks such as these occur. There almost always exist a minimum of two paths for communications flow to and from the customer. Many times, strategic project planning is accomplished between the customer and contractor at a level above the respective project managers. This type of situation can have a strongly demoralizing effect.

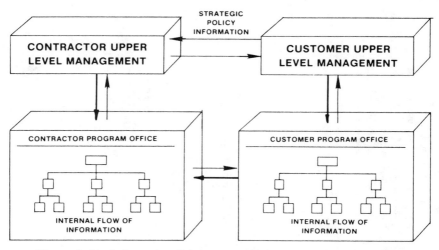

Figure 5–11. Information flow pattern from contractor program office.

5.16 COMMUNICATION TRAPS

Projects are run by communications. The work is defined by the communications tool known as the work breakdown structure. Actually, this is the easy part of communications, where everything is well defined. Unfortunately, project managers cannot document everything they wish to say or relate to other people, regardless of the level in the company. The worst possible situation occurs when an outside customer loses faith in the contractor. When a situation of mistrust prevails, the logical sequence of events would be:

- More documentation
- More interchange meetings
- Customer representation on your site

In each of these situations, the project manager becomes severely overloaded with work. This situation can also occur in-house when a line manager begins to mistrust a project manager, or vice versa. There may suddenly appear an exponential increase in the flow of paperwork, and everyone is writing "protection" memos. Previously, everything was verbal.

Communication traps occur most frequently with customer–contractor relationships. The following are examples of this:

- Phase I of the program has just been completed successfully. The customer, however, was displeased because he had to wait three weeks to a month after all tests were completed before the data were presented. For Phase II, the customer is insisting that his people be given the raw data at the same time your people receive it.
- The customer is unhappy with the technical information that is being given by the project manager. As a result, he wants his technical people to be able to communicate with your technical people on an individual basis without having to go through the project office.
- You are a subcontractor to a prime contractor. The prime contractor is a little nervous about what information you might present during a technical interchange meeting where the customer will be represented, and therefore wants to review all material before the meeting.
- You are a subcontractor to a prime contractor. During negotiations between the customer and the prime contractor, your phone rings. You find out that it is the customer asking for certain information.
- The customer has asked to have a customer representative office set up in the same building as the project office.
- During an interchange meeting with the customer, one of your company's

functional employees presents data to the customer and concludes with the remarks, "I personally disagree with our company's solution to this problem, and I think that the company is all wet in their approach. Let me show you my solution to this problem."

- Functional employees are supposed to be experts. In front of the customer (or even your top management) an employee makes a statement that you the project manager do not believe is completely true or accurate.
- On Tuesday morning, the customer's project manager calls your project manager and asks him a question. On Tuesday afternoon, the customer's project engineer calls your project engineer and asks him the same question.

Communication traps can also occur between the project office and line managers. Below are several examples:

- The project manager can hold too many "useless" team meetings.
- The project manager can hold too few team meetings.
- People refuse to make decisions, and ultimately the team meetings are flooded with agenda items that are irrelevant.
- Last month, Larry completed an assignment as an assistant project manager on an activity where the project manager kept him continuously informed as to project status. Now, Larry is working for a project manager who tells him only what he needs to know to get the job done.

In a project environment, the line manager is not part of any project team, otherwise he would spend 40 hours per week simply attending team meetings. Therefore, how does the line manager learn of the true project status? Written memos will not do it. The information must come first hand from either the project manager or the assigned functional employee. Line managers would rather hear it from the project manager because line employees have the tendency to censor bad news from the respective line manager. Line managers must be provided true status by the project office. Consider the following example:

John is a functional support manager with fourteen highly competent individuals beneath him. John's main concern is performance. He has a tendency to leave scheduling and cost problems up to the project managers. During the past two months, John has intermittently received phone calls and casual visits from upper-level management and senior executives asking him about his department's costs and schedules on a variety of projects. Although he can answer almost all of the performance questions, he has found great difficulty in responding to time and cost questions. John is a little nervous that if this situation continues it may affect his evaluation and merit pay increase.

Sometimes, project managers expect too much from their employees during problem-solving or brainstorming sessions, and communications become inhibited. There are several possible causes for having unproductive team meetings:

- Because of superior–subordinate relationships (i.e., pecking orders), creativity is inhibited.
- Criticism and ridicule have a tendency to inhibit spontaneity.
- Pecking orders, unless adequately controlled, can inhibit teamwork and problem solving.
- All seemingly crazy or unconventional ideas are ridiculed and eventually discarded. Contributors do not wish to contribute anything further.
- Many lower-level people, who could have good ideas to contribute, feel inferior and, therefore, refuse to contribute
- Meetings are dominated by upper-level management personnel.
- The meetings are held at an inappropriate place and time.
- Many people are not given adequate notification of meeting time and subject matter.

5.17 PROVERBS

Below are twenty project management proverbs that show you what can go wrong:[20]

- You cannot produce a baby in one month by impregnating nine women.
- The same work under the same conditions will be estimated differently by ten different estimators or by one estimator at ten different times.
- The most valuable and least used word in a project manager's vocabulary is "NO."
- You can con a sucker into committing an unreasonable deadline, but you can't bully him into meeting it.
- The more ridiculous the deadline, the more it costs to try to meet it.
- The more desperate the situation, the more optimistic the situatee.
- Too few people on a project can't solve the problems—too many create more problems than they solve.
- You can freeze the user's specs but he won't stop expecting.
- Frozen specs and the abominable snowman are alike: they are both myths, and they both melt when sufficient heat is applied.
- The conditions attached to a promise are forgotten, and the promise is remembered.
- What you don't know hurts you.

---

20. Source unknown.

- A user will tell you anything you ask about—nothing more.
- Of several possible interpretations of a communication, the least convenient one is the only correct one.
- What is not on paper has not been said.
- No major project is ever installed on time, within budget, with the same staff that started it.
- Projects progress quickly until they become 90 percent complete; then they remain at 90 percent complete forever.
- If project content is allowed to change freely, the rate of change will exceed the rate of progress.
- No major system is ever completely debugged; attempts to debug a system inevitably introduce new bugs that are even harder to find.
- Project teams detest progress reporting because it vividly demonstrates their lack of progress.
- Parkinson and Murphy are alive and well—in your project.

5.18 MANAGEMENT POLICIES AND PROCEDURES

Although each project manager has the authority and responsibility to establish project policies and procedures, they must fall within the general guidelines established by top management. Table 5–5 identifies sample top-management guidelines. Guidelines can also be established for planning, scheduling, controlling, and communications.

PROBLEMS

5–1 A project manager finds that he does not have direct reward power over salaries, bonuses, work assignments, or project funding for members of the project team with whom he interfaces. Does this mean that he is totally deficient in reward power? Explain your answer.

5–2 For each of the remarks made below, what types of interpersonal influences could exist?

a. "I've had good working relations with Department X. They like me and I like them. I can usually push through anything ahead of schedule."
b. A research scientist was temporarily promoted to project management for an advanced state-of-the-art effort. He was overheard making the following remark to a team member: "I know it's contrary to department policy, but the test must be conducted according to these criteria or else the results will be meaningless."

5–3 Do you agree or disagree that scientists and engineers are likely to be more creative if they feel that they have sufficient freedom in their work? Can this condition backfire?

5–4 Should the amount of risk and uncertainty in the project have a direct bearing upon how much authority is granted to a project manager?

5-5 Some projects are directed by project managers who have only monitoring authority. These individuals are referred to as influence project managers. What kind of projects would be under their control? What organizational structure might be best for this?

5-6 As a project nears termination, the project manager may find that the functional people are more interested in finding a new role for themselves than in giving their best to the current situation. How does this relate to Maslow's hierarchy of needs, and what should the project manager do?

5-7 Richard M. Hodgetts ("Leadership Techniques in the Project Organization," *Academy of Management Journal*, June 1968, pp. 211-219) conducted a survey on aerospace, chemical, construction, and state government workers as to whether they would rate the following leadership techniques as very important, important or not important:

- Negotiation
- Personality and/or persuasive ability
- Competence
- Reciprocal favors

How do you think each industry answered the questionnaires?

5-8 Robert D. Doering ("An Approach Toward Improving the Creative Output of Scientific Task Teams," *IEEE Transactions on Engineering Management*, February 1973, pp. 29-31) commented that:

The team leader's role is crucial. He is directly involved and must know the individual team member well, not only in terms of their technical capabilities but also in terms of how they function when addressing a problem as part of a group. The technical competence of a potential team member can usually be determined from information about previous assignments, but it is not so easy to predict and control the individual's interaction within and with a new group, since it is related to the psychological and social behavior of each of the other members of the group as a whole. What the leader needs is a tool to measure and characerize the individual members so that he can predict their interactions and structure his task team accordingly.

Is such a test possible for people working in a project environment? Are there any project organizational forms that would be conducive for such testing?

5-9 Project managers consider authority and funding as being very important in gaining support. Functional personnel, however, prefer friendship and work assignments. How can these two outlooks be related to the theories of Maslow and McGregor?

5-10 Lloyd A. Rogers ("Guidelines for Project Management Teams," *Industrial Engineering*, December 1974, p. 12. Published and copyright 1974 by the American Institute of Industrial Engineers Inc., Norcross, GA 30092) has commented that:

The technical planners, whether they are engineers or systems analysts, must be experts at designing the system, but seldom do they recognize the need to "put on

Table 5-5. General Management Guidelines.

PROGRAM MANAGER	FUNCTIONAL MANAGER	RELATIONSHIP
GENERAL	*GENERAL*	*GENERAL*
The program manager is responsible for overall program direction, control, and coordination; and is the principal contact with the program management of the customer.	The functional organization managers are responsible for supporting the program manager in the performance of the contract(s) and in accordance with the terms of the contract(s) and are accountable to their cognizant managers for the total performance.	The program manager determines what will be done: he obtains, through the assigned program team members, the assistance and concurrence of the functional support organizations in determining the definitive requirements and objectives of the program.
To achieve the program objectives, the program manager utilizes the services of the functional organizations in accordance with the prescribed division policies and procedures affecting the functional organizations.		The functional organizations determine *how* the work will be done.
He establishes program and technical policy as defined by management policy.	The functional support organizations perform all work within their functional areas for all programs within the cost, schedule, quality, and specifications established by contract for the program so as to assist the program manager in achieving the program objectives.	The program manager operates within prescribed division policies and procedures except where requirements of a particular program necessitate deviations or modifications as approved by the general manager. The functional support organizations provide strong, aggressive support to the program managers.
The program manager is responsible for the progress being made as well as the effectiveness of the total program.		
Integrates research, development, production, procurement, quality assurance, product support, test, and financial and contractual aspects.	The functional support organization management seeks out or initiates innovations, methods, improvements, or other means that will enable that function to better schedule commitments, reduce cost, improve quality, or otherwise render exemplary performance as approved by the program manager.	The program manager relies on the functional support program team members for carrying out specific program assignments.
Approves detailed performance specifications, pertinent physical characteristics and functional design criteria to meet the programs development or operational requirements.		Program managers and the functional support program team members are jointly responsible for ensuring that unresolved conflicts between
Ensures preparation of, and approves, overall plan, budgets, and work statements essential to the integration of system elements.		

Directs the preparation and maintenance of a time, cost, and performance schedule to ensure the orderly progress of the program.

Coordinates and approves subcontract work statement, schedules, contract type, and price for major "buy" items.

Coordinates and approves vendor evaluation and source selections in conjunction with procurement representative to the program team.

Program decision authority rests with the program manager for all matters relating to his assigned program, consistent with division policy and the responsibilities assigned by the general manager.

requirements levied on functional organizations by different program managers are brought to the attention of management.

Program managers do not make decisions that are the responsibility of the functional support organizations as defined in division policies and procedures and/or as assigned by the general manager.

Functional organization managers do not request decisions of a program manager that are not within the program manager's delineated authority and responsibility and that do not affect the requirements of the program.

Functinal organizations do not make program decisions that are the responsibility of the program manager. Joint participation in problem solution is essential to providing satisfactory decisions that fulfill overall program and company objectives, and is accomplished by the program manger and the assigned program team members.

In arriving at program decisions, the program manager obtains the assistance and concurrence of cognizant functional support managers, through the cognizant program team member, since they are held accountable for their support of each program and for overall division functional performance.

another hat" when system design specifications are completed and design the project control or implementation plan. If this is not done, setting a project completion target date or a set of management checkpoint milestones is done by guesswork at best. Management will set the checkpoint milestones, and the technical planners will hope they can meet the schedule.

How can this planning problem be effectively resolved on a continuing basis?

5-11 What kind of working relationships would result if the project manager had more reward power than the functional managers?

5-12 For each of the following remarks, state the possible situation and accompanying assumptions that you would make.

a. "A good project manager should manage by focusing on keeping people happy."
b. "A good project manager must be willing to manage tension."
c. "The responsibility for the success or failure rests with upper-level management. This is their baby."
d. Remarks by functional employee: "What if I fail on this project? What can he (the project manager) do to me?"

5-13 Can each of the following situations lead to failure?

a. Lack of expert power
b. Lack of referent power
c. Lack of reward and punishment power
d. Not having sufficient authority

5-14 One of your people comes into your office and states that he has a technical problem and would like your assistance by making a phone call.

a. Is this managing or doing?
b. Does your answer depend upon who must be called? (That is, is it possible that authority relationships may have to be considered?)

5-15 On the LRC, can we structure the responsibility column to primary and secondary responsibilities?

5-16 Discuss the meaning of each of the two poems listed below:

- We shall have to evolve
  Problem solvers galore
  Since each problem they solve
  Creates ten problems more.
  —*Source Unknown*

- Jack and Jill went up the hill*
  To fetch a pail of water

---

*Stacer Holcomb, OSD (SA), as quoted in *The C/E Newsletter,* publication of the cost effectiveness section of the Operations Research Society of America, Vol. 2, No. 1, January 1967.

Jack fell down and broke his crown
And Jill came tumbling after.

Jack could have avoided this awful lump
By seeking alternative choices
Like installing some pipe and a great big pump
And handing Jill the invoices.

5-17 What is the correct way for a project manager to invite line managers to attend team meetings?

5-18 Can a project manager sit and wait for things to happen, or should he cause things to happen?

5-19 The company has just hired a fifty-four-year-old senior engineer who holds two masters degrees in engineering disciplines. The engineer is quite competent and has worked well as a loner for the past twenty years. This same engineer has just been assigned to the R&D phase of your project. You, as project manager or project engineer, must make sure that this engineer works as a team member with other functional employees, not as a loner. How do you propose to accomplish this? If the individual persists in wanting to be a loner, should you fire him?

5-20 Suppose the linear responsibility chart is constructed with the actual names of the people involved, rather than just their titles. Should this chart be given to the customer?

5-21 How should a functional manager handle a situation where the project manager:

a. Continuously cries wolf concerning some aspect of the project when, in fact, the problem either does not exist or is not as severe as the project manager makes it out to be?
b. Refuses to give up certain resources that are no longer needed on the project?

5-22 How do you handle a project manager or project engineer who continually tries to "bite off more than he can chew"? If he were effective at doing this, at least temporarily, would your answer change?

5-23 A functional manager says that he has fifteen people assigned to work on your project next week (according to the project plan and schedule). Unfortunately, you have just learned that the prototype is not available and that these fifteen people will have nothing to do. Now what? Who is at fault?

5-24 Manpower requirements indicate that a specific functional pool will increase sharply from eight to seventeen people over the next two weeks and then drop back to eight people. Should you question this?

5-25 Below are several sources from which legal authority can be derived. State whether or not each source provides the project manager with sufficient authority from which he can effectively manage the project.

a. The project or organizational charter
b. The project manager's position in the organization
c. The job description and specifications for project managers
d. Policy documents
e. The project manager's "executive" rank
f. Dollar value of the contract
g. Control of funds

5–26   Is This Managing or Doing?

MANAGING	DOING	
_____	_____	1. Making a call with one of your people to assist him in solving a technical problem.
_____	_____	2. Signing a check to approve a routine expenditure
_____	_____	3. Conducting the initial screening interview of a job applicant.
_____	_____	4. Giving one of your experienced people your solution to a new problem without first asking for his recommendation.
_____	_____	5. Giving your solution to a recurring problem that one of your new people has just asked you about.
_____	_____	6. Conducting a meeting to explain to your people a new procedure.
_____	_____	7. Phoning a department to request help in solving a problem that one of your people is trying to solve.
_____	_____	8. Filling out a form to give one of your people a pay increase.
_____	_____	9. Explaining to one of your people why he is receiving a merit pay increase.
_____	_____	10. Deciding whether to add a position.
_____	_____	11. Asking one of your people what he thinks about an idea you have that will affect your people.
_____	_____	12. Transferring a desirable assignment from employee A to employee B because employee A did not devote the necessary effort.
_____	_____	13. Reviewing regular written reports to determine your people's progress toward their objectives.
_____	_____	14. Giving a regular progress report by phone to your supervisor.
_____	_____	15. Giving a tour to an important visitor from outside of your organization.
_____	_____	16. Drafting an improved layout of facilities.

MANAGING	DOING	
_____	_____	17. Discussing with your key people the extent to which they should use staff services during the next year.
_____	_____	18. Deciding what your expense-budget request will be for your area of responsibility.
_____	_____	19. Attending a professional or industrial meeting to learn detailed technical developments.
_____	_____	20. Giving a talk on your work activities to a local community group.

From *Manage More by Doing Less,* By Raymond O. Leon, p. 4. Copyright © 1971 by McGraw-Hill, Inc., New York. Used with permission of Mc-Graw-Hill Book Company.

5-27 Below are three broad statements describing the functions of management. For each statement, are we referring to upper-level management, project management, or functional management?

a. Acquire the best available assets and try to improve them.
b. Provide a good working environment for all personnel.
c. Make sure that all resources are applied effectively and efficiently such that all constraints are met, if possible.

5-28 Decide whether you agree or disagree that, in the management of people, the project manager:

- Must convert mistakes into learning experiences.
- Acts as the lubricant that eases the friction (i.e., conflicts) between the functioning parts.

5-29 Functional employees are supposed to be the experts. A functional employee makes a statement that the project manager does not believe is completely true or accurate. Should the project manager support the team member? If so, for how long? Does your answer depend upon who the remarks are being addressed to, such as upper-level management or the customer? At what point should a project manager stop supporting his team members?

5-30 Below are four statements: two statements describe a function, and two others describe a purpose. Which statements refer to project management and which refer to functional management?

- Function
  - Reduce or eliminate uncertainty
  - Minimization and assessment of risk
- Purpose
  - Create the environment (using transformations)
  - Perform decision making in the transformed environment

5-31 Manager A is a department manager with thirty years of experience in the company. For the last several years, he has worn two hats and acted as both project manager and functional manager on a variety of projects. He is an expert in his field.

The company has decided to incorporate formal project management and has established a project management department. Man B, a thirty-year-old employee with three years of experience with the company, has been assigned as project manager. In order to staff his project, Man B has requested from Manager A that Man C (a personal friend of Man B) be assigned to the project as the functional representative. Man C is twenty-six years old and has been with the company for two years. Manager A agrees to the request and informs Man C of his new assignment, closing with the remarks, "This project is yours all the way. I don't want to have anything to do with it. I'll be too busy with paperwork as the result of our new organizational structure. Just send me a memo once in a while telling me what's happening."

During the project kickoff meeting it became obvious to both Man B and Man C that the only person with the necessary expertise was Manager A. Without the support of Manager A, the time duration for project completion could be expected to double.

This situation is ideal for role-playing. Put yourself in the place of Manager A, Man B, and Man C and discuss the reasons for your actions. How can this problem be overcome? How do you get Manager A to support the project? Who should inform upper-level management of this situation? When should upper-level management be informed? Would any of your answers change if Man B and Man C were not close friends?

5–32 Is it possible for a product manager to have the same degree of tunnel vision that a project manager has? If so, under what circumstances?

5–33 Your company has a policy that employees can participate in an educational tuition reimbursement program, provided that the degree obtained will benefit the company and that the employee's immediate superior gives his permission. As a project manager, you authorize George, your assistant project manager who reports directly to you, to take courses leading to an M.B.A. degree.

Midway through your project, you find that overtime is required on Monday and Wednesday evenings, the same two evenings that George has classes. George cannot change the evenings that his classes are offered. You try without success to reschedule the overtime to early mornings or other evenings. According to company policy, the project office must supervise all overtime. Since the project office consists of only you and George, you must perform the overtime if George does not. How should you handle this situation? Would your answer change if you thought that George might leave the company after receiving his degree?

5–34 Establishing good interface relationships between the project manager and functional manager can take a great deal of time, especially during the conversion from a traditional to a project organizational form. Below are five statements that represent the different stages in the development of a good interface relationship. Place these statements in the proper order, and discuss the meaning of each one.

a. The project manager and functional manager meet face-to-face and try to work out the problem.
b. Both the project and functional managers deny that any problems exist between them.

c. The project and functional managers begin formally and informally to anticipate the problems that can occur.

d. Both managers readily admit responsibility for several of the problems.

e. Each manager blames the other for the problem.

5-35 John is a functional support manager with fourteen highly competent individuals beneath him. John's main concern is performance. He has a tendency to leave scheduling and cost problems up to the project managers. During the past two months, John has intermittently received phone calls and casual visits from upper-level management and senior executives asking him about his department's costs and schedules on a variety of projects. Although he can answer almost all of the performance questions, he has experienced great difficulty in responding to time and cost questions. John is a little apprehensive that if this situation continues, it may affect his evaluation and merit pay increase. What are John's alternatives?

5-36 Projects have a way of providing a "chance for glory" for many individuals. Unfortunately, they quite often give the not-so-creative individual an opportunity to demonstrate his incompetence. Examples would include the designer who always feels that he has a better way of laying out a blueprint, or the individual who intentionally closes a door when asked to open it, or vice versa. How should a project manager handle this situation? Would your answer change if the individual were quite competent but always did the opposite just to show his individuality? Should these individuals be required to have close supervision? If close supervision is required, should it be the responsibility of the functional manager, the project office, or both?

5-37 Are there situations in which a project manager can wait for long-term changes instead of an immediate response to actions?

5-38 Is it possible for functional employees to have performed a job so long or so often that they no longer listen to the instructions given by the project or functional managers?

5-39 On Tuesday morning, the customer's project manager calls the subcontractor's project manager and asks him a question. On Tuesday afternoon, the customer's project engineer calls the contractor's project engineer and asks him the same question. How do you account for this? Could this be "planned" by the customer?

5-40 Below are eight common methods that project and functional employees can use to provide communications:

a.	Counseling sessions	e.	Project office memo
b.	Telephone conversation	f.	Project office directive
c.	Individual conversation	g.	Project team meeting
d.	Formal letter	h.	Formal report

For each of the following actions, select one and only one means of communication from the above list that you would utilize in accomplishing the action:

1. Defining the project organizational structure to functional managers

2. Defining the project organizational structure to team members
3. Defining the project organizational structure to executives
4. Explaining to a functional manager the reasons for conflict between his employee and your assistant project managers
5. Requesting overtime because of schedule slippages
6. Reporting an employee's violation of company policy
7. Reporting an employee's violation of project policy
8. Trying to solve a functional employee's grievance
9. Trying to solve a project office team member's grievance
10. Directing employees to increase production
11. Directing employees to perform work in a manner that violates company policy
12. Explaining the new indirect project evaluation system to project team members
13. Asking for downstream functional commitment of resources
14. Reporting daily status to executives or the customer
15. Reporting weekly status to executives or the customer
16. Reporting monthly or quarterly status to executives or the customer
17. Explaining the reason for the cost overrun
18. Establishing project planning guidelines
19. Requesting a vice president to attend your team meeting
20. Informing functional managers of project status
21. Informing functional team members of project status
22. Asking a functional manager to perform work not originally budgeted for
23. Explaining customer grievances to your people
24. Informing employees of the results of customer interchange meetings
25. Requesting that a functional employee be removed from your project because of incompetence

5–41 Last month, Larry completed an assignment as chief project engineer on Project X. It was a pleasing assignment. Larry, and all of the other project personnel, were continually kept informed (by the project manager) concerning all project activities. Larry is now working for a new project manager who tells his staff only what they have to know in order to get their job done. What can Larry do about this situation? Can this be a good situation?

5–42 Phase I of a program has just been completed successfully. the customer however, was displeased because he always had to wait three weeks to a month after all tests were complete before data were supplied by the contractor.

For Phase II of the program, the customer is requiring that advanced quality control procedures be adhered to. This permits the customer's quality control people to observe all testing and obtain all of the raw data at the same time the contractor does. Is there anything wrong with this arrangement?

5–43 You are a subcontractor to Company Z, who in turn is the prime contractor to Company Q. Before any design review or technical interchange meeting, Company Z requires that they review all material to be presented both in-house and with Company Q prior to the meeting. Why would a situation such as this occur? Is it beneficial?

5–44 Referring to Problem 5–44, during contract negotiations between Company Q and Company Z, as project manager for the subcontractor you are sitting in your office when the phone rings. It is Company Q requesting information to support their negotiation position. Should you provide them with the information?

5–45 How does a project manager find out if the project team members from the functional departments have the authority to make decisions?

5–46 One of your functional people has been assigned to perform a certain test and document the results. For two weeks you "hound" this individual only to find out that he is continually procrastinating on work in another program. You later find out from one of his co-workers that he hates to write. What should you do?

5–47 During a crisis, you find that all of the functional managers as well as the team members are writing letters and memos to you, whereas previously everything was verbal. How do you account for this?

5–48 Below are several problems that commonly occur in project organizations. State, if possible, the effect that each problem could have upon communications and time management:

  a. People tend to resist exploration of new ideas
  b. People tend to mistrust each other in temporary management situations.
  c. People tend to protect themselves.
  d. Functional people tend to look at day-to-day activities rather than long-range efforts.
  e. Both functional and project personnel often look for individual rather than group recognition.
  f. People tend to create win-or-lose positions.

5–49 How can executives obtain loyalty and commitments from horizontal and vertical personnel in a project organizational structure?

5–50 What is meant by polarization of communications? What are the most common causes?

5–51 Many project managers contend that project team meetings are flooded with agenda items, many of which may be irrelevant. How do you account for this?

5–52 Paul O. Gaddis ("The Project Manager," *Harvard Business Review,* May–June 1959, p. 90 Copyright © 1959 by the President and Fellows of Harvard College. All rights reserved) has stated that:
In learning to manage a group of professional employees, the usual boss–subordinate relationship must be modified. Of special importance, the how—the details or methods of work performance by a professional employee—should be established by the employee. It follows that he must be given the facts necessary to permit him to develop a rational understanding of the why of tasks assigned to him.

How would you relate this information to the employee?

5–53 The customer has asked to have a customer representative office set up in the same building as the project office. As project manager, you put the customer's office at the opposite end of the building from where you are, and on a different floor. The customer states that he wants his office next to yours. Should this be permitted, and, if so, under what conditions?

5–54 During an interchange meeting with the customer, one of the functional personnel makes a presentation stating that he personally disagrees with the company's solution to the particular problem under discussion and that the company is "all wet" in its approach. How do you, as a project manager, handle this situation?

5–55 Do you agree or disagree with the statement that documenting results "forces" people to learn?

5–56 Should a project manager encourage the flow of problems to him? If yes, should he be selective in which ones to resolve?

5–57 Is it possible for a project manager to hold too few project review meetings?

5–58 If all projects are different, should there exist a uniform company policies and procedures manual?

5–59 Of the ten items below, which are considered as part of directing and which are controlling?

- a. Supervising
- b. Communicating
- c. Delegating
- d. Evaluating
- e. Measuring
- f. Motivating
- g. Coordinating
- h. Staffing
- i. Counseling
- j. Correcting

5–60 Which of the following items is not considered to be one of the seven M's of Management?

- a. Manpower
- b. Money
- c. Machines
- d. Methods
- e. Materials
- f. Minutes
- g. Mission

5–61 Match the following leadership styles (source unknown):

1. Management by inaction   _____   a. Has an executive who

2. Management by detail   ———
3. Management by invisibility   ———
4. Management by consensus   ———
5. Management by manipulation ———
6. Management by rejection   ———
7. Management by survival   ———
8. Management by despotism   ———
9. Management by creativity   ———
10. Management by leadership   ———

      manages with flair, wisdom and vision. He listens to his men, prods them, and leads them.

b. Grows out of fear and anxiety.

c. Can be fair or unfair, effective or ineffective, legitimate or illegitimate. Some people are manipulators of other for power. People are not puppets.

d. Is the roughly negative style. Executive always has ideas; devil's advocate. Well-prepared proponents can win—so such a boss can be stimulating.

e. Has an executive who needs every conceivable fact; is methodical and orderly; often is timid, inappropriate, or late.

f. Is good as long as it is based on reality. The executive has a trained instinct.

g. Has an executive who will do anything to survive, the jungle fighter. If it is done constructively, the executive will build instead of destroy.

h. Is totalitarian. There are no clashes of ideas. The organization moves. Creative people flee. Employees always know who is boss.

i. Has an executive who is not around, has good subordinates, and works in an office, off-stage.

j. Can be important in dealing with the unknown (R&D projects). Subordinates are independent and powerful. This style could be a substitute for decision-making It is important for setting policy.

CASE STUDY: WEBSTER INDUSTRIAL CONTROLS

Webster Industrial Controls (WIC) is a thirty-two-year-old company which manufactures quality industrial control systems for aerospace, defense, construction, electronics, and nuclear components. In 1975, WIC incorporated formal project management, by decree. On December 19, 1978, the author visited WIC (the name is fictitious) to ascertain some of the major problem areas affecting successful project management operations. Several of WIC's personnel were interviewed. All of the questions discussed revolved about three major areas of concern:

- What are the major problems with current WIC operation?
- What are the major weaknesses with the current organizational structure, the project managers, and the functional managers?
- What kind of training would you like to see developed here at WIC in order to help you perform your job better and to improve your working relationships with other project management personnel?

Below are the responses to these questions. They have been edited somewhat for conciseness.

Q. What are the major problems with current WIC operations?

A1. *Scheduling:* "Many people, both in project management and production, do not understand why we have such a terrible problem in scheduling activities. Sure, our people understand the necessity for getting the order out as fast as possible in order to meet customer requirements, but there are severe environmental factors. The government has tied our hands with requirements on qualified customer vendors."

A2. "Qualifying a vendor means qualifying in terms of safety. This leads us to other questions. Does our vendor have design control? Has the vendor made these parts obsolete? How do we get vendor commitment? We spend $25–50K per product before we can call it qualified."

A3. "All vendors who have input also have changing situations. We have to write test procedure acceptance criteria, often under adverse conditions. If the control system is all right, then the point of release to manufacturing will be six months to a year. That's after three to four years in design. Also, how do we incorporate information on aging to show that the theoretical life of a nuclear control system is forty years? I wish I knew."

A1. *Priorities:* "There is lack of communication about how and why priorities can continuously shift. Manufacturing has the greatest concern. Priorities in manufacturing are related to the dollar value of the contract, usually through the marketing group and the project manager. Although there are several reasons for establishing a priority, the most common cause is with penalty or liquidated damages (i.e., failure to perform on a given date because the customer has people waiting to work and the equipment is not yet available)."

A2. "We have good channels to the upper levels of the organization for priority setting. But this doesn't resolve our problem. How do we keep people motivated with a shifting priority environment? Maybe we can't help it in our environment, but at least explaining the rationale to our people might ease some of the tension."

A1. *Conflicting Instructions to Manufacturing:* "This creates real havoc in our organization, and results from a lack of information, untimely information, wrong data, or incomplete engineering. The result is that manufacturing blames engineering, stating that it's engineering's fault (possibly because of incorrect drawings and wrong parts), and engineering blames manufacturing for making it wrong and not ordering the parts in time.

"When this occurs, we usually just get our heads together and hash it out. If penalty clauses are included as part of the contract, or any other clause that may require special attention, the usual result is weekly team meetings. Now time management becomes a problem. Perhaps there are better ways to handle this."

A2. "We have a very poor monitoring and control system. Not only are we tied down with too much paperwork, but the value of this paperwork always forces me to ask whether or not it is really necessary. Less than 50 percent of our orders go out without a final push. Here we are designing industrial control systems, and we have no system that functions on its own.

"Fortunately we've been successful because we have an easy access to upper-level management. They usually get totally involved and try to give us immediate resolution."

A3. "Planning is poor, at best. Sometimes, marketing provides a very, very poor forecast and everyone has to live with it. This becomes a problem when our new project managers are at a low level on the learning curve. Manufacturing sometimes doesn't know the status of a piece of equipment until it physically appears in front of them."

A4. "We cannot control resources unless we have planning and know what's coming. I don't know what's coming until I see it on the floor. What happened to proper planning?"

Q. What are the major weaknesses with the current organizational structure, the project managers, and the functional managers?

A1. "I've been here several years, and I have no idea about how project management is supposed to work. Who has what authority, responsibility, how, when . . .?"

A2. "Project managers cannot be successful unless they know the total picture, especially manufacturing operations. Perhaps they should spend some time there. Project engineers are not allowed to track activities in the production area. I'm not sure this is the way the project management system is supposed to work. There must be a better way to get total control of resources."

A3. "We have an extremely weak information system and poor feedback. Manufacturing does not want the project engineer in their domain in order to get feedback. They claim that the PM prevents people from working. The system shouldn't work this way. We have to get these people together to iron out their differences."

A4. "I've often wondered if there's better way to control our paperwork, especially engineering change notices (ECNs). These ECNs are very, very unmanageable. Who is responsible for chairing configuration management? What are the requirements? Nobody seems to know."

Q. What kind of training would you like to see developed here at WIC in order to help you perform your job better and to improve your working relationships with other project management personnel?

A1. "What is project management? I don't know. Why do the project engineers report to marketing, but have little authority in manufacturing? Is this the way the system should work?"

A2. "Section supervisors and group leaders now act as interface agents between department managers and project personnel. If they have to supervise more than five or six people, the system may break down. Is there a better way?"

A3. "Once a system is shipped, in effect, parts distribution becomes the customer interface. Aren't we therefore project managers? We should also be trained in project management."

A4. "Project management has a pecking order—not enough pull. Are there better ways of establishing authority and responsibility relationships?"

A5. "There is a lack of communications. Much information is not said or understood. How well do we listen? Perhaps people don't listen or just have a parochial view."

A6. "We must understand priorities and conflict resolution as well as why urgency is needed."

A7. "Interpersonal skills—from A to Z. Can this and attitude problems be taught or does it come with on-the-job training? How do we keep a cool head in stress situations? Can we teach professionalism and positive reaction?"

A8. "What is project management? I don't know. I lost track about two years ago. We've made too many changes, and nobody knows what's going on."

A9. "I want to know the flow of paperwork. It's very difficult to become dedicated if you're kept in the dark."

A10. "The biggest problem is paperwork. We overcomplicate things by doing it serially instead of in parallel. Perhaps this is why we can't ship as fast as the customer would like."

A11. "Project managers are not technical specialists. Our project managers need formal training in project management. As far as I know, they've had none."

A12. "How can I do my job if I don't know who the players are?"

A13. "There is a logic to decisions, but people just don't listen. They build up roadblocks."

A14. "What is a cost-control system? The PM doesn't know where he stands costwise on a project? That shouldn't be. We need help."

A15. "Should our project managers be customer or cost-oriented? When should we compromise? Most PMs are at the extremes. The best ones know when to give and take. Can this be learned?"

A16. "We in engineering are instructed to keep out of manufacturing. So, we have less information as to how manufacturing works."

A17. "PMs do not understand the operation of each department. That's a mistake in project management. Also, the PMs are very weak in planning and do not close the feedback loops. The result is scramble time. We need better planning and control of our resources. We need a cadet indoctrination program for ongoing people. Our people can read black and white, but not gray. They have strong tunnel vision. I'm not sure if this is good or bad."

A18. "We've had project management training programs in the past where everyone walked out saying that it was a fine program. Unfortunately, it was a failure because our people could not relate the information to their everyday job. Don't you make the same mistake."

CASE STUDY: PROJECT MANAGEMENT AT LIBERTY CONSTRUCTION[21]

Background

The stockholders' report for 1960 made it clear that Liberty Construction was a company to reckon with. The company had grown from 50 people back in 1955 to 400 people in 1960. Although Liberty had evolved primarily as an industrial facilities contractor, their business base expanded in commercial buildings, office buildings, production plants, chemical plants, and even private housing. This rapid expansion was attributed mainly to Liberty's ability to work with the customer.

As Liberty began to grow, they found it more and more difficult to coordinate efforts using the traditional structure. Planning and scheduling were accomplished with great difficulty. A new organizational structure was needed.

In 1964, Liberty adopted the classical matrix structure so that individuals could be shared. The project engineering function now included project management as well as project engineering. For the most part, each project engineer was assigned full-time to one and only one project. The project engineering positions were primarily administrative and included all customer communication. In effect, the project engineer could also serve as a customer representative if the customer did not have one.

The project engineer worked closely with the functional team members, by providing direction and answering questions. When in doubt, the project engineer would coordinate with the functional manager so that conflicting direction would not be given to the functional team member.

By 1967, Liberty found themselves in a position of having their project engineers consistently arguing with the functional managers over resources and priorities. Furthermore, because key individuals were being shared on as many as four projects at one time, the project engineers felt that they did not have total accountability for a given project. In 1968, Liberty sponsored a series of in-house seminars in hopes that this would lead to better working relationships between the project engineers and the functional design groups. Below are the seven basic questions and answers that resulted from the seminars.

Questions and Answers

1. Q—Does a project engineer need more legal authority over the project group?

A—The group consensus was that the project engineer has enough "legal' (organizational) authority.
Amplifying remarks were:

  a. A "partnership" of the design and project groups must be established.
  b. It is important for the project engineers to clarify goals for the purpose of minimizing conflict.
  c. If all project engineers would do a better job of using "tools" that they already have, this would be sufficient authority. Some of the tools mentioned were:
    —improved communications
    —using motivational techniques
    —creating a better team "climate"

2. Q—The Project Engineer has responsibility for leading a given project but does not have authority over the "who" does it and "how" it is to be done. In what ways is this a problem?

A—Some of the problems associated with having responsibilities for a project without complete authority over the "how" and "who" questions occur:

  a. In a situation whereby the project engineer becomes demotivated as a result of his authority being diluted, and as a result of organizational confusion, the group becomes demotivated.
  b. If the project engineer does not exercise what authority he already has when needed.
  c. If low-quality or low-performer people are assigned to project.

3. Q—"How" and "who" decisions are made by design. Can project engineers be involved in these decisions?

A—The group concluded that the project manager can be involved in "how" and "who" decisions by reviewing any conflicts with design group people and, in extreme cases, by reviewing problems with the manager of project engineering.
Specifically, the group talked in detail about "who" problems. Some of the solutions to the problems offered were:

  a. Before a project is formalized, the project manager should make recommendations for lead people with design section managers.

b. During the design stage of a project, changing key design people is a serious consideration and should be avoided whenever possible.

c. The key to resolving "who" problems is to work with design supervision first, and if the problem has significant impact on the success of the project and cannot be resolved with design supervision, then the problem should be reviewed with the manger of project engineering.

4. Q—"What" has to be done and "when" it has to be done decisions are made by project engineers. How should these be communicated to the "who" group?

A—Not discussed in detail. However, from the research conclusions presented, it should be evident that it's critically important for project engineers to involve key design people in "what" and "when" decisions, assuming the project engineer does this and "stays close' to design people on "what" and "when" problems. The project engineer can keep such problems from creating conflicts.

5. Q—Different project engineers create different human relations "climates" on their projects. What are some of the techniques that can be used to control this?

A—The general conclusion relative to Question 5 was that project engineers can create a positive project team climate by balancing overall goals with specific project demands and needs (such as evaluating people and development of people).
Group discussions centered around the need for the project engineers to emphasize mutual goals (design, project, etc.), and to de-emphasize those areas where there may be conflict.

6. Q—What is an appropriate project communication concerning:
    —rating people (design and project)?
    —feedback to people on project (successes) failures in the field?

A—It was suggested that design personnel assigned to project teams should be evaluated by the project engineer. In the event design management does not request such feedback, it is suggested that project engineers routinely evaluate project people. It was also suggested that project engineers be rated by design management. (Example of an evaluation form is shown in Table 5–6). Techniques for providing feedback for project personnel regarding success and failures of projects in the field were considered:
    —the need for project engineers to emphasize successes was discussed.
    —evaluating new field problems and their successful completion, the project engineer might use a variety of feedback techniques: individually, to several individuals, to the total group, or to section managers.
    — letters commending individual or group efforts by project engineers were mentioned as a technique for social recognition.

7. Q—How are project engineer decisions "validated" by project team members?

A—Not discussed in detail. However, from the research presented, "participation" of project team members in project decisions seems to be the key.

Table 5–6. Project Work Assignment Appraisal.

EMPLOYEE'S NAME _____ DATE _____

PROJECT TITLE _____ JOB NO. _____

ASSIGNMENT _____TIME ON JOB _____

For each item below, select a number between zero and five according to the following:

> 0 = not applicable
> 1 = outstanding
> 2 = excellent
> 3 = good or average
> 4 = adequate or acceptable
> 5 = inadequate or unacceptable

I TECHNICAL ABILITY
☐ Ability to meet quality of work standards
☐ Ability to meet quantity of work standards
☐ Ability to apply technical judgment
☐ Time and cost consciousness
☐ Safety consciousness

II HUMAN RELATIONS
☐ Job attitude
☐ Communicative skills
☐ Ability to work with others
☐ Cooperation
☐ Personality
☐ Loyalty to the company

III PROBLEM-SOLVING ABILITY
☐ Originality
☐ Adaptability
☐ Judgment
☐ Thoroughness

IV SELF-MOTIVATION
☐ Willingness to accept responsibility or accountability
☐ Ambitious
☐ Vigor
☐ Likes work challenge

V MANAGERIAL RESPONSIBILITIES
☐ Planning
☐ Organizing
☐ Directing
☐ Motivating employees

VI WORK HABITS
☐ Attendance at meetings
☐ Punctuality
☐ Housekeeping
☐ Stays at desk

VII IN COMPARISON TO HIS CONTEMPORARIES, I WOULD RATE THIS EMPLOYEE
☐ Top 10%
☐ Top 25%
☐ Average
☐ Bottom 25%
☐ Bottom 10%

Table 5-6. Project Work Assignment Appraisal. (*Continued*)

VIII ADDITIONAL COMMENTS

_____
_____
_____
_____
_____
_____
_____

Although the group seminar did provide some relief for many of the dilemmas, there still existed many problems that created conflicts. The majority of the conflicts revolved about the fact that the project engineer did not have total responsibility for the project because he did not have any control over the functional team members. For example, when a buyer might be working on more than one project at a time, the project engineer would then have to compete with other projects for the services of this buyer.

Product Management

In 1972, Liberty's management decided that the only realistic means of reducing conflicts would be to reorganize. Liberty went to the product organizational form in hopes that the project engineer would be able to achieve total responsibility, accountability, and control over those resources that would be needed. Liberty's management decided that all projects could be categorized as either industrial construction, home/office construction, government construction, or special projects. Each of these four "product lines" would be headed up by a team manager. Each team manager had the same eight functional departments beneath him.

Each team manager was responsible for approximately sixty people. This included the project engineers. There was some concern that the best technical specialists would be assigned to the special projects team. Top-level management, however, made it clear that there would be an equal division of the key people. All employees reported directly to the team managers and indirectly to the project engineers. The project engineers, however, had authority delegated to them by the team manager to utilize those people resources within their team as they saw fit. In theory, the new system looked like a matrix organizational structure within a product organizational form.

Each team manager was responsible for keeping two of the eight disciplines current with technology, the same two disciplines in all teams. In addition, the team managers would be responsible for evaluating all functional team members, regardless of their discipline.

The case writer interviewed the four team managers, the project engineers, and the functional (group) engineers as to how they foresaw the new organizational form and whether or not they felt that the problems that existed under the matrix would be carried over.

Interview with Project Engineers

Q. What problems do you see carrying over into the new system?

A. *Planning:* "Many times we're not even sure what our planning needs are, and this tends to create havoc. Sometimes it's our fault, but quite often the customer doesn't even know what he wants. This makes it difficult for us to work with the functional team members because we always end up replanning. The result is that the functional people may have lost confidence in us and therefore do not believe that the plan is any good. One functional guy once told me, 'Why should we plan at all? Nobody follow it anyway.'

"If we had good planning that everyone had confidence in, then we could play 'what if' games and develop contingency plans."

A. *Communications:* "We have to establish better communications with our design people. They're the people that make our system a success. Unfortunately, it's not easy working with design people and establishing a good communications network. It's difficult for a project engineer to become successful until after he has established credibility with functional people. To do this, a project engineer must make the first contact and show some interest in what they're doing. Of course, this can backfire because quite often the functional team members think that we're sticking our nose into their business and that we're going to tell them how to do their job. I guess they have a right to feel this way. This is a carry over from the matrix.

"Many times I tell our functional people everything I know about the project but I still get the feeling that they think that I'm holding something back.

"A good project engineer is a manager, not a doer. Most of his time he is caught up in paperwork and some red tape. Sometimes I consider myself as a highpriced clerk. I wish we (project engineers) could lighten some of the load we put on our design people in the way of writing reports. If our design people think they have to do a lot of writing, perhaps they should have my job for a while.

"We need a more dedicated effort on our projects. I think the only way we can do it is by developing better communications channels, both up as well as down.

"Many of our design people have poor communicative skills. They cannot write well, read, or sometimes even understand what they've read. I guess this is typical of engineers. I'm used to it now and am willing to help them out whenever I can. I just hope when I do this that they don't think that I'm trying to do their job for them."

Q. What kind of working relationships would you like to see develop between the project engineer and the team manager?

A. "Team managers should be managers, not doers. Their job should be administrative, for the most part. We must remember, however, that the team managers are still engineers, and damn good ones at that. I would like to see them act as consultants, not only to our team personnel, but to the other teams as well.

"The team managers have the authority to establish their own team policies, procedures, and standards as they see fit (I assume as long as though they conform to Liberty's policies, procedures, and rules). The team managers could easily end up telling the design people how to structure their work. This could put the project engineer in a position of responsibility without authority. I'd like to see the team managers funnel their work through us. In the new system, team managers are like the old functional managers, but tied up more with administrative duties."

Q. How do you feel about having new hirers attached to your project? Do you feel that you have a responsibility for on-the-job training?

A. "Somebody's got to do it. Sure, I'd prefer having seasoned veterans. But a good project engineer assumes that whatever people are assigned to him have the technical ability."

Interview With Group Engineers

Q. What are the biggest problems that you would like to see overcome by the new system?

A. *Planning:* "I've seen several packages that are total disasters from the start. I think there is a discontinuity of effort and lack of willingness of the project engineer and the customer to do good planning. Our project engineers might need refresher courses in industrial construction, but I don't think that this is a big problem. The 'biggy' is probably that the customer hasn't done any good planning and keeps coming up with different ideas. I wish our P.E.'s would keep us more informed about the total picture. I think it would give us a better understanding of their job and improve our relationships.

"Many times we do poor planning beause we have to come up with too much information too quickly. Because of the amount of changes we end up making, we should develop schedules as we go along.

"Someday, just someday, I'd like to have some kind of feedback or appraisal of how good our engineering package is. Contrary to popular belief, several of us group engineers are interested . . . I should say dedicated . . . to the total project."

A. *Communications:* "Up, down, sideways, and inside out! We have severe interdisciplinary commuications problems. There are some activities that can be handled by more than one group . . . at least this is the way it was in the old system. Overlapping efforts occurred because poor planning left several 'fuzzy areas' that could not be completely resolved until halfway through the job. Hopefully, the new system will alleviate this.

"I'd like somebody to tell me how much money I'm spending in doing my job. A little feedback wouldn't hurt.

"The best P.E.'s are those that have developed good communications channels with us but keep their nose out of our business and 'stop trying to help.'"

A. *Loss of Flexibility:* "I'm worried that the new system is trying to isolate and define more responsibility. This may be bad if it results in less flexibility for us. We're at the mercy of the team managers in the new system. I can see them tell us, 'Do it my way; use this procedure; use this standard; etc.' What happens if I'm transferred or just temporarily assigned to another group? We could very easily have a loss of learning between groups and teams. The team managrs have a great deal more responsibility in the new system. I can sympathize with their problem of having to control technology in all four teams, of which only one reports to them directly."

Q. How do you foresee the role of the team managers?

A. *Procedures and Standards:* "Everyone has the tendency of wanting people to conform to their own standards. Sure, we here in the functional groups would like to use our own policies and procedures, but we do understand that one of the responsibilities of the team manager is to develop team procedures. This could pose a problem if each team manager has a different procedure for his team. I don't think I'd be very happy being temporarily assigned to another team and then finding a change in the way I'm supposed to do my job.

"I sure as hell hope that the team managers consult the project engineers before policies and procedures are developed. How can anyone expect the functional people to be motivated toward the successful accomplishment of a project when it is obvious that there's a conflict in procedures between the team manager and the project engineer?"

A. *Character of the Team Manager:* "Sometimes I'm not sure that the right man is placed in the right position around here. Upper-level management must look at the ability of a team manager to interact with his people. We have conflicts in our group. Most of our conflicts are probably personality-related. For this reason he must be able to interact. I don't care if he's the world's greatest engineer. If he can't interact with us (and the P.E.'s) then I question whether or not he'll be effective. This boils down to the proverbial question, 'Should people be assigned according to system characteristics or people characteristics?' I have complete confidence in all four team managers. But, if one were weak, I think the new system could easily handle it by having good project engineers available. They (P.E.'s) will be the guys who should make this new system go. I wonder what will happen if a team manager gets promoted? I don't think it will be easy for someone to walk in and fill his shoes. The team managers we have now have an advantage that they've worked the old system and are coming on board at the beginning of the new system so that they can have some say about how the system should be designed and operated. A new man, promoted into a team manager's slot, might not be able to readily adapt to this situation. He (the new manager) will have to work closely with the other three team managers. In the ideal situation, I'd like to see all four team managers think as one. For this reason, I feel that the team managers will probably have some say about who gets promoted to the vacant position when one exists. I'm not so sure that we'll always be able to fill this vacancy from within."

A. *Promotion and Evaluation:* "The big disadvantage I see about the new system is that we've lost our opportunity to excel. We had this chance in the old system, but it looks like it will be difficult to do in the new one.

"I can see a problem in that functional members might be worried about being evaluated by a team manager who doesn't understand their discipline. How can a team manager trained in, say, electronics effectively evaluate the performance of, say, a civil engineer or a piping engineer?

"I expect our team manager to show favoritism during evaluation. Everyone has their favorites. I do think that, overall, everyone will get a fair shake."

Q. Do you think that keeping in touch with technology will suffer in the new system?

A. "No. Each team manager is responsible for keeping two functional group disciplines (i.e., civil and mechanical) up to date with technology. If he does his job, then this effort will consume a great deal of time. And even if he slacks off, I'm not worried because the company has always been good about providing in-house seminars and letting us travel to out-of-house seminars and conferences."

Interview With Team Managers

Q. Do you expect to spend a great deal of your time resolving conflicts?

A. "I want the P.E. to come to me only as a last resort."

A. "I need all information flowing up, especially problems, even if they are resolved by the P.E., so that I can understand them (the people) better and they can understand me."

A. "I expect to have disagreements with the P.E.'s. But even though we have disagreements, we must have mutual respect for each other's opinion."

Q. What do you foresee as some of your biggest problems?

A. *Personnel Evaluation:* "In order for evaluation to be effective, the team managers must talk to one another in order to be consistent. This will probably be the secret to our success. I'm sure the functional people are worried about how we'll end up evaluating those whose disciplines we are not totally familiar with. We're aware of their concern."

Q. Do you have many people who would rather be managers than engineers?

A. "Yes, we have some. We have both a technical ladder and a management performance ladder. People can go back and forth on both, provided they commit. Some of our people place more emphasis on title than on salary."

CASE STUDY: WYNN COMPUTER EQUIPMENT (WCE)

In 1965, Joseph Wynn began building computer equipment in a small garage behind his house. By 1982, WCE was a $1 billion a year manufacturing organization employing 900 people. The major success found by WCE has been attributed to the nondegreed workers who have stayed with WCE over the past 15 years. The nondegreed personnel account for 80 percent of the organization. Both the salary structure and fringe benefit packages are well above the industry average.

CEO Presentation

In February 1982, the new vice president and general manager made a presentation to his executive staff outlining the strategies he wished to see implemented to improve productivity.

Our objective for the next twelve months is to initiate a planning system with the focus on strategic, developmental, and operational plans that will assure continued success of WCE and support for our broad objectives. Our strategy is a four-step process:

- To better clarify expectations and responsibility
- To establish cross-functional goals and objectives
- To provide feedback and performance results to all employees in each level of management
- To develop participation through teamwork

The senior staff will merely act as a catalyst in developing long- and short-term objectives. Furthermore, the senior staff will participate and provide direction and leadership in formulating an integrated manufacturing strategy that is both technology- and human-resources-driven. The final result should be an integrated project plan that will:

- Push decision-making down
- Trust the decision of peers and people in each organization
- Eliminate committee decisions

Emphasis should be on communications that will build and convey ownership in the organization and a *we* approach to surfacing issues and solving problems.

In April 1982, a team of consultants interviewed a cross section of Wynn personnel to determine the "pulse" of the organization. The following information was provided:

- "We have a terrible problem in telling our personnel (both project and functional) exactly what is expected on the project. It is embarrassing to say that we are a computer manufacturer and we do not have any computerized planning and control tools."
- "Our functional groups are very poor planners. We, in the project office, must do the planning for them. They appear to have more confidence in and pay more attention to our project office schedules than to their own."
- "We have recently purchased a $65,000 computerized package for planning and controlling. It is going to take us quite a while to educate our people. In order to interface with the computer package, we must use a work breakdown structure. This is an entirely new concept for our people."
- "We have a lack of team spirit in the organization. I'm not sure if it is simply the result of poor communications. I think it goes further than that. Our priorities get shifted on a weekly basis, and this produces a demoralizing effect. As a result, we cannot get our people to live up to either their old or new commitments."

- "We have a very strong mix of degreed and nondegreed personnel. All new, degreed personnel must 'prove' themselves before officially accepted by the non-degreed personnel. We seem to be splitting the organization down the middle. Technology has become more important than loyalty and tradition and, as a result, the nondegreed personnel, who believe themselves to be the backbone of the organization, now feel cheated. What is a proper balance between experience and new blood?"

- "The emphasis on education shifts with each new executive. Our nondegreed personnel obviously are paying the price. I wish I knew what direction the storm is coming from."

- "My department does not have a data base to use for estimating. Therefore, we have to rely heavily upon the project office for good estimating. Anyway, the project office never gives us sufficient time for good estimating so we have to ask other groups to do our scheduling for us."

- "As line manager, I am caught between the rock and the hard spot. Quite often, I have to act as the project manager and line manager at the same time. When I act as the project manager I have trouble spending enough time with my people. In addition, my duties also include supervising outside vendors at the same time."

- "My departmental personnel have a continuous time management problem because they are never full-time on any one project, and all of our projects never have 100 percent of the resources they need. How can our people ever claim ownership?"

- "We have trouble in conducting up-front feasibility studies to see if we have a viable product. Our manufacturing personnel have poor interfacing with advanced design."

- "If we accept full project management, I'm not sure where the project managers should report. Should we have one group of project managers for new processes/products and a second group for continuous (or old) processes/products? Can both groups report to the same person?"

CASE STUDY: THE TROPHY PROJECT

The ill-fated Trophy Project was in trouble right from the start. Reichart, who had been an assistant project manager, was involved with the project from its conception. When the Trophy Project was accepted by the company, Reichart was assigned as the project manager. The program schedules started to slip from day one, and expenditures were excessive. Reichart found that the functional managers were charging direct labor time to his project but working on their own "pet" projects. When Reichart complained of this, he was told not to meddle in the functional manager's allocation of resources and budgeted expenditures. After approximately six months, Reichart was requested to make a progress report directly to corporate and division staffs.

Reichart took this opportunity to bare his soul. The report substantiated that the project was forecasted to be one complete year behind schedule. Reichart's staff, as supplied by the line managers, was inadequate to stay at the required pace, let alone make up any time that had already been lost. The estimated cost at completion at this interval showed a cost overrun of at least 20 percent. This was Reichart's first opportunity to tell his story to people who were in a position to correct the situation. The result of Reichart's frank, candid evaluation of the Trophy Project was very predictable. Nonbelievers finally saw the light, and the line managers realized that they had a role to play in the completion of the project. Most of the problems were now out in the open and could be corrected by providing adequate staffing and resources. Corporate staff ordered immediate remedial action and staff support to provide Reichart a chance to bail out his program.

The results were not at all what Reichart had expected. He no longer reported to the project office; he now reported directly to the operations manager. Corporate staff's interest in the project became very intense, requiring a 7:00 A.M. meeting every Monday morning for complete review of the project status and plans for recovery. Reichart found himself spending more time preparing paperwork, reports, and projections for his Monday morning meetings than he did administering the Trophy Project. The main concern of corporate was to get the project back on schedule. Reichart spent many hours preparing the recovery plan and establishing manpower requirements to bring the program back onto the original schedule.

Group staff, in order to more closely track the progress of the Trophy Project, assigned an assistant program manager. The assistant program manager determined that a sure cure for the Trophy Project would be to computerize the various problems and track the progress through a very complex computer program. Corporate provided Reichart with twelve additional staff members to work on the computer program. In the meantime, nothing changed. The functional managers still did not provide adequate staff for recovery, assuming that the additional manpower Reichart had received from corporate would accomplish that task.

After approximately $50,000 was spent on the computer program to track the problems, it was found that the program objectives could not be handled by the computer. Reichart discussed this problem with a computer supplier and found that $15,000 more was required for programming and additional storage capacity. It would take two months for installation of the additional storage capacity and the completion of the programming. At this point, the decision was made to abandon the computer program.

Reichart was now a year and a half into the program with no prototype units completed. The program was still nine months behind schedule with the overrun projected at 40 percent of budget. The customer had been receiving his reports on a timely basis and was well aware of the fact that the Trophy Project was behind schedule. Reichart had spent a great deal of time with the customer explaining the problems and the plan for recovery. Another problem that Reichart had to contend with was that the vendors who were supplying components for the project were also running behind schedule.

On Sunday morning, while Reichart was in his office putting together a report for the client, a corporate vice president came into his office. "Reichart," he said, "in any project I look at the top sheet of paper and the man whose name appears at the top of the sheet is the one I hold responsible. For this project your name appears at the top of the sheet. If you cannot bail this thing out, you are in serious trouble in this corporation." Reichart did not know which way to turn or what to say. He had no control over the functional managers who were creating the problems, but he was the person who was being held responsible.

After another three months the customer, becoming impatient, realized that the Trophy Project was in serious trouble and requested that the division general manager and his entire staff visit the customer's plant to give a progress and "get well" report within a week. The division general manager called Reichart into his office and said, "Reichart, go visit our customer. Take three or four functional line people with you and try to placate him with whatever you feel is necessary." Reichart and four functional line people visited the customer and gave a four-and-a-half-hour presentation defining the problems and the progress to that point. The customer was very polite and even commented that it was an excellent presentation, but the content was totally unacceptable. The program was still six to eight months late, and the customer demanded progress reports on a weekly basis. The customer made arrangements to assign a representative in Reichart's department to be "on-site" at the project on a daily basis and to interface with Reichart and his staff as required. After this turn of events, the program became very hectic.

The customer representative demanded constant updates and problem identification and then became involved in attempting to solve these problems. This involvement created many changes in the program and the product in order to eliminate some of the problems. Reichart had trouble with the customer and did not agree with the changes to the program. He expressed his disagreement vocally when, in many cases, the customer felt the changes were at no cost. This caused a deterioration of the relationship between client and producer.

One morning Reichart was called into the division general manager's office and introduced to Mr. "Red" Baron. Reichart was told to turn over the reins of the Trophy Project to Red immediately. "Reichart, you will be temporarily reassigned to some other division within the corporation. I suggest you start looking outside the company for another job." Reichart looked at Red and asked, "Who did this? Who shot me down?"

Red was program manager on the Trophy Project for approximately six months, after which, by mutual agreement, he was replaced by a third project manager. The customer reassigned his local program manager to another project. With the new team the Trophy Project was finally completed one year behind schedule and at a 40 percent cost overrun.

CASE STUDY: STARR AIR FORCE BASE (SAFB)

"You have to remember when looking at SAFB that we have a military structure superimposed on top of a government structure, which, in turn, is superimposed on top of a civilian traditional structure. In addition, we have some sort of project management structure on top of everything. Military personnel get rotated through this maze of interrelationships every two or three years, but the civilian population have to endure it forever. Living with it isn't the problem as long as we understand it, and how it should work. I've been here at SAFB for over 15 years, and I don't think that I fully understand the organization."

History

From its inception in the late 1940s, Starr Air Force Base has historically been a leader in high-technology electronic R&D activities.The majority of the base's military and technical civilian personnel have advanced degrees in technical disciplines. The working atmosphere at SAFB appears to be much more cordial than at other installations because engineers notoriously are interested more in work challenge than in organizational structures, empire-building, and internal politics.

Observations

In the summer of 1981, several employees (GS–9 through GS–15) were interviewed concerning their views of project management at SAFB. The comments that follow indicate their feelings.*

"We must realize that project management here at SAFB is different than in private industry. Industry, especially in project-driven organizations, has profits as their primary concern. SAFB is somewhere between a project- and non-project-driven organization with emphasis on efficiency, productivity, visibility, and mobility rather than profits."

"There are also major differences in the work flow and project size. Most of our projects are in the $200K–$300K range with very few over $1 million. We use project management (with horizontal work flow) primarily to develop an RFP. After the RFP is developed, we seem to have functional control of the project, where a line employee acts as the project monitor. Actually, we are more likely to appear as contract monitors rather than project managers."

"The biggest frustration here appears to be authority. Authority rests with the division managers, especially for the distribution of funds. The branch is responsible for task performance, and section chiefs have responsibility for work units. Although we do have some projects that operate on a horizontal line, most of our projects are controlled at the section level, especially after the RFP is prepared."

"Perhaps the biggest source of frustration in authority is in the civilian–military interface. It is pretty obvious that all of the authority rests with the military, regardless of the reporting level of the civilian project manager. Military personnel sit on the top of our organization, and we have a well-established 'staircase' of management from the bottom up. Unfortunately, the staircase does not work from the top down because many of our military personnel (especially at the top) believe themselves to be the true project managers and meddle in the lower levels of the organization. It is a shame that these senior military types don't realize the damage that they inflict with their meddling and violating of the civilian structures. Sometimes, I believe that the best qualifications for a military leader at SAFB would be a degree in some discipline other than engineering."

"We occasionally have projects that are large enough to support a project office. The project offices generally report to division heads. However, there are projects where the project office fell under the control of a technical advisor."

"Another serious problem is the promotion policy and cycle. Our lower-level people are frustrated with the basic system, but the upper-level personnel are frustrated by the promotion system. Technical expertise does not appear to be a criterion for pro-

---

*Several of these comments have been modified for clarity.

motion. Visibility appears to be most important. Many of our employees are volunteering for project management and project engineering positions so that they can become more visible to top management. The idea is simple: if you continuously make briefings to top management concerning the status of your project, then the executive staff will get to know you on a first-name basis, and your chances for promotion may be greater."

"I wish I knew how industry manages their projects. I would like nothing better than to be able to assist them in time of trouble. Unfortunately, I do not know when, where, or how to interface properly, especially when trade-offs are necessary. Sometimes the person which I interface with in industry sits pretty low in the organization and needs upper-level management approval for decisions. This creates additional frustration."

"Industry seems to have us between the rock and the hard spot once we award them the contract. We do not appear to have any kind of forward financing in order to keep the contractors honest. We must expend all of the funds or lose them. As a result, when the contractor says that he has expended all of the hours or money, work stops, and perhaps there will be no final report. We also have no effective way to evaluate the past performance of contractors who are now bidding."

"Many of our people are technical experts in some engineering discipline, but lack ability or training in other pertinent areas such as cost analysis or proposal preparation. This holds true for proposal evaluation as well as proposal preparation. We place too much emphasis on dollars rather than on performance. We continuously avoid looking at the procurement cycle. Sometimes we have just two weeks to evaluate six-month proposals. Some of our own people have developed a laziness syndrome in detailing information and communications. We consistently look for the easiest way to estimate, and this forces us to make a linear burn rate assumption rather than to look at past history. I simply don't understand why we aren't using some sort of data base."

"Our system has an inherent weakness in that we have bottom-up planning rather than top-down planning. As a result, we (especially top military personnel) shuffle priorities without a strong technical base. Our priority system appears to be directly related to the quantity of paperwork. Since many of our people simply track projects, we spend a lot of time and effort on paperwork. I'm not sure how much tracking is professional. It will take strong leadership to back away from all of this paperwork."

"I don't think that we actually have people here who are project managers, at least not according to industrial definitions. Some of our engineers are program element managers, but do not evaluate. They simply monitor (and sometimes control) funds. Some of our engineers act as consultants to other labs while acting as project element managers."

"My boss gets no feedback from the project office or lead engineer as to my performance on the project. Some people get absolutely no rewards or recognition for work done well. We need recognition ('fill in the squares') for promotion. Also, if we were to go to some kind of merit system based upon performance, we would still need horizonal as well as vertical performance evaluation."

"Our strength here is our technological base. I'm not sure that we can be pushed into projects without sacrificing technology."

"Many of our projects are in 'virgin' territory, and even our line managers lack the necessary information. How do we break into new areas/ground? How do we perform risk assessment here? How do we find the right projects and put manpower on the right work? Many of our best ideas originate in the depths of the working area but still require upper-level approval."

"I would like to see project management at SAFB where project managers could be equivalent to division heads or at least a GS–14. That would eliminate some of the 'log jam' that we have in the GS–12 through GS–14 slots. Under this type of arrangement we can train people to become professional project managers by creating a separate line function for perhaps up to ten full-time project managers. If an employee wants a vertical rather than horizontal career, he can go back to a line function/ position for vertical promotion."

"This concept of creating a line group of project managers has an interesting application. Within industry, project management is an ideal way to give people exposure to the operation of the entire company. Perhaps we can employ that concept here at SAFB. Any person aspiring to become a branch or division manager must first have a tour of duty in project management before fulfilling this position. Therefore, branch and division managers will become knowledgeable in total SAFB operations rather than their own line group. This type of training would be invaluable for military personnel as well as civilian person and would be compatible with the SPO training provided at Wright-Patterson Air Force Base."

"If we try to implement any change like this at SAFB, will we need approval at the AFSC level? Will this change have to be made at all agencies of AFSC?"

"Conflicts cannot be resolved at the lower levels of management. By decree, any issue must go upstairs, and we end up getting help that we don't want or need."

"If we go to project management, we'll have trouble with the military because they also must be visible for promotion. Military personnel will probably take the key project management slots and leave the crumbs for us. Lately, military officers have taken over some of the key (branch and division) postions formerly held by civilians. This creates frustration for civilians because it limits their career progression."

"Most industrial companies have three career paths: technical, line management, and project management. Here, at SAFB, we recognize only the first two, with the third one being implied."

"Can we set up project management as though it is a mini SPO?"

"How can we prevent micro-management by our senior personnel?"

"Sometimes I have been given a direct order by military officers not to report any bad news on projects because the officers are fearful that bad news on projects may have a serious impact on their evaluation for promotion. So we conceal the bad news until the officer gets rotated to another assignment, and then the replacement gets greeted with a surprise."

In-house Training

Two hundred hours of in-house training programs on project management were scheduled for 1981–82 in order to introduce both military and civilian personnel to the discipline of project management. Prior to the seminar, forty-eight employees were asked to rank the twenty-one topics that were to be covered during the seminars. The results are shown in Exhibit 5–1.

Job Descriptions

One of the major difficulties in going to a project management line organization is in developing job descriptions for the various GS grade levels. Exhibits 5–2 through 5–5 show the current job descriptions of various GS grades for electronic engineers. The difficulty is in the creation of job descriptions for various levels of project management/project engineering. Using Exhibits 5–2 through 5–5 as the basis, how can we create meaningful job descriptions that distinguish between the responsibilities of various project management pay grades?

Exhibit 5–1.

Results of the project management course outline questionnaire are shown below. Forty-eight people were asked to rank the twenty-one elements in the questionnaire on a scale of 1 through 5, with 5 being the top choice.

RANK	TOPIC	TOTAL POINTS
1	Managing total resources	220
2	Program scheduling	209
3	Project management bottlenecks	203
4	Planning and organizing work	196
5	Communications	187
6	Human resources management	182
7	Pricing: the final phase of planning	179
8	Preparing proposals and bids	179
9	Expectations and interface	175
10	Cost control	173
11	Project management concepts	171
12	The evaluation process	171
13	The selection process	170
14	Total interface relationships	169
15	Negotiations	168
16	Definitions and job descriptions	165
17	Network scheduling	164
18	Conflicts	164
19	Computerized project planning	159
20	Organizational structures	153
21	Case studies	152

Exhibit 5–2. GS–7 Electronics Engineer.

I. DUTIES AND RESPONSIBILITIES:
1. Designs electronic equipment of moderate complexity that forms a part of a system. Uses higher mathematics such as algebra and calculus in establishing design characteristics and parameters.
2. Makes comprehensive studies of existing techniques and equipment in use and by a search and study of pertinent engineering data and technical reports for possible application to assignments.
3. Makes evaluations and prepares reports on findings involving design, construction, and final performance of a specific task. Makes recommendations and decisions that affect the program with regard to evaluation of new equipment and new developments.
4. Evaluates equipment in relation to other portions of overall task by devising test procedures, compiling and evaluating test data. Makes engineering modifications of assigned equipment or of associated equipment as a result of analysis of test results.
5. Constructs breadboard models of circuitry for use in investigation and analyses of circuits. Selects types and layout of chassis for best electrical and mechanical effect. Exercises initiative in obtaining design criteria for existing literature. Uses judgment in selecting circuit best suited for the particular need.
6. Meets with engineers within the laboratory to explain work accomplished.
7. Receives classroom and on-the-job training related to assigned field of work.

II. CONTROLS OVER WORK:
Works under close guidance and instruction from supervisor who gives oral or written instructions pertaining to work assignments. Work is reviewed often for technical adequacy and accuracy through discussion on written progress reports.

Exhibit 5–3. GS–9 Electronics Engineer.

I. DUTIES AND RESPONSIBILITIES:
1. Analyzes problems, studies technical literature and existing technology, and discusses with supervisor or other personnel having experience in assigned area to obtain information pertaining to problem area.
2. Compiles basic technical data for the preparation of necessary specifications, exhibits, and exhibit revisions, stating technical requirements, tests, and test procedures required in accordance with AFSC directives.
3. Evaluates bid proposals of prospective contractors to determine contractor best qualified to accomplish work. Recommends contractor most suitable for the particular contract taking into consideration proposed approach to problem, personnel, and facilities to be expended. Attends bidders conferences to explain the requirements of the contractor and to answer questions pertaining thereto.
4. Administers engineering aspects of contract by evaluating suitability of technique and components proposed by contractor an proposed deviations fom specification requirements. Evaluates and reports on contractor's progress and recommends major changes or authorized minor changes.

5. Designs and constructs breadboard models and runs tests in validating engineering or scientific concepts applicable to assignment. Analyzes test data and recommends changes in approach to supervisor. These recommendations may influence the design of equipment/techniques in the experimental stages.
6. Attends test runs and evaluates test data before recommending acceptance of equipment/techniques. Writes or approves technical manual outlining operating techniques of equipment.
7. Attends meetings with representatives of SAFB and other Centers, contractors, and universities in gathering and dispensing technical information for application to assigned area.
8. Receives classroom and on-the-job training related to assigned field of work.

II. CONTROLS OVER WORK:

Receives work assignments from supervisor or higher grade employee who provides guidance on problems arising and determines effectiveness of results in meeting requirements. Receives on-the-job training, including instruction and guided practice in performing duty assignments. classroom training is evaluated through discussion/written progress reports. Guidelines are in the form of technical pamphlets, articles, textbooks, techniques, and advances in the field.

Exhibit 5–4. GS–11 Electronics Engineer.

I. DUTIES AND RESPONSIBILITIES:

1. Exercises initiative and originality in analyzing requirements, determining problem areas, and establishing approaches for solution to engineering problems. Investigates and analyzes all possible sources of data in assigned field to determine the feasibility, utility, and accuracy of these sources as related to assigned problems. Researches technical literature for new or existing equipment and/or techniques to determine possible application to assignments, or recommends modifications of the techniques that can be applied. Makes recommendations and decisions as a result of analysis and investigations on techniques and/or equipment that can be utilized as developed to meet AF requirements. Uses initiative and originality in analyzing requirements, determining problems.
2. Determines contractor services required to develop equipment/techniques as assigned. Writes engineering exhibits for the work to be performed on contract; reviews and evaluates technical proposals received from interested contractors; recommends those qualified to perform work based on their technical capabilities. Administers technical portion of contract by monitoring work performed at contractor's plant. This entails observing experiments being conducted, discussing methods being utilized, and/or determining alternate methods to alleviate unsatisfactory progress. Evaluates progress reports and final engineering report prepared by the contractor to ensure that contractual requirements are met. Plans and conducts acceptance test; approves or disapproves contractual effort on the basis of equipment performance and compliance with contractual requirements.
3. Submits budget estimates to supervisor for future work to be accomplished in

accordance with known requirements. Prepares documentation including technical plans and estimates of funds, manpower, facilities to accomplish the programs using the AFSC Program Management instruction guidelines.

4. Attends conferences with personnel of universities, operational commands, other Center and government agencies to discuss present and contemplated applied research efforts in assigned area, present results of experimentation, and obtain and/or exchange information for application to problems.

5. Writes technical memorandums, reports, and papers, outlining development of techniques and/or equipment to resolve technical problems; specifies approaches taken, results achieved, test administered, data accumulated, correlations and evaluations made, and conclusions reached. Makes specific recommendations based on peculiar data taken in tests that is unexplainable and should be investigated.

II. CONTROLS OVER WORK:

Receives general work assignments from supervisor. Objectives, time limitations, priorities, and unusual problems are dscussed and resolved by supervisor. Work is reviewed upon completion for compliance with overall objectives and conformances to established engineering practices and branch policy. Guidelines are established policies, precedents, engineering techniques, and standard and technical reports and textbooks.

III. OTHER SIGNIFICANT FACTS:

Requires a thorough understanding of engineering techniques and theory gained through four years of engineering training in a recognized college or university, or training equivalent in type, scope, and thoroughness. Travel by military aircraft is required in accomplishment of assignments.

Exhibit 5–5. GS–14 Electronics Engineer.

I. DUTIES AND RESPONSIBILITIES:

1. Serves as the SAFB technical focal point and lead engineer for the development of a secure, efficient system. Conceives, plans, formulates, and guides applied research, techniques, and analysis studies. This involves the development of advanced/improved components. Resolutions of problem areas represent significant advances in the state-of-the-art and pave the way for extensive related developments and/or eventually result in a new technique or practical device.

2. Conducts detailed scientific studies and investigations on exceptionally difficult scientific problems. Assumes complete technical responsibility for formulating plans and hypotheses, interpreting findings, and carrying them through to completion. Serves as group leader in generating ideas and studies to be pursued by personnel within the section.

3. Authors technical papers of new and complex techniques and devices specifying analysis and evaluation from an advanced technological point of view. These papers are of considerable interest to the professional community in that the contributed inventions, designs, or techniques involved are of material significance in the solution of critical problems for application to R&D

programs. Outlines development or design problems, approaches taken, results achieved, tests performed, data accumulated, correlations and evaluations made, and conclusions reached. Exercises considerable scientific skill and authoritative knowledge of conventional and unconventional techniques.

4. Provides technical guidance and advisory services in assigned areas to SAFB personnel, other Centers, and other military and civil agencies engaged in similar or related technical areas; specifies techniques and design criteria to be used to maximize the efficiency of new and novel strategic command and control systems/techniques.

5. Serves as Air Force representative on mission analysis studies, technical committees, and teams of service and interservice high-level personnel for the purposes of evaluating technical approaches, guiding and/or recommending optimum technology as required. Analyzes reports or literature emanating from studies, techniques investigation, and systems design in association with keeping abreast of other technological source documentation, to ascertain a well-directed continuous technological flow toward immediate and long-range goals. Identifies areas and initiates action where redirection is deemed advisable.

6. Studies and evaluates scientific and engineering proposals submitted by contractor personnel containing radically new or novel approaches, criteria, techniques, and engineering design. Renders scientific judgments; recommends modifications and alterations, and/or determines feasibility of approaches and design features and the desirability an acceptability of such proposals.

7. Visits contractor's plant and universities to discuss technical requirements and objectives of research and development projects and to review progress of contractual work. Provides technical guidance and instructs contractors to vary the emphasis being placed on different phases of the program; establishes trends to be followed on controversial programs; resolves technical differences and makes decisions when modifications or selection of different modes of approach is required to meet desired objective. These decisions are often precedent-setting and are the basis for planning future research and development.

8. Attends symposia in professional engineering fields of interest to branch to exchange information on work performed. Conducts studies on specific programs that may arise from general requirements placed on the division to meet new requirements, or result from changing field operational concepts. Recognizes problems needing solution, and recommends possible method of solution.

9. Represents the Center at conferences with personnel of other Centers.

10. Maintins continuous review and analysis of applicable research and development programs of SAFB, other Centers, Defense Department, and civilian agencies and the operational requirements received from higher headquarters to determine research and development effort required and ensure that latest state-of-the-art is reflected in SAFB effort to meet Air Force operational requirements.

11. Serve as group leader and exercises technical control over personnel engaged

in in-house and contractual efforts to develop new and novel concepts which are necessary for the successful exploitation of strategic command and control.

II. CONTROLS OVER WORK:

Works under general administrative supervision of section chief. Briefs superior on the status of planning and plan accomplishments. Work is reviewed for conformance with broad directives and policy; technical findings and recommendations are accepted as authoritative and conclusive. Although precedents are practically nonexistent for the major portion of assignments, guidelines are available in the form of broad requirements and policy statements received from higher headquarters.

III. OTHER SIGNIFICANT FACTS:

Requires a thorough understandig of engineering/scientific techniques and methods gained though four years of engineering/scientific training in a recognized college or university, or training equivalent in type, scope, and thoroughness, and several years of experience in specialized areas.

CASE STUDY: LEADERSHIP EFFECTIVENESS (A)

Instructions

This form is concerned with a comparison of personal supervisory styles. Indicate your preference to the two alternatives after each item by writing appropriate figures in the blanks. Some of the alternatives may seem equally attractive or unattractive to you. Nevertheless, please attempt to choose the alternative that is relatively more characteristic of you. For each question given, you have three (3) points that you may distribute in any of the following combinations:

A. If you agree with alternative (a) and disagree with (b), write 3 in the top blank and 0 in the bottom blank.

    a. _3_

    b. _0_

B. If you agree with (b) and disagree with (a), write:

    a. _0_

    b. _3_

C. If you have a slight preference for (a) over (b), write:

    a. _2_

    b. _1_

D. If you have a slight preference for (b) over (a), write:

    a. _1_

    b. _2_

Important—Use only the combinations shown above. Try to relate each item to your own personal experience. Please make a choice from every pair of alternatives.

1. On the job, a project manager should make a decision and . . .

   a. _____ tell his team to carry it out.

   b. _____ "tell" his team about the decision and then try to "sell" it.

2. After a project manager has arrived at a decision . . .

   a. _____ he should try to reduce the team's resistance to his decisions by indicating what they have to gain.

   b. _____ he should provide an opportunity for his team to get a fuller explanation of his ideas.

3. When a project manager presents a problem to his subordinates . . .

   a. _____ he should get suggestions from them and then make a decision.

   b. _____ he should define it and request the group make a decision.

4. A project manager . . .

   a. _____ is paid to make all the decisions affecting the work of his team.

   b. _____ should commit himself in advance to assist in implementing whatever decision his team selects when they are asked to solve a problem.

5. A project manager should . . .

   a. _____ permit his team an opportunity to exert some influence on decisions but reserves final decisions for himself.

   b. _____ participate with his team in group decision-making but attempt to do so with a minimum of authority.

6. In making a decision concerning the work situation, a project manager should . . .

   a. _____ present his decision and ideas and engage in a "give-and-take" session with his team to allow them to fully explore the implications of the decision.

   b. _____ present the problem to his team, get suggestions, and then make a decision.

7. A good work situation is one in which the project manager . . .

   a. _____ "tells" his team about a decision and then tries to "sell" it to them.

   b. _____ calls his team together, presents a problem, defines the problem, and requests they solve the problem with the understanding he will support their decision(s).

8. A well-run project will include . . .

   a. _____ efforts by the project manager to reduce the team's resistance to his decisions by indicating what they have to gain from them.

   b. _____ "give-and-take" sessions to enable the project manager and team to explore more fully the implications of the project manager's decisions.

9. A good way to deal with people in a work situation is . . .

   a. _____ to present to your team, problems as they arise; get suggestions and then make a decision.

   b. _____ to permit the team to make decisions, with the understanding that the project manager will assist in implementing whatever decision they make.

10. A good project manager is one who takes . . .

    a. _____ the responsibility for locating problems and arriving at solutions, then tries to persuade his team to accept them.

    b. _____ the opportunity to collect ideas from his team about problems, then he makes his decision.

11. A project manager . . .

    a. _____ should make the decisions in his organization and tell his team to carry them out.

    b. _____ should work closely with his team in solving problems, and attempt to do so with a minimum of authority.

12. To do a good job, a project manager should . . .

    a. _____ present solutions for his team's reaction.

    b. _____ present the problem and collect from the team suggested solutions, then make a decision based on the best solution offered.

13. A good method for a project manager is . . .

    a. _____ to "tell" and then try to "sell" his decision.

    b. _____ define the problem for his team, then pass them the right to make decisions.

14. On the job, a project manager . . .

    a. _____ need not give consideration to what his team will think or feel about his decisions.

    b. _____ should present his decisions and engage in a "give-and-take" session to enable everyone concerned to explore, more fully, the implications of the decision.

15. A project manager . . .

   a. _____ should make all decisions himself.

   b. _____ should present the problem to his team, get suggestions, and then make a decision.

16. It is good . . .

   a. _____ to permit the team an opportunity to exert some influence on decisions, but the project manager should reserve final decisions for himself.

   b. _____ for the project manager to participate with his team in group decision-making with as little authority as possible.

17. The project manager who gets the most from his team is the one who . . .

   a. _____ exercises direct authority.

   b. _____ seeks possible solutions from them and then makes a decision.

18. An effective project manager should . . .

   a. _____ make the decisions on his project and tell his team to carry them out.

   b. _____ make the decisions and then try to persuade his team to accept them.

19. A good way for a project manager to handle work problems is to . . .

   a. _____ implement decisions without giving any consideration to what his team will think or feel.

   b. _____ permit the team an opportunity to exert some influence on decisions but reserve final decision for himself.

20. Project managers . . .

   a. _____ should seek to reduce the team's resistance to their decisions by indicating what they have to gain from them.

   b. _____ should seek possible solutions from their team when problems arise and then make a decision from the list of alternatives.

CASE STUDY: LEADERSHIP EFFECTIVENESS (B)

The Project

Your company has just won a contract for an outside customer. The contract is for one year, broken down as follows: R&D: six months; prototype testing: one month; manufacturing: five months. In addition to the risks involved in the R&D stage, both your management and the customer have stated that there absolutely will be no tradeoffs on time, cost, or performance.

LEADERSHIP QUESTIONNAIRE
Tabulation Form

	1	2	3	4	5
1	a	b			
2		a	b		
3				a	b
4	a				b
5			a		b
6			a	b	
7		a			b
8		a	b		
9				a	b
10	a		b		
11	a				b
12			a	b	
13		a			b
14	a		b		
15	a			b	
16			a		b
17	a			b	
18	a	b			
19	a		b		
20		a		b	
TOTAL					

LEADERSHIP GUIDE

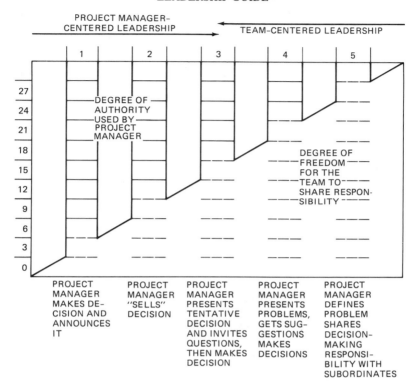

| PROJECT MANAGER MAKES DECISION AND ANNOUNCES IT | PROJECT MANAGER "SELLS" DECISION | PROJECT MANAGER PRESENTS TENTATIVE DECISION AND INVITES QUESTIONS, THEN MAKES DECISION | PROJECT MANAGER PRESENTS PROBLEMS, GETS SUGGESTIONS, MAKES DECISIONS | PROJECT MANAGER DEFINES PROBLEM SHARES DECISION-MAKING RESPONSIBILITY WITH SUBORDINATES |

When you prepared the proposal six months ago, you planned and budgeted for a full time staff of five people, in addition to the functional support personnel. Unfortunately, due to limited resources, your staff (i.e., the project office) will be as follows:

Tom: An excellent engineer, somewhat of a prima donna, but has worked very well with you on previous projects. You specifically requested Tom and were fortunate to have him assigned, although your project is not regarded as a high priority. Tom is recognized as both a technical leader and expert, and is considered as perhaps the best engineer in the company. Tom will be full-time for the duration of the project.

Bob: Started with the company a little over a year ago, and may be a little "green behind the ears." His line manager has great expectations for him in the future but, for the time being, wants you to give him on-the-job-training as a project office team member. Bob will be full-time on your project.

Carol: She has been with the company for twenty years and does an acceptable job. She has never worked on your projects before. She is full-time on the project.

George: He has been with the company for six years, but has never worked on any of your projects. His superior tells you that he will be only half-time on your project until he finishes a crash job on another project. He should be available for full-time work in a month or two. George is regarded as an outstanding employee.

Management informs you that there is nobody else available to fill the fifth position. You'll have to spread the increased work load over the other members. Obviously, the customer may not be too happy about this.

In each situation which follows, circle the best answer. The grading system will be provided later.

Remember: these staff individuals are "dotted" to you and "solid" to their line manager, although they are in your project office.

Situation 1: The project office team members have been told to report to you this morning. They have all received your memo concerning the time and place of the kickoff meeting. However, they have not been provided any specific details concerning the project except that the project will be at least one year in duration. For your company, this is regarded as a long-term project. A good strategy for the meeting would be:

  A. The team must already be self-motivated or else they would not have been assigned. Simply welcome them and assign homework.
  B. Motivate the employees by showing them how they will benefit; esteem, pride, self-actualization. Minimize discussion on specifics.
  C. Explain the project and ask them for their input. Try to get them to identify alternatives and encourage group decision making.
  D. Identify the technical details of the project; the requirements, performance standards, and expectations.

Situation 2: You give the team members a copy of the winning proposal and a "confidential" memo describing the assumptions and constraints you considered in developing the proposal. You tell your team to review the material and be prepared to perform detailed planning at the meeting you have scheduled for the following Monday. During Monday's planning meeting, you find that Tom (who has worked with you before) has established a take-charge role and has done some of the planning that should have been the responsibility of other team members. You should:

  A. Do nothing. This may be a beneficial situation. However, you may wish to ask if the other project office members wish to review Tom's planning.
  B. Ask each team member individually how they feel about Tom's role. If they complain, have a talk with Tom.
  C. Ask each team member to develop their own schedules and then compare results.
  D. Talk to Tom privately about the long-term effects of his behavior.

Situation 3: Your team appears to be having trouble laying out realistic schedules which will satisfy the customer's milestones. They keep asking you pertinent questions and seem to be making the right decisions, but with difficulty.

A. Do nothing. If the team is good, they will eventually work out the problem.
B. Encourage the team to continue but give some ideas as to possible alternatives. Let them solve the problem.
C. Become actively involved and help the team solve the problem. Supervise the planning until completion.
D. Take charge yourself and solve the problem for the team. You may have to provide continuous direction.

Situation 4: Your team has taken an optimistic approach to the schedule. The functional managers have reviewed the schedules and have sent your team strong memos stating that there is no way that they can support your schedules. Your team's morale appears to be very low. Your team expected the schedules to be returned for additional iterations and tradeoffs, but not with such harsh words from the line managers. You should:

A. Take no action. This is common to these types of projects and the team must learn to cope.
B. Call a special team meeting to discuss the morale problem and ask the team for recommendations. Try to work out the problem.
C. Meet with each team member individually to reinforce their behavior and performance. Let them know how many other times this has occurred and been resolved through tradeoffs and additional iterations. State your availability to provide advice and support.
D. Take charge and look for ways to improve morale by changing the schedules.

Situation 5: The functional departments have begun working, but are still criticizing the schedules. Your team is extremely unhappy with some of the employees assigned out of one functional department. Your team feels that these employees are not qualified to perform the required work. You should:

A. Do nothing until you are absolutely sure (with evidence) that the assigned personnel cannot perform as needed.
B. Sympathize with your team and encourage them to live with this situation until an alternative is found.
C. Assess the potential risks with the team and ask for their input and suggestions. Try to develop contingency plans if the problem is as serious as the team indicates.
D. Approach the functional manager and express your concern. Ask to have different employees assigned.

Situation 6: Bob's performance as a project office team member has begun to deteriorate. You are not sure whether he simply lacks the skills, cannot endure the pressure, or cannot assume part of the additional work that resulted from the fifth position in the project being vacant. You should:

A. Do nothing. The problem may be temporary and you cannot be sure that there is a measurable impact on the project.
B. Have a personal discussion with Bob, seek out the cause, and ask him for a solution.
C. Call a team meeting and discuss how productivity and performance are decreasing. Ask the team for recommendations and hope Bob gets the message.
D. Interview the other team members and see if they can explain Bob's actions lately. Ask the other members to assist you by talking to Bob.

Situation 7: George, who is half-time on your project, has just submitted for your approval his quarterly progress report for your project. After your signature has been attained, the report is sent to senior management and the customer. The report is marginally acceptable and not at all what you would have expected from George. George apologizes to you for the report and blames it upon his other project, which is in its last two weeks. You should:

A. Sympathize with George and ask him to rewrite the report.
B. Tell George that the report is totally unacceptable and will reflect upon his ability as a project office team member.
C. Ask the team to assist George in redoing the report since a bad report reflects upon everyone.
D. Ask one of the other team members to rewrite the report for George.

Situation 8: You have completed the R&D stage of your project and are entering phase II: Prototype testing. You are entering month seven of the twelve month project. Unfortunately, the results of phase I: R&D indicate that you were too optimistic in your estimating for phase II and a schedule slippage of at least two weeks is highly probable. The customer may not be happy. You should:

A. Do nothing. These problems occur and have a way of working themselves out. The end date of the project can still be met.
B. Call a team meeting to discuss the morale problem resulting from the slippage. If morale is improved, the slippage may be overcome.
C. Call a team meeting and seek ways of improving productivity for phase II. Hopefully, the team will come up with alternatives.
D. This is a crisis and you must exert strong leadership. You should take control and assist your team in identifying alternatives.

Situation 9: Your rescheduling efforts have been successful. The functional managers have given you adequate support and you are back on schedule. You should:

A. Do nothing. Your team has matured and is doing what they are paid to do.
B. Try to provide some sort of monetary or nonmonetary reward for your team. (i.e., management-granted time off or a dinner team meeting.)
C. Provide positive feedback/reinforcement for the team and search for ideas for shortening phase III.

D. Obviously, your strong leadership has been effective. Continue this role for the phase III schedule.

Situation 10: You are now at the end of the seventh month and everything is proceeding as planned. Motivation appears high: You should:

A. Leave well enough alone.
B. Look for better ways to improve the functioning of the team. Talk to them and make them feel important.
C. Call a team meeting and review the remaining schedules for the project. Look for contingency plans.
D. Make sure the team is still focusing on the goals and objectives of the project.

Situation 11: The customer unofficially informs you that his company has a problem and may have to change the design specifications before production actually begins. This would be a catastrophe for your project. The customer wants a meeting at your plant within the next seven days. This will be the customer's first visit to your plant. All previous meetings were informal and at the customer's facilities, with just you and the customer. This meeting will be formal. To prepare for the meeting, you should:

A. Make sure the schedules are updated and assume a passive role since the customer has not officially informed you of his problem.
B. Ask the team to improve productivity before the customer's meeting. This should please the customer.
C. Call an immediate team meeting and ask the team to prepare an agenda and identify the items to be discussed.
D. Assign specific responsibilities to each team member for preparation of handout material for the meeting.

Situation 12: Your team is obviously not happy with the results of the customer interface meeting because the customer has asked for a change in design specifications. The manufacturing plans and manufacturing schedules must be developed anew. You should:

A. Do nothing. The team is already highly motivated and will take charge as before.
B. Reemphasize the team spirit and encourage your people to proceed. Tell them that nothing is impossible for a good team.
C. Roll up your shirt sleeves and help the team identify alternatives. Some degree of guidance is necessary.
D. Provide strong leadership and close supervision. Your team will have to rely upon you for assistance.

Situation 13: You are now in the ninth month. while your replanning is going on (as a result of changes in the specifications), the customer calls and asks for an assessment of the risks in cancelling this project right away and starting another one. You should:

A. Wait for a formal request. Perhaps you can delay long enough for the project to finish.

B. Tell the team that their excellent performance may result in a follow-on contract.

C. Call a team meeting to assess the risks and look for alternatives.

D. Accept strong leadership for this and with *minimum,* if any, team involvement.

Situation 14: One of the functional managers has asked for your evaluation of all of his functional employees currently working on your project (excluding project office personnel). Your project office personnel appear to be working closer with the functional employees than you are. You should:

A. Return the request to the functional manager since this is not part of your job description.

B. Talk to each team member individually telling them how important their input is and ask for their evaluations.

C. As a team, evaluate each of the functional team members, and try to come to some sort of agreement.

D. Do not burden your team with this request. You can do it yourself.

Situation 15: You are in the tenth month of the project. Carol informs you that she has the opportunity to be the project leader for an effort starting in two weeks. She has been with the company for twenty years and this is her first opportunity as a project leader. She wants to know if she can be released from your project. You should:

A. Let Carol go. You do not want to stand in the way of her career advancement.

B. Ask the team to meet in private and conduct a vote. Tell Carol you will abide by the team vote.

C. Discuss the problem with the team since they must assume the extra work load, if necessary. Ask for their input into meeting the constraints.

D. Counsel her and explain how important it is for her to remain. You are already short-handed.

Situation 16: Your team informs you that one of the functional manufacturing managers has built up a brick wall around his department and all information requests must flow through him. The brick wall has been in existence for two years. Your team members are having trouble with status reporting, but always get the information after catering to the functional manager. You should:

A. Do nothing. This is obviously the way the line manager wants to run his department. Your team is getting the information they need.

B. Ask the team members to use their behavioral skills in obtaining the information.

C. Call a team meeting to discuss alternative ways of obtaining the information.

D. Assume strong leadership and exert your authority by calling the line manager and asking for the information.

Situation 17: The executives have given you a new man to replace Carol for the last two months of the project. Neither you nor your team have worked with this man before. You should:

A. Do nothing. Carol obviously filled him in on what he should be doing and what is involved in the project.
B. Counsel the new man individually, bring him up to speed, and assign him Carol's work.
C. Call a meeting and ask each member to explain their role on the project to the new man.
D. Ask each team member to talk to this man as soon as possible and help him come on board. Request that individual conversations be used.

Situation 18: One of your team members wants to take a late afternoon course at the local college. Unfortunately, this course may conflict with his workload. You should:

A. Postpone your decision. Ask the employee to wait until the course is offered again.
B. Review the request with the team member and discuss the impact on his performance.
C. Discuss the request with the team and ask for the team's approval. The team may have to cover for this employee's workload.
D. Discuss this individually with each team member to make sure that the task requirements will still be adhered to.

Situation 19: Your functional employees have used the wrong materials in making a production run test. The cost to your project was significant, but absorbed in a small "cushion" which you saved for emergencies as this. Your team members tell you that the test will be rerun without any slippage of the schedule. You should:

A. Do nothing. Your team seems to have the situation well under control.
B. Interview the employess that created this problem and stress the importance of productivity and following instructions.
C. Ask your team to develop contingency plans for this situation should it happen again.
D. Assume a strong leadership role for the rerun test to let people know your concern.

Situation 20: All good projects must come to an end, usually with a final report. Your project has a requirement for a final report. This final report may very well become the basis for follow-on work. You should:

A. Do nothing. Your team has things under control and knows that a final report is needed.
B. Tell your team that they have done a wonderful job and there is only one more task to do.
C. Ask your team to meet and provide an outline for the final report.
D. You must provide some degree of leadership for the final report, at least the structure. The final report could easily reflect on your ability as a manager.

Fill in the table below. The answers appear in Appendix D.

Situation	Answer	Points	Situation	Answer	Points
1			11		
2			12		
3			13		
4			14		
5			15		
6			16		
7			17		
8			18		
9			19		
10			20		
				TOTAL	

CASE STUDY: MOTIVATIONAL QUESTIONNAIRE

On the next several pages, you will find 40 questions concerning what motivates you and how you try to motivate others. Beside each question, circle the number that corresponds to your opinion. In the example below, your choice would have been "Slightly Agree."

−3	Strongly Disagree
−2	Disagree
−1	Slightly Disagree
0	No Opinion
(+1)	Slightly Agree
+2	Agree
+3	Strongly Agree

Example: (−3, −2, −1, 0, +1, +2, +3)
The row of numbers from −3 to +3 will be used later for evaluating the results.

Part 1

The following 20 questions involve *what motivates you*. Please answer each of the following twenty questions as honestly as possible. Mark the appropriate answer which you think is correct, *not* the answer which you think the instructor is looking for:

1. My company pays me a reasonable salary for the work that I do.
   -3 -2 -1 0 $+1$ $+2$ $+3$

2. My company believes that every job that I do can be considered as a challenge.
   -3 -2 -1 0 $+1$ $+2$ $+3$

3. The company provides me with the latest equipment (i.e., hardware, software, etc.) so I can do my job effectively.
   -3 -2 -1 0 $+1$ $+2$ $+3$

4. My company provides me with recognition for work well done.
   -3 -2 -1 0 $+1$ $+2$ $+3$

5. Seniority on the job, job security, and vested rights are provided by the company.
   -3 -2 -1 0 $+1$ $+2$ $+3$

6. Executives provide managers with feedback of strategic or long-range information that may affect the manager's job.
   -3 -2 -1 0 $+1$ $+2$ $+3$

7. My company provides off-hour clubs and organizations so that employees can socialize, as well as sponsoring social events.
   -3 -2 -1 0 $+1$ $+2$ $+3$

8. Employees are allowed to either set their own work/performance standards or to at least approve/review standards set for them by management.
   -3 -2 -1 0 $+1$ $+2$ $+3$

9. Employees are encouraged to maintain membership in professional societies and/or attend seminars and symposiums on work-related subjects.
   -3 -2 -1 0 $+1$ $+2$ $+3$

10. The company often reminds me that the only way to have job security is to compete effectively in the marketplace.
    -3 -2 -1 0 $+1$ $+2$ $+3$

11. Employees that develop a reputation for "excellence" are allowed to further enhance their reputation, if job-related.
    -3 -2 -1 0 $+1$ $+2$ $+3$

12. Supervisors encourage a friendly, cooperative working environment for employees	−3	−2	−1	0	+1	+2	+3
13. My company provides me with a detailed job description, identifying my role and responsibilities.	−3	−2	−1	0	+1	+2	+3
14. My company gives *automatic,* wage and salary increases for the employees.	−3	−2	−1	0	+1	+2	+3
15. My company gives me the opportunity to do what I do best.	−3	−2	−1	0	+1	+2	+3
16. My job gives me the opportunity to be truly creative, to the point where I can solve complex problems.	−3	−2	−1	0	+1	+2	+3
17. My efficiency and effectiveness is improving because the company provided me with better physical working conditions (i.e., lighting, low noise, temperature, restrooms, etc.).	−3	−2	−1	0	+1	+2	+3
18. My job gives me constant self-development.	−3	−2	−1	0	+1	+2	+3
19. Our supervisors have feelings for employees rather than simply treating them as "inanimate tools."	−3	−2	−1	0	+1	+2	+3
20. Participation in the company's stock option/retirement plan is available to employees.	−3	−2	−1	0	+1	+2	+3

Part 2

Questions 21–40 involve how project managers motivate team members. Again, it is important that your answers honestly reflect the way you think that *you,* as project manager, try to motivate employees. Do *not* indicate the way others or the instructor might recommend motivating the employees. Your thoughts are what are important in this exercise.

21. Project managers should encourage employees to take advantage of company benefits as stock option plans and retirement plans.	−3	−2	−1	0	+1	+2	+3
22. Project managers should make sure that team members have a good work environment (i.e., heat, lighting, low noise, restrooms, cafeteria, etc.).	−3	−2	−1	0	+1	+2	+3
23. Project managers should assign team members work that can enhance each team member's reputation.	−3	−2	−1	0	+1	+2	+3

24. Project managers should create a   −3 −2 −1 0 +1 +2 +3
relaxed, cooperative environment for
the team members.

25. Project managers should *continuously*   −3 −2 −1 0 +1 +2 +3
remind the team that job security is a
function of competitiveness, staying
within constraints, and good customer
relations.

26. Project managers should try to   −3 −2 −1 0 +1 +2 +3
convince team members that each
new assignment is a challenge.

27. Project managers should be willing to   −3 −2 −1 0 +1 +2 +3
reschedule activities, if possible,
around the team's company and
out-of-company social functions.

28. Project managers should continuously   −3 −2 −1 0 +1 +2 +3
remind employees of how they will
benefit, monetarily, by successful
performance on your project.

29. Project managers should be willing to   −3 −2 −1 0 +1 +2 +3
"pat people on the back" and provide
recognition where applicable.

30. Project managers should encourage   −3 −2 −1 0 +1 +2 +3
the team to maintain constant
self-development with each
assignment.

31. Project managers should allow team   −3 −2 −1 0 +1 +2 +3
members to set their own standards,
where applicable.

32. Project managers should assign work   −3 −2 −1 0 +1 +2 +3
to functional employees according to
seniority on the job.

33. Project managers should allow team   −3 −2 −1 0 +1 +2 +3
members to use the informal, as well
as formal, organization to get work
accomplished.

34. As a project manager, I would like to   −3 −2 −1 0 +1 +2 +3
control the salaries of the full-time
employees on my project.

35. Project managers should share   −3 −2 −1 0 +1 +2 +3
information with the team. This
includes project information which
may not be directly applicable to the
team member's assignment.

36. Project managers should encourage   −3 −2 −1 0 +1 +2 +3
the team to be creative and to solve
their own problems.

37. Project managers should provide detailed job descriptions for team members, outlining the team member's role and responsibility. −3 −2 −1 0 +1 +2 +3

38. Project managers should give each team member the opportunity to do what the team member can do best. −3 −2 −1 0 +1 +2 +3

39. Projects managers should be willing to interact informally with the team members and get to know them as long as there exists sufficient time on the project. −3 −2 −1 0 +1 +2 +3

40. Most of the employees on my project earn a salary commensurate with their abilities. −3 −2 −1 0 +1 +2 +3

Part 1 Scoring Sheet (What Motivates You?)

Each circled answer in questions 1–20 had a corresponding column value between −3 and +3. In the appropriate spaces below, place the corresponding value between −3 and +3 beside each question.

Basic Needs	*Safety Needs*	*Belonging Needs*
#1 _____	#5 _____	#7 _____
#3 _____	#10 _____	#9 _____
#14 _____	#13 _____	#12 _____
#17 _____	#20 _____	#19 _____
Total _____	Total _____	Total _____

Esteem/Ego Needs	*Self-Actualization Needs*
#4 _____	#2 _____
#6 _____	#15 _____
#8 _____	#16 _____
#11 _____	#18 _____
Total _____	Total _____

Transfer your total score in each category to the table on page 346 by placing an "X" in the appropriate area for motivational needs, and then do the same for the table on p. 346.

Part 2 Scoring Sheet (How Do You Motivate?)

Each circled answer in Questions 21–40 had a corresponding column value between −3 and +3. In the appropriate spaces below, place the corresponding value between −3 to +3 beside each question.

Basic Needs

#22 _____
#28 _____
#34 _____
#40 _____
Total _____

Safety Needs

#21 _____
#25 _____
#32 _____
#37 _____
Total _____

Belonging Needs

#24 _____
#27 _____
#33 _____
#39 _____
Total_____

Esteem/Ego Needs

#23 _____
#29 _____
#31 _____
#35 _____
Total _____

Self-Actualization Needs

#26 _____
#30 _____
#36 _____
#38 _____
Total _____

Transfer your total score in each category to the table on p. 346 by placing an "X" in the appropriate area for motivational needs:

Questions 1–20

	Points																								
Needs	−12	−11	−10	−9	−8	−7	−6	−5	−4	−3	−2	−1	0	+1	+2	+3	+4	+5	+6	+7	+8	+9	+10	+11	+12
Self-Actualization																									
Esteem/Ego																									
Belonging																									
Safety																									
Basic																									

Questions 21–40

	Points																								
Needs	−12	−11	−10	−9	−8	−7	−6	−5	−4	−3	−2	−1	0	+1	+2	+3	+4	+5	+6	+7	+8	+9	+10	+11	+12
Self-Actualization																									
Esteem/Ego																									
Belonging																									
Safety																									
Basic																									

6
Time Management

6.0 INTRODUCTION

Managing projects within time, cost, and performance is easier said than done. The project management environment is extremely turbulent, and is composed of numerous meetings, report writing, conflict resolution, continuous planning and replanning, communications with the customer, and crisis management. Ideally, the effective project manager is a manager, not a doer. But in the "real world," project managers often find themselves compromising their time between managing and doing, mainly because of the uncertain nature of the project environment.

In such situations, it is extremely critical that the project manager effectively manage his own time. It is often said that if the project manager cannot control his own time (see Figure 6–1) then he will control nothing else on the project. Disciplined time management is one of the keys to effective project management. Figures 6–2 and 6–3 represent the lack of disciplined time management.

6.1 UNDERSTANDING TIME MANAGEMENT[1]

For most people, time is a resource which, when lost or misplaced, is gone forever. For a project manager, however, time is more of a constraint, and effective time management principles must be employed to make it a resource.

Most executives prefer to understaff projects, with the mistaken belief (or should we say, hope) that the project manager will assume the additional work load. Unfortunately, this is easier said than done. The project manager may already be heavily burdened with meetings, report preparation, internal and external communications, conflict resolution, and planning/replanning for crises. And yet, each project manager somehow manages to manipulate his time so that the work will get done.

Inexperienced project managers often work large amounts of overtime, with the faulty notion that this is the only way to get the job done. While this may be

---

1. Sections 6.1, 6.2, and 6.3 have been adapted from David Cleland and Harold Kerzner, *Engineering Team Management,* Van Nostrand Reinhold, New York, 1986, Chapter 8.

Figure 6-1. Time management.

Figure 6-2. Effective time management?

Figure 6–3. Effective time management?

true, experienced personnel soon learn to delegate tasks and how to employ effective time management principles.

The major problem with time management is getting people to realize that there exists a time management problem and that solutions are possible. The following questions should make the reader realize that each of us has room for improvement.

- Do you have trouble completing work within the allocated deadlines?
- How long can you work at your desk before being interrupted? How many interruptions are there each day?
- Do you have a procedure for handling interruptions?
- If you need a large block of uninterrupted time, is it available? With or without overtime?
- How do you handle drop-in visitors and phone calls?
- How is incoming mail handled?
- Are you accomplishing more or less than you were three months ago? Six months ago?
- How difficult is it for you to say no?
- How do you approach detail work?
- Do you perform work that should be handled by your subordinates?
- Do you have sufficient time each day for personal interests?

- Do you still think about your job when away from the office?
- Do you make a list of things to do? If yes, is the list prioritized?
- Does your schedule have some degree of flexibility?
- Do you have established procedures for routine work?

While it may not be possible to cope with all of these questions, the more one can deal with, the greater the opportunity for the project manager to convert time from being a constraint to becoming a resource.

6.2 TIME ROBBERS

Project managers are not merely managers, but are doers as well. As a result, they suffer from the time robbers of both the managers and the doers. If the project manager is not careful, and overemphasizes his role as a doer rather than a manager, the impact of time robbers may become monumental.

The most challenging problem facing the project manager is his inability to say no. Consider the situation in which an employee comes into your office with a problem. The employee may be sincere when he says that he simply wants your advice but, more often than not, the employee wants to take the monkey off of his back and put it onto yours. If the latter is, in fact, the real truth, then the employee's problem is now *your* problem.

The correct way to handle a situation such as this is to first screen out the problems with which you do not wish to get involved. Second, if the situation does necessitate your involvement, then you must make sure that when the employee leaves your office, the employee realizes that the problem is still his, not yours. Third, if you find that the problem will require your continued attention, remind the employee that all future decisions will be joint decisions and that the problem will still be on the employee's shoulders. Once employees realize that they cannot put their problems on your shoulders, then they soon learn how to make decisions and your time demands may ease up.

There are numerous time robbers in the project management environment. These include:

- Incomplete work
- A job poorly done that must be done over
- Poor communications channels
- Uncontrolled telephone calls
- Casual visitors
- Waiting for people
- Failure to delegate, or unwise delegation
- Lack of adequate responsibility and commensurate authority
- Poor functional performance
- Changes without direct notification/explanation
- Lack of authorization to make judgment decisions
- Poor functional status reporting
- Inability to use one's full potential

- Poor retrieval systems
- Lack of information in a ready-to-use format
- Day-to-day administration
- Spending more time than anticipated in answering questions
- Lack of sufficient clerical support
- Late appointments
- Impromptu tasks
- Union grievances
- Having to explain "thinking" to superiors
- Too many levels of review
- Too many people in a small area
- Office casual conversations
- Misplaced information
- Sorting mail
- Record keeping
- Shifting priorities
- Indecision or delaying decisions
- Procrastination
- Proofreading correspondence
- Setting up appointments
- Too many meetings
- Monitoring delegated work
- Unclear roles/job descriptions
- Unnecessary crisis intervention
- Overcommitted outside activities
- Executive meddling
- Budget adherence requirements
- Poorly educated customers
- Need to get involved in details to get job done
- Not enough proven or trustworthy managers
- Vague goals and objectives
- Lack of a job description
- Too many people involved in minor decision making
- Lack of technical knowledge
- Disorganization of superiors
- Overeducated for daily tasks
- Work overload
- Unreasonable time constraints
- Lack of commitment from higher authorities
- Not being responsible for the full scope
- Indecision on the part of higher management
- Too much travel
- Lack of adequate project management tools
- Poor functional communications/writing skills
- Departmental "buck-passing"
- Meetings with executives
- Inability to relate to peers in a personal way
- Rush into decisions/beat the deadlines
- People being overpaid for their work
- Lack of reward ("a pat on the back can do wonders")
- Expecting too much from one's people and oneself
- Multiple time constraints
- Nonsupportive family
- Company political power struggles
- Going from crisis to crisis
- Conflicting directives
- Line management acting as a "father" figure
- Fire drills
- Lack of privacy
- Lack of challenge in job duties
- P.M. not involved/unknowledgeable about decision making
- Bureaucratic roadblocks ("ego")
- Empire-building line managers

- No communication between sales and engineering
- Too much work for one person to handle effectively
- Excessive paperwork
- Lack of clerical/administrative support
- Work load growing faster than capacity
- Dealing with unreliable subcontractors
- Reeducating project managers
- Lack of new business
- Personnel not willing to take risks
- Demand for short-term results
- Lack of long-range planning
- Being overdirected
- Changing company systems, which requires relearning
- Overreacting management
- Poor lead time on projects
- Disregard for company or personal things
- Documentation (reports/red tape)
- Large number of projects
- Inadequate or inappropriate requirements
- Desire for perfection
- Lack of dedication by technical experts
- Poor salary compared to contemporaries
- Lack of project organization
- Constant pressure
- Constant interruptions
- Problems coming in waves
- Severe home constraints
- Project monetary problems
- Shifting of functional personnel
- Lack of employee discipline
- Lack of qualified manpower

Sometimes, the project manager's inability to effectively handle a time robber will create additional time robbers. Consider the following list of "how not to get something done."[2]

- Profess not to have the answer. That lets you out of having any answer.
- Say that we must not move too rapidly. That avoids the necessity of getting started.
- For every proposal, set up an opposite and conclude that the middle ground (no motion whatever) represents the wisest course of action.
- When in a tight place, say something that the group cannot understand.
- Look slightly embarrassed when the problem is brought up. Hint that it is in bad taste, or too elementary for mature consideration, or that any discussion of it is likely to be misinterpreted by outsiders.
- Say that the problem cannot be separated from other problems. Therefore, no problem can be solved until all other problems have been solved.

---

2. Source Unknown

- Point out that those who see the problem do so because they are unhappy—rather than vice versa.
- Ask what is meant by the question. When it is sufficiently clarified, there will be no time left for the answer.
- Move away from the problem into endless discussion of various ways to study it.
- Put off recommendations until every related problem has been definitely settled by scientific research.
- Carry the problem into other fields; show that it exists everywhere; hence everyone will just have to live with it.
- Introduce analogies and discuss them rather than the problem.
- Explain and clarify over and over again what you have already said.
- As soon as any proposal is made, say that you have been doing it for 10 years.
- Wait until some expert can be consulted.
- Say, "That is not on the agenda; we'll take it up later." this may be extended ad infinitum.
- Conclude that we have all clarified our thinking on the problem, even though no one has thought of any way to solve it.
- Point out that some of the greatest minds have struggled with this problem, implying that it does us credit to have even thought of it.

6.3 TIME MANAGEMENT FORMS

There are two basic forms which project managers and project engineers can use for practicing better time management. The first form is the "to do" pad as shown in Figure 6–4. The project manager or secretary prepares the list of things to do. The project manager then decides which activities he must perform himself and assigns the appropriate priorities.

The activities with the highest priorities are then transferred to the "daily calender log," as shown in Figure 6–5. The project manager assigns these activities to the appropriate time blocks based upon his own energy cycle. Unfilled time blocks are then used for unexpected crises or for lower-priority activities.

If there are more priority elements than time slots, the project manager may try to schedule well in advance. This is normally not a good practice, because it is very easy to create a backlog of high-priority activities to such a degree that schedule slippages are inevitable. In addition, an activity which today may be a "B" priority could easily become an "A" priority in a day or two. The moral here is do not postpone until tomorrow what you or your team can do today.

Date _____				
Activities	Priority	Started	In Process	Completed

Figure 6–4. "To do" pad.

Date _____		
Time	Activity	Priority
8:00–9:00		
9:00–10:00		
10:00–11:00		
11:00–12:00		
12:00–1:00		
1:00–2:00		
2:00–3:00		
3:00–4:00		
4:00–5:00		

Figure 6–5. Daily calendar log.

6.4 INTRODUCTION TO STRESS AND BURNOUT[3]

Everyone who works knows that on-the-job pressure is one of the major sources of stress in daily life. Project managers are subject to stress due to several different facets of their jobs. This can manifest itself in a variety of ways, such as:

1. Being tired: Being tired is a result of being drained of strength and energy, perhaps through physical exertion, boredom, or impatience. The definition here applies more to a short-term, rather than long-term, effect. Typical causes for feeling tired include meetings, report-writing, and other forms of document preparation.

2. Feeling depressed: Feeling depressed is an emotional condition usually characterized by discouragement or a feeling of inadequacy. There are several sources of depression in a project environment: Management or the client considers your report unacceptable, you are unable to get timely resources assigned, the technology is not available, or the constraints of the project are unrealistic and may not be met.

A state of depression in a project environment is usually the result of a situation which is beyond the control or capabilities of the project manager. This situation can exist indefinitely because the project manager has a great deal of responsibility and very little authority, and has no direct control over the staffing or assignment of personnel.

3. Having a good day: For most people, having a good day implies that something has gone right. In a project management environment, every project may be inherently different, and a good day may simply be the result of the project manager's ability to attack and resolve difficult problems, even if the final result is detrimental to the project. Sometimes it is truly amazing how decision making and looking at the "means to the end" rather than the end itself equals a good day. An experienced project manager once commented: "If I sit at my desk and do not have problems to resolve, then I go out and look for (or even create) problems to solve. That's my definition of having a good day."

4. Being physically exhausted: Project managers are both managers and doers. It is quite common for project managers to perform a great deal of the work themselves, either because they consider the assigned personnel unqualified to perform the work or because the project manager is impatient and considers himself capable of performing the work faster. In addition, project managers often work a great deal of "self-inflicted" overtime.

---

3. The remaining sections have been adapted from Mary Khosh and Harold Kerzner, "Stress and Burnout in Project Management," presented at the Annual Seminar/Symposium on Project Management, sponsored by the Project Management Institute, Philadelphia, October 8–10, 1984.

5. Being emotionally exhausted: The most common cause of emotional exhaustion is report writing and the preparation of handouts for interchange meetings. Sometimes the project manager finds himself performing these functions for line personnel, but more often than not, line employees procrastinate and force this function upon project managers. Since data preparation is a continuous project function, one might expect this effect to occur frequently.

6. Being happy: Happiness generally suggests a feeling of pleasure and contentment. Most project managers view project management as a lifetime profession and are usually quite happy, even under situations of stress. A senior construction project manager commented on why he has not accepted a promotion to vice-president: "I can take my children and grandchildren into 10 countries in the world and show them projects which I either built or helped build. What do I show them as a vice-president? My bank account? The size of my office? The stockholder's report?" Obviously, not all people would respond like this. The work challenge associated with the project environment is a strong driving force toward happiness. There are very few positions where an employee can see an activity through from beginning to end.

7. Wiped out: Feeling wiped out is normally a combination of physical and emotional exhaustion. It is a short-term, rather than long-term, effect and may be caused by short spurts of intense overtime; nearness of deadlines on the time, cost, and performance constraints; or simply lengthy customer review meetings.

8. Burned out: Being burned out is more than just a feeling; it is a condition. Being burned out implies that one is totally exhausted, both physically and emotionally, and that rest, recuperation, or vacation time may not remedy the situation. The most common cause is prolonged overtime, or the need thereof, and an inability to endure or perform under continuous pressure and stress. The solution is almost always a change in job assignment, preferably with another company.

Burnout can occur almost overnight, often with very little warning. In one company, a project manager who was managing a high-technology project (and was on the fast track in the organization) burned out and accepted a job as the manager of quality control for a small company that manufactures brooms. In the termination interview, the project manager stated that his reason for leaving was because he felt burned out.

9. Being unhappy: There are several factors which produce unhappiness in project management. Such factors include highly optimistic planning, unreasonable expectations by management, management cutting resources because of a "buy-in," or simply customer demands for additional data items. A major source of unhappiness is the frustration caused by having limited authority which is not commensurate with the assigned responsibility.

10. Feeling run down: Feeling run down is a temporary condition caused by exhaustion, overwork, or simply poor physical conditioning. The run-down

feeling usually occurs following "panics," especially as one nears the project constraints.

11. Feeling trapped: The most common situation where project managers feel trapped is when they have no control over the assigned resources on the project and feel as though they are at the mercy of the line managers. Employees tend to favor the manager who can offer them the most rewards, and that is usually the line manager. Providing the project manager with some type of direct reward power can remedy the situation.

Another instance of feeling trapped is when the project manager and line managers work together to develop realistic costs and schedules for a proposal and senior management arbitrarily slashes the price to remain competitive. Now, if the project is awarded to the company, the project manager feels trapped into accepting constraints which are not really his.

12. Feeling worthless: Feeling worthless implies that one is without worth or merit, that is, valueless. This situation occurs when project managers feel that they are managing projects beneath their dignity. Most project managers look forward to the death of their project right from the onset, and expect their next project to be more important, perhaps twice the cost, and more complex. Unfortunately, there are always situations where one must take a step backwards.

13. Being weary: Being weary is a combination of several of the previous feelings. This includes tiredness, lack of energy, worn out, and perhaps impatient. Weariness is usually the transition stage between being tired and being burned out.

14. Being troubled: The two major causes for a project manager to be troubled are optimistic planning (which has since turned "sour") and approaching the constraints of the project with little hope for correction. The latter case is not a really serious problem, because most project managers pride themselves on their ability to perform trade-offs.

15. Feeling resentful and disillusioned about people: This situation occurs most frequently in the project manager's dealings (i.e., negotiations) with the line managers. During the planning stage of a project, line managers often make promises concerning future resource commitments, but renege on their promises during execution. Disillusionment then occurs and can easily develop into serious conflict. Another potential source of these feelings is when line managers appear to be making decisions which are not in the best interest of the project.

16. Feeling week and helpless: A weak and helpless feeling is a common result of feeling disillusioned. Again, the cause of this feeling depends upon the working relationship that project managers have with executives and line managers.

17. Feeling hopeless: The most common sources of hopelessness are R&D projects where the ultimate objective is beyond the reach of the employee or

even of the state-of-the art technology. Hopelessness means showing no signs of a favorable outcome. Hopelessness is more a result of the performance constraint than of time or cost.

18. Feeling rejected: Feeling rejected can be the result of a poor working relationship with executives, line managers, or clients. Rejection often occurs when people with authority feel that their options or opinions are better than those of the project manager. Rejection has a demoralizing effect upon the project manager because he feels that he is the "president" of the project and the true "champion" of the company.

19. Feeling optimistic: Almost all project managers feel optimistic, even in time of trouble. Project managers often have more faith in themselves and others than other people perceive. Optimism is usually a desired trait in a project manager.

20. Feeling energetic: The work challenge created by the project environment usually brings with it an energetic feeling, where the individual accepts the daily challenge of problem solving and troubleshooting. The exact degree of energy may depend, of course, upon the time of day, the day of the week, or simply the age of the project manager.

21. Feeling anxious: Almost all project managers have some degree of "tunnel vision," where they look forward to the end of the project, even when the project is in its infancy. This anxious feeling is not only to see the project end, but to see it completed successfully.

Stress is not necessarily negative. Without certain amounts of stress, reports would never get written or distributed, time deadlines would never be met, and in fact, no one would ever even get to work on time. Stress not only serves to energize and motivate, but can also be a powerful force resulting in illness and even fatal disease, and must be understood and managed if it is to be controlled and utilized for constructive purposes.

The mind, body, and emotions are not the separate entities they were once thought to be. They are one integrated system. One affects the other, sometimes in a positive way, and sometimes in a negative way. Stress becomes detrimental only when it is prolonged beyond what an individual can comfortably handle. In as project environment, with continuously changing requirements, impossible deadlines, and each project being considered as a unique entity in itself, we must ask, How much prolonged stress can a project manager handle comfortably?

Business people deal with these stresses in different ways. It is not unusual to find high-powered, successful executives "dropping out" and buying farms in Vermont. Nor is it unusual to find a project manager turning bicycle shop owner or house painter. When questioned, they will often say that they did it because the pressures of their old jobs "weren't worth it."

Others are opting for early retirement at age 55 rather than continue to face the pressures of a demanding job. They may have successfully moved in their career to a point of having responsibility for large projects involving millions of dollars and interfacing with all kinds of people. However, by then they might prefer not to take on another vast project. They often reach a plateau or develop a neurotic suspicion that every subordinate is competing for their job. In project management, peers may become subordinates. Responsibility increases threefold. Project managers may be caught in a vise of conflicting demands: demands from above to get more done with fewer people, and demands to work harder and longer to meet time constraints.

6.5 STRESS IN PROJECT MANAGEMENT

The factors that serve to make any occupation especially stressful are: responsibility without the authority or ability to exert control, a necessity for perfection, the pressure of deadlines, role ambiguity, role conflict, role overload, the crossing of organizational boundaries, responsibility for the actions of subordinates, and the necessity to keep up with the information explosions or technological breakthroughs. Project managers have all of these factors included in their jobs.

A project manager has his resources controlled by line management, yet the responsibilities of bringing a project to completion by a prescribed deadline are his. A project manager may be told to increase the work output, while the work force is simultaneously being cut. Project managers are expected to get work out on schedule, but are often not permitted to pay overtime. One project manager described it this way: "I have to implement plans I didn't design, but if the project fails, I'm responsible."

Project managers, unlike line managers or top executives, do not have the power or facilities to accomplish many of their objectives alone. They must depend on superiors, subordinates, and peers for the cooperation and efforts to make their projects successful, as they are constantly crossing organizational boundaries. maintaining these three levels of interpersonal relationships is a juggling game that may make a consistent pattern of behavior almost impossible.

The project manager's superior is interested only in what is accomplished and may not be interested in hearing the specifics of how it was accomplished. The executive will hand down a list of required results, but it is the project manager's responsibility to translate that list into an organized system of behaviors that will produce the desired results. Whereas some levels of management have accessibility to a scapegoat if desired performance is not reached, the project manager has to assume full responsibility. He is evaluated on the results of the total operation and is solely responsible for whatever happens.

Additional high-intensity stressors in project management include unrealistic and inflexible time, cost, and performance constraints, unrealistic customer and environmental constraints, no direct input into the staffing process, no direct control or authority over resources after the project begins, no control over subordinates salaries, and having to share key personnel with other projects.

The stresses of project management may seem excessive for whatever rewards the position may offer. However, the project manager who is aware of the stresses inherent in the job and knows stress management techniques can face this challenge objectively and make it a rewarding experience.

6.6 TIME MANAGEMENT SURVEY

In March/April 1981, a survey was conducted of more than 300 project managers in twenty-four different industries to identify the problems that exist in trying to obtain effective project time management.[4] The survey was conducted with written questionnaires and personal interviews. Fifteen areas were investigated:

- Employee's background (age, project time span, and dollar value of project)
- Energy level per day
- Energy level per week
- Daily/weekly work schedule
- Overtime
- Productivity
- Meetings
- Time robbers
- Time away from desk
- Priorities
- Communications
- Conflict management
- Planning/replanning
- Community service
- Delegation

Table 6–1 identifies the survey base for the questionnaires. The respondents were surveyed according to gender, average age, project time span, and dollar value of project. The seventeen industries shown in Table 6–1 were representative of the survey. Most of the projects fell into the one- to two-year time

---

4. Although we refer to the respondents as project managers, the list also includes assistant project manager, project engineers, and other project office personnel.

Table 6-1. Survey Base.

INDUSTRY	NUMBER OF PEOPLE		AVERAGE AGE, YEARS	SPAN OF PROJECTS	VALUE OF PROJECTS
	MALE	FEMALE			
Utilities (electric)	9	2	40–45	2 mos–4 yrs	$2–200M
Automotive equipment	39	0	35–40	1–7 yrs	1–100M
Utilities (telephone)	10	0	35–40	1 mo–2 yrs	10K–500K
Oil	10	0	35–50	1–5 yrs	25M–2.5B
Banking	5	3	25–30	2 wks–6 mos	10K–100K
Manufacturing	7	0	25–35	6 mos–1 yr	1–9M
Construction	57	2	30–40	6 mos–5 yrs	1M–500M
Communications	9	0	30–35	6 mos–2 yrs	50K–25M
Computers	2	1	25–30	6 mos–2 yrs	100K–175K
Steel	7	1	25–30	3 mos–1 yr	10K–1M
Chemical	4	0	30–40	3 mos–1 yr	25K–5M
Government	38	3	45–55	3 mos–2 yrs	100K–25M
Batteries	10	0	30–35	6 mos–1 yr	100K–2M
Rubber	3	0	45–50	2 mos–1 yr	100K–500K
Nuclear	4	1	30–35	6 mos–5 yrs	100K–50M
Consulting (engineering)	9	0	30–35	1 mo–2 yrs	25K–500K
Health care	7	3	30–35	1 mo–3 yrs	25K–2M

period except for banking and manufacturing. The banking projects were predominantly data-processing-oriented, and the manufacturing projects were capital-equipment projects for modification and improvement of existing facilities. This accounts for the relatively short time periods.

The average age of the project managers appears to be consistent with published data.[5,6] The average age of all project managers appears to fall in the 30–40 years range. The younger project managers are usually found in computer-oriented projects, such as in banking. Two surprises were found in the age brackets. In manufacturing companies today the trend is to give more responsibility to the younger manufacturing engineers for the capital equipment projects, and the steel industry appears to be hiring younger project managers and providing them with sufficient training in project management. Unfortunately, the sample size of the survey in these two areas makes these statements more assumptions than facts.

It should be mentioned that in some project-driven organizations such as construction, the project managers are generally older than the 30–40 years

5. Harold Kerzner, "Formal Training for Project Managers," *Project Management Quarterly,* June 1979, pp. 38–44.
6. Harold Kerzner, "The Educational Path to Training Systems Managers," *Journal of Systems Management,* December 1978, pp. 23–27.

identified in Table 6–1. The 30–40 years reported reflects ages of project office personnel and assistant project managers.

Energy Level per Day

The exact amount of energy that an employee possesses is usually a function of such variables as fatigue, efficiency of work, concentration, amount of work, listlessness, eagerness, and alertness. Unfortunately, these individual energy flow variables are extremely difficult to measure. Because of the difficulty in measuring these paramenters, the project managers were asked simply to rate their energy level per hour (per work day) on a scale from 1 to 10, with 10 being the best rating. Figure 6–6 illustrates the average energy cycle. Most respondents identified a primary and a secondary peak.

The energy cycle per day per industry is identified in Table 6–2. Most employees identified primary and secondary peaks as in Figure 6–6, with the first peak at 9–11 A.M. and the second peak at 1–4 P.M. However, there were some unusual results. Both NASA and construction project managers identified their secondary peaks as being higher than their primary peaks, a suggestion that these people do their more productive work in the afternoon rather than the morning. Another interesting result is in the magnitude of the energy level. Several respondents indicated that they never achieve an energy level of 10. Generally, project-driven organizations and those that use well-established historical standards for work appear to have the highest overall levels of energy.

All employees identified a minimum level at noon, the time for their lunch hour. However, because some employees work through lunch, the energy levels were never assigned a scale value of 1. Probably the most interesting result was that most project managers and project engineers know their own energy cycle. Many people believe, for example, that they do their most effective writing in the morning and save their reading for the afternoon. It is very important to know one's own energy cycle.

Energy Cycle per Week

Most employees do not perform at the same energy level each day of the week. In order to verify this, the respondents were asked again to rate their energy on a scale of 1 to 10, but for each day of the week. The results are shown in Table 6–3. Most respondents felt that their peak performance days were Wednesday and Thursday. Construction and oil industries had the highest overall energy level per week.

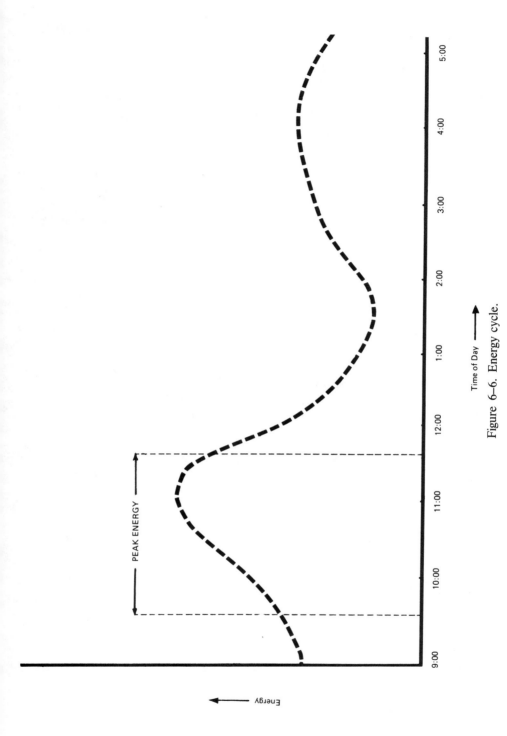

Figure 6–6. Energy cycle.

363

Table 6-2. Energy Cycle per Day (8 A.M. to 5 P.M.).

INDUSTRY TYPE	FIRST PEAK		MINIMUM		2ND PEAK	
	TIME	RANGE	TIME	RANGE	TIME	RANGE
NASA	9–12	8.6–9.2	8–9, 12–1	7.7	1–3	9.2
EDP	9–12	8.75	12–1	6.5	2–4	8.6
Auto manu. (primary)	9–11	8.0–8.3	12–1	7.0	2–3, 4–5	8.1
Auto manu. (subcontractors)	9–11	9.5	12–1	3.3	1–3	8.75
Construction*	8–11	8.6	12–1	6.2	1–3	8.75
Construction**	7–4	8.5	—	—	—	—
Oil	9–11	9.4	12–1	6.2	2–5	8.1
Primary batteries	9–11	8.4	12–1	5.2	1–2	7.0
Manu. engineering	9–12	9.0–9.2	12–1	7.5	1–5	7.8–8.0
Government	9–10	9.60	12–1	5.9	2–4	7.7–7.8
Others	10–12	8.8	12–1	5.4	2–4	7.2

*These personnel felt that their energy fluctuated per hour.
**These personnel felt that their energy cycle was virtually constant for the entire day.

Several people identified energy levels for Saturday and Sunday because of the necessity for overtime. In most cases, the energy level for Saturday was lower than that of the weekdays, and Sunday was lower than Saturday. Surprisingly, respondents from the automobile manufacturers, manufacturing engineering, and construction industries stated that they maintain at least 90% of their peak energy on Saturday. Unfortunately, there was no discussion as to whether this was due to mandatory workload, overtime pay, or other such arguments. However, the high Sunday energy level for the construction respondents

Table 6-3. Energy Cycle per Week.

INDUSTRY	MONDAY	TUESDAY	WEDNESDAY	THURSDAY	FRIDAY	SATURDAY	SUNDAY
NASA	8.25	9.25	9.75	9.63	7.14	5.0	
EDP	7.1	8.7	8.65	8.85	8.2	7.4	5.0
Auto. manu. (primary)	8.1	8.2	7.5	8.1	8.6	8.9	6.9
Auto. manu. (subcontractors)	8	9	9	8.7	7		
Construction	8.6	8.8	8.8	9.1	8.9	8.0	7.8
Oil	8.2	9.5	9.5	9.5	8.1		
Primary batteries	6.7	8.4	8.5	7.9	6.0	4.3	3.5
Manu. engineering	7.3	8.4	8.9	9.0	8.5	8.3	6.9
Others	8.1	8.9	8.6	8.1	6.4	3.8	

indicates that, at least for the construction industry, the pressure of the time, cost, and performance constraints make prolonged overtime a necessity, and employees are expected to perform at a high energy level continuously.

Daily/Weekly Work Schedule

The majority of the people surveyed began work between 7:30 and 8:00 A.M. and finished between 4:00 and 5:00 P.M. Several government employees operated on a flex-time schedule. This meant that their energy cycle per day had to be adjusted to a common starting time. The employees who were under the flex-time system were required to work a minimum of 8.5 hours per day and *must* be in the plant between 9:00 A.M. and 3:30 P.M. (core time). The employees could begin their workday any time between 7:00 and 9:00 A.M. With the adjustment of a common starting point due to flex-time, almost all government employees exhibited the daily energy cycle shown in Table 6–2.

This concept of flex-time is often used in project management. For example, it is common for East Coast companies to have their procurement specialists maintain a noon to 8:30 P.M. work day so as to coincide with the normal work day of West Coast distributors and vendors. Remote-location projects often create a need for flex-time for home office communications.

Overtime

Project-driven organizations tend to require a great deal of overtime due to underemployment, rather than to have to terminate people because of overemployment. These companies believe that if you have sufficient resources for all of your projects, then your organization is overstaffed. Non-project-driven organizations also require overtime but not to the same degree as in the project-driven organization. When respondents were asked about overtime, the following responses were obtained:

- Ninety percent of the government project managers worked an average of 4–8 hours of overtime per week.
- Almost 100 percent of the construction workers claimed that overtime was a necessity, at 14.9 hours per week.
- The oil industry project managers equated the necessity and amount of overtime with the size of the project.
- Automotive equipment manufacturers and primary batteries managers also equated overtime with the size of the project, and said that overtime is usually required on all of the large projects.
- Health care/health services personnel work an average of 6 hours of overtime per week on their data processing/MIS projects.

- Nuclear power personnel stated that overtime is required on 50 percent of their projects, and the overtime is usually accomplished on Saturdays rather than weekdays.

Overtime can be good for the company as long as productivity levels are maintained. However, if overtime is prolonged, then employees may end up giving the same output in twelve hours that they would produce in a normal eight-hour day. In addition, if the overtime is prolonged, employees may get used to the overtime pay and may "create" the need for additional overtime if they feel that the additional money may be terminated.

Productivity

An individual can have a large amount of energy, but the productive use of this energy may be low. The average employee is usually productive about six hours in an eight-hour work day. The reason for this 70–80 percent productivity level is that various items "steal" time needed for the completion of a task. The following such items were identified by project managers:[7]

- Lack of information in a ready format
- Phone calls
- Day-to-day administration
- Spending more time than anticipated in answering questions
- Lack of sufficient clerical support
- Late appointments
- Impromptu tasks
- Unscheduled appointments or "drop-ins"
- Union grievances
- Having to explain "thinking" to superiors
- Too many levels of review
- Too many people in a small area
- Office casual conversations

The last two items require further clarification. More and more organizations are finding that white collar productivity is directly related to the working environment. If employees are provided a relatively secluded place to work, productivity will increase. A company employing 1,700 people found that their

---

7. This list is in addition to the "time robbers" identified elsewhere.

white collar productivity was five hours out of a nine-hour day. This low productivity was attributed to the fact that the employees' desks were so close together that casual conversations were continuously occurring, and employees had to work overtime to get their normal work load completed.

Table 6–4 shows the way that the various project managers and project office personnel responded to questions about effective productive hours per day. The majority of the people felt that they were productive at least six hours per day. Productivity lower than this is probably the result of increased time robbers, or an inability to handle time robbers.

Most of the respondees felt that their productivity was at least the same on overtime. However, several comments were made that prolonged or continuous overtime would have a direct bearing on efficiency.

Meetings

Meetings become a way of life in project management and project engineering. Unfortunately, meetings can become unproductive and a total waste of time, especially if the project manager:

- Spends too much time on trivial items
- Neglects sending out an agenda
- Holds too many team meetings
- Holds too few team meetings
- Neglects inviting personnel with decision-making authority

Table 6–4. Productivity per Day.

INDUSTRY	PRODUCTIVE HOURS PER DAY							
	2 HRS	3 HRS	4 HRS	5 HRS	6 HRS	7 HRS	8 HRS	9 HRS
Rubber/chemical			5.6%*		33.3%	11.1%	22.2%	27.8%
Government			10.0	40.0	40.0	10.0		
Automotive equipment					20.0	40.0	40.0	
Automotive (subcontracts)	6.25		12.5	12.5	37.5	12.5	18.75	
Construction					75.0	25.0		
Health care				44.4	55.6			
Utilities (electrical)					50.0	20.0	30.0	
Banking					100**			
Batteries				33.3	33.3	33.4		

*Percentage of industry personnel selecting this choice.
**Only average figures available.

If functional employees are unhappy with the way that the project is progressing, they can easily tie up valuable time in team meetings by arguing about trivial items. This is often the case when team members wish to avoid making a decision. Team meetings are ideal for routine activities such as schedule updating and status reporting. However, if decision making is necessary, the project manager may have a problem because the functional team members may not have the authority to make a decision without first checking with their line managers. The project managers *must* learn, at the beginning of the project, which team members actually represent their line groups in decision making. One employee responded: "A letter would be just as effective as a team meeting but would require less time. Many meetings are just communications, not decision-making."

Functional managers would like nothing better than to be able to attend project team meetings, but they do not have the time. Functional managers argue that they cannot spend two hours or more in a project team meeting simply to participate in a fifteen-minute conversation. If the project manager sends out an agenda and identifies the approximate time when each major topic will be discussed, then he may find more decision-makers attending his meetings, and the meetings can easily become more productive.

Table 6–5 lists seven industry responses regarding the amount of time per week spent in meetings and how productive the meetings are. In general, the project-driven organizations appear to spend more time in meetings than the non-project-driven organizations, and the productivity of the former meetings seems to be higher. This may be attributed to the pressure of the project-driven organization as well as the experience and maturity of the project-driven organization.

Team meetings are supposedly meetings of the mind where information giving and receiving and listening take place. Unfortunately, many meetings are conducted using the methodology of Figure 6–7. Unless they are effective,

Table 6–5. Meetings.

INDUSTRY	APPROX. HOURS PER WEEK	PRODUCTIVITY LEVEL OF MEETINGS
Oil	10	No response
NASA	6–11	75%
Government	8	75%
Batteries	1	50%
Automotive	1	50%
Health care (MIS)	13	No response
Nuclear	8	80%

Figure 6–7. How to conduct an effective meeting.

team meetings become time management pitfalls. The project manager must ensure that meetings are valuable and necessary for the exchange of information. General guidelines for conducting effective meetings are given in Chapter 5 (Section 5.12).

Time Robbers

In the previous discussions, identification was made of the most common time robbers in a project environment. These included:

- Incomplete work
- Jobs done over
- Delayed decisions
- Poor communications
- Telephone calls

- Casual visits
- Waiting for people
- Failure to delegate
- Poor retrieval system
- Others

The project managers were queried as to which of these time robbers commonly occur on their projects, and how much time is usually spent per week on each time robber. The results are shown in Table 6-6. Delayed decisions and poor communications were the most commonly identified items. Most of the industries appear to have two or three predominant time robbers, except for the construction project managers.

Most respondents identified "other" items that detracted from their performance. Seventy percent of the major automotive equipment manufacturer respondents identified such items. The following "other" items were listed in this survey:

- Lack of information in a ready format
- Too many people in a small area

Table 6-6. Time Robbers Analysis.*

	INDUSTRIES								
TIME ROBBERS	AUTOMOTIVE EQUIPMENT	AUTOMOTIVE SUBCONTRACTORS	CONSTRUCTION	UTILITIES (ELECTRICAL)	NASA	BATTERIES	COMMUNICATIONS	OTHERS	RANGE OF HOURS PER WEEK
Incomplete work	40%	40%	30%	50%	30%	40%	70%	50%	1–2
Jobs done over	40	70	10	50	50	30	60	50	1–5
Delayed decisions	80	100	50	90	100	60	80	70	1–4
Poor communication	50	80	50	80	50	80	70	70	1–10
Telephone calls	70	100	30	40	20	60	70	60	½–10
Casual visits	50	70	20	60	30	40	30	40	½–5
Waiting for people	70	70	50	30	40	70	70	60	½–5
Failure to delegate	20	30	10	60	20	10	30	20	2–5
Poor retrieval system	30	50	40	20	30	20	70	30	1–5
Others	70	10	20	20	30	10	10	10	1–3

*Table identifies percentage of the respondees that selected each item.

- Casual office conversations
- Day-to-day administration
- Spending more time than anticipated answering questions
- Lack of sufficient clerical support
- Late appointments
- Impromptu tasks
- Having to explain thinking to superiors
- Too many levels of review
- Union grievances

Several project managers felt that they should be divorced from the parent company's administrative responsibilities. Although this point may be arguable, the author contends that all projects are still attached to the parent company administratively, and that project personnel must assume their share of responsibility for company administrative requirements.

Also shown in Table 6–6 is the average number of hours spent per week on each time robber. This identifies the magnitude of the time management problem. One project manager in the nuclear power industry estimated that he spends fourteen hours per week on the job robbers. If 30 to 40 percent of his time is spent on the time robbers, then this limits him to a maximum of 70 percent productivity in each time period. Another project manager felt that time robbers are simply part of a project manager's responsibility: "I'm not sure that I have a lot of time robbers, just a lot of work."

Time Away from Desk

The project managers were asked to identify how much time they spend away from their desk. The results are shown in Table 6–7. The majority of the

Table 6–7. Time Away from Desk.

INDUSTRY	TIME AWAY FROM DESK, %												
	0	1–3	5	10	15	20	25	30	35	40	50	60	70
Oil			10%*	20%	10%	10%	10%	10%		20%		10%	
Chemical/ rubber	10		10	25	10	5		20		20			
Government	5	45		10	5	15	5			5			
NASA			10	15	5	10	15	10	5	10	15		5
Construction	5		20	5	35	5	10			10	5	5	
Batteries			10	10	30	30	10				10		
Health care			25	75									

*Percentage of industry respondees that selected this time

respondents indicated that 5 to 30 percent of their time is spent away from their desk on such items as:

- Vendor visits/communications
- Team meetings
- Time robbers
- Traveling
- Supervising functional work

Priorities

The purpose of the priorities question was to determine how project priorities were established, and by whom. Here, we are referring to the activities on the project, not necessarily for new projects. Most of the project managers were at either one end of the spectrum or the other; namely, either they establish the priorities, or top management does it. The following responses were typical of the survey results:

- Oil industry: 100 percent of project managers felt that they establish their own priorities.
- Construction industry: Priorities are established by either the customer or in-house top-level management.
- Primary batteries: Priorities are established by either the results of the cost–benefit analysis or top-level management.
- Nuclear: Project managers set all priorities, but 50 percent do it with top management approval.
- Health care: "Everyone except the project managers appears to be establishing the priorities."

The majority of the project managers appeared to be unfamiliar with the methods used by top management to establish priorities.

Communications

The project managers were asked how they prefer to communicate on the project, and were asked to select from these forms of communication:

- Written formal
- Written informal
- Oral formal
- Oral informal

Several respondents felt that they could not answer the question without specifying whether the communications were with superiors, subordinates, or the client. The results are shown in Table 6–8. Most people seemed to prefer oral communications, especially informal ones.

As part of the survey, the project managers were asked how much time they spend each week trying to resolve conflicts. The results are shown in Table 6–9. It was anticipated that the project managers in project-driven organizations would spend more time resolving conflicts than those in non-project-driven organizations. The results of the survey, however, are not conclusive enough to support this hypothesis.

Planning/Replanning Time

The project managers were asked how many hours they spend each week either planning (originally unplanned) project activities for a project already started, or replanning current activities. The results are shown in Table 6–10. Most project managers felt that at least ten hours per week are spent on planning/replanning. Several project managers tried to distinguish between planning and replanning, and commented that planning requires at least twice as much time as replanning. However, it was felt that some of these people may have misunderstood the nature of the question.

Table 6.8 Communications.

					INDUSTRY			
COMMUNICATIONS WITH:	COMMUNICATIONS FORM:	OIL	ELECTRIC UTILITIES	NASA	AUTOMOTIVE	BATTERIES	BANKING	CONSTRUCTION
Superior	Written formal		20	26	42	23	50	
	Written informal		18	23	10	23		50
	Oral formal		15	20	27	16		
	Oral informal		47	31	21	38	50	50
Subordinate	Written formal	20	20	26	19	23	50	
	Written informal		18	23	35	23		50
	Oral formal		15	20	11	16		
	Oral informal	80	47	31	35	38	50	50
Client	Written formal				42			50
	Written informal				3			
	Oral formal				28			50
	Oral informal				27			

Table 6–9. Conflict Management Time.

INDUSTRY	AVERAGE HOURS PER WEEK RESOLVING CONFLICTS
Rubber/chemical	2
Oil	10
Electric utilities	9.9
NASA	4.3
Automotive	6.3
Construction	13.8
Banking (MIS)	12
Health care	10
Communications	12
Government	6

Table 6–10. Planning/Replanning Time.

INDUSTRY	AVERAGE HOURS PER WEEK SPENT PLANNING/REPLANNING PROJECT
Oil	10
Construction	3 (small projects), 10 (large projects)
NASA	6
Automotive	4.8
Banking	14.4
Health care	10
Communications	12.4
Government	8

Community Service

People in a project environment, especially project managers, have very little if any time available for community service work. The average response for all industries was approximately four hours per week spent in such work, with most of that time going to religious organizations. There was no distinction in the responses between project- and non-project-driven organizations.

Delegation

The project managers were asked what percentage of their own work they try to delegate to subordinates. The results are shown in Table 6–11. Most project managers said that they try to delegate as much work as possible while delegating virtually no authority. Ideally, if the project manager delegated all of the work, the result would resemble Figure 6–8. Unfortunately, there will always be paperwork to create the situation shown in Figure 6–9.

Table 6–11. Delegation Time.

INDUSTRY	PERCENTAGE OF PROJECT MANAGER'S WORK LOAD DELEGATED
Rubber/chemical	18
Oil	57
Electrical utility	20–70, varies with project
Construction	22
Banking	40
Health care	20
Communications	80 administrative/20 technical
Government	25
NASA	56

We can now summarize the major time management problems for the project managers. These include:

- Meetings (8 hours/week, from Table 6–5)
- Time robbers (10 hours/week, from Table 6–6)[8]
- Conflicts (12 hours/week, from Table 6–9)
- Planning/replanning (10 hours/week, from Table 6–10)

Summing up these hours, we find that it is entirely possible for project managers to spend 40 hours or more each week on these problems—a calculation that neglects the possibility that the project manager's overall efficiency may be only 70 to 80 percent!

6.7 EFFECTIVE TIME MANAGEMENT

There are several techniques that project managers can practice in order to make better use of their time:[9]

- Delegate.
- Follow the schedule.
- Decide fast.
- Decide who should attend.
- Learn to say no.
- Start now.

---

8. This assumes that 50 percent of the time robbers will occur, requiring the mean time from Table 6–6.
9. Source unknown.

Figure 6–8. Project management: effective resource utilization.

Figure 6–9. Is paperwork bottling you up?

- Do the tough part first.
- Travel light.
- Work at travel stops.
- Avoid useless memos.
- Refuse to do the unimportant.
- Look ahead.
- Ask: Is this trip necessary?
- Know your energy cycle.
- Control telephone time.
- Send out the meeting agenda.
- Shut off in-house visits.
- Overcome procrastination.
- Manage by exception.

As we learned in Chapter 5, the project manager, to be effective, must establish time management rules and then ask himself four questions:

- Rules for time management
  - Conduct a time analysis (time log).
  - Plan solid blocks for important things.
  - Classify your activities.
  - Establish priorities.
  - Establish opportunity cost on activities.
  - Train your system (boss, subordinate, peers).
  - Practice delegation.
  - Practice calculated neglect.
  - Practice management by exception.
  - Focus on opportunities—not on problems.
- Questions
  - What am I doing that I don't have to be doing at all?
  - What am I doing that can be done better by someone else?
  - What am I doing that could be done sufficiently well by someone else?
  - Am I establishing the right priorities for my activities?

The following recommendations are given to project managers:

- Know the weekly and daily energy cycle of your people as well as your own. Be sure to assign or perform work that is compatible with this energy cycle.
- If you have employees who come and go on flex-time schedules, be sure to account for this arrangement in assigning work and understanding their energy cycle.

- Understand the productivity levels of your people, and make sure that the project's performance standards are compatible with the productivity level of your people.
- Do not schedule overtime unnecessarily unless you know that overtime is needed and that efficiency will be maintained. It is possible for employees to "save themselves for overtime" and thereby produce the same work in twelve hours that they would in eight hours.
- Try to monitor your own work load closely and see if there is any work that does not have to be done effectively by someone else. If necessary, refuse to do the unimportant work. Avoid procrastination and try to work on the most difficult tasks first. Start now and look for ways to buy additional time. Be prepared to make quick decisions.
- Do not schedule meetings unless they are cost-effective and necessary. Assist your people in preparation for the meeting. Prepare an agenda and make sure that key personnel are informed well in advance of any major problems to be discussed.
- Conduct the meeting effectively and efficiently. Start the meeting on time, get right to the point, and end the meeting on time. Try to get all attendees to express their views, and avoid prolonged discussions of trivial tasks.
- Decide whether or not it is absolutely necessary for you to attend a given meeting, especially if it requires travel time. If travel time is required, be prepared to work at travel stops.
- Try to minimize the amount of time you spend away from your desk. Be willing to delegate. Plan solid blocks of time for important work. Classify your objectives, and get to the point at once. Learn how to say no. Be willing to delegate and employ the management-by-exception concept.
- Time robbers can destroy a good project schedule. Control telephone time and be willing to let your secretary take messages. Get rid of casual visitors. If necessary, find a way to work in seclusion.
- Establish proper priorities for yourself, your project, and your people.
- Avoid time-consuming communication processes. Avoid memos. If memos or letters are necessary, make them short and summary-type in nature. If you have lengthy reports to read, it is best to take them with you on long trips.
- Train your boss, peers, and subordinates on how to work with you. Be willing to assert your rights.
- If conflict resolution is necessary, obtain the necessary information as fast as possible and make a decision. Establishing procedures for conflict resolution may be helpful.
- Follow your schedules closely, especially items on the critical path. You may find it necessary to monitor critical items yourself rather than wait for periodic feedback.

- Be willing to delegate work to subordinates and peers. Do not try to be a "nice guy" and do it all yourself, lest you place yourself in the position of doing work that is normally the responsibility of the functional departments or other project office personnel.

Project managers typically understand well the role of the project manager at project conception, but seem to forget it during project execution. This loss of understanding, which creates time management problems for the project manager, is usually caused by the project manager's:

- Waiting for someone else to make a decision that is his own responsibility.
- Neglecting to "keep his door open" and "walk the halls" to find out what's going on.
- Neglecting to use the experts correctly and trying to do it all himself.
- Being concerned about his previous technical discipline or profession rather than the best interest of the company.
- Being too interested in methods rather than in results.
- Trying to do the work himself rather than to delegate it to someone working slower.
- Wasting time in project team meetings discussing one-on-one problems.
- Failing to recognize that his boss is there to help.

Project managers must understand that even though they have the authority, responsibility, and accountability for a project, there are still parent company administrative duties that must be accepted. These items are usually additional work that the project manager has not considered.

Project management may not be the best system for managing resources, but it is better than anything we have had in the past. Effective time management may very well be the most important weapon in the project manager's arsenal for obtaining proper resource control.

6.8 MANAGEMENT PITFALLS

The project environment offers numerous opportunities for project managers and team members to get into trouble, above and beyond time management traps. These problem-causing activities are referred to as management pitfalls. Common types of management pitfalls are:

- Lack of planning
- Lack of self-control (knowing oneself)
- Activity traps

- Managing vs. doing
- People vs. task skills
- Ineffective communications
- Management bottlenecks

These management pitfalls are discussed in detail in Chapter 5 (Section 5.12), to which the reader is referred.

6.9 PROJECT COMMUNICATIONS

Proper communications are vital to project success. The subject of communications was discussed in Chapter 5 (Section 5.12) and will be reviewed only briefly here.

The four types of communication are:

- Written formal
- Written informal
- Oral formal
- Oral informal

Noise, from our own personality screens and from our perception screens, may distort or destroy information, causing ambiguity. Such ambiguity:

- Causes us to hear what we want to hear.
- Causes us to hear what the group wants.
- Causes us to relate to past experiences without being discriminatory.
- Causes situations like those depicted in Figure 6–10.

The reader should consult Section 5.13 for the six simple steps for communicating, techniques used to improve communication, and barriers to communication.

These admonitions from Section 5.13 are well worth repeating:

- Don't assume that the message you sent will be received in the form you sent it.
- The swiftest and most effective communications take place among people with common points of view. The manager who fosters a good relationship with his associates will have little difficulty in communicating with them.
- Communications must be established early in the project.

AS PROPOSED BY THE PROJECT SPONSOR

AS SPECIFIED IN THE PROJECT REQUEST

AS DESIGNED BY THE ENGINEER

AS PRODUCED BY MANUFACTURING

AS INSTALLED AT THE USER'S SITE

WHAT THE USER WANTED

Figure 6–10. A breakdown in communications. (Source unknown.)

Communication is also listening (see Figure 6–11). The advantages of being a good listener, both professionally and personally, are that:

- Subordinates know you are sincerely interested.
- You obtain feedback.
- Employee acceptance is fostered.

Figure 6–11. Listen to everything.

Ask yourself these questions:

- Do I make it easy for employees to talk to me?
- Am I sympathetic to their problems?
- Do I attempt to improve human relations?
- Do I make an extra effort to remember names and faces?

6.10 PROJECT MANAGEMENT BOTTLENECKS

Poor communications can produce communications bottlenecks, in both the parent and client organizations. The most common problems in information flow were discussed in Chapter 5 (see Section 5.15). Table 5–4 shows typical communications policies that can be employed to avoid bottlenecks.

PROBLEMS

6–1 Should time robbers be added to direct labor standards for pricing out work?

6–2 Is it possible for a project manager to improve his time management skills by knowing the "energy cycle" of his people? Can this energy cycle be a function of the hour of the day, day of the week, or whether or not overtime is required?

CASE STUDY: THE RELUCTANT WORKERS

Tim Aston had changed employers three months ago. His new position was project manager. At first he had stars in his eyes about becoming the best project manager that his company had ever seen. Now, he wasn't sure if project management was worth the effort. He made an appointment to see Phil Davies, director of project management.

Tim Aston: "Phil, I'm a little unhappy about the way things are going. I just can't seem to motivate my people. Every day, at 4:30 P.M., all of my people clean off their desks and go home. I've had people walk out of late afternoon team meetings because they were afraid that they'd miss their car pool. I have to schedule morning team meetings."

Phil Davies: "Look Tim. You're going to have to realize that in a project environment, people think that they come first and that the project is second. This is a way of life in our organizational form."

Tim Aston: "I've continuously asked my people to come to me if they have problems. I find that the people do not think that they need help and, therefore, do not want it. I just can't get my people to communicate more."

Phil Davies: "The average age of our employees is about forty-six. Most of our people have been here for twenty years. They're set in their ways. You're the first person that we've hired in the past three years. Some of our people may just resent seeing a thirty-year-old project manager."

Tim Aston: "I found one guy in the accounting department who has an excellent head on his shoulders. He's very interested in project management. I asked his boss if he'd release him for a position in project management, and his boss just laughed at me, saying something to the effect that as long as that guy is doing a good job for him, he'll never be released for an assignment elsewhere in the company. His boss seems more worried about his personal empire than he does in what's best for the company.

"We had a test scheduled for last week. The customer's top management was planning on flying in for first-hand observations. Two of my people said that they had programmed vacation days coming, and that they would not change, under any conditions. One guy was going fishing and the other guy was planning to spend a few days working with fatherless children in our community. Surely, these guys could change their plans for the test."

Phil Davies: "Many of our people have social responsibilities and outside interests. We encourage social responsibilities and only hope that the outside interests do not interfere with their jobs.

"There's one thing you should understand about our people. With an average age of forty-six, many of our people are at the top of their pay grades and have no place to go. They must look elsewhere for interests. These are the people you have to work with and motivate. Perhaps you should do some reading on human behavior."

CASE STUDY: TIME MANAGEMENT FOR PROJECT MANAGERS

Effective time management is one of the most difficult chores facing even the most experienced managers. For a manager who manages well-planned repetitive tasks, effective time management can be accomplished without very much pain. But for a project manager who must plan, schedule, and control resources and activities on unique, one-of-a-kind projects or tasks, effective time management may not be possible because of the continuous stream of unexpected problems that develop.

This exercise is designed to make you aware of the difficulties of time management both in a traditional organization as well as in a project environment. Before beginning the exercise, you must make the following assumptions concerning the nature of the project:

- You are the project manager on a project for an outside customer.
- The project is estimated at $3.5 million with a timne span of two years.
- The two year time span is broken down into three phases: Phase I—one year, beginning February 1. Phase II—six months; Phase III—six months. You are now at the end of Phase I. (Phases I and II overlap by approximately two weeks. You are now in the Monday of the next to the last week of Phase I.) Almost all of the work has been completed.
- Your project employs between 35 to 60 people, depending upon the phase that you are in.

- You, as the project manager, have three full-time assistant project managers that report directly to you in the project office; an assistant project manager each for engineering, cost control, and manufacturing. (Material procurement is included as part of the responsibilities of the manufacturing assistant project manager.)
- Phase I appears to be proceeding within the time, cost, and performance constraints.
- You have a scheduled team meeting for each Wednesday from 10–12 a.m. The meeting will be attended by all project office team members and the functional team members from all participating line organizations. Line managers are not team members and therefore do not show up at team meetings. It would be impossible for them to show up at the team meetings for all projects and still be able to function as a line manager. Even when requested, they may not show up at the team meeting because it is not effective time management for them to show up for a two hour meeting simply to discuss ten minutes of business. (Disregard the possibility that a team meeting agenda could resolve this problem.)

It is now Monday morning and you are home eating breakfast, waiting for your car pool to pick you up. As soon as you enter your office, you will be informed about problems, situations, tasks, and activities which have to be investigated. Your problem will be to accomplish effective time management for this entire week based upon the problems and situations that occur.

You will take each day one at a time. You will be given 10 problems and/or situations that will occur for each day, and the time necessary for resolution. You must try to optimize your time for each of the next five days and get the maximum amount of productive work accomplished. Obviously, the word "productive" can take on several meanings. You must determine what is meant by productive work. For the sake of simplicity, let us assume that your energy cycle is such that you can do eight hours of productive work in an eight hour day. You do not have to schedule idle time, except for lunch. However, you must be aware that in a project environment, the project manager occasionally becomes the catch-all for all work that line managers, line personnel, and even executives do not feel like accomplishing.

Following the 10 tasks for each day, you will find a worksheet which breaks down each day into half-hour blocks between 9:00 a.m. and 5:00 p.m. Your job will be to determine which of the tasks you wish to accomplish during each half-hour block. The following assumptions are made in scheduling work:

- Because of car pool requirements, overtime is not permitted.
- Family commitments for the next week prevent work at home. Therefore, you will not schedule any work after 5:00 p.m.
- The project manager is advised of the 10 tasks as soon as he arrives at work.

The first step in the solution to the exercise is to establish the priorities for each activity based upon:

- *Priority A:* This activity is urgent and must be completed today. (However, some A priorities can be withheld until the team meeting.)

- *Priority B:* This activity is important but not necessarily urgent.
- *Priority C:* This activity can be delayed, perhaps indefinitely.

Fill in the space after each activity as to the appropriate priority. next, you must determine which of the activities you have time to accomplish for this day. You have either seven or seven and one-half hours to use for effective time management, depending upon whether you want a half-hour or a full hour for lunch.

You have choices as to how to accomplish each of the activities. These choices are shown below:

- You can do the activity yourself. (Symbol = Y)
- You can delegate the responsibility to one of your assistant project managers (Symbol = D). If you use this technique, you can delegate only one hour's work of *your* work to each of your assistants without incurring a penalty. The key word here is that you are delegating *your work*. If the task that you wish to delegate is one which the assistant project manager would normally perform, then it does *not* count toward the one hour's worth of your work. This type of work is transmittal work and will be discussed below. For example, if you wish to delegate five hours of work to one of your assistant project managers and four of those hours are activities which would normally be his responsibility, then no penalty will be assessed. You are actually transmitting four hour and delegating one. You may assume that whatever work you assign to an assistant project manager will be completed on the day it is assigned, regardless of the priority.
- Many times, the project manager and his team are asked to perform work which is normally the responsibility of someone else, say an executive or a line manager. As an example, a line employee states that he doesn't have sufficient time to write a report and he wants you to do it, since you are the project manager. These types of requests can be returned to the requestor since they normally do not fall within the project manager's responsibilities. You may therefore, select one of the following four choices:
  - You can return the activity request back to the originator, whether line manager, executive, or subordinate, since it is not your responsibility (Symbol = R). Of course, you might want to do this activity, if you have time, in order to build up good will with the requestor.
  - Many times, work that should be requested of an assistant project manager is automatically sent to the project manager. In this case, the project manager will automatically transmit this work to the appropriate assistant project manager. (Symbol = T) As before, if the project manager feels that he has sufficient time available or if his assistants are burdened, he may wish to do the work himself. work which is normally the responsibility of an assistant project manager is transmitted, not delegated. Thus the project manager can transmit four hours of work (T) and still delegate one hour of work (D) to the same assistant project manager without incurring any penalty.
  - You can postpone work from one day to the next (Symbol = P). As an example, you decide that you want to accomplish a given Monday activity but do not have sufficient time. You can postpone the activity until Tuesday.

If you do not have sufficient time on Tuesday, you may then decide to transmit (T) the activity to one of your assistants, delegate (D) the activity to one of your assistants, return (R) the activity to the requestor or postpone (P) the activity another day. Postponing activities can be a trap. On Monday you decide to postpone a Category B priority. On Tuesday, the activity may become a category A priority and you have no time to accomplish it. If you make a decision to postpone an activity from Monday to Tuesday and find that you have made a mistake by not performing this activity on Monday, you *cannot* go back in time and correct the situation.

- You can simply consider the activity as unnecessary and avoid doing it. (Symbol = A)

After you have decided which activities you will perform each day, place them in the appropriate time slot based upon your own energy cycle. Later we will discuss energy cycles and the order of the activities accomplished each day. You will find one worksheet for each day. The worksheets follow the 10 daily situations and/or problems.

Repeat the procedure for each of the five days. Remember to keep track of the activities that are carried over from the previous days. Several of the problems can be resolved by more than one method. If you are thoroughly trapped between two or more choices on setting priorities or modes of resolution, then write a note or two to justify your answer in space beneath each activity.

Scoring System

Briefly look at the worksheet for one of the days. Under the column labelled "priority," the 10 activities for each day will be listed. You must first identify the priorities for each activity. Next, under the column labelled "method," you must select the method of accomplishment according to the legend at the bottom of the page. At the same time, you must fill in the activities you wish to perform yourself under the "accomplishment" column in the appropriate time slot because your method for accomplishment may be dependent upon whether or not you have sufficient time to accomplish the activity.

Notice that there is a space provided for you to keep track of activities that have been carried over. This means that if you have three activities on Monday's list that you wish to carry over until Tuesday, then you must turn to Tuesday's work plan and record these activities so that you will not forget.

You will not score any points until you complete Friday's work plan. Using the scoring sheets which follow Friday's work plan, you can return to the daily work plans and fill in the appropriate points. You will receive either positive points or negative points for each decision that you make. Negative points should be subtracted when calculating totals.

After completing the work plans for all five days, fill in the summary work plan which follows and be prepared to answer the summary questions.

You will not be told at this time how the scoring points will be awarded because it may impact your answers.

Turn the page and begin when ready.

Monday's Activities

Activity	Description	Priority
1.	The detailed schedules for Phase II must be updated prior to Thursday's meeting with the customer. (Time = 1 hr)	_____
2.	The manufacturing manager calls you and states that he cannot find a certain piece of equipment for tomorrow's production run test. (Time = ½ hr)	_____
3.	The local university has a monthly distinguished lecturer series scheduled for 3–5 p.m. today. You have been directed by the vice-president to attend and hear the lecture. The company will give you a car. Driving time to the university is one hour. (Time = 3 hrs)	_____
4.	A manufacturer's representative wants to call on you today to show you why his product is superior to the one that you are now using. (Time = ½ hr)	_____
5.	You must write a two-page weekly status report for the vice-president. Report is due on his desk by 1:00 p.m. Wednesday. (Time = 1 hr)	_____
6.	A vice-president calls you and suggests that you contact one of the other project managers about obtaining a uniform structure for the weekly progress reports. (Time = ½ hr)	_____
7.	A functional manager calls to inform you that, due to a schedule slippage on another project, your beginning milestones on Phase II may slip to the right because his people will not be available. He wants to know if you can look at the detailed schedules and modify them. (Time = 2 hrs)	_____
8.	The director of personnel wants to know if you have reviewed the three resumes that he sent you last week. He would like your written comments by quitting time today. (Time = 1 hr)	_____
9.	One of your assistant project managers asks you to review a detailed Phase III schedule which appears to have errors. (Time = 1 hr)	_____
10.	The procurement department calls with a request that you tell them approximately how much money you plan to spend on raw materials for Phase III. (Time = ½ hr)	_____

WORK PLAN

Day ___Monday___

Priority			Method	
Activity	Priority	Points	Method of Accomplishment	Points
1				
2				
3				
4				
5				
6				
7				
8				
9				
10				
Total			Total	

Accomplishment		
Time	Activity	Points
9:00–9:30		
9:30–10:00		
10:00–10:30		
10:30–11:00		
11:00–11:30		
11:30–12:00		
12:00–12:30		
12:30–1:00		
1:00–1:30		
1:30–2:00		
2:00–2:30		
2:30–3:00		
3:00–3:30		
3:30–4:00		
4:00–4:30		
4:30–5:00		
Total		

Activities Postponed Until Today	Today's Priority

Points	
Priority Points	
Method Points	
Accomplishment Points	
Today's Points	

Legend
Method of Accomplishment:
Y = you
D = delegate
T = transmit
R = return
A = avoid
P = postpone

Tuesday's Activities

Activity	Description	Priority
11.	A functional manager calls you wanting to know if his people should be scheduled for overtime next week. (Time = ½ hr)	_____
12.	You have a safety board meeting today from 1–3 p.m. and must review the agenda. (Time = 2½ hrs)	_____
13.	Because of an impending company cash flow problem, your boss has asked you for the detailed monthly labor expenses for the next three months. (Time = 2 hrs)	_____
14.	The vice-president has just called to inform you that two congressmen will be visiting the plant today and you are requested to conduct the tour of the facility from 3–5 p.m. (Time = 2 hrs)	_____
15.	You have developed a new policy for controlling overtime costs on Phase II. You must inform your people either by memo, phone, or team meeting. (Time = ½ hr)	_____
16.	You must sign and review 25 purchase order requisitions for Phase III raw materials. It is company policy that the project manager sign all forms. Almost all of the items require a three month lead time. (Time = 1 hr)	_____
17.	The engineering division manager has asked you to assist one of his people this afternoon in the solution of a technical problem. You are not required to do this. It would be as a personal favor for the Engineering manager, a man whom you reported to for the six years that you were an engineering functional manager. (Time = 2 hrs)	_____
18.	The data processing department manager informs you that the company is trying to eliminate unnecessary reports. He would like you to tell him which reports you can do without. (Time = ½ hr)	_____
19.	The assistant project manager for cost informs you that he does not know how to fill out the revised corporate project review form. (Time = ½ hr)	_____
20.	One of the functional managers wants an immediate explanation of why the scope of effort for Phase II was changed this late into the project and why he wasn't informed. (Time = 1 hr)	_____

WORK PLAN   Day____Tuesday_____

Priority			Method				Accomplishment		
Activity	Priority	Points	Method of Accomplishment	Points		Time	Activity	Points
11						9:00–9:30		
12						9:30–10:00		
13						10:00–10:30		
14						10:30–11:00		
15						11:00–11:30		
16						11:30–12:00		
17						12:00–12:30		
18						12:30–1:00		
19						1:00–1:30		
20						1:30–2:00		
Total			Total			2:00–2:30		
						2:30–3:00		
						3:00–3:30		
						3:30–4:00		
						4:00–4:30		
						4:30–5:00		
						Total		

Activities Postponed Until Today	Today's Priority

Points	
Priority Points	
Method Points	
Accomplishment Points	
Today's Points	

Legend
Method of Accomplishment:
Y = you
D = delegate
T = transmit
R = return
A = avoid
P = postpone

Wednesday's Activities

Activity	Description	Priority
21.	A vice-president calls you stating that he has just read the rough draft of your Phase I report and wants to discuss some of the conclusions with you before the report is submitted to the customer on Thursday. (Time = 2 hrs)	_____
22.	The reproduction department informs you that they are expecting the final version of the in-house quarterly report for your project by noon today. The report is on your desk waiting for final review. (Time = 1 hr)	_____
23.	The manufacturing department manager calls to say that they may have to do more work than initially defined for in Phase II. A meeting is requested. (Time = 1 hr)	_____
24.	Quality control sends you a memo stating that, unless changes are made, they will not be able to work with the engineering specifications developed for Phase III. A meeting will be required with all assistant project managers in attendance. (Time = 1 hr)	_____
25.	A functional manager calls to tell you that the raw data from yesterday's tests are terrific and invites you to come up to the laboratory and see the results yourself. (Time = 1 hr)	_____
26.	Your assistant project manager is having trouble resolving a technical problem. The functional manager wants to deal with you directly. This problem must be resolved by Friday or else a major Phase II milestone might slip. (Time = 1 hr)	_____
27.	You have a technical interchange meeting with the customer scheduled for 1–3 p.m. on Thursday, and must review the handout before it goes to publication. The reproduction department has requested at least 12 hours notice. (Time = 1 hr)	_____
28.	You have a weekly team meeting from 10–12 a.m. (Time = 2 hrs)	_____
29.	You must dictate minutes to your secretary concerning your weekly team meeting which is held on Wednesday 10–12 a.m. (Time = ½ hr)	_____
30.	A new project problem has occurred in the manufacturing area and your manufacturing functional team members are reluctant to make a decision. (Time = 1 hr)	_____

WORK PLAN

Day _____Wednesday_____

Priority			Method	
Activity	Priority	Points	Method of Accomplishment	Points
21				
22				
23				
24				
25				
26				
27				
28				
29				
30				
Total			Total	

Accomplishment		
Time	Activity	Points
9:00–9:30		
9:30–10:00		
10:00–10:30		
10:30–11:00		
11:00–11:30		
11:30–12:00		
12:00–12:30		
12:30–1:00		
1:00–1:30		
1:30–2:00		
2:00–2:30		
2:30–3:00		
3:00–3:30		
3:30–4:00		
4:00–4:30		
4:30–5:00		
Total		

Activities Postponed Until Today	Today's Priority

Points	
Priority Points	
Method Points	
Accomplishment Points	
Today's Points	

Legend
Method of Accomplishment:
Y = you
D = delegate
T = transmit
R = return
A = avoid
P = postpone

Thursday's Activities

Activity	Description	Priority
31.	The electrical engineering department informs you that they have completed some Phase II activities ahead of schedule and want to know if you wish to push any other activities to the left. (Time = 1 hr)	_____
32.	The assistant project manager for cost informs you that the corporate overhead rate is increasing faster than anticipated. If this continues, severe costs overruns will occur in Phases II and III. A schedule and cost review is necessary. (Time = 2 hrs)	_____
33.	Your insurance man is calling to see if you wish to increase your life insurance. (Time = ½ hr)	_____
34.	You cannot find one of last week's manufacturing line manager's technical reports as to departmental project status. You'll need it for the customer technical interchange meeting. (Time = ½ hr)	_____
35.	One of your car pool members wants to talk to you concerning next Saturday's golf tournament. (Time = ½ hr)	_____
36.	A functional manager calls to inform you that, due to a change in his division's workload priorities, people with the necessary technical expertise may not be available for next week's Phase II tasks. (Time = 2 hrs)	_____
37.	An employee calls you stating that he is receiving conflicting instructions from one of your assistant project managers and his line manager. (Time = 1 hr)	_____
38.	The customer has requested bimonthly instead of monthly team meetings for Phase II. You must decide whether or not to add an additional project office team member to support the added workload. (Time = ½ hr)	_____
39.	Your secretary reminds you that you must make a presentation to the Rotary Club tonight on how your project will affect the local economy. You must prepare your speech. (Time = 2 hrs)	_____
40.	The bank has just called you concerning your personal loan. The information is urgent to get loan approval in time. (Time = ½ hr)	_____

WORK PLAN

Day____Thursday____

Priority			Method		Accomplishment		
Activity	Priority	Points	Method of Accomplishment	Points	Time	Activity	Points
31					9:00–9:30		
32					9:30–10:00		
33					10:00–10:30		
34					10:30–11:00		
35					11:00–11:30		
36					11:30–12:00		
37					12:00–12:30		
38					12:30–1:00		
39					1:00–1:30		
40					1:30–2:00		
Total			Total		2:00–2:30		
					2:30–3:00		
					3:00–3:30		
					3:30–4:00		
					4:00–4:30		
					4:30–5:00		
					Total		

Activities Postponed Until Today	Today's Priority

Points	
Priority Points	
Method Points	
Accomplishment Points	
Today's Points	

Legend
Method of Accomplishment:
Y = you
D = delegate
T = transmit
R = return
A = avoid
P = postpone

Friday's Activities

Activity	*Description*	*Priority*
41.	An assistant project manager has asked for your solution to a recurring problem. (Time = ½ hr)	_____
42.	A functional employee is up for a merit review. You must fill out a brief checklist form and discuss it with the employee. The form must be on the functional manager's desk by next Tuesday. (Time = ½ hr)	_____
43.	the personnel department wants you to review the summer vacation schedule for your project office personnel. (Time = ½ hr)	_____
44.	The vice-president calls you into his office stating that he has seen the excellent test results from this week's work, and feels that a follow-on contract should be considered. He wants to know if you can develop reasonable justification for requesting a follow-on contract at this early date. (Time = 1 hr)	_____
45.	The travel department says that you'll have to make your own travel arrangements for next month's trip to one of the customers, since you are taking a planned vacation trip in conjunction with the customer visit. (Time = ½ hr)	_____
46.	The personnel manager has asked if you would be willing to conduct a screening interview for an applicant who wants to be an assistant project manager. The applicant will be available this afternoon from 1–2 p.m. (Time = 1 hr)	_____
47.	Your assistant project manager wants to know why you haven't approved his request to take MBA courses this quarter. (Time = ½ hr)	_____
48.	Your assistant project manager wants to know if he has the authority to visit vendors without informing procurement. (Time = ½ hr)	_____
49.	You have just received your copy of *Engineering Review Quarterly* and would like to look it over. (Time = ½ hr)	_____
50.	You have been asked to make a statement before the grievance committee (this Friday, 10–12 a.m.) because one of the functional employees has complained about working overtime on Sunday mornings. You'll have to be in attendance for the entire meeting. (Time = 2 hrs)	_____

WORK PLAN   Day____Friday_____

Priority			Method			Accomplishment		
Activity	Priority	Points	Method of Accomplishment	Points		Time	Activity	Points
41						9:00–9:30		
42						9:30–10:00		
43						10:00–10:30		
44						10:30–11:00		
45						11:00–11:30		
46						11:30–12:00		
47						12:00–12:30		
48						12:30–1:00		
49						1:00–1:30		
50						1:30–2:00		
Total			Total			2:00–2:30		
						2:30–3:00		
						3:00–3:30		
						3:30–4:00		
						4:00–4:30		
						4:30–5:00		
						Total		

Activities Postponed Until Today	Today's Priority

Points	
Priority Points	
Method Points	
Accomplishment Points	
Today's Points	

Legend
Method of Accomplishment:
Y = you
D = delegate
T = transmit
R = return
A = avoid
P = postpone

Rationale and Point Awards

In the answers which follow, your recommendations may differ from those of the author because of the type of industry or the nature of the project. You will be given the opportunity to defend your answers at a later time.

(a) If you selected the correct priority according to the table on the following page, then the following system should be employed for awarding points:

Priority	Points
A	10
B	5
C	3

(b) If you selected the correct accomplishment mode according to the table on the following page, then the following system should be employed for assigning points:

Method of Accomplishment	Points
Y	10
T	10
P	8
D	8
A	6

(c) You will receive 10 bonus points for each correctly postponed or delayed activity accomplished during the team meeting.

(d) You will receive 5 points for each half hour time slot in which you perform a Priority A activity (one which is correctly identified as priority A).

(e) You will receive a 10 point penalty for any activity which is split.

(f) You will receive a 20 point penalty for each Priority A or B activity not accomplished by you or your team by Friday at 5:00 p.m.

Activity	*Rationale*
1.	The updating of schedules, especially for Phase II, should be of prime importance because of the impact on functional resources. These schedules can be delegated to assistant project managers. However, with a team meeting scheduled for Wednesday, it should be an easy task to update the schedules when all of the players are present. The updating of the schedules should *not* be delayed until Thursday. Sufficient time must be allocated for close analysis and reproduction services.
2.	This must be done immediately. Your assistant project manager for manufacturing should be able to handle this activity.
3.	You must handle this yourself.
4.	Here, we assume that the representative is available only today. The assistant project managers can handle this activity. This activity may be important if you were unaware of this vendor's product.

Activity (continued)   *Rationale* (continued)

5.   This could be delegated to your assistants provided that you allow sufficient time for personal review on Wednesday.

6.   Delaying this activity for one more week should not cause any problems. This activity can be delegated.

7.   You must take charge at once.

8.   Even though your main concern is the project, you still must fulfill your company's administrative requirements.

9.   This can be delayed until Wednesday's team meeting, especially since these are Phase III schedules. However, there is no guarantee that line people will be ready or knowledgeable to duscuss phase III this early. You will probably have to do this yourself.

10.   The procurement request must be answered. Your assistant project manager for manufacturing should have this information available.

11.   This is urgent and should *not* be postponed until the team meeting. Good project managers will give functional managers as much information as possible as early as possible for resource control. This task can be delegated to the assistant project managers, but it is not recommended.

12.   This belongs to the project manager. The agenda review and the meeting can be split, but it is not recommended.

13.   This must be done immediately. The results could severely limit your resources (especially if overtime would normally be required). Although your assistant project managers will probably be involved, the majority of the work is yours.

14.   Most project managers hate a request like this but know that such situations as this are inevitable.

15.   Project policies should be told by the project manager himself. Policy changes should be announced as early as possible. Team meetings are appropriate for such actions.

16.   Obviously, the project manager must do this task himself. Fortunately, there is sufficient time if the lead times are accurate.

17.   The priority of this activity is actually your choice, but an A priority is preferred if you have time. This activity cannot be delegated.

18.   This activity must be done, but the question is when. Parts of this task can be delegated, but the final decision must be made by the project manager.

19.   Obviously you must do this yourself. Your priority, of course, depends upon the deadline on the corporate project review form.

20.   The project manager must perform this activity immediately.

21.   Top level executives from both the customer and contractor often communicate project status among themselves. Therefore, since the conclusions in the report reflect corporate policy, this activity should be accomplished immediately.

22.   The reproduction department considers each job as a project and therefore you should try not to violate their milestones. This activity can be delegated, depending upon the nature of the report.

Activity (continued)   *Rationale* (continued)

23. This could have a severe impact on your program. Although you could delegate this to one of your assistants, you should do this yourself because of the ramifications.
24. This must be done and the team meeting is the ideal place.
25. You, personally, should give the functional manager the courtesy of showing you his outstanding results. However, it is not a high priority and could even be delegated or postponed since you'll see the data eventually.
26. The question here is the importance of the problem. The problem must be resolved by Thursday in case an executive meeting needs to be scheduled to establish company direction. Waiting until the last minute can be catastrophic here.
27. The project manager should personally review all data presented to the customer. Check Thursday's schedule. Did you forget the interchange meeting?
28. This is your show.
29. This should be done immediately. Nonparticipants need to know the project status. The longer you wait, the greater the risk that you will neglect something important. This activity can be delegated, but it is not recommended.
30. You may have to solve this yourself even though you have an assistant project manager for manufacturing. The decision may impact the schedule and milestones.
31. Activities as this do not happen very often. But when they do, the project manager should make the most of them, as fast as he can. These are gold mine activities. They can be delegated, but not postponed.
32. If this activity is not accomplished immediately, the results can be catastrophic. Regardless of the project manager's first inclination to delegate, this activity should be done by the project manager himself.
33. This activity can be postponed or even avoided, if necessary.
34. Obviously, if the report is that important, then your assistant project managers should have copies of the report and the activity can be delegated.
35. This activity should be discussed in the car pool, not on company time.
36. This is extremely serious. The line manager would probably prefer to work directly with the project manager on this problem.
37. This is an activity which you should handle. Transmitting this to one of your assistants may aggravate the situation further. Although it is possible that this activity could be postponed, it is highly unlikely that time would smooth out the conflict.
38. This is a decision for the project manager. Extreme urgency may not be necessary.
39. Project managers also have a social responsibility.
40. The solution to this activity is up for grabs. Most companies realize

Priority/Accomplishment Mode

ACTIVITY	Monday PRIOR.	Monday ACCOM.	Tuesday PRIOR.	Tuesday ACCOM.	Wednesday PRIOR.	Wednesday ACCOM.	Thursday PRIOR.	Thursday ACCOM.	Friday PRIOR.	Friday ACCOM.
1	B	D,Y,T,P	B	D,Y,T,P	A	D,Y,T				
2	A	D,Y,T								
3	A	Y								
4	A/B	D,Y,T								
5	B	D,Y,P	B	D,Y,P	A	D,Y				
6	B	D,Y,P	B	D,Y,P	B	D,Y,P	B	D,Y,P	B	D,Y,P
7	A	Y								
8	A	Y								
9	B	Y,P	B	Y,P	A	Y				
10	B	Y,T,P	B	Y,T,P	B	Y,T,P	B	Y,T,P	B	Y,T,P
11			A	D,Y,T						
12			A	Y						
13			A	Y,P						
14			A	Y						
15			B	P,Y	A	Y				
16			B	Y,P	B	Y,P	B	Y,P	B	Y,P
17			C	A,Y						
18			B/C	D,Y,P	B	D,Y,P	B	D,Y,P	B	D,Y,P
19			A/B	Y,P	A/B	Y,P	A/B	Y,P	A/B	Y,P
20			A	Y						
21					A	Y				
22					A	D,Y				
23					A	D,Y,T				

(continued)

Row	1	2	3	4	5	6
24					Y	A
25	Y,T,P,R	B	Y,T,P,D	B	Y,T,P,D	B
26			Y	A	Y	B
27					Y	A
28					Y	A
29					Y,D	A
30					Y,T	A
31			Y,D	A		
32			Y	A		
33	Y,P	C	Y,P	C		
34			Y,T	A		
35	A,P	C	A,P	C		
36			Y,T	A		
37			Y	A		
38	Y,P	B	Y,P	B		
39			Y	A		
40			Y	A		
41	R	A/B				
42	Y,P	B				
43	Y,P,D	B				
44	Y	A				
45	Y,P	B				
46	Y,T,D	A				
47	Y	A				
48	Y,T,P,D,R	B				
49	Y,P,A	C				
50	Y	A				

Activity (continued)   *Rationale* (continued)

that employees occasionally need company time to complete personal business.

41.   Why is he asking you about a recurring problem? How did he solve it last time? Let him do it again.

42.   You must do this personally, but it can wait until Monday.

43.   This activity is not urgent and can be accomplished by your assistant project managers.

44.   This could be your lucky day.

45.   Although most managers would prefer to delegate this activity to their secretary, it is really the responsibility of the project manager since it involves personal business.

46.   This is an example of an administrative responsibility which is required of all personnel regardless of the job title or management level. This activity must be accomplished today, if time permits.

47.   Although you might consider this as a B priority or one which can be postponed, you must remember that your assistant project manager considers this as an A priority anbd would like an answer today. You are morally obligated to give him the answer today.

48.   Why can't he get the answer himself? Whether or not you handle this activity might depend on the priority and how much time you have available.

49.   How important is it for you to review the publication?

50.   This is mandatory attendance on your behalf. You have total responsibility for all overtime scheduled on your project. You may wish to bring one of your assistant project managers with you for moral support.

Now take the total points for each day and complete the following table:

SUMMARY WORK PLAN	
Day	Points
Monday	
Tuesday	
Wednesday	
Thursday	
Friday	
Total	

Conclusions and Summary Questions:

1. Project managers have a tendency to want to carry the load themselves, even if it means working 60 hours a week. You were told to do everything within your normal working day. But, as a potentially good project manager, you probably

have the natural tendency of wanting to postpone some work until a later date so that you can do it yourself. Doing the activities, when they occur, even through transmittal or delegation, is probably the best policy. You might wish to do the game again at a later time and see if you can beat your present score. Only this time, try to do as many tasks as possible on each day, even if it means delegation.

2. Several of the activities were company, not project, requests. Project managers have a tendency to avoid administrative responsibilities unless it deals directly with their project. This process of project management "tunnel vision" can lead to antagonism and conflicts if the proper attitude is not developed on the part of the project manager. This can easily carry down to his assistants as well.

3. Several of the activities could have been returned to the requestor. However, in a project environment where the project manager cannot be successful without the functional manager's support, most project managers would never turn away a line employee's request for assistance.

4. make a list of the activities where your answers differ from those of the answer key and where you feel that there exists sufficient justification for your interpretation.

5. Quite often self-productivity can be increased by knowing one's own energy cycle. Are your more important meetings in the mornings or afternoons? What time of day do you perform your most productive work? When do you do your best writing? Does your energy cycle vary according to the day of the week?

7
Conflicts

7.0 INTRODUCTION

In discussing the project environment, we have purposely avoided discussion of what may be the single most important characteristic of the project environment: conflicts. Opponents of project management assert that the major reason why many companies avoid changeover to a project management organizational structure is either fear or an inability to handle the resulting conflicts. Conflicts are a way of life in a project structure and can generally occur at any level in the organization, usually the result of conflicting objectives.

The project manager has often been described as a conflict manager. In many organizations the project manager continually fights fires and crises evolving from conflicts, and delegates the day-to-day responsibility of running the project to the project team members. Although this is not the best situation, it cannot always be prevented from occurring, especially after organizational restructuring or the initiation of projects requiring new resources.

The ability to handle conflicts requires an understanding of why conflicts occur. Four questions can be asked, the answers to which should be beneficial in handling, and possibly preventing, conflicts.

- What are the project objectives and can they be in conflict with other projects?
- Why do conflicts occur?
- How do we resolve conflicts?
- Is there any type of preliminary analysis that could identify possible conflicts before they occur?

7.1 OBJECTIVES

Each project identified as such by management must have at least one objective. The objectives of the project must be made known to all project personnel and all managers, at every level of the organization. If this information is not communicated accurately, then it is entirely possible that upper-level managers, project managers, and functional managers may all have a different interpretation of the ultimate objective, a situation that invites conflicts to occur. As an example, Company X has been awarded a $100,000 government contract for surveillance of a component that appears to be fatiguing. Top management might view the objective of this project to be the discovery of the cause of the fatigue and elimination of it in future component production. This might give Company X a "jump" on the competition. The division manager might just view it as a means of keeping people employed, with no follow-on possibilities. The department manager can consider the objective as either another job that has to be filled, or a means of establishing new surveillance technology. The department manager, therefore, can staff the necessary positions with any given degree of expertise, depending upon the importance and definition of the objective.

Projects are established with objectives in mind. Project objectives must be:

- Specific, not general
- Not overly complex
- Measurable, tangible, and verifiable
- Realistic and attainable
- Established within resource bounds
- Consistent with resources available or anticipated
- Consistent with organizational plans, policies, and procedures

Unfortunately, the above characteristics are not always evident, especially if we consider that the project might be unique to the organization in question. As an example, research and development projects sometimes start out general, rather than specific. Research and development objectives are reestablished as time goes on because the initial objective may not be attainable. As an example, Company Y believes that they can develop a high-energy rocket-motor propellant. A proposal is submitted to the government, and, after a review period, the contract is awarded. However, as is the case with all R&D projects, there always exists the question of whether the objective is attainable within time, cost, and performance constraints. It might be possible to achieve the initial objective, but at an incredibly high production cost. In this case, the specifications of the propellant (i.e., initial objectives) may be modified so as to align them closer to the available production funds.

Reestablishment of objectives occurs most frequently during the definition phase of system/project development. If resources are not available, then alternatives must be considered. This type of analysis exists during the initial stages of feasibility studies, construction, design, and estimates, and new faculty and equipment purchases.

Once the total project objective is set, subobjectives are defined in order that cost and performance may be tracked. (This procedure will be described in later chapters.) Subobjectives are a vital link in establishing proper communications between the project and functional managers. In a project environment employees are evaluated according to accomplishment, rather than to how they spend their time. Since the project manager has temporarily assigned personnel, many of whom may have never worked for him either part-time or full-time, it is vital that employees have clearly defined objectives and subobjectives. In order to accomplish this effectively, without wasting valuable time, employees should have a part in setting their own objectives and subobjectives.

Many projects are directed and controlled using a management-by-objective approach based upon effective project/functional communications and working relations as stated above. The philosophy of management by objectives:

- Is proactive rather than reactive management.
- Is results-oriented emphasizing accomplishment.
- Focuses on change to improve individual and organizational effectiveness.

Management by objectives is a systems approach for aligning project goals with organizational goals, project goals with the goals of other subunits of the organization, and project goals with individual goals. Furthermore, management by objectives (MBO) can be regarded as a:

- Systems approach to planning and obtaining project results for an organization.
- Strategy of meeting individual needs at the same time that project needs are met.
- Method of clarifying what each individual and organizational unit's contribution to the project should be.

MBO professes to have a framework that can promote the effective utilization of time and other project resources. Many organizations, however, do not utilize the MBO philosophy. Whether or not MBO is utilized, project objectives must be set.

- If you do not have the right objectives, you may not have any idea of whether or not you are on the right road.
- Without objectives it is difficult to measure results against prior expectations.
- Objectives are utilized to determine individual goals that will provide maximum effectiveness of the whole.

7.2 THE CONFLICT ENVIRONMENT

In the project environment, conflicts are inevitable. However, as described in Chapter 5, conflicts and their resoution can be planned for. For example, conflicts can easily develop out of a situation where members of a group have a misunderstanding of each other's roles and responsibilities. Through documentation, such as the linear responsibility charts, it is possible to establish formal organizational procedures (either at the project level or company-wide). Resolution means collaboration in which people must rely upon one another. Without this, mistrust will prevail and activity documentation can be expected to increase.

The most common type of conflicts involve:

- Manpower resources
- Equipment and facilities
- Capital expenditures
- Costs
- Technical opinions and trade-offs
- Priorities
- Administrative procedures
- Scheduling
- Responsibilities
- Personality clashes

Each of these conflicts can vary in relative intensity over the life cycle of a project. The relative intensity can vary as a function of:

- Getting closer to project constraints
- Having only two constraints instead of three (i.e., time and performance, but not cost)
- The project life cycle itself
- The person whom the conflict is with

Sometimes conflict is "meaningful" and produces beneficial results. These meaningful conflicts should be permitted to continue as long as project constraints are not violated and beneficial results are being received. An example of this would be two technical specialists arguing that each has a better way of solving a problem, and each trying to find additional supporting data for his hypothesis.

Some conflicts are inevitable and continuously reoccur. As an example, let us consider the raw material and finished goods inventory. Manufacturing wants the largest possible inventory of raw materials on hand so as not to shut down production; sales and marketing want the largest finished goods inventory so that customer demands will be met; and, finally, finance and accounting want the smallest raw material and finished goods inventory so the books will look better and no cash flow problems will occur.

Conflicts appear differently depending on the organizational structure. In the traditional structure, conflict should be avoided; in the project structure, conflict is part of change and therefore inevitable. In the traditional structure, conflict is the result of troublemakers and egoists; in the project structure, conflict is determined by the structure of the system and relationship among components. In the traditional structure, conflict is bad; in the project structure, conflict may be beneficial.

Conflicts can occur with anyone and over anything. Some people contend that personality conflicts are the most difficult to resolve. Below are several situations. The reader might consider what he or she would do if placed in the situations.

- Two of your functional team members appear to have personality clashes and almost always assume opposite points of view during decision making. They are both from the same line organization. Conflicts are inevitable.
- Two of your line managers continuously argue as to who should perform a certain test. You know that this situation exists, and that the department managers are trying to work it out themselves, often with great pain. However, you are not sure for how long they will be able to resolve the problem themselves.
- Manufacturing says that they cannot produce the end item according to engineering specifications.
- R&D quality control and manufacturing operations quality control argue as to who should perform a certain test on an R&D project. R&D postulates that it is their project, and manufacturing argues that it will eventually go into production and that they wish to be involved as early as possible.
- During contract negotiations, a disagreement occurs. The vice-president of Company A orders his director of finance, the contract negotiator, to break off negotiations with Company B because the contract negotiator for Company B does not report directly to a vice-president.
- Mr. X is the project manager of a $65 million project of which $1 million is subcontracted out to another company in which Mr. Y is the project manager. Mr. X does not consider Mr. Y as his counterpart and continuously communicates with the director of engineering in Mr. Y's company.

Ideally, the project manager should report high enough so that he can get timely assistance in resolving conflicts. Unfortunately, this is easier said than done. Therefore, project managers must plan for conflict resolution. As examples of this:

- The project manager might wish to concede on a low-intensity conflict if he knows that a high-intensity conflict is expected to occur at a later point in the project.
- Jones Construction Company has recently won a $120 million effort for a local company. The effort includes three separate construction projects, each one beginning at the same time. Two of the projects are 24 months in duration, and the third one is 36 months. Each project has its own project manager. When resource conflicts occur between the projects, the customer is usually called in.
- Richard is a department manager who must supply resources to four different projects. Although each project has an established priority, the project managers continuously argue that departmental resources are not being allocated effectively. Richard now holds a monthly meeting with all four of the project managers and lets them determine how the resources should be allocated.

Many executives feel that the best way of resolving conflicts is by establishing priorities. This may be true as long as priorities are not continuously shifted around. As an example, Minnesota Power and Light establishes priorities as:

- Level 0: no completion date
- Level 1: to be completed on or before a specific date
- Level 2: to be completed on or before a given fiscal quarter
- Level 3: to be completed within a given year

This type of technique will work as long as we do not have a large number of projects in any one group, say Level 1. How would we then distinguish between projects?

Executives are responsible for establishing priorities and often make the mistake of *not* telling the project managers the reasons for the priority level. There may be sound reasons for concealing this information, but this practice should be avoided whenever possible.

The most common factors influencing the establishment of project priorities include:

- The technical risks in development

- The risks that the company will incur, financially or competitively
- The nearness of the delivery date and the urgency
- The penalties that can accompany late delivery dates
- The expected savings, profit increase, and return on investment
- The amount of influence that the customer possesses, possibly due to the size of the project
- The impact on other projects
- The impact on affiliated organizations
- The impact on a particular product line

The ultimate responsibility for establishing priorities rests with top-level management. Yet even with priority establishment, conflicts still develop. David Wilemon has identified several reasons why conflicts still occur:[1]

- The greater the diversity of disciplinary expertise among the participants of a project team, the greater the potential for conflict to develop among members of the team.
- The lower the project manager's degree of authority, reward, and punishment power over those individuals and organizational units supporting his project, the greater the potential for conflict to develop.
- The less the specific objectives of a project (cost, schedule, and technical performance) are understood by the project team members, the more likely it is that conflict will develop.
- The greater the role ambiguity among the participants of a project team, the more likely it is that conflict will develop.
- The greater the agreement on superordinate goals by project team participants, the lower the potential for detrimental conflict.
- The more the members of functional areas perceive that the implementation of a project management system will adversely ursurp their traditional roles, the greater the potential for conflict.
- The lower the percent need for interdependence among organizational units supporting a project, the greater the potential for dysfunctional conflict.
- The higher the managerial level within a project or functional area, the more likely it is that conflicts will be based upon deep-seated parochial resentments. By contrast, at the project or task level, it is more likely that cooperation will be facilitated by task orientation and professionalism that a project requires for completion.

---

1. David L. Wilemon, "Managing Conflict in Temporary Management Situations," *The Journal of Management Studies,* 1973, pp. 282–296.

7.3 MANAGING CONFLICT

Temporary management situations produce conflicts. This is a natural occurrence resulting from the differences in the organizational behavior of individuals, the differences in the way that functional and project managers view the work required, and the lack of time necessary for project managers and functional personnel to establish ideal working relationships.

Regardless of how well planning is developed, project managers must be willing to operate in an environment that is characterized by constant and rapid change. This turbulent environment can be the result of changes in the scope of work, a shifting of key project and functional personnel due to new priorities, and other unforeseen developments. The success or failure of a project manager is quite often measured by the ability to deal with change.

In contrast to the functional manager who works in a more standardized and predictable environment, the project manager must live with constant change. In his effort to integrate various disciplines across functional lines, he must learn to cope with the pressures of the changing work environment. He has to foster a climate that promotes the ability of his personnel to adapt to this continuously changing work environment. Demanding compliance to rigid rules, principles, and techniques is often counter-productive. In such situations, an environment conducive to effective project management is missing and the project leader too often suffers the same fate as heart-transplant patients—rejection![2]

There is no one single method that will suffice for managing all conflicts in temporary management situations because:

- There exist several types of conflicts.
- Each conflict can assume a different relative intensity over the life cycle of the project.

The detrimental aspects of these conflicts can be minimized if the project manager can anticipate their occurrence and understand their composition. The prepared manager can then resort to one of several conflict resolution modes in order to more effectively manage the disagreements that can occur.[3]

Thamhain and Wilemon surveyed 150 project managers on conflict man-

2. H. S. Dugan, H. J. Thamhain, and D. L. Wilemon, "Managing Change in Project Management," *Proceedings of the Ninth Annual International Seminar/Symposium on Project Management,* Chicago, October 22–26, 1977, pp. 178–188.
3. The remainder of Section 7.3 is devoted to Hans J. Thamhain and David L. Wilemon, "Conflict Management in Project Life Cycles," *Sloan Management Review,* Summer 1975, pp. 31–50. Reprinted by permission.

agement. Their research tried to determine the type and magnitude of the particular type of conflict which is most common at specific life-cycle stages, regardless of the particular nature of the project. For the purpose of their paper the authors stated the following definitions:

Conflict is defined as the behavior of an individual, a group, or an organization which impedes or restricts (at least temporarily) another party from attaining its desired goals. Although conflict may impede the attainment of one's goals, the consequences may be beneficial if they produce new information which, in turn, enhances the decision-making process. By contrast, conflict becomes dysfunctional if it results in poor project decision-making, lengthy delays over issues which do not importantly affect the outcome of the project, or a disintegration of the team's efforts.[4]

The study presented in their paper was part of an ongoing and integrated research effort on conflict in the project-oriented work environment.[4-8]

Project managers frequently indicate that one of the requirements for effective performance is the ability to effectively manage various conflicts and disagreements that invariably arise in task accomplishment. While several research studies have reported on the general nature of conflict in project management, few studies have been devoted to the cause and management of conflict in specific project life-cycle stages. If project managers are aware of some of the major causes of disagreements in the various project life-cycle phases, there is a greater likelihood that the detrimental aspects of these potential conflict situations can be avoided or minimized.

This study first investigates the mean intensity of seven potential conflict determinants frequently thought to be prime causes of conflict in project management. Next, the intensity of each conflict determinant is viewed from the perspective of individual project life-cycle stages. An examination is then made of various conflict-handling modes used by project managers which leads to a number of suggestions for minimizing the detrimental effects of conflict over the project life cycle.

4. H. J. Thamhain and D. L. Wilemon, "Conflict Management in Project-Oriented Work Environments," *Proceedings of the Sixth International Meeting of the Project Management Institute,* Washington, D.C., September 18–21, 1974.
5. "Diagnosing Conflict Determinants in Project Management," *IEEE Transactions on Engineering Management,* Vol. 22, 1975, pp. 35–44.
6. D. L. Wilemon and J. P. Cicero, "The Project Manager—Anomalies and Ambiguities," *Academy of Management Journal,* Fall 1970, pp. 269–282.
7. D. L. Wilemon, "Project Management Conflict: A View From Apollo," *Proceedings of the Third Annual Symposium of the Project Management Institute,* Houston, Texas, October 1971.
8. D. L. Wilemon, "Project Management and its Conflicts: A View From Apollo," *Chemical Technology,* Vol. 2, No. 9, 1972, pp. 527–534.

Research Design

Approximately 150 managers from a variety of technology-oriented companies were asked to participate in this comprehensive research project. A usable sample of 100 project managers was eventually selected for this study.

A questionnaire was used as the principal data collection instrument. In addition, discussions were held with a number of project managers on the subject under investigation to supplement the questionnaire data and the resulting conclusions. This process proved helpful in formulating a number of recommendations for minimizing detrimental conflicts.

The development of the questionnaire relied on several pilot studies. It was designed to measure values on three variables: (1) the average intensity of seven potential conflict determinants over the entire project life cycle; (2) the intensity of each of the seven conflict sources in the four project life-cycle phases; and (3) the conflict resolution modes used by project managers.

Mean Conflict Intensity

The average conflict intensity perceived by the project managers was measured for various conflict sources and for various phases of the project life cycle. Project managers were asked to rank the intensity of conflict they experienced for each of seven potential conflict sources on a standard four-point scale. The seven potential sources are:

- *Conflict over Project Priorities.* The views of project participants often differ over the sequence of activities and tasks that should be undertaken to achieve successful project completion. Conflict over priorities may occur not only between the project team and other support groups but also within the project team.
- *Conflict over Administrative Procedures.* A number of managerial and administrative-oriented conflicts may develop over how the project will be managed; i.e., the definition of the project manager's reporting relationships, definition of responsibilities, interface relationships, project scope, operational requirements, plan of execution, negotiated work agreements with other groups, and procedures for administrative support.
- *Conflict over Technical Opinions and Performance Trade-offs.* In technology-oriented projects, disagreements may arise over technical issues, performance specifications, technical trade-offs, and the means to achieve performance.
- *Conflict over Manpower Resources.* Conflicts may arise around the staffing of the project team with personnel from other functional and staff support areas or from the desire to use another department's personnel for

project support even though the personnel remain under the authority of their functional or staff superiors.

- *Conflict over Cost.* Frequently, conflict may develop over cost estimates from support areas regarding various project work breakdown packages. For example, the funds allocated by a project manager to a functional support group might be perceived as insufficient for the support requested.
- *Conflict over Schedules.* Disagreements may develop around the timing, sequencing, and scheduling of project-related tasks.
- *Personality Conflict.* Disagreements may tend to center on interpersonal differences rather than on "technical" issues. Conflicts often are "ego-centered."

Intensity of Specific Conflict Sources by Project Life-Cycle Stage

The conflict intensity experienced by project managers for each source over the four life-cycle stages was measured on a special grid. The x-axis of the grid identifies four standard life-cycle phases: project formation, project build-up, main program phase, and phaseout. The y-axis delineates the seven potential sources of conflict. The respondents were asked to indicate on a standard four-point scale the intensity of the conflict they experienced for each of the seven potential sources of conflict within each of the four project life-cycle stages.

Conflict-Handling Modes

A number of research studies indicate that managers approach and resolve conflicts by utilizing various conflict resolution modes. Blake and Mouton,[9] for example, have delineated five modes for handling conflicts:

- *Withdrawal.* Retreating or withdrawing from an actual or potential disagreement.
- *Smoothing.* De-emphasizing or avoiding areas of difference and emphasizing areas of agreement.
- *Compromising.* Bargaining and searching for solutions that bring some degree of satisfaction to the parties in a dispute. Characterized by a "give-and-take" attitude.
- *Forcing.* Exerting one's viewpoint at the potential expense of another. Often characterized by competitiveness and a win/lose situation.
- *Confrontation.* Facing the conflict directly which involves a problem-solv-

---

9. R. R. Blake and J. S. Mouton, *The Managerial Grid* (Houston: Gulf Publishing, 1964).

ing approach whereby affected parties work through their disagreements.[10]

Aphorisms or statements of folk wisdom were used as surrogates for each conflict resolution mode.[11] The project managers were asked to rank the accuracy of each proverb in terms of how accurately it reflected the actual way in which they handled disagreements in the project environment. Fifteen proverbs were selected to match the five conflict-handling modes identified by Blake and Mouton.[12,13] This analysis provides an insight into the perceived conflict-handling mode of the project managers.

Analysis of Results

The results of the study are presented in three parts.

Mean Conflict Intensity over the Project Life Cycle

The mean intensity experienced for each of the potential conflict sources over the entire life of projects is presented in Figure 7-1. As indicated, relative to other situations, disagreements over schedules result in the most intense conflict over the total project. Scheduling conflicts often occur with other support departments over whom the project manager may have limited authority and control. Scheduling problems and conflicts also often involve disagreements and differing perceptions of organizational departmental priorities. For example, an issue urgent to the project manager may receive a low-priority treatment from support groups and/or staff personnel because of a different priority structure in the support organization. Conflicts over schedules frequently result from the technical problems and manpower resources.

Conflict over project priorities ranked second highest over the project life

---

10. For a fuller description of these definitions, see R. J. Burke, "Methods of Resolving Interpersonal Conflict," *Personnel Administration,* July–August 1969, pp. 48–55. Also see H. J. Thamhain and D. L. Wilemon, "Conflict Management in Project-Oriented Work Environments," *Proceedings of the Sixth International Meeting of the Project Management Institute,* Washington, D.C., September 18–21, 1974.

11. Specifically, the measurements rely on the research of P. R. Lawrence and J. W. Lorsch, "New Management Job: The Integrator," *Harvard Business Review,* November–December 1967, pp. 142–152.

12. See Ref. 9.

13. These proverbs have been used in other research of a similar nature to avoid the potential bias that might be introduced otherwise by the use of social science jargon. For further details, see R. J. Burke, "Methods of Managing Superior–Subordinate Conflict," *Canadian Journal of Behavioral Science,* Vol. 2, No. 2, 1970, pp. 124–135.

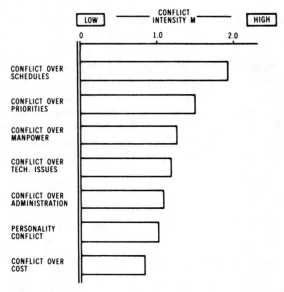

Figure 7–1. Mean conflict intensity profile over project life cycle. (Source: Hans J. Thamhain and David L. Wilemon, "Conflict Management in Project Life Cycles," *Sloan Management Review,* Summer 1975, pp. 31–50. Reprinted by permission.)

cycle. In our discussions with project managers, many indicated that this type of conflict frequently develops because the organization did not have prior experience with a current project undertaking. Consequently, the pattern of project priorities may change from the original forecast, necessitating the reallocation of crucial resources and schedules, a process that is often susceptible to intense disagreements and conflicts. Similarly, priority issues often develop into conflict with other support departments whose established schedules and work patterns are disturbed by the changed requirements.

Conflict over manpower resources was the third most important source of conflict. Project managers frequently lament when there is little "organizational slack" in terms of manpower resources, a situation in which they often experience intense conflicts. Project managers note that most of the conflicts over personnel resources occur with those departments who either assign personnel to the project or support the project internally.

The fourth strongest source of conflict involved disagreements over technical opinions and trade-offs. Often the groups who support the project are primarily responsible for technical inputs and performance standards. The project manager, on the other hand, is accountable for the cost, schedule, and performance objectives. Since support areas are usually responsible for only parts of the project, they may not have the broad management overview of the total project. The project manager, for example, may be presented with a technical problem. Often he must reject the technical alternative owing to cost or schedule restraints. In other cases, he may find that he disagrees with the opinions of others on strictly technical grounds.

Conflict over administrative procedures ranked fifth in the profile of seven conflict sources. It is interesting to note that most of the conflict over administrative procedures that occurs is almost uniformly distributed with functional departments, project personnel, and the project manager's superior.[14] Examples of conflict originating over administrative issues may involve disagreements over the project manager's authority and responsibilities, reporting relationships, administrative support, status reviews, or interorganizational interfacing. For the most part, disagreements over administrative procedures involve issues of how the project manager will function and how he relates to the organization's top management.

Personality conflict was ranked low in intensity by the project managers. Our discussions with project managers indicated that while the intensity of personality conflicts may not be as high as some of the other sources of conflict, they are among the most difficult to deal with effectively. Personality issues also may be obscured by communication problems and technical issues. A support person, for example, may stress the technical aspect of a disagreement with the project manager when, in fact, the real issue is a personality conflict.

Cost, like schedules, is often a basic performance measure in project management. As a conflict source, cost ranked lowest. Disagreements over cost frequently develop when project managers negotiate with other departments who will perform subtasks on the project. Project managers with tight budget constraints often want to minimize cost, while support groups may want to maximize their part of the project budget. In addition, conflicts may occur as a result of technical problems or schedule slippages which may increase costs.

Conflict Sources and Intensity in the Project Life Cycle

While it is important to examine some of the principal determinants of conflict from an aggregate perspective, more specific and useful insights can be gained by exploring the intensity of various conflict sources in each life-cycle stage, namely, project formation, project build-up, main program phase, and phaseout. See Figure 7–2.

---

14. See Thamhain and Wilemon in Ref. 10.

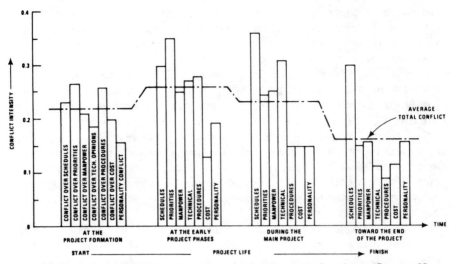

Figure 7–2. Relative intensity of conflict over the life cycle of projects. (Source: Hans J. Thamhain and David L. Wilemon, "Conflict Management in Project Life Cycles," *Sloan Management Review,* Summer 1975, pp. 31–50. Reprinted by permission.)

1. *Project Formation.* As Figure 7–2 illustrates, during the project formation state, the following conflict sources listed in order of rank were found:[15]

1. Project priorities
2. Administrative procedures
3. Schedules
4. Manpower
5. Cost
6. Technical
7. Personality

Unique to the project formation phase are some characteristics not typical of the other life-cycle stages. The project manager, for example, must launch his

---

15. Conflict intensity is computed as the total frequency (F) × magnitude (M) product of conflict experienced within the sample of project managers, when $0 \leq M \leq 3$. For example, if the average conflict intensity experienced by project managers on schedules with all interfaces was M = 1.65 (considerable) and F = 14% of all project managers indicated that "most" of this conflict occurred during the project formation phase, then "conflict over schedules" would be M × F = 1.65 × 0.14 = 0.23 during project formation.

project within the larger "host" organization. Frequently, conflict develops between the priorities established for the project and the priorities that other line and staff groups believe important. To eliminate or minimize the detrimental consequences that could result, project managers need to carefully evaluate and plan for the impact of their projects on the groups that support them. This should be accomplished as early as possible in the program life cycle. The source of conflict ranked second was administrative procedures, which are concerned with several critically important management issues; for example: How will the project organization be designed? Who will the project manager report to? What is the authority of the project manager? Does the project manager have control over manpower and material resources? What reporting and communication channels will be used? Who establishes schedules and performance specifications? Most of these areas are negotiated by the project manager, and conflict frequently occurs during the process. To avoid prolonged problems over these issues, it is important to clearly establish these procedures as early as possible.

Schedules typify another area where established groups may have to accommodate the newly formed project organization by adjusting their own operations. Most project managers attest that this adjustment is highly susceptible to conflict, even under ideal conditions, since it may involve a reorientation of present operating patterns and "local" priorities in support departments. These same departments might be fully committed to other projects. For similar reasons, negotiations over support personnel and other resources can be an important source of conflict in the project formation stage. Thus, effective planning and negotiation over these issues at the beginning of a project appear important.

2. *Project Build-up.* The conflict sources for the project build-up are listed below in order of rank:

1. Project priorities
2. Schedules
3. Administrative procedures
4. Technical
5. Manpower
6. Personality
7. Cost

Disagreements over project priorities, schedules, and administrative procedures continue as important determinants of conflict. Some of these sources of conflict appear as an extension from the previous program phase. Additional conflicts surface during negotiations with other groups in the build-up phase. It is interesting to note that while schedules ranked third in conflict intensity in the project formation phase, they are the second major conflict determinant in the build-up phase. Many of the conflicts over schedules arise in the first phase because of the disagreements that develop over the establishment of schedules. By contrast, in the build-up phase, conflict may develop over the enforcement of schedules according to objectives of the overall project plan.

An important point is that conflict over administrative procedures becomes less intense in the build-up phase, indicating the diminishing magnitude and frequency of administrative problems. It also appears that it is important to resolve potential conflicts, such as administrative disagreements, in the earlier phase of a project to avoid a replication of the same problems in the more advanced project life-cycle phases.

Conflict over technical issues also becomes more pronounced in the build-up phase, rising from the sixth-ranked conflict source in the project formation phase to fourth in the build-up phase. Often this results from disagreements with a support group that cannot meet technical requirements or wants to enhance the technological input for which it is responsible. Such action can adversely affect the project manager's cost and schedule objectives.

Project managers emphasized that personality conflicts are particularly difficult to handle. Even apparently small and infrequent personality conflicts might be more disruptive and detrimental to overall program effectiveness than intense conflicts over nonpersonal issues, which can often be handled on a more rational basis. Many project managers also indicated that conflict over cost in the build-up phase generally tends to be low for two primary reasons. First, conflict over the establishment of cost targets does not appear to create intense conflicts for most project managers. Second, some projects are not yet mature enough in the build-up phase to cause disagreements over cost between the project manager and those who support him.

3. *Main Program.* The main program phase reveals a different conflict pattern. The seven potential causes of conflict are listed in rank order below:

1. Schedules
2. Technical
3. Manpower
4. Priorities
5. Procedures
6. Cost
7. Personality

In the main program phase, the meeting of schedule commitments by various support groups becomes critical to effective project performance. In complex task management, the interdependency of various support groups dealing with complex technology frequently gives rise to slippages in schedules. When several groups or organizations are involved, this in turn can cause a "whiplash" effect throughout the project. In other words, a slippage in schedule by one group may affect other groups if they are on the critical path of the project.

As noted, while conflicts over schedules often develop in the earlier project phases, they are frequently related to the establishment of schedules. In the main program phase, our discussions with project managers indicated that conflicts frequently develop over the "management and maintenance" of schedules. The latter, as indicated in Figure 7–2, produces more intense conflicts.

Technical conflicts are also one of the most important sources of conflict in the main program phase. There appear to be two principal reasons for the rather high level of conflict in this phase. First, the main program phase is often characterized by the integration of various project subsystems for the first time, such as configuration management. Owing to the complexities involved in this integration process, conflicts frequently develop over lack of subsystem integration and poor technical performance of one subsystem, which may, in turn, affect other components and subsystems. Second, the fact that a component can be designed in prototype does not always assure that all the technical anomalies will be eliminated. In extreme cases, the subsystem may not even be producible in the main program phase. Such problems can severely impact the project and generate intense conflicts. Disagreements also may arise in the main program phase over reliability and quality control standards, various design problems, and testing procedures. All these problems can severely impact the project and cause intense conflicts for the project manager.

Manpower resources ranked third as a determinant of conflict. The need for manpower reaches the highest levels in the main program phase. If support groups also are providing personnel to other projects, severe strains over manpower availability and project requirements frequently develop.

Conflict over priorities continued its decline in importance as a principal cause of conflict. Again, project priorities tend to be a form of conflict most likely to occur in the earlier project phases. Finally, administrative procedures, cost, and personality were about equal as the lowest-ranked conflict sources.

4. *Phaseout.* The final stage, project phaseout, illustrates an interesting shift in the principal cause of conflict. The ranking of the conflict sources in this final project phase are:

1. Schedules
2. Personality
3. Manpower
4. Priorities
5. Cost
6. Technical
7. Procedures

Schedules are again the most likely form of conflict to develop in project phaseout. Project managers frequently indicated that many of the schedule slippages that developed in the main program phase tended to carry over to project phaseout. Schedule slippages often become cumulative and impact the project most severely in the final stage of a project.

Somewhat surprisingly, personality conflict was the second ranked source of conflict. It appears that much of the personality-oriented conflict can be explained in two ways. First, it is not uncommon for project participants to be tense and concerned with future assignments. Second, project managers frequently note that interpersonal relationships may be quite strained during this period owing to the pressure on project participants to meet stringent schedules, budgets, and performance specifications and objectives.

Somewhat related to the personality issue are the conflicts that arise over manpower resources, the third-ranked conflict source. Disagreements over manpower resources may develop due to new projects phasing in, hence creating competition for personnel during the critical phaseout stage. Project managers, by contrast, also may experience conflicts over the absorption of surplus manpower back into the functional areas where they impact the budgets and organizational variables.

Conflict over priorities in the phaseout stage often appears to be directly or indirectly related to competition with other project start-ups in the organization. Typically, newly organized projects or marketing support activities might require urgent, short-notice attention and commitments that have to be squeezed into tight schedules. At the same time, personnel might leave the project organization prematurely because of prior commitments that conflict with a slipped schedule on the current project or because of a sudden opportunity for a new assignment elsewhere. In either case, the combined pressure on schedules, manpower, and personality creates a climate that is highly vulnerable to conflicts over priorities.

As noted in Figure 7–2, cost, technical, and administrative procedures tend to be ranked lowest as conflict sources. Cost, somewhat surprisingly, was not a major determinant of conflict. Discussions with project personnel suggest that while cost control can be troublesome in this phase, intense conflicts usually do not develop. Most problems in this area develop gradually and provide little ground for arguments.[16] The reader should be cautioned, however, that the low

---

16. Depending on the work environment and particular business there might be various reasons why conflicts over cost are low. First, some of the project components may be purchased externally on a fixed-fee basis. In such cases the contractor would bear the burden of costs. Second, costs are one of the most difficult project variables to control throughout the life cycle of a project, and budgets are frequently adjusted for increase in material and manpower costs over the life of the project. These incremental cost adjustments frequently eliminate some of the "sting" in cost when they exceed the original estimates of the project manager. Moreover, some projects in the high-technology area are managed on a cost-plus basis. In some of these projects precise cost estimates cannot always be rigidly adhered to.

level of conflict is by no means indicative of the importance of cost performance to overall rating of a project manager. During discussions with top management, it was repeatedly emphasized that cost performance is one of the key evaluation measures in judging the performance of project managers.

Technical and administrative procedures ranked lowest in project phaseout. When a project reaches this stage, most of the technical issues are usually resolved. A similar argument holds for administrative procedures.

A graphical summary of the relative conflict intensity over the four conflict stages is provided in Figure 7–3. The diagram, an abstract of Figures 7–1 and 7–2, shows the change of relative conflict intensity over the project life for each of the seven conflict sources.

It is important to note that while a determinant conflict may be ranked relatively low in a specific life-cycle stage, it can, nevertheless, cause severe problems. A project manager, for example, may have serious ongoing problems with schedules throughout his project, but a single conflict over a technical issue can be equaly detrimental and could jeopardize his performance to the same extent as schedule slippages. This point should be kept in mind in any discussion on project management conflict. Moreover, problems may develop that are virtually "conflict-free" (i.e., technological anomalies or problems with suppliers)

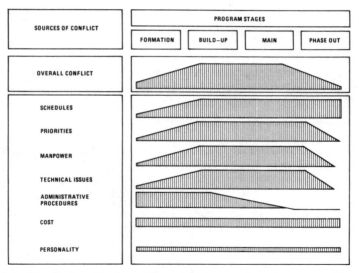

Figure 7–3. Trend of conflict intensity over the four project life-cycle stages. (Source: Hans J. Thamhain and David L. Wilemon, "Conflict Management in Project Life Cycles," *Sloan Management Review*, Spring 1975, pp. 31–50. Reprinted by permission.)

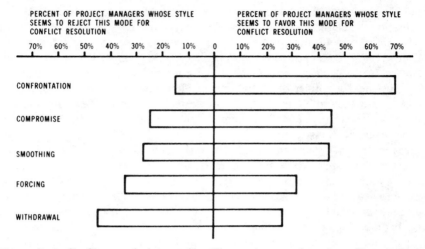

Figure 7–4. Conflict resolution profile. The various modes of conflict resolution actually used to manage conflict in project-oriented work environments. (Source: Hans J. Thamhain and David L. Wilemon, "Conflict in Project Life Cycles," *Sloan Management Review,* Summer 1975, pp. 31–50. Reprinted by permission.)

but may be just as troublesome to the project manager as any of the conflict issues discussed.

The problem that now should be addressed is how these various conflict sources and the situations they create are managed.

Conflict-handling Modes

The investigation into the conflict-handling modes of project managers developed a number of interesting patterns. The actual style of project managers was determined from their scores on the aphorisms. As indicated in Figure 7–4, confrontation was most frequently utilized as a problem-solving mode. This mode was favored by approximately 70 percent of the project managers.[17] The compromise approach which is characterized by trade-offs and a give-and-take

---

17. Quantitatively, this means that 70 percent of the project managers in the sample indicated that the proverbs that are representative of this mode (i.e., confrontation) describe the actual way the manager is resolving conflict "accurately" or "very accurately" as related to his project situations.

attitude ranked second, followed by smoothing. Forcing and withdrawal ranked as the fourth and fifth most favored resolution modes, respectively.

In terms of the most and least favored conflict resolution modes, the project managers had similar rankings for the conflict-handling method used between him and his personnel, his superior, and his functional support departments except in the cases of confrontation and compromise. While confrontation was the most favored mode for dealing with superiors, compromise was more favored in handling disagreements with functional support departments. The various modes of conflict resolution used by project managers are summarized in the profile of Figure 7–4.

Implications

A number of ideas evolved for improving conflict management effectiveness in project-oriented environments from this research. As the data on the mean conflict intensities indicate, the three areas most likely to cause problems for the project manager over the entire project cycle are disagreements over schedules, project priorities, and manpower resources. One reason these areas are apt to produce more intense disagreements is that the project manager may have limited control over other areas that have an important impact on these areas particularly the functional support departments. These three areas (schedules, project priorities, and manpower resources) require careful surveillance throughout the life cycle of a project. To minimize detrimental conflict, intensive planning prior to actually launching of the project is recommended. Planning can help the project manager anticipate many potential sources of conflict before they occur. Scheduling, priority setting, and resource allocation require effective planning to avoid problems later in the project. In our discussions with project managers who have experienced problems in these areas, almost all maintain that these problems frequently originate from lack of effective pre-project planning.

Managing projects involves managing change. It is not our intention to suggest that all such problems can be eliminated by effective planning. A more realistic view is that many potential problems can be minimized. There always will be random, unpredictable situations that defy forecasting in project environments.

Some specific suggestions are summarized in Table 7–1. The table provides an aid to project managers in recognizing some of the most important sources of conflict that are most likely to occur in various phases of projects. The table also suggests strategies for minimizing their detrimental consequences.

As one views the seven potential sources of disagreements over the life of a project, the dynamic nature of each conflict source is revealed. Frequently, areas that are most likely to foster disagreements early in a project become less

Table 7-1. Major Conflict Source and Recommendations for Minimizing Dysfunctional Consequences.

PROJECT LIFE CYCLE PHASE	CONFLICT SOURCE	RECOMMENDATIONS
Project formation	Priorities	Clearly defined plans. Joint decision-making and/or consultation with affected parties.
	Procedures	Develop detailed administrative operating procedures to be followed in conduct of project. Secure approval from key administrators. Develop statement of understanding or charter.
	Schedules	Develop schedule commitments in advance of actual project commencement.
		Forecast other departmental priorities and possible impact on project.
Buildup phase	Priorities	Provide effective feedback to support areas on forecasted project plans and needs via status review sessions.
	Schedules	Schedule work breakdown packages (project subunits) in cooperation with functional groups.
	Procedures	Contingency planning on key administrative issues.
Main program	Schedules	Continually monitor work in progress. Communicate results to affected parties.
		Forecast problems and consider alternatives.
		Identify potential "trouble spots" needing closer surveillance.
	Technical	Early resolution of technical problems.
		Communication of schedule and budget restraints to technical personnel.
		Emphasize adequate, early technical testing.
		Facilitate early agreement on final designs.
	Manpower	Forecast and communicate manpower requirements early.
	Manpower	Establish manpower requirements and priorities with functional and staff groups.
Phaseout	Schedules	Close schedule monitoring in project life cycle.
		Consider reallocation of available manpower to critical project areas prone to schedule slippages.
		Attain prompt resolution of technical issues which may impact schedules.
	Personality and Manpower	Develop plans for reallocation of manpower upon project completion.
		Maintain harmonious working relationships with project team and support groups. Try to loosen up "high-stress" environment.

Source: Hans J. Thamhain and David L. Wilemon, "Conflict Management in Project Life Cycles," *Sloan Management Review,* Summer 1975, pp. 31–50. Reprinted by permission.

likely to induce severe conflicts in the maturation of a project. Administrative procedures, for example, continually lose importance as an intense source of conflict during project maturation. By contrast, personality conflict, which ranks lowest in the project formation stage, is the second most important source of conflict in project phaseout. In summary, it is posited that if project managers are aware of the importance of each potential conflict source by project life cycle, then more effective conflict minimization strategies can be developed.

In terms of the means by which project managers handle conflicts and disagreements, the data revealed that the confrontation or problem-solving mode was the most frequent method utilized. While our study did not attempt to explore the effectiveness of each mode separately, in an earlier research project Burke[18] suggests that the confrontation approach is the most effective conflict-handling mode.[19]

In some contrast to studies of general management, the findings of our research in project-oriented environments suggest that it is less important to search for a best mode of effective conflict management. It appears to be more significant that project managers, in their capacity as integrators of diverse organizational resources, employ the full range of conflict resolution modes. While confrontation was found as the ideal approach under most circumstances, other approaches may be equally effective depending upon the situational content of the disagreement. Withdrawal, for example, may be used effectively as a temporary measure until new information can be sought, or to "cool off" a hostile reaction from a colleague. As a basic long-term strategy, however, withdrawal may actually escalate a disagreement if no resolution is eventually sought.[20]

In other cases, compromise and smoothing might be considered an effective strategy by the project manager, if it does not severely affect the overall project objectives. Forcing, on the other hand, often proves to be a win/lose mode. Even though the project manager may win over a specific issue, effective working arrangements with the "forced" party may be jeopardized in future relationships. Nevertheless, some project managers find that forcing is the only viable mode in some situations. Confrontation of the problem-solving mode may actually encompass all conflict-handling modes to some extent. A project

---

18. R. J. Burke, "Methods of Resolving Interpersonal Conflict," *Personnel Administration,* July–August 1969, pp. 48–55.

19. Although Burke's study was conducted on general management personnel, it offers an interesting comparison to our research. Burke's paper notes that "Compromising" and "Forcing" were effective in 11.3 percent and 24.5 percent of the cases, while "Withdrawal" or "Smoothing" approaches were found mostly ineffective in the environment under investigation.

20. H. J. Thamhain and D. L. Wilemon, "Conflict Management in Project-Oriented Work Environments," *Proceedings of the Sixth International Meeting of the Project Management Institute,* Washington, D.C., September 1974, pp. 18–21.

manager, for example, in solving a conflict may use withdrawal, compromise, forcing, and smoothing to eventually get an effective resolution. The objective of confrontation, however, is to find a solution to the issue in question whereby all affected parties can live with the eventual outcome.

In summary, conflict is fundamental to complex task management. It is important not only for project managers to be cognizant of the potential sources of conflict, but also to know when in the life cycle of a project they are most likely to occur. Such knowledge can help the project manager avoid the detrimental aspects of conflict and maximize its beneficial aspects. Conflict can be beneficial when disagreements result in the development of new information that can enhance the decision-making process. Finally, when conflicts do develop, the project manager needs to know the advantages and disadvantages of each resolution mode for conflict resolution effectiveness.

7.4 CONFLICT RESOLUTION

Although each project within the company may be inherently different, the company may wish to have the resulting conflicts resolved in the same manner. The four most common methods are:

1. The development of company-wide conflict resolution policies and procedures
2. The establishment of project conflict resolutions procedures during the early planning activities
3. The use of hierarchical referral
4. The requirement of direct contact

With each of the above methods, the project manager may still select any of the conflict resolution modes discussed in the previous section.

Many companies have attempted to develop company-wide policies and procedures for conflict resolution. Results have shown that this method is doomed to failure because each project is different and not all conflicts can be handled the same way. Furthermore, project managers, by virtue of their individuality, and sometimes differing amounts of authority and responsibility, prefer to resolve conflicts in their own fashion.

A second method for resolving conflicts, and one that is often very effective, is to "plan" for conflicts during the planning activities. This can be accomplished through the use of linear responsibility charts. Planning for conflict resolution is similar to the first method except that each project manager can develop his own policies, rules, and procedures.

Hierarchical referral for conflict resolution, in theory, appears as the best method because neither the project manager nor the functional manager will dominate. Under this arrangement, the project and functional managers agree that for a proper balance to exist. Their common superior must resolve the conflict in order to protect the company's best interest. Unfortunately, this is not a realistic course of action because the common superior cannot be expected to continually resolve lower-level conflicts. Going to the "well" too often gives the impression that the functional and project managers cannot resolve their own problems.

The last method is direct contact, which is an outgrowth of the policies and procedures methods where established guidelines dictate that conflicting parties meet face to face and resolve their disagreement. Unfortunately, this method does not always work and, if continually stressed, can result in conditions where individuals will either suppress the identification of problems or develop new ones during confrontation.

Many conflicts can be either reduced or eliminated by constant communication of the project objectives to the team members. Many times this continual repetition will prevent individuals from going too far into the "wrong" and thus avoid the creation of a conflict situation.

7.5 UNDERSTANDING SUPERIOR, SUBORDINATE, AND FUNCTIONAL CONFLICTS[21]

In order for the project manager to be effective, an understanding of how to work with the various employees who must interface with the project is necessary. These various employees include upper-level management, subordinate project team members, and functional personnel. Quite often, especially when conflicts are possible, the project manager must demonstrate an ability for continuous adaptability by creating a different working environment with each group of employees. The need for this was shown in the previous section by the fact that the relative intensity of conflicts can vary in the life cycle of a project.

The type and intensity of conflicts can also vary with the type of employee whom the project manager must interface with, as shown in Figure 7–5. Both conflict causes and sources are rated according to relative conflict intensity. Any conflict that the project manager has with a functional manager can also occur with the functional employee, and vice versa. The data in Figure 7–5 were obtained for a 75 percent confidence level.

In the previous section we discussed the five basic resolution modes for handling conflicts. The specific type of resolution mode that a project manager will

---

21. The majority of this section, including the figures, has been adapted from *Seminar in Project Management Workbook,* © 1977 by Hans J. Thamhain. Reproduced by permission of Dr. Hans J. Thamhain.

CONFLICT CAUSES	SOURCES: CONFLICTS OCCURRED MOSTLY WITH					
	FUNCTIONAL MANAGERS	FUNCTIONAL PERSONNEL	BETWEEN PROJECT PERSONNEL	SUPERIORS	SUBORDINATES	RELATIVE CONFLICT INTENSITY
SCHEDULES	■	■				HIGH
PRIORITIES	■	■	■			
MANPOWER	■	■				
TECHNICAL	■	■	■			
PROCEDURES	■	■		■	■	
PERSONALITY	■	■	■	■	■	
COSTS	■	■		■		LOW

HIGH ◄——— RELATIVE CONFLICT INTENSITY ———► LOW

Figure 7–5. Relationship between conflict causes and sources.

use might easily depend upon whom the conflict is with, as shown in Figure 7–6. The data in Figure 7–6 do not necessarily show the modes that project managers would prefer, but rather identify the modes that will increase or decrease the potential conflict intensity. For example, although project managers consider, in general, that withdrawal is their least favorite mode, it can be used quite effectively with functional managers. In dealing with superiors, project managers would rather be ready for an immediate compromise than for face-to-face confrontation which could easily result in having the resolution forced in the favor of upper-level management.

Figure 7–7 identifies the various influence styles that project managers find effective in helping to reduce potential conflicts. Penalty power, authority, and expertise are considered as strongly unfavorable associations with respect to low conflicts. As expected, work challenge and promotions (if the project manager has the authority) are strongly favorable associations with his personnel.

Therefore, for the project manager to be truly effective, he or she should understand not only what types of conflicts are possible in the various stages of the life cycle, but with whom these conflicts can occur and how to deal with them effectively.

(The figure shows only those associations which are statistically significant at the 95 percent level)

INTENSITY OF CONFLICT PERCEIVED BY PROJECT MANAGERS (P.M.)	ACTUAL CONFLICT RESOLUTION STYLE				
	FORCING	CONFRONTA-TION	COMPROMISE	SMOOTHING	WITHDRAWAL
BETWEEN P.M. AND HIS PERSONNEL	■	▲	▲	▲	■
BETWEEN P.M. AND HIS SUPERIOR		■	▲		
BETWEEN P.M. AND FUNCTIONAL SUPPORT DEPARTMENTS	■	■			▲

▲ STRONGLY FAVORABLE ASSOCIATION WITH REGARD TO LOW CONFLICT ($-\ \tau$)

■ STRONGLY UNFAVORABLE ASSOCIATION WITH REGARD TO LOW CONFLICT ($+\ \tau$)

*KENDALL τ CORRELATION

Figure 7-6. Association between perceived intensity of conflict and mode of conflict resolution.*

(The figure shows only those associations which are statistically significant at the 95 percent level)

INTENSITY OF CONFLICT PERCEIVED BY PROJECT MANAGER (P.M.)	INFLUENCE METHODS AS PERCEIVED BY PROJECT MANAGERS						
	EXPERTISE	AUTHORITY	WORK CHALLENGE	FRIENDSHIP	PROMOTION	SALARY	PENALTY
BETWEEN P.M. AND HIS PERSONNEL	■	■	▲		▲		■
BETWEEN P.M. AND HIS SUPERIOR			▲				■
BETWEEN P.M. AND FUNCTIONAL SUPPORT DEPARTMENTS		■					■

▲ STRONGLY FAVORABLE ASSOCIATION WITH REGARD TO LOW CONFLICT ($-\ \tau$)

■ STRONGLY UNFAVORABLE ASSOCIATION WITH REGARD TO LOW CONFLICT ($+\ \tau$)

*KENDALL τ CORRELATION

Figure 7-7. Association between influence methods of project manager and their perceived conflict intensity.*

7.6 THE MANAGEMENT OF CONFLICTS[22]

Good project managers realize that conflicts are inevitable and that procedures or techniques must be developed for their resolution. If the project manager is not careful, he or she could easily worsen the conflict by not knowing how to manage it. Once a conflict occurs, the project manager must observe certain preliminaries, including:

- Studying the problem and collecting all available information
- Developing a situational approach or methodology
- Setting the appropriate atmosphere or climate

In setting the appropriate atmosphere, the project manager must establish a willingness to participate for himself as well as the other participants. The manager must clearly state the objectives of the forthcoming meeting, establish the credibility of the meeting, and sanction the meeting.

If a confrontation meeting is necessary between conflicting parties, then the project manager should be aware of the logical steps and sequence of events that should be taken. These include:

- Setting the climate: establishing a willingness to participate
- Analyzing the images (How do you see yourself and others, and how do they see you?)
- Collecting the information: getting feelings out in the open
- Defining the problem: defining and clarifying all positions
- Sharing the information: making the information available to all
- Setting the appropriate priorities: developing working sessions for setting priorities and time tables
- Organizing the group: forming cross-functional problem-solving groups
- Problem solving: obtaining cross-functional involvement, securing commitments, and setting the priorities and time table
- Developing the action plan: getting commitment
- Implementing the work: taking action on the plan
- Following up: obtaining feedback on the implementation for the action plan

---

22. See Ref. 21.

Once the conflict has been defined and a meeting is necessary, the project manager or team leader should understand the conflict minimization procedures. These include:

- Pausing and thinking before reacting
- Building trust
- Trying to understand the conflict motives
- Keeping the meeting under control
- Listening to all involved parties
- Maintaining a give-and-take attitude
- Educating others tactfully on your views
- Be willing to say when you were wrong
- Not acting as a superman and level the discussion only once in a while

We can now sum up these actions by defining the role of the effective manager in conflict problem solving. The effective manager:

- Knows the organization
- Listens with understanding rather than evaluation
- Clarifies the nature of the conflict
- Understands the feelings of others
- Suggests the procedures for resolving differences
- Maintains relationships with disputing parties
- Facilitates the communications process
- Seeks resolutions

PROBLEMS

7-1   Is it possible to establish formal organizational procedures (either at the project level or company-wide) for the resolution of conflicts? If a procedure is established, what can go wrong?

7-2   Under what conditions would a conflict result between members of a group over misunderstandings of each other's roles?

7-3   Is it possible to have a situation in which conflicts are not effectively controlled, and yet have a decision-making process that is not lengthy or cumbersome?

7-4   If conflicts develop into a situation where mistrust prevails, would you expect activity documentation to increase or decrease? Why?

7-5   If a situation occurs that can develop into meaningful conflict, should the project manager let the conflict continue as long as it produces beneficial contributions, or should he try to resolve it as soon as possible?

7-6   Consider the following remarks made by David L. Wilemon ("Managing Conflict in Temporary Management Situations," *Journal of Management Studies,* October 1973, p. 296):

The value of the conflict produced depends upon the effectiveness of the project manager in promoting beneficial conflict while concomitantly minimizing its potential dysfunctional aspects. A good project manager needs a "sixth sense" to indicate when conflict is desirable, what kind of conflict will be useful, and how much conflict is optimal for a given situation. In the final analysis he has the sole responsibility for his project and how conflict will impact the success or failure of his project.

Based upon these remarks, would your answer to Problem 7–5 change?

7-7.   Mr. X is the project manager of a $65 million project of which $1 million is subcontracted out to another company in which Mr. Y is project manager. Unfortunately, Mr. X does not consider Mr. Y as his counterpart and continually communicates with the Director of Engineering in Mr. Y's company. What type of conflict is that, and how should it be resolved?

7-8   Contract negotiations can easily develop into conflicts. During a disagreement, the vice-president of Company A ordered his director of finance, the contract negotiator, to break off contract negotiations with Company B because the contract negotiator of Company B did not report directly to a vice-president. How can this situation be resolved?

7-9   For each part below there are two statements; one represents the traditional view and the other the project organizational view. Identify each one.

   a. Conflict should be avoided; conflict is part of change and is therefore inevitable.
   b. Conflict is the result of trouble-makers and egoists; conflict is determined by the structure of the system and the relationship among components.
   c. Conflict may be beneficial; conflict is bad.

7-10   Using the modes for conflict resolution defined in Section 7–3, which would be strongly favorable and strongly unfavorable for resolving conflicts between:

   a. Project manager and his project office personnel?
   b. Project manager and the functional support departments?
   c. Project manager and his superiors?
   d. Project manager and other project managers?

7-11   Which influence methods should increase and which should decrease the opportunities for conflict between the following:

   ● Project manager and his project office personnel?
   ● Project manager and the functional support departments?
   ● Project manager and his superiors?
   ● Project manager and other project managers?

7-12   Would you agree or disagree with the statement that "Conflict resolution through collaboration needs trust; people must rely upon one another."

7–13. Davis and Lawrence (*Matrix,* Addison-Wesley, 1977) identify several situations common to the matrix that can easily develop into conflicts. For each situation, what would be the recommended cure?

    a. Compatible and incompatible personnel must work together
    b. Power struggles break the balance of power
    c. Anarchy
    d. Groupitis (people confuse matrix behavior with group decision-making)
    e. A collapse during economic crunch
    f. Decision strangulation processes
    g. Forcing the matrix organization to the lower organizational levels
    h. Navel-gazing (spending time ironing out internal disputes instead of developing better working relationships with the customer)

7–14 Determine the best conflict resolution mode for each of the following situations:

    a. Two of your functional team members appear to have personality clashes and almost always assume opposite points of view during decision making. Personality conflicts appear inevitable.
    b. R&D quality control and manufacturing operations quality control continually argue as to who should perform testing on an R&D project. R&D postulates that it's their project, and manufacturing argues that it will eventually go into production and that they wish to be involved as early as possible.
    c. Two functional department managers continually argue as to who should perform a certain test. You know that this situation exists, and that the department managers are trying to work it out themselves, often with great pain. However, you are not sure that they will be able to resolve the problem themselves.

7–15 Forcing a confrontation to take place assures that action will be taken. Is it possible that, by using force, a lack of trust among the participants will develop?

7–16. With regard to conflict resolution, should it matter to whom in the organization the project manager reports?

7–17. One of the most common conflicts in an organization occurs with raw materials and finished goods. Why would finance/accounting, marketing/sales, and manufacturing have disagreements?

7–18 Explain how the relative intensity of a conflict can vary as a function of:

    a. Getting closer to the actual constraints
    b. Having only two constraints instead of three (i.e., time and performance, but not cost)
    c. The project life cycle
    d. The person whom the conflict is with

7–19 The conflicts shown in Figure 7–1 identify the relative intensity as perceived in project-driven organizations. Would this list be arranged differently for non-project-driven organizations?

7-20 Consider the responses made by the project managers in Figures 7–5 through 7–7. Which of their choices do you agree with, and which do you disagree with? Justify your answers.

7-21 As a good project manager, you try to plan for conflict avoidance. You now have a low-intensity conflict with a functional manager and, as in the past, handle the conflict with confrontation. If you knew that there would be a high-intensity conflict shortly thereafter, would you be willing to use the withdrawal mode for the low-intensity conflict in order to lay the groundwork for the high-intensity conflict?

7-22 Jones Construction Company has recently won a $120 million effort for a local company. The effort includes three separate construction projects, each one beginning at the same time. Two of the projects are 18 months in duration and the third one is 30 months. Each project has its own project manager. How do we resolve conflicts when each project may have a different priority but they are all for the same customer?

7-23 Minnesota Power and Light establishes priorities as follows:

Level 0: no priority
Level 1: to be completed on or before a specific date
Level 2: to be completed on or before a given fiscal quarter
Level 3: to be completed within a given year

How do you feel about this system of establishing priorities?

7-24 Richard is a department manager who must supply resources to four different projects. Although each project has an established priority, the project managers continually argue that departmental resources are not being allocated effectively. Richard has decided to have a monthly group meeting with all four of the project managers and to let them determine how the resources should be allocated. Can this technique work? If so, under what conditions?

CASE STUDY: FACILITIES SCHEDULING AT MAYER MANUFACTURING

Eddie Turner was elated with the good news that he was being promoted to section supervisor in charge of scheduling all activities in the new engineering research laboratory. The new laboratory was a necessity for Mayer Manufacturing. The engineering, manufacturing, and quality control directorates were all in desperate need of a new testing facility. Upper-level management felt that this new facility would alleviate many of the problems that previously existed.

The new organizational structure (as shown in Exhibit 7–1) required a change in policy over use of the laboratory. The new section supervisor, upon approval from his department manager, would have full authority for establishing priorities for the use of the new facility. The new policy change was a necessity because upper-level management felt that there would be inevitable conflict between manufacturing, engineering, and quality control.

After one month of operations, Eddie Turner was finding his job impossible. Eddie has a meeting with Gary Whitehead, his department manager.

Exhibit 7–1. Mayer Manufacturing Organizational Structure.

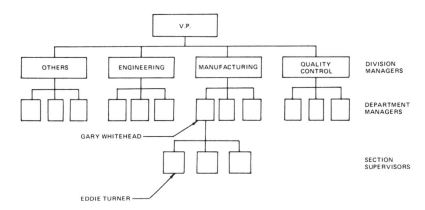

Eddie: "I'm having a hell of a time trying to satisfy all of the department managers. If I give engineering prime time use of the facility, then quality control and manufacturing say that I'm playing favorites. Imagine that! Even my own people say that I'm playing favorites with other directorates. I just can't satisfy everyone."

Gary: "Well, Eddie, you know that this problem comes with the job. You'll get the job done."

Eddie: "The problem is that I'm a section supervisor and have to work with department managers. These department managers look down on me like I'm their servant. If I were a department manager, then they'd show me some respect. What I'm really trying to say is that I would like you to send out the weekly memos to these department managers telling them of the new priorities. They wouldn't argue with you like they do with me. I can supply you with all the necessary information. All you'll have to do is to sign your name."

Gary: "Determining the priorities and scheduling the facilities is your job, not mine. This is a new position and I want you to handle it. I know you can because I selected you. I do not intend to interfere."

During the next two weeks, the conflicts got progressively worse. Eddie felt that he was unable to cope with the situation by himself. The department managers did not respect his authority delegated to him by his superiors. For the next two weeks, Eddie sent memos to Gary in the early part of the week asking whether or not Gary agreed with the priority list. There was no response to the two memos. Eddie then met with Gary to discuss the deteriorating situation.

Eddie: "Gary, I've sent you two memos to see if I'm doing anything wrong in establishing the weekly priorities and schedules. Did you get my memos?"

Gary: "Yes, I received your memos. But as I told you before, I have enough problems to worry about without doing your job for you. If you can't handle the work let me know and I'll find someone who can."

Eddie returned to his desk and contemplated his situation. Finally, he made a decision. Next week he was going to put a signature block under his for Gary to sign, with carbon copies for all division managers. "Now, let's see what happens," remarked Eddie.

CASE STUDY: SCHEDULING THE SAFETY LAB

"Now see here, Tom, I understand your problem well," remarked Dr. Polly, Director of the Research Laboratories. "I pay you a good salary to run the Safety Labs. That salary also includes doing the necessary scheduling to match our priorities. Now, if you can't handle the job, I'll get someone who can."

Tom: "Every Friday morning your secretary hands me a sheet with the listing of priorities for the following week. Once, just once, I'd like to sit in on the director's meeting and tell you people what you do to us in the Safety Lab when you continually shuffle around the priorities from week to week.

"On Friday afternoons, my people and I meet with representatives from each project to establish the following week's schedules."

Dr. Polly: "Can't you people come to an agreement?"

Tom: "I don't think you appreciate my problem. Two months ago, we all sat down to work out the lab schedule. Project X-13 had signed up to use the lab last week. Now, mind you, they had been scheduled for the past two months. But the Friday before they were to use it, your new priority list forced them to reschedule the lab at a later date, so that we could give the use of the lab to a higher-priority project. We're paying an awful lot of money for idle time and the redoing of network schedules. Only the project managers on the top-priority projects end up smiling after our Friday meetings."

Dr. Polly: "As I see your problem, you can't match long-range planning with the current priority list. I agree that it does create conflicts for you. But you have to remember that we, upstairs, have many other conflicts to resolve. I want that one solved at your level, not mine."

Tom: "Every project we have requires use of the Safety Lab. This is the basis for our problem. Would you consider letting us modify your priority list with regard to the Safety Lab?"

Dr. Polly: "Yes, but you had better have the agreement of all of the project managers. I don't want them coming to see me about your scheduling problems."

Tom: "How about if I let people do long-range scheduling for the lab, say for three out of the four weeks each month? The fourth week will be for the priority projects."

Dr. Polly: "That might work. You had better make sure that each project manager informs you immediately of any schedule slippages so that you can reschedule accordingly. From what I've heard, some of the project managers don't let you know until the last minute."

Tom: "That has been part of the problem. Just to give you an example, Project VX-161 was a top-priority effort and had the lab scheduled for the first week in March. I was never informed that they had accelerated their schedule by two weeks. They walked into my office and demanded use of the lab for the third week in February. Since they had the top priority, I had to grant them their request. However, Project BP-3 was planning on using the lab during that week and was bumped back three weeks. That cost them a pile of bucks in idle time pay and, of course, they're blaming me."

Dr. Polly: "Well Tom, I'm sure you'll find a solution to your problem."

CASE STUDY: TELESTAR INTERNATIONAL

On November 15, 1978, The Department of Energy Resources awarded Telestar a $475,000 contract for the developing and testing of two waste treatment plants. Telestar had spent the better part of the last two years developing waste treatment technology under their own R&D activities. This new contract would give Telestar the opportunity to "break into a new field," that of waste treatment.

The contract was negotiated at a firm-fixed price. Any cost overruns would have to be incurred by Telestar. The original bid was priced out at $847,000. Telestar's management, however, wanted to win this one. The decision was made that Telestar would "buy in" at $475,000 so that they could at least get their foot into the new marketplace.

The original estimate of $847,000 was very "rough" because Telestar did not have any good man-hour standards, in the area of waste treatment, upon which to base their man-hour projections. Corporate management was willing to spend up to $400,000 of their own funds in order to compensate the bid of $475,000.

By February 15, 1979, costs were increasing to such a point where overrun would be occurring well ahead of schedule. Anticipated costs to completion were now $943,000. The project manager decided to stop all activities in certain functional departments, one of which was structural analysis. The manager of the structural analysis department strongly opposed the closing out of the work order prior to the testing of the first plant's high-pressure pneumatic and electrical systems.

Structures Manager: "You're running a risk if you close out this work order. How will you know if the hardware can withstand the stresses that will be imposed during the test? After all, the test is scheduled for next month and I can probably finish the analysis by then."

Project Manager: "I understand your concern, but I cannot risk a cost overrun. My boss expects me to do the work within cost. The plant design is similar to one that we have tested before, without any structural problems being detected. On this basis I consider your analysis as unnecessary."

Structures Manager: "Just because two plants are similar does not mean that they will be identical in performance. There can be major structural deficiencies."

Project Manager: "I guess the risk is mine."

Structures Manager: "Yes, but I get concerned when a failure can reflect upon the integrity of my department. You know, we are performing on schedule and within the time and money budgeted. You're setting a bad example by cutting off our budget without any real justification."

Project Manager: "I understand your concern, but we must pull out all stops when overrun costs are inevitable."

Structures Manager: "There's no question in my mind that this analysis should be completed. However, I'm not going to complete it on my overhead budget. I'll reassign my people tomorrow. Incidentally, you had better be careful; my people are not very happy to work for a project that can be canceled immediately. I may have trouble getting volunteers next time."

Project Manager: "Well, I'm sure you'll be able to adequately handle any future work. I'll report to my boss that I have issued a work stoppage order to your department."

During the next month's test, the plant exploded. Post analysis indicated that the failure was due to a structural deficiency.

a. Who is at fault?
b. Should the structures manager have been dedicated enough to continue the work on his own?
c. Can a functional manager, who considers his organization as strictly support, still be dedicated to total project success?

CASE STUDY: THE PROBLEM WITH PRIORITIES

For the past several years, Kent Corporation had achieved remarkable success in winning R&D contracts. The customers were pleased with the analytical capabilities of the R&D staff at Kent Corporation. Theoretical and experimental results were usually within 95 percent agreement. But many customers still felt that 95 percent was too low. They wanted 98–99 percent.

In 1973, Kent updated their computer facility by renting an IBM-370 computer. The increased performance with the new computer encouraged the R&D group to attempt to convert from two-dimensional to three-dimensional solutions to their theoretical problems. Almost everyone except the director of R&D thought that this would give better comparison between experimental and theoretical data.

Kent Corporation had tried to develop the computer program for three-dimensional solutions with their own internal R&D programs, but the cost was too great. Finally, after a year of writing proposals, Kent Corporation convinced the federal government to sponsor the project. The project was estimated at $750,000, to begin January 2, 1975 and to be completed by December 20, 1975. Dan McCord was selected as project manager. Dan had worked with the EDP department on other projects and knew the people and the man-hour standards.

Kent Corporation was big enough to support one hundred simultaneous projects. With so many projects in existence at one time, continual reshuffling of resources was necessary. The corporation directors met every Monday morning to establish project priorities. Priorities were not enforced unless project and functional managers could not agree upon the allocation and distribution of resources.

Because of the R&D director's persistence, the computer project was given a low priority. This posed a problem for Dan McCord. The computer department manager refused to staff the project with his best people. As a result, Dan had severe scepticism about the success of the project.

In July, two other project managers held a meeting with Dan to discuss the availability of the new computer model.

"We have two proposals which we're favored to win, providing that we can state in our proposal that we have this new computer model available for use," remarked one of the project managers.

"We have a low priority and, even if we finish the job on time, I'm not sure of the quality of work because of the people we have assigned," said Dan.

"How do you propose we improve our position?" asked a project manager.

"Let's try to get in to see the Director of R&D," asserted Dan.

"And what are we going to say in our defense?" asked one of the project managers.

CASE STUDY: HANDLING CONFLICT IN PROJECT MANAGEMENT

The next several pages contain a six-part case study in conflict management. Read the instructions carefully on how to keep score and use the boxes below as the worksheet for recording your choice and the group's choice; after the case study has been completed, your instructor will provide you with the proper grading system for recording your scores.

Part 1: Facing the Conflict

As part of his first official duties, the new department manager informs you by memo that he has changed his input and output requirements for the MIS project (on which you are the project manager) because of several complaints by his departmental employees. This is contradictory to the project plan that you developed with the previous manager and are currently working toward. The department manager states that he has already discussed this with the vice-president and general manager, a man to whom both of you report, and feels that the former department manager made a poor decision and did not get sufficient input from the employees who would be using the system as to the best system specifications. You telephone him and try to convince him to hold off on his request for change until a later time, but he refuses.

Changing the input/output requirements at this point in time will require a major revision and will set back total system implementation by three weeks. This will also impact other department managers who expect to see this system operational according to the original schedule. You can explain this to your superiors, but the increased

LINE	PART	PERSONAL		GROUP	
		CHOICE	SCORE	CHOICE	SCORE
1	1. Facing the Conflict				
2	2. Understanding Emotions	////		////	
3	3. Establishing Communications				
4	4. Conflict Resolution	////		////	
5	5. Understanding you choices				
6	6. Interpersonal Influences				
	TOTAL	////		////	

project costs will be hard to absorb. The potential cost overrun might be difficult to explain at a later date.

At this point you are somewhat unhappy with yourself at having been on the search committee that found this department manager and especially at having recommended him for this position. You know that something must be done, and the following are your alternatives:

A. You can remind the department manager that you were on the search committee that recommended him and then ask him to return the favor, since he "owes you one."

B. You can tell him that you will form a new search committee to replace him if he doesn't change his position.

C. You can take a tranquilizer and then ask your people to try to perform the additional work within the original time and cost constraints.

D. You can go to the vice-president and general manager and request that the former requirements be adhered to, at least temporarily.

E. You can send a memo to the department manager explaining your problem and asking him to help you find a solution.

F. You can tell the department manager that your people cannot handle the request and his people will have to find alternate ways of solving their problems.

G. You can send a memo to the department manager requesting an appointment, at his earliest convenience, to help you resolve your problem.

H. You can go to the department manager's office later that afternoon and continue the discussion further.

I. You can send him a memo telling him that you have decided to use the old requirements but will honor his request at a later time.

Although other alternatives exist, assume that these are the only ones open to you at the moment. Without discussing the answer with your group, record the letter representing your choice in the appropriate space on line 1 of the worksheet under personal choice.

As soon as all of your group have finished, discuss the problem as a group and determine that alternative that the group considers to be best. Record this answer on line 1 of the worksheet under group choice. Allow ten minutes for this part.

Part 2: Understanding Emotions

Never having worked with this department manager before, you try to predict what his reactions will be when confronted with the problem. Obviously, he can react in a variety of ways:

a. He can *accept* your solution in its entirety without asking any questions.
b. He can discuss some sort of justification in order to *defend* his position.
c. He can become extremely annoyed with having to discuss the problem again and demonstrate *hostility*.
d. He can demonstrate a willingness to *cooperate* with you in resolving the problem.
e. He can avoid making any decision at this time by *withdrawing* from the discussion.

		YOUR CHOICE					GROUP CHOICE				
		ACC	DEF	HOST	COOP	WITH	ACC	DEF	HOST	COOP	WITH
A.	I've given my answer. See the general manager if you're not happy.										
B.	I understand your problem. Let's do it your way.										
C.	I understand your problem, but I'm doing what is best for my department.										
D.	Let's discuss the problem. Perhaps there are alternatives.										
E.	Let me explain to you why we need the new requirements.										
F.	See my section supervisors. It was their recommendation.										
G.	New managers are supposed to come up with new and better ways, aren't they?										

In the table on p. 443 are several possible statements that could be made by the department manager when confronted with the problem. Without discussion with your group, place a checkmark beside the appropriate emotion that could describe this statement. When each member of the group has completed his choice, determine the group choice. Numerical values will be assigned to your choices in the discussion that will follow. Do not mark the worksheet at this time. Allow ten minutes for this part.

Part 3: Establishing Communications

Unhappy over the department manager's memo and the resulting follow-up phone conversation, you decide to walk in on the department manager. You tell him that you will have a problem trying to honor his request. He tells you that he is too busy with his own problems of restructuring his department and that your schedule and cost problems are of no concern to him at this time. You storm out of his office, leaving him with the impression that his actions and remarks are not in the best interest of either the project or the company.

The department manager's actions do not, of course, appear to be those of a dedicated manager. He should be concerned more about what's in the best interest of the company. As you contemplate the situation, you wonder if you could have received a better response from him had you approached him differently. In other words, what is your best approach to opening up communications between you and the department manager? From the list of alternatives shown below, and working alone, select the alternative which best represents how you would handle this situation. When all members of the group have selected their personal choices, repeat the process and make a group choice. Record your personal and group choices on line three of the worksheet.

A. Comply with the request and document all results so that you will be able to defend yourself at a later date in order to show that the department manager should be held accountable.

B. Immediately send him a memo reiterating your position and tell him that at a later time you will reconsider his new requirements. Tell him that time is of the utmost importance, and you need an immediate response if he is displeased.

C. Send him a memo stating that you are holding him accountable for all cost overruns and schedule delays.

D. Send him a memo stating you are considering his request and that you plan to see him again at a later date to discuss changing the requirements.

E. See him as soon as possible. Tell him that he need not apologize for his remarks and actions, and that you have reconsidered your position and wish to discuss it with him.

F. Delay talking to him for a few days in hopes that he will cool off sufficiently and then see him in hopes that you can reopen the discussions.

G. Wait a day or so for everyone to cool off and then try to see him through an appointment; apologize for losing your temper, and ask him if he would like to help you resolve the problem.

Allow ten minutes for this part.

Part 4: Conflict Resolution Modes

Having never worked with this manager before, you are unsure about which conflict resolution mode would work best. You decide to wait a few days and then set up an appointment with the department manager without stating what subject matter will be discussed. You then try to determine what conflict resolution mode appears to be dominant based upon the opening remarks of the department manager. Neglecting the fact that your conversation with the department manager might already be considered as confrontation, for each statement shown below, select the conflict resolution mode that the *department manager* appears to prefer. After each member of the group has recorded his personal choices, determine the group choices. Numerical values will be attached to your answers at a later time.

Allow ten minutes for this part.

a. *Withdrawal* is retreating from a potential conflict.
b. *Smoothing* is emphasizing areas of agreement and de-emphasizing areas of disagreement.
c. *Compromising* is the willingness to give and take.
d. *Forcing* is directing the resolution in one direction or another, a win-or-lose position.
e. *Confrontation* is a face-to-face meeting to resolve the conflict.

	PERSONAL CHOICE					GROUP CHOICE				
	WITH	SMOOTH	COMP	FORC	CONF	WITH	SMOOTH	COMP	FORC	CONF
A. The requirements are my decision, and we're doing it my way.										
B. I've thought about it and you're right. We'll do it your way.										
C. Let's discuss the problem. Perhaps there are alternatives.										
D. Let me again explain why we need the new requirements.										
E. See my section supervisors; they're handling it now.										
F. I've looked over the problem and I might be able to ease up on some of the requirements.										

Part 5: Understanding Your Choices

Assume that the department manager has refused to see you again to discuss the new requirements. Time is running out, and you would like to make a decision before the costs and schedules get out of hand. From the list below, select your personal choice, and then after each group member is finished, find a group choice.

A. Disregard the new requirements, since they weren't part of the original project plan.

B. Adhere to the new requirements, and absorb the increased costs and delays.

C. Ask the vice-president and general manager to step in and make the final decision.

D. Ask the other department managers who may realize a schedule delay to try to convince this department manager to ease his request or even delay it.

Record your answer on line 5 of the worksheet. Allow five minutes for this part.

Part 6: Interpersonal Influences

Assume that upper-level management resolves the conflict in your favor. In order to complete the original work requirements you will need support from this department manager's organization. Unfortunately, you are not sure as to which type of interpersonal influence to use. Although you are considered as an expert in your field, you fear that this manager's functional employees may have a strong allegiance to the department manager and not want to adhere to your requests. Which of the following interpersonal influence styles would be best under the given set of conditions?

A. You threaten the employees with penalty power by telling them that you will turn in a bad performance report to their department manager.

B. You can use reward power and promise the employees a good evaluation, possible promotion, and increased responsibilities on your next project.

C. You can continue your technique of trying to convince the functional personnel to do your bidding because you are the expert in the field.

D. You can try to motivate the employees to do a good job by convincing them that the work is challenging.

E. You can make sure that they understand that your authority has been delegated to you by the vice-president and general manager and that they must do what you say.

F. You can try to build up friendships and off-work relationships with these people and rely on referent power.

Allow ten minutes for completion of this part.

The solution to this exercise appears in Appendix C.

8
Special Topics

8.0 INTRODUCTION

Some situations or special topics could be discussed in every chapter. However, since most of the special topics span several chapters, the information will be condensed here for the sake of clarity. The special topics will include:

- Rewards and evaluation
- Managing small projects
- Managing mega projects
- Using project management for strategic planning
- R&D project management
- Ethics in project management

8.1 PERFORMANCE MEASUREMENT ON THE HORIZONTAL LINE

When functional employees are assigned to a new project, their first concern is that their functional manager be informed when they have performed well on their new assignment. A good project manager will make it immediately clear to all new functional employees that if they perform well in the project, then he (the project manager) will inform the functional manager of their progress and achievements. This assumes that the functional manager is not providing close supervision over the functional employees and is, instead, passing on some of the responsibility to the project manager—a common situation in project management organizational structures. Obviously, if the functional manager has a small span of control and/or sufficient time to monitor closely the work of his subordinates, then the project manager's need for indirect reward power is minimal.

Many good projects as well as project management structures have failed because of the inability of the system to evaluate properly the functional employee's performance. This problem is, unfortunately, one of the most often overlooked trouble spots in project management.

In a project management structure, there are basically six ways that a functional employee can be evaluated on a project:

- *The project manager prepares a written, confidential evaluation and gives it to the functional manager.* The functional manager will evaluate the validity of the project manager's comments and prepare his own evaluation. Only the line manager's evaluation is shown to the employee. The use of confidential forms is not preferred because, first, it may be contrary to government regulations, and, second, it does not provide the necessary feedback for an employee to improve.
- *The project manager prepares a nonconfidential evaluation and gives it to the functional manager.* The functional manager prepares his own evaluation form and shows both evaluations to the functional employee. This is the technique preferred by most project and functional managers. However, there are several major difficulties with this technique. If the functional employee is an average or below-average worker, and if this employee is still to be assigned to this project after his evaluation, then the project manager might rate the employee as above average simply to prevent any sabotage or bad feelings downstream. In this situation, the functional manager might want a confidential evaluation instead, knowing that the functional employee will see both evaluation forms. Functional employees tend to blame the project manager if they receive a below-average merit pay increase, but give credit to the functional manager if the increase is above average. The best bet here is for the project manager periodically to tell the functional employees how well they are doing, and to give them an honest appraisal. Several companies that use this technique allow the project manager to show the form to the line manager first (to avoid conflict later) and then show it to the employee.
- *The project manager provides the functional manager with an oral evaluation of the employee's performance.* Although this technique is commonly used, most functional managers prefer documentation on employee progress. Again, lack of feedback may prevent the employee from improving.
- *The functional manager makes the entire evaluation without any input from the project manager.* In order for this technique to be effective, the functional manager must have sufficient time to supervise each subordinate's performance on a continual basis. Unfortunately, most functional managers do not have this luxury because of their broad span of control and must therefore rely heavily upon the project manager's input.
- *The project manager makes the entire evaluation for the functional manager.* This technique can work if the functional employee spends 100 per-

cent of his time on one project, or if he is physically located at a remote site where he cannot be observed by his functional manager.

- *All project and functional managers jointly evaluate all project functional employees at the same time.* This technique should be limited to small companies with fewer than fifty or so employees; otherwise the evaluation process might be time-consuming for key personnel. A bad evaluation will be known by everyone.

In five of the six techniques, the project manager has either a direct or an indirect input into the employee's evaluation process.

Since most project managers prefer written, nonconfidential evaluations, we must determine what the evaluation forms look like and when the functional employee will be evaluated. The indirect evaluation process will be time-consuming. This is of paramount importance on large projects where the project manager may have as many as 200 part-time functional employees assigned to his activities.

The evaluation forms can be filled out either when the employee is up for evaluation or after the project is completed. If the evaluation form is to be filled out when the employee is eligible for promotion or a merit increase, then the project manager should be willing to give an *honest* appraisal of the employee's performance. Of course, the project manager should not fill out the evaluation form if he has not had sufficient time to observe the employee at work.

The evaluation form can be filled out at the termination of the project. This, however, may produce a problem in that the project may end the month after the employee is considered for promotion. The advantage of this technique is that the project manager may have been able to find sufficient time both to observe the employee in action and to see the output.

Figure 8–1 represents, in a humorous way, how project personnel perceive the evaluation form. Unfortunately, the evaluation process is very serious and can easily have a severe impact on an individual's career path with the company even though the final evaluation rests with the functional manager.

Figure 8–2 shows a simple type of evaluation form on which the project manager identifies the best description the employee's performance. The project manager may or may not make additional comments. This type of form is generally used whenever the employee is up for evaluation, provided that the project manager has had sufficient time to observe the employee's performance.

Figure 8–3 shows another typical form that can be used to evaluate an employee. In each category, the employee is rated on a subjective scale. In order to minimize time and paper work, it is also possible to have a single evaluation form at project termination for evaluation of all employees. This is shown in Figure 8–4. All employees are rated in each category on a scale of one to five. Totals are obtained to provide a relative comparison of employees.

PERFORMANCE FACTORS	EXCELLENT (1 OUT OF 15)	VERY GOOD (3 OUT OF 15)	GOOD (8 OUT OF 15)	FAIR (2 OUT OF 15)	UNSATISFACTORY (1 OUT OF 15)
	FAR EXCEEDS JOB REQUIREMENTS	EXCEEDS JOB REQUIREMENTS	MEETS JOB REQUIREMENTS	NEEDS SOME IMPROVEMENT	DOES NOT MEET MINIMUM STANDARDS
QUALITY	LEAPS TALL BUILDINGS WITH A SINGLE BOUND	MUST TAKE RUNNING START TO LEAP OVER TALL BUILDING	CAN ONLY LEAP OVER A SHORT BUILDING OR MEDIUM ONE WITHOUT SPIRES	CRASHES INTO BUILDING	CANNOT RECOGNIZE BUILDINGS
TIMELINESS	IS FASTER THAN A SPEEDING BULLET	IS AS FAST AS A SPEEDING BULLET	NOT QUITE AS FAST AS A SPEEDING BULLET	WOULD YOU BELIEVE A SLOW BULLET?	WOUNDS HIMSELF WITH THE BULLET
INITIATIVE	IS STRONGER THAN A LOCOMOTIVE	IS STRONGER THAN A BULL ELEPHANT	IS STRONGER THAN A BULL	SHOOTS THE BULL	SMELLS LIKE A BULL
ADAPTABILITY	WALKS ON WATER CONSISTENTLY	WALKS ON WATER IN EMERGENCIES	WASHES WITH WATER	DRINKS WATER	PASSES WATER IN EMERGENCIES
COMMUNICATIONS	TALKS WITH GOD	TALKS WITH ANGELS	TALKS TO HIMSELF	ARGUES WITH HIMSELF	LOSES THE ARGUMENT WITH HIMSELF

Figure 8–1. Guide to performance appraisal.

Obviously, evaluation forms such as Figure 8–4 have severe limitations, as a one-to-one comparison of all project functional personnel is of little value if the employees are from different departments. How can a project engineer be compared to a cost accountant? If the project engineer receives a total score of forty and the cost accountant receives a score of thirty, does this mean that the project engineer is of more value or a better employee? Employees should have the right to challenge any item in a nonconfidential evaluation form.

Several companies are using this form by assigning coefficients of importance to each topic. For example, under a topic of technical judgment, the project engineer might have a coefficient of importance of 0.90, whereas the cost accountant's coefficient might be 0.25. These coefficients could be reversed for a topic on cost consciousness. Unfortunately, such comparisons have questionable validity, and this type of evaluation form is usually of a confidential nature.

Even though the project manager fills out an evaluation form, there is no guarantee that the functional manager will believe the project manager's evaluation. There are always situations in which the project and functional man-

EMPLOYEE'S NAME

DATE

PROJECT TITLE

JOB NUMBER

EMPLOYEE ASSIGNMENT

EMPLOYEE'S TOTAL TIME TO DATE ON PROJECT

EMPLOYEE'S REMAINING TIME ON PROJECT

TECHNICAL JUDGEMENT:

☐ Quickly reaches sound conclusions   ☐ Usually makes sound conclusions   ☐ Marginal decision making ability   ☐ Needs technical assistance   ☐ Makes faulty conclusions

WORK PLANNING:

☐ Good planner   ☐ Plans well with help   ☐ Occasionally plans well   ☐ Needs detailed instructions   ☐ Cannot plan at all

COMMUNICATIONS:

☐ Always understands instructions   ☐ Sometimes needs clarification   ☐ Always needs clarifications   ☐ Needs follow-up   ☐ Needs constant instruction

ATTITUDE:

☐ Always job interested   ☐ Shows interest most of the time   ☐ Shows no job interest   ☐ More interested in other activities   ☐ Does not care about job

COOPERATION:

☐ Always enthusiastic   ☐ Works well until job is completed   ☐ Usually works well with others   ☐ Works poorly with others   ☐ Wants it done his/her way

WORK HABITS:

☐ Always project oriented   ☐ Most often project oriented   ☐ Usually consistent with requests   ☐ Works poorly with others   ☐ Always works alone

ADDITIONAL COMMENTS: _____

Figure 8–2. Project work assignment appraisal.

agers disagree as to either quality or direction of work. This disagreement can easily alienate the project manager so that he will recommend a poor evaluation regardless of how well the employee has performed. If a functional employee spends most of his time working alone, the project manager may give an average evaluation even if the employee's performance is superb. Also the project manager may know the employee personally and allow personal feelings to influence his decision.

Another problem may exist in the situation where the project manager is a "generalist," say at a grade 7 level, and requests that the functional manager assign his best employee to the project. The functional manager agrees to the request and assigns his best employee, a grade 10 specialist. One solution to this problem is to have the project manager evaluate the expert only in certain

EMPLOYEE'S NAME

DATE

PROJECT TITLE

JOB NUMBER

EMPLOYEE ASSIGNMENT

EMPLOYEE'S TOTAL TIME TO DATE ON PROJECT   EMPLOYEE'S REMAINING TIME ON PROJECT

	EXCELLENT	ABOVE AVERAGE	AVERAGE	BELOW AVERAGE	INADEQUATE
TECHNICAL JUDGEMENT					
WORK PLANNING					
COMMUNICATIONS					
ATTITUDE					
COOPERATION					
WORK HABITS					
PROFIT CONTRIBUTION					

ADDITIONAL COMMENTS _____

Figure 8–3. Project work assignment appraisal.

categories such as communications, work habits, and problem solving, but not in the area of his technical expertise. The functional manager might be the only person qualified to evaluate functional personnel on technical abilities and expertise.

As a final note, it is sometimes argued that functional employees should have some sort of indirect input into a project manager's evaluation. This raises rather interesting questions as to how far we can go with the indirect evaluation procedure.

From a top-management perspective, the indirect evaluation process brings with it several headaches. Wage and salary administrators readily accept the necessity for using different evaluation forms for white-collar and blue-collar workers. But now, we have a situation in which there can be more than one type of evaluation system for white-collar workers alone. Those employees who work in project-driven functional departments will be evaluated directly and indirectly, but based upon formal procedures. Employees who charge their time to overhead accounts and non-project-driven departments might simply be evaluated by a single, direct evaluation procedure.

PROJECT TITLE	JOB NUMBER
EMPLOYEE ASSIGNMENT	DATE

CODE:

EXCELLENT = 5
ABOVE AVERAGE = 4
AVERAGE = 3
BELOW AVERAGE = 2
INADEQUATE = 1

NAMES	TECHNICAL JUDGEMENT	WORK PLANNING	COMMUNICATIONS	ATTITUDE	COOPERATION	WORK HABITS	PROFIT CONTRIBUTION	SELF MOTIVATION	TOTAL POINTS

Figure 8–4. Project work assignment appraisal.

Many wage and salary administrators contend that they cannot live with a white-collar evaluation system and therefore have tried to combine the direct and indirect evaluation forms into one, as shown in Figure 8–5. Some administrators have even gone so far as to adopt a single form company-wide, regardless of whether an individual is a white- or blue-collar worker.

The design of the employee's evaluation form depends upon what evaluation

I. EMPLOYEE INFORMATION:

1. NAME_____ 2. DATE OF EVALUATION_____

3. JOB ASSIGNMENT _____ 4. DATE OF LAST EVALUATION _____

5. PAY GRADE _____ _____

6. EMPLOYEE'S IMMEDIATE SUPERVISOR _____

7. SUPERVISOR'S LEVEL: ☐ SECTION ☐ DEPT. ☐ DIVISION ☐ EXECUTIVE

II. EVALUATOR'S INFORMATION:

1. EVALUATOR'S NAME _____

2. EVALUATOR'S LEVEL: ☐ SECTION ☐ DEPT. ☐ DIVISION ☐ EXECUTIVE

Figure 8–5. Job evaluation.

3. RATE THE EMPLOYEE ON THE FOLLOWING:

	EXCELLENT	VERY GOOD	GOOD	FAIR	POOR
ABILITY TO ASSUME RESPONSIBILITY					
WORKS WELL WITH OTHERS					
LOYAL ATTITUDE TOWARD COMPANY					
DOCUMENTS WORK WELL AND IS BOTH COST AND PROFIT CONSCIOUS					
RELIABILITY TO SEE JOB THROUGH					
ABILITY TO ACCEPT CRITICISM					
WILLINGNESS TO WORK OVERTIME					
PLANS JOB EXECUTION CAREFULLY					
TECHNICAL KNOWLEDGE					
COMMUNICATIVE SKILLS					
OVERALL RATING					

4. RATE THE EMPLOYEE IN COMPARISON TO HIS CONTEMPORARIES:

LOWER 10%	LOWER 25%	LOWER 40%	MIDWAY	UPPER 40%	UPPER 25%	UPPER 10%

5. RATE THE EMPLOYEE IN COMPARISON TO HIS CONTEMPORARIES:

SHOULD BE PROMOTED AT ONCE	PROMOTABLE NEXT YEAR	PROMOTABLE ALONG WITH CONTEMPORARIES	NEEDS TO MATURE IN GRADE	DEFINITELY NOT PROMOTABLE

6. EVALUATOR'S COMMENTS: _____

_____

_____

SIGNATURE _____

III. CONCURRENCE SECTION:

1. NAME _____

2. POSITION: ☐ DEPARTMENT ☐ DIVISION ☐ EXECUTIVE

3. CONCURRENCE ☐ AGREE ☐ DISAGREE

4. COMMENTS: _____

_____

_____

_____

SIGNATURE _____

IV. PERSONNEL SECTION: (to be completed by the Personnel Department only)

| 6/79 |
| 6/78 |
| 6/77 |
| 6/76 |
| 6/75 |
| 6/74 |
| 6/73 |
| 6/72 |
| 6/71 |
| 6/70 |

| LOWER 10% | LOWER 25% | LOWER 40% | MIDWAY | UPPER 40% | UPPER 25% | UPPER 10% |

V. EMPLOYEE'S SIGNATURE_____ DATE: _____

Figure 8–5. Job evaluation. (*continued*)

method or procedure is being used. Generally speaking, there are nine methods available for evaluating personnel:

- Essay appraisal
- Graphic rating scale
- Field review
- Forced-choice review
- Critical incident appraisal
- Management by objectives
- Work standards approach
- Ranking methods
- Assessment center

Descriptions of these methods can be found in almost any text on wage and salary administration. Which method is best suited for a project-driven organizational structure? To answer this question, we must analyze the characteristics of the organizational form as well as those of the personnel who must perform there. As an example, project management can be described as an arena of conflict. Which of the above evaluation procedures can best be used to evaluate an employee's ability to work and progress in an atmosphere of conflict? Figure 8–6 compares the above nine evaluation procedures against the six most common project conflicts. This type of analysis must be carried out for all variables and characteristics that describe the project management environment. Most compensation managers would agree that the management by objectives (MBO) technique offers the greatest promise for a fair and equi-

	Essay Appraisal	Graphic Rating Scale	Field Review	Forced-Choice Review	Critical Incident Appraisal	Management By Objectives	Work Standards Approach	Ranking Methods	Assessment Center
Conflict over schedules	●	●		●	●		●	●	
Conflict over priorities	●	●		●	●		●	●	
Conflict over technical issues	●			●			●		
Conflict over administration	●	●	●	●			●	●	●
Personality conflict	●	●		●			●		
Conflict over cost	●		●	●	●		●	●	●

Circles define areas where evaluation technique may be difficult to implement.

Figure 8–6. Rating evaluation techniques against types of conflict.

table evaluation of all employees. Although MBO implies that functional employees will have a say in establishing their own goals and objectives, this may not be the case. In project management, maybe the project manager or functional manager will set the objectives, and the functional employee will be told that he has to live with that. Obviously, there will be advantages and disadvantages to whatever evaluation procedures are finally selected.

Having identified the problems with employee evaluation in a project environment, we can now summarize the results and attempt to predict the future. Project managers must have some sort of either direct or indirect input into an employee's evaluation. Without this, project managers may find it difficult to motivate people adequately on the horizontal line. The question is, of course, how should this input take place? Most wage and salary administrators appear to be pushing for a single procedure to evaluate all white-collar employees. At the same time, however, administrators recognize the necessity for an indirect input by the project manager and, therefore, are willing to let the project and functional managers (and possibly functional personnel) determine the exact method of input, which can be different for each employee and each project. This implies that the indirect input might be oral for one employee and written for another, with both employees reporting to the functional manager. Although this technique may seem confusing, it may be the only viable alternative for the future.

Sometimes, project management can create severe evaluation problems. As an example, Gary has been assigned as a part-time assistant project manager. He must function as both an assistant project manager and a functional employee. In addition, Gary reports both vertically to his functional manager and horizontally to a project manager. As part of his project responsibilities, Gary must integrate activities between his department and two other departments within his division. His responsibilities also include writing a nonconfidential performance evaluation for all functional employees from all three departments who are assigned to his project. Can Gary effectively and honestly evaluate functional employees in his own department, people with whom he will be working side by side when the project is over? The answer to this question is no; the project manager should come to the rescue. If Gary were the project manager instead of the assistant project manager, then the line manager should come to his rescue.

8.2 FINANCIAL COMPENSATION AND REWARDS[1]

Proper financial compensation and rewards are important to the morale and motivation of people in any organization. Projects are no exception. However,

---

1. Adapted from Harold Kerzner and Hans J. Thamhain, *Project Management for the Small and Medium-Sized Business* (New York: Van Nostrand Reinhold, 1983), pp. 315–324.

there are several issues that often make it necessary to treat compensation practices of project personnel separately from the rest of the organization:

- *Job classification and job descriptions* for project personnel are usually not compatible with those existing for other professional jobs. It is often difficult to pick an existing classification and adopt it to project personnel. Without proper adjustment, the small amount of formal authority of the project and the small number of direct reports may distort the position level of project personnel in spite of their broad range of business responsibilities.
- *Dual accountability* and dual reporting relationships of project personnel raise the question of who should assess performance and control the rewards.
- *Bases for financial rewards* are often difficult to establish, quantify, and administer. The criteria for "doing a good job" are difficult to quantify.
- *Special compensations* for overtime, extensive travel, or living away from home should be considered in addition to bonus pay for preestablished results. Bonus pay is a particularly difficult and delicate issue because often many people contribute to the results of such incentives. Discretionary bonus practices can be demoralizing to the project team.

Some specific guidelines are provided in this book to help business managers to establish compensation systems for their project organizations. The foundations of these compensation practices are based on four systems: (1) job classification, (2) base pay, (3) performance appraisals, and (4) merit increases.

Job Classifications and Job Descriptions

Every effort should be made to fit the new classifications for project personnel into the existing standard classification that has already been established for the organization.

The first step is to define job titles for various project personnel and their corresponding responsibilities. Titles are very noteworthy. They imply certain responsibilities, position power, organizational status, and pay level. Furthermore, titles may indicate certain functional responsibilities, as does, for example, the title of task manager.[2] Therefore, titles should be carefully selected and each of them supported by a formal job description.

---

2. In most organizations the title of task manager indicates being responsible for managing the technical content of a project subsystem within a functional unit, having dual accountabilities to the functional superior and the project office.

Table 8—1. Sample Job Description.

JOB DESCRIPTION; LEAD PROJECT
ENGINEER OF PROCESSOR DEVELOPMENT

OVERALL RESPONSIBILITY:

Responsible for directing the technical development of the new Central Processor including managing the technical personnel assigned to this development. The Lead Project Engineer has dual responsibility, (1) to his/her functional superior for the technical implementation and engineering quality and (2) to the project manager for managing the development within the established budget and schedule.

SPECIFIC DUTIES AND RESPONSIBILITIES:

1. Provide necessary program direction for planning, organizing, developing and integrating the engineering effort, including establishing the specific objectives, schedules and budgets for the processor subsystem.
2. Provide technical leadership for analyzing and establishing requirements, preliminary designing, designing, prototyping and testing of the processor subsystem.
3. Divide the work into discrete and clearly definable tasks. Assign tasks to technical personnel within the Lead Engineer's area of responsibility and other organizational units.
4. Define, negotiate and allocate budgets and schedules according to the specific tasks and overall program requirements.
5. Measure and control cost, schedule and technical performance against program plan.
6. Report deviations from program plan to program office.
7. Replan trade-off and redirect the development effort in case of contingencies such as to best utilize the available resources toward the overall program objectives.
8. Plan, maintain and utilize engineering facilities to meet the long-range program requirements.

QUALIFICATIONS:

1. Strong technical background in state-of-the-art central processor development.
2. Prior task management experience with proven record for effective cost and schedule control of multi-disciplinary technology-based task in excess of SIM.
3. Personal skills to lead, direct and motivate senior engineering personnel.
4. Excellent communication skills, both orally and in writing.

The job description provides the basic charter for the job and the individual in charge of it. Therefore, the job description should be written not just for one individual but more generically for all individuals who fit the respective job classification. A good job description is brief and concise, not exceeding one page. Typically, it is broken down into three sections: (1) overall responsibilities, (2) specific duties, and (3) qualifications. A sample job description is given in Table 8–1.

Base-Pay Classifications and Incentives

After the job descriptions have been developed, one can delineate pay classes consistent with the responsibilities and accountabilities for business results. If left to the personnel specialist, these pay scales often have a tendency to slip toward the lower end of an equitable compensation. This is understandable because, on the surface, project positions look less senior than their functional counterparts, as formal authority over resources and direct reports are often less necessary for project positions than for traditional functional positions. The impact of such a skewed compensation system is that the project organization will attract less qualified personnel than the functional units. Moreover, project management may be seen as an inferior career that at best may serve as a stepping stone for getting into functional management.

Many companies that have struggled with this problem have solved it by (1) working out compensation schemes as a team of senior managers and personnel specialists, and (2) applying criteria of responsibility and business/profit accountablility to setting pay sales for project personnel in accord with other jobs in their organization. Once the proper range of compensation has been set, fine-tuning is a built-in feature. That is, managers who are hiring can choose a salary from the established range based on their judgment of actual position responsibilities, the candidate's qualifications, the available budget, and other considerations. Valuable guidance and perspective can be obtained from the personnel specialist.

Performance Appraisals

Traditionally, the purpose of the performance appraisal is to:

- Assess the employee's work performance, preferably against preestablished objectives
- Provide a justification for salary actions
- Establish new goals and objectives for the next review period
- Identify and deal with work-related problems
- Serve as a basis for career discussions

In reality, however, the first two objectives are in conflict. As a result, traditional performance appraisals essentially become a salary discussion with the objective to justify subsequent managerial actions.[3] In addition, discussions dominated by salary actions are usually not conducive for future goal setting, problem solving, or career planning.

In order to get around this dilemma, many companies have separated the salary discussion from the other parts of the performance appraisal. Moreover,

---

3. For detailed discussions, see The Conference Board, *Matrix Organizations of Complex Businesses,* 1979; plus some basic research by H. H. Meyer, E. Kay, and J. R. P. French, "Split Roles in Performance Appraisal," *Harvard Business Review,* January–February 1965.

successful managers have carefully considered the complex issues involved and have built a performance appraisal system solidly based on content, measurability, and source of information.

The first challenge is in content, that is, to decide "what to review" and "how to measure performance." Modern management practices try to individualize accountability as much as possible. Furthermore, subsequent incentive or merit increases are tied to profit performance. Although most companies apply these principles to their project organizations, they do it with a great deal of skepticism. Practices are often modified to assure balance and equity for jointly performed responsibilities. A similar dilemma exists in the area of profit accountability. The comment of a project manager at the General Electric Company is typical of the situation faced by business managers: "Although I am responsible for business results of a large program, I really can't control more than 20% of its cost." Acknowledging the realities, organizations are measuring performance of their *project managers,* in at least two areas:

- *Business results* as measured by profits, contribution margin, return on investment, new business, and income; also, on-time delivery, meeting contractual requirements, and within-budget performance.
- *Managerial performance* as measured by overall project management effectiveness, organization, direction and leadership, and team performance.

The first area applies only if the *project manager* is indeed responsible for business results such as contractual performance or new business acquisitions. Many project managers work with company-internal sponsors, such as a company-internal new product development or a feasibility study. In these cases, producing the results within agreed-on schedule and budget constraints becomes the primary measure of performance. The second area is clearly more difficult to assess. Moreover, if handled improperly, it will lead to manipulation and game playing. Table 8–2 provides some specific measures of project management performance. Whether the sponsor is company-internal or external, project managers are usually being assessed on how long it took to organize the team, whether the project is moving along according to agreed-on schedules and budgets, and how closely they meet the global goals and objectives set by their superiors.

On the other side of the project organization, *resource managers* or *project personnel* are being assessed primarily on their ability to direct the implementation of a specific project subsystem:

- *Technical implementation* as measured against requirements, quality, schedules, and cost targets.

Table 8-2. Performance Measures for Project Managers.

WHO PERFORMS APPRAISAL:
Functional superior of project manager
SOURCE OF PERFORMANCE DATA:
Functional superior, resource managers, general managers
PRIMARY MEASURES:
1. Project manager's success in leading the project toward preestablished global objectives
   - Target costs
   - Key milestones
   - Profit, net income, return on investment, contribution margin
   - Quality
   - Technical accomplishments
   - Market measures, new business, follow-on contract
2. Project manager's effectiveness in overall project direction and leadership during all phases, including establishing:
   - Objectives and customer requirements
   - Budgets and schedules
   - Policies
   - Performance measures and controls
   - Reporting and review system

SECONDARY MEASURES:
1. Ability to utilize organizational resources
   - Overhead cost reduction
   - Working with existing personnel
   - Cost-effective make-buy decisions
2. Ability to build effective project team
   - Project staffing
   - Interfunctional communications
   - Low team conflict complaints and hassles
   - Professionally satisfied team members
   - Work with support groups
3. Effective project planning and plan implementation
   - Plan detail and measurability
   - Commitment by key personnel and management
   - Management involvement
   - Contingency provisions
   - Reports and reviews
4. Customer/client satisfaction
   - Perception of overall project performance by sponsor
   - Communications, liaison
   - Responsiveness to changes
5. Participation in business management
   - Keeping management informed of new project/product/business opportunities
   - Bid proposal work
   - Business planning, policy development

ADDITIONAL CONSIDERATIONS:
1. Difficulty of tasks involved
   - Technical tasks
   - Administrative and organizational complexity
   - Multidisciplinary nature
   - Staffing and start-up

Table 8–2. Performance Measures for Project Managers. (*Continued*)

---

2. Scope of the project
    - Total project budget
    - Number of personnel involved
    - Number of organizations and subcontractors involved
3. Changing work environment
    - Nature and degree of customer changes and redirections
    - Contingencies

- *Team performance* as measured by ability to staff, build an effective task group, interface with other groups, and integrate among various functions.

Specific performance measures are shown in Table 8–3. In addition, the actual project performance of both project managers and their resource personnel should be assessed on the conditions under which it was achieved: the degree of task difficulty, complexity, size, changes, and general business conditions.

Finally, one needs to decide who is to perform the performance appraisal and to make the salary adjustment. Where dual accountabilities are involved, good practices call for inputs from both bosses. Such a situation could exist for project managers who report functionally to one superior but are also accountable for specific business results to another person. While dual accountability of project managers is an exception for most organizations, it is common for project resource personnel who are responsible to their functional superior for the quality of the work and to their project manager for meeting the requirements within budget and schedule. Moreover, resource personnel may be shared among many projects. Only the functional or resource manager can judge overall performance of resource personnel.

Merit Increases and Bonuses

Professionals have come to expect merit increases as a reward for a job well done. However, under inflationary conditions, which we have experienced for many years, pay adjustments seldom keep up with cost-of-living increases. To deal with this salary compression and to give incentive for management performance, companies have introduced bonuses uniformly to all components of their organizations. The problem is that these standard plans for merit increases and bonuses are based on individual accountability while project personnel work in teams with shared accountabilities, responsibilities, and controls. It is usually very difficult to credit project success or failure to a single individual or a small group.

Table 8-3. Performance Measures for Project Personnel.

WHO PERFORMS APPRAISAL:
Functional superior of project person
SOURCE OF PERFORMANCE DATA;
Project manager and resource managers
PRIMARY MEASURES:
1. Success in directing the agreed-on task toward completion
   - Technical implementation according to requirements
   - Quality
   - Key milestones/schedules
   - Target costs, design-to-cost
   - Innovation
   - Trade-offs
2. Effectiveness as a team member or team leader
   - Building effective task team
   - Working together with others, participation, involvement
   - Interfacing with support organizations and subcontractors
   - Interfunctional coordination
   - Getting along with others
   - Change orientation
   - Making commitments

SECONDARY MEASURES:
1. Success and effectiveness in performing functional tasks in addition to project work in accordance with functional charter
   - Special assignments
   - Advancing technology
   - Developing organization
   - Resource planning
   - Functional direction and leadership
2. Administrative support services
   - Reports and reviews
   - Special task forces and committees
   - Project planning
   - Procedure development
3. New business development
   - Bid proposal support
   - Customer presentations
4. Professional development
   - Keeping abreast in professional field
   - Publications
   - Liaison with society, vendors, customers and educational institutions

ADDITIONAL CONSIDERATIONS:
1. Difficulty of tasks involved
   - Technical challenges
   - State-of-the-art considerations
   - Changes and contingencies
2. Managerial responsibilities
   - Task leader for number of project personnel
   - Multi-functional integration

Table 8–3. Performance Measures for Project Personnel. (*Continued*)

- Budget responsibility
- Staffing responsibility
- Specific accountabilities
3. Multi-project involvement
   - Number of different projects
   - Number and magnitude of functional task and duties
   - Overall work load

Most managers with these dilemmas have turned to the traditional remedy of the performance appraisal. If done well, the appraisal should provide particular measures of job performance that assess the level and magnitude at which the individual has contributed to the success of the project, including the managerial performance and team performance components. Therefore, a properly designed and executed performance appraisal that includes input from all accountable management elements, and the basic agreement of the employee with the conclusions, is a sound basis for future salary reviews. Often more important than the actual increase is the size of the salary adjustment relative to that of other employees. Equitable pay for performance and position is crucial to employee morale and satisfactory productivity, a very important area that deserves careful management attention.

8.3 EFFECTIVE PROJECT MANAGEMENT IN THE SMALL BUSINESS ORGANIZATION

The acceptance of project management in large companies has been relatively easy because of the abundance of published literature identifying its potential pitfalls and problems. The definition of a small project could be:

- Total duration is usually three to twelve months.
- Total dollar value is $5,000 to $1.5 million (upper limit is usually capital equipment projects).
- There is continuous communication between team members, and no more than three or four cost centers are involved.
- Manual rather than computerized cost control may be acceptable.
- Project managers work closely with functional personnel and managers on a daily basis, so time-consuming detail reporting is not necessary.
- The work breakdown structure does not go beyond level three.

Here, we are discussing project management in both small companies and small organizations within a larger corporation. In small organizations, major differences from large companies must be accounted for:

● *In small companies, the project manager has to wear multiple hats and may have to act as a project manager and line manager at the same time.* Large companies may have the luxury of a single full-time project manager for the duration of a project. Smaller companies may not be able to afford a full-time project manager and therefore may require that functional managers wear two hats. This poses a problem in that the functional managers may be more dedicated to their own functional unit than to the project, and the project may suffer. There is also the risk that when the line manager also acts as project manager, then the line manager may keep the best resources for his own project. The line manager's project may be a success at the expense of all the other projects that he must supply resources for.

In the ideal situation, the project manager works horizontally and has project dedication, whereas the line manager works vertically and has functional (or company) dedication. If the working relationship between the project and functional managers is a good one, then decisions will be made in a manner that is in the best interest of both the project and the company. Unfortunately, this may be difficult to accomplish in small companies when an individual wears multiple hats.

● *In a small company, the project manager handles multiple projects, perhaps each with a different priority.* In large companies, project managers normally handle only one project at a time. Handling multiple projects becomes a serious problem if the priorities are not close together. For this reason, many small companies avoid the establishment of priorities for fear that the lower-priority activities will never be accomplished.

● *In a small company, the project manager has limited resources.* In a large company, if the project manager is unhappy with resources that are provided, he may have the luxury of returning to the functional manager to either demand or negotiate for other resources. In a small organization, the resources assigned may be simply the only resources available.

● *In a small company, project managers must generally have a better understanding of interpersonal skills than in a larger company.* This is a necessity because a project manager in the small company has limited resources and must provide the best motivation that he can.

● *In the smaller company, the project manager generally has shorter lines of communications.* In small organizations project managers almost always report to a top-level executive, whereas in larger organizations the project managers can report to any level of management. Small companies tend to have fewer levels of management.

● *Small companies do not have a project office.* Large companies, especially in aerospace or construction, can easily support a project office of twenty to thirty people, whereas in the smaller company the project manager may have to be the entire project office. This implies that the project manager in a small company may be required to have more general and specific information about all company activities, policies, and procedures than his counterparts in the larger companies.

● *In a small company, there may be a much greater risk to the total company with the failure of as little as one project.* Large companies may be able to afford the loss of a multi-million-dollar program, whereas the smaller company may be in serious financial trouble. For example, a machine tool company in the Midwest has almost 70 percent of its business generated by one of the big three automotive manufacturers. The risk to the small company occurs when one project represents a large percentage of its business. Thus many smaller companies avoid bidding on projects that could place the company in such a delicate position; for, with the acceptance of such a project, the company would have to either hire additional resources or give up some of its smaller accounts.

● *In a small company, there might be tighter monetary controls but with less sophisticated control techniques.* Because the smaller company incurs greater risk with the failure (or cost overrun) of as little as one project, costs are generally controlled much more tightly and more frequently than in larger companies. However, the smaller companies generally rely upon manual or partially computerized systems, whereas the larger organizations rely heavily upon sophisticated software packages. Today, more and more small companies are being forced to completely computerize their cost control procedures to adhere to requirements imposed by customers and prime contractors.

● *In a small company, there usually exists more upper-level management interference.* This is expected because in the small company there is a much greater risk with the failure of a single project. In addition, executives in smaller companies "meddle" more than executives in larger companies, and quite often delegate as little as possible to project managers.

● *Evaluation procedures for individuals are usually easier in a smaller company.* This holds true because the project manager gets to know the people better, and, as stated above, there exists a greater need for interpersonal skills on the horizontal line in a smaller company.

● *In a smaller company, project estimating is usually more precise and based upon either history or standards.* This type of planning process is usually manual as opposed to computerized. In addition, functional managers in a small company usually feel obligated to live up to their commitments, whereas in the larger companies, much more lip service is given.

The arguments presented here are not necessarily meant to discourage the small company, but to identify problems that may have to be encountered and resolved. Project management, when implemented correctly, will generate a smoother flow of work and better control of resources, on both horizontal and vertical lines.

8.4 MEGA PROJECTS

Mega projects may have a different set of rules and guidelines from those of smaller projects. For example, in large projects:

- Vast amounts of people may be required, often for short or intense periods of time.
- Continuous organizational restructuring may be necessary as each project goes through a different life-cycle phase.
- The matrix and project organizational form may be used interchangeably.
- The following elements are critical for success.
  - Training in project management
  - Rules and procedures clearly defined
  - Communications at all levels
  - Quality front-end planning

Many companies dream of winning mega project contracts only to find disaster rather than a pot of gold. The difficulty in managing mega projects stems mainly from resource restraints:

- Lack of available on-site workers (or local labor forces)
- Lack of skilled workers
- Lack of properly trained on-site supervision
- Lack of raw materials

As a result of such problems, the company immediately assigns its best employees to the mega project, thus creating severe risks for the smaller projects, many of which could lead to substantial follow-on business. Overtime is usually required, on a prolonged basis, and this results in lower efficiency and unhappy employees.

As the project schedule slips, management hires additional home-office personnel to support the project. By the time that the project is finished, the total organization is overstaffed, many smaller customers have taken their business elsewhere, and the company finds itself in the position of needing another mega project in order to survive and support the existing staff.

Mega projects are not always as glorious as people think they are. Organizational stability, accompanied by a moderate growth rate, may be more important than quantum steps to mega projects. The lesson here is that mega projects should be left to those companies that have the facilities, expertise, resources, and management know-how to handle the situation.

8.5 STRATEGIC PLANNING USING A MATRIX

The matrix structure is an organizational form for project management that, as the name implies, is designed to handle projects primarily in a project-driven company. Matrix management has been used successfully to handle all types of projects ranging from small feasibility studies to massive, mega-dollar construction projects. The matrix structure knows no bounds, whether they be size, dollar, time, or other limiting factors.

Only recently has the matrix structure been considered applicable for strategic planning efforts, although it has long been known as a highly organic organizational methodology capable of responding rapidly to an ever changing environment. The advantages and disadvantages of the matrix are well known and can be found in most texts on project management.

Several questions need to be answered before executives will consider adoption of the matrix for strategic planning. The remainder of this section deals with those questions.

Is Strategic Planning a Project?

Project management using a matrix is an effort to obtain the most effective and efficient utilization of resources while attempting to achieve an objective within the constraints of time, cost, and performance or technology. If it is to fit into the somewhat rigid matrix model, strategic planning must be considered as a project. If this is the case, then the goals and objectives of the strategic plan must be clearly identified, together with any limiting factors such as time, cost, and performance.

Project managers historically prefer to work in concrete rather than abstract notation, and to implement a plan that they themselves have developed. Being forced to work with vague generalities may very well be contrary to the project manager's entire world of experience.

> *Moral:* If strategic planning is to be performed using a matrix, then, in general, the strategic planning methodology must change to be adaptable to the existing matrix, not vice versa.

To Whom Should the Project Manager Report?

The level at which the project manager reports cannot be discussed without considering executive control of the matrix. Mature matrix organizations usually identify a separate line function for project managers, and the head of the line function is an executive with the title of manager or director of project management. We must remember, however, that the manager of project managers and his functional project managers are more operational planners than strategic planners. Therefore, forcibly placing a strategic planning project manager in their midst may result in the project manager's not getting the support that he needs.

Generally speaking, strategic planning can take place at three levels in the organization:

- Corporate
- Divisional
- Functional

Corporate planning is geared to total "portfolio" planning, and, in this case, the project manager would report directly to a corporate executive or corporate staff. At the divisional level, strategic planning is equivalent to business strategy planning, whereas, at the functional level, strategic planning becomes synonymous with "strategic programming," a concept that some consider extremely close to operational planning. At the divisional or functional level, strategic planners should report no lower than to the divisional staff, especially if a matrix structure already exists within the organization. If a project management line group does not already exist, then it may be acceptable to have project managers reporting at different levels and still have a good operational matrix.

Since the growth and survivability of the organization may very well depend upon the success of the strategic plan, the strategic planning project manager must have *at least* the same level of authority as the other project managers. Functional groups, especially in manufacturing, are often nearsighted and assign their best resources to those projects that can be expected to yield immediate profits. Therefore, project managers involved in strategic planning may find it more difficult to obtain qualified functional resources than do the operational project managers.

> *Moral:* Strategic planning project managers should report high in the organization and *must* have sufficient authority to obtain qualified resources.

One final note should be made here concerning the dedication and commitment of project managers. History has shown that the success of project management is based upon the motivational behavior of the project manager when he gets to see an entire project from birth to death. Seeing the results of one's efforts is probably the strongest motivational force in any form of project/matrix management. Therefore, project managers involved in strategic planning should be allowed to participate in the execution stage of the plan as well as the formulation stage. Dedication and commitment follow naturally from ownership, and ownership cannot be achieved without active participation during the implementation phase. This could, however, prove to be a problem area if the strategic planning time frame is too long.

At the beginning of this section, we stated that the strategic planning matrix is similar to the operational matrix in that project managers can report to several levels of management on the same project. The operational matrix is designed to "force" conflicts to be resolved at the lower levels of the company, thus freeing executives for more vital concerns. For the most part, this philosophy is acceptable. However, there are some conflicts that must be brought to the attention of senior executives. It may be catastrophic during the strategic planning process to remove the executive from conflict resolution. This is yet another good reason for having the project managers report high up.

> *Moral:* Conflicts that arise during the strategic planning process should be made known to executive management rather than buried within the organization.

How Do the Executive and the Project Manager Interface?

Planning, be it strategic, operational, or tactical, is a function that should be performed by managers, not for them. If the executive wishes to delegate some of the planning activities to a project manager, then the executives must be aware of the project manager's strengths and weaknesses with regard to strategic planning. Consider a planning logic such as this:[4]

- Environmental Analysis
  - Where are we?
  - How and why did we get here?
- Setting Objectives
  - Is this where we want to be?
  - Where would we like to be? In a year? In five years?
- List Alternative Strategies
  - Where will we go if we continue as before?
  - Is that where we want to go?
  - How could we get to where we want to go?
- List Threats and Opportunities
  - What might prevent us from getting there?
  - What might help us to get there?
- Prepare Forecasts
  - Where are we capable of going?
  - What do we need to take us where we want to go?
- Select Strategy Portfolio
  - What is the best course for us to take?
  - What are the potential benefits?
  - What are the risks?
- Prepare Action Programs
  - What do we need to do?
  - When do we need to do it?
  - How will we do it?
  - Who will do it?
- Monitor and Control
  - Are we on course? If not, why?
  - What do we need to do to be on course?
  - Can we do it?

The first stage, environmental analysis, can be easily accomplished by the project manager. If the project manager has been with the company for, say, five or more years, then this information should be readily available. Additionally, the information could be obtained from talking to other managers or from stockholder reports.

Setting project objectives has never been the responsibility of a project manager. In general project management, objectives are prepared by executives or

---

4. Harold Kerzner, *Project Management for Executives* (New York: Van Nostrand Reinhold, 1982), p. 326.

user groups, and the project then introduces these objectives as part of the statement/scope of work. This same philosophy holds true for strategic planning.

The next three stages—list alternative strategies, list threats and opportunities, and prepare forecasts—can be accomplished by the project managers because the methodology for accomplishing them is usually part of every project. The project manager must understand the environmental factors such as legal, social, economic, technological, and political constraints. He must understand the characteristics of his own industry, including the strategic variables. (These variables may have to be defined by the executives and may vary from company to company even within the same industry.) The project manager must be able to predict future changes in the environment and the criteria against which success will be measured.

Stage 6 is the selection of the strategy portfolio. This stage requires the answering of such questions as:[5]

- Is the strategy identifiable, and has it been made clear in words or practice?
- Does the strategy exploit full domestic and international environmental opportunities?
- Is the strategy consistent with corporate competence (including effective management) and resources, both present and projected?
- Are the program's major policies and provisions internally consistent?

It should be obvious that these questions require strong executive involvement. This stage cannot be delegated to the project manager.

Stage 7, on the other hand, can be performed solely by the project manager as long as the project manager realizes the action plan is long-term and may be based upon environmental factors that have yet to be completely defined. Preparing the action plan includes:

- Identification of the tasks and their sequencing
- Identification of the decisions to be made
- Identification of the information requirements
- Identification of the constraints
- Identification of the monitoring and control system

---

5. Adapted from Kenneth R. Andrews, *The Concept of Corporate Strategy*, (Homewood, Illinois: Dow Jones-Irwin, 1971), pp. 36–42.

Stage 8, monitoring and control, can be accomplished entirely by the project manager. This stage involves such concerns as:

- Coordination through the chain of command
- Comparison of actual to projected data with explanations of the deviations
- Assigning responsibility for each task
- Evaluating performance and, if possible, providing rewards

Control also includes feedback. The feedback mechanism to executives must be more rapid and well structured than general feedback because the information may cause the executive to realign his thinking. This may result in a raising or lowering of expectations, a shift in the business emphasis, or an effort to minimize risk by obtaining a better balance, say through acquisitions or divestitures.

> *Moral:* Strategic project planning, whether or not a matrix is used, requires an extremely close working relationship between executives and project managers, especially during execution.

When matrix management first came into existence, it was used predominantly for relatively short-term activities that had definable goals and objectives. As projects grew in size and complexity, the matrix was used for long-range as well as short-range project planning. Unfortunately, many experienced project managers who were asked to perform strategic planning within a matrix considered strategic planning to be the same as long-range planning. There are several major differences, and, if the project manager is not aware of them, the results may be disastrous:[6]

- Long-range planning is merely a projection of current operations into the future, not necessarily the direction in which you want to go.
- In long-range planning, plans determine the direction rather than vice versa.
- In long-range planning, objectives are usually defined in financial terms only.
- In long-range planning, we can get so involved with the precision of the plans and the estimates that we no longer know if we are taking the direction we want.

6. Adapted from Benjamin B. Tregoe and John W. Zimmerman, *Top Management Strategy* (New York: Simon and Schuster, 1980), pp. 23–27.

- Long-range planning is based upon optimistic functional estimates.
- Long-range planning is based upon well-structured environmental assumptions.
- Long-range planning is inflexible unless a crisis exists.
- Long-range planning is merely an extension of short-range planning.

Strategic planning can be accomplished using a matrix if, and only if, the project manager understands the difference between strategic and long-range planning. This is yet another reason for close executive involvement.

In a matrix organization, there are usually formal procedures for project selection and initiation, and many times active CEO involvement may not be necessary. For strategic planning, however, there is a need for active CEO involvement:[7]

- The CEO must initiate the planning process himself by giving his general endorsement, preferably in writing. Without this endorsement, the project manager may find that line executives and managers do not believe that the executive is committed and therefore hesitate to participate, thinking that the process is not real.
- The CEO should identify his own goals and aspirations. If this is not done, line executives and managers may decide to waste time by sitting in holding patterns waiting for the CEO to declare himself.
- Without CEO involvement, line managers may try to take the easy way out by not allocating sufficient time to strategic planning. When this occurs, functional groups will tend to preserve the status quo of their own group in addition to favoring their own group during planning. When a line manager chooses the easy way out, most of his planning is simply linear extrapolation of previous years' data.

Most people readily accept the fact that executive involvement is mandatory in all types of planning, even if it is merely for approvals. However, during the implementation stage there are major differences between a general project and a strategic planning project. In general projects, executive involvement during project implementation is in a rather passive role as long as the project manager is providing the executive with meaningful data as to project status.

Lack of executive involvement during the implementation stage of a strategic planning project can lead to disastrous results. Strategic plans generally do not have well-structured details for line managers to follow; so line man-

---

7. Peter Lorange, *Corporate Planning: An Executive Viewpoint,* © 1980, pp. 257–262. Adapted by permission of Prentice-Hall, Inc., Englewood Cliffs, New Jersey.

agers may find it easy to keep their best resources for other functional activities and "pull the wool over the eyes of the project manager." With respect to authority, the project manager may need much more (documented) authority during implementation in order to consolidate functional strategic packages through cross-functional involvement.

Because strategic plans are not necessarily well structured, the project manager may have to continuously redefine new time spans for project control. In a matrix organization this might not work well because mature matrix structures are based upon a highly mechanistic approach to monitoring and control. A fluctuating time reference on one project may not be readily meshed with a rigid time reference on all of the other projects.

Finally, in most matrix organizations the project manager may not have the authority to provide rewards and incentives. Executives, on the other hand, may wish to provide these rewards and incentives so that line personnel will think more in long-range rather than short-range terms. This is another good reason for executive involvement during implementation.

> *Moral:* Strategic goals and objectives must be established before planning begins; otherwise short-term thinking takes over.

> *Moral:* Goals for the planners must be identified in order to guard against nonessentials.

> *Moral:* Top-management involvement may very well be the single most important variable in strategic planning.

> *Moral:* The matrix structure stresses people-to-people contact, thus producing a fast response.

> *Moral:* The most overlooked variable in strategic planning is the company's future spending plans.

> *Moral:* Test the assumptions of functional personnel for pessimism and optimism.

> *Moral:* Strategic planning must be divorced from crisis management and firefighting.

When Does the Project Manager Communicate?

One of the advantages of matrix management is the development of both horizontal and vertical channels of communication. In motivating people performing in a matrix, a major strength is to keep them well-informed as to the status of the project, in addition to how well their specific job fits into the overall picture. Project managers try to articulate as much as possible to the employees to get them motivated, dedicated, and committed to the horizontal line in the matrix.

For a strategic planning project, the project manager must know when *not* to articulate the strategy to personnel below the executive level. Proprietary information leaks can cause a company to lose its competitive edge. If the strategy were to drain all of the cash out of an obsolete business (or even a "cash cow") or to sell one of the divisions, there would undoubtedly be strong resistance by lower-level personnel, as well as a lack of commitment.

> *Moral:* In strategic planning, project managers must realize that, more often than not, articulating corporate strategy to lower-level personnel may prove detrimental. This may be contrary to the way the project manager has performed on previous projects.

How is the Matrix Used for Resource Control?

Previously, we showed that matrix management can be applied to strategic planning. The question, of course, is whether or not resources can be employed effectively in a strategic planning project as in other projects. Two major problems must be considered. First, a matrix structure should not be set up strictly for strategic planning projects. If the matrix is not already in existence and being used for daily operation, it is doubtful that personnel will understand it and accept it. Second, it may be a mistake to create a matrix within a matrix just for strategic planning or to create a separate external strategic planning matrix. Strategic planning must be fitted to the existing matrix for effective resource control.

The matrix is designed to share key people on an as-needed basis so that each project will benefit from the use of these key people. Without matrix control, the strategic planning process may become costly because key people will be utilized full-time. In addition, line managers may be reluctant to release their key people from the daily operations for full-time strategic planning assignments. This is particularly true in production activities where manufacturing managers generally express more interest in immediate than in downstream profits.

Table 8–4 summarizes the changes that have to be considered in using a matrix for strategic planning. Each X in the right-hand column identifies a change that may be necessary. Without these changes, it is unlikely that matrix management and strategic planning can be married.

8.6 R&D PROJECT MANAGEMENT

One of the most difficult tasks in any organization is the management of R&D activities. These R&D activities are usually headed by scientists, engineers, managers, employees, or even executives. All of these people, at one time or another, may act as R&D project managers. They start out with an idea and are asked to lay out a detailed schedule, cost summary, set of specifications, and resource requirements so that the idea can become a reality. Unfortunately, this is easier said than done.

Project management is an attempt to obtain more efficient utilization of resources within an organization by getting work to flow horizontally as well as vertically. Furthermore, all projects must be completed within the constraints of time, cost, and performance. If the project is for an outside customer, then there exists a fourth constraint—good customer relations. Without proper training and understanding, R&D project managers might easily manage their projects within time, cost, and performance, but alienate the outside customer to such a degree that follow-on (or production-type) contracts are nonexistent.

R&D personnel were probably the first true project managers in the world. Unfortunately, very little training was available until the vanguard of modern project management occurred in the late fifties in aerospace, defense, and construction companies. Even today, twenty-five years later, very little project management training is provided for R&D personnel.

R&D personnel are technically trained perfectionists who believe that cost and time are unimportant when it comes to improving the state of the art. R&D personnel would rather crawl on their hands and knees and beg for more

Table 8–4. Analysis of Changes Needed in Using the Matrix for Strategic Planning.

	NO CHANGE NEEDED	SOME CHANGE NEEDED
Communication with executive management		X
Communication with line management	X	
Identifying planning variables		X
Understanding organizational structures	X	
Location of the project manager		X
Objective-setting		X
CEO involvement		X
Feedback to executive management		X
Conflict resolution		X
Resource control	X	
Use of experienced project manager		X
Negotiation for qualified resources	X	
Dedication of the project manager	X	
Monitoring and control		X
Integrating work cross-functionally	X	
Continuous replanning		X
Continuous reassessing of constraints		X
Flexibility in trade-offs		X
Ability to provide rewards		X

money and time than admit defeat on an R&D project. The more degrees an individual has, the more reluctant he is to accept defeat.

R&D personnel have been stereotyped and subjected to more criticism than any other employees, even engineers. R&D personnel are considered to be egocentric, spoon-fed, coddled individuals sitting in small corners of laboratories, who are provided with hand calculators so that they can get excited once in a while. The stereotypical R&D project managers avoid people-contact whenever possible. They cannot communicate well, write reports, or make presentations. They are illiterate except when it comes to complex graphs and equations. And yet they are consistently placed in charge of projects. In most project-driven organizations, there is usually strong representation of former project managers in top echelons of management, but how many senior corporate executives or CEOs have come out of the R&D ranks? Could it be that this inappropriate stereotyping has prevented R&D personnel from rising to the top?

The R&D Environment

Very few people in an organization truly understand the R&D environment and the problems facing the R&D project manager. We continuously ask the R&D project manager to achieve an objective that even science fiction writers haven't thought of, and that requires technology that hasn't been discovered yet. We further ask him to lay out a detailed schedule, with established milestones and predetermined costs set forth by some executive, and then inform him that he may have trouble obtaining the resources that he needs.

After he establishes his schedule, executives change the milestones because the schedule affects their Christmas bonuses. And when the project finally gets on track, marketing pushes the end milestone to the left because they wish to have earlier introduction of the project into the marketplace in order to either beat or keep up with the competition.

The project manager therefore finds that he must do his work in seclusion, avoiding meddling from executives, marketing, and manufacturing. The avoidance of the manufacturing group ultimately leads to the R&D project manager's downfall because he finds out too late that manufacturing cannot mass-produce the item according to the R&D specifications. Who gets blamed? The R&D project manager, of course! He should have been communicating with everyone.

The R&D environment might very well be the most difficult and turbulent environment in which to manage a project. The remainder of this section will describe this problem in R&D project management in hopes that readers will better appreciate those individuals who accept R&D project management as a career.

Detail Scheduling: Fact or Fantasy?

Scheduling activities for R&D projects is extremely difficult because of the problems mentioned above. Many R&D people believe that if you know how long it will take to complete an objective, you do not need R&D. Most R&D

schedules are not detailed but are composed of major milestones where executives can decide whether or not additional money or resources should be committed. Some executives and R&D managers believe in this philosophy:

> I'll give you "so much time" to get an answer.

In R&D project management, failure is often construed as an acceptable answer.

There are two schools of thought on R&D scheduling, depending of course upon the type of project, time duration, and resources required. The first school involves tight R&D scheduling. This may occur if the project is a one-person activity. R&D personnel are generally highly optimistic and believe that they can do anything. Therefore, they tend to lay out rather tight, optimistic schedules. This type of optimism is actually a good trait. Where would we be without it? How many projects would be prematurely canceled without optimistic R&D personnel?

Tight schedules occur mostly on limited-resource projects. Project managers tend to avoid tight schedules if they feel that there exists a poor "window" in the functional organization for a timely commitment of resources. Also R&D personnel know that in time of crisis or firefighting on manufacturing lines, which are yielding immediate profits, they may lose their key functional project employees, perhaps for an extended period.

The second school of thought believes that R&D project management is not mechanical like other forms of project management; so all schedules must be loose. Scientists do not like or want tight structuring because they feel that they cannot be creative without having sufficient freedom to do their job. Many good results have been obtained from spinoffs and other activities where R&D project managers have deviated from predetermined schedules. Of course, too much freedom can spell disaster because the individual might try to be overly creative and "reinvent the wheel."

This second school says that R&D project managers should not focus on limited objectives. Rather, the project manager should be able to realize that other possible objectives can be achieved with further exploration of some of the activities.

Two special types of projects are generally performed without any schedules: the "grass roots" project and the "bootleg" project. Each type is simply an idea that, with one or two good data points, could become a full-blown, well-funded activity. The major difference between the two is that the grass roots project is normally funded with some sort of "seed" money, whereas the bootleg project is accomplished piecemeal and on the sly. With the bootleg project, employees charge their time to other activities while performing the bootleg R&D.

Working with Executives

Executives earn high salaries because they can perform long-range planning and formulate policy. In general project management executive meddling is a way of life because of conflict resolution and the continuing need to reassess project priorities. In R&D, the problem of executive meddling becomes more pronounced because, in addition to the above reasons for his involvement, the executive might still consider himself to be a technical specialist or might develop a sense of executive pride of ownership because the project was his idea. If an executive continually provides technical advice, it is entirely possible that an atmosphere of stifled creativity will develop. If the executive is considered to be an expert in the field, then everyone, including the R&D project manager, may let the executive do it all—and both the project and the executive's duties may suffer.

There is nothing wrong with an executive's demonstrating pride of ownership for a project as long as he does not assert that "this project will be mine, all the way," and meddle continuously. The R&D project manager should still be permitted to run the show with timely, structured feedback of information to the executive. If executives meddle continuously, then the R&D project manager may adopt a policy of "avoidance management," in which executives are continuously avoided unless problems arise.

In general project management, executives should actively interface a project only during the conception and planning stages. The same holds true in R&D project management but with much more emphasis on the conceptual stage than the planning stage. The executive should work closely with the R&D project manager in defining the:

- Needs
- Requirements
- Objectives
- Success factors
- Realistic end date

The executive should then step out of the way and let the R&D project manager establish his own timetable. One cannot expect executive meddling to be entirely eliminated from R&D activities because each R&D activity could easily have a direct bearing upon the strategic planning that the executive must perform as part of his daily routine.

R&D activities have a direct bearing on the organization's strategic planning. Executives should therefore provide some sort of feedback to R&D managers. The following comments were made by an R&D project manager:

I know that there is planning going on now for activities which I will be doing three months from now. How should I plan for this? I don't have any formal or informal data on planning as yet. What should I tell my boss?

Executives should not try to understaff the R&D function. Forcing R&D personnel and project managers to work on too many projects at once can drastically reduce creativity. This does not imply that personnel should be used on only one project at a time. Most companies do not have this luxury. However, this situation of multi-project project management should be carefully monitored.

Finally, executives must be very careful about how much control they exercise over R&D project managers. Too much control can drastically reduce bootleg research, and, in the long run, the company may suffer.

Working with Marketing

In most organizations, either R&D drives marketing, or marketing drives R&D. The latter is more common. Well-managed organizations maintain a proper balance between marketing and R&D. Marketing-driven organizations can create havoc, especially if marketing continuously requests information faster than R&D can deliver, and if bootleg R&D is eliminated. In this case, all R&D activities must be approved by marketing. In some organizations, R&D funding comes out of the marketing budget.

In order to stimulate creativity, R&D should have control over at least a portion of its own budget. This is a necessity because not all R&D activities are designed to benefit marketing. Some activities are intended simply to improve technology or create a new way of doing business.

Marketing support, if needed, should be available to all R&D projects, whether they originate in marketing or R&D. An R&D project manager at a major food manufacturer made the following remarks:

A few years ago, one of our R&D people came up with an idea and I was assigned as the project manager. When the project was completed, we had developed a new product, ready for market introduction and testing. Unfortunately, R&D does not maintain funds for the market testing of a new product. The funds come out of marketing. Our marketing people either did not understand the product or placed it low on their priority list. We, in R&D, tried to talk to them. They were reluctant to test the new product because the project was our idea. Marketing lives in their own little world. To make a long story short, last year one of our competitors introduced the same product into the market place. Now, instead of being the leader, we are playing catch-up. I know R&D project managers are not trained in market testing, but what if marketing refuses to support R&D-conceived projects? What can we do?

Several organizations today have R&D project managers reporting directly to a new business group, business development group, or marketing. Engineering-oriented R&D project managers continually express their displeasure at being evaluated for promotion by someone in marketing who may not understand the technical difficulties in managing an R&D project. Yet, executives have valid arguments for this arrangement, asserting that the high-technology R&D project managers are so in love with their project that they don't know how and when to cancel it. Marketing executives contend that projects should be canceled when:

- Costs become excessive, causing product cost to be noncompetitive.
- Return on investment will occur too late.
- Competition is too stiff and not worth the risk.

and so on. Of course, the question arises, "Should marketing have a vote in the cancellation of each R&D project or only those that are marketing-driven?" Some organizations cancel projects with the consensus of the project team.

Location of the R&D Function

R&D project management in small organizations is generally easier than similar functions in large organizations. In small companies, there usually exists a single R&D group responsible for all R&D activities. In large companies, each division may have its own R&D function. The giant corporations try to encourage decentralized R&D under the supervision of a central research (or corporate research) group. The following problems were identified by a central research group project manager:

- I have seen parallel projects going on at the same time.
- We have a great duplication of effort because each division has their own R&D and Quality Control functions. We have a very poor passing of information between divisions.
- Central research was originally developed to perform research functions which could not be effectively handled by the divisions. Although we are supposed to be a service group, we still bill each division for the work we do for them. Some pay us and some don't. Last year, several divisions stopped using us because they felt that it was cheaper to do the work

themselves. Now, we are funded entirely by corporate and have more work than we can handle. Everyone can think of work for us to do when it is free.

Priority-Setting

Priorities create colossal managerial headaches for the R&D project manager because R&D projects are usually prioritized on a different list from all of the other projects. Functional managers must now supply resources according to two priority lists. Unfortunately, the R&D priority list is usually not given proper attention.

As an example of this, the director of R&D of a Fortune 25 corporation made the following remarks:

> Each of our operating divisions have their own R&D projects and priorities. Last year corporate R&D had a very high R&D project geared toward cost improvement in the manufacturing areas. Our priorities were based upon the short run requirements. Unfortunately, the operating divisions that had to supply resources to our project felt that the benefits would not be received until the long run and therefore placed support for our project low on their priority list.

Communication of priorities is often a problem in the R&D arena. Setting of priorities on the divisional level may not be passed down to the departmental level, and vice versa. We must have early feedback of priorities so that functional managers can make their own plans.

Written Communications

R&D project managers are no different from other project managers in that they are expected to have superior writing skills but actually do not. R&D project managers quickly become prolific writers if they feel that they will receive recognition through their writings.

Most R&D projects begin with a project request form that includes a feasibility study and cost–benefit analysis. The report can vary from five to fifty pages. The project manager must identify benefits that the company will receive if it allocates funds to this activity. In many non-R&D activities project managers are not required to perform such feasibility studies.

Because of the lack of professional writing skills, executives should try to reduce the number of interim reports, since report writing can seriously detract the individual from more important R&D functions. In addition, most interim reports are more marketing-oriented than R&D-oriented.

Many of today's companies have weekly or bimonthly status review meetings where each R&D project manager provides a five-minute (or shorter) oral briefing on the status of his project, without getting involved in technical details. Of course, at project completion or termination, a comprehensive written report is still required.

Salaries and Performance Evaluation

R&D groups have one of the highest salaries ranges in a company. R&D groups are generally the first to establish a dual-ladder system where employees can progress on a technical pay scale to high salary positions without having to accept a position in management. In the R&D environment, it is quite common for some functional employees to be at a higher salary level than the R&D project manager or even their own functional managers. This arrangement is necessary in order to maintain a superior technical community and to select managers based upon their managerial expertise, not technical superiority.

The R&D group of a Fortune 25 corporation recently adopted a dual-ladder system and found that it created strange problems. Several scientists began fighting over the size of their office, type of desk, and who should have their own secretaries.

The evaluation process of R&D personnel can be very difficult. R&D project managers can have either direct or indirect control over an employee's evaluation for promotion. Generally speaking, project managers, even R&D project managers, can only make recommendations to the functional managers, who in turn assess the validity of the recommendations and make the final assessments. Obviously, not all R&D projects are going to produce fruitful results. In such a case, should the employee be graded down because the project failed? This is a major concern to managers.

Motivation

R&D project managers have no problem with self-motivation, especially on one-person projects. But how does a project manager motivate project team members, especially when you, the R&D project manager, may have no say in the performance or evaluation? How do you get all of your employees to focus on the correct information? How do you motivate employees when their time is fragmented over several activities? How can you prevent employees from picking up bad habits that can lead to missed opportunities?

R&D project managers would rather motivate employees through work challenge and by demonstrating their own expertise. Most R&D project managers prefer not to use formal authority. One R&D project manager summed up his problem as follows:

I have only implied authority and cannot always force the project partic-ipants to perform my way. We have used task forces both effectively and ineffectively. We are always confronted with authority and priority prob-lems when it comes to motivating people. Functional managers resent R&D project managers who continuously demonstrate their project authority. Our best results are obtained when the task force members visualize this project as part of their own goals.

Executives must take a hard look at how they are managing their R&D projects. In general, all R&D personnel are project managers and should be trained accordingly, as any other project manager would be. If executives wish to develop an organization that will retain superior personnel and stimulate creativity and freedom, then they must recognize the need for effective orga-nizational communications and alleviate meddling by marketing and the exec-utive level of the organization. R&D project managers are actually the archi-tects of the conceptual phase of the corporation's long-range plans, and it appears that their value to the organization finally is being recognized by management.

Management[8]

The primary responsibility for success in any organization is in its manage-ment. Possibly in research and development, more than any other function, true success depends upon upper-level management and other functional managers rather than its own functional management. This dependence on other levels of management is a result of the information and resources required by the R&D function being supplied by other organizational units, which, for exam-ple, establish organizational needs for R&D, influence program priorities, con-trol budgets, and coordinate activities outside the R&D structure. Since most upper-level and functional management is not familiar with the systems approach, especially in small companies, the perspective of line and staff man-agement is greatly influenced by functional parochialism and consideration of R&D as a cost center rather than a profit center. In part, this view of R&D as a cost center leads to a commonly implied, if not expressed, feeling that "in good times, who needs R&D because we are successful in what we are doing, and, in bad times, who can afford it?" Another important factor affecting the way management views R&D is the short-term perspective of most of today's managers. Concern for short-term profits rather than long-term objectives such

---

8. The remainder of Section 8.6 has been adapted from a course paper by Dr. John J. Miller, "Problems of Informal Project Management in R&D in Small Companies."

as growth and diversification has a considerable impact on the programs and priorities recommended and supported by functional management. In many cases, functional parochialism and short-term perspectives are reinforced by empire-building attitudes and possibly feelings of inferiority. These attitudes and feelings are, generally, more pronounced when a functional manager has risen from the ranks. This type of manager, although very experienced, may be afraid of new technology and dependent on closefisted control that has been successful in the past.

Within this environment, the R&D manager or director in the traditional organizational structure must be a strong individual. An informal project management system requires that the manager of the R&D organization provide a forceful representation of the function within the company. However, this requires an individual who can conduct a critical balancing game. If the manager is too forceful, he will alienate the organization. Projects that must interface with other functions will receive little assistance or support from these functions. If the R&D manager is weak, the direction of projects will be essentially controlled by the functional groups. R&D projects would then tend to be very short-term. There would be many more support programs oriented toward process and quality control. The balancing game played by the manager or director of R&D becomes very time-consuming, and little time is left for technical and administrative responsibilities. In fact, much of the manager's time is spent justifying and rejustifying R&D programs to other functional groups.

Coordination

A nonstructured or informal approach to project management has a major shortcoming in that coordination between R&D and other functional groups cannot be formally established. There is no structure for this formal coordination. Cooperation and assistance from other functional groups on R&D projects is a "beg, borrow, or steal" situation. Although cooperation on programs cannot be effectively mandated even in a formal project management structure, the problem is magnified in an informal project system. Two major factors hinder effective cooperation and coordination in the informal project management system. First, there is little preplanned communication with the functional units. Therefore, the functional units have little knowledge of the project objectives or understanding of how the project, if successful, fits into the goals and objectives of the company. Second, there is no higher authority designated to encourage the coordination of R&D and functional units or to provide conflict resolution.

Training

A handicap of the informal project management approach is that its users lack training and development in project management concepts. There is little or no emphasis on systems theory, systems analysis, and systems management. Without this type of knowledge and training, it is difficult for users of the informal project management approach to obtain or maintain a successful track record, especially in the critical area of the transfer of technology from the laboratory to production. This lack of emphasis on systems and project management concepts is also, at least in many cases, reflected by a lack of concern for the thorough development of the individuals employed in the R&D department. Generally, professional development is focused only on technical areas. Training in nontechnical areas is usually not encouraged and may, in fact, be discouraged. This applies not only to formal training programs, but to informal in-house training programs. This is one reason why technically oriented individuals in the R&D environment have little familiarity with business strategies and business tools. Without some of these business basics, the individuals in the R&D unit can be severely handicapped. First, the R&D project leaders must depend on others in the organization for basic business and financial analyses. Second, communication with administration and other functional units is thwarted, since the individuals involved do not speak the same language. Not only might the technical people not understand the type of information required for business analyses, but also comments made by the engineers or scientists might easily be misinterpreted by the business analysts. Finally, persons with little business background or experience have little chance for advancement outside the R&D environment. This can be an especially difficult problem in a small company where chances for advancement are few and far between. Opportunity for advancement can enhance the spirit of the organization and motivation of employees.

Some individuals within this environment will attempt to learn on their own about the operation of other units or functions of the organization and basic business tools; but, in spite of this type of initiative, learning in such an atmosphere is slow. Unfortunately, these efforts may be interpreted by R&D management and other functional managers as overaggressiveness or meddling. Further self-learning may then be quickly discouraged.

Planning

One of the most crucial aspects of management in any organization is planning. With an informal project management approach in the R&D organization, planning may not be optimized. Without a systems approach, planning tends to be segmented, with concentration on aspects of the projects that can be accomplished within the R&D unit. Little effort is applied to involving functional units in the planning process, and there is a general lack of integration of the project plans with the operational units.

Although R&D projects are difficult to plan and schedule because of the large number of unknowns, planning in R&D units of small companies tends to be very short-term, for only one to twelve months. Without formal planning tools, such as statement of work, work breakdown schedules, linear responsibility charts, and PERT networks, planning tends to be simplified, but important details, responsibilities, and interfaces may easily be omitted. In certain respects the shorter-range planning, although not identifying the need for future resources, does not commit resources to a schedule that is or can be very tentative. There actually may be an advantage to short-term planning, since project plans that interface with other functional units can be more realistic with respect to the amount of support needed, amount and type of work to be done, and schedules, although the functional personnel must have sufficient notification of plans or needs to be able to act and react to these plans without undue strain on their schedules and resources. Of course, this advantage can be utilized in a formal planning procedure by constant updating of plans and schedules so that the functional units are aware of the progress of the project, especially as their work or assistance comes into the near-term planning horizon.

A common mistake made during the planning phase in the informal type of project management is that the functional managers are not included in the planning of the project, even when the project involves work performed in their department. Time, costs, and procedures may be established for the functional department by the project manager without input from the functional manager. The functional manager can be difficult to work with, once he learns that someone else has planned his involvement and that he is supposed to adhere to these plans.

Communications

Lack of effective communications may be a major reason why R&D does not include functional managers in project planning, and why, once plans are established and approved, functional managers are not aware of the progress of a project. There is no doubt that functional managers need to be aware of potential and real changes in schedules, resources, and work scope that may affect their department. Without effective communications neither the project manager nor the functional manager knows what the other is doing, or what the current problems are. In fact, planning, coordination, and management cannot be performed effectively and efficiently without effective communications. However, communication on the horizontal or project level is not the only problem that the informal project management system has; all communication with upper management is filtered through the director of R&D. This may be an effective route for upward communication, but in downward communication two problems are common. First, because R&D is often considered a necessary evil, much of the information on business plans and strategies is not communicated to R&D. Second, since the director of R&D is the filter of downward-moving information from upper management, he may omit information he feels is not important or does not want his people to know. This lack of information on what the company is doing or going to do has a negative effect on the morale of the R&D group. Moreover, the reverse may also be true—R&D may have to toot their horn instead of relying on the results to "speak for themselves."

Problem Solutions

A number of the problems presented could be markedly improved or resolved by adopting a formal project management organizational structure in the entire company or just in the R&D unit. The R&D organization is probably an excellent proving ground for the introduction of project management to the company. A major reorganization such as the introduction of project management, preferably as a matrix type of structure, is a difficult task. The implementation of such a reorganization must be carefully planned, and a formal implementation program must be prepared. Generally, the success of such a major organizational change will depend not only on effective planning and implementation, but also on the degree of commitment of upper management. A well-planned project management approach should include solutions to the problems present in informal project management.

Although this discussion has centered on the problems commonly present in informal project management in small-company R&D laboratories, many successful projects can be, and have been, completed in this environment. Efforts by individuals to solve or minimize these problems personally have produced very acceptable program results. However, in these cases, success depends on the management skills of the individual and his or her understanding of the business environment. Personal experience indicates that many scientists and engineers, especially those involved in development projects, are at least cognizant of many of the business considerations that can affect the implementation of their development projects, such as costs, acceptable vs. superior performance, and time constraints.[9] This observation may be influenced by the small-company environment that allows one to obtain a good perspective of the entire business more easily than in a larger company. In fact, the small company may be a good training environment for project managers because of this more accessible vista of the overall organization, and because, since resources are usually limited, the small-company engineer or scientist must be more self-

---

9. This observation is in conflict with the observations of Harold Kerzner, "The R&D Project Manager," *Project Management Quarterly,* June 1981, pp. 20–24.

OBLIGATIONS	TO WHOM OWED						
	EMPLOYER	CLIENT/CUSTOMER	TEAM MEMBERS	STUDENT/APPRENTICE	PROFESSIONAL SOCIETY	PUBLIC IN GENERAL	GOVERNMENT
1. Support Code of Ethics					X		
2. Support Professional Society					X		
3. Guard Privileged Information	X	X					
4. Accept Responsibility for Actions	X	X	X	X	X	X	X
5. Proper Use of Authority	X		X	X			
6. Maintain Expertise in State-of-Art	X	X	X	X	X		
7. Build and Maintain Public Confidence					X		
8. Support, Respect and Abide by Laws						X	X
9. Avoid Gift Exchange	X	X					
10. Conservation of Resources (Productivity)	X	X				X	
11. Avoid Conflict of Interest	X	X					
12. Equal Opportunity Employment						X	
13. Health and Safety			X			X	
14. Promote Project Management Profession					X		
15. Honesty in Dealing With Employer and Client	X	X					
16. Professional Interface	X	X	X	X	X	X	

Figure 8–7. Ethics obligation matrix.

reliant and learn to perform a number of varied skills using a wide range of tools.

8.7 CODE OF ETHICS

Professional organizations such as the Project Management Institute are taking a serious look at developing the requirements for a professional project manager. In a recent paper by Ireland, Pike, and Schrock, this subject was described by an ethics obligation matrix (see Figure 8–7) and a code of ethics (see Table 8–5).[10] The reader can expect to see more published literature in the near future on topics such as this.

---

10. L. R. Ireland, W. J. Pike, and J. L. Schrock, "Ethics for Project Managers," *Proceedings of the 1982 PMI Seminar/Symposium on Project Management,* Toronto, Ontario, Canada, pp. II-E-5, 6.

Table 8–5. Code of Ethics for Project Managers.

PREAMBLE: Project Managers, in the pursuit of their profession, affect the quality of life for all people in our society. Therefore, it is vital that Project Managers conduct their work in an ethical manner to earn and maintain the confidence of team members, colleagues, employees, clients and the public.

ARTICLE I: Project Managers shall maintain high standards of personal and professional conduct.

    a. Accept responsibility for their actions.

    b. Undertake projects and accept responsibility only if qualified by training or experience, or after full disclosure to their employers or clients of pertinent qualifications.

    c. Maintain their professional skills at the state-of-the-art and recognize the importance of continued personal development and education.

    d. Advance the integrity and prestige of the profession by practicing in a dignified manner.

    e. Support this code and encourage colleagues and co-workers to act in accordance with this code.

    f. Support the professional society by actively participating and encouraging colleagues and co-workers to participate.

    g. Obey the laws of the country in which work is being performed.

ARTICLE II: Project Managers shall, in their work:

    a. Provide the necessary project leadership to promote maximum productivity while striving to minimize costs.

    b. Apply state-of-the-art project management tools and techniques to ensure schedules are met and the project is appropriately planned and coordinated.

    c. Treat fairly all project team members, colleagues and co-workers, regardless of race, religion, sex, age or national origin.

    d. Protect project team members from physical and mental harm.

    e. Provide suitable working conditions and opportunities for project team members.

    f. Seek, accept and offer honest criticism of work, and properly credit the contribution of others.

    g. Assist project team members, colleagues and co-workers in their professional development.

ARTICLE III: Project Managers shall, in their relations with employers and clients:

    a. Act as faithful agents or trustees for their employers or clients in professional or business matters.

    b. Keep information on the business affairs or technical processes of an employer or client in confidence while employed, and later, until such information is properly released.

    c. Inform their employers, clients, professional societies or public agencies of which they are members or to which they may make any presentations, of any circumstances that could lead to a conflict of interest.

    d. Neither give nor accept, directly or indirectly, any gift, payment or service of more than nominal value to or from those having business relationships with their employers or clients.

    e. Be honest and realistic in reporting project cost, schedule and performance.

ARTICLE IV: Project Managers shall, in fulfilling their responsibilities to the community:

    a. Protect the safety, health and welfare of the public and speak out against abuses in those areas affecting the public interest.

    b. Seek to extend public knowledge and appreciation of the project management profession and its achievements.

PROBLEMS

8-1 Beta Company has decided to modify its wage and salary administration program whereby line managers are evaluated for promotion and merit increases based upon how well they have lived up to the commitments that they made to the project managers. What are the advantages and disadvantages of this approach?

8-2 How should a project manager handle a situation in which the functional employee (or functional manager) appears to have more loyalty to his profession, discipline, or expertise than to the project? Can a project manager also have this loyalty, say, on an R&D project?

8-3 Most wage and salary administrators contend that project management organizational structures must be "married" to the personnel evaluation process because personnel are always concerned with how they will be evaluated. Furthermore, converting from a traditional structure to a project management structure cannot be accomplished without first considering performance evaluation. What are your feelings on this?

8-4 As part of the evaluation process for functional employees, each project manager submits a written, confidential evaluation report to the employee's department manager who, in turn, makes the final judgment. The employee is permitted to see only the evaluation from his department manager. Assume that the average department merit increase is 7 percent, and that the employee could receive the merit increases shown. How would he respond in each case?

PROJECT MANAGER'S EVALUATION	MERIT INCREASE, %	Credit or Blame to		REASON
		P.M.	Fct.Mgr.	
Excellent	5			
Excellent	7			
Excellent	9			
Average	5			
Average	7			
Average	9			
Poor	5			
Poor	7			
Poor	9			

8-5 Should the evaluation form in Figure 8-4 be shown to the employees?

8-6 Does a functional employee have the right to challenge any items in the project manager's nonconfidential evaluation form?

8–7 Some people contend that functional employees should be able to evaluate the effectiveness of the project manager after project termination. Design an evaluation form for this purpose.

8–8 Some executives feel that evaluation forms should not include cooperation and attitude. The executives feel that a functional employee will always follow the instructions of the functional manager, and therefore attitude and cooperation are unnecessary topics. Does this kind of thinking also apply to the indirect evaluation forms that are filled out by the project managers?

8–9 Consider a situation in which the project manager (a generalist) is asked to provide an evaluation of a functional employee (a specialist). Can the project manager effectively evaluate the functional employee on technical performance? If not, then what information can the project manager base his evaluation upon? Can a grade 7 generalist evaluate a grade 12 specialist?

8–10 Gary has been assigned as a part-time, assistant project manager. Gary's duties are split between assistant project management and being a functional employee. In addition, Gary reports both vertically to his functional manager and horizontally to a project manager. As part of his project responsibilities, Gary must integrate activities between his department and two other departments within his division. His responsibilities also include writing a nonconfidential performance evaluation for all functional employees from all three departments that are assigned to his project. Can Gary effectively and honestly evaluate functional employees in his own department, people with whom he will be working side by side when the project is over? Should the project manager come to his rescue? Suppose Gary is a part-time project manager instead of a part-time assistant project manager. Can anyone come to his rescue now?

8–11 The following question was asked of executives: How do you know when to cut off research? The answers given: That's a good question, a very good question, and some people don't know when to cut it off. You have to have a feel; in some cases it depends upon how much resource you have and whether you have enough resources to take a chance on sustaining research which may appear to be heading for a dead end. You don't know sometimes whether you're heading down the wrong path or not; sometimes it's pretty obvious you ought to shift directions—you've gone about as far as you can or you've taken it far enough that you can demonstrate to your own satisfaction that you just can't get there from here, or it's going to be very costly. You may discover that there are more productive ways to get around the barrier; you're always looking for faster ways. And it depends entirely on how creative the person is, whether he has tunnel vision, a very narrow vision, or whether he is fairly flexible in his conceptual thinking so that he can conceive of better ways to solve the problem. Discuss the validity of these remarks.

8–12 In a small company, can a functional manager act as director of engineering and director of project management at the same time?

8–13 In 1982, an electrical equipment manufacturer decentralized the organization, allowing each division manager to set priorities for the work in his division. The division manager of the R&D division selected as his number one priority project the development of low-cost methods for manufacturing. This project required support from the manufacturing division. The division manager for manufacturing did not assign proper resources, claiming that the results of such a project would not be realized for at least five years, and that he (the manufacturing manager) was worried only about the immediate profits. Can this problem be resolved and divisional decentralization still be maintained?

8–14   The executives of a company that produces electro-optical equipment for military use found it necessary to implement project management using a matrix. The project managers reported to corporate sales, and the engineers with the most expertise were promoted to project engineering. After the first year of operation, it became obvious to the executives that the engineering functional managers were not committed to the projects. The executives then made a critical decision. The functional employees selected by the line managers to serve on projects would report as a solid line to the project engineer and dotted to the line manager. The project engineers, who were selected for their technical expertise, were allowed to give technical direction and monetary rewards to the employees. Can this situation work? What happens if an employee has a technical question? Can he go to his line manager? Should the employees return to their former line managers at project completion? What are the authority/responsibility problems with this structure? What are the long-term implications?

8–15   Consider the four items listed on page 141 describing what happens when a matrix goes out of control. Which of these end up creating the greatest difficulty for the company? for the project managers? for the line managers? for executives?

8–16   As a functional employee, the project manager tells you, "Sign these prints or I'll fire you from this project." How should this situation be handled?

8–17   How efficient can project management be in a unionized, immobile manpower environment?

8–18   Corporate salary structures and limited annual raise allocations often prevent proper project management performance rewards. Explain how each of the following could serve as motivational factors:

A. Job satisfaction
B. Personal recognition
C. Intellectual growth

CASE STUDY: PRODUCT MANAGEMENT AT COSTA PHARMACEUTICAL LABORATORIES

The pharmaceutical industry is considered to be one of the most competitive industries in business today. Numerous companies, both major and minor, compete to gain a share of the billions of dollars spent worldwide on health care services.

Costa Laboratories, headquartered in Chicago, Illinois, is one of the ten largest pharmaceutical houses in the world. The corporation consists of eight divisions employing more than 25,000 people and had sales of $1.5 billion in 1977.

The Pharmaceutical Products Division of Costa is the third largest division with sales of $250 million. Primary products of the division consist of anti-anxiety agents, anti-hypertensive agents for controlling blood pressure, anti-epileptic drugs, hematinics, and vitamins.

In June 1978 the division underwent a reorganization that affected various marketing and promotional functions within the division. Previously, the various functions of pricing, product management, advertising, market research, and sample promotion existed as separate service centers, with staff members reporting to their respective department heads. While the system worked efficiently in terms of each function, management felt it lacked one element for truly multidisciplined strategic planning: cohesion. The resources of each of these service departments were not always equally or immediately available to a particular business unit.

Inevitably, this tended to create problems because of competing priorities. With the budgets of each of the service centers under separate control, there were natural inhibitions on transferring or allocating resources across functional boundaries as needs arose. Simply stated, there was no common accountability for the activities or objectives of the various service units.

Thus, basic to the reorganization process was the formation of new business planning units called "strategic planning centers." The purpose of each center was to undertake and assume responsibility for the strategic business and promotional planning of an assigned group of products. The strategic planning center, utilizing the concept of zero-based budgeting, was designed to give each unit both authority and responsibility for allocation of resources to strategies and media that would best accomplish the unit's profit goal. It was the responsibility of the planning center to analyze the various strategies and develop action plans based on the current realities of the marketplace.

The reorganization of the key elements of the division also had the effect of broadening the authority and responsibility of the product manager, now referred to as a "business unit manager."

Under the previous system, the product manager lacked the authority to coordinate the activities of supporting departments in order to direct them toward the established objective of effective product promotion. Instead the manager was faced with a chain-of-command-type situation. The essential departments of market research, advertising, manufacturing, distribution, and sample promotion were reached only through their respective managers or vice-presidents, who weighted requests in terms of priorities and, most specifically, budget expenditures to complete the requested projects.

The previous system often led to such situations as: incomplete and late marketing research data due to communication problems over the type and amount needed; advertising that projected the wrong theme or used improper copy, creating regulatory problems with the Food and Drug Administration; manufacturing and distribution problems when a new product was sold to retailers by the sales force with no stock available in the distribution centers to be shipped to them; and the failure of drug samples to be sent out to the sales force for promotion to the medical community. Such situations combined with competing departmental priorities developed into a system that supported frustration, and the inability of departments to view an objective in comprehensive terms rather than in terms of specific departmental contributions to an objective.

The reorganization of the divisional structure was intended to broaden the authority of the product manager under the business unit concept.

Under the new concept, the organizational structure included the following persons within the strategic planning center:

1. Director of strategic planning
2. Business unit manager (product manager)
3. Promotion manager
4. Pricing assistant
5. Marketing research assistant
6. Medical liaison
7. Manufacturing liaison
8. Sales liaison

Within this framework, the business unit manager reports to the director of strategic planning for all activities conducted within the unit itself. The unit or product manager coordinates the activities of advertising under the promotion manager, pricing under the pricing assistant, marketing research under the auspices of the market research assistant, medical under the director of the medical department, and contact with the sales department under a sales liaison. Because of the nature of Costa's products the manager must also be aware of the activities of the regulatory department.

Specifically, the relationship of the business unit manager to the various departments within the unit is as follows:

1. *Pricing.* Within the framework of pricing, the business unit manager has several duties. He is responsible for determining and updating factory costs of products; he must monitor profit margins and adjust retail prices when factory costs threaten to reduce the margin; he must monitor competitive product pricing so as to maintain near parity with highly competitive products; and he is responsible for segmentation of pricing between retail, wholesale, and government customers. The product manager not only works closely with the pricing assistant for the above requirements, but he also maintains active communication with pricing in competitive bidding situations. With the intense competition becoming keener daily, many large-volume pharmaceuticals are being put up for bid by hospital (nonprofit) and government customers. It is the role of the unit manager and the pricing assistant to accept or reject bids in the context of profit potential in terms of factory cost vs. dollars realized from the bid, potential for retail sales as a result of a patient obtaining a refilled prescription on a drug that was first given in a hospital, etc. In addition, they must analyze when the drug was sold on bid, the type and size of the customer requesting the bid, and the status of competition in terms of who they are and what prices they are offering.

   Primary responsibility in pricing belongs to the pricing assistant, but all efforts are coordinated by the unit manager, who accepts or rejects pricing recommendations. In turn, many decisions of a pricing nature (e.g., acceptance of a large-volume bid) have an effect on manufacturing, specifically product planning. Often these effects are changes in product forecasts and necessitate changes in product priorities. This requires involvement between the unit manager and manufacturing in order to reset those priorities.

Normally, a business unit manager interacts with manufacturing only in terms of unit forecasts that control production schedules, product specifications and quality assurance, inventory control, and production capacity questions. However, the manufacturing liaison also works closely with the unit manager to handle any sudden manufacturing problems, such as with equipment, that could significantly affect product throughput. The business manager provides essential manufacturing cost information when the unit manager begins to consider aspects of a new product or line extension.

2. *Advertising.* Within the framework of advertising, the unit manager works closely with the advertising promotion manager. The promotion manager is responsible for aspects of product promotion dealing with advertising, most often of the medical journal type, and the creation of sales aids used by the sales force. The promotion manager, often a creative artist, uses ideas suggested by the unit manager along with his own to create effective advertising that will convey a sales message to the medical community in an ethical and acceptable manner and reinforce the message communicated by the field sales force. In addition, the promotion manager creates sales aids or detail booklets, which contain medical product information, for use by the sales force with the medical community. Last, the promotion manager has the responsibility of coordinating the promotional budget with the business unit manager for all assigned products. Twice yearly the managers draw up and review promotional budgets to ensure that proper expenditures are being carried out according to the promotional plan, and to readjust any factors of advertising, etc., that are not falling within the scope of the market plan. Final coordination and control of advertising and promotion rest with the business unit manager.

3. *Marketing research.* To formulate, implement, and receive feedback from a marketing plan, the unit manager relies heavily on data obtained by market research. Foremost among the many duties that the business unit manager has is the maintenance and improvement of a product's share of market. The manager constantly strives for better methods to increase market share and relies heavily on market research for usable information. Market research uses a variety of tools, for example, surveys of physicians on a particular product. This type of information can allow the unit manager to judge the efficacy of a promotional theme in terms of physician recall from sales force calls and journal advertising. Market research can also describe competitive activity in terms of efficacy and depth of promotion as these relate to increases or decreases of sales force calls, sample mailings and regular mailings, along with an estimate of total dollars spent on each category.

Other areas essential to the unit manager and provided by market research include a statistical picture of the manager's product category, specifically the increase or decrease of a pharmaceutical category, for example, the antibiotic market. It also can portray how a particular product is faring against competition in terms of increase or decrease of market share, the number of new prescriptions written for a particular product, and the segmentation of a product category into retail and hospital markets.

Last, marketing research can provide valuable information to the unit manager when new products or line extensions are being considered. In early stages, a prime consideration for a new product is the state of the product category (increasing or decreasing) and the conclusion that a new product can gain a good share of market and be profitable. Marketing research can provide the essential information so the unit manager can make an informed decision.

4. *Medical department.* All printed material of a promotional nature must be approved by the medical department for authenticity, accuracy, and compliance to FDA standards. Handling requests for documentation and information from the medical community on a variety of medical subjects is also the responsibility of the medical department. The business unit manager must have all promotional material approved by the medical department before it can be sent to the sales force. This material is reviewed for content accuracy under generally accepted medical guidelines enforced by the FDA. The medical department will either approve promotional materials or return them for restructuring with appropriate comments. In addition, the product manager relies on the medical department to handle complex medical questions from the medical community and often uses these as indications of physician interest in the promotional message. Last, the medical department and the product manager must work together closely during periods of clinical studies for a new product. The outcome of clinical studies can be the basis for either committing large sums of money to formulating a new product marketing plan or scrapping a potential product.

In the medical department the unit manager has the ability to coordinate efforts, but cannot exercise direct authority. The manager lacks in-depth medical knowledge and must accept the expert opinions of the physicians and scientists he is working with.

5. *Regulatory affairs.* For the safety of consumers, the FDA maintains rigid standards for all aspects of pharmaceutical company operations from manufacturing to sales. The regulatory department evaluates the accuracy of promotional materials, that is, advertising and sales force promotional aids. It reviews all such material and must give written approval before these can be released for general use. In addition, the department monitors the medical package inserts required for all drugs to ensure correctness and adherence to FDA standards.

The involvement of the product manager with the regulatory department is not extensive, but because strict compliance to FDA regulations is required, the manager must constantly be aware of the actions, if any, that regulatory is taking.

6. *Sales.* The unit manager's interaction with the sales department is crucial. Sales are the culmination of all efforts by the product manager and all other supportive departments. The sales effort determines if the forecasts for the success of a product are fulfilled. Product management and sales management can clash over promotional themes, sizes or samples, pricing, bids, stock situations,

and promotional priorities, but they must reach some agreement or the product is a failure.

Basically the product manager must "sell" his promotional program to the managers of the sales department. Usually this involves discussion and compromise. But the final promotional effort must be supported by both product and sales management.

In dealing with the sales department, the product manager interacts with a variety of individuals. He works with a vice-president of sales, a director of sales, numerous regional and district managers, the salesmen themselves, and persons involved in sales training. The manager is truly one individual who must be able to motivate many. The old saying of "give us the tools to sell with" is in proper context here. The product manager does provide the tools to sell with—everything from promotional materials up to the design of sales samples. The manager needs feedback on programs from the sales department in order to alter ineffective programs, react quickly to competition, and maintain a consistency in materials and ideas. The result of all this effort by the product manager is successful programs that lead to sales increases.

It should be obvious that the role of the product manager is diverse. It is the manager's responsibility to formulate the market plans for products by drawing upon the skills and resources of supportive departments. The market plans serve as a baseline from which to formulate promotional ideas. The plans must take into account important areas such as the status of a particular pharmaceutical product category in terms of growth potential, competitive activity and methodology for coping with it, descriptions of key customers, the final promotional budget, a complete layout of planned promotional activities, and expected results based on short- and long-range forecasting.

The product manager also plays a key role in forecasting long- and short-range goals. Working with market research, manufacturing, and pricing, the manager is responsible for setting objectives both of a tactical and long-range nature. These objectives consist of forecasting gross dollar sales, percent share of market, unit sales, and percent of market served in relation to market share. These forecasts in turn are used for corporate long-range planning in terms of gross dollar sales, capital expenditure requests by manufacturing to meet demand for increased unit sales, and formulation of specific dollar budgets for use by various departments based on total percentages of sales.

One of the most important roles of the product manager is the creation of new product ideas. In a survey of the market, the manager often recognizes a need for a specific product. With supportive departments, the manager formulates preliminary information on market potential, competitive products, estimated gain of market share for a product based on price parity or price undercut, manufacturing costs with profit margin, new product requirements of the FDA, and time periods required to market the product.

Product managers bring together their own ideas and those of others into a cohesive, goal-oriented plan of action. They must maintain a clear view of objectives and must often clear away the confusion created by the meshing of efforts of unrelated departments. They must communicate the objective, clarify its purpose, and then motivate others to help them reach it. At all times, it will be the job of the manager to train individuals in various departments to work effectively toward an objective.

CASE STUDY: AMERICAN ELECTRONICS INTERNATIONAL

On February 13, 1976, American Electronics International (AEI) was awarded a $30 million contract for R&D and production qualification for an advanced type of guidance system. During an experimental program that preceded this award and was funded by the same agency, AEI identified new materials with advanced capabilities, which could easily replace existing field units. The program, entitled The Mask Project, would be thirty months in length, requiring the testing of fifteen units. The Mask Project was longer than any other project that AEI had ever encountered. AEI personnel were now concerned about what kind of staffing problems there would be.

Background

In June 1974, AEI won a one-year research project for new material development. Blen Carty was chosen as project manager. He had twenty-five years of experience with the company in both project management and project engineering positions. During the past five years Blen had successfully performed as the project manager on R&D projects.

AEI used the matrix approach to structuring project management. Blen was well aware of the problems that can be encountered with this organizational form. When it became apparent that a follow-on contract would be available, Blen felt that functional managers would be reluctant to assign key personnel full-time to his project and lose their services for thirty months. Likewise, difficulties could be expected in staffing the project office.

During the proposal stage of the Mask Project, a meeting was held with Blen Carty, John Wallace, the director of project management, and Dr. Albert Runnels, the director of engineering. The purpose of the meeting was to satisfy a customer requirement that all key project members be identified in the management volume of the proposal.

John Wallace: "I'm a little reluctant to make any firm commitment. By the time your program gets off of the ground, four of our other projects are terminating, as well as several new projects starting up. I think it's a little early to make firm selections."

Blen Carty: "But we have a proposal requirement. Thirty months is a long time to assign personnel for. We should consider this problem now."

Dr. Runnels: "Let's put the names of our top people into the proposal. We'll add several Ph.D.'s from our engineering community. That should beef up our management volume. As soon as we're notified of contract go-ahead, we'll see who's available and make the necessary assignments. This is a common practice in the industry."

Completion of the Material Development Project

The material development program was a total success. From its inception, everything went smoothly. Blen staffed the project office with Richard Flag, a Ph.D. in engineering, to serve as project engineer. This was a risky move at first, because Richard had been a research scientist during his previous four years with the company. During the development project, however, Richard demonstrated that he could divorce himself from R&D and perform the necessary functions of a project engineer assigned to the project office. Blen was pleased with the way that Richard controlled project costs and directed activities.

Richard had developed excellent working relations with development lab personnel and managers. Richard permitted lab personnel to work at their own rate of speed provided that schedule dates were kept. Richard spent ten minutes each week with each of the department managers informing them of the status of the project. The department managers liked this approach because they received first-hand (nonfiltered) information concerning the total picture, not necessarily on their own activities, and because they did not have to spend "wasted hours" in team meetings.

When it became evident that a follow-up contract might be available, Blen spent a large percentage of his time traveling to the customer, working out the details for future business. Richard then served as both project manager and project engineer.

The customer's project office was quite pleased with Richard's work. Information, both good and bad, was transmitted as soon as it became available. Nothing was hidden or disguised. Richard became familiar with all of the customer's project office personnel through the monthly technical interchange meetings.

At completion of the material development project, Blen and John decided to search for project office personnel and make recommendations to upper-level management. Blen wanted to keep Richard on board as chief project engineer. He would be assigned six engineers and would have to control all engineering activities within time, cost, and performance. Although this would be a new experience for him, Blen felt that he could easily handle it.

Unfortunately, the grapevine was saying that Larry Gilbert was going to be assigned chief project engineer for the Mask Project.

Selection Problems

On November 15, Dr. Runnels and Blen Carty had a meeting to select the key members of the project team.

Dr. Runnels: "Well Blen, the time has come to decide on your staff. I want to assign Larry Gilbert as Chief Engineer. He's a good man and has 15 years experience. What are your feelings on that?"

Blen Carty: "I was hoping to keep Richard Flag on. He has performed well, and the customer likes working with him."

Dr. Runnels: "Richard does not have the experience necessary for that position. We can still assign him to Larry Gilbert and keep him in the project office."

Blen Carty: "I'd like to have Larry Gilbert working for Richard Flag, but I don't suppose that we'd ever get approval to have a grade 9 engineer working for a grade 7 engineer. Personally, I'm worried about Gilbert's ability to work with people. He has been so regimented in his ways that our people in the functional units have refused to work with him. He treats them as kids, always walking around with a big stick. One department manager said that if Gilbert becomes the boss, then it will probably result in cutting the umbilical cord between the project office and his department. His people refuse to work for a dictator. I have heard the same from other managers."

Dr. Runnels: "Gilbert gets the job done. You'll have to teach him how to be a theory Y manager. You know, Blen, we don't have very many grade 9 engineering positions in this company. I think we should have a responsibility to our employees. I can't demote Gilbert into a lower slot. If I were to promote Flag, and the project gets canceled, where would I reassign him? He can't go back to functional engineering. That would be a step down."

Blen Carty: "But Gilbert is so set in his ways. He's just totally inflexible. In addition, thirty months is a long time to maintain a project office. If he 'screws up' we'll never be able to replace positions in time without totally upsetting the customer. There seems to be an awful lot of people volunteering to work on the Mask Project. Is there anyone else available?"

Dr. Runnels: "People always volunteer for long-duration projects because it gives them a feeling of security. This even occurs among our dedicated personnel. Unfortunately we have no other grade 9 engineers available. We could reassign one from another program, but I hate to do it. Our engineers like to carry a project through from start to finish. I think you had better spend some time with the functional managers making sure that you get good people."

Blen Carty: "I've tried that and am having trouble. The functional managers will not surrender their key people full time for thirty months. One manager wants to assign two employees to our project so that they can get on-the-job training. I told him that this project is considered as 'strategic' by our management and that we must have good people. The manager just laughed at me and walked away."

Dr. Runnels: "You know, Blen, you cannot have all top people. Our other projects must be manned. Also, if you were to use all seasoned veterans, the cost would exceed what we put into the proposal. You're just going to have to make do with what you can get. Prepare a list of the people you want and I'll see what I can do."

As Blen left the office, he wondered if Dr. Runnels would help him in obtaining key personnel.

    a. Whose responsibility is it to staff the office?
    b. What should be Blen Carty's role as well as that of Dr. Runnels?
    c. Should Larry Gilbert be assigned?
    d. How would you negotiate with the functional managers?

9
The Variables for Success

9.0 INTRODUCTION

Project management cannot succeed unless the project manager is willing to employ the systems approach to project management by analyzing those variables that lead to success and failure. This chapter will briefly discuss the dos and don'ts of project management as well as provide a "skeleton" checklist of the key success variables. The following four topics will be included:

- Predicting success
- Project management effectiveness
- Expectations
- Force field analysis

9.1 PREDICTING PROJECT SUCCESS

One of the most difficult tasks is predicting whether the project will be successful. Most goal-oriented managers look only at the time, cost, and performance parameters. If an out-of-tolerance condition exists, then additional analysis is required to identify the cause of the problem. Looking only at time, cost, and performance might identify immediate contributions to profits, but will not identify whether or not the project itself was managed correctly. This takes on paramount importance if the survival of the organization is based upon a steady stream of successfully managed projects. Once or twice a program manager might be able to force a project to success by continually swinging a large baseball bat. After a while, however, either the effect of the big bat will become tolerable, or people will avoid working on his projects.

Project success is often measured by the "actions" of three groups: the project manager and team; the parent organization; and finally the customer's organization. There are certain actions that the project manager and team can take in order to stimulate project success. These actions include:

- Insist upon the right to select key project team members.
- Select key team members with proven track records in their fields.

- Develop commitment and a sense of mission from the outset.
- Seek sufficient authority and a projectized organizational form.
- Coordinate and maintain a good relationship with the client, parent, and team.
- Seek to enhance the public's image of the project.
- Have key team members assist in decision making and problem solving.
- Develop realistic cost, schedule, and performance estimates and goals.
- Have back-up strategies in anticipation of potential problems.
- Provide a team structure that is appropriate, yet flexible and flat.
- Go beyond formal authority to maximize influence over people and key decisions.
- Employ a workable set of project planning and control tools.
- Avoid overreliance on one type of control tool.
- Stress the importance of meeting cost, schedule, and performance goals.
- Give priority to achieving the mission or function of the end item.
- Keep changes under control.
- Seek to find ways of assuring job security for effective project team members.

In Chapter 4 we stated that a project cannot be successful unless it is recognized as a project and has the support of top-level management. Top-level management must be willing to commit company resources and provide the necessary administrative support so that the project easily adapts to the company's day-to-day routine of doing business. Furthermore, the parent organization must develop an atmosphere conducive to good working relationships between the project manager, parent organization, and client organization.

With regard to the parent organization, there exist several variables that can be used to evaluate parent organization support. These variables include:

- A willingness to coordinate efforts
- A willingness to maintain structural flexibility
- A willingness to adapt to change
- Effective strategic planning
- Rapport maintenance
- Proper emphasis on past experience
- External buffering
- Prompt and accurate communications
- Enthusiastic support
- Identification to all concerned parties that the project does, in fact, contribute to parent capabilities

The mere identification and existence of these variables do not guarantee project success in dealing with the parent organization. Instead, it implies that there exists a good foundation to work with so that if the project manager and team, and the parent organization, take the appropriate actions, project success is likely. The following actions must be taken:

- Select at an early point, a project manager with a proven track record of technical skills, human skills, and administrative skills (in that order) to lead the project team.
- Develop clear and workable guidelines for the project manager.
- Delegate sufficient authority to the project manager, and let him make important decisions in conjunction with key team members.
- Demonstrate enthusiasm for and commitment to the project and team.
- Develop and maintain short and informal lines of communication.
- Avoid excessive pressure on the project manager to win contracts.
- Avoid arbitrarily slashing or ballooning project team's cost estimate.
- Avoid "buy-ins."
- Develop close, not meddling, working relationships with the principal client contact and project manager.

Both the parent organization and the project team must employ proper managerial techniques to ensure that judicious and adequate, but not excessive, use of planning, controlling, and communications systems can be made. These proper management techniques must also include preconditioning, such as:

- Clearly established specifications and designs
- Realistic schedules
- Realistic cost estimates
- Avoidance of "buys-ins"
- Avoidance of overoptimism

The client organization can have a great deal of influence on project success by minimizing team meetings, making rapid responses to requests for information, and simply letting the contractor "do his thing" without any interference. The variables that exist for the client organization include:

- A willingness to coordinate efforts
- Rapport maintenance
- Establishment of reasonable and specific goals and criteria
- Well-established procedures for changes
- Prompt and accurate communications
- Commitment of client resources
- Minimization of red tape
- Providing sufficient authority to the client contact (especially for decision making)

With these variables as the basic foundation, it should be possible to:

- Encourage openness and honesty from the start from all participants.
- Create an atmosphere that encourages healthy competition, but not cut-throat situations or "liars" contests.
- Plan for adequate funding to complete the entire project.
- Develop clear understandings of the relative importance of cost, schedule, and technical performance goals.
- Develop short and informal lines of communication and a flat organizational structure.
- Delegate sufficient authority to the principal client contact, and allow prompt approval or rejection of important project decisions.
- Reject "buy-ins."
- Make prompt decisions regarding contract award or go ahead.
- Develop close, not meddling, working relationships with project participants.
- Avoid arms-length relationships.
- Avoid excessive reporting schemes.
- Make prompt decisions regarding changes.

By combining the relevant actions of the project team, parent organization, and client organization, we can identify the fundamental lessons for management. These include:

- When starting off in project management, plan to go all the way.
  - Recognize authority conflicts—resolve.
  - Recognize change impact—be a change agent.
- Match the right people with the right jobs.
  - No system is better than the people who implement it.
- Allow adequate time and effort for laying out the project groundwork and defining work:
  - Work breakdown structure
  - Network planning
- Ensure that work packages are the proper size:
  - Manageable, with organizational accountability
  - Realistic in terms of effort and time
- Establish and use planning and control systems as the focal point of project implementation.
  - Know where you're going.
  - Know when you've gotten there.
- Be sure information flow is realistic.
  - Information is the basis for problem solving and decision making.
  - Communication "pitfalls" are the greatest contributor to project difficulties.

- Be willing to replan—do so.
  - The best-laid plans can often go astray.
  - Change is inevitable.
- Tie together responsibility, performance, and rewards:
  - Management by objectives
  - Key to motivation and productivity
- Long before the project ends, plan for its end:
  - Disposition of personnel
  - Disposal of material and other resources
  - Transfer of knowledge
  - Closing out work orders
  - Customer/contractor financial payments and reporting

The last lesson, project termination, has been the downfall for many good project managers. As projects near completion, there is a natural tendency to minimize costs by transferring people as soon as possible and by closing out work orders. This often leaves the project manager with the responsibility for writing the final report and transferring raw materials to other programs. Many projects require one or two months after work completion simply for administrative reporting and final cost summary.

Having defined project success, we can now identify some of the major causes for the failure of project management:

- Selection of a concept that is not applicable. Since each application is unique, selecting a project that does not have a sound basis, or forcing a change when the time is not appropriate, can lead to immediate failure.
- Selection of the wrong person as project manager. The individual selected must be a manager, not a doer. He must place emphasis on all aspects of the work, not merely the technical.
- Upper management that is not supportive. Upper management must concur in the concept and must behave accordingly.
- Inadequately defined tasks. There must exist an adequate system for planning and control such that a proper balance between cost, schedule, and technical performance can be maintained.
- Misused management techniques. There exists the inevitable tendency in technical communities to attempt to do more than is initially required by contract. Technology must be watched, and individuals must buy only what is needed.
- Project termination that is not planned. By definition, each project must stop. Termination must be planned so that the impact can be identified.

It is often said that more can be learned from failure than from success. The lessons that can be learned from project failure include:[1]

- When starting off in project management, plan to go all the way.
- Don't skimp on the project manager's qualifications.
- Do not spare time and effort in laying out the project groundwork and defining work.
- Ensure that the work packages in the project are of proper size.
- Establish and use network planning techniques, having the network as the focal point of project implementation.
- Be sure that the information flow related to the project management system is realistic.
- Be prepared to replan jobs continually to accommodate frequent changes on dynamic programs.
- Whenever possible, tie together responsibility, performance, and rewards.
- Long before a project ends, provide some means for accommodating the employees' personal goals.
- If mistakes in project implementation have been made, make a fresh try.

9.2 PROJECT MANAGEMENT EFFECTIVENESS[2]

Project managers interact continuously with upper-level management, perhaps more so than with functional managers. Not only the success of the project, but even the career path of the project manager can depend upon the working relationships and expectations established with upper-level management. There are four key variables in measuring the effectiveness of dealing with upper-level management. These variables are credibility, priority, accessibility, and visibility:

- Credibility
  - Credibility comes from the image of a sound decision-maker.
  - It is normally based upon experience in a variety of assignments.
  - It is refueled by the manager and the status of his project.
  - Making success visible to others increases credibility.
  - To be believable, emphasize facts rather than opinions.
  - Give credit to others; they may return this favor.

---

1. Ivars Avots, "Why Does Project Management Fail?" *California Management Review*, Vol. 12, 1969, pp. 77–82.
2. This section and Section 9.3 have been adapted from *Seminar in Project Management Workbook*, copyright 1977 by Hans J. Thamhain. Reproduced by permission of Dr. Hans J. Thamhain.

- Priority
  - Sell the specific importance of the project to the objectives of the total organization.
  - Stress the competitive aspect, if relevant.
  - Stress changes for success.
  - Secure testimonial support from others—functional departments, other managers, customers, independent sources.
  - Emphasize "spin-offs" that may result from projects.
  - Anticipate "priority problems."
  - Sell priority on a one-to-one basis.
- Accessibility
  - Accessibility involves the ability to communicate directly with top management.
  - Show that your proposals are good for the total organization, not just the project.
  - Weigh the facts carefully; explain the pros and cons.
  - Be logical and polished in your presentations.
  - Become personally known by members of top management.
  - Create a desire in the "customer" for your abilities and your project.
  - Make curiosity work for you.
- Visibility
  - Be aware of the amount of visibility you really need.
  - Make a good impact when presenting the project to top management.
  - Adopt a contrasting style of management when feasible and possible.
  - Use team members to help regulate the visibility you need.
  - Conduct timely "informational" meetings with those who count.
  - Use available publicity media.

9.3 EXPECTATIONS

In the project management environment, the project managers, team members, and upper-level managers each have expectations of what their relationships should be with the other parties. To illustrate this, top management expects project managers to:

- Assume total accountability for the success or failure to provide results.
- Provide effective reports and information.
- Provide minimum organizational disruption during the execution of a project.
- Present recommendations, not just alternatives.

- Have the capacity to handle most interpersonal problems.
- Demonstrate a self-starting capacity.
- Demonstrate growth with each assignment.

At first glance, it may appear that these qualities are expected of all managers, not necessarily project managers. But this is not true. The first four items are different. The line managers are not accountable for total project success, just for that portion performed by their line organization. Line managers can be promoted on their technical ability, not necessarily on their ability to write effective reports. Line managers cannot disrupt an entire organization, but the project manager can. Line managers do not necessarily have to make decisions, just provide alternatives and recommendations.

Just as top management has expectations of project managers, project managers have certain expectations of top management. Project management expects top management to:

- Provide clearly defined decision channels.
- Take actions on requests.
- Facilitate interfacing with support departments.
- Assist in conflict resolution.
- Provide sufficient resources/charter.
- Provide sufficient strategic/long-range information.
- Provide feedback.
- Give advice and stage-setting support.
- Define expectations clearly.
- Provide protection from political infighting.
- Provide the opportunity for personal and professional growth.

The project team also has expectations from their leader, the project manager. The project team expects the project manager to:

- Assist in the problem-solving process by coming up with ideas.
- Provide proper direction and leadership.
- Provide a relaxed environment.
- Interact informally with team members.
- Stimulate the group process.
- Facilitate adoption of new members.
- Reduce conflicts.
- Defend the team against outside pressure.
- Resist changes.
- Act as the group spokesperson.
- Provide representation with higher management.

In order to provide high task efficiency and productivity, a project team should have certain traits and characteristics. A project manager expects the project team to:

- Demonstrate membership self-development.
- Demonstrate the potential for innovative and creative behavior.
- Communicate effectively.
- Be committed to the project.
- Demonstrate the capacity for conflict resolution.
- Be results-oriented.
- Be change-oriented.
- Interface effectively and with high morale.

Team members want, in general, to fill certain primary needs. The project manager should understand these needs before demanding that the team live up to his expectations. Members of the project team need:

- A sense of belonging
- Interest in the work itself
- Respect for the work being done
- Protection from political infighting
- Job security and job continuity
- Potential for career growth

Project managers must remember that team members may not always be able to verbalize these needs, but they do exist nevertheless.

9.4 FORCE FIELD ANALYSIS

Project managers must live in a dynamic environment in which constant and rapid change becomes a way of life. To operate effectively under these circumstances, the project manager must be able to diagnose the situation, design alternatives that will remedy it, provide the necessary leadership so that these changes can be implemented, and develop an atmosphere that helps the employees to adapt readily to these changes.

One of the early pioneers in developing theories for managing change was Kurt Lewin.[3] Lewin believed that at any point in time during the life cycle of

---

3. Kurt Lewin, "Frontiers in Group Dynamics," *Human Relations,* Vol. 1, No. 1, 1947; Also, *Field Theory in Social Science* (New York: Harper, 1951).

a project there will exist driving forces that will push the project toward success and restraining forces that may induce failure. In a steady-state environment, the driving and restraining forces are in balance. However, if the driving forces increase or the restraining forces decrease, whether they act independently or together, change is likely to take place. The formal analysis of these forces is commonly referred to as force field analysis. This type of analysis can be used to:[4]

- Monitor the project team and measure potential deficiencies.
- Audit the project on an ongoing basis.
- Involve project personnel, which can be conducive to team-building.
- Measure the sensitivity of proposed changes.

Current studies in force field analysis have been conducted by Dugan et al.,[5] whose research involved 125 project managers in approximately seventy different technology-oriented companies. The research study and questionnaire were personally explained to the participating project managers to minimize potential communications problems.

The researchers obtained information in several areas, including:

- Personal drive, motivation, and leadership
- Team motivation
- Management support
- Functional support
- Technical expertise
- Project objectives
- Financial resources
- Client support and commitment

The research study categorized each of the above areas according to project life-cycle phase. However, for simplicity's sake, only a brief synopsis of each of these areas will be presented. The reader is directed to the reference article for a more detailed description.

Personal drive, motivation, and leadership were found to provide the strongest driving forces, and were important attributes of the project manager and team members and important in all project life-cycle phases. The lack of personal drive, motivation, and leadership was found to result in strong restraining

---

4. See note 3 above.
5. H. S. Dugan, H. J. Thamhain, and D. L. Wilemon, "Managing Change in Project Management," *Proceedings of the Ninth Annual International Seminar/Symposium on Project Management,* The Project Management Institute, 1977, pp. 178–188.

forces. The force field analysis gave the following results for personal drive, motivation, and leadership:

- Driving forces:
  - Desire for accomplishment
  - Interest in project
  - Work challenge
  - Group acceptance
  - Common objectives
  - Experience in task management
  - Providing proper direction
  - Assistance in problem solving
  - Team builder
  - Effective communications
- Restraining forces:
  - Inexperienced project leader
  - Uncertain roles
  - Lack of technical knowledge
  - Personality problems
  - Lack of self-confidence and credibility
  - Poor project control
  - First project management experience

Team motivation was identified as having the strongest overall influence on project success, and as an important factor in all phases of the project. Team motivation was a strong driver and, if lacking, became a strong restraint. The following results for team motivation were found:

- Driving forces:
  - Good interpersonal relations
  - Desire to achieve
  - Expertise
  - Common goal
  - Integration of team and project objectives
  - Agreement and distribution of work
  - Clear role definition
  - Professional interest in project
  - Challenge of project
  - Project visibility and rewards
- Restraining forces:
  - Poor team organization
  - Communication barriers

- Poor leadership
- Uncertain rewards
- Uncertain objectives
- Resistance to project management approach
- Little commitment or ownership in project
- Team members overloaded
- Limited prior team experience
- Unequal talent distribution

Management support was found to have important driving and restraining qualities, and was associated with all project phases. The following results were obtained:

- Driving forces:
  - Sufficient resources
  - Proper priorities
  - Authority delegation
  - Management interest
- Restraining forces:
  - Unclear objectives
  - Insufficient resources
  - Changing priorities
  - Insufficient authority/charter
  - Management indifference
  - Poor direction
  - Excessive preoccupation with minor details
  - Wanting support
  - Unresponsive management
  - Continuous change in scope
  - Poor project organization

Functional support was identified as important during project buildup, main phase, and phaseout, as well as being a must for successful project completion. Functional support was impacted by top-management support, funding, and organizational structure. The forces behind functional support were found to be:

- Driving forces:
  - Clear goals and priorities
  - Proper planning
  - Adequate task integrators
- Restraining forces:

- Priority conflicts
- Funding restraints
- Poor project organization
- Resistance to project objectives
- Unclear roles

Technical expertise was particularly important during project formation and buildup. The forces identified were:

- Driving forces:
  - Ability to manage technology
  - Prior track record
  - Low-risk project
- Restraining forces:
  - Lack of technical information
  - Unexpected technical problems
  - Inability to cope with change

Project objectives were most important during project formation and start-up. The forces identified were:

- Driving forces:
  - Clear goals
  - Clear expectations/responsibilities
  - Clear interface relationships
  - Clear specifications
  - Workable project plan
- Restraining forces:
  - Conflict over objectives (i.e., no project plan)
  - Customer uncertainties
  - Power plays
  - Technical problems

The last two items are financial resources and client support and commitment. Under *financial resources* are:

- Driving forces:
  - Necessary financial resources
  - Financial control capability
- Restraining forces:
  - Budget restraints
  - Lack of authority to commit funds

- Manpower problems
- Facilities unavailable
- Insufficient planning

Under *client support* and *commitment* are:

- Driving forces:
  - Good working relations
  - Clear objectives
  - Timely client feedback
  - Client support and commitment
  - Regular meetings/reviews
  - Help and concern
- Restraining forces:
  - Lacking information on client needs
  - Lacking sustained interest
  - Conflict within client organization
  - Changing requirements
  - Funding problems

The authors then summarized their results as follows:

- Implications for project managers
  - Understand interaction of organizational and behavioral elements to build an effective team.
  - Show concern for team members—know their needs.
  - Provide work challenge.
  - Communicate objectives clearly.
  - Plan effectively and early in the project cycle.
  - Establish a contingency plan.
- Implications for top management
  - Poor organizational climate has a negative effect on project performance.
  - Project leader abilities are crucial to effective project management. Program management selection should be careful considered. Formal training and development may be necessary.
  - Senior management support is important.
  - Clearly defined decision channels and priorities may improve operating effectiveness with functional departments.
  - Smooth project startup and phaseout procedures help to ease personnel problems and power plays.

PROBLEMS

9-1 What is an effective working relationship between project managers themselves?

9-2 Must everyone in the organization understand the "rules of the game" for project management to be effective?

9-3 Defend the statement that the first step in making project management work must be a complete definition of the boundaries across which the project manager must interact.

10
Working with Executives

10.0 INTRODUCTION

In any project management environment, project managers must continuously interface with executives during both the planning and execution stages. Unless the project manager understands the executive's role and thought process, a poor working relationship will develop. In order to understand the executive–project interface, four topics will be discussed:

- The project sponsor
- The in-house representatives
- Selling executives on project management
- Executives reassess matrix management

10.1 THE PROJECT SPONSOR

In Section 9.3, we discussed the expectations of and for executives. They are:

- Project planning
- Conflict resolution
- Priority-setting
- Acting as the project sponsor

The first three items are easily recognized. The fourth, acting as the project sponsor, is primarily for communications with customers/clients. Project–customer communications can take place at three levels in the organization:

- Executive to executive
- Project office to project office
- Technician to technician

Figure 10–1 shows the structured communications flow. Usually the formal communication goes from project office to project office, and the informal com-

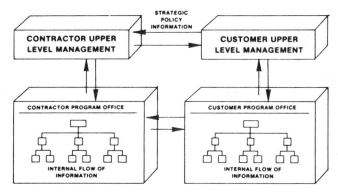

Figure 10–1. Information flow pattern from contractor program office.

munication is from executive to executive. Figure 10–2 shows the role and activities of the project sponsor, the primary one being the executive–client contact. From the contractor's organization, the project sponsor ensures that the correct information is reaching executives in the customer's organization; that is, there is no filtering of information by the customer's project office. From the customer's point of view, the project sponsor should make sure that the customer's money is being spent wisely. The project sponsor will normally transmit cost status information to the customer with the schedule and performance data coming from the project manager. The need for the project sponsor

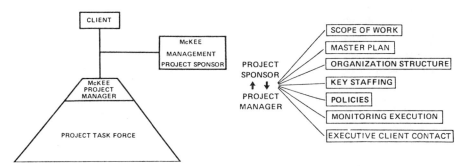

Figure 10–2. The project sponsor. (Source: L. J. Weber, W. Riethmeier, A. F. Westergard, and K. O. Hartley, "The Project Sponsor's View," *Proceedings of the Ninth Annual Seminar/Symposium on Project Management,* Presented by the Project Management Institute, Chicago, Illinois, 1977, p. 70.)

is easily identified if we look at the client's checklist for evaluating the contractor's decision-making capability:[1]

What Contractor Decision-making Patterns Can Be Expected?
- Assignment and retention of top engineers?
- Modification of manpower loading schedules to achieve efficiency; to achieve technical performance; to achieve progress payments?
- Selection of cost–performance trade-offs favoring performance?
- Stress incentives to personnel?
- Control of overhead charges?
- Receive top management attention?
- Prepare timely and clear cost/schedule reports?
- Maintain high level of interpersonal communications in planning and problem solving?
- Place little vs. great emphasis on cost control?
- Show commitment to meeting the client's needs?

Most project sponsors are vice-presidents or higher in the organization. Sometimes, even the chairman of the board will act as the sponsor, as was the case for a Cleveland Corporation that was soliciting business from a new source. For the first project, the project manager reported "solid" to the vice-president but "dotted" to the board chairman. This reporting procedure was done to impress upon the customer that the contractor considered the project to be very important. Any executive, regardless of the size of the company, may find it necessary to act as a project sponsor in addition to his other duties. The one exception is usually found in construction companies with the vice-president of operations because such an arrangement there would create a conflict of interest.

Figure 10–3 represents a situation where there were two project sponsors for one project. Alpha Company received a $25 million prime contractor project from the Air Force and subcontracted out $2 million to Beta Company. The project manager in Alpha Company earned a salary of $70,000 per year and refused to communicate directly with the project manager of Beta Company because his salary was only $35,000 per year. After all, as one executive said, "Elephants don't communicate with mice." The Alpha Company project manager then sought out someone in his salary range to act as the project sponsor, and the burden fell upon the director of engineering.

The Alpha Company project manager reported to an Air Force colonel. The

---

1. Joseph P. Guiltinan, "Contractor Motivations, Constraints and Decision-Making Patterns: Implications for Project Management," *Project Management Quarterly*, Vol. VIII, No. 2, June 1977, p. 20.

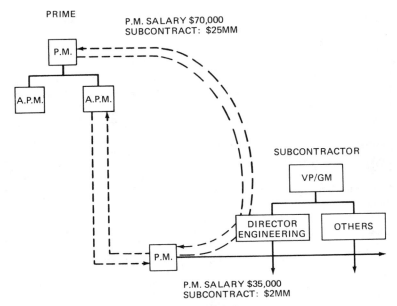

Figure 10–3. Multiple project sponsors.

Air Force colonel considered his counterpart in Beta Company to be the vice-president and general manager. Here, power and title were more important than the $100,000 differential in their salaries. Thus there was one project sponsor for the prime contractor and a second project sponsor for the customer.

In some industries, such as construction, the project sponsor is identified in the proposal, and everyone realizes this. Unfortunately there are situations where the project-sponsor role is "hidden," and the project manager may not realize that this communication is taking place.

10.2 THE IN-HOUSE REPRESENTATIVES

On high-risk, high-priority projects or during periods of mistrust, customers may wish to place in-house representatives in the contractor's plant. These in-house representatives do not always appear as in Figure 10–4. (The in-house representative is the one on top!) These representatives, if treated properly, are like additional project office personnel who are not supported by your budget. They are invaluable resources for reading rough drafts of reports and making recommendations as to how their company may wish to see the report organized.

Figure 10–4. The in-house representative.

In-house representatives are normally not situated in or near the contractor's project office because of the project manager's need for some degree of privacy. The exception to the rule would be in the design phase of a construction project, where it is imperative to design what the customer wants and to obtain quick decisions and approvals.

Most in-house representatives know where their authority begins and ends. Some companies demand that in-house representatives have a project office escort when touring the plant, talking to functional employees, or simply observing the testing and manufacturing of components.

Contrary to popular belief, it is possible to have an in-house representative removed from the company because of a disruptive nature. This removal usually requires strong support from the project sponsor in the contractor's shop. The important point to be made here is that executives and project sponsors must maintain proper contact with and control over the in-house representatives, perhaps more so than the project manager.

10.3 SELLING EXECUTIVES ON PROJECT MANAGEMENT

Executives of the 1980s are much more inquisitive about matrix implementation than their predecessors were, even though the advantages and disadvantages of matrix structures have been published extensively in the literature. This section deals with questions asked of the author by executives. Usually the executives questioned the author in a closed session, as quite often executives do not wish functional employees to hear either such questions or their answers. In each of these cases, the executives were contemplating a change to a matrix organizational structure. When reading the questions, it is important to understand that executives of the 1980s are operating under greater pressure and more risk and uncertainty than the executives of either the 1960s or the 1970s, and therefore must be "sold" on the project management approach.[2]

- *Can our people be part-time project managers?* The nature of the question suggests that the executives wanted to manage the projects within the existing resource base of the company. The answer to the question depends, of course, upon the size, nature, and complexity of the project. It is generally better to have a full-time project manager responsible for several small projects than to have many part-time project managers. Executives, as well as functional personnel, will never be convinced that the matrix will work until they see it in action. Therefore, it is strongly recommended that the first few projects be "breakthrough" projects with full-time project managers. This implies that, initially, these project managers will be staff to a top-level manager rather than within a newly developed line group for project managers.
- *If we go to project (matrix) management, must we increase resources, especially the number of project managers?* The reason for this question is obvious, namely that the executives do not wish to increase the manpower base or overhead rate. Matrix management is designed to get better control of functional resources such that more work can be completed in less time, with less money, and with potentially fewer people. Unfortunately, these results may not become evident for a year or two.

Initially, executives prefer to select project managers from within the organization with the argument that project managers must know the people and

---

2. It should be noted that the conceptual phase of project management implementation begins with functional managers who identify the need for project management because of their problems with resource control. The next step, therefore, is to sell top management on the concept. This is usually best accomplished through outside consultants, whom executives trust to give an impartial view.

the operation of the organization. Even today, some companies require that all project managers first spend at least eighteen months in the functional areas prior to becoming project managers. However, there are also good reasons for filling project management positions from outside the company. Sometimes newly transferred project managers still maintain loyal ties to their former functional department, and impartial project decision-making is not possible.

Let's assume that we set up a separate staff function called project admin- istration that is staff to one of our executives. Can we then use our func- tional people as part-time project managers who report vertically to a line manager and horizontally to project administration? With proper prepa- ration and training, most employees can learn how to report effectively to multiple managers. However, the process is more complicated if the employee acts as a project manager and functional employee at the same time. When a conflict occurs over what is best for the horizontal or the vertical line, the employee will usually bend in the direction that will put more pay into his pocket. In other words, if the (part-time or perhaps even full-time) project manager always makes decisions in the best interest of his line manager, the project will suffer. The most practical way to solve this problem is to let the functional employee act as a part-time assistant project manager rather than as a part-time project manager because now the functional employee has someone else to plead his case for him, and he is no longer caught in the middle.

This question has serious impacts on how employees are treated. If an employee reports to multiple managers and some managers treat him as though he is Theory Y while others treat him as Theory X, decisions will almost always be made in favor of the Theory Y managers. People who report to multiple managers must understand that, even if they are Theory Y employ- ees, in time of crisis they will be treated as though they are Theory X. This type of understanding and training must be given to all employees who perform in a project environment.

Which vice-president should be responsible for the project administration function? Assuming that the company does not want to create a separate position for a vice-president of projects, we must find out whether or not there exists a dominant percentage of people (on all projects) who come from one major functional group. If, say, 60 to 70 percent of all project employees come from engineering, then the vice-president for engineering should also control the project administration function because there now exists a common superior for the resolution of the majority of project con- flicts. Having to go up two or three levels of management to find a common superior for conflict resolution can create a self-defeating attitude within the matrix.

The assignment will become more difficult if functional dominance does not exist. We must now decide who dominates the decision-making process of the company (i.e., is the company marketing-driven, engineering-driven, etc.?). The project administrative function will then fall under the control of this line function. Without either of these degrees of dominance and assuming a project-driven organization, it is not uncommon to find all project managers reporting under marketing with the vice-president for marketing acting as the project sponsor.

Is it true that most project managers consider their next step to be that of a vice-president? Most project managers view the organization of the company with the project managers on top and executives performing horizontally. Therefore, project managers already consider themselves to be executives on the project and naturally expect their next step to be as executives in the company.

However, we should mention that many project managers are so in love with their jobs that money is not an important factor, and they may wish to stay in project management. Project managers are self-motivated by work challenge and therefore many have refused top-level promotions because they did not consider the work to be as challenging at this level, in comparison with project management.

- *Can we give our employees (especially engineers) a rotation period of six to eighteen months in the project office and then return them to the functional departments, where they should be more well-rounded individuals with a better appreciation and understanding of project management?* On paper, this technique looks good and may have some merit. But in the real world, the results may be disastrous. There are four detrimental effects of this arrangement. First, employees who know that they will be returning to their line function will not be dedicated to project management and will still try to maintain a strong allegiance to their line function. The result, of course, will be that the project will suffer. Second, when the employee knows that his assignment is temporary and brief, he usually walks the straight and narrow path and avoids risk whenever possible. Risky decisions are left to other project office personnel or even his replacement. Third, depending upon the rate at which technology changes, the employee may find himself technically obsolete when he returns to his functional group. The fourth and last point is the most serious. The employee may find himself so attracted to the project management function that he wants to stay. If the company forces him to return to his functional department, there is always the risk that the employee will update his resume and begin reading the job-market section of the Tuesday *Wall Street Journal.* Simply stated, a company should not place people in project management unless the company is willing to offer these people a career path there.

- *How much control should a project manager have over costs and budgets?* Executives in the areas of accounting and finance are very reluctant to delegate total cost control to project managers. Project managers cannot be effective unless they have the right to control costs by opening and closing work orders in accordance with the established project plan. However, if the project manager redirects the project activities in a manner that causes a major deviation in the cash flow position of the project, then he must coordinate his activities with top management in order to prevent a potential company cash flow problem.

- *What role should a project manager have in strategic and operational planning?* First of all, project managers are concerned primarily with the immediate execution of an operational plan. Therefore, they are operational planners. However, because of the company-wide knowledge that the project manager obtains on functional operations and integration, he becomes an invaluable asset to the executives during strategic planning, but primarily as a resource person. Project managers are not known for their corporate strategic planning posture, but for their strategic project planning capability.

- *What working relationships should exist between executives and the project manager?* The answer to this question involves two things: internal meddling and customer communications. Executives are expected to work closely with the project manager and take an active role during the conceptual and planning stages of a project. However, after the project enters the implementation phase, active participation by executives equates to executive meddling and can do more harm than good. After planning is completed, executives should step back and let the project manager run the show. There will still be structured feedback from the project office to the executive, and the executive will still be actively involved in priority-setting and conflict resolution. The exception to this occurs when the executive is required to act as the project sponsor, as shown in Figure 10–2. In this case, the client wants to be sure that his project is receiving executive attention and feels confident when he sees one of the contractor's executives looking over the project. The project sponsor exists primarily as the executive–client contact link but can also serve as an invaluable staff resource.

Executives must not be blinded by the partial success they may achieve with executive meddling during the early days of matrix implementation. The overall, long-term effect on the company could be disastrous if executives feel that they can effectively control vertical and horizontal resources at the same time.

Where do we find good project managers? First of all, project management is both an art and a science. The science aspect includes the quantitative tools and techniques for planning, scheduling, and controlling. The art aspect involves dealing with a wide variety of people. The science portion can be learned in the classroom, whereas the art portion can come only from on-the-job experience. Perhaps the most important characteristics are interpersonal skills and communicative skills.

Most companies have qualified people within the organization, and often they produce disastrous results by "forcing" such people to unwillingly accept a project management assignment. Project management generally works best if it is a voluntary assignment, which usually brings with it loyalty and dedication. Unfortunately, many people enter project management without fully understanding the job description of the project manager. If employees are promoted into project management and then "want out" or fail, the company may have no place for them at their new salary. Sometimes it is better to transfer employees to project management laterally, under the stipulation that rewards will follow if they produce.

- *What percentage of a total project budget should be available for project management and administrative support?* The answer to this question depends upon the nature of the project. Management support may run from a low of 2 percent to a high of 15 percent.
- *My company has fifty projects going on at once. The project managers handle multiple projects, each with a different priority, and can report to anyone in the company. Will a matrix give better control?* The matrix will alleviate a lot of these problems, provided that all of the project managers report to one line group. This will give uniform control of projects and will make it easier to establish priorities. If it becomes necessary to get better control over the project managers, then the projects should be grouped according to the customer or to similar technologies, not necessarily dollar value.
- *In a matrix, people are often assigned full-time to a project. What happens if a functional manager complains that pulling a good employee out of his department will leave a large gap?* In a matrix the employee is still physically and administratively attached to his functional group. And even with a full-time project assignment, the employee will probably still find

sufficient slack time to assist in another project, even if only in a consultant capacity.

- *On some of our projects the first step is a cost–benefit analysis to see if the project is a feasible undertaking. Who will do this in a matrix?* On some projects, the job-related characteristics are more important than the project manager's personal characteristics. In this case, it may be better to have project managers who are trained in this area rather than having the cost–benefit analysis performed by another group. Project managers should be actively involved in any planning or decision making that may be bottom-line-oriented.
- *How do we make sure that everyone in the company knows what the priorities are?* Priorities should be transmitted to both the project and functional departments through the traditional structure within the matrix. Even with the establishment of priorities, project managers will still fight for what they believe to be in the best interest of their project. This is to be expected. Initially, during the implementation of the matrix, it may be necessary to have all priorities documented.

There is a risk within the matrix that the slippage of as little as one project could cause reestablishment of all other project priorities. Even though some project managers may control their project so closely that they can obtain daily status reports, continuously changing priorities on a daily or even weekly basis can destroy the functioning of the matrix because the functional managers may now be forced to continually shift resources from project to project.

> *We have had an explosion of operations support systems (the Minicomputer Era). How do we manage these projects? Can we use matrix management?* Matrix management works best for projects that cut across more than one functional group. Multi-functional MIS and data base packages can be very effectively managed using a matrix. Banks are a prime example of industries where matrix management may exist primarily for such projects.

One major risk should be considered. There is always controversy over whether the programmers or the users should be the project managers. The usual arguments are that the programmers don't understand the user's needs and the user doesn't understand why it takes so long to write a program. Many companies have established a project management group to handle such conflicts. Each project is headed by a project manager and two assistant project managers, one from programming and one to represent the users. Conflicts and problems are now resolved horizontally rather than vertically. In this situation, it is possible for one project manager to handle several projects at once.

- *How does top management control the responsibilities that each person will have on a project?* Neither top management nor project management controls the responsibilities. The functional managers still control their own people. Project managers can fill out a linear responsibility chart (LRC) to make sure that every work breakdown structure element is accounted for. However, the functional managers should still approve the amount of authority and responsibility that the project manager wishes to delegate to functional employees. The reason for this is that the project manager should not be able to upgrade functional employees without the consent of the functional manager. The exception would be the project office personnel, who may report full-time to the project manager and also be evaluated by him. During the implementation phase of a matrix, the executives may wish to be actively involved in the LRC establishment, since, in fact, it is part of the planning process, and executives are expected to be closely associated with the project at this time.

- *How do we ensure effective and timely communications to all levels?* The project manager, being the focal point for all project activities, should be able to provide timely project information to everyone, including executives, at a faster rate than the traditional structure itself. The ability to provide effective and timely communications should be part of every project manager's job description.

- *How do we get top management committed to project management?* Regardless of how much literature exists in the area of effective project management, executives will not become committed until they see the system operating effectively and producing the expected dollar value of profit on the bottom line of the project. In order to effectively observe and comprehend the problems, executives must understand their new role in a project management environment and should attend the same "therapy" training sessions as middle management.

- *We need an awful lot of front-end work (i.e., planning) on projects. We are living in a world of limited resources. We need commitments from our people, not just promises. How do we get that?* When the functional managers realize that project management is designed for them, and not for executives or project managers, then the functional managers will start giving commitments that they will live up to. The functional managers must be convinced that the matrix is not simply an attempt on the part of the project manager to control the functional manager's empire, but that in fact the project manager and matrix exist to support the functional managers in getting better control over their own resources such that future commitments can be kept.

- *How do we resolve problems in which there is a lack of knowledge of project team members concerning their own roles?* The responsibility here rests on the shoulders of both the project and functional managers. Planning tools, such as the linear responsibility charts, can be used, but the "bottom line" is still effective communications. This is why one of the major prerequisites for a project manager is to be an effective communicator and integrator.

- *How do we convince people to disclose problems and not bury them?* In a matrix organization, the critical point is the project/functional interface. Both the project and functional managers must be willing to disclose problems and ask for help, especially on the horizontal line. When the project manager gets into trouble, he goes first to the functional manager to discuss project resources. When the functional manager gets into trouble, he goes to the project manager seeking additional time, additional funding, or a change in specifications. Project personnel must realize that the project is a team effort, and everyone should pitch in when problems occur.

Many people refuse to reveal problems for fear that the identification of the problem will be reflected in their evaluation for promotion. The matrix structure is designed not only to put forth the best team for accomplishing the objectives, but also to resolve problems. Because the matrix approach encourages the sharing of key people, employees may find that the best corporate resources are now available to assist them temporarily.

Executives and functional managers must encourage people to bring forth problems, especially during matrix implementation. This encouragement should probably be done orally, with personal contact, rather than through memos.

- *Is it true that if we go to a matrix, many of our functional people will start communicating directly with our customers?* When you have a matrix structure, customers are very reluctant to have all information flow from your project office to their project office for fear that your project office is filtering the information. Therefore, the customer may request (or even demand) that his technical people be permitted to talk to your technical people on a one-on-one basis. This should be permitted as long as the customer fully understands that:
  - Functional employees reflect their own personal opinion. Official company position can come only through the project office or through the project sponsor.
  - Functional employees cannot commit to additional work which may be beyond the scope of the contract. Any changes in work must be approved by the project office.

Functionally, employees should contact the project office after each communication and relate to the project office what was discussed. The project office will then consider whether or not a memo should be written to document the results of the discussion.

The purpose of the question–answer session is to convince the executives that a change might be for the better. With matrix management styles, the following are the most common arguments that executives give for avoiding change:[3]

- Why Change?
  - I must be doing something right to get where I am. I may have to start working differently. Can I succeed?
- Balance of Power
  - I understand the balance of power and my role within top management. Why change it? I might lose my present power.
- Loss of Control
  - I presently generate change on projects and in policy areas. Why change it? I won't be able to control recommended changes.
- Need for Contact with Projects
  - I will lose my ability to perceive appropriate adjustments in organization policies when I lose detail involvement in projects. Why change it?
- Excessive Delegation
  - It is not good practice to have key decisions delegated below the top men. Why change?
- Coordination
  - Coordination responsibility is a key management job. Why delegate it to project managers?

If the executives are willing to accept change, then the next step is to discuss the methods for implementation. The executives must understand the following strategies and tactics for implementation to be effective:

- Top management must delegate authority and responsibility to the project manager.
- Top management must delegate total cost control to the project manager.
- Top management must rely upon the project manager for total project planning and scheduling.

---

3. Adapted from John M. Tettemer, "Keeping Your Boss Happy While Implementing Project Management—A Management View," *Proceedings of the Tenth Annual Seminar/Symposium of the Project Management Institute,* Los Angeles, October 8–11, 1978, pp. IA-1 through IA-4; reproduced by permission of the Project Management Institute.

- Only the project managers must fully understand advanced scheduling techniques such as PERT/CPM. This may require additional training. Functional managers may use other scheduling techniques for resource control.
- Top management must encourage functional managers to resolve problems and conflicts at the lowest organizational levels and not always run "upstairs."
- Top management must not consider functional departments as merely support groups for a project. Functional departments still control the company resources, and, contrary to popular belief, the project managers actually work for the functional managers, not vice versa.
- Top management must provide sufficient training for functional employees on how to report to and interact with multiple project managers.
- Top management must take an interest in how project management should work.
- Top management must not fight among themselves as to who should control the project management function.

The project manager also has strategies and tactics that should be understood during implementation. The following key points should be carefully considered by the project manager:[4]

- Breakthrough Project
  - Start with a breakthrough project that the administration can keep pace with in the new project management format.
- Traditional Information for Top Management
  - The new project manager must be sure that traditional types of functional and project information are available to top management for traditional problem solving. He should take this information forward voluntarily, ahead of top management's knowledge of the problem, preferably more quickly than the traditional line of communication.
- Retention of Power
  - Allow every administrator to retain his traditional power within the hierarchy during the implementation phase.
- Policy Recommendations
  - Project managers should carefully and thoughtfully develop only policy recommendations that can be easily accepted by the administration as

---

4. Adapted from John M. Tettemer, "Keeping Your Boss Happy While Implementing Project Management—A Management View," *Proceedings of the Tenth Annual Seminar/Symposium of the Project Management Institute,* Los Angeles, October 8–11, 1978, pp. IA-1 through IA-4; reproduced by permission of the Project Management Institute.

being in concert with the organization's goals and objectives, and that are easy to implement and readily accepted by those outside the organization.
- Slow Down
  - It is necessary for project managers to push for change but not at a rate that in itself builds opposition.
- Schedules Aren't the End of the World
  - Project managers should keep schedules and other tools in the background of their involvement with top management. (The tools of project management are of far less interest to top management than the results obtained through them.)
- Decode All Information
  - It is extremely important that project managers decode all their reporting documents to meet the style of the executive with whom they are trying to communicate.
- Use Broad Perspective
  - Project managers should be sure to recommend as general policy changes only those items that are applicable to a broad range of projects. Exceptions should be clearly indicated as exceptions to meet clearly defined project objectives.

It should be readily apparent from these key points that during implementation the project managers could easily frighten executives to such a degree that all thoughts of matrix implementation will be forgotten.

The last point that should be emphasized is that some executives face "blockages" even after the implementation phase is completed. These executive blockages may be avoided as follows:

- Top management directly interfaces a project only during its idea development and planning phases. Once the project is initiated, the executives should maintain a monitoring perspective via structured feedback from the project manager.
- Top management still establishes corporate direction and must make sure that the project managers fully understand its meaning.
- Top management must try to control environmental factors that may be beyond the control of the project manager. These factors include such items as external communications, joint-venture relationships, providing internal support, and providing environmental ongoing intelligence.
- Top management must have confidence in the project managers and must be willing to give them both difficult and easy projects.
- Top management must understand that in order for work to flow horizontally in a company, a "dynamic" organizational structure is necessary.

Not all activities can flow in parallel with the main activities of the company.

- Upper-level management must not want to take an active role in this "new" concept called project management.
- Upper-level management must be familiar with their new responsibilities and interface relationships in a project environment.

There is no sure-fire method today for the successful acceptance and implementation of matrix management. The best approach appears to be an early education process (including questions and answers) whereby executives, project managers, and functional personnel will be willing at least to give the system a chance. This type of early educational approach may be acceptable to all types of companies and in all industries where the matrix is applicable.

PROBLEMS

10–1 Should age have a bearing upon how long it takes an executive to accept project management?

10–2 You have been called in by the executive management of a major utility company and asked to give a "selling" speech on why the company should go to project management. What are you going to say? What areas will you stress? What questions would you expect the executives to ask? What fears do you think the executives might have?

10–3 Some executives would prefer to have their project managers become tunnel-vision workaholics, with the project managers falling in love with their jobs and living to work instead of working to live. How do you feel about this?

10–4 Project management is designed to make effective and efficient use of resources. Most companies that adopt project management find it easier to under-employ and schedule overtime than to overemploy and either lay people off or drive up the overhead rate. A major electrical equipment manufacturer contends that with proper utilization of the project management concept, the majority of the employees who leave the company through either termination or retirement do not have to be replaced. Is this rationale reasonable?

10–5 The director of engineering services of R. P. Corporation believes that a project organizational structure of some sort would help resolve several of his problems. As part of the discussion, the director has made the following remarks: "All of our activities (or so-called projects if you wish) are loaded with up-front engineering. We have found in the past that time is the important parameter, not quality control or cost. Sometimes we rush into projects so fast that we have no choice but to cut corners, and, of course, quality must suffer."

What questions, if any, would you like to ask before recommending a project organizational form? Which form will you recommend?

10–6 How should a project manager react when he finds inefficiency in the functional lines? Should executive management become involved?

10–7 An electrical equipment manufacturing company has just hired you to conduct a three-day seminar on project management for sixty employees. The president of the company asks you to have lunch with him on the first day of the seminar. During lunch, the executive remarks, "I inherited the matrix structure when I took over. Actually I don't think it can work here, and I'm not sure how long I'll support it." How should you continue at this point?

10–8 Should project managers be permitted to establish prerequisites for top management regarding standard company procedures?

10–9 During the implementation of project management, you find that line managers are reluctant to release any information showing utilization of resources in their line function. How should this situation be handled, and by whom?

10–10 Corporate engineering of a large corporation usually assumes control of all plant expansion projects in each of its plants for all projects over $25 million. For each case below, discuss the ramifications of this, assuming that there are several other projects going on in each plant at the same time as the plant expansion project.

   a. The project manager is supplied by corporate engineering and reports to corporate engineering, but all other resources are supplied by the plant manager.
   b. The project manager is supplied by corporate but reports to the plant manager for the duration of the project.
   c. The plant manager supplies the project manager, and the project manager reports "solid" to corporate and "dotted" to the plant manager for the duration of the project.

10–11 An aircraft company requires seven years from initial idea to full production of a military aircraft. Consider the following facts: engineering design requires a minimum of two years of R&D; manufacturing has a passive role during this time; and engineering builds their own prototype during the third year.

   a. To whom in the organization should the program manager, project manager, and project engineering report? Does your answer depend upon the life-cycle phase?
   b. Can the project engineers be "solid" to the project manager and still be authorized by the engineering vice-president to provide technical direction?
   c. What should be the role of marketing?
   d. Should there be a project sponsor?

10–12 Does a project sponsor have the right to have an in-house representative removed from his company?

10–13 An executive once commented that his company was having trouble managing projects, not because of a lack of tools and techniques, but because they (employees) did not know how to manage what they had. How does this relate to project management?

10-14 Ajax National is the world's largest machine tool equipment manufacturer. Their success is based upon the experience of their personnel. The majority of their department managers are 45–55-year-old, nondegreed people who have come up from the ranks. Ajax has just hired several engineers with bachelor's and master's degrees to control the project management and project engineering functions. Can this pose a problem? Are advanced-degreed people required because of the rapid rate of change of technology?

10-15 When does project management turn into overmanagement?

10-16 Brainstorming at United Central Bank (Part I): As part of the 1979 strategic policy plan for United Central Bank, the president, Joseph P. Keith, decided to embark upon weekly "brainstorming meetings" in hopes of developing creative ideas that could lead to solutions to the bank's problems. The bank's executive vice-president would serve as permanent chairman of the brainstorming committee. Personnel representation would be randomly selected under the constraint that 10 percent must be from division managers, 30 percent from department managers, 30 percent from section level supervisors, and the remaining 30 percent from clerical and nonexempt personnel. President Keith further decreed that the brainstorming committee would criticize all ideas and submit only those that successfully passed the criticism test to upper-level management for review.

After six months, with only two ideas submitted to upper-level management (both ideas were made by division managers), Joseph Keith formed an inquiry committee to investigate the reasons for the lack of interest by the brainstorming committee participants. Which of the following statements might be found in the inquiry committee report? (More than one answer is possible.)

a. Because of superior, subordinate, subordinate relationships (i.e., pecking orders), creativity is inhibited.
b. Criticism and ridicule have a tendency to inhibit spontaneity.
c. Good managers can become very conservative and unwilling to stick their necks out.
d. Pecking orders, unless adequately controlled, can inhibit teamwork and problem solving.
e. All seemingly crazy or unconventional ideas were ridiculed and eventually discarded.
f. Many lower-level people, who could have good ideas to contribute, felt inferior

g. Meetings were dominated by upper-level management personnel.
h. The meetings were held at an inappropriate place and time.
i. Many people were not given adequate notification of meeting time and subject matter.

10-17 Brainstorming at United Central Bank (Part II): After reading the inquiry committee report, President Keith decided to reassess his thinking about brainstorming by listing the advantages and disadvantages. What are the arguments for and against brainstorming? If you were Joseph Keith, would you vote for or against the continuation of the brainstorming sessions?

10-18 Brainstorming at United Central Bank (Part III): President Keith evaluated all of the data and decided to give the brainstorming committee one more chance. What changes can Joseph Keith implement in order to prevent the previous problems from recurring?

10-19 Explain the meaning of the following proverb: "The first ninety percent of the work is accomplished with ninety percent of the budget. The second ninety percent of the work is accomplished with the remaining ten percent of the budget."

10-20 You are a line manager, and two project managers (each reporting to a divisional vice-president) enter your office soliciting resources. Each project manager claims that his project is top-priority as assigned by his own vice-president. How should you, as the line manager, handle this situation? What are the recommended solutions to keep this situation from recurring repeatedly?

10-21 Figure 10–5 shows the organizational structure for a new Environmental Protection Agency project. Alpha Company was one of three subcontractors chosen for the contract. Because this was a new effort, the project manager reported "dotted" to the board chairman, who was acting as the project sponsor. The vice-president was the immediate superior to the project manager.

Because the project manager did not believe that Alpha Company maintained the expertise to do the job, he hired an outside consultant from one of the local colleges. Both the EPA and the prime contractor approved of the consultant, and the consultant's input was excellent.

The project manager's superior, the vice-president, disapproved of the consultant, continuously arguing that the company had the expertise internally. How should you, the project manager, handle this situation?

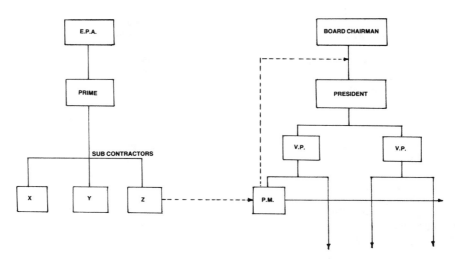

Figure 10–5. Organizational chart for EPA project.

10-22 You are the customer for a twelve-month project. You have team meetings scheduled with your subcontractor on a monthly basis. The contract has a contractual requirement to prepare a 25–30 page handout for each team meeting. Are there any benefits for you, the customer, to see these handouts at least 3–4 days prior to the team meeting?

10-23 You have a work breakdown structure which is detailed to level 5. One level 5 work package requires that a technical subcontractor be selected to support one of the technical line organizations. Who should be responsible for customer-contractor communications: the project office or line manager? Does your answer depend upon the life cycle phase? The level of the WBS? Project manager's "faith" in the line manager?

10-24 Should a client have the right to communicate directly to the project staff (i.e., project office) rather than directly to the project manager, or should this be at the discretion of the project manager?

CASE STUDY: THE BLUE SPIDER PROJECT[5]

"This is impossible! Just totally impossible! Ten months ago I was sitting on top of the world. Upper-level management considered me one of the best, if not the best engineer in the plant. Now look at me! I have bags under my eyes, I haven't slept soundly in the last six months, and here I am, cleaning out my desk. I'm sure glad they gave me back my old job in engineering. I guess I could have saved myself a lot of grief and aggravation had I not accepted the promotion to project manager."

History

Gary Anderson had accepted a position with Parks Corporation right out of college. With a Ph.D. in mechanical engineering, Gary was ready to solve the world's most traumatic problems. At first, Parks Corporation offered Gary little opportunity to do the pure research which he eagerly wanted to undertake. However, things soon changed. Parks grew into a major electronics and structural design corporation during the big boom of the late fifties and early sixties when the Department of Defense (DoD) contracts were plentiful.

Parks Corporation grew from a handful of engineers to a major DoD contractor, employing some 6,500 people. During the recession of the late sixties, money became scarce and major layoffs resulted in lowering the employment level to 2,200 employees. At that time, Parks decided to get out of the R&D business and compete as a low-cost production facility while maintaining an engineering organization solely to support production requirements.

After attempts at virtually every project management organizational structure, Parks Corporation selected the matrix form. Each project had a program manager

---

5. Copyright © 1978 by Harold Kerzner.

who reported to the director of program management. Each project also maintained an assistant project manager, normally a project engineer, who reported directly to the project manager and indirectly to the director of engineering. The program manager spent most of his time worrying about cost and time, whereas the assistant program manager worried more about technical performance.

With the poor job market for engineers, Gary and his colleagues began taking coursework toward an M.B.A. degree should the job market deteriorate further.

In 1975, with the upturn in DoD spending, Parks had to change its corporate strategy. Parks had spent the last seven years bidding on the production phase of large programs. But now, with the new evaluation criteria set forth for contract awards, those companies winning the R&D and qualification phases had a definite edge on being awarded the production contract. The production contract was where the big profits could be found. In keeping with this new strategy, Parks began to beef up its R&D engineering staff. By 1978, Parks had increased in size to 2,700 employees. The increase was mostly in engineering. Experienced R&D personnel were difficult to find for the salaries that Parks was offering. Parks was, however, able to lure some employees away from the competitors, but relied mostly upon the younger, inexperienced engineers fresh out of college.

With the adoption of this corporate strategy, Parks Corporation administered a new wage and salary program that included job upgrading. Gary was promoted to senior scientist, responsible for all R&D activities performed in the mechanical engineering department. Gary had distinguished himself as an outstanding production engineer during the past several years, and management felt that his contribution could be extended to R&D as well.

In January 1978, Parks Corporation decided to compete for Phase I of the Blue Spider Project, an R&D effort that, if successful, could lead into a $500 million program spread out over twenty years. The Blue Spider Project was an attempt to improve the structural capabilities of the Spartan Missile, a short-range tactical missile used by the Army. The Spartan Missile was exhibiting fatigue failure after six years in the field. This was three years less than what the original design specifications called for. The Army wanted new materials that could result in a longer age life for the Spartan Missile.

Lord Industries was the prime contractor for the Army's Spartan Program. Parks Corporation would be a subcontractor to Lord if they could successfully bid and win the project. The criteria for subcontractor selection were based not only on low bid, but also on technical expertise as well as management performance on other projects. Park's management felt that they had a distinct advantage over most of the other competitors because they had successfully worked on other projects for Lord Industries.

The Blue Spider Project Kickoff

On November 3, 1977, Henry Gable, the director of engineering, called Gary Anderson into his office.

Henry Gable: "Gary, I've just been notified through the grapevine that Lord will be issuing the RFP for the Blue Spider Project by the end of this month, with a thirty-day response period. I've been waiting a long time for a project like this to come along so that I can experiment with some new ideas that I have. This project is going to be my baby all the way! I want you to head up the proposal team. I think it must be an engineer. I'll make sure that you get a good proposal manager to help you. If we start working now, we can get close to two months of research in before proposal submittal. That will give us a one-month's edge on our competitors."

Gary was pleased to be involved in such an effort. He had absolutely no trouble in getting functional support for the R&D effort necessary to put together a technical proposal. All of the functional managers continually remarked to Gary that, "This must be a biggy. The director of engineering has thrown all of his support behind you."

On December 2, the RFP was received. The only trouble area that Gary could see was that the technical specifications stated that all components must be able to operate normally and successfully through a temperature range of $-65°$ F to $145°$ F. Current testing indicated the Parks Corporation's design would not function above $130°$ F. An intensive R&D effort was conducted over the next three weeks. Everywhere Gary looked, it appeared that the entire organization was working on his technical proposal.

A week before the final proposal was to be submitted, Gary and Henry Gable met to develop a company position concerning the inability of the preliminary design material to be operated above $130°$ F.

Gary Anderson: "Henry, I don't think it is going to be possible to meet specification requirements unless we change our design material or incorporate new materials. Everything I've tried indicates we're in trouble."

Henry Gable: "We're in trouble only if the customer knows about it. Let the proposal state that we expect our design to be operative up to $155°$ F. That'll please the customer."

Gary Anderson: "That seems unethical to me. Why don't we just tell them the truth?"

Henry Gable: "The truth doesn't always win proposals. I picked you to head up this effort because I thought that you'd understand. I could have just as easily selected one of our many moral project managers. I'm considering you for program manager after we win the program. If you're going to pull this conscientious crap on me like the other project managers do, I'll find someone else. Look at it this way; later we can convince the customer to change the specifications. After all, we'll be so far downstream that he'll have no choice."

After two solid months of sixteen-hour days, the proposal was submitted. On February 10, 1978 Lord Industries announced that Parks Corporation would be awarded the Blue Spider Project. The contract called for a ten-month effort, negotiated at $2.2 million at a firm-fixed price.

Selecting the Project Manager

Following contract award, Henry Gable called Gary in for a conference.

Henry Gable: "Congratulations Gary! You did a fine job. The Blue Spider Project has great potential for ongoing business over the next ten years, provided that we perform well during the R&D phase. Obviously you're the most qualified person in the plant to head up the project. How would you feel about a transfer to program management?"

Gary: "I think it would be a real challenge. I could make maximum use of the M.B.A. degree I earned last year. I've always wanted to be in program management."

Henry Gable: "Having several master's degrees, or even doctorate's for that matter, does not guarantee that you'll be a successful project manager. There are three requirements for effective program management: you must be able to communicate both in writing and orally; you must know how to motivate people; and you must be willing to give up your car pool. The last one is extremely important in that program managers must be totally committed and dedicated to the program, regardless of how much time is involved.

"But this is not the reason why I asked you to come here. Going from project engineering to program management is a big step. There are only two places you can go from program management; up the organization or out the door. I know of very, very few engineers that failed in program management and were permitted to return."

Gary: "Why is that? If I'm considered to be the best engineer in the plant, why can't I return to engineering?"

Henry Gable: "Program management is a world of its own. It has its own formal and informal organizational ties. Program managers are outsiders. You'll find out. You might not be able to keep the strong personal ties you now have with your fellow employees. You'll have to force even your best friends to comply with your standards. Program managers can go from program to program, but functional departments remain intact.

"I'm telling you all this for a reason. We've worked well together the past several years. But if I sign the release so that you can work for Grey in Program Management, you'll be on your own, like hiring into a new company. I've already signed the release. You still have some time to think about it."

Gary: "One thing I don't understand. With all of the good program managers we have here, why am I given this opportunity?"

Henry Gable: "Almost all of our program managers are over forty-five years old. This resulted from our massive layoffs several years ago when we were forced to lay off the younger, inexperienced program managers. You were selected because of your age and because all of our other program managers have worked on only production-type programs. We need someone at the reins who knows R&D. Your counterpart at Lord Industries will be an R&D type. You have to fight fire with fire.

"I have an ulterior reason for wanting you to accept this position. Because of the division of authority between program management and project engineering, I need someone in program management whom I can communicate with concerning R&D work. The program managers we have now are interested only in time and cost. We need a manager who will bend over backwards to get performance also. I think you're that man. You know the commitment we made to Lord when we submitted that proposal. You have to try to achieve that. Remember, this program is my baby. You'll get all the support you need. I'm tied up on another project now. But when it's over, I'll be following your work like a hawk. We'll have to get together occasionally and discuss new techniques.

"Take a day or two to think it over. If you want the position, make an appointment to see Elliot Grey, the director of program management. He'll give you the same speech I did. I'll assign Paul Evans to you as chief project engineer. He's a seasoned veteran and you should have no trouble working with him. He'll give you good advice. He's a good man."

The Work Begins

Gary accepted the new challenge. His first major hurdle occurred in staffing the project. The top priority given to him to bid the program did not follow through for staffing. The survival of Parks Corporation depended upon the profits received from the production programs. In keeping with this philosophy Gary found that engineering managers (even his former boss) were reluctant to give up their key people to the Blue Spider Program. However, with a little support from Henry Gable, Gary formed an adequate staff for the program.

Right from the start Gary was worried that the test matrix called out in the technical volume of the proposal would not produce results that could satisfy specifications. Gary had a milestone, ninety days after go-ahead, to identify the raw materials that could satisfy specification requirements. Gary and Paul Evans held a meeting to map out their strategy for the first few months.

Gary Anderson: "Well Paul, we're starting out with our backs against the wall on this one. Any recommendations?"

Paul Evans: "I also have my doubts in the validity of this test matrix. Fortunately, I've been through this before. Gable thinks this is his project and he'll sure as hell try to manipulate us. I have to report to him every morning at 7:30 A.M. with the raw data results of the previous day's testing. He wants to see it before you do. He also stated that he wants to meet with me alone.

"Lord will be the big problem. If the test matrix proves to be a failure, we're going to have to change the scope of effort. Remember, this is an FFP contract. If we change the scope of work and do additional work in the earlier phases of the program, then we should prepare a trade-off analysis to see what we can delete downstream so as to not overrun the budget."

Gary Anderson: "I'm going to let the other project office personnel handle the administrating work. You and I are going to live in the research labs until we get some results. We'll let the other project office personnel run the weekly team meetings."

For the next three weeks Gary and Paul spent virtually twelve hours per day, seven days a week, in the research and development lab. None of the results showed any promise. Gary kept trying to set up a meeting with Henry Gable but always found him unavailable.

During the fourth week, Gary, Paul, and the key functional department managers met to develop an alternate test matrix. The new test matrix looked good. Gary and his team worked frantically to develop a new workable schedule that would not have impact on the second milestone, which was to occur at the end of 180 days. The second milestone was the final acceptance of the raw materials and preparation of production runs of the raw materials to verify that there would be no scale-up differences between lab development and full-scale production.

Gary personally prepared all of the technical handouts for the interchange meeting. After all, he would be the one presenting all of the data. The technical interchange meeting was scheduled for two days. On the first day, Gary presented all of the data, including test results, and the new test matrix. The customer appeared displeased with the progress to date and decided to have their own in-house caucus that evening to go over the material that was presented.

The following morning the customer stated their position: "First of all, Gary, we're quite pleased to have a project manager who has such a command of technology. That's good. But every time we've tried to contact you last month, you were unavailable or had to be paged in the research laboratories. You did an acceptable job presenting the technical data, but the administrative data was presented by your project office personnel. We, at Lord, do not think that you're maintaining the proper balance between your technical and administrative responsibilities. We prefer that you personally give the administrative data and your chief project engineer present the technical data.

"We did not receive any agenda. Our people like to know what will be discussed, and when. We also want a copy of all handouts to be presented at least three days in advance. We need time to scrutinize the data. You can't expect us to walk in here blind and make decisions after seeing the data for ten minutes.

"To be frank, we feel that the data to date are totally unacceptable. If the data do not improve, we will have no choice but to issue a work stoppage order and look for a new contractor. The new test matrix looks good, especially since this is a firm-fixed-price contract. Your company will burden all costs for the additional work. A trade-off with later work may be possible, but this will depend upon the results presented at the second design review meeting, ninety days from now.

"We have decided to establish a customer office at Parks to follow your work more closely. Our people feel that monthly meetings are insufficient during R & D activities. We would like our customer representative to have daily verbal meetings with you or your staff. He will then keep us posted. Obviously, we had expected to review much more experimental data than you have given us.

"Many of our top quality engineers would like to talk directly to your engineering community, without having to continually waste time by having to go through the project office. We must insist upon this last point. Remember, your effort may be only $2.2 million, but our total package is $100 million. We have a lot more at stake than you people do. Our engineers do not like to get information that has been filtered by the project office. They want to help you.

"And last, don't forget that you people have a contractual requirement to prepare complete minutes for all interchange meetings. Send us the original for signature before going to publication."

Although Gary was unhappy with the first team meeting, especially with the requests made by Lord Industries, he felt that they had sufficient justification for their comments. Following the team meeting, Gary personally prepared the complete minutes. "This is absurd," thought Gary. "I've wasted almost one entire week doing nothing more than administrative paperwork. Why do we need such detailed minutes? Can't a rough summary just as well suffice? Why is it that customers want everything documented? That's like an indication of fear. We've been completely cooperative with them. There has been no hostility between us. If we've gotten this much paperwork to do now, I hate to imagine what it will be like if we get into trouble."

A New Role

Gary completed and distributed the minutes to the customer as well as to all key team members.

For the next five weeks testing went according to plan, or at least Gary thought that it had. The results were still poor. Gary was so caught up in administrative paperwork that he hadn't found time to visit the research labs in over a month. On a Wednesday morning, Gary entered the lab to observe the morning testing. Upon arriving in the lab, Gary found Paul Evans, Henry Gable, and two technicians testing a new material, JXB-3.

Henry Gable: "Gary, your problems will soon be over. This new material, JXB-3, will permit you to satisfy specification requirements. Paul and I have been testing it for two weeks. We wanted to let you know, but were afraid that if the word leaked out to the customer that we were spending his money for testing materials that were not called out in the program plan, then he would probably go crazy and might cancel the contract. Look at these results. They're super!"

Gary Anderson: "Am I supposed to be the one to tell the customer now? This could cause a big wave."

Henry Gable: "There won't be any wave. Just tell them that we did it with our own IR&D funds. That'll please them because they'll think we're spending our own money to support their program."

Before presenting the information to Lord, Gary called a team meeting to present the new data to the project personnel. At the team meeting, one functional manager spoke out: "This is a hell of a way to run a program. I like to be kept informed about everything that's happening here at Parks. How can the project office expect to get support out of the functional departments if we're kept in the dark until the very last minute? My people have been working with the existing materials for the last two months and you're telling us that it was all for nothing. Now you're giving us a material that's so new that we have no information on it whatsoever. We're now going to have to play catch-up, and that's going to cost you plenty."

One week before the 180-day milestone meeting, Gary submitted the handout package to Lord Industries for preliminary review. An hour later the phone rang.

Customer: "We've just read your handout. Where did this new material come from? How come we were not informed that this work was going on? You know, of course, that our customer, the Army, will be at this meeting. How can we explain this to them? We're postponing the review meeting until all of our people have analyzed the data and are prepared to make a decision.

"The purpose of a review or interchange meeting is to exchange information when *both* parties have familiarity with the topic. Normally, we (Lord Industries) require almost weekly interchange meetings with our other customers because we don't trust them. We disregarded this policy with Parks Corporation based upon past working relationships. But with the new state of developments, you have forced us to revert to our previous position, since we now question Parks Corporation's integrity in communicating with us. At first we believed this was due to an inexperienced program manager. Now, we're not sure."

Gary Anderson: "I wonder if the real reason we have these interchange meetings isn't to show our people that Lord Industries doesn't trust us. You're creating a hell of a lot of work for us, you know."

Customer: "You people put yourself in this position. Now you have to live with it."

Two weeks later Lord reluctantly agreed that the new material offered the greatest promise. Three weeks later the design review meeting was held. The Army was definitely not pleased with the prime contractor's recommendation to put a new untested material into a multi-million-dollar effort.

The Communications Breakdown

During the week following the design review meeting Gary planned to make the first verification mix in order to establish final specifications for selection of the raw materials. Unfortunately, the manufacturing plans were a week behind schedule, primarily because of Gary, since he had decided to reduce costs by accepting the responsibility for developing the bill of materials himself.

A meeting was called by Gary to consider rescheduling of the mix.

Gary Anderson: "As you know we're about a week to ten days behind schedule. We'll have to reschedule the verification mix for late next week."

Production Manager: "Our resources are committed until a month from now. You can't expect to simply call a meeting and have everything reshuffled for the Blue Spider Program. We should have been notified earlier. Engineering has the responsibility for preparing the bill of materials. Why aren't they ready?"

Engineering Integration: "We were never asked to prepare the bill of materials. But I'm sure that we could get it out if we work our people overtime for the next two days."

Gary: "When can we remake the mix?"

Production Manager: "We have to redo at least 500 sheets of paper every time we reschedule mixes. Not only that, we have to reschedule people on all three shifts. If we are to reschedule your mix, it will have to be performed on overtime. That's going to increase your costs. If that's agreeable with you, we'll try it. But this will be the first and last time that production will bail you out. There are procedures that have to be followed."

Testing Engineer: "I've been coming to these meetings since we kicked off this program. I think I speak for the entire engineering division when I say that the role that the director of engineering is playing in this program is suppressing individuality among our highly competent personnel. In new projects, especially those involving R&D, our people are not apt to stick their necks out. Now our people are becoming ostriches. If they're impeded from contributing, even in their own slight way, then you'll probably lose them before the project gets completed. Right now I feel that I'm wasting my time here. All I need are minutes of the team meetings and I'll be happy. Then I won't have to come to these pretend meetings anymore."

The purpose of the verification mix was to make a full-scale production run of the material to verify that there would be no material property changes in scale-up from the small mixes made in the R&D laboratories. After testing, it became obvious that the wrong lots of raw materials were used in the production verification mix.

A meeting was called by Lord Industries for an explanation of why the mistake had occurred and what the alternatives were.

Lord: "Why did the problem occur?"

Gary: "Well, we had a problem with the bill of materials. The result was that the mix had to be made on overtime. And when you work people on overtime, you have to be willing to accept mistakes as being a way of life. The energy cycles of our people are slow during the overtime hours."

Lord: "The ultimate responsibility has to be with you, the program manager. We, at Lord, think that you're spending too much time doing and not enough time managing. As the prime contractor, we have a hell-of-a-lot more at stake than you do. From now on we want documented weekly technical interchange meetings and closer interaction by our quality control section with yours."

Gary: "These additional team meetings are going to tie up our key people. I can't spare people to prepare handouts for weekly meetings with your people."

Lord: "Team meetings are a management responsibility. If Parks does not want the Blue Spider Program, I'm sure we can find another subcontractor. All you (Gary) have to do is give up taking the material vendors to lunch and you'll have plenty of time for handout preparation."

Gary left the meeting feeling as though he had just gotten raked over the coals. For the next two months, Gary worked sixteen hours a day, almost every day. Gary did not want to burden his staff with the responsibility of the handouts, so he began preparing them himself. He could have hired additional staff, but with such a tight budget, and having to remake the verification mix, cost overruns appeared inevitable.

As the end of the seventh month approached, Gary was feeling pressure from within Parks Corporation. The decision-making process appeared to be slowing down and Gary found it more and more difficult to motivate his people. In fact, the grapevine was referring to the Blue Spider Project as a loser, and some of his key people acted as though they were on a sinking ship.

By the time the eighth month rolled around, the budget had nearly been expended. Gary was tired of doing everything himself. "Perhaps I should have stayed an engineer," thought Gary. Elliot Grey and Gary Anderson had a meeting to see what could be salvaged. Grey agreed to get Gary additional corporate funding to complete the project. "But performance must be met, since there is a lot riding on the Blue Spider Project," asserted Grey. He called a team meeting to identify the program status.

Gary: "It's time to map out our strategy for the remainder of the program. Can engineering and production adhere to the schedule that I have laid out before you?"

Team Member: Engineering: "This is the first time that I've seen this schedule. You can't expect me to make a decision in the next ten minutes and commit the resources of my department. We're getting a little unhappy being kept in the dark until the last minute. What happened to effective planning?"

Gary: "We still have effective planning. We must adhere to the original schedule, or at least try to adhere to it. This revised schedule will do that."

Team Member: Engineering: "Look Gary! When a project gets in trouble it is usually the functional departments that come to the rescue. But if we're kept in the dark, then how can you expect us to come to your rescue? My boss wants to know, well in advance, every decision that you're contemplating with regard to our departmental resources. Right now, we . . ."

Gary: "Granted, we may have had a communications problem. But now we're in trouble and have to unite forces. What is your impression as to whether your department can meet the new schedule?"

Team Member: Engineering: "When the Blue Spider Program first got in trouble, my boss exercised his authority to make all departmental decisions regarding the program himself. I'm just a puppet. I have to check with him on everything."

Team Member: Production: "I'm in the same boat, Gary. You know we're not happy having to reschedule our facilities and people. We went through this once before. I also have to check with my boss before giving you an answer about the new schedule."

The following week the verification mix was made. Testing proceeded according to the revised schedule, and it looked as though the total schedule milestones could be met, provided that specifications could be adhered to.

Because of the revised schedule, some of the testing had to be performed on holidays. Gary wasn't pleased with asking people to work on Sundays and holidays, but had no choice, since the test matrix called for testing to be accomplished at specific times after end-of-mix.

A team meeting was called on Wednesday to resolve the problem of who would work on the holiday, which would occur on Friday, as well as staffing Saturday and Sunday. During the team meeting Gary became quite disappointed. Phil Rodgers, who had been Gary's test engineer since the project started, was assigned to a new project that the grapevine called Gable's new adventure. His replacement was a relatively new man, only eight months with the company. For an hour and a half, the team members argued about the little problems and continually avoided the major question, stating that they would have to first coordinate commitments with their boss. It was obvious to Gary that his team members were afraid to make major decisions and therefore "ate up" a lot of time on trivial problems.

On the following day, Thursday, Gary went to see the department manager responsible for testing, in hopes that he could use Phil Rodgers this weekend.

Department Manager: "I have specific instructions from the boss (director of engineering) to use Phil Rodgers on the new project. You'll have to see the boss if you want him back."

Gary Anderson: "But we have testing that must be accomplished this weekend. Where's the new man you assigned yesterday?"

Department Manager: "Nobody told me you had testing scheduled for this weekend. Half of my department is already on an extended weekend vacation, including Phil Rodgers and the new man. How come I'm always the last to know when we have a problem?"

Gary Anderson: "The customer is flying down his best people to observe this weekend's tests. It's too late to change anything. You and I can do the testing."

Department Manager: "Not on your life. I'm staying as far away as possible from the Blue Spider Project. I'll get you someone, but it won't be me. That's for sure!"

The weekend's testing went according to schedule. The raw data were made available to the customer under the stipulation that the final company position would be announced at the end of next month, after the functional departments had a chance to analyze it.

Final testing was completed during the second week of the ninth month. The initial results looked excellent. The materials were within contract specifications, and although they were new, both Gary and Lord's management felt that there would be little difficulty in convincing the Army that this was the way to go. Henry Gable visited Gary and congratulated him on a job well done.

All that now remained was the making of four additional full-scale verification mixes in order to determine how much deviation there would be in material properties between full-sized production-run mixes. Gary tried to get the customer to concur (as part of the original trade-off analysis) that two of the four production runs could be deleted. Lord's management refused, insisting that contractual requirements must be met at the expense of the contractor.

The following week, Elliot Grey called Gary in for an emergency meeting concerning expenditures to date.

Elliot Grey: "Gary, I just received a copy of the financial planning report for last quarter in which you stated that both the cost and performance of the Blue Spider Project were 75 percent complete. I don't think you realize what you've done. The target profit on the program was $200,000. Your memo authorized the vice-president and general manager to book 75 percent of that, or $150,000, for corporate profit spending for stockholders. I was planning on using all $200,000 together with the additional $300,000 I personally requested from corporate headquarters to bail you out. Now I have to go back to the vice-president and general manager and tell them that we've made a mistake and that we'll need an additional $150,000."

Gary Anderson: "Perhaps I should go with you and explain my error. Obviously, I take all responsibility."

Elliot Grey: "No, Gary. It's our error, not yours. I really don't think you want to be around the general manager when he sees red at the bottom of the page. It takes an act of God to get money back once corporate books it as profit. Perhaps you should reconsider project engineering as a career instead of program management. Your performance hasn't exactly been sparkling, you know."

Gary returned to his office quite disappointed. No matter how hard he worked, the bureaucratic red tape of project management seemed to always do him in. But late that afternoon, Gary's disposition improved. Lord Industries called to say that, after consultation with the Army, Parks Corporation would be awarded a sole-source contract for qualification and production of Spartan Missile components using the new longer-life raw materials. Both Lord and the Army felt that the sole-source contract was justified, provided that continued testing showed the same results, since Parks Corporation had all of the technical experience with the new materials.

Gary received a letter of congratulations from corporate headquarters, but no additional pay increase. The grapevine said that a substantial bonus was given to the director of engineering.

During the tenth month, results were coming back from the accelerated aging tests performed on the new materials. The results indicated that although the new materials would meet specifications, the age life would probably be less than five years. These numbers came as a shock to Gary. Gary and Paul Evans had a conference to determine the best strategy to follow.

Gary Anderson: "Well, I guess we're now in the fire instead of the frying pan. Obviously, we can't tell Lord Industries about these tests. We ran them on our own. Could the results be wrong?"

Paul Evans: "Sure, but I doubt it. There's always margin for error when you perform accelerated aging tests on new materials. There can be reactions taking place which we know nothing about. Furthermore, the accelerated aging tests may not even correlate well with actual aging. We must form a company position on this as soon as possible."

Gary Anderson: "I'm not going to tell anyone about this, especially Henry Gable. You and I will handle this. It will be my throat if word of this leaks out. Let's wait until we have the production contract in hand."

Paul Evans: "That's dangerous. This has to be a company position, not a project office position. We had better let them know upstairs."

Gary Anderson: "I can't do that. I'll take all responsibility. Are you with me on this?"

Paul Evans: "I'll go along. I'm sure I can find employment elsewhere when we open Pandora's Box. You had better tell the department managers to be quiet also."

Two weeks later, as the program was winding down into the testing for the final verification mix and final report development, Gary received an urgent phone call asking him to report immediately to Henry Gable's office.

Henry Gable: "When this project is over, you're through. You'll never hack it as a program manager, or possibly a good project engineer. We can't run projects around here without honesty and open communications. How the hell do you expect top management to support you when you start censoring bad news to the top? I don't like surprises. I like to get the bad news from the program managers and project engineers, not second-hand from the customer. And of course, we cannot forget the cost overrun. Why didn't you take some precautionary measures?"

Gary Anderson: "How could I when you were asking our people to do work such as accelerated aging tests that would be charged to my project and was not part of program plan? I don't think that I'm totally the blame for what's happened."

Henry Gable: "Gary, I don't think its necessary to argue the point any further. I'm willing to give you back your old job, in engineering. I hope you didn't lose too many friends while working in program management. Finish up final testing and the program report. Then I'll reassign you."

Gary returned to his office and put his feet up on the desk. "Well," thought Gary, "perhaps I'm better off in engineering. At least I can see my wife and kids once in a while." As Gary began writing the final report, the phone rang:

Functional Manager: "Hello Gary. I just thought I'd call to find out what charge number you want us to use for experimenting with this new procedure to determine accelerated age life."

Gary Anderson: "Don't call me! Call Gable. After all, the Blue Spider Project is his baby."

CASE STUDY: GREYSON CORPORATION

Greyson Corporation was formed in 1940 by three scientists from the University of California. The major purpose of the company was research and development for advanced military weaponry. Following World War II Greyson became a leader in the field of Research and Development. By the mid 1950s, Greyson employed over 200 scientists and engineers.

The fact that Greyson handled only R&D contracts was advantageous. First of all, all of the scientists and engineers were dedicated to R&D activities, not having to share their loyalties with production programs. Second, a strong functional organization was established. The project management function was the responsibility of the functional manager whose department would perform the majority of the work. Working relationships between departments were excellent.

By the late fifties Greyson was under new management. Almost all R&D programs called for establishment of qualification and production planning as well. As a result, Greyson decided to enter into the production of military weapons as well, and capture some of the windfall profits of the production market. This required a major reorganization from a functional to a matrix structure. Personnel problems occurred, but none that proved major catastrophies.

In 1964 Greyson entered into the aerospace market with the acquisition of a subcontract for the propulsion unit of the Hercules Missile. The contract was projected at $200 million over a five-year period, with excellent possibilities for follow-on work. Between 1964 and 1968 Greyson developed a competent technical staff composed mainly of young, untested college graduates. The majority of the original employees who were still there were in managerial positions. Greyson never had any layoffs. In addition, Greyson had excellent career development programs for almost all employees.

Between 1967 and 1971 the Department of Defense procurement for new Weapon Systems was on the decline. Greyson relied heavily on their two major production programs, Hercules and Condor II, both of which gave great promise for continued procurement. Greyson also had some thirty smaller R&D contracts as well as two smaller production contracts for hand weapons.

Because R&D money was becoming scarce, Greyson's management decided to phase out many of the R&D activities and replace them with lucrative production contracts. Greyson believed that they could compete with anyone in regard to low-cost production. Under this philosophy, the R&D community was reduced to minimum levels necessary to support in-house activities. The director of engineering froze all hiring except for job-shoppers with special talents. All nonessential engineering personnel were transferred to production units.

In 1972, Greyson entered into competition with Cameron Aerospace Corporation for development, qualification, and testing of the Navy's new Neptune Missile. The competition was an eight-motor shoot-off during the last ten months of 1973. Cameron Corporation won the contract owing to technical merit. Greyson Corporation, however, had gained valuable technical information in rocket motor development and testing. The loss of the Neptune Program made it clear to Greyson's management that aerospace technology was changing too fast for Greyson to maintain a passive position. Even though funding was limited, Greyson increased the technical staff and soon found great success in winning research and development contracts.

By 1975, Greyson had developed a solid aerospace business base. Profits had increased by 30 percent. Greyson Corporation expanded from a company with 200 employees in 1964 to 1,800 employees in 1975. The Hercules Program, which began in 1964, was providing yearly follow-on contracts. All indications projected a continuation of the Hercules Program through 1982.

Cameron Corporation, on the other hand, had found 1975 a difficult year. The Neptune Program was the only major contract that Cameron Corporation maintained. The current production buy for the Neptune Missile was scheduled for completion in August 1975 with no follow-on work earlier than January 1976. Cameron Corporation anticipated that overhead rates would increase sharply prior to next buy. The cost per motor would increase from $55,000 to $75,000 for a January procurement, $85,000 for a March procurement, and $125,000 for an August procurement.

In February 1975, the Air Force asked Greyson Corporation if they would be interested in submitting a sole-source bid for production and qualification of the Neptune Missile. The Air Force considered Cameron's position as uncertain, and wanted to maintain a qualified vendor should Cameron Corporation decide to get out of the aerospace business.

Greyson submitted a bid of $30 million for qualification and testing of thirty Neptune motors over a thirty-month period beginning in January 1976. Current testing of the Neptune Missile indicated that the minimum motor age life would extend through January 1979. This meant that production funds over the next 30 months could be diverted toward requalification of a new vendor and still meet production requirements for 1979.

In August of 1975, upon delivery of the last Neptune Rocket to the Air Force, Cameron Corporation announced that without an immediate production contract for Neptune follow-on work it would close its door and get out of the aerospace business. Cameron Corporation invited Greyson Corporation to interview all of their key employees for possible work on the Neptune Requalification Program.

Greyson hired thirty-five of Cameron's key people to begin work in October 1975. The key people would be assigned to ongoing Greyson programs to become familiar with Greyson methods. Greyson's lower-level management was very unhappy about bringing in these thirty-five employees for fear that they would be placed in slots that could have resulted in promotions for some of Greyson's people. Management then decreed that these thirty-five people would work solely on the Neptune Program, and other vacancies would be filled, as required, from the Hercules and Condor II programs. Greyson estimated that the cost of employing these thirty-five people was approximately $150,000 per month, almost all of which was being absorbed through overhead. Without these thirty-five people, Greyson did not believe that they would have won the contract as sole-source procurement. Other competitors could have "grabbed" these key people and forced an open bidding situation.

Because of the increased overhead rate, Greyson maintained a minimum staff to prepare for contract negotiations and document preparation. To minimize costs, the directors of engineering and program management gave the Neptune program office the authority to make decisions for departments and divisions that were without representation in the program office. Top management had complete confidence in the program office personnel because of their past performance on other programs and years of experience.

In December 1975, the Department of Defense announced that spending was being curtailed sharply and that funding limitations made it impossible to begin the qualification program before July 1976. To make matters worse, consideration was being made for a compression of the requalification program to twenty-five motors in a twenty-month period. However, long-lead funding for raw materials would be available.

After lengthy consideration, Greyson decided to maintain its present position and retain the thirty-five Cameron employees by assigning them to in-house programs. The

Neptune program office was still maintained for preparations to support contract negotiations, rescheduling of activities for a shorter program, and long-lead procurement.

In May of 1976, contract negotiations began between the Navy and Greyson. At the beginning of contract negotiations, the Navy stated the three key elements for negotiations:

1. Maximum funding was limited to the 1975 quote for a 30-motor/30-month program.
2. The amount of money available for the last six months of 1976 was limited to $3.7 million.
3. The contract would be cost plus incentive fee (CPIF).

After three weeks of negotiations there appeared a stalemate. The Navy contended that the production manhours in the proposal were at the wrong level on the learning curves. It was further argued that Greyson should be a lot "smarter" now because of the thirty-five Cameron employees and because of experience learned during the 1971 shoot-off with Cameron Corporation during the initial stages of the Neptune Program.

Since the negotiation teams could not agree, top level management of the Navy and Greyson Corporation met to iron out the differences. An agreement was finally reached on a figure of $28.5 million. This was $1.5 million below Greyson's original estimate to do the work. Management, however, felt that, by "tightening our belts," the work could be accomplished within budget.

The program began on July 1, 1976 with the distribution of the department budgets by the program office. Almost all of the department managers were furious. Not only were the budgets below their original estimates, but the thirty-five Cameron employees were earning salaries above the department mean salary, thus reducing total manhours even further. Almost all department managers asserted that cost overruns would be the responsibility of the program office and not the individual departments.

By November 1976, Greyson was in trouble. The Neptune Program was on target for cost but 35 percent behind for work completion. Department managers refused to take responsibility for certain tasks that were usually considered to be joint department responsibilities. Poor communication between program office and department managers provided additional discouragement. Department managers refused to have their employees work on Sunday.

Even with all this, program management felt that catch-up was still possible. The thirty-five former Cameron employees were performing commendable work equal to their counterparts on other programs. Management considered that the potential cost overrun situation was not in the critical stage, and that more time should be permitted before considering corporate funding.

In December 1976, the Department of Defense announced that there would be no further buys of the Hercules Missile. This announcement was a severe blow to Greyson's management. Not only were they in danger of having to lay off 500 employees, but overhead rates would rise considerably. There was an indication last year that there would be no further buys, but management did not consider the indications positive enough to require corporate strategy changes.

Although Greyson was not unionized, there was a possibility of a massive strike if

Greyson career employees were not given seniority over the thirty five former Cameron employees in case of layoffs.

By February, 1977, the cost situation was clear:

1. The higher overhead rates threatened to increase total program costs by $1 million on the Neptune Program.
2. Because the activities were behind schedule, the catch-up phases would have to be made in a higher salary and overhead rate quarter, thus increasing total costs further.
3. Inventory costs were increasing. Items purchased during long-lead funding were approaching shelf-life limits. Cost impact might be as high as $1 million.

The vice-president and general manager considered the Neptune Program critical to the success and survival of Greyson Corporation. The directors and division heads were ordered to take charge of the program. The following options were considered:

1. Perform overtime work to get back on schedule.
2. Delay program activities in hopes that the Navy can come up with additional funding.
3. Review current material specifications in order to increase material shelf-life, thus lowering inventory and procurement costs.
4. Begin laying off noncritical employees.
5. Purchase additional tooling and equipment (at corporate expense) so that schedule requirements can be met on target.

On March 1, 1977, Greyson gave merit salary increases to the key employees on all in-house programs. At the same time, Greyson laid off 700 employees, some of whom were seasoned veterans. By March 15, Greyson employees formed a union and went out on strike.

CASE STUDY: MIS PROJECT MANAGEMENT AT FIRST NATIONAL BANK

During the last five years, First National Bank (FNB) has been one of the fastest-growing banks in the Midwest. The holding company of the bank has been actively involved in purchasing small banks thoughout the state of Ohio. This expansion and the resulting increase of operations had been attended by considerable growth in numbers of employees and in the complexity of the organizational structure. In five years the staff of the bank has increased by 35 percent, and total assets have grown by 70 percent. FNB management is eagerly looking forward to a change in the Ohio banking laws that will allow statewide branch banking.

ISD History

Data processing at FNB has grown at a much faster pace than the rest of the bank. The systems and programming staff grew from twelve in 1970 to over seventy-five during the first part of 1977. Because of several future projects, the staff is expected to increase by 50 percent during the next two years.

Prior to 1972, the information services department reported to the executive vice-president of the Consumer Banking and Operations Division. As a result, the first banking applications to be computerized were in the demand deposit, savings, and consumer credit banking areas. The computer was seen as a tool to speed up the processing of consumer transactions. Little effort was expended to meet the informational requirements of the rest of the bank. This caused a high-level conflict, since each major operating organization of the bank did not have equal access to systems and programming resources. The management of FNB became increasingly aware of the benefits that could accrue from a realignment of the bank's organization into one that would be better attuned to the total information requirements of the corporation.

In 1972 the Information Services Division (ISD) was created. ISD was removed from the Consumer Banking Operations Division to become a separate division reporting directly to the president. An organization chart depicting the Information Services Division is shown in Exhibit 10–1.

Priorities Committee

During 1972 the Priorities Committee was formed. It consists of the chief executive officer of each of the major operating organizations whose activities are directly affected by the need for new or revised information systems. The Priorities Committee was established to ensure that the resources of systems and programming personnel and computer hardware would be used only on those information systems that can best be cost-justified. Divisions represented on the committee are included in Exhibit 10–2.

Exhibit 10–1. Information Services Division Organization Chart.

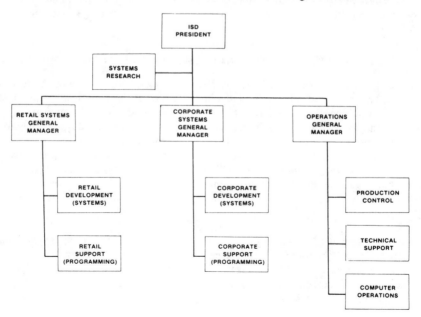

Exhibit 10–2. First National Bank Organization Chart.

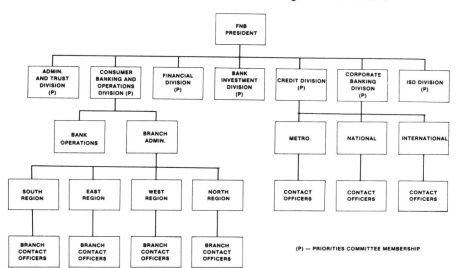

The Priorities Committee meets monthly to reaffirm previously set priorities and rank new projects introduced since the last meeting. Bank policy states that the only way to obtain funds for an information development project is to submit a request to the Priorities Committee and have it approved and ranked in overall priority order for the bank. Placing potential projects in ranked sequence is done by the senior executives. The primary document used for Priorities Committee review is called the project proposal.

The Project Proposal Life Cycle

When a user department determines a need for the development or enhancement of an information system, it is required to prepare a draft containing a statement of the problem from its functional perspective. The problem statement is sent to the president of ISD who authorizes systems research (see Exhibit 10–1) to prepare an impact statement. This impact statement will include a general overview from ISD's perspective of:

- Project feasibility
- Project complexity
- Conformity with long-range ISD plans
- Estimated ISD resource commitment
- Review of similar requests
- Unique characteristics/problems
- Broad estimate of total costs

The problem and impact statements are then presented to the members of the Priorities Committee for their review. The proposals are preliminary in nature, but they permit the broad concept (with a very approximate cost attached to it) to be reviewed by the executive group to see if there is serious interest in pursuing the idea. If the interest level of the committee is low, then the idea is rejected. However, if the Priorities Committee members feel the concept has merit, they authorize the systems research group of ISD to prepare a full-scale project proposal that contains:

- A detailed statement of the problem
- Identification of alternative solutions
- Impact of request on:
  - User division
  - ISD
  - Other operating divisions
- Estimated costs of solutions
- Schedule of approximate task duration
- Cost/benefit analysis of solutions
- Long-range implications
- Recommended course of action

After the project proposal is prepared by systems research, the user sponsor must review the proposal and appear at the next Priorities Committee meeting to speak in favor of the approval and priority level of the proposed work. The project proposal is evaluated by the committee and either dropped, tabled for further review, or assigned a priority relative to ongoing projects and available resources.

The final output of a Priorities Committee meeting is an updated list of project proposals in priority order with an accompanying milestone schedule that indicates the approximate time span required to implement each of the proposed projects.

The net result of this process is that the priority setting for systems development is done by a cross-section of executive management; it does not revert by default to data processing management. Priority setting, if done by data processing, can lead to misunderstanding and dissatisfaction by sponsors of the projects that did not get ranked high enough to be funded in the near future. The project proposal cycle at FNB is included in Exhibit 10–3. Once a project has risen to the top of the ranked priority list, it is assigned to the appropriate systems group for systems definition, system design and development, and system implementation.

The time spent by systems research in producing impact statements and project proposals is considered to be overhead by ISD. No systems research time is directly charged to the development of information systems.

Project Life Cycle

As noted before, the systems and programming staff of ISD has increased in size rapidly and is expected to expand 50 percent during the next two years. As a rule, most new employees have previous data processing experience and training in various systems methodologies. ISD management recently implemented a project management system dedicated to providing a uniform step-by-step methodology for the development of management information systems. All project work is covered by tasks that

Exhibit 10–3. The Project Proposal Cycle.

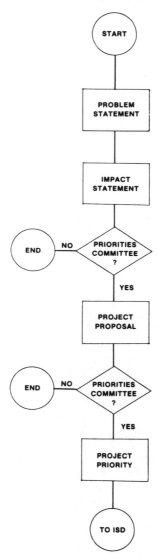

make up the information project development life cycle at FNB. The subphases used by ISD in the project life cycle are:

1. Systems Definition
   a. Project plan
   b. User requirements

    c. Systems definition
    d. Advisability study
2. Systems Design and Development
    a. Preliminary systems design
    b. Subsystems design
    c. Program design
    d. Programming and testing
3. System Implementation
    a. System implementation
    b. System test
    c. Production control turnover
    d. User training
    e. System acceptance

Project Estimating

The project management system contains a list of all normal tasks and subtasks (over 400) to be performed during the life cycle of a development project. The project manager must examine all the tasks to determine if they apply to his project. He must insert additional tasks if required and delete tasks that do not apply. The project manager next estimates the amount of time (in hours) to complete each task of each subphase of the project life cycle.

The estimating process of the project management system uses a "moving window" concept. ISD management feels that detailed cost estimating and time schedules are only meaningful for the next subphase of a project, where the visibility of the tasks to be performed is quite clear. Beyond that subphase, a more summary method of estimating is relied upon. As the project progresses, new segments of the project gain visibility. Detailed estimates are made for the next major portion of the project, and summary estimates are done beyond that until the end of the project.

Estimates are performed at five intervals during the project life cycle. When the project is first initiated, the funding is based on the original estimates, which are derived from the list of normal tasks and subtasks. At this time, the subphases through the advisability study are estimated in detail, and summary estimates are prepared for the rest of the tasks in the project. Once the project has progressed through the advisability study, the preliminary systems design is estimated in detail, and the balance of the project is estimated in a more summary fashion. Estimates are conducted in this manner until the systems implementation plan is completed and the scope of the remaining subphases of the project is known. This multiple estimating process is used because it is almost impossible at the beginning of many projects to be certain of what the magnitude of effort will be later on in the project life cycle.

Funding of Projects

The project plan is the official document for securing funding from the sponsor in the user organization. The project plan must be completed and approved by the project manager before activity can begin on the user requirements subphase (1b). An initial stage in developing a project plan includes the drawing of a network that identifies each of the tasks to be done in the appropriate sequence for their execution. The project plan must include a milestone schedule, a cost estimate, and a budget request. It is submitted to the appropriate general manager of systems and programming for review so that an understanding can be reached of how the estimates were prepared and why the costs and schedules are as shown. At this time the general manager can get an idea of the quantity of systems and programming resources required by the project. The general manager next sets up a meeting with the project manager and the user sponsor to review the project plan and obtain funding from the user organization.

The initial project funding is based on an estimate that includes a number of assumptions concerning the scope of the project. Once certain key milestones in the project have been achieved, the visibility on the balance of the project becomes much clearer, and reestimates are performed. The reestimates may result in refunding if there has been a significant change in the project. The normal milestone refunding points are as follows:

1. After the advisability study (1d)
2. After the preliminary systems design (2a)
3. After the program design (2c)
4. After system implementation (3a)

The refunding process is similar to the initial funding with the exception that progress information is presented on the status of the work and reasons are given to explain deviations from project expenditure projections. A revised project plan is prepared for each milestone refunding meeting.

During the systems design and development stage, design freezes are issued by the project manager to users announcing that no additional changes will be accepted to the project beyond that point. The presence of these design freezes is outlined at the beginning of the project. Following the design freeze, no additional changes will be accepted unless the project is reestimated at a new level and approved by the user sponsor.

System Quality Reviews

The key element in ensuring user involvement in the new system is the conducting of quality reviews. In the normal system cycles at FNB, there are ten quality reviews, seven of which are participated in jointly by users and data processing personnel, and three of which are technical reviews by data processing personnel only. An important side benefit of this review process is that users of a new system are forced to become involved in and are permitted to make a contribution to the systems design.

Each of the quality review points coincides with the end of a subphase in the project life cycle. The review must be held at the completion of one subphase to obtain authorization to begin work on the tasks of the next subphase of the project.

All tasks and subtasks assigned to members of the project team should end in some "deliverable" for the project documentation. The first step in conducting a quality review is to assemble the documentation produced during the subphase for distribution to the Quality Review Board. The Quality Review Board consists of between two and eight people who are appointed by the project manager with the approval of the project sponsor and the general manager of systems and programming. The minutes of the quality review meeting are written either to express "concurrence" with the subsystem quality or to recommend changes to the system that must be completed before the next subphase can be started. By this process the system is fine-tuned to the requirements of the members of the review group at the end of each subphase in the system. The members of the Quality Review Board charge their time to the project budget.

Quality review points and review board make-up are as follows:

Review	*Review Board*
User requirements	User oriented
Systems definition	User oriented
Advisability study	User oriented
Preliminary systems design	User oriented
Subsystems design	Users and D.P.
Program design	D.P.
Programming and testing	D.P.
System implementation	User oriented
System test	User oriented
Production control turnover	D.P.

To summarize, the quality review evaluates the quality of project subphase results, including design adequacy and proof of accomplishment in meeting project objectives. The review board authorizes work to progress based upon their detailed knowledge that all required tasks and subtasks of each subphase have been successfully completed and documented.

Project Team Staffing

Once a project has risen to the top of the priority list, the appropriate manager of systems development appoints a project manager from his staff of analysts. The project manager has a short time to review the project proposal created by systems research before developing a project plan. The project plan must be approved by the general manager of systems and programming and the user sponsor before the project can be funded and work started on the user requirements subphase.

The project manager is "free" to spend as much time as required in reviewing the project proposal and creating the project plan; however, his time is "charged" to the project at a rate of $26 per hour. The project manager must negotiate with his "supervisor," the manager of systems development, to obtain the required systems analysts for the project, starting with the user requirements subphase. The project manager must obtain programming resources from the manager of systems support. Schedule delays caused by a lack of systems or programming resources are to be communicated to the general manager by the project manager. All ISD personnel working on a project charge their time at a rate of $26 per hour. All computer time is billed at a rate of $64 per hour.

There are no user personnel on the project team; all team members are from ISD.

Corporate Data Base

John Hart had for several years seen the need to use the computer to support the corporate marketing effort of the bank. Despite the fact that the majority of the bank's profits were from corporate customers, most information systems effort was directed at speeding up transactions handling for small unprofitable accounts.

Mr. Hart had extensive experience in the Corporate Banking Division of the bank. He realized the need to consolidate information about corporate customers from many areas of the bank into one "corporate data base." From this information corporate banking services could be developed not only to better serve the corporate customers, but also to contribute heavily to the profit structure of the bank through repricing of services.

The absence of a corporate data base meant that no one individual knew what total banking services a corporate customer was using, because corporate services are provided by many banking departments. It was also impossible to determine how profitable a corporate customer was to the bank. Contact officers did not have regularly scheduled calls. They serviced corporate customers almost on a hit-and-miss basis. Unfortunately, many customers were "sold" on a service because they walked in the door and requested it. Mr. Hart felt that there was a vast market of untapped corporate customers in Ohio who would purchase services from the bank if they were contacted and "sold" in a professional manner. A corporate data base could be used to develop corporate profiles to help contact officers sell likely services to corporations.

Mr. Hart knew that data about corporate customers were being processed in many departments of the bank, but mainly in the following divisions:

- Corporate Banking
- Corporate Trust
- Consumer Banking

He also realized that much of the information was processed in manual systems, some was processed by time-sharing at various vendors, and other information was computerized in many internal information systems.

The upper management of FNB must have agreed with Mr. Hart because in December of 1976 the Corporate Marketing Division was formed with John Hart as its executive vice-president. Mr. Hart was due to retire within the year but was honored to be selected for the new position. He agreed to stay with the bank until "his" new system was "off the ground." He immediately composed a problem statement and sent it to the ISD. Systems research compiled a preliminary impact statement. At the next Priorities Committee meeting, a project proposal was authorized to be done by systems research.

The project proposal was completed by systems research in record time. Most information was obtained from Mr. Hart. He had been thinking about the systems requirements for years and possessed vast experience in almost all areas of the bank. Other user divisions and departments were often "too busy" when approached for information. A common reply to a request for information was "the project is John's baby; he knows what we need."

The project proposal as prepared by systems research recommended the following:

- Interfaces should be designed to extract information from existing computerized systems for the corporate data base (CDB).
- Time-sharing systems should be brought in-house to be interfaced with the CDB.
- Information should be collected from manual systems to be integrated into the CDB on a temporary basis.
- Manual systems should be consolidated and computerized, potentially causing a reorganization of some departments.
- Information analysis and flow for all departments and divisions having contact with corporate customers should be coordinated by the Corporate Marketing Division.
- All corporate data base analysis should be done by the Corporate Marketing Division staff, using either a user-controlled report writer or interactive inquiry.

The project proposal was presented at the next Priorities Committee meeting where it was approved and rated as the highest-priority MIS development project in the bank. Mr. Hart became the user sponsor for the CDB project.

The project proposal was sent to the manager of corporate development, who appointed Jim Gunn as project manager from the staff of analysts in corporate development. Jim Gunn was the most experienced project manager available. His prior experience consisted of successful projects in the Financial Division of the bank.

Jim reviewed the project proposal and started to work on his project plan. He was aware that the corporate analyst group was presently understaffed but was assured by his manager, the manager of corporate development, that resources would be available for the user requirements subphase. He had many questions concerning the scope of the project and the interrelationship between the Corporate Marketing Division and the other users of corporate marketing data. But each meeting with Mr. Hart ended with the same comment: "This is a waste of time. I've already been over this with systems research. Let's get moving." Jim also was receiving pressure from the general manager to "hurry up" with the project plan. Jim therefore quickly prepared his project plan, which included a general milestone schedule for subphase completion, a general cost estimate, and a request for funding. The project plan was reviewed by the general manager and signed by Mr. Hart.

Jim Gunn anticipated the need to have four analysts assigned to the project and went to his manager to see who was available. He was told that two junior analysts were available now and another analyst should be free next week. No senior analysts were available. Jim notified the general manager that the CDB schedule would probably be delayed because of a lack of resources, but received no response.

Jim assigned tasks to the members of the team and explained the assignments and the schedule. Since the project was understaffed, Jim assigned a heavy load of tasks to himself.

During the next two weeks the majority of the meetings set up to document user requirements were canceled by the user departments. Jim notified Mr. Hart of the problem and was assured that steps would be taken to correct the problem. Future meetings with the users in the Consumer Banking and Corporate Banking Divisions became very hostile. Jim soon discovered that many individuals in these divisions did not see the need for the corporate data base. They resented spending their time in meetings documenting the CDB requirements. They were afraid that the CDB project would lead to a shift of many of their responsibilities and functions to the Corporate Marketing Division.

Mr. Hart was also unhappy. The CDB team was spending more time than was budgeted in documenting user requirements. If this trend continued, a revised budget would have to be submitted to the Priorities Committee for approval. He was also growing tired of ordering individuals in the user departments to keep appointments with the CDB team. Mr. Hart could not understand the resistance to his project.

Jim Gunn kept trying to obtain analysts for his project but was told by his manager that none were available. Jim explained that the quality of work done by the junior analysts was not "up to par" because of lack of experience. Jim complained that he could not adequately supervise the work quality because he was forced to complete many of the analysis tasks himself. He also noted that the quality review of the user requirements subphase was scheduled for next month, making it extremely critical that experienced analysts be assigned to the project. No new personnel were assigned to the project. Jim thought about contacting the general manager again to explain his need for more experienced analysts, but did not. He was due for a semi-yearly evaluation from his manager in two weeks.

Even though he knew the quality of the work was below standards, Jim was determined to get the project done on schedule with the resources available to him. He drove both himself and the team very hard during the next few weeks. The quality review of the user requirements subphase was held on schedule. Over 90 percent of the assigned tasks had to be redone before the Quality Review Board would sign-off on the review. Jim Gunn was "removed" as project manager.

Three senior analysts and a new project manager were assigned to the CDB project. The project received additional funding from the Priorities Committee. The user requirements subphase was completely redone despite vigorous protests from the Consumer Banking and Corporate Banking divisions.

Within the next three months the following events happened:

- The new project manager resigned to accept a position with another firm.
- John Hart took early retirement.
- The CDB project was "tabled."

CORWIN CORPORATION

By June 1983, Corwin Corporation had grown into a $150 million per year corporation with an international reputation for manufacturing low-cost, high-quality rubber components. Corwin maintained more than a dozen different product lines, all of which were sold as off-the-shelf items in department stores, hardware stores, and automotive parts distributors. The name "Corwin" was now synonymous with "quality." This provided management with the luxury of having products that maintained extremely long life cycles.

Organizationally, Corwin had maintained the same structure for more than fifteen years. (See Exhibit 10–4.) The top management of Corwin Corporation was highly conservative and believed in a marketing approach to find new markets for existing product lines rather than to explore for new products. Under this philosophy, Corwin maintained a small R&D group whose mission was simply to evaluate state-of-the-art technology and its application to existing product lines.

Corwin's reputation was so good that they continually received inquiries about the manufacturing of specialty products. Unfortunately, the conservative nature of Corwin's management created a "do not rock the boat" atmosphere opposed to taking any type of risks. A management policy was established to evaluate all specialty-product requests. The policy required the answering of the following questions:

- Will the specialty product provide the same profit margin (20 percent) as existing product lines?
- What is the total projected profitability to the company in terms of follow-on contracts?
- Can the specialty product be developed into a product line?
- Can the specialty product be produced with minimum disruption to existing product lines and manufacturing operations?

These stringent requirements forced Corwin to no-bid more than 90 percent of all specialty product inquiries.

Corwin Corporation was a marketing-driven organization although manufacturing often had different ideas. Almost all decisions were made by marketing with the exception of product pricing and estimating, which was a joint undertaking between manufacturing and marketing. Engineering was considered as merely a support group to marketing and manufacturing.

For specialty products, the project managers would always come out of marketing

Exhibit 10–4. Organizational Chart for Corwin Corporation.

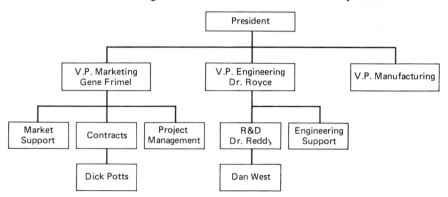

even during the R&D phase of development. The company's approach was that if the specialty product should mature into a full product line, then there should be a product line manager assigned right at the onset.

The Peters Company Project

In 1980, Corwin accepted a specialty product assignment from Peters Company because of the potential for follow-on work. In 1981 and 1982 and again in 1983 profitable follow-on contracts were received, and a good working relationship developed, despite Peters's reputation for being a difficult customer to work with.

On December 7, 1982, Gene Frimel, the vice-president of marketing at Corwin received a rather unusual phone call from Dr. Frank Delia, the marketing vice-president at Peters Company.

Delia: "Gene, I have a rather strange problem on my hands. Our R&D group has $250,000 committed for research toward development of a new rubber product material, and we simply do not have the available personnel or talent to undertake the project. We have to go outside. We'd like your company to do the work. Our testing and R&D facilities are already overburdened."

Frimel: "Well, as you know Frank, we are not a research group even though we've done this once before for you. And furthermore, I would never be able to sell our management on such an undertaking. Let some other company do the R&D work and then we'll take over on the production end."

Delia: "Let me explain our position on this. We've been 'burned' several times in the past. Projects like this generate several patents, and the R&D company almost always requires that our contracts give them royalties or first refusal for manufacturing rights."

Frimel: "I understand your problem, but it's not within our capabilities. This project, if undertaken, could disrupt parts of our organization. We're already operating lean in engineering."

Delia: "Look Gene! The bottom line is this: we have complete confidence in your manufacturing ability to such a point that we're willing to commit to a five-year production contract if the product can be developed. That makes it extremely profitable for you."

Frimel: "You've just gotten me interested. What additional details can you give me?"

Delia: "All I can give you is a rough set of performance specifications that we'd like to meet. Obviously, some trade-offs are possible."

Frimel: "When can you get the specification sheet to me?"

Delia: "You'll have it tomorrow morning. I'll ship it overnight express."

Frimel: "Good! I'll have my people look at it, but we won't be able to get you an answer until after the first of the year. As you know, our plant is closed down for the last two weeks in December, and most of our people have already left for extended vacations."

Delia: "That's not acceptable! My management wants a signed, sealed, and delivered contract by the end of this month. If this is not done, corporate will reduce our budget for 1983 by $250,000 thinking that we've 'bitten off more than we can chew.' Actually, I need your answer within forty-eight hours so that I'll have some time to find another source."

Frimel: "You know, Frank, today is December 7, Pearl Harbor Day. Why do I feel as though the sky is about to fall in?"

Delia: "Don't worry Gene! I'm not going to drop any bombs on you. Just remember, all that we have available is $250,000, and the contract must be a firm-fixed-price effort. We anticipate a six-month project with $125,000 paid upon contract signing and the balance at project termination."

Frimel: "I still have that ominous feeling, but I'll talk to my people. You'll hear from us with a go or no-go decision within forty-eight hours. I'm scheduled to go on a cruise in the Caribbean, and my wife and I are leaving this evening. One of my people will get back to you on this matter."

Gene Frimel had a problem. All bid and no-bid decisions were made by a four-man committee composed of the president and the three vice-presidents. The president and the vice-president for manufacturing were on vacation. Frimel met with Dr. Royce, the vice-president of engineering, and explained the situation.

Royce: "You know, Gene, I totally support projects like this because it would help our technical people grow intellectually. Unfortunately, my vote never appears to carry any weight."

Frimel: "The profitability potential as well as the development of good customer relations makes this attractive, but I'm not sure we want to accept such a risk. A failure could easily destroy our good working relationship with Peters Company."

Royce: "I'd have to look at the specification sheets before assessing the risks, but I would like to give it a shot."

Frimel: "I'll try to reach our president by phone."

By late afternoon, Frimel was fortunate enough to be able to contact the president and received a reluctant authorization to proceed. The problem now was how to prepare a proposal within the next two to three days and be prepared to make an oral presentation to Peters Company.

Frimel: "The boss gave his blessing, Royce, and the ball is in your hands. I'm leaving for vacation, and you'll have total responsibility for the proposal and presentation. Delia wants the presentation this weekend. You should have his specification sheets tomorrow morning."

Royce: "Our R&D Director, Dr. Reddy, left for vacation this morning. I wish he were here to help me price out the work and select the project manager. I assume that, in this case, the project manager will come out of engineering rather than marketing."

Frimel: "Yes, I agree. Marketing should not have any role in this effort. It's your baby all the way. And as for the pricing effort, you know our bid will be for $250,000. Just work backwards to justify the numbers. I'll assign one of our contracting people to assist you in the pricing. I hope I can find someone who has experience in this type of effort. I'll call Delia and tell him we'll bid it with an unsolicited proposal."

Royce selected Dan West, one of the R&D scientists, to act as the project leader. Royce had severe reservations about doing this without the R&D director, Dr. Reddy, being actively involved. With Reddy on vacation, Royce had to make an immediate decision.

On the following morning, the specification sheets arrived and Royce, West, and Dick Potts, a contracts man, began preparing the proposal. West prepared the direct labor man-hours, and Royce provided the costing data and pricing rates. Potts, being completely unfamiliar with this type of effort, simply acted as an observer and provided legal advice when necessary. Potts allowed Royce to make all decisions even though the contracts man was considered the official representative of the president.

Finally completed two days later, the proposal was actually a ten-page letter that simply contained the cost summaries (see Exhibit 10–5) and the engineering intent. West estimated that *thirty tests* would be required. The test matrix described only the test conditions for the first five tests. The remaining twenty-five test conditions would be determined at a later date, jointly by Peters and Corwin personnel.

On Sunday morning, a meeting was held at Peters Company, and the proposal was accepted. Delia gave Royce a letter-of-intent authorizing Corwin Corporation to begin working on the project immediately. The final contract would not be available for signing until late January, and the letter-of-intent simply stated that Peters Company would assume all costs until such time that the contract was signed or the effort terminated.

West was truly excited about being selected as the project manager and being able to interface with the customer, a luxury that was usually given only to the marketing personnel. Although Corwin Corporation was closed for two weeks over Christmas, West still went into the office to prepare the project schedules and to identify the support he would need in the other areas, thinking that if he presented this information to management on the first day back to work, they would be convinced that he had everything under control.

Exhibit 10–5. Proposal Cost Summaries.

Direct labor and support	$ 30,000
Testing (30 tests at $2,000 each)	60,000
Overhead at 100%	90,000
Materials	30,000
G&A (General & administrative, 10%)	21,000
Total	$231,000
Profit	19,000
Total	$250,000

The Work Begins . . .

On the first working day in January 1983, a meeting was held with the three vice-presidents and Dr. Reddy to discuss the support needed for the project. (West was not in attendance at this meeting, although all participants had a copy of his memo.)

Reddy: "I think we're heading for trouble in accepting this project. I've worked with Peters Company previously on R&D efforts, and they're tough to get along with. West is a good man, but I would never have assigned him as the project leader. His expertise is in managing internal rather than external projects. But, no matter what happens, I'll support West the best I can."

Royce: "You're too pessimistic. You have good people in your group and I'm sure you'll be able to give him the support he needs. I'll try to look in on the project every so often. West will still be reporting to you for this project. Try not to burden him too much with other work. This project is important to the company."

West spent the first few days after vacation soliciting the support that he needed from the other line groups. Many of the other groups were upset that they had not been informed earlier and were unsure as to what support they could provide. West met with Reddy to discuss the final schedules.

Reddy: "Your schedules look pretty good, Dan. I think you have a good grasp on the problem. You won't need very much help from me. I have a lot of work to do on other activities, so I'm just going to be in the background on this project. Just drop me a note every once in a while telling me what's going on. I don't need anything formal. Just a paragraph or two will suffice."

By the end of the third week, all of the raw materials had been purchased, and initial formulation and testing were ready to begin. In addition, the contract was ready for signature. The contract contained a clause specifying that Peters Company had the right to send an in-house representative into Corwin Corporation for the duration of the project. Peters Company informed Corwin that Patrick Ray would be the in-house representative, reporting to Delia, and would assume his responsibilities on or about February 15.

By the time Pat Ray appeared at Corwin Corporation, West had completed the first three tests. The results were not what was expected, but gave promise that Corwin was heading in the right direction. Pat Ray's interpretation of the tests was completely opposite to that of West. Ray thought that Corwin was "way off base," and redirection was needed.

Ray: "Look Dan! We have only six months to do this effort and we shouldn't waste our time on marginally acceptable data. These are the next five tests I'd like to see performed."

West: "Let me look over your request and review it with my people. That will take a couple of days, and, in the meanwhile, I'm going to run the other two tests as planned."

Ray's arrogant attitude bothered West. However, West decided that the project was too important to "knock heads" with Ray and simply decided to "cater" to Ray the best he could. This was not exactly the working relationship that West expected to have with the in-house representative.

West reviewed the test data and the new test matrix with engineering personnel, who felt that the test data were inconclusive as yet and preferred to withhold their opinion until the results of the fourth and fifth tests were made available. Although this displeased Ray, he agreed to wait a few more days if it meant getting Corwin Corporation "on the right track."

The fourth and fifth tests appeared to be marginally acceptable just as the first three were. Corwin's engineering people analyzed the data and made their recommendations.

West: "Pat, my people feel that we're going in the right direction and that our path has greater promise than your test matrix."

Ray: "As long as we're paying the bills, we're going to have a say in what tests are conducted. Your proposal stated that we would work together in developing the other test conditions. Let's go with my test matrix. I've already reported back to my boss that the first five tests were failures and that we're changing the direction of the project."

West: "I've already purchased $30,000 worth of raw materials. Your matrix uses other materials and will require additional expenditures of $12,000."

Ray: "That's your problem. Perhaps you shouldn't have purchased all of the raw materials until we agreed on the complete test matrix."

During the month of February, West conducted fifteen tests, all under Ray's direction. The tests were scattered over such a wide range that no valid conclusions could be drawn. Ray continued sending reports back to Delia confirming that Corwin was not producing beneficial results and there was no indication that the situation would reverse itself. Delia ordered Ray to take any steps necessary to ensure a successful completion of the project.

Ray and West met again as they had done for each of the past forty-five days to discuss the status and direction of the project.

Ray: "Dan, my boss is putting tremendous pressure on me for results, and thus far I've given him nothing. I'm up for promotion in a couple of months and I can't let this project stand in my way. It's time to completely redirect the project."

West: "Your redirection of the activities is playing havoc with my scheduling. I have people in other departments who just cannot commit to this continual rescheduling. They blame me for not communicating with them when, in fact, I'm embarrassed to."

Ray: "Everybody has their problems. We'll get this problem solved. I spent this morning working with some of your lab people in designing the next fifteen tests. Here are the test conditions."

West: "I certainly would have liked to be involved with this. After all, I thought I was the project manager. Shouldn't I have been at the meeting?"

Ray: "Look, Dan! I really like you, but I'm not sure that you can handle this project. We need some good results immediately, or my neck will be stuck out for the next four months. I don't want that. Just have your lab personnel start on these tests, and we'll get along fine. Also, I'm planning on spending a great deal of time in your lab area. I want to observe the testing personally and talk to your lab personnel."

West: "We've already conducted twenty tests, and you're scheduling another fifteen tests. I priced out only thirty tests in the proposal. We're heading for a cost-overrun condition."

Ray: "Our contract is a firm-fixed-price effort. Therefore, the cost overrun is your problem."

West met with Dr. Reddy to discuss the new direction of the project and potential cost overruns. West brought along a memo projecting the costs through the end of the third month of the project. (See Exhibit 10–6.)

Dr. Reddy: "I'm already overburdened on other projects and won't be able to help you out. Royce picked you to be the project manager because he felt that you could do the job. Now, don't let him down. Send me a brief memo next month explaining the situation, and I'll see what I can do. Perhaps the situation will correct itself."

During the month of March, the third month of the project, West received almost daily phone calls from the people in the lab stating that Pat Ray was interfering with their job. In fact, one phone call stated that Ray had changed the test conditions from what was agreed upon in the latest test matrix. When West confronted Ray on his meddling, Ray asserted that Corwin personnel were very unprofessional in their attitude and that he thought this was being carried down to the testing as well. Furthermore, Ray demanded that one of the functional employees be removed immediately from the project because of incompetence. West stated that he would talk to the employee's department manager. Ray, however, felt that this would be useless and said, "Remove him or else!" The functional employee was removed from the project.

By the end of the third month, most Corwin employees were becoming disenchanted with the project and were looking for other assignments. West attributed this to Ray's

Exhibit 10–6. Projected Cost Summary at the End of the Third Month.

	ORIGINAL PROPOSAL COST SUMMARY FOR SIX MONTH PROJECT	TOTAL PROJECT COSTS PROJECTED AT END OF THIRD MONTH
Direct labor/support	$ 30,000	$ 15,000
Testing	60,000 (30 tests)	70,000 (35 tests)
Overhead	90,000 (100%)	92,000 (120%)*
Materials	30,000	50,000
G&A	21,000 (10%)	22,700 (10%)
	$231,000	$249,700

*Total engineering overhead was estimated at 100%, whereas the R&D overhead was 120%.

**Exhibit 10–7. Estimate of Total
Project Completion Costs.**

Direct labor/support	$ 47,000*
Testing (60 tests)	120,000
Overhead (120%)	200,000
Materials	70,000
G&A	47,000
	$517,000
Peters contract	250,000
Overrun	$267,000

*Includes Dr. Reddy.

harassment of the employees. To aggravate the situation even further, Ray met with Royce and Reddy, and demanded that West be removed and a new project manager be assigned.

Royce refused to remove West as project manager, and ordered Reddy to take charge and help West get the project back on track.

Reddy: "You've kept me in the dark concerning this project, West. If you want me to help you, as Royce requested, I'll need all the information tomorrow, especially the cost data. I'll expect you in my office tomorrow morning at 8:00 A.M. I'll bail you out of this mess."

West prepared the projected cost data for the remainder of the work and presented the results to Dr. Reddy. (See Exhibit 10–7.) Both West and Reddy agreed that the project was now out of control, and severe measures would be required to correct the situation, in addition to more than $250,000 in corporate funding.

Reddy: "Dan, I've called a meeting for 10:00 A.M. with several of our R&D people to completely construct a new test matrix. This is what we should have done right from the start."

West: "Shouldn't we invite Ray to attend this meeting? I'm sure he'd want to be involved in designing the new test matrix."

Reddy: "I'm running this show now, not Ray!! Tell Ray that I'm instituting new policies and procedures for in-house representatives. He's no longer authorized to visit the labs at his own discretion. He must be accompanied by either you or me. If he doesn't like these rules, he can get out. I'm not going to allow that guy to disrupt our organization. We're spending our money now, not his."

West met with Ray and informed him of the new test matrix as well as the new policies and procedures for in-house representatives. Ray was furious over the new turn of events and stated that he was returning to Peters Company for a meeting with Delia.

On the following Monday, Frimel received a letter from Delia stating that Peters

Company was officially canceling the contract. The reasons given by Delia were as follows:

1. Corwin had produced absolutely no data that looked promising.
2. Corwin continuously changed the direction of the project and did not appear to have a systematic plan of attack.
3. Corwin did not provide a project manager capable of handling such a project.
4. Corwin did not provide sufficient support for the in-house representative.
5. Corwin's top management did not appear to be sincerely interested in the project and did not provide sufficient executive-level support.

Royce and Frimel met to decide upon a course of action in order to sustain good working relations with Peters Company. Frimel wrote a strong letter refuting all of the accusations in the Peters letter, but to no avail. Even the fact that Corwin was willing to spend $250,000 of their own funds had no bearing upon Delia's decision. The damage was done. Frimel was now thoroughly convinced that a contract should not be accepted on "Pearl Harbor Day."

11
Planning

11.0 INTRODUCTION

The most important responsibilities of a project manager are planning, integrating, and executing plans. Almost all projects, because of their relatively short duration and often prioritized control of resources, require formal, detailed planning. The integration of the planning activities is necessary because each functional unit may develop its own planning documentation with little regard for other functional units.

Planning, in general, can best be described as the function of selecting the enterprise objectives and establishing the policies, procedures, and programs necessary for achieving them. Planning in a project environment may be described as establishing a predetermined course of action within a forecasted environment. The project's requirements set the major milestones, and the line managers hope that they can meet them. If the line manager cannot commit because the milestones are perceived as unrealistic, the project manager may have to develop alternatives, one of which may be to move the milestones. Upper-level management must become involved in the selection of alternatives during the planning stage. Planning is, of course, decision making, since it involves choosing among alternatives. Planning is a required management function to facilitate the comprehension of complex problems involving interacting factors.

The project manager is the key to successful project planning. It is desirable that the project manager be involved from project conception through execution. Project planning must be *systematic, flexible* enough to handle unique activities, *disciplined* through reviews and controls, and capable of accepting *multifunctional* inputs. Successful project managers realize that project planning is an iterative process and must be performed throughout the life of the project.

One of the objectives of project planning is to completely define all work required (possibly through the development of a documented project plan) so that it will be readily identifiable to each project participant. This is a necessity in a project environment because:

- If the task is well understood prior to being performed, much of the work can be preplanned.

- If the task is not understood, then during the actual task execution more knowledge is learned that, in turn, leads to changes in resource allocations, schedules, and priorities.
- The more uncertain the task, the greater the amount of information that must be processed in order to ensure effective performance.

These considerations are important in a project environment because each project can be different from the others, requiring a variety of different resources, but having to be performed under time, cost, and performance constraints with little margin for error. Figure 11-1 identifies the type of project planning required to establish an effective monitoring and control system. The boxes in the upper portion of the curve represent the planning activities, and the lower portion identifies the "tracking" or monitoring of the planned activities.

Without proper planning, programs and projects can start off "behind the eight ball" because of poorly defined requirements during the initial planning phase. Below is a list of the typical consequences of poor planning:

- Project initiation
- Wild enthusiasm
- Disillusionment
- Chaos
- Search for the guilty
- Punishment of the innocent
- Promotion of the nonparticipants
- Definition of the requirements

Obviously, the definition of the requirements should have been the first step. There are four basic reasons for project planning:

- To eliminate or reduce uncertainty
- To improve efficiency of the operation
- To obtain a better understanding of the objectives
- To provide a basis for monitoring and controlling work

There are involuntary and voluntary reasons for planning. Involuntary reasons can be internally mandatory functions of the organizational complexity and an organizational lag in response time; or they can be externally correlated to environmental fluctuations, uncertainty, and discontinuity. The voluntary reasons for planning are attempts to secure efficient and effective operations.

Planning is decision making based upon futurity. It is a continuous process of making entrepreneurial decisions with an eye to the future, and methodically

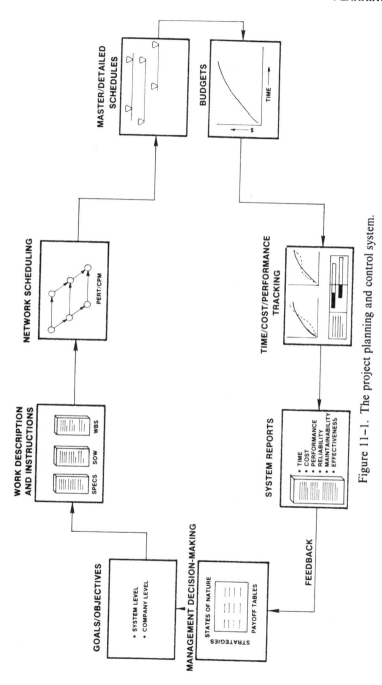

Figure 11-1. The project planning and control system.

organizing the effort needed to carry out these decisions. Furthermore, systematic planning allows an organization to set goals. The alternative to systematic planning is decision making based upon history. This generally results in reactive management leading to crisis management, conflict management, and firefighting.

11.1 GENERAL PLANNING

Planning is determining what needs to be done, by whom, and by when, in order to fulfill one's assigned responsibility. There are nine major components of the planning phase:

- Objective: a goal, target, or quota to be achieved by a certain time
- Program: the strategy to be followed and major actions to be taken in order to achieve or exceed objectives
- Schedule: a plan showing when individual or group activities or accomplishments will be started and/or completed
- Budget: planned expenditures required to achieve or exceed objectives
- Forecast: a projection of what will happen by a certain time
- Organization: design of the number and kinds of positions, along with corresponding duties and responsibilities, required to achieve or exceed objectives
- Policy: a general guide for decision making and individual actions
- Procedure: a detailed method for carrying out a policy
- Standard: a level of individual or group performance defined as adequate or acceptable

Several of these factors require additional comment. Forecasting what will happen may not be easy, especially if predictions of environmental reactions are required. For example, planning is customarily defined as either strategic, tactical, or operational. Strategic planning is generally for five years or more, tactical can be for one to five years, and operational is the here and now of six months to one year. Although most projects are operational, they can be considered as strategic, especially if spin-offs or follow-up work is promising. Forecasting also requires an understanding of strengths and weaknesses as found in:

- The competitive situation
- Marketing
- Research and development
- Production
- Financing

- Personnel
- The management structure

If project planning is strictly operational, then these factors may be clearly definable. However, if strategic or long-range planning is necessary, then the future economic outlook can vary, say, from year to year, and replanning must be accomplished at regular intervals because the goals and objectives can change. (The procedure for this can be seen in Figure 11–1.)

The last three factors, policies, procedures, and standards, can vary from project to project because of their uniqueness. Each project manager can establish project policies, provided that they fall within the broad limits set forth by top management. Policies are predetermined general courses or guides based upon the following principles:[1]

- Subordinate policies are supplementary to superior policies.
- Policies are based upon known principles in the operative areas.
- Policies should be complementary for coordination.
- Policies should be definable, understandable, and preferably in writing.
- Policies should be both flexible and stable.
- Policies should be reasonably comprehensive in scope.

Project policies must often conform closely to company policies, and are usually similar in nature from project to project. Procedures, on the other hand, can be drastically different from project to project, even if the same activity is performed. For example, the signing off of manufacturing plans may require different signatures on two selected projects even though the same end-item is being produced.

Planning varies at each level of the organization. At the "individual" level, planning is required so that cognitive simulation can be established before irrevocable actions are taken. At the "working group or functional level," planning must include:

- Agreement on purpose
- Assignment and acceptance of individual responsibilities
- Coordination of work activities
- Increased commitment to group goals
- Lateral communications

---

1. Edwin Flippo and Gary Munsinger, *Management,* 3rd edition (Boston: Allyn and Bacon, 1975), p. 83.

At the "organizational or project" level, planning must include:

- Recognition and resolution of group conflict of goals
- Assignment and acceptance of group responsibilities
- Increased motivation and commitment to organizational goals
- Vertical and lateral communications
- Coordination of activities between groups

The logic of planning requires answers to several questions in order for the alternatives and constraints to be fully understood. An outline for a partial list of questions would include:

- Prepare environmental analysis
  - Where are we?
  - How and why did we get here?
- Set objectives
  - Is this where we want to be?
  - Where would we like to be? In a year? In five years?
- List alternative strategies
  - Where will we go if we continue as before?
  - Is that where we want to go?
  - How could we get to where we want to go?
- List threats and opportunities
  - What might prevent us from getting there?
  - What might help us to get there?
- Prepare forecasts
  - Where are we capable of going?
  - What do we need to take us where we want to go?
- Select strategy portfolio
  - What is the best course for us to take?
  - What are the potential benefits?
  - What are the risks?
- Prepare action programs
  - What do we need to do?
  - When do we need to do it?
  - How will we do it?
  - Who will do it?
- Monitor and control
  - Are we on course? If not, why?
  - What do we need to do to be on course?
  - Can we do it?

One of the most difficult activities in the project environment is to keep the planning on target. Below are typical procedures that can assist project managers during planning activities:

- Let functional managers do their own planning. Too often operators are operators, planners are planners, and never the twain shall meet.
- Establish goals before you plan. Otherwise short-term thinking takes over.
- Set goals for the planners. This will guard against the nonessentials and places your effort where there is pay-off.
- Stay flexible. Use people-to-people contact, and stress fast response.
- Keep a balanced outlook. Don't overreact, and position yourself for an upturn.
- Welcome top-management participation. Top management has the capability to make or break a plan, and may just well be the single most important variable.
- Beware of future spending plans. This may eliminate the tendency to underestimate.
- Test the assumptions behind the forecasts. This is necessary because professionals are generally too optimistic. Do not depend solely upon one set of data.
- Don't focus on today's problems. Try to get away from crisis management and fire-fighting.
- Reward those who dispel illusions. Avoid the Persian messenger syndrome (i.e., beheading the bearer of bad tidings). Reward the first to come forth with bad news.

11.2 IDENTIFYING STRATEGIC PROJECT VARIABLES

For long-range or strategic projects, the project manager must continuously monitor the external environment in order to develop a well-structured program that can stand up under pressure. These environmental factors play an integral part in planning. The project manager must be able to identify and evaluate these strategic variables in terms of the future posture of the organization with regard to constraints on existing resources.

In the project environment, strategic project planning is performed at the horizontal hierarchy level, with final approval by upper-level management. There are three basic guidelines for strategic project planning:

- Strategic project planning is a job that should be performed by managers, not for them.
- It is extremely important that upper-level management maintain a close involvement with project teams, especially during the planning phase.

- Successful strategic planning must define the authority, responsibility, and roles of the strategic planning personnel.

For the project to be successful, all members of the horizontal team must be aware of those strategic variables that can influence the success or failure of the project plan. The analysis begins with the environment, subdivided as internal, external, and competitive, as shown below:

- Internal environment
  - Management skills
  - Resources
  - Wage and salary levels
  - Government freeze on jobs
  - Minority groups
  - Layoffs
  - Sales forecasts
- External environment
  - Legal
  - Political
  - Social
  - Economic
  - Technological
- Competitive environment
  - Industry characteristics
  - Company requirements and goals
  - Competitive history
  - Present competitive activity
  - Competitive planning
    - Return on investment
    - Market share
    - Size and variety of product lines
  - Competitive resources

Once the environmental variables are defined, the planning process continues with the following:

- Identification of company strengths and weaknesses
- Understanding personal values of top management
- Identification of opportunities
- Definition of product market
- Identification of competitive edge
- Establishment of goals, objectives, and standards
- Identification of resource deployment

Complete identification of all strategic variables is not easily obtainable at the program level. Internal, or operating, variables are readily available to program personnel by virtue of the structure of the organization. The external variables are normally tracked under the perceptive eyes of top management. This presents a challenge for the organization of the system. In most cases, those in the horizontal hierarchy of a program are more interested in the current operational plan than in external factors and tend to become isolated from the environment after the program begins, losing insight into factors influencing the rapidly changing external variables in the process. Proper identification of these strategic variables requires that communication channels be established between top management and the project office.

Top-management support must be available for identification of strategic planning variables so that effective decision making can occur at the program level. The participation of top management in this regard has not been easy to implement. Many top-level officers consider this process a relinquishment of some of their powers and choose to retain strategic variable identification for the top levels of management.

The systems approach to management does not attempt to decrease top management's role in strategic decision making. The maturity, intellect, and wisdom of top management cannot be replaced. Ultimately, decision making will always rest at the upper levels of management, regardless of the organizational structure.

Identification and classification of the strategic variables are necessary to establish relative emphasis, priorities, and selectivity among the alternatives, to anticipate the unexpected, and to determine the restraints and limitations of the program. Universal classification systems are nonexistent because of the varied nature of organizations and projects. However, variables can be roughly categorized as internal and external, as shown in Table 11–1.

A survey of fifty companies was conducted to determine if lower-level and middle management, as well as project managers, knew what variables in their own industry were considered by top management as important planning variables. The following results were obtained:[2]

- Top management considered fewer variables as being strategic than did middle managers.
- Middle management and top management in project-driven companies had better agreement on strategic variable identification than did managers in non-project-driven companies.

---

2. Harold Kerzner, "Survey of Strategic Planning Variables," unpublished report, Project/Systems Management Research Institute, Baldwin-Wallace College, 1977.

Table 11–1. Strategic Planning Variables in the Tire Industry.

INTERNAL	EXTERNAL
● Operating	● Operating
● Product changes	● Customer requirements
● Volume (economies of scale)	● Capacity of plants
● Wages vs. automation	● Borrowing expenses
● R&D	● Technological advances
● Legal	● Legal
● Product quality	● OSHA noise levels
● Union and safety considerations	● Product liabilities
	● DoT requirements
● Economic	● Economic
● Market indicators	● Forecast of industry
● Division of market	● Inventory (on hand/dealers)
● Production runs (timing)	● Steel and chemical output
● Pricing/promotion policy	● Competition
● Sociopolitical	● Sociopolitical
● Allocation of resources	● Produce what is profitable
● Raw material price/availability	● Primarily third world
● Feasibility of exporting	● Threat of imports
● Productivity levels	● Stability of free market

- Top executives within the same industry differed as to the identification of strategic variables, even within companies having almost identical business bases.
- Very little attempt was made by top management to quantify the risks involved with each strategic variable.

As an example of the differences between the project manager and upper-level management, consider the six strategic variables, listed below, that are characteristic of the machine tool industry:

- Business markets and business cycles
- Product characteristics
- Pricing and promotion policies
- Technology changes
- Labor force and available skills
- Customer organization restructuring

Both project managers and upper-level management agreed upon the first four variables. The last two were identified by upper-level management. Since many products are now made of materials other than steel, the question arises as to the availability of qualified workers. This poses a problem in that many customers perform a make-or-buy analysis before contracting with machine tool companies. The machine tool companies surveyed felt that it is the responsibility of upper-level management to communicate continuously with all customers to ascertain if they are contemplating developing or enlarging their machine tool capabilities. Obviously, the decision of a prime customer to develop its own machine shop capabilities could have a severe impact on the contractor's growth potential, business base, and strategic planning philosophy.

11.3 LIFE CYCLE PHASES

Project planning takes place at two levels. The first level is the corporate cultural approach; the second method is the individual's approach. The corporate cultural approach breaks the project down into life cycle phases, such as those shown in Table 2–7. The life cycle phase approach is *not* an attempt to put handcuffs on the project manager but to provide a methodology for uniformity in project planning. Many companies, including government agencies, prepare checklists of activities which should be considered in each phase. These checklists are for consistency in planning. The project manager can still exercise his own planning initiatives within each phase.

A second benefit of life cycle phases is control. At the end of each phase there is a meeting between the project manager, sponsor, senior management, and even the customer, to assess the accomplishments of this life cycle phase and to get approval for the next phase. These meetings are often called critical design reviews, "on-off ramps," and "gates." In some companies, these meetings are used to firm up budgets and schedules for the follow-on phases. In addition to monetary considerations, life cycle phases can be used for manpower deployment and equipment/facility utilization. Some companies go so far as to prepare project management policy and procedure manuals where all information is subdivided according to life cycle phasing.

Consider a company which utilizes the following life cycle phases:

- Conceptualization
- Feasibility
- Preliminary planning
- Detail planning
- Execution
- Testing and commissioning

The conceptualization phase includes brainstorming and common sense and involves two critical factors: (1) Identify and define the problem; and (2) Identify and define potential solutions.

In a brainstorming session, *all* ideas are recorded and none are discarded. The brainstorming session works best if there is no formal authority present and if the time duration is no more than 30 to 60 minutes. Sessions over 60 minutes in length will produce ideas that may begin to resemble science fiction.

The feasibility study phase considers the technical aspects of the conceptual alternatives and provides a firmer basis on which to decide whether or not to undertake the project.

The purpose of the feasibility phase is to:

- Plan the project development and implementation activities.
- Estimate the probable elapsed time, staffing, and equipment requirements.
- Identify the probable costs and consequences of investing in the new project.

If practical, the feasibility study results should evaluate the alternative conceptual solutions along with associated benefits and costs.

The objective of this step is to provide management with the predictable results of implementing a specific project and to provide generalized project requirements. This, in the form of a feasibility study report, is used as the basis on which to decide whether or not to proceed with the costly requirements, development, and implementation phases.

User involvement during the feasibility study is critical. The user must supply much of the required effort and information, and, in addition, must be able to judge the impact of alternative approaches. Solutions must be operationally, technically, and economically feasible. Much of the economic evaluation must be substantiated by the user. Therefore, the primary user must be highly qualified and intimately familiar with the workings of the organization and should come from the line operation.

The feasibility study also deals with the technical aspects of the proposed project and requires the development of conceptual solutions. Considerable experience and technical expertise are required to gather the proper information, analyze it, and reach practical conclusions.

Improper technical or operating decisions made during this step may go undetected or unchallenged throughout the remainder of the process. In the worst case, such an error could result in the termination of a valid project—or the continuation of a project that is not economically or technically feasible.

In the feasibility study phase, it is necessary to define the project's basic approaches and its boundaries or scope. A typical feasibility study checklist might include:

- Summary level:
  - Evaluate alternatives

- Evaluate market potential
- Evaluate cost effectiveness
- Evaluate producibility
- Evaluate technical base
- Detail level:
  - A more specific determination of the problem.
  - Analysis of the state-of-the-art technology
  - Assessment of in-house technical capabilities
  - Test validity of alternatives
  - Quantify weaknesses and unknowns
  - Conduct tradeoff analysis on time, cost, and performance
  - Prepare initial project goals and objectives
  - Prepare preliminary cost estimates and development plan

The end result of the feasibility study is a management decision on whether to terminate the project or to approve its next phase. Although management can stop the project at several later phases, the decision is especially critical at this point, because later phases require a major commitment of resources. All too often, management review committees approve the continuation of projects merely because termination at this point might cast doubt on the group's judgment in giving earlier approval.

The decision made at the end of the feasibility study should identify those projects that are to be terminated. Once a project is deemed feasible and is approved for development, it must be prioritized with previously approved projects waiting for development (given a limited availability of capital or other resources). As development get under way, management is given a series of checkpoints to monitor the project's actual progress as compared to the plan.

The third life cycle phase is either preliminary planning or "defining the requirements." This is the phase where the effort is officially defined as a project. In this phase, we should consider the following:

- General scope of the work
- Objectives and related background
- Contractor end item performance requirements
- Reference to related studies, documentation, and specifications
- Data items (documentation)
- Support equipment for contract end item
- Customer-furnished property, facilities, equipment, and services
- Customer-furnished documentation
- Schedule of performance
- Exhibits, attachments, and appendices

These elements can be condensed into four core documents, as will be shown in Section 11.5. Also, it should be noted that the word "customer" can be an internal customer, such as the user group or your own executives.

The table below shows the percentage of *direct* labor hours/dollars that are spent in each phase:

PHASE	PERCENT OF DIRECT LABOR DOLLARS
Conceptualization	5
Feasibility study	10
Preliminary planning	15
Detail planning	20
Execution	40
Commissioning	10

The interesting fact from this table is that as much as 50 percent of the direct labor hours and dollars can be spent before execution begins. The reason for this is simple: quality must be planned for and designed in. Quality cannot be inspected into the project. Companies that spend less than these percentages usually find quality problems in execution.

11.4 UNDERSTANDING PARTICIPANTS' ROLES

Planning simply does not happen by itself. Companies that have histories of successful plans also have employees who fully understand their role in the planning process. Good up-front planning may not eliminate the need for changes, but may reduce the number of changes required. The responsibilities of the major players are as follows:

- Project manager will define:
  - Goals and objectives
  - Major milestones
  - Requirements
  - Ground rules and assumptions
  - Time, cost, and performance constraints
  - Operating procedures
  - Administrative policy
  - Reporting requirements
- Line manager will define:
  - Detailed task descriptions to implement objectives, requirements, and milestones
  - Detailed schedules and manpower allocations to support budget and schedule
  - Identification of areas of risk, uncertainty, and conflict
- Senior management (project sponsor) will:

- Act as the negotiator for disagreements between project and line management
- Provide clarification of critical issues
- Provide communication link with customer's senior management

Successful planning requires that project, line, and senior management are in agreement with the plan.

11.5 PROJECT PLANNING

Successful project management, whether it be in response to an in-house project or a customer request, must utilize effective planning techniques. The quantitative and qualitative tools for project planning must be identified (see Figure 11-2). From a systems point of view, management must make effective utilization of resources. This effective utilization over several different types of projects requires a systematic plan in which the entire company is considered as one large network subdivided into smaller ones.

The first step in total program scheduling is understanding the project objectives. These goals may be to develop expertise in a given area, to become competitive, to modify an existing facility for later use, or simply to keep key personnel employed.

The objectives are generally not independent; they are all interrelated, both

Figure 11-2. Tools for project planning.

implicitly and explicitly. Many times it is not possible to satisfy all objectives. At this point, management must prioritize the objectives as to which are strategic and which are not.

Once the objectives are clearly defined, four questions must be considered:

- What are the major elements of the work required to satisfy the objectives, and how are these elements interrelated?
- Which functional divisions will assume responsibility for accomplishment of these objectives and the major-element work requirements?
- Are the required corporate and organizational resources available?
- What are the information flow requirements for the project?

If the project is large and complex, then careful planning and analysis must be accomplished by both the direct- and indirect-labor-charging organizational units. The project organizational structure must be designed to fit the project; work plans and schedules must be established so that maximum allocation of resources can be made; resource costing and accounting systems must be developed; and a management information and reporting system must be established.

Effective total program planning cannot be accomplished unless all of the necessary information becomes available at project initiation. These information requirements are:

- The statement of work (SOW)
- The project specifications
- The milestone schedule
- The work breakdown structure (WBS)

The statement of work (SOW) is a narrative description of the work to be accomplished. It includes the objectives of the project, a brief description of the work, the funding constraint if one exists, and the specifications and schedule. The schedule is a "gross" schedule and includes such things as the:

- Start date
- End date
- Major milestones
- Written reports (data items)

Written reports should always be identified so that if functional input is required, the functional manager will assign an individual who has writing skills. After all, it is no secret who would write the report if the line people did not.

The last major item is the work breakdown structure. The WBS is the breaking down of the statement of work into smaller elements so that better visibility and control will be obtained. Each of these planning items will be described in the following sections.

11.6 THE STATEMENT OF WORK

The statement of work (SOW) is a narrative description of the work required for the project. The complexity of the SOW is determined by the desires of top management, the customer, and/or the user groups. For projects internal to the company, the SOW is prepared by the project office with input from the user groups. The reason for this is that user groups tend to write in such scientific terms that only the user groups understand their meaning. Since the project office is usually composed of personnel with writing skills, it is only fitting that the project office prepare the SOW and submit it to the user groups for verification and approval.

For projects external to the organization, as in competitive bidding, the contractor may have to prepare the SOW for the customer because the customer may not have a team of people trained in SOW preparation. In this case, as before, the contractor would submit the SOW to the customer for approval. It is also quite common for the project manager to rewrite a customer's SOW so that the contractor's line managers can price out the effort.

In a competitive bidding environment, the reader should be aware of the fact that there are two SOWs—the SOW used in the proposal and a contract statement of work (CSOW). There might also be a proposal WBS and a contract work breakdown structure (CWBS). Special care must be taken by contract and negotiation teams that all discrepancies between the SOW/WBS and CSOW/CWBS are discovered, or additional costs may be incurred. A good (or winning) proposal is *no guarantee* that the customer or contractor understands the SOW. For large projects, fact-finding is usually required before final negotiations because it is *essential* that both the customer and the contractor understand and agree upon the SOW, what work is required, what work is proposed, the factual basis for the costs, and other related elements. In addition, it is imperative that there be agreement between the final CSOW and CWBS.

SOW preparation is not as easy as it sounds. Consider the following:

- The SOW says that you are to conduct a *minimum* of fifteen tests to determine the material properties of a new substance. You price out twenty tests just to "play it safe." At the end of the fifteenth test, the customer says that the results are not conclusive and that you must run another fifteen tests. The cost overrun is $40,000.

- The Navy gives you a contract in which the SOW states that the prototype must be tested in "water." You drop the prototype into a swimming pool to test it. Unfortunately, the Navy's definition of "water" is the Atlantic Ocean, and it costs you $1 million to transport all of your test engineers and test equipment to the Atlantic Ocean.
- You receive a contract in which the SOW says that you must transport goods across the country using "aerated" boxcars. You select boxcars that have open tops so that air can flow in. During the trip, the train goes through an area of torrential rains, and the goods are ruined. The customer wanted boxcars that were aerated from below. The court is currently deciding who should be blamed for misinterpretation of the word "aerated."

The above three examples show that misinterpretations of the SOW can result in losses of hundreds of millions of dollars a year. Common causes of misinterpretation are:

- Mixing tasks, specifications, approvals, and special instructions
- Using imprecise language ("nearly," "optimum," "approximately," etc.)
- No pattern, structure, or chronological order
- Wide variation in size of tasks
- Wide variation in how to describe details of the work
- Failing to get third-party review

Today, both private industry and government agencies are developing manuals on SOW preparation. The following has been adapted from a NASA publication on SOW preparation:[3]

- The project manager or his designees should review the documents that authorize the project and define its objectives, and also review contracts and studies leading to the present level of development. As a convenience, a bibliography of related studies should be prepared together with samples of any similar SOWs, and compliance specifications.
- A copy of the WBS should be obtained. At this point coordination between the CWBS elements and the SOW should commence. Each task element of the preliminary CWBS should be explained in the SOW, and related coding should be used.
- The project manager should establish a SOW preparation team consisting of personnel he deems appropriate from the program or project office who

3. Adapted from *Statement of Work Handbook* NHB5600.2, National Aeronautics and Space Administration, February 1975.

are experts in the technical areas involved, and representatives from procurement, financial management, fabrication, test, logistics, configuration management, operations, safety, reliability and quality assurance, plus any other area that may be involved in the contemplated procurement.

- Before the team actually starts preparation of the SOW, the project manager should brief program management as to the structure of the preliminary CWBS and the nature of the contemplated SOW. This briefing is used as a baseline from which to proceed further.

- The project manager may assign identified tasks to team members and identify compliance specifications, design criteria, and other requirements documentation that must be included in the SOW and assign them to responsible personnel for preparation. Assigned team members will identify and obtain copies of specifications and technical requirements documents, engineering drawings, and results of preliminary and/or related studies that may apply to various elements of the proposed procurement.

- The project manager should prepare a detailed checklist showing the mandatory items and the selected optional items as they apply to the main body or the appendixes of the SOW.

- The project manager should emphasize the use of preferred parts lists; standard subsystem designs, both existing and under development; available hardware in inventory; off-the-shelf equipment; component qualification data; design criteria handbooks; and other technical information available to design engineers to prevent deviations from the best design practices.

- Cost estimates (manning requirements, material costs, software requirements, etc.) developed by the cost-estimating specialists should be reviewed by SOW contributors. Such reviews will permit early trade-off consideration on the desirability of requirements that are not directly related to essential technical objectives.

- The project manager should establish schedules for submission of coordinated SOW fragments from each task team member. He must assure that these schedules are compatible with the schedule for the RFP issuance. The statement of work should be prepared sufficiently early to permit full project coordination and to ensure that all project requirements are included. It should be completed in advance of RFP preparation.

SOW preparation manuals also contain guides for editors and writers:[4]

- Every SOW that exceeds two pages in length should have a table of contents conforming to the CWBS coding structure. There should rarely be

---

4. Ibid.

items in the SOW that are not shown on the CWBS; however, it is not absolutely necessary to restrict items to those cited in the CWBS.

- Clear and precise task descriptions are essential. The SOW writer should realize that his or her efforts will have to be read and interpreted by persons of varied background (such as lawyers; buyers; engineers; cost estimators; accountants; and specialists in production, transportation, security, audit, quality, finance, and contract management). A good SOW states precisely the product or service desired. The clarity of the SOW will affect administration of the contract, since it defines the scope of work to be performed. Any work that falls outside that scope will involve new procurement with probable increased costs.

- The most important thing to keep in mind when writing a SOW is the most likely effect the written work will have upon the reader. Therefore, every effort must be made to avoid ambiguity. All obligations of the government should be carefully spelled out. If approval actions are to be provided by the government, set a time limit. If government-furnished equipment (GFE) and/or services, etc., are to be provided, state the nature, condition, and time of delivery if feasible.

- Remember that any provision that takes control of the work away from the contractor, even temporarily, may result in relieving the contractor of responsibility.

- In specifying requirements, use active rather than passive terminology. Say that the contractor shall conduct a test rather than that a test should be conducted. In other words, when a firm requirement is intended, use the mandatory term "shall" rather than the permissive term "should."

- Limit abbreviations to those in common usage. Provide a list of all pertinent abbreviations and acronyms at the beginning of the SOW. When using a term for the first time, spell it out and show the abbreviation or acronym in parentheses following the word or words.

- When it is important to define a division of responsibilities between the contractor, other agencies, etc., a separate section of the SOW (in an appropriate location) should be included to delineate such responsibilities.

- Include procedures. When immediate decisions cannot be made, it may be possible to include a procedure for making them (e.g., "as approved by the contracting officer," or "the contractor shall submit a report each time a failure occurs").

- Do not overspecify. Depending upon the nature of the work and the type of contract, the ideal situation may be to specify results required or end-items to be delivered and let the contractor propose his best method.

- Describe requirements in sufficient detail to assure clarity, not only for legal reasons, but for practical application. It is easy to overlook many details. It is equally easy to be repetitious. Beware of doing either. For every piece of deliverable hardware, for every report, for every immediate action, do not specify that something be done "as necessary." Rather, specify whether the judgment is to be made by the contractor or by the government. Be aware that these types of contingent actions may have an impact on price as well as schedule. Where expensive services, such as technical liaison, are to be furnished, do not say "as required." Provide a ceiling on the extent of such services, or work out a procedure (e.g., a level of effort, pool of man-hours) that will ensure adequate control.

- Avoid incorporating extraneous material and requirements. They may add unnecessary cost. Data requirements are common examples of problems in this area. Screen out unnecessary data requirements, and specify only what is essential and when. It is recommended that data requirements be specified separately in a data requirements appendix or equivalent.
- Do not repeat detailed requirements or specifications that are already spelled out in applicable documents. Instead, incorporate them by reference. If amplification, modification, or exceptions are required, make specific reference to the applicable portions and describe the change.

Some preparation documents also contain checklists for SOW preparation.[5] A checklist is furnished below to provide considerations that SOW writers should keep in mind in preparing statements of work:

- Is the SOW (when used in conjunction with the preliminary CWBS) specific enough to permit a contractor to make a tabulation and summary of manpower and resources needed to accomplish each SOW task element?
- Are specific duties of the contractor stated so he will know what is required, and can the contracting officer's representative, who signs the acceptance report, tell whether the contractor has complied?
- Are all parts of the SOW so written that there is no question as to what the contractor is obligated to do, and when?
- When it is necessary to reference other documents, is the proper reference document described? Is it properly cited? Is all of it really pertinent to the task, or should only portions be referenced? Is it cross-referenced to the applicable SOW task element?
- Are any specifications or exhibits applicable in whole or in part? If so, are they properly cited and referenced to the appropriate SOW element?
- Are directions clearly distinguishable from general information?

---

5. Ibid.

- Is there a time-phased data requirement for each deliverable item? If elapsed time is used, does it specify calendar or work days?
- Are proper quantities shown?
- Have headings been checked for format and grammar? Are subheadings comparable? Is the text compatible with the title? Is a multidecimal or alpha-numeric numbering system used in the SOW? Can it be cross-referenced with the CWBS?
- Have appropriate portions of procurement regulations been followed?
- Has extraneous material been eliminated?
- Can SOW task/contract line items and configuration item breakouts at lower levels be identified and defined in sufficient detail so they can be summarized to discreet third-level CWBS elements?
- Have all requirements for data been specified separately in a data requirements appendix or its equivalent? Have all extraneous data requirements been eliminated?
- Are security requirements adequately covered if required?
- Has its availability to contractors been specified?

Finally, there should be a management review of the SOW preparation and interpretation:[6]

During development of the Statement of Work, the project manager should ensure adequacy of content by holding frequent reviews with project and functional specialists to determine that technical and data requirements specified do conform to the guidelines herein and adequately support the common system objective. The CWBS/ SOW matrix should be used to analyze the SOW for completeness. After all comments and inputs have been incorporated, a final team review should be held to produce a draft SOW for review by functional and project managers. Specific problems should be resolved and changes made as appropriate. A final draft should then be prepared and reviewed with the program manager, contracting officer, or with higher management if the procurement is a major acquisition. The final review should include a briefing on the total RFP package. If other program offices or other Government agencies will be involved in the procurement, obtain their concurrence also.

11.7 PROJECT SPECIFICATIONS

A specification list as shown in Table 11–2 may be separately identified or called out as part of the statement of work. Specifications are used for man-hour, equipment, and material estimates. Small changes in a specification can cause large cost overruns.

---

6. *Statement of Work Handbook* NHB5600.2, National Aeronautics and Space Administration, February 1975.

Another reason for identifying the specifications is to make sure that there are no surprises for the customer downstream. The specifications should be the most current revision. It is not uncommon for a customer to hire outside agencies to evaluate the technical proposal and to make sure that the proper specifications are being used.

Specifications are, in fact, standards for pricing out a proposal. If specifications either do not yet exist or are not necessary, then work standards should be included in the proposal. The work standards can also appear in the cost volume of the proposal. Labor justification back-up sheets may or may not be included in the proposal, depending upon RFP/RFQ requirements.

11.8 MILESTONE SCHEDULES

Project milestone schedules contain such information as:

- Project start date
- Project end date
- Other major milestones
- Data items (deliverables or reports)

Project start and end dates, if known, must be included. Other major milestones such as review meetings, prototype available, procurement, testing, and so on, should also be identified. The last topic, data items, is often overlooked. There are two good reasons for preparing a separate schedule for data items. First, the separate schedule will indicate to line managers that personnel with writing skills may have to be assigned. Second, data items require direct-labor man-hours for writing, typing, editing, proofing, retyping, graphic arts, and reproduction. Many companies identify on the data item schedules the approximate number of pages per data item, and each data item is priced out at a cost per page, say $100/page. Pricing-out data items separately often induces customers to require fewer reports.

11.9 WORK BREAKDOWN STRUCTURE

The successful accomplishment of both contract and corporate objectives requires a plan that defines all effort to be expended, assigns responsibility to a specially identified organizational element, and establishes schedules and budgets for the accomplishment of the work. The preparation of this plan is the responsibility of the program manager, who is assisted by the program team assigned in accordance with program management system directives. The detailed planning is also established in accordance with company budgeting policy before contractual efforts are initiated.

Table 11—2. Specification for Statement of Work.

DESCRIPTION	SPECIFICATION NO.
Civil	100 (Index)
• Concrete	101
• Field equipment	102
• Piling	121
• Roofing and siding	122
• Soil testing	123
• Structural design	124
Electrical	200 (Index)
• Electrical testing	201
• Heat tracing	201
• Motors	209
• Power systems	225
• Switchgear	226
• Synchronous generators	227
HVAC	300 (Index)
• Hazardous environment	301
• Insulation	302
• Refrigeration piping	318
• Sheetmetal ductwork	319
Installation	400 (Index)
• Conveyors and chutes	401
• Fired heaters and boilers	402
• Heat exchangers	403
• Reactors	414
• Towers	415
• Vessels	416
Instruments	500 (Index)
• Alarm systems	501
• Control valves	502
• Flow instruments	503
• Level gages	536
• Pressure instruments	537
• Temperature instruments	538
Mechanical Equipment	600 (Index)
• Centrifugal pumps	601
• Compressors	602
• High-speed gears	603
• Material handling equipment	640
• Mechanical agitators	641
• Steam turbines	642
Piping	700 (Index)
• Expansion joints	701
• Field pressure testing	702
• Installation of piping	703
• Pipe fabrication specs	749
• Pipe supports	750
• Steam tracing	751

Table 11-2. Specification for Statement of
Work. (*Continued*)

DESCRIPTION	SPECIFICATION NO.
Project Administration	800 (Index)
● Design drawings	801
● Drafting standards	802
● General requirements	803
● Project coordination	841
● Reporting procedure	842
● Vendor data	843
Vessels	900 (Index)
● Fireproofing	901
● Painting	902
● Reinforced tanks	948
● Shell and tube heat exchangers	949
● Steam boilers	950
● Vessel linings	951

In planning a project, the project manager must structure the work into small elements that are:

● Manageable, in that specific authority and responsibility can be assigned.
● Independent, or with minimum interfacing with and dependence on other ongoing elements.
● Integratable so that the total package can be seen.
● Measurable in terms of progress.

The first major step in the planning process after project requirements definition is the development of the work breakdown structure (WBS). The WBS is the single most important element because it provides a common framework from which:

● The total program can be described as a summation of subdivided elements.
● Planning can be performed.
● Costs and budgets can be established.
● Time, cost, and performance can be tracked.
● Objectives can be linked to company resources in a logical manner.
● Schedules and status-reporting procedures can be established.
● Network construction and control planning can be initiated.
● The responsibility assignments for each element can be established.

The work breakdown structure acts as a vehicle for breaking the work down into smaller elements, thus providing a greater probability that every major and minor activity will be accounted for. Although a variety of work breakdown structures exist, the most common is the six-level indentured structure shown below:

Level	Description
1	Total program
2	Project
3	Task
4	Subtask
5	Work package
6	Level of effort

Level 1 is the total program and is composed of a set of projects. The summation of the activities and costs associated with each project must equal the total program. Each project, however, can be broken down into tasks, where the summation of all tasks equals the summation of all projects, which, in turn, comprises the total program. The reason for this subdivision of effort is simply ease of control. Program management therefore becomes synonymous with the integration of activities, and the project manager acts as the integrator, using the work breakdown structure as the common framework.

Careful consideration must be given to the design and development of the WBS. From Figure 11–3, the work breakdown structure can be used to provide the basis for:[7]

- The responsibility matrix
- Network scheduling
- Costing
- Risk analysis
- Organizational structure
- Coordination of objectives
- Control (including contract administration)

The upper three levels of the WBS are normally specified by the customer (if part of an RFP/RFQ) as the summary levels for reporting purposes. The lower levels are generated by the contractor for in-house control. Each level serves a vital purpose: level 1 is generally used for the authorization and release of all work, budgets are prepared at level 2, and schedules are prepared at level 3. Certain characteristics can now be generalized for these levels:

---

7. Paul Mali, *Managing by Objectives*, (New York: John Wiley, 1972), p. 163.

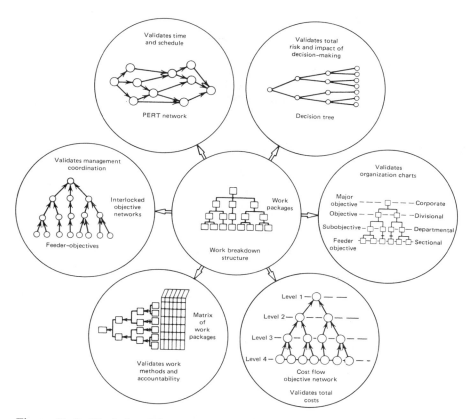

Figure 11–3. Work breakdown structure for objective control and evaluation. (Source: Paul Mali, *Managing by Objectives,* New York: John Wiley and Sons, 1972, p. 163.)

- The top three levels of the WBS reflect integrated efforts and should not be related to one specific department. Effort required by departments or sections should be defined in subtasks and work packages.
- The summation of all elements in one level must be the sum of all work in the next lower level.
- Each element of work should be assigned to one and only one level of effort. For example, the construction of the foundation of a house should be included in one project (or task), not extended over two or three. (At level 5, the work packages should be identifiable and homogeneous.)
- The WBS must be accompanied by a description of the scope of effort required, or else only those individuals who issue the WBS will have a

complete understanding of what work has to be accomplished. It is common practice to reproduce the customer's statement of work as the description for the WBS.

- It is often the best policy for the project manager, regardless of his technical expertise, to allow all of the line managers to assess the risks in the SOW. After all, the line managers are usually the recognized experts in the organization.

In setting up the work breakdown structure, tasks should:

- Have clearly defined start and end dates.
- Be usable as a communications tool in which results can be compared with expectations.
- Be estimated on a "total" time duration, not when the task must start or end.
- Be structured so that a minimum of project office control and documentation (i.e., forms) is necessary.

For large projects, planning will be time-phased at the work package level of the WBS. The work package has the following characteristics:

- Represents units of work at the level where the work is performed.
- Clearly distinguishes one work package from all others assigned to a single functional group.
- Contains clearly defined start and end dates that are representative of physical accomplishment.
- Specifies a budget in terms of dollars, man-hours, or other measurable units.
- Limits the work to be performed to relatively short periods of time to minimize the work-in-process effort.

Table 11–3 shows a simple work breakdown structure with the associated numbering system following the work breakdown structure. The first number represents the total program (in this case, it is represented by 01), the second number represents the project, and the third number identifies the task. Therefore, number 01-03-00 represents project 3 of program 01, whereas 01-03-02 represents task 2 of project 3. This type of numbering system is not standard; each company may have its own system, depending on how costs are to be controlled.

The preparation of the work breakdown structure is not easy. The WBS is a communications tool, providing detailed information to different levels of management. If it does not contain enough levels, then the integration of activities may prove difficult. If too many levels exist, then unproductive time will

**Table 11–3. Work Breakdown Structure for
New Plant Construction and Start-up.**

Program: New Plant Construction and Start-up	01-00-00
Project 1: Analytical Study	01-01-00
Task 1: Marketing/Production Study	01-01-01
Task 2: Cost Effectiveness Analysis	01-01-02
Project 2: Design and Layout	01-02-00
Task 1: Product Processing Sketches	01-02-01
Task 2: Product Processing Blueprints	01-02-02
Project 3: Installation	01-03-00
Task 1: Fabrication	01-03-01
Task 2: Set-up	01-03-02
Task 3: Testing and Run	01-03-03
Project 4: Program Support	01-04-00
Task 1: Management	01-04-01
Task 2: Purchasing Raw Materials	01-04-02

be made to have the same number of levels for all projects, tasks, and so on. Each major work element should be considered by itself. Remember, the WBS establishes the number of required networks for cost control.

For many programs, the work breakdown structure is established by the customer. If the contractor is required to develop a WBS, then certain guidelines must be considered. A partial list is as follows:

● The complexity and technical requirements of the program (i.e., the statement of work)
● The program cost
● The time span of the program
● The contractor's resource requirements
● The contractor's and customer's internal structure for management control and reporting
● The number of subcontracts

Applying these guidelines serves only to identify the complexity of the program. These data must then be subdivided and released, together with detailed information, to the different levels of the organization. The WBS should follow specified criteria because, although preparation of the WBS is performed by the program office, the actual work is performed by the doers, not the planners. Both the doers and the planners must be in agreement as to what is expected. A sample listing of criteria for developing a work breakdown structure is shown below:

● The WBS and work description should be easy to understand.
● All schedules should follow the WBS.

- No attempt should be made to subdivide work arbitrarily to the lowest possible level. The lowest level of work should not end up having a ridiculous cost in comparison to other efforts.
- Since scope of effort can change during a program, every effort should be made to maintain flexibility in the WBS.
- The WBS can act as a list of discrete and tangible milestones so that everyone will know when the milestones were achieved.
- The level of the WBS can reflect the "trust" you have in certain line groups.
- The WBS can be used to segregate recurring from nonrecurring costs.
- Most WBS elements (at the lowest control level) range from 0.5 to 2.5 percent of the total project budget.

From a cost control point of view, cost analysis down to the fifth level is advantageous. However, it should be noted that the cost required to prepare cost analysis data to each lower level may increase exponentially, especially if the customer requires data to be presented in a specified format that is not part of the company's standard operating procedures. The level 5 work packages are normally for in-house control only. Some companies bill customers separately for each level of cost reporting below level 3.

The WBS can be subdivided into subobjectives with finer divisions of effort as we go lower into the WBS. By defining subobjectives, we add greater understanding and, it is hoped, clarity of action for those individuals who will be required to complete the objectives. Whenever work is structured, understood, and easily identifiable and within the capabilities of the individuals, there will almost always exist a high degree of confidence that the objective can be reached.

Work breakdown structures can be used to structure work for reaching such objectives as lowering cost, reducing absenteeism, improving morale, and lowering scrap factors. The lowest subdivision now becomes an end-item or subobjective, not necessarily a work package as described here. However, since we are describing project management, for the remainder of the text we will consider the lowest level as the work package.

Once the WBS is established and the program is "kicked off," it becomes a very costly procedure to either add or delete activities, or change levels of reporting because of cost control. Many companies do not give careful forethought to the importance of a properly developed WBS, and ultimately they risk cost control problems downstream. One important use of the WBS is that it serves as a cost control standard for any future activities that may follow on or just may be similar. One common mistake made by management is the combining of direct support activities with administrative activities. For example, the department manager for manufacturing engineering may be required to provide administrative support (possibly by attending team meetings) throughout the duration of the program. If the administrative support is spread out over each of the projects, a false picture is obtained as to the actual hours needed to accomplish each project in the program. If one of the projects should be canceled, then the support man-hours for the total program would be reduced when, in fact, the administrative and support functions may be constant, regardless of the number of projects and tasks.

Quite often work breakdown structures accompanying customer RFPs contain much more scope of effort as specified by the statement of work than the existing funding will support. This is done intentionally by the customer in hopes that a contractor may be willing to "buy in." If the contractor's price exceeds the customer's funding limitations, then the scope of effort must be reduced by eliminating activities from the WBS. By developing a separate project for administrative and indirect support activities, the customer can easily modify his costs by eliminating the direct support activities of the canceled effort.

Before we go on, there should be a brief discussion of the usefulness and applicability of the WBS system. Many companies and industries have been successful in managing programs without the use of work breakdown structures, especially on repetitive-type programs. However, even as this text is being prepared, more and more companies are entering diversified project areas where some fundamentally common basis is needed for organizational synergy. The development of the WBS system will fulfill this need.

As was the case with the SOW, there are also preparation guides for the WBS:[8]

- Develop the WBS structure by subdividing the total effort into discrete and logical subelements. Usually a program subdivides into projects, major systems, major subsystems, and various lower levels until a manageable-size element level is reached. Wide variations may occur, depending upon the type of effort (e.g., major systems development, support services, etc.). Include more than one cost center and more than one contractor if this reflects the actual situation.
- Check the proposed WBS and the contemplated efforts for completeness, compatibility, and continuity.
- Determine that the WBS satisfies both functional (engineering–manufacturing–test) and program/project (hardware, services, etc.) requirements, including recurring and nonrecurring costs.

8. Source: *Handbook for Preparation of Work Breakdown Structures*, NHB5610.1, National Aeronautics and Space Administration, February 1975.

- Check to determine if the WBS provides for logical subdivision of all project work.
- Establish assignment of responsibilities for all identified effort to specific organizations.
- Check the proposed WBS against the reporting requirements of the organizations involved.

There are also checklists that can be used in the preparation of the WBS:[9]

- Develop a preliminary WBS to not lower than the top three levels for solicitation purposes (or lower if deemed necessary for some special reason).
- Assure that the contractor is required to extend the preliminary WBS in response to the solicitation, to identify and structure all contractor work to be compatible with his organization and management system.
- Following negotiations, the CWBS included in the contract should not normally extend lower than the third level.
- Assure that the negotiated CWBS structure is compatible with reporting requirements.
- Assure that the negotiated CWBS is compatible with the contractor's organization and management system.
- Review the CWBS elements to ensure correlation with:
  - The specification tree
  - Contract line items
  - End-items of the contract
  - Data items required
  - Work statement tasks
  - Configuration management requirements
- Define CWBS elements down to the level where such definitions are meaningful and necessary for management purposes (WBS dictionary).
- Specify reporting requirements for selected CWBS elements if variations from standard reporting requirements are desired.
- Assure that the CWBS covers measurable effort, level of effort, apportioned effort, and subcontracts, if applicable.
- Assure that the total costs at a particular level will equal the sum of the costs of the constituent elements at the next lower level.

On simple projects, the WBS can be constructed as a "tree diagram" (see Figure 11–4) or according to the logic flow. In Figure 11–4, the tree diagram can follow the work or even the organizational structure of the company (i.e.,

---

9. Ibid.

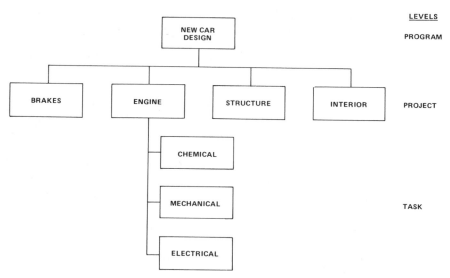

Figure 11-4. WBS tree diagram.

division, department, section, unit). The second method is to create a logic flow (see Figure 12-17) and cluster certain elements to represent tasks and projects. In the tree method, lower-level functional units may be assigned to one and only one work element, whereas in the logic flow method the lower-level functional units may serve several WBS elements.

11.10 ROLE OF THE EXECUTIVE IN PLANNING

Many project managers view the first critical step in planning as obtaining the support of top management because once it becomes obvious to the functional managers that top management is expressing an interest in the project, they (the functional managers) are more likely to respond favorably to the project team's request for support, partly to protect themselves.

Executives are also responsible for selecting the project manager, and the person chosen should have planning expertise. Not all technical specialists are good planners. As Rogers points out:[10]

The technical planners, whether they are engineers or systems analysts, must be experts at designing the system, but seldom do they recognize the need to "put on

10. Lloyd A. Rogers, "Guidelines for Project Management Teams," *Industrial Engineering,* December 12, 1974. Published and copyright 1974 by the American Institute of Industrial Engineers, Inc., Norcross, Georgia 30092.

another hat" when system design specifications are completed and design the project control or implementation plan. If this is not done, setting a project completion target date of a set of management checkpoint milestones is done by guesswork at best. Management will set the checkpoint milestones, and the technical planners will hope they can meet the schedule.

Executives must not arbitrarily set unrealistic milestones and then "force" line managers to fulfill them. Both project and line managers should try to adhere to unrealistic milestones, but if a line manager says he cannot, executives should comply because the line manager is supposedly the expert. Sometimes, executives lose sight of what they are doing. As an example, a bank executive took the six-month completion date milestone and made it three months. The project and line managers rescheduled all of the other projects to reach this milestone. The executive then did the same thing on three other projects, and again the project and line managers came to his rescue. The executive began to believe that the line people did not know how to estimate and that they probably loaded up every schedule with "fat." So, the executive changed the milestones on all of the other projects to what his "gut feeling" told him was realistic. The reader can imagine the chaos that followed.

Executives should interface with project and line personnel during the planning stage in order to define the requirements and establish reasonable deadlines. Executives must realize that creating an unreasonable deadline may require the reestablishment of priorities, and, of course, changing priorities can push milestones backward instead of forward.

11.11 THE PLANNING CYCLE

In section 2.7, we stated that perhaps the most important reason for structuring projects into life-cycle phases is to provide management with control of the critical decision points in order to:

- Avoid commitment of major resources too early
- Preserve future options
- Maximize benefits of each project in relation to all other projects
- Assess risks

On long-term projects, phasing can be overdone, with resultant extra costs and delays in achieving objectives. To prevent such a situation, many project-driven companies resort to other types of systems, such as a management cost and control system (MCCS). No program or project can be efficiently organized and managed without some form of management cost and control sys-

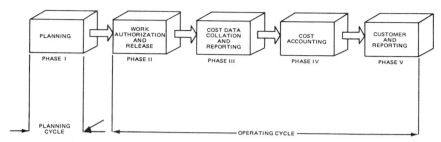

Figure 11-5. Phases of a management cost and control system.

tem. Figure 11-5 shows the five phases of a management cost and control system. The first phase constitutes the planning cycle, and the next four phases identify the operating cycle.

Figure 11-6 shows the activities included in the planning cycle. The work breakdown structure serves as the initial control from which all planning emanates. The WBS acts as a vital artery for both communications and operations, not only for the planning cycle, but for all other phases as well. A comprehensive analysis of management cost and control systems will be presented in Chapter 15.

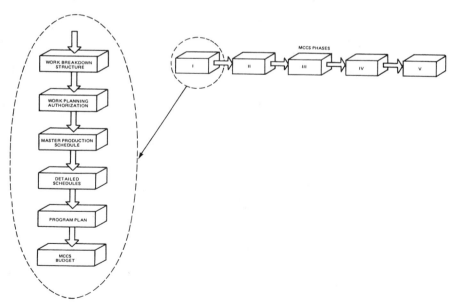

Figure 11-6. The planning cycle of a management cost and control system.

11.12 WORK PLANNING AUTHORIZATION

After receipt of a contract, some form of authorization is needed before work can begin, even in the planning stage. Both work authorization and work planning authorization are used to release funds, but for different purposes. Work planning authorization releases funds (primarily for functional management) so that scheduling, costs, budgets, and all other types of plans can be prepared prior to the release of operational cycle funds, which hereafter shall be referred to simply as work authorization. Both forms of authorization require the same paperwork. In many companies this work authorization is identified as a sub-divided work description (SWD), which is a narrative description of the effort to be performed by the cost center (division-level minimum). This package establishes the work to be performed, the period of performance, and possibly the maximum number of hours available. The SWD is multi-purpose in that it can be used to release contract funds, authorize planning, describe activities as identified in the WBS, and, last but not least, release work.

The SWD is one of the key elements in the planning of a program as shown in Figure 11–6. Contract control and administration releases the contract funds by issuing a SWD which sets forth general contractual requirements and authorizes program management to proceed. Program management issues the SWD to set forth the contractual guidelines and requirements for the functional units. The SWD specifies how the work will be performed, which functional organizations will be involved, and who has what specific responsibilities, and authorizes the utilization of resources within a given time period.

The SWD authorizes both the program team and functional management to begin work. As shown in Figure 11–6, the SWD provides direct input to Phase II of the MCCS. Phase I and Phase II can and do operate simultaneously because it is generally impossible for program office personnel to establish plans, procedures, and schedules without input from the functional units.

The subdivided work description package is used by the operating organizations to further subdivide the effort defined by the WBS into small segments or work packages.

Many people contend that if the data in the work authorization document are different from what was originally defined in the proposal, the project is in trouble right at the start. This may not be the case because most projects are priced-out assuming "unlimited" resources, whereas the hours and dollars in the work authorization document are based upon "limited" resources. This situation is common for companies that thrive on competitive bidding.

11.13 WHY DO PLANS FAIL?

No matter how hard we try, planning is not perfect, and sometimes plans fail (Figure 11–7). Typical reasons why plans fail include:

- Corporate goals are not understood at the lower organizational levels.
- Plans encompass too much in too little time.
- Financial estimates were poor.
- Plans were based upon insufficient data.
- No attempt was made to systematize the planning process.
- Planning was performed by a planning group.
- No one knows the ultimate objective.
- No one knows the staffing requirements.
- No one knows the major milestone dates, including written reports.
- Project estimates are best guesses, and are not based upon standards or history.
- Not enough time was given for proper estimating.
- No one bothered to see if there would be personnel available with the necessary skills.
- People are not working toward the same specifications.
- People are consistently shuffled in and out of the project with little regard for schedule.

Why do these situations occur, and who should be blamed? If corporate goals are not understood, it is because corporate executives were negligent in providing the necessary strategic information and feedback. If a plan fails

Figure 11–7. Why always on my project?

because of extreme optimism, then the responsibility lies with both the project and line managers for not assessing risk. Project managers should ask the line managers if the estimates are optimistic or pessimistic, and expect an honest answer. Erroneous financial estimates are the responsibility of the line manager. If the project fails because of a poor definition of the requirements, then the project manager is totally at fault.

Project managers must be willing to accept failure. Sometimes, a situation occurs that can lead to failure, and the problem rests with either upper-level management or some other group. As an example, consider the major utility company with a planning group that prepares budgets (with the help of functional groups) and selects projects to be completed within a given time period. A project manager on one such project discovered that the project should have started "last month" in order to meet the completion date. In cases like this, project managers will not become dedicated to the projects unless they are active members during the planning and know what assumptions and constraints were considered in development of the plan.

Sometimes, the project manager is part of the planning group and as part of a feasibility study is asked to prepare, with the assistance of functional managers, a schedule and cost summary for a project that will occur three years downstream, if it is approved at all. Suppose that three years downstream the project is approved. How does the project manager get functional managers to accept the schedule and cost summary that they themselves prepared three years before? It cannot be done because technology may have changed, people may be working higher or lower on the learning curve, and salary and raw material escalation factors are inaccurate.

Sometimes project plans fail because simple details are forgotten or overlooked. Examples of this might be:

- Neglecting to tell a line manager early enough that the prototype is not ready and that rescheduling is necessary.
- Neglecting to see if the line manager can still provide additional employees for the next two weeks because it was possible to do so six months ago.

Sometimes plans fail because the project manager "bites off more than he can chew," and then something happens, such as his becoming ill. Even if the project manager is effective at doing a lot of the work, overburdening is unnecessary. Many projects have failed because the project manager was the only one who knew what was going on, and then got sick.

11.14 STOPPING PROJECTS

There are always situations in which projects have to be stopped. Below are several reasons for stopping:

- Final achievement of the objectives
- Poor initial planning and market prognosis
- A better alternative having been found
- A change in the company interest and strategy
- Allocated time having been exceeded
- Budgeted costs having been exceeded
- Key people having left the organization
- Personal whims of management
- Problem too complex for the resources available

Today most of the reasons why projects are not completed on time and cost are behavioral rather than quantitative considerations. They include:

- Poor morale
- Poor human relations
- Poor labor productivity
- No commitment by those involved in the project

The last item appears to be the cause of the first three items in many situations.

Once the reasons for cancellation are defined, the next problem concerns how to stop the project. Some of the ways are:

- Orderly planned termination
- The "hatchet" (withdrawal of funds and removal of personnel)
- Reassignment of people to higher priority
- Redirection of efforts toward different objectives
- Burying it or letting it die on the vine (i.e., not taking any official action)

There are three major problem areas to be considered in stopping projects:

- Worker morale
- Reassignment of personnel
- Adequate documentation and wrap-up

Sometimes executives do not realize the relationship between projects, and what happens if one is canceled prematurely. As an example, the following remarks were made by an executive concerning data processing operations:

When 75%–80% of the resource commitment is obtained, there is the point of no return and the benefits to be obtained from the project are anticipated. However, project costs, once forecast, are seldom adjusted during the project life cycle. Adjustments, when made, are normally to increase costs prior to or during conversion.

Increases in cost are always in small increments and usually occur when the corporation is "committed," i.e., 75%–80% of the actual costs are expended; however, total actual costs are not known until the project is over. . . .

Projects can and sometimes should be cancelled at any point in the project life cycle. Projects are seldom cancelled because costs exceed forecasts. More often, resources are drained from successful projects. The result of the action is the corporation as a whole becomes marginally successful in bringing all identified projects on line. One might assume individual projects can be analyzed to determine which projects are successful and which are unsuccessful. However, the corporate movement of resources makes the determination difficult without elaborate computer systems. For example, as Project A appears to be successful, resources are diverted to less successful Project B. The costs associated with Project A increase dramatically as all remaining activities become critical to Project A completion. Increasing costs for Project A are associated with overtime, traveling, etc. Costs for Project B are increasing at a straight time rate and more activities are being accomplished because more manpower can be expended. Often resources, particularly manpower working on Project B, are charged to Project A because the money is in the budget for Project A. The net result is Projects A and B overrun authorized budgets by about the same percentage. In the eyes of top corporate management, neither project team has done well nor have the teams performed poorly. This mediocrity in performance is often the goal of corporate project management technique.

11.15 HANDLING PROJECT PHASEOUTS AND TRANSFERS[11]

By definition, projects have an end point. Closing-out is a very important phase in the project life-cycle, which should follow particular disciplines and procedures with the objective of:

- Effectively bringing the project to a closure according to agreed-on contractual requirements.
- Preparing for the transition of the project into the next operational phase, such as from production to field installation, field operation, or training.
- Analyzing overall project performance with regard to financial data, schedules, and technical efforts.
- Closing the project office; transferring or selling off all resources originally assigned to the project, including personnel.
- Identifying and pursuing follow-on business.

Although most project managers are completely cognizant of the necessity for proper planning for project startup, many project managers neglect planning for project termination. Planning for project termination includes:

---

11. Adapted from Harold Kerzner and Hans J. Thamhain, *Project Management for the Small and Medium-Sized Business* (New York: Van Nostrand, 1983), pp. 325–329.

- Transferring responsibility
- Documenting results
- Satisfying contractual requirements
- Releasing resources
  - Reassignment of project office team members
  - Disposition of functional personnel
  - Disposition of materials
- Closing out work orders
- Preparing for financial payments

Project success or failure often depends on management's ability to handle personnel issues properly during this final phase. If job assignments beyond the current project look undesirable or uncertain to project team members, a great deal of anxiety and conflict may develop that diverts needed energy to job hunting, foot dragging, or even sabotage. Another problem is that project personnel engage in job searches on their own and may leave the project prematurely. This creates a glaring void that is often difficult to patch, always costing additional time and money and often eroding the already strained morale of the remaining project team.

Given the business realities, it is often difficult to transfer project personnel under ideal conditions for all parties involved. However, some suggestions are delineated below that can increase organizational effectiveness in closing out a project and can minimize personal stress for all parties involved:

- Carefully plan the project close-out on the part of both project and functional managers. Use a checklist to assist in the preparation of the close-out plan.
- Establish a simple project close-out procedure that identifies the major steps and responsibilities.
- Treat the close-out phase like any other project with clearly delineated tasks, agreed-on responsibilities, schedules, budgets, and deliverable items or results.
- Understand the interaction of behavioral and organizational elements in order to build an environment conducive to teamwork during this final project phase.
- Emphasize the overall goals, applications, and utilities of the project as well as its business impact. This will boost the morale of the team and enhance the desire to participate up to final closure and success.
- Secure top-management involvement and support.
- Be aware of conflict, fatigue, shifting priorities, and technical or logistic problems. Try to identify and deal with these problems when they start to develop. Maintaining an effective flow of communications is the key to the

ability to manage these problems. Regularly scheduled status meetings can be an important vehicle for maintaining effective communications.

- If at all possible, keep project personnel informed of upcoming job opportunities. Resource managers should discuss and negotiate new assignments with their personnel and, ideally, start involving their people already in the next project.
- Be aware of rumors. If a reorganization or layoff is inevitable at the end of a project, the situation should be described in a professional manner. If it is left to the imagination, project personnel will make the worst assumptions, resulting in a demoralized team, work slowdowns, and sporadic departure of key team members.
- Assign a contract administrator dedicated to company-oriented projects. He/she will protect your financial position and business interests by following through on customer sign-offs and final payment.

11.16   DETAILED SCHEDULES AND CHARTS

The scheduling of activities is the first major requirement of the program office after program go-ahead. The program office normally assumes full responsibility for activity scheduling if the activity is not too complex. For large programs, functional management input is required before scheduling can be completed. Depending on program size and contractual requirements, it is not unusual for the program office to maintain, at all times, a program staff member whose responsibility is that of a scheduler. This individual continuously develops and updates activity schedules to provide a means of tracking program work. The resulting information is then supplied to the program office personnel, functional management, and team members, and, last but not least, is presented to the customer.

Activity scheduling is probably the single most important tool for determining how company resources should be integrated so that synergy is produced. Activity schedules are invaluable for projecting time-phased resource utilization requirements as well as providing a basis for visually tracking performance. Most programs begin with the development of schedules so that accurate cost estimates can be made. The schedules serve as master plans from which both the customer and management have an up-to-date picture of operations.

Certain guidelines should be followed in the preparation of schedules, regardless of the projected use or complexity:

- All major events and dates must be clearly identified. If a statement of work is supplied by the customer, then those dates shown on the accompanying schedules must be included. If for any reason the customer's milestone dates cannot be met, then the customer should be notified immediately.

- The exact sequence of work should be defined through a network in which interrelationships between events can be identified.
- Schedules should be directly relatable to the work breakdown structure. If the WBS is developed according to a specific sequence of work, then it becomes an easy task to identify work sequences in schedules using the same numbering system as in the WBS. The minimum requirement should be to show where and when all tasks start and finish.
- All schedules must identify the time constraints and, if possible, should identify those resources required for each event.

Although these four guidelines relate to schedule preparation, they do not define how complex the schedules should be. Before preparing schedules, three questions should be considered:

- How many events or activities should each network have?
- How much of a detailed technical breakdown should be included?
- Who is the intended audience for this schedule?

Most organizations develop multiple schedules: summary schedules for management and planners and detailed schedules for the doers and lower-level control. The detailed schedules may be strictly for interdepartmental activities. Program management must approve all schedules down through the first three levels of the work breakdown structure. For lower-level schedules (i.e., detailed interdepartmental) program management may or may not request a sign of approval.

The need for two schedules is clear. According to Martin:[12]

In larger complicated projects, planning and status review by different echelons are facilitated by the use of detailed and summary networks. Higher levels of management can view the entire project and the interrelationships of major tasks without looking into the detail of the individual subtasks. Lower levels of management and supervision can examine their parts of the project in fine detail without being distracted by those parts of the project with which they have no interface.

One of the most difficult problems to identify in schedules is a hedge position. A hedge position is a situation in which the contractor may not be able to meet a customer's milestone date without incurring a risk, or may not be able to

12. Charles Martin, *Project Management: How to Make It Work,* (New York: AMACOM, a Division of American Management Associations, 1976), p. 137.

meet activity requirements following a milestone date because of contractual requirements. To illustrate a common hedge position, consider Example 11-1 below.

Example 11-1. Condor Corporation is currently working on a project that has three phases: design, development, and qualification of a certain component. Contractual requirements with the customer specify that no components will be fabricated for the development phase until the design review meeting is held following the design phase. Condor has determined that if they do not begin component fabrication prior to the design review meeting, then the second and third phases will slip. Condor is willing to accept the risk that should specifications be unacceptable during the design review meeting, the costs associated with preauthorization of fabrication will be incurred. How should this be shown on a schedule? (The problems associated with performing unauthorized work are not being considered here.)

The solution to Example 11-1 is not an easy one. Condor must play an honest game and show on the master production schedule that component fabrication will begin early, at the contractor's risk. This should be followed up by a contractual letter in which both the customer and contractor understand the risks and implications.

Example 11-1 also raises the question of whether this hedge position could have been eliminated with proper planning. Hedge positions are notorious for occurring in research and development or design phases of a program. Condor's technical community, for example, may have anticipated that each component could be fabricated in one week based on certain raw materials. If new raw materials were required or a new fabrication process had to be developed, it is then possible that the new component fabrication time could have increased from one week to two or three weeks, thus creating an unanticipated hedge position.

Detailed schedules are prepared for almost every activity. It is the responsibility of the program office to marry all of the detailed schedules into one master schedule to verify that all activities can be completed as planned. The preparation sequence for schedules (and also for program plans) is shown in Figure 11-8. The program office submits a request for detailed schedules to the functional managers. The request may be in the form of a planning work authorization document. The functional managers then prepare summary schedules, detailed schedules, and, if time permits, interdepartmental schedules. Each functional manager then reviews his schedules with the program office. The program office, together with the functional program team members, integrates all of the plans and schedules and verifies that all contractual dates can be met.

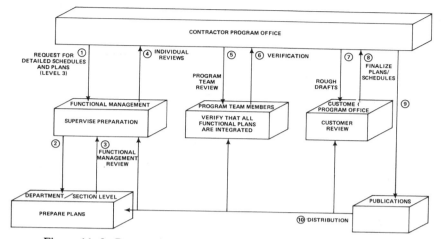

Figure 11–8. Preparation sequence for schedules and program plans.

Before the schedules are submitted to publications, rough drafts of each schedule and plan should be reviewed with the customer. This procedure accomplishes the following:

- Verifies that nothing has fallen through the crack.
- Prevents immediate revisions to a published document and can prevent embarrassing moments.
- Minimizes production costs by reducing the number of early revisions.
- Shows customers early in the program that you welcome their help and input into the planning phase.

After the document is published, it should be distributed to all program office personnel, functional team members, functional management, and the customer.

The exact method of preparing the schedules is usually up to the individual performing the activity. All schedules, however, must be approved by the program office. The schedules are normally prepared in a format that is suitable to both the customer and contractor and is easily understood by all. The schedules may then be used in-house as well as for customer review meetings, in which case the contractor can "kill two birds with one stone" by tracking cost and performance on the original schedules. Examples of detailed schedules are shown in Chapter 13.

In addition to the detailed schedules, the program office, with input provided by functional management, must develop organizational charts. The organizational charts tell all active participants in the project who has responsibility for each activity. (Examples were shown in Section 4.10.) The organizational charts display the formal (and often the informal) lines of communication.

The program office may also establish linear responsibility charts (LRCs). In spite of the best attempts by management, many functions in an organization may overlap between functional units. Also, management might wish to have the responsibility for a certain activity given to a functional unit that normally would not have that responsibility. This is a common occurrence on short-duration programs where management desires to cut costs and red tape.

Care must be taken that project personnel do not forget the reason why the schedule was developed. The primary objective of detailed schedules is usually to coordinate activities into a master plan in order to complete the project with the:

- Best time
- Least cost
- Least risk

Of course, the objective can be constrained by:

- Calendar completion dates
- Cash or cash flow restrictions
- Limited resources
- Approvals

There are also secondary objectives of scheduling:

- Studying alternatives
- Developing an optimal schedule
- Using resources effectively
- Communicating
- Refining the estimating criteria
- Obtaining good project control
- Providing for easy revisions

11.17 MASTER PRODUCTION SCHEDULING

The release of the planning SWD, as shown in Figure 11-6, authorizes the manufacturing units to prepare a master production schedule from which detailed analysis of the utilization of company resources can be seen and tracked.

Master production scheduling is not a new concept. Earliest material control systems used a "quarterly ordering system" to produce a master production schedule (MPS) for plant production. This system uses customer order backlogs to develop a production plan over a three-month period. The production plan is then exploded manually to determine what parts must be purchased or manufactured at the proper time. However, rapidly changing customer requirements and fluctuating lead times, combined with a slow response to these changes, can result in the disruption of master production scheduling.[13]

Master Production Schedule Definition

A master production schedule is a statement of what will be made, how many units will be made, and when they will be made. It is a production plan, not a sales plan. The MPS considers the total demand on a plant's resources, including finished product sales, spare (repair) part needs, and interplant needs. The MPS must also consider the capacity of the plant and the requirements imposed on vendors. Provisions are made in the overall plan for each manufacturing facility's operation. All planning for materials, manpower, plant, equipment, and financing for the facility is driven by the master production schedule.

Objectives of the MPS

Objectives of master production scheduling are:

- To provide top management with a means to authorize and control manpower levels, inventory investment, and cash flow.
- To coordinate marketing, manufacturing, engineering, and finance activities by a common performance objective.
- To reconcile marketing and manufacturing needs.
- To provide an overall measure of performance.
- To provide data for material and capacity planning.

The development of a master production schedule is a very important step in a planning cycle. Master production schedules directly tie together personnel, materials, equipment, and facilities as shown in Figure 11-9. Master production schedules also identify key dates to the customer, should he wish to visit the contractor during specific operational periods.

---

13. The master production schedule is being discussed here because of its importance in the planning cycle. The MPS cannot be fully utilized without effective inventory control procedures.

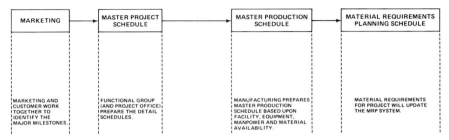

Figure 11–9. Material requirements planning interrelationships.

11.18 PROGRAM PLAN

Fundamental to the success of any project is documented planning in the form of a program plan. In an ideal situation, the program office can present the functional manager with a copy of the program plan and simply say "accomplish it." The concept of the program plan came under severe scrutiny during the 1960s when the Department of Defense required all contractors to submit detailed planning to such extremes that many organizations were wasting talented people by having them serve as writers instead of doers. Since then, because of the complexity of large programs, requirements imposed on the program plan have been eased.

For large and often complex programs, customers may require a program plan that documents all activities within the program. The program plan then serves as a guideline for the lifetime of the program and may be revised as often as once a month, depending upon the circumstances and the type of program (i.e., research and development programs require more revisions to the program plan than manufacturing or construction programs). The program plan provides the following framework:

- Eliminates conflicts between functional managers.
- Eliminates conflicts between functional management and program management.
- Provides a standard communications tool throughout the lifetime of the program. (It should be geared to the work breakdown structure.)
- Provides verification that the contractor understands the customer's objectives and requirements.
- Provides a means for identifying inconsistencies in the planning phase.
- Provides a means for early identification of problem areas and risks so that no surprises occur downstream.
- Contains all of the schedules defined in Section 11.14 as a basis for progress analysis and reporting.

Development of a program plan can be time-consuming and costly. The input requirements for the program plan depend on the size of the project and the integration of resources and activities. All levels of the organization participate. The upper levels provide summary information, and the lower levels provide the details. The program plan, like activity schedules, does not preclude departments from developing their own planning.

The program plan must identify how the company resources will be integrated. Finalization of the program is an iterative process similar to the sequence of events for schedule preparation, shown in Figure 11–8. Since the program plan must explain the events in Figure 11–8, additional iterations are required, which can cause changes in a program. This can be seen in Figure 11–10.

The program plan is a standard from which performance can be measured, not only by the customer, but by program and functional management as well. The plan serves as a cookbook for the duration of the program by answering these questions for all personnel identified with the program:

- What will be accomplished?
- How will it be accomplished?
- Where will it be accomplished?
- When will it be accomplished?
- Why will it be accomplished?

The answers to these questions force both the contractor and the customer to take a hard look at:

- Program requirements
- Program management
- Program schedules
- Facility requirements
- Logistic support
- Financial support
- Manpower and organization

The program plan is more than just a set of instructions. It is an attempt to eliminate crisis by preventing anything from "falling through the crack." The plan is documented and approved by both the customer and the contractor to determine what data, if any, are missing and the probable resulting effect. As the program matures, the program plan is revised to account for new or missing data. The most common reasons for revising a plan are:

- "Crashing" activities to meet end dates

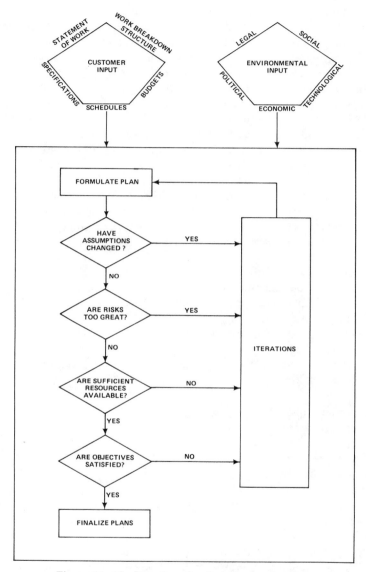

Figure 11–10. Iterations for the planning process.

- Trade-off decisions involving manpower, scheduling, and performance
- Adjusting and leveling manpower requests

Maturity of a program usually implies that crisis will decrease. Unfortunately, this is not always the case.

The makeup of the program plan may vary from contractor to contractor.[14] Most program plans can be subdivided into four main sections: introduction, summary and conclusions, management, and technical. The complexity of the information is usually up to the discretion of the contractor, provided that customer requirements, as may be specified in the statement of work, are satisfied.

The introductory section contains the definition of the program and the major parts involved. If the program follows another, or is an outgrowth of similar activities, this is indicated, together with a brief summary of the background and history behind the project.

The summary and conclusion section identifies the targets and objectives of the program and includes the necessary "lip service" on how successful the program will be and how all problems can be overcome. This section must also include the program master schedule showing how all projects and activities are related. The total program master schedule should include the following:

- An appropriate scheduling system (bar charts, milestone charts, network, etc.)
- A listing of activities at the project level or lower
- The possible interrelationships between activities (can be accomplished by logic networks, critical path networks or PERT networks)
- Activity time estimates (a natural result of the item above)

The summary and conclusion chapter is usually the second section in the program plan so that upper-level customer management can have a complete overview of the program without having to search through the technical information.

The management section of the program plan contains procedures, charts, and schedules as follows:

- The assignment of key personnel to the program is indicated. This usually refers only to the program office personnel and team members, since under

---

14. Cleland and King define fourteen subsections for a program plan. This detail appears more applicable to the technical and management volumes of a proposal. They do, however, provide a more detailed picture than presented here. See David I. Cleland and William R. King, *Systems Analysis and Project Management* (New York: McGraw-Hill, 1975), pp. 371–380.

normal operations these will be the only individuals interfacing with customers.

- Manpower, planning, and training are discussed to assure customers that qualified people will be available from the functional units.
- A linear responsibility chart might also be included to identify to customers the authority relationships that will exist in the program.

Situations exist in which the management section may be omitted from the proposal. For a follow-up program, the customer may not require this section if management's positions are unchanged. Management sections are also not required if the management information was previously provided in the proposal or if the customer and contractor have continuous business dealings.

The technical section may include as much as 75 to 90 percent of the program plan, especially if the effort includes research and development. The technical section may require constant updating as the program matures. The following items can be included as part of the technical section:

- A detailed breakdown of the charts and schedules used in the program master schedule, possibly including schedule/cost estimates.
- A listing of the testing to be accomplished for each activity. (It is best to include the exact testing matrices.)
- Procedures for accomplishment of the testing. This might also include a description of the key elements in the operations or manufacturing plans as well as a listing of the facility and logistic requirements.
- Identification of materials and material specifications. (This might also include system specifications.)
- An attempt to identify the risks associated with specific technical requirements (not commonly included). This assessment tends to scare management personnel who are unfamiliar with the technical procedures, so it should be omitted if at all possible.

The program plan, as used here, contains a description of all phases of the program. For many programs, especially large ones, detailed planning is required for all major events and activities. Table 11-4 identifies the type of individual plans that may be required in place of a (total) program plan. However, the amount of detail must be controlled, for too much paperwork can easily inhibit successful management of a program.

The program plan, once agreed upon by the contractor and customer, is then used to provide program direction. This is shown in Figure 11-11. If the program plan is written clearly, then any functional manager or supervisor should be able to identify what is expected of him.

The program plan should be distributed to each member of the program

Table 11–4. Types of Plans.

TYPE OF PLAN	DESCRIPTION
Budget	How much money is allocated to each event?
Configuration management	How are technical changes made?
Facilities	What facilities resources are available?
Logistics support	How will replacements be handled?
Management	How is the program office organized?
Manufacturing	What are the time-phase manufacturing events?
Procurement	What are my sources? Should I make or buy? If vendors are not qualified, how shall I qualify them?
Quality assurance	How will I guarantee specifications will be met?
Research/development	What are the technical activities?
Scheduling	Are all critical dates accounted for?
Tooling	What are my time-phased tooling requirements?
Training	How will I maintain qualified personnel?
Transportation	How will goods and services be shipped?

team, all functional managers and supervisors interfacing with the program, and all key functional personnel. The program plan does not contain all of the answers, for if it did, there would be no need for a program office. The plan serves merely as a guide.

One final note need be mentioned concerning the legality of the program plan. The program plan may be specified contractually to satisfy certain requirements as identified in the customer's statement of work. The contractor retains the right to decide how to accomplish this, unless, of course, this is also identified in the SOW. If the SOW specifies that quality assurance testing will be accomplished on fifteen end-items from the production line, then fifteen is the minimum number that must be tested. The program plan may show that twenty-five items are to be tested. If the contractor develops cost overrun problems, he may wish to revert to the SOW and test only fifteen items. Contractually, he may do this without informing the customer. In most cases, however, the customer is notified, and the program is revised.

11.19 TOTAL PROJECT PLANNING

The difference between the good project manager and the poor project manager is often described in one word: planning. Unfortunately, people have a poor definition of what project planning actually involves. Project planning involves planning for:

- Schedule development
- Budget development
- Project administration (see Section 5.3)

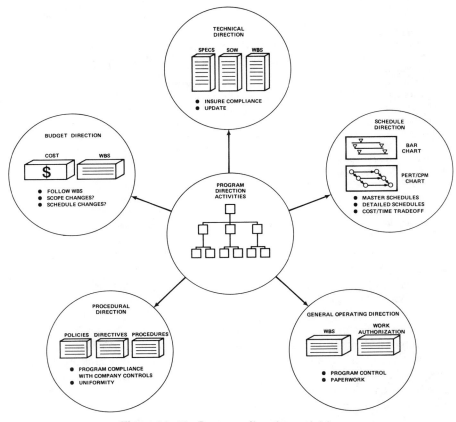

Figure 11–11. Program direction activities.

- Leadership styles (interpersonal influences; see Section 5.4)
- Conflict management (see Chapter 7)

The first two items involve the quantitative aspects of planning. Planning for project administration includes the development of the linear responsibility chart.

Although each project manager has the authority and responsibility to establish project policies and procedures, they must fall within the general guidelines established by top management. Guidelines can also be established for planning, scheduling, controlling, and communications.

Linear responsibility charts can result from customer-imposed requirements above and beyond normal operations. For example, the customer may require as part of his quality control requirements that a specific engineer supervise and approve all testing of a certain item, or that another individual approve all data released to the customer over and above program office approval. Customer requirements similar to those identified above require LRCs and can cause disruptions and conflicts within an organization.

Several key factors affect the delegation of authority and responsibility both from upper-level management to project management, and from project management to functional management. These key factors include:

- The maturity of the project management function
- The size, nature, and business base of the company
- The size and nature of the project
- The life cycle of the project
- The capabilities of management at all levels

Once agreement has been reached on the project manager's authority and responsibility, the results may be documented to clearly delineate that role regarding:

- Focal position
- Conflict between the project manager and functional managers
- Influence to cut across functional and organizational lines
- Participation in major management and technical decisions
- Collaboration in staffing the project
- Control over allocation and expenditure of funds
- Selection of subcontractors
- Rights in resolving conflicts
- Input in maintaining the integrity of the project team
- Establishment of project plans
- Provisions for a cost-effective information system for control
- Provisions for leadership in preparing operational requirements
- Maintenance of prime customer liaison and contact
- Promotion of technological and managerial improvements
- Establishment of project organization for the duration
- Elimination of red tape

Documenting the project manager's authority is necessary in some situations because:

- All interfacing must be kept as simple as possible.
- The project manager must have the authority to "force" functional managers to depart from existing standards and possibly incur risk.
- Gaining authority over those elements of a program that are not under the project manager's control is essential. This is normally achieved by earning the respect of the individuals concerned.

- The project manager should not attempt to fully describe the exact authority and responsibilities of the project office personnel or team members. Problem solving rather than role definition should be encouraged.

Although documenting project authority is undesirable, it may be a necessary prerequisite, especially if project initiation and planning require a formal project chart. In such a case, a letter such as that shown in Table 11–5 may suffice.

Power and authority are often discussed as though they are hand-in-hand. Authority comes from people above you, perhaps by delegation, whereas power comes from people below you. You can have authority without power or power without authority.

In a traditional organizational structure, most individuals maintain position power. The higher up you sit, the more power you have. But in project management, the reporting level of the project might be irrelevant, especially if a project sponsor exists. In project management, the project manager's power base emanates from his/her

- Expertise (technical or managerial)
- Credibility with employees
- Sound decision-making ability

The last item is usually preferred. If the project manager is regarded as a sound decision-maker, then the employees normally give the project manager a great deal of power over them.

Leadership styles refer to the interpersonal influence modes that a project manager can use. Project managers may have to use several different leadership styles, depending upon the makeup of the project personnel. Conflict management is important because if the project manager can predict what conflicts will occur and when they are most likely to occur, he may be able to plan for the resolution of the conflicts through project administration.

Figure 11–12 shows the complete project planning phase for the quantitative portions. The object, of course, is to develop a project plan that shows complete distribution of resources and the corresponding costs. The figure represents an iterative process. The project manager begins with a coarse (arrow diagram) network and then decides upon the work breakdown structure. The WBS is essential to the arrow diagram and should be constructed so that reporting elements and levels are easily identifiable. Eventually, there will be an arrow diagram and detailed chart for each element in the WBS. If there exists too much detail, the project manager can refine the diagram by combining all logic into one plan and can then decide upon the work assignments. There is a risk here that, by condensing the diagrams as much as possible, there may be a loss

Table 11–5. Project Charter.
ELECTRODYNAMICS
12 Oak Avenue
CLEVELAND, OHIO 44114

11 June 1983

TO: DISTRIBUTION
FROM: L. WHITE, EXECUTIVE VICE PRESIDENT
SUBJECT: PROJECT CHARTER FOR THE ACME PROJECT

Mr. Robert L. James has been assigned as the Project Manager for the Acme Project.
RESPONSIBILITY:

Mr. James will be responsible for ensuring that all key milestones are met within the time, cost, and performance constraints of his project, while adhering to proper quality control standards. Furthermore, the project manager must work closely with line managers to ensure that all assigned resources are used effectively and efficiently, and that the project is properly staffed.

Additionally, the project manager will be responsible for:

1. All formal communications between the customer and contractor.
2. Preparation of a project plan that is realistic, and acceptable by both the customer and contractor.
3. Preparation of all project data items.
4. Keeping executive management informed as to project status through weekly (detailed) and monthly (summary) status reporting.
5. Ensuring that all functional employees and managers are kept informed as to their responsibilities on the project and all revisions imposed by the customer or parent organization.
6. Comparing actual to predicted cost and performance, and taking corrective action when necessary.
7. Maintaining a plan that continuously displays the project's time, cost, and performance as well as resource commitments made by the functional managers.

AUTHORITY:

To ensure that the project meets its objectives, Mr. James is authorized to manage the project and issue directives in accordance to the policies and procedures section of the company's *Project Management Manual.* Additional directives may be issued through the office of the executive vice-president.

The program manager's authority also includes:

1. Direct access to the customer on all matters pertaining to the Acme Project.
2. Direct access to Electrodynamics' executive management on all matters pertaining to the Acme Project.
3. Control and distribution of all project dollars, including procurement, such that company and project cash flow limitations are adhered to.
4. To revise the project plan as needed, and with customer approval.
5. To require periodic functional status reporting.
6. To monitor the time, cost, and performance activities in the functional departments and ensure that all problems are promptly identified, reported, and solved.
7. To cut across all functional lines and to interface with all levels of management as necessary to meet project requirements.
8. To renegotiate with functional managers for changes in personal assignments.
9. Delegating responsibilities and authority to functional personnel, provided that the line manager is in approval that the employee can handle this authority/responsibility level.

Any questions regarding the above policies should be directed to the undersigned.

L. White
Executive Vice-President

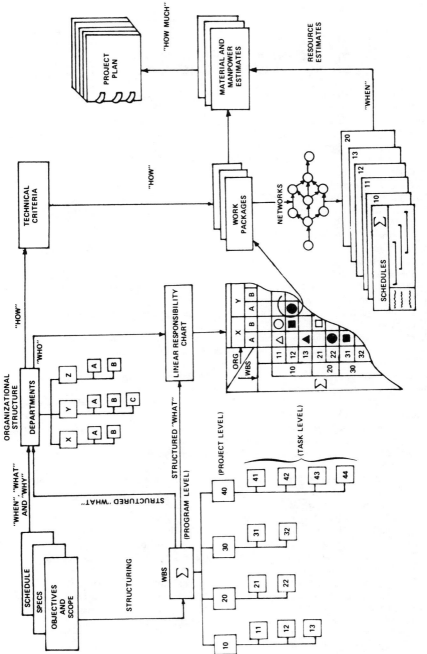

Figure 11–12. Project planning.

of clarity. Finally, as shown in Figure 11–12, all the charts and schedules can be integrated into one summary-level figure. This can be accomplished at each WBS level until the desired plan is achieved.

Finally, project, line, and executive management must analyze other internal and external variables before finalizing these schedules. A partial listing of these variables would include:

- Introduction or acceptance of the product in the marketplace
- Present or planned manpower availability
- Economic constraints of the project
- Degree of technical difficulty
- Manpower availability
- Availability of personnel training
- Priority of the project

In small companies and projects, certain items in Figure 11–12 may be omitted, such as the LRCs.

11.20 MANAGEMENT CONTROL

Because the planning phase provides the fundamental guidelines for the remainder of the project, careful management control must be established. In addition, since planning is an ongoing activity for a variety of different programs, management guidelines must be established on a company-wide basis in order to achieve unity and coherence.

All functional organizations and individuals working directly or indirectly on a program are responsible for identifying, to the program manager, scheduling and planning problems that require corrective action during both the planning cycle and the operating cycle. The program manager bears the ultimate and final responsibility for identifying requirements for corrective actions. Management policies and directives are written specifically to assist the program manager in defining the requirements. Without clear definitions during the planning phase, many projects run off into a variety of directions.

Many companies establish planning and scheduling management policies for the project and functional managers, as well as a brief description of how they should interface. Table 11–6 identifies a typical management policy for planning and requirements, and Table 11–7 describes scheduling management policies.

11.21 THE PROJECT MANAGER—LINE MANAGER INTERFACE

The utilization of management controls, such as those outlined in Section 11.18, does not necessarily guarantee successful project planning. Good project

Table 11–6. Planning and Requirements Policies.

PROGRAM MANAGER	FUNCTIONAL MANAGER	RELATIONSHIP
Plans and Requirements Requests the preparation of the program master schedules and provides for integration with the division composite schedules. Defines work to be accomplished through preparation of the subdivided work description package. Provides program guidance and direction for the preparation of program plans that establish program cost, schedule, and technical performance; and that define the major events and tasks to ensure the orderly progress of the program.	*Plans and Requirements* Develops the details of the program plans and requirements in conjunction with the program manager. Provides proposal action in support of program manager requirements and the program master schedule. With guidance furnished by the program manager, participates in the preparation of program plans, schedules, and work release documents which cover cost, schedule, and technical performance; and which define major events and tasks. Provides supporting detail plans and schedules.	*Plans and Requirements* Program planning and scheduling is a functional specialty; the program manager utilizes the services of the specialist organizations. The specialists retain their own channels to the general manager but must keep the program manager informed. Program planning is also a consultative operation and is provided guidelines by the program manager. Functional organizations initiate supporting plans for program manager approval, or react to modify plans to maintain currency. Functional organizations also initiate planning studies involving trade-offs and alternative courses of action for presentation to the program manager.
Establishes priorities within the program. Obtains relative program priorities between programs managed by other programs from the director, program management, manager, marketing and product development, or the general manager as specified by the policy.	Negotiates priorities with program managers for events and tasks to be performed by his organization.	The program manager and program team members are oriented to his program, whereas the functional organizations and the functional managers are "function" and multi-program oriented. The orientation of each director, manager, and team member

must be mutually recognized to preclude unreasonable demands and conflicting priorities. Priority conflicts that cannot be resolved must be referred to the general manager.

Make-or-buy concurrence and approvals are obtained in accordance with current Policies and Procedures.

Conducts analysis of contractual data requirements. Develops data plans including contractor data requirements list and obtains program manager approval.

Remains alert to new contract requirements, government regulations and directives that might affect the work, cost, or management of his organization on any program.

Provides the necessary make-or-buy data; substantiates estimates and recommendations in the area of functional specialty.

Prepares the program bill of material.

Approves program contractual data requirements.

Remains alert to new contract requirements, government regulations and directives that might affect the work, cost, or management of the program.

Provides early technical requirements definitions, and substantiates make-or-buy recommendations. Participates in the formulation of the make-or-buy plan for the program.

Approves the program bill of material for need and compliance with program need and requirements.

Directs data management including maintenance of current and historical files on programmed contractual data requirements.

Table 11-7. Scheduling Policies.

PROGRAM MANAGER	FUNCTIONAL MANAGER	RELATIONSHIP
Scheduling Provides contractual data requirements and guidance for construction of program master schedules.	*Scheduling* The operations directorate shall construct the program master schedule. Data should include but not be limited to engineering plans, manufacturing plans, procurement plans, test plans, quality plans, and provide time spans for accomplishment of work elements defined in the work breakdown structure to the level of definition visible in the planned subdivided work description package.	*Scheduling* The operations directorate constructs the program master schedule with data received from functional organizations and direction from the program manager. Operations shall coordinate program master schedule with functional organizations and secure program manager's approval prior to release.
Concurs with detail schedules constructed by functional organizations. Provides corrective action decisions and direction as required at any time a functional organization fails to meet program master schedule requirements or when, by analysis, performance indicated by detail schedule monitoring threatens to impact the program master schedule.	Constructs detail program schedules and working schedules in consonance with program manager-approved program master schedule. Secures program manager concurrence and forwards copies to the program manager.	Program manager monitors the functional organizations detail schedules for compliance with program master schedules and reports variance items that may impact division operations to the director, program management.

planning, as well as other project functions, requires a good working relationship between the project and line managers. At this interface:[15]

- The project manager answers these questions:
  - What is to be done? (using the SOW, WBS)

15. Adapted from *Systems Analysis and Project Management* by David I. Cleland and William R. King, p. 237. Copyright © 1968, 1975 by McGraw-Hill. Used with permission of McGraw-Hill Book Company.

- When will the task be done? (using the summary schedule)
- Why will the task be done? (using the SOW)
- How much money is available? (using the SOW)
- The line manager answers these questions:
  - How will the task be done? (i.e., technical criteria)
  - Where will the task be done? (i.e., technical criteria)
  - Who will do the task? (i.e., staffing)

Project managers may be able to tell line managers "how" and "where," provided that the information appears in the SOW as a requirement for the project. Even then, the line manager can take exception based upon his technical expertise.

Figures 11–13 and 11–14 show what can happen when project managers overstep their bounds. In Figure 11–13, the manufacturing manager built a brick wall to keep the project managers away from his personnel because the project managers were telling his line people how to do their job. In Figure 11–14, the subproject managers (for simplicity's sake, equivalent to project engineers) would have, as their career path, promotions to APMs. Unfortunately, the APMs still felt that they were technically competent enough to give technical direction, and this created havoc for the engineering managers.

The simplest solution to all of these problems is for the project manager to provide the technical direction *through* the line managers. After all, the line managers are supposedly the true technical experts.

11.22 FAST-TRACKING

Sometimes, no matter how well we plan, something happens which causes havoc on the project. Such is the case when either the customer or management changes the project's constraints. Consider Figure 11–15 and let us asume that the execution time for the construction of the project is one year. To prepare the working drawings and specifications down through level five of the WBS would require an additional 35 percent of the expected execution time and if a feasibility study is required, then an additional 40 percent will be added on. In other words, if the execution phase of the project is one year, then the entire project is almost two years.

Now, let us assume that management wishes to keep the end date fixed but the start date is delayed because of lack of adequate funding. How can this be accomplished *without* sacrificing the quality? The answer is to fast-track the project. Fast-tracking a project is when activities that are normally done in series are done in parallel. An example of this is when construction begins before detail design is completed. (See Table 2–7 on life cycle phases, on p. 85).

Fast-tracking a job can accelerate the schedule but requires that additional risks be taken. If the risks materialize, then either the end date will slip or

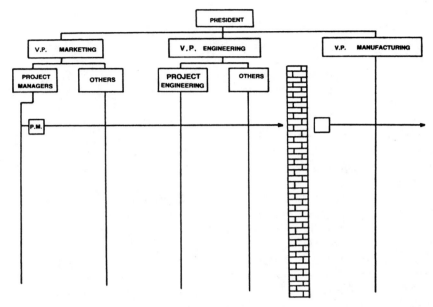

Figure 11–13. The brick wall.

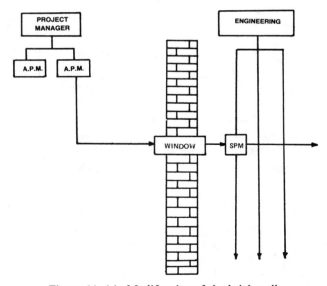

Figure 11–14. Modification of the brick wall.

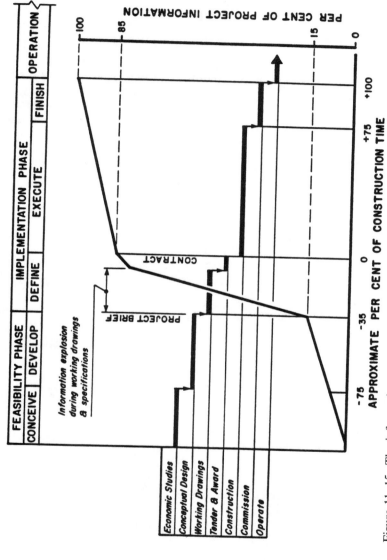

Figure 11–15. The information explosion. (*Source: Cost Control of Capital Projects*, R. M. Wideman, A.E.W. Services of Canada, Vancouver, B.C. 1983, p. 22.

expensive rework will be needed. Almost all project-driven companies fast-track projects. The danger, however, is when fast-tracking becomes a "way of life" on all projects.

11.23   CONFIGURATION MANAGEMENT

One of the most critical tools employed by a project manager is configuration management or configuration change control. As projects progress downstream through the various life-cycle phases, the cost of engineering changes can grow boundlessly. It is not uncommon for companies to bid on proposals at 40 percent below their own cost hoping to make up the difference downstream with engineering changes. It is also quite common for executives to "encourage" project managers to seek out engineering changes because of their profitability.

Configuration management is a control technique, through an orderly process, for formal review and approval of configuration changes. If properly implemented, configuration management provides

- Appropriate levels of review and approval for changes
- Focal points for those seeking to make changes
- A single point of input to contracting representatives in the customer and contractors office for approved changes

At a minimum, the configuration control committee should include representation from the customer, contractor, and line group initiating the change. Discussions should answer the following questions:

- What is the cost of the change?
- Do the changes improve quality?
- Is the additional cost for this quality justifiable?
- Is the change necessary?
- Is there an impact on the delivery date?

Changes cost money. Therefore, it is imperative that configuration management be implemented correctly. The following steps can enhance the implementation process:

- Define the starting point or "baseline" configuration
- Define the "classes" of changes
- Define the necessary controls or limitations on both the customer and contractor

- Identify policies and procedures, such as
  - Board chairman
  - Voters/alternatives
  - Meeting time
  - Agenda
  - Approval forums
  - Step-by-step processes
  - Expedition processes in case of emergencies

Effective configuration control will be pleasing to both the customer and contractor. Overall benefits will include:

- Better communication among staff
- Better communication with the customer
- Better technical intelligence
- Reduced confusion for changes
- Screening of frivolous changes
- Providing a paper trail

As a final note, it must be understood that configuration control, as used here, is not a replacement for design review meetings or customer interface meetings. These meetings are still an integral part of all projects.

PROBLEMS

11–1   Under what conditions would each of the following either not be available or not be necessary for initial planning?

a. Work breakdown structure
b. Statement of work
c. Specifications
d. Milestone schedules

11–2   What planning steps should precede total program scheduling? What steps are necessary?

11–3   How does a project manager determine how complex to make a program plan or how many schedules to include?

11–4   Can objectives always be identified and scheduled?

11–5   Can a WBS always be established for attaining an objective?

11–6   Who determines the work necessary to accomplish an objective?

11–7   What role does a functional manager play in establishing the first three levels of the WBS?

11-8 Should the length of a program have an impact on whether or not to set up a separate project or task for administrative support? How about for raw materials?

11-9 Is it possible for the WBS to be designed so that resource allocation is easier to identify?

11-10 If the scope of effort of a project changes during execution of activities, what should be the role of the functional manager?

11-11 What types of conflicts can occur during the planning cycle, and what modes should be used for their resolution?

11-12 What would be the effectiveness of Figure 11-3 if the work packages were replaced by tasks?

11-13 Under what situations or projects would work planning authorization not be necessary?

11-14 On what types of projects could hedge positions be easily identified on a schedule?

11-15 Can activities 5 and 6 of Figure 11-8 be eliminated? What risks does a project manager incur if these activities are eliminated?

11-16 Where in the planning cycle should responsibility charts be prepared? Can you identify this point in Figure 11-8?

11-17 For each one of the decision points in Figure 11-10, who makes the decision? Who must input information? What is the role of the functional manager and the functional team member? Where are strategic variables identified?

11-18 Consider a project in which all project planning is performed by a group. After all planning is completed, including the program plan and schedules, a project manager is selected. Is there anything wrong with this arrangement? Can it work?

11-19 How do the customer and contractor know if each one completely understands the statement of work, the work breakdown structure, and the program plan?

11-20 Should a good project plan formulate methods for anticipating problems?

11-21 Some project managers schedule staff meetings as the primary means for planning and control. Do you agree with this philosophy?

11-22 Paul Mali (*Management by Objectives*, New York: John Wiley, 1972, p. 12) defines MBO as a five-step process:

- Finding the objective
- Setting the objective
- Validating the objective
- Implementing the objective
- Controlling and reporting status of the objective

How can the work breakdown structure be used to accomplish each of the above steps? Would you agree or disagree that the more levels that the WBS contains, the greater the understanding and clarity of those steps necessary to complete the objectives?

11-23 Many textbooks on management state that you should plan like you work, by doing one thing at a time. Can this same practice be applied at the project level, or must a project manager plan all activities at once?

11-24 Is it true that project managers set the milestones and functional managers hope they can meet them?

11-25 You have been asked to develop a work breakdown structure for a project. How should you go about accomplishing this? Should the WBS be time-phased, department-phased, division-phased, or some combination?

11-26 You have just been instructed to develop a schedule for introducing a new product into the marketplace. Below are the elements that must appear in your schedule. Arrange these elements into a work breakdown structure (down through level 3), and then draw the arrow diagram. You may feel free to add additional topics as necessary.

- Production layout
- Market testing
- Analyze selling cost
- Analyze customer reactions
- Storage and shipping costs
- Select salesmen
- Train salesmen
- Train distributors
- Literature to salesmen
- Literature to distributors
- Print literature
- Sales promotion
- Sales manual
- Trade advertising

- Review plant costs
- Select distributors
- Lay out artwork
- Approve artwork
- Introduce at trade show
- Distribute to salesmen
- Establish billing procedure
- Establish credit procedure
- Revise cost of production
- Revise selling cost
- Approvals*
- Review meetings*
- Final specifications
- Material requisitions

(*Approvals and review meetings can appear several times.)

11-27 Once a project begins, a good project manager will set up checkpoints. How should this be accomplished? Will it matter what the duration of the project is? Can checkpoints be built into a schedule? If so, how should they be identified?

11-28 Detailed schedules (through WBS levels 3, 4, 5, . . .) are prepared by the functional managers. Should these schedules be shown to the customer?

11-29 The project startup phase is complete, and you are now ready to finalize the operational plan. Below are six steps that are often part of the finalization procedure. Place them in the appropriate order.

1. Draw diagrams for each individual WBS element.
2. Establish the work breakdown structure and identify the reporting elements and levels.
3. Create a coarse (arrow-diagram) network and decide upon the WBS.
4. Refine the diagram by combining all logic into one plan. Then decide upon the work assignments.

5. If necessary, try to condense the diagram as much as possible without losing clarity.
6. Integrate diagrams at each level until only one exists. Then begin integration into higher WBS levels until the desired plan is achieved.

11-30 Below are seven factors that must be considered before finalizing a schedule. Explain how a base case schedule can change as a result of each of these:

- Introduction or acceptance of the product in the marketplace
- Present or planned manpower availability
- Economic constraints of the project
- Degree of technical difficulty
- Manpower availability
- Availability of personnel training
- Priority of the project

11-31 You are the project manager of a nine-month effort. You are now in the fifth month of the project and are more than two weeks behind schedule, with very little hope of catching up. The dam breaks in a town near you, and massive flooding and mudslides take place. Fifteen of your key functional people request to take off three days from the following week to help fellow church members dig out. Their functional managers, bless their hearts, have left the entire decision up to you. Should you let them go?

11-32 Once the functional manager and project manager agree on a project schedule, who is responsible for getting the work performed? Who is accountable for getting the work performed? Why the difference, if any?

11-33 Discuss the validity of the following two statements on authority:

a. A good project manager will have more authority than his responsibility calls for.
b. A good project manager should not hold a subordinate responsible for duties that he (the project manager) does not have the authority to enforce.

11-34 Below are twelve instructions. Which are best described as planning, and which are best described as forecasting?

a. Give a complete definition of the work.
b. Lay out a proposed schedule.
c. Establish project milestones.
d. Determine the need for different resources.
e. Determine the skills required for each WBS task or element.
f. Change the scope of the effort and obtain new estimates.
g. Estimate the total time to complete the required work.
h. Consider changing resources.
i. Assign appropriate personnel to each WBS element.

j. Reschedule project resources.
k. Begin scheduling the WBS elements.
l. Change the project priorities.

11-35 A major utility company has a planning group that prepares budgets (with the help of functional groups) and selects the projects to be completed within a given time period. You are assigned as a project manager on one of the projects and find out that it should have been started "last month" in order to meet the completion date. What can you, the project manager, do about this? Should you delay the start of the project to replan the work?

11-36 The director of project management calls you into his office and informs you that one of your fellow project managers has had a severe heart attack midway through a project. You will be taking over his project, which is well behind schedule and overrunning costs. The director of project management then "orders" you to complete the project within time and cost. How do you propose to do it? Where do you start? Should you shut down the project to replan it?

11-37 Planning is often described as establishing, budgeting, scheduling, and resource allocation. Identify these four elements in Figure 11-1.

11-38 A company is undertaking a large development project that requires that a massive "blueprint design tree" be developed. What kind of WBS outline would be best to minimize the impact of having two systems, one for blueprints and one for WBS work?

11-39 A company allows each line organization to perform its own procurement activities (through a centralized procurement office) as long as the procurement funds have been allocated during the project planning phase. The project office does not sign off on these functional procurement requisitions and may not even know about them. Can this system work effectively? If so, under what conditions?

11-40 As part of a feasibility study you are asked to prepare, with the assistance of functional managers, a schedule and cost summary for a project that will occur three years downstream, if the project is approved at all. Suppose that three years downstream the project is approved. How does the project manager get functional managers to accept the schedule and cost summary that they themselves prepared three years before?

11-41 "Expecting Trouble." Good project managers know what type of trouble can occur at the various stages in the development of a project. The activities on the left indicate the various stages of a project. The list on the right identifies major problems. For each item on the left, select all of those items on the right that are applicable.

1. Request for proposal _____
2. Submittal to customer _____
3. Contract award _____
4. Design review meetings _____

5. Testing the product _____
6. Customer acceptance _____

a. Engineering does not request manufacturing input for end-item producibility.
b. Poorly defined work breakdown structure.
c. Customer does not fully realize the impact that a technical change will have upon cost and schedule.
d. Time and cost constraints are not compatible with the state-of-the-art.

e. Poor project/functional interface definition.
f. Improper systems integration had created conflicts and a communications breakdown.
g. Several functional managers did not realize that they were responsible for certain risks.
h. The impact of design changes is not systematically evaluated.

11–42 Table 11–8 identifies 26 steps in project planning and control. Identified below is a description of each of the 26 steps. Using this information, fill-in columns 1 and 2 (column 2 is a group response). After your instructor provides you with column 3, fill-in the remainder of the table.

1. *Develop the linear responsibility chart:* This chart identifies the work breakdown structure and assigns specific authority/responsibility to various individuals as groups in order to be sure that all WBS elements are accounted for. The linear responsibility chart can be prepared with either the titles or names of the individuals. Assume that this is prepared after you negotiate for

Table 11–8.

ACTIVITY	DESCRIPTION	COLUMN 1: YOUR SEQUENCE	COLUMN 2: GROUP SEQUENCE	COLUMN 3: EXPERT'S SEQUENCE	COLUMN 4: DIFFERENCE BETWEEN 1 & 3	COLUMN 5: DIFFERENCE BETWEEN 2 & 3
1.	Develop linear responsibility chart					
2.	Negotiate for qualified functional personnel					
3.	Develop specifications					
4.	Determine means for measuring progress					
5.	Prepare final report					

Table 11-8. (*Continued*)

ACTIVITY	DESCRIPTION	COLUMN 1: YOUR SEQUENCE	COLUMN 2: GROUP SEQUENCE	COLUMN 3: EXPERT'S SEQUENCE	COLUMN 4: DIFFERENCE BETWEEN 1 & 3	COLUMN 5: DIFFERENCE BETWEEN 2 & 3
6.	Authorize departments to begin work					
7.	Develop work breakdown structure					
8.	Close out functional work orders					
9.	Develop scope statement and set objectives					
10.	Develop gross schedule					
11.	Develop priorities for each project element					
12.	Develop alternative courses of action					
13.	Develop PERT network					
14.	Develop detailed schedules					
15.	Establish functional personnel qualifications					
16.	Coordinate ongoing activities					
17.	Determine resource requirements					
18.	Measure progress					
19.	Decide upon a basic course of action					
20.	Establish costs for each WBS element					
21.	Review WBS costs with each functional manager					
22.	Establish a project plan					
23.	Establish cost variances for base case elements					
24.	Price out WBS					
25.	Establish logic network with checkpoints					
26.	Review "base case" costs with director					

qualified personnel, so that you know either the names or capabilities of those individuals who will be assigned.

2. *Negotiate for qualified functional personnel:* Once the work is decided upon, the project manager tries to identify the qualifications for the desired personnel. This then becomes the basis for the negotiation process.

3. *Develop specifications:* This is one of the four documents needed to initially define the requirements of the project. Assume that these are either performance or material specifications, and are provided to you at the initial planning stage by either the customer or the user.

4. *Determine the means for measuring progress:* Before the project plan is finalized and project execution can begin, the project manager must identify the means for measuring progress; specificially, what is meant by an out-of-tolerance condition and what are the tolerances/variances/thresholds for each WBS base case element?

5. *Prepare the final report:* This is the final report to be prepared at the termination of the project.

6. *Authorize departments to begin work:* This step authorizes departments to begin the actual execution of the project, *not* the planning. This step occurs generally after the project plan has been established, finalized, and perhaps even approved by the customer or user group. This is the initiation of the work orders for project implementation.

7. *Develop the work breakdown structure:* This is one of the four documents required for project definition in the early project planning stage. Assume that WBS is constructed using a bottom-up approach. In other words, the WBS is constructed from the logic network (arrow diagram) and checkpoints which will eventually become the basis for the PERT/CPM charts. (See Activity 25).

8. *Close out functional work orders:* This is where the project manager tries to prevent excessive charging to his project by closing out the functional work orders (i.e., Activity 6) as work terminates. This includes cancelling all work orders except those needed to administer the termination of the project and the preparation of the final report.

9. *Develop scope statement and set objectives:* This is the statement of work and is one of the four documents needed in order to identify the requirements of the project. Usually, the WBS is the structuring of the statement of work.

10. *Develop gross schedule:* This is the summary or milestone schedule needed at project initiation in order to define the four requirements documents for the project. The gross schedule includes start and end dates (if known), other major milestones, and data items.

11. *Develop priorities for each project element:* After the base case is identified and alternative courses of action are considered (i.e., contingency planning), the project team performs a sensitivity analysis for each element of the WBS. This may require assigning priorities for each WBS element, and the highest priorities may *not* necessarily be assigned to elements on the critical path.

12. *Develop alternative courses of action:* Once the base case is known and detailed courses of action (i.e., detailed scheduling) are prepared, project

managers conduct "what if" games to develop possible contingency plans.

13. *Develop PERT network:* This is the finalization of the PERT/CPM network and becomes the basis from which detailed scheduling will be performed. The logic for the PERT network can be conducted earlier in the planning cycle (See Activity 25), but the finalization of the network, together with the time durations, are usually based upon who has been (or will be) assigned, and the resulting authority/responsibility of the individual. In other words, the activity time duration is a function not only of the performance standard, but also of the individual's expertise and authority/responsibility.

14. *Develop detailed schedules:* These are the detailed project schedules, and are constructed from the PERT/CPM chart and the capabilities of the assigned individuals.

15. *Establish functional personnel qualifications:* Once senior management reviews the base case costs and approves the project, the project manager begins the task of conversion from rough to detail planning. This includes identification of the required resources, and then the respective qualifications.

16. *Coordinate ongoing activities:* These are the ongoing activities for project execution, not project planning. These are the activities that were authorized to begin in Activity 6.

17. *Determine resource requirements:* After senior management approves the estimated base case costs obtained during rough planning, detailed planning begins by determining the resource requirements, including human resources.

18. *Measure progress:* As the project team coordinates on-going activities during project execution, the team monitors progress and prepares status reports.

19. *Decide upon a basic course of action:* Once the project manager obtains the rough cost estimates for each WBS element, the project manager puts together all of the pieces and determines the basic course of action.

20. *Establish costs for each WBS element:* After deciding upon the base case, the project manager establishes the base case cost for each WBS element in order to prepare for the senior management pricing review meeting. These costs are usually the same as those which were provided by the line managers.

21. *Review WBS costs with each functional manager:* Each functional manager is provided with the WBS and told to determine his role and price out his functional involvement. The project manager then reviews the WBS costs to make sure that everything was accounted for and without duplication of effort.

22. *Establish project plan:* This is the final step in detail planning. Following this step, project execution begins. (Disregard the situation where project plan development can be run concurrently with project execution.)

23. *Establish cost variances for base case elements:* Once the priorities are known for each base case element, the project manager establishes the allowable cost variances which will be used as a means for measuring progress. Cost reporting is minimum as long as the actual costs remain within these allowable variances.

24. *Price out the WBS:* This is where the project manager provides each functional manager with the WBS for initial activity pricing.

25. *Establish logic network with checkpoints:* This is the bottom-up approach that is often used as the basis for developing both the WBS and later the PERT/CPM network.
26. *Review "base case" costs with Director:* Here the project manager takes the somewhat rough costs obtained during the WBS functional pricing and review and seeks management's approval to begin detail planning.

11–43 Consider the work breakdown structure shown in Figure 11–16. Can the project be managed off of this one sheet of paper assuming that, at the end of each month, the project manager also receives a cost and percent complete summary?

CASE STUDY: THE TWO-BOSS PROBLEM

On May 15, 1977, Brian Richards was assigned full-time to Project Turnbolt by Fred Taylor, manager of the thermodynamics department. All work went smoothly for four and one-half of the five months necessary to complete this effort. During this period of successful performance Brian Richards had good working relations with Edward Compton (the Turnbolt Project Engineer) and Fred Taylor.

Fred treated Brian as a Theory Y employee. Once a week Fred and Brian would chat about the status of Brian's work. Fred would always conclude their brief meeting with, "You're doing a fine job, Brian. Keep it up. Do anything you have to do to finish the project."

During the last month of the project Brian began receiving conflicting requests from the project office and the department manager as to the preparation of the final report. Compton told Brian Richards that the final report was to be assembled in viewgraph format (i.e., "bullet" charts) for presentation to the customer at the next technical interchange meeting. The project did not have the funding necessary for a comprehensive engineering report.

The theromodynamics department, on the other hand, had a policy that all engineering work done on new projects would be documented in a full and comprehensive report. This new policy was implemented about one year ago when Fred Taylor became department manager. Rumor had it that Fred wanted formal reports so that he could put his name on them and either publish or present them at technical meetings. All work performed in the thermodynamics department required Taylor's signature before it could be released to the project office as an official company position. Upper-level management did not want their people to publish and therefore did not maintain a large editorial or graphic arts department. Personnel desiring to publish had to get the department manager's approval and, upon approval, had to prepare the entire report themselves, without any "overhead" help. Since Taylor had taken over the reins as department head, he had presented three papers at technical meetings.

A meeting was held between Brian Richards, Fred Taylor, and Edward Compton.

Edward: "I don't understand why we have a problem? All the project office wants is a simple summary of the results. Why should we have to pay for a report that we don't want or need?"

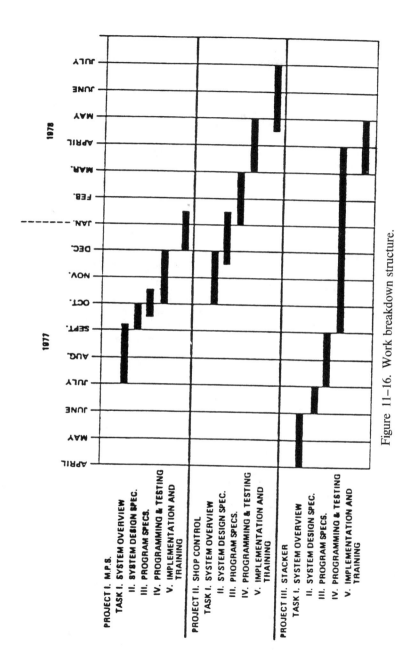

Figure 11–16. Work breakdown structure.

Fred: "We have professional standards in this department. All work that goes out must be fully documented for future use. I purposely require that my signature be attached to all communications leaving this department. This way we obtain uniformity and standardization. You project people must understand that, although you can institute your own project policies and procedures (within the constraints and limitations of company policies and procedures), we department personnel also have standards. Your work must be prepared within our standards and specifications."

Edward: "The project office controls the purse strings. We (the project office) specified that only a survey report was necessary. Furthermore, if you want a more comprehensive report, then you had best do it on your own overhead account. The project office isn't going to foot the bill for your publications."

Fred: "The customary procedure is to specify in the program plan the type of report requested from the departments. Inasmuch as your program plan does not specify this, I used my own discretion as to what I thought you meant."

Edward: "But I told Brian Richards what type of report I wanted. Didn't he tell you?"

Fred: "I guess I interpreted the request a little differently from what you had intended. Perhaps we should establish a new policy that all program plans must specify reporting requirements. This would alleviate some of the misunderstandings, especially since my department has several projects going on at one time. In addition, I am going to establish a policy for my department that all requests for interim, status, or final reports be given to me directly. I'll take personal charge of all reports."

Edward: "That's fine with me! And for your first request I'm giving you an order that I want a survey report, not a detailed effort."

Brian: Well, since the meeting is over, I guess I'll return to my office (and begin updating my resumé just in case)."

CASE STUDY: PROJECT OVERRUN

The Green Company production project was completed three months behind schedule and at a cost overrun of approximately 60 percent. Following submittal of the final report, Phil Graham, the director of project management, called a meeting to discuss the problems encountered on the Green Project.

Phil Graham: "We're not here to point the finger at anyone. We're here to analyze what went wrong and to see if we can develop any policies and/or procedures that will prevent this from happening in the future. What went wrong?"

Project Manager: "When we accepted the contract, Green did not have a fixed delivery schedule for us to go by because they weren't sure when their new production plant would be ready to begin production activities. So, we estimated 3,000 units per month for months five through twelve of the project. When they found that the production plant would be available two months ahead of schedule, they asked us to accelerate our production activities. So, we put all of our production people on overtime in order to satisfy their schedule. This was our mistake, because we accepted a fixed delivery date and budget before we understood everything."

Functional Manager: "Our problem was that the customer could not provide us with a fixed set of specifications, because the final set of specifications depended upon the OSHA and EPA requirements which could not be confirmed until initial testing of the new plant. Our people, therefore, were asked to commit to man-hours before specifications could be reviewed.

"Six months after project go-ahead, Green Company issued the final specifications. We had to remake 6,000 production units because they did not live up to the new specifications."

Project Manager: "The customer was willing to pay for the remake units. This was established in the contract. Unfortunately, our contract people didn't tell me that we were still liable for the penalty payments if we didn't adhere to the original schedule."

Phil Graham: "Don't you feel that misinterpretation of the terms and conditions is your responsibility?"

Project Manager: "I guess I'll have to take some of the blame."

Functional Manager: "We need specific documentation on what to do in case of specification changes. I don't think that our people realize that user approval of specifications is not a contract agreed to in blood. Specifications can change, even in the middle of a project. Our people must understand that, as well as the necessary procedures for implementing change."

Phil Graham: "I've heard that the functional employees on the assembly line are grumbling about the Green Project. What's their gripe?"

Functional Manager: "We were directed to cut out all overtime on all projects. But when the Green Project got into trouble, overtime became a way of life. For nine months, the functional employees on the Green Project had as much overtime as they wanted. This made the functional employees on other projects very unhappy.

"To make matters worse, the functional employees got used to a big take-home paycheck and started living beyond their means. When the project ended, so did their overtime. Now, they claim that we should give them the opportunity for more overtime. Everybody hates us."

Phil Graham: "Well, now we know the causes of the problem. Any recommendations for cures and future prevention activities?"

12
Program Evaluation and Review Technique (PERT)

12.0 INTRODUCTION

Management is continually seeking new and better control techniques to cope with the complexities, masses of data, and tight deadlines that are characteristic of many industries and their highly competitive environments today, as well as seeking better methods for presenting technical and cost data to customers.

Four integrated project management techniques have come into prominence since World War II. The most recent of these techniques are the program evaluation and review technique (PERT), the critical path method (CPM), and variations of them. Of somewhat earlier origin is the line of balance (LOB),* which was introduced in 1941, and of course, the Gantt chart has long been used in industry.

Perhaps the best known of all the relatively new techniques is the program evaluation and review technique. PERT has several distinguishing characteristics:

- It forms the basis for all planning and predicting; provides management with the ability to plan for best possible use of resources to achieve a given goal within time and cost limitations.
- It provides visibility and enables management to control "one-of-a-kind" programs as opposed to repetitive situations.
- It helps management handle the uncertainties involved in programs by answering such questions as to how time delays in certain elements influence project completion, where slack exists between elements, and what elements are crucial to meet the completion date. This provides management with a means for evaluating alternatives.

---

*Line of balance is more applicable to manufacturing operations for production line activities. However, it can be used for project management activities where a finite number of deliverables must be produced in a given time period. The reader need only refer to the multitude of texts on production management for more information on this technique.

- It provides a basis for obtaining the necessary facts for decision making.
- It utilizes a so-called time network analysis as the basic method to determine manpower, material, and capital requirements as well as providing a means for checking progress.
- It provides the basic structure for reporting information.

PERT was originally developed in 1958 and 1959 to meet the needs of the "Age of Massive Engineering" where the techniques of Taylor and Gantt were inapplicable. The Special Projects Office of the U.S. Navy, concerned with performance trends on large military development programs, introduced PERT on its Polaris Weapon System in 1958, after the technique had been developed with the aid of the management consulting firm of Booz, Allen, and Hamilton. Since that time, PERT has spread rapidly throughout almost all industries. At about the same time the Navy was developing PERT, the DuPont Company initiated a similar technique known as the critical path method (CPM), which also has spread widely, and is particularly concentrated in the construction and process industries.

In the early 1960s, the basic requirements of PERT/time as established by the Navy were as follows:

- All of the individual tasks to complete a given program must be visualized in a clear-enough manner to be put down in a network, which is comprised of events and activities; i.e., follow the work breakdown structure.
- Events and activities must be sequenced on the network under a highly logical set of ground rules that allow the determination of important critical and subcritical paths. Networks can have up to one hundred or more events, but not less than ten or twenty.
- Time estimates must be made for each activity of the network on a three-way basis. Optimistic, most likely, and pessimistic elapsed-time figures are estimated by the person(s) most familiar with the activity involved.
- Critical path and slack times are computed. The critical path is that sequence of activities and events whose accomplishment will require the greatest expected time.

A big advantage of PERT is the kind of planning required to create a major network. Network development and critical path analysis reveal interdependencies and problem areas that are neither obvious nor well defined by other planning methods. The technique therefore determines where the greatest effort should be made for a project to stay on schedule.

The second advantage of PERT is that one can determine the probability of meeting specified deadlines by development of alternative plans. If the decision-maker is statistically sophisticated, he can examine the standard deviations and the probability of accomplishment data. If there exists a minimum of uncertainty, one may use the single-time approach, of course, while retaining the advantage of network analysis.

A third advantage is the ability to evaluate the effect of changes in the program. For example, PERT can evaluate the effect of a contemplated shift of resources from the less critical activities to the activities identified as probable bottlenecks. Other resources and performance trade-offs may also be evaluated. PERT/CPM can also evaluate the effect of a deviation in the actual time required for an activity from what had been predicted.

Finally, PERT allows a large amount of sophisticated data to be presented in a well-organized diagram from which both contractor and customer can make joint decisions.

PERT, unfortunately, is not without its disadvantages. The complexity of PERT adds to the implementation problems. There exist more data requirements for a PERT-organized MCCS reporting system than for most others. PERT, therefore, becomes an item that is expensive to maintain and is utilized most often on large, complex programs.

In recent years, many companies have taken a hard look at the usefulness of PERT on small projects. The literature contains many diversified approaches toward applying PERT to other than large and complex programs. The result has been the PERT/LOB procedures, which, when applied properly, can do the following job:

- Cut project costs and reduce time scale
- Coordinate and expedite planning
- Eliminate idle time
- Provide better scheduling and control of subcontractor activities
- Develop better troubleshooting procedures
- Cut the time required for routine decisions, but allow more time for decision-making

Even with these advantages, many companies should ask themselves whether or not they actually need PERT. Incorporation of PERT may not be easy, even if canned software packages are available. One of the biggest problems with incorporating PERT occurred in the 1960s when the Department of Defense requested that DoD customers adopt PERT/cost for relating cost and schedules. This resulted in the expenditure of considerable cost and effort on behalf of the contractor to overcome the numerous cost-accounting problems. Many contractors eventually went to two sets of books; one set was for program control (which was in compliance with standard company cost control procedures), and a second set was created for customer reporting. Therefore, before accepting a PERT system, management must perform a trade-off study to determine if the results are worth the cost.

An in-depth study of PERT/CPM would require a course or two by itself. The intent of this chapter is to familiarize the reader with the terminology, capability, and applications of PERT/CPM. For a more detailed description, the reader should consult the literature.[1-4] Several texts are available that also combine PERT with project management. (Weist and Levy provide an eighteen-page bibliography of PERT-related topics.[4])

12.1 NETWORK FUNDAMENTALS

The major discrepancy with Gantt, milestone, or bubble charts is the inability to show the interdependencies between events and activities. These interdependencies must be identified so that a master plan can be developed that provides an up-to-date picture of operations at all times and is easily understood by all.

Interdependencies are shown through the construction of networks. Network analysis can provide valuable information for planning, integration of plans, time studies, scheduling, and resource management. The primary purpose of network planning is to eliminate the need for crisis management by providing a pictorial representation of the total program. The following management information can be obtained from such a representation:

- Impact of late starts
- Impact of early starts
- Cost of a crash program
- Slippage in planning

Networks are composed of events and activities. An event is defined as the starting or ending point for a group of activities, and an activity is the work required to proceed from one event or point in time to another. Figure 12–1 shows the standard nomenclature for PERT networks. The circles represent events, and arrows represent activities. The numbers in the circles signify the specific events or accomplishments. The number over the arrow specifies the time needed (hours, days, months), to go from event 6 to event 3. The events need not be numbered in any specific order. However, event 6 must take place before event 3 can be completed (or begin). In Figure 12–2 (a), event 26 must

---

1. Joseph G. Moder and Cecil R. Phillips, *Project Management with CPM and PERT* (New York: Van Nostrand Reinhold, 1964, 1970).

2. Russell D. Archibald and R. L. Villoria, *Network-Based Management Systems* (New York: John Wiley, 1967).

3. Robert W. Miller, *Schedule, Cost and Project Control with PERT* (New York: McGraw-Hill, 1963).

4. J. D. Weist and F. K. Levy, *A Management Guide to PERT/CPM,* (Englewood Cliffs, New Jersey: Prentice-Hall, 1977).

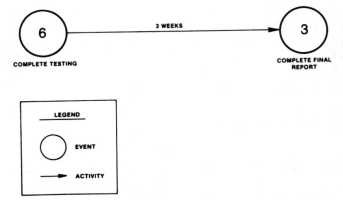

Figure 12-1. Standard PERT nomenclature.

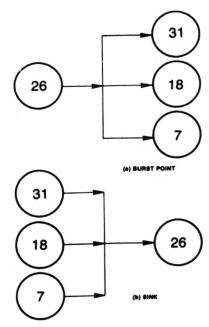

Figure 12-2. PERT sources (burst points) and sinks.

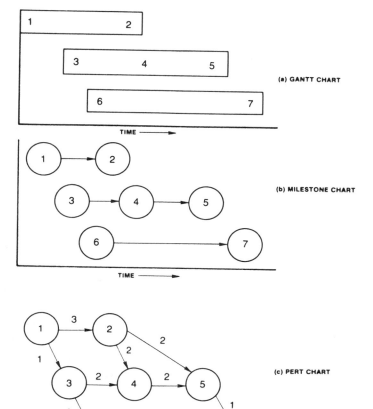

Figure 12–3. Conversion from bar chart to PERT chart.

take place prior to events 7, 18, and 31. In Figure 12–2 (b), the opposite holds true, and events 7, 18, and 31 must take place prior to event 26. Figure 12–2 (b) is similar to "and gates" used in logic diagrams.*

Elsewhere we have summarized the advantages and disadvantages of Gantt and milestone charts. These charts, however, can be used to develop the PERT network, as shown in Figure 12–3. The bar chart in Figure 12–3 (a) can be

---

*PERT diagrams can, in fact, be considered as logic diagrams. Many of the symbols used in PERT have been adapted from logic flow nomenclature.

Table 12–1. Sequence of Events.

ACTIVITY	TITLE	IMMEDIATE PREDECESSORS	ACTIVITY TIME, WEEKS
1–2	A	—	1
2–3	B	A	5
2–4	C	A	2
3–5	D	B	2
3–7	E	B	2
4–5	F	C	2
4–8	G	C	3
5–6	H	D,F	2
6–7	I	H	3
7–8	J	E,I	3
8–9	K	G,J	2

converted to the milestone chart in Figure 12–3 (b). By then defining the relationship between the events on different bars in the milestone chart, we can construct the PERT chart in Figure 12–3 (c).

PERT is basically a management planning and control tool. It can be considered as a road map for a particular program or project in which all of the major elements (events) have been completely identified together with their corresponding interrelations.* PERT charts are often constructed from back to front because, for many projects, the end-date is fixed and the contractor has front-end flexibility.

One of the purposes of constructing the PERT chart is to determine how much time is needed to complete the project. PERT, therefore, uses time as a common denominator to analyze those elements that directly influence the success of the project, namely, time, cost, and performance. The construction of the network requires two inputs. First, a selection must be made as to whether the events represent the start or the completion of an activity. Event completions are generally preferred. The next step is to define the sequence of events, as shown in Table 12–1, which relates each event to its immediate predecessor. Large projects can easily be converted into PERT networks once the following questions are answered:

● What job immediately precedes this job?
● What job immediately follows this job?
● What jobs can be run concurrently?

*These events in the PERT charts should be broken down to at least the same reporting levels as defined in the work breakdown structure.

Figure 12–4 shows a typical **PERT** network. The bold line in Figure 12–4 represents the critical path, which is established by the longest time span through the total system of events. The critical path is composed of events 1– 2–3–5–6–7–8–9. The critical path is vital for successful control of the project because it tells management two things:

- Because there is no slack time in any of the events on this path, any slip-page will cause a corresponding slippage in the end-date of the program unless this slippage can be recovered during any of the downstream events (on the critical path).
- Because the events on this path are the most critical for the success of the project, management must take a hard look at these events in order to improve the total program.

Using **PERT/CPM** we can now identify the earliest possible dates on which we can expect an event to occur, or an activity to start or end. There is nothing overly mysterious about this type of calculation, but without a network analysis the information might be hard to obtain.

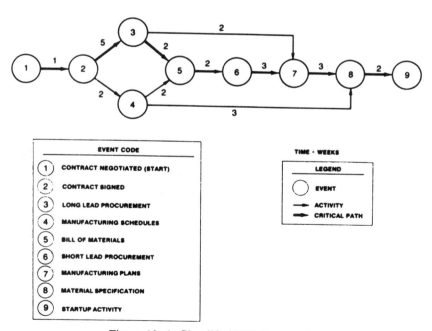

Figure 12–4. Simplified **PERT** network.

12.2   SLACK TIME

Since there exists only one path through the network that is the longest, the other paths must be either equal in length to or shorter than that path. Therefore, there must exist events and activities that can be completed before the time when they are actually needed. The time differential between the scheduled completion date and the required date to meet critical path is referred to as the slack time. From Figure 12–4, event 4 is not on the critical path. To go from event 2 to event 5 on the critical path requires seven weeks taking the route 2–3–5. If route 2–4–5 is taken, only four weeks are required. Therefore, event 4, which requires two weeks for completion, should begin anywhere from zero to three weeks after event 2 is complete. During these three weeks, management might find another use for the resources of people, money, equipment, and facilities required to complete event 4.

The critical path is vital for resource scheduling and allocation because the project manager, with coordination from the functional manager, can reschedule those events not on the critical path for accomplishment during other time periods when maximum utilization of resources can be achieved, provided that the critical path time is not extended. This type of rescheduling through the use of slack times provides for a better balance of resources throughout the company, and may possibly reduce project costs by eliminating idle or waiting time.

Slack can be defined as the difference between the latest allowable date and the earliest expected date based upon the nomenclature below:

T_E = the earliest time (date) on which an event can be expected to take place
T_L = the latest date on which an event can take place without extending the completion date of the project
Slack time = $T_L - T_E$

The calculation for slack time is performed for each event in the network as shown in Figure 12–5, by identifying the earliest expected date and the latest starting date. For event 1, $T_L - T_E = 0$. Event 1 serves as the reference point for the network and could just as easily have been defined as a calendar date. As before, the critical path is represented as a bold line. The events on the critical path have no slack (i.e., $T_L = T_E$) and provide the boundaries for the noncritical path events.* Since event 2 is critical, $T_L = T_E = 3 + 7 = 10$ for event 5. Event 6 terminates the critical path with a completion time of 15 weeks.

---

*There are special situations where the critical path may include some slack. These cases will not be considered here.

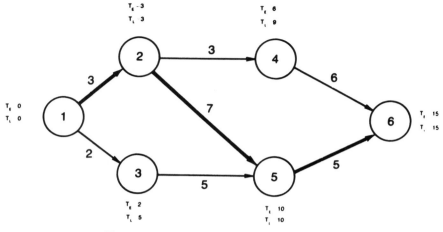

Figure 12–5. PERT network with slack time.

The earliest time for event 3, which is not on the critical path, would be two weeks ($T_E = 0 + 2 = 2$), assuming that it started as early as possible. The latest allowable date is obtained by subtracting the time required to complete the activity from events 3 to 5 from the latest starting date of event 5. Therefore, T_L (for event 3) $= 10 - 5 = 5$ weeks. Event 3 can now occur anywhere between weeks 2 and 5 without interfering with the scheduled completion date of the project. This same procedure can be applied to event 4, in which case $T_E = 6$ and $T_L = 9$.

Figure 12–5 contains a simple PERT network, and therefore the calculation of slack time is not too difficult. For complex networks containing multiple paths, the earliest starting dates must be found by proceeding from start to finish through the network, while latest allowable starting date must be calculated by working backward from finish to start.

The importance of knowing exactly where the slack exists cannot be overstated. Proper use of slack time permits better technical performance. Donald Marquis has observed that those companies making proper use of slack time were 30 percent more successful than the average in completing technical requirements.[5]

Because of these slack times, PERT networks are often not plotted with a time scale. Planning requirements, however, can require that PERT charts be reconstructed with time scales, in which case a decision must be made as to

---

5. Donald Marquis, "Ways of Organizing Projects," *Innovation,* 1969.

whether we wish early or late time requirements for slack variables. This is shown in Figure 12–6 for comparison with total program costs and manpower planning . Early time requirements for slack variables are utilized in this figure.

The earliest times and late times can be combined to determine the probability of successfully meeting the schedule. A sample of the required information is shown in Table 12–2. The earliest and latest times are considered as random variables. The original schedule refers to the schedule for event occurrences that were established at the beginning of the project. The last column in Table 12–2 gives the probability that the earliest time will not be greater than the original schedule time for this event. The exact method for determining this probability, as well as the variances, will be described in Section 12.5.

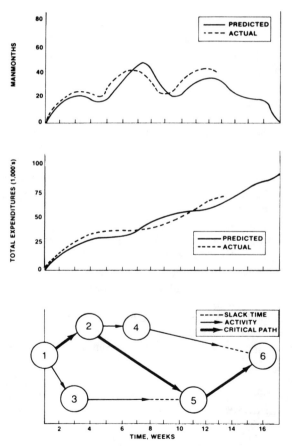

Figure 12–6. Comparison models for a time-phased PERT chart.

Table 12-2. PERT Control Output Information.

EVENT NUMBER	EARLIEST TIME		LATEST TIME		SLACK	ORIGINAL SCHEDULE	PROBABILITY OF MEETING SCHEDULE
	EXPECTED	VARIANCE	EXPECTED	VARIANCE			

12.3 NETWORK REPLANNING

Once constructed, the PERT/CPM charts provide the framework from which detailed planning can be initiated and costs can be controlled and tracked. Many iterations, however, are normally made during the planning phase before the PERT/CPM chart is finished. Figure 12–7 shows this iteration process. The slack times form the basis from which additional iterations, or network replanning, can be performed. Network replanning is performed either at the conception of the program in order to reduce the length of the critical path, or during the program, should the unexpected occur. If all were to go according

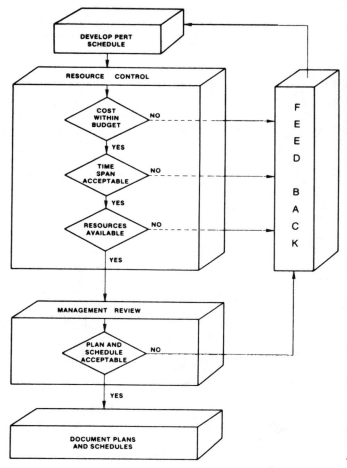

Figure 12–7. Iteration process for PERT schedule development.

to schedule, then the original PERT/CPM chart would be unchanged for the duration of the project. But, how many programs or projects follow an exact schedule from start to finish?

Suppose that activities 1–2 and 1–3 in Figure 12–5 require manpower from the same functional unit. Upon inquiry by the project manager, the functional manager asserts that he can reduce activity 1–2 by one week if he shifts resources from activity 1–3 to activity 1–2. Should this happen, however, activity 1–3 will increase in length by one week. Reconstructing the PERT/CPM network as shown in Figure 12–8, the length of the critical path is reduced by one week, and the corresponding slack events are likewise changed.

Unfortunately, not all PERT/CPM networks permit such easy rescheduling of resources. Project managers should make every attempt to reallocate resources so as to reduce the critical path, provided that the slack was not intentionally planned as a safety valve.

Transferring resources from slack paths to more critical paths is only one method for reducing expected project time. Four other methods are available:

- Elimination of some parts of the project
- Addition of more resources
- Substitution of less time-consuming components or activities
- Parallelization of activities

Under the ideal situation, the project start and end dates are fixed, and performance within this time scale must be completed within the guidelines described by the statement of work. Should the scope of effort have to be

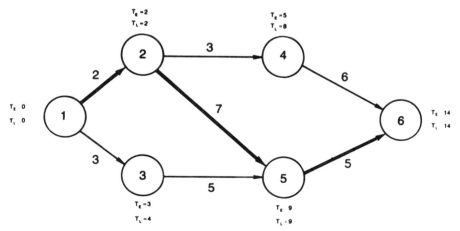

Figure 12–8. Network replanning of Figure 12–5.

reduced in order to meet other requirements, the contractor incurs a serious risk in that the project may be canceled, or performance expectations may no longer be possible.

Adding resources is not always possible. If the activities requiring these added resources also call for certain expertise, then the contractor may not have qualified or experienced employees, and may avoid the risk. The contractor might still reject this idea, even if time and money were available for training new employees, because upon project termination he might not have any other projects to which to assign these additional people. However, if the project is the construction of a new facility, then the labor-union pool may be large enough that additional experienced manpower can be hired.

Parallelization of activities can be regarded as accepting a risk by assuming that a certain event can begin in parallel with a second event that would normally be in sequence with it. This is shown in Figure 12–9. One of the biggest headaches at the beginning of any project is the purchasing of tooling and raw materials. As shown in Figure 12–9, four weeks can be saved by sending out purchase orders after contract negotiations are completed, but before the one-

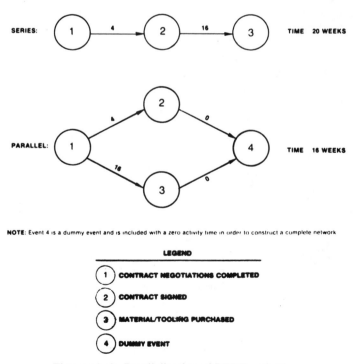

NOTE: Event 4 is a dummy event and is included with a zero activity time in order to construct a complete network

LEGEND

(1) CONTRACT NEGOTIATIONS COMPLETED

(2) CONTRACT SIGNED

(3) MATERIAL/TOOLING PURCHASED

(4) DUMMY EVENT

Figure 12–9. Parallelization of PERT activities.

month waiting period necessary to sign the contract. Here the contractor incurs a risk. Should the effort be canceled or the statement of work change prior to the signing of the contract, the customer incurs the cost of the termination liability expenses from the vendors. This risk is normally overcome by the issuance of a long-lead procurement letter immediately following contract negotiations.

There are two other types of risk that are common. In the first situation, engineering has not yet finished the prototype, and manufacturing must order the tooling in order to keep the end-date fixed. In this case, engineering may finally design the prototype to fit the tooling. In the second situation, the subcontractor finds it difficult to perform according to the original blueprints. In order to save time, the customer may allow the contractor to work without blueprints, and the blueprints are then changed to represent the as-built end-item.

Because of the complexities of large programs, network replanning becomes an almost impossible task when analyzed on total program activities. It is often better to have each department or division develop its own PERT/CPM networks, upon approval by the project office, and based upon the work breakdown structure. The individual PERT charts are then integrated into one master chart to identify total program critical paths, as shown in Figure 12–10. The

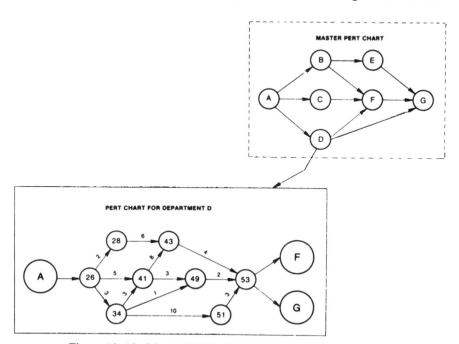

Figure 12–10. Master PERT chart breakdown by department.

reader should not infer from Figure 12–10 that department D does not interact with other departments or that department D is the only participant for this element of the project.

Segmented PERT charts can also be used when a number of contractors work on the same program. Each contractor (or subcontractor) develops his own PERT chart. It then becomes the responsibility of the prime contractor to integrate all of the subcontractors' PERT charts to ensure that total program requirements can be met.

12.4 ESTIMATING ACTIVITY TIME

Determining the elapsed time between events requires that the responsible functional managers evaluate the situation and submit their best estimates. The calculations for critical paths and slack times in the previous sections were based upon these best estimates.

In this ideal situation, the functional manager would have at his disposal a large volume of historical data from which to make his estimates. Obviously, the more historical data available, the more reliable the estimate. Many programs, however, include events and activities that are nonrepetitive. In this case, the functional managers must submit their estimates using three possible completion assumptions:

- *Most optimistic completion time.* This time assumes that everything will go according to plan and with a minimal amount of difficulties. This should occur approximately 1 percent of the time.
- *Most pessimistic completion time.* This time assumes that everything will not go according to plan and that the maximum potential difficulties will develop. This should also occur approximately 1 percent of the time.
- *Most likely completion time.* This is the time that, in the mind of the functional manager, would most often occur should this effort be reported over and over again.*

Before these three times can be combined into a single expression for expected time, two assumptions must be made. The first assumption is that the standard deviation, σ, is one-sixth of the time requirement range. This assumption stems from probability theory where the end points of a curve are three standard deviations from the mean. The second assumption requires that the

---

*It is assumed that the functional manager performs all of the estimating. The reader should be aware that there are exceptions where the program or project office would do their own estimating.

probability distribution of time required for an activity be expressible as a beta distribution.[6]

The expected time between events can be found from the expression:

$$t_e = \frac{a + 4m + b}{6}$$

where

t_e = expected time
a = most optimistic time
b = most pessimistic time
m = most likely time

As an example, if $a = 3$, $b = 7$, and $m = 5$ weeks, then the expected time, t_e, would be 5 weeks. This value for t_e would then be used as the activity time between two events in the construction of a PERT chart. This method for obtaining best estimates contains a large degree of uncertainty. If we change the variable times to $a = 2$, $b = 12$, and $m = 4$ weeks, then t_e will still be 5 weeks. The latter case, however, has a much higher degree of uncertainty because of the wider spread between the optimistic and pessimistic times. Care must be taken in the evaluation of risks in the expected times.

12.5 ESTIMATING TOTAL PROGRAM TIME

In order to calculate the probability of completing the project on time, the standard deviations of each activity must be known. This can be found from the expression:

$$\sigma_{t_e} = \frac{b - a}{6}$$

where σ_{t_e} is the standard deviation of the expected time, t_e. Another useful expression is the variance, v, which is the square of the standard deviation. The variance is primarily useful for comparison to the expected values. However, the standard deviation can be used just as easily, except that we must identify whether it is a one, two, or three sigma limit deviation. Figure 12–11 shows

---

6. See Hillier F. S. and Lieberman G. J., *Introduction to Operations Research* (San Francisco: Holden-Day, 1967), p. 229.

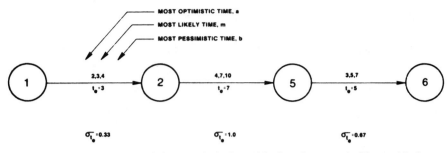

Figure 12–11. Expected time analysis for critical path events in Figure 12–5.

the critical path of Figure 12–5, together with the corresponding values from which the expected times were calculated, as well as the standard deviations. The total path standard deviation is calculated by the square root of the sum of the squares of the activity standard deviations using the following expression:

$$\sigma_{\text{total}} = \sqrt{\sigma^2_{1-2} + \sigma^2_{2-5} + \sigma^2_{5-6}}$$
$$= \sqrt{(0.33)^2 + (1.0)^2 + (0.67)^2}$$
$$= 1.25$$

From probability and statistics, there exists a 68 percent chance of completion within one standard deviation, 95 percent within two standard deviations, and 99 percent within three standard deviations. This is shown in Table 12–3. The key element in Table 12–3 is the outer range for each of the percentages. If there appears the possibility that the project might be extended beyond the expected fifteen weeks, then additional costs (which may not have been accounted for in the budget) will undoubtedly occur, and cost overruns will be inevitable.

Table 12–3. Statistical Estimates of Total Time (Weeks).

SIGMA LIMIT	PERCENTAGE	EXPRESSION	RANGE
1	68	15 ± 1.25	13.75–16.25
2	95	15 ± 2.50	12.50–17.50
3	99	15 ± 3.75	11.25–18.75

12.6 TOTAL PERT/CPM PLANNING

Before we continue, it is necessary to discuss the methodology for preparing PERT schedules. PERT scheduling is a six-step process. Steps one and two begin with the project manager laying out a list of activities to be performed and then placing these activities in order of precedence, thus identifying the interrelationships. These charts drawn by the project manager are called either logic charts, arrow diagrams, work flow, or simply networks. The arrow diagrams will look like Figure 12–5 with two exceptions: the activity time is not identified, and neither is the critical path.

Step three is reviewing the arrow diagrams with the line managers (i.e., the true experts) in order to obtain their assurance that neither too many nor too few activities are identified, and that the interrelationships are correct.

In step four the functional manager converts the arrow diagram to a PERT chart by identifying the time duration for each activity. It should be noted here that the time estimates that the line managers provide are based upon the *assumption of unlimited resources* because the calendar dates have not yet been defined.

Step five is the first iteration on the critical path. It is here that the project manager looks at the critical calendar dates in the definition of the project's requirements. If the critical path does not satisfy the calendar requirements, then the project manager must try to shorten the critical path using methods explained in Section 12.3 or asking the line managers to take the "fat" out of their estimates.

Step six is often the most overlooked step. Here the project manager places calendar dates on each event in the PERT chart, thus converting from planning under unlimited resources to planning with *limited resources*. Even though the line manager has given you a time estimate, there is no guarantee that the correct resources will be available when needed. That is why this step is crucial. If the line manager cannot commit to the calendar dates, then replanning will be necessary. Most companies that survive on competitive bidding lay out proposal schedules based upon unlimited resources. After contract award, the schedules are analyzed again because the company now has limited resources. After all, how can a company bid on three contracts simultaneously and put a detailed schedule into each proposal if it is not sure how many contracts, if any, it will win? For this reason customers require that formal project plans and schedules be provided thirty to ninety days after contract award.

Finally, PERT replanning should be an ongoing function during project execution. The best project managers are those individuals who continually try to assess what can go wrong and perform perturbation analysis on the schedule. (This should be obvious because the constraints and objectives of the project can change during execution.) Primary objectives on a schedule are:

- Best time
- Least cost
- Least risk

Secondary objectives include:

- Studying alternatives
- Optimum schedules
- Effective use of resources
- Communications
- Refinement of the estimating process
- Ease of project control
- Ease of time or cost revisions

Obviously, these objectives are limited by such constraints as:

- Calendar completion
- Cash or cash flow restrictions
- Limited resources
- Management approvals

12.7 CRASH TIMES

In the preceding sections, no distinction was made between PERT and CPM. The basic difference between PERT and CPM lies in the ability to calculate percent complete. PERT is used in R&D or just development activities where percent complete determination is almost impossible. Therefore, PERT is event-oriented rather than activity-oriented. In PERT, funding is normally provided for each milestone (i.e., event) achieved because incremental funding along the activity line has to be based upon percent complete. CPM, on the other hand, is activity-oriented because, in activities such as construction, percent complete along the activity line can be determined. CPM can be used as an arrow diagram network without PERT. The difference between the two methods lies in the environments in which each one evolved and how each one is applied. According to Archibald and Villoria:[7]

the environmental factors which had an important role in determining the elements of the CPM techniques were:

(a) Well-defined projects
(b) One dominant organization

---

7. R. D. Archibald and R. L. Villoria, *Network-Based Management Systems (PERT/CPM)* (New York: John Wiley, 1967), p. 14.

(c) Relatively small uncertainties

(d) One geographical location for a project

The CPM (activity-type network) has been widely used in the process industries, in construction, and in single-project industrial activities. Common problems include no place to store early arrivals of raw materials and project delays for late arrivals.

Using strictly the CPM approach, project managers can consider the cost of speeding up, or crashing, certain phases of a project. In order to accomplish this, it is necessary to calculate a crashing cost per unit time as well as the normal expected time for each activity. CPM charts, which are closely related to PERT charts, allow visual representation of the effects of crashing. There are these requirements:

- For a CPM chart, the emphasis is on activities, not events. Therefore, the PERT chart should be redrawn with each circle representing an activity rather than an event.
- In CPM, both time and cost of each activity are considered.*
- Only those activities on the critical path are considered, starting with the activities for which the crashing cost per unit time is the lowest.

Figure 12–12 shows a CPM network with the corresponding crash time for all activities both on and off the critical path. The activities are represented by circles and include an activity identification number and the estimated time. The costs expressed in the figure are usually direct costs only.

To determine crashing costs we begin with the lowest weekly crashing cost, activity A, at $2,000 per week. Although activity C has a lower crashing cost, it is not on the critical path. Only critical path activities are considered for crashing. Activity A will be the first to be crashed for a maximum of two weeks at $2,000 per week. The next activity to be considered would be F at $3,000 per week for a maximum of three weeks. These crashing costs are additional expenses above the normal estimates.

A word of caution concerning the selection and order of the activities that are to crash: There is a good possibility that as each activity is crashed, a new critical path will be developed. This new path may or may not include those elements that were bypassed because they were not on the original critical path.

Returning to Figure 12–12 (and assuming that no new critical paths are

---

*Although PERT considers mainly time, modifications through PERT/cost analysis can be made to consider the cost factors.

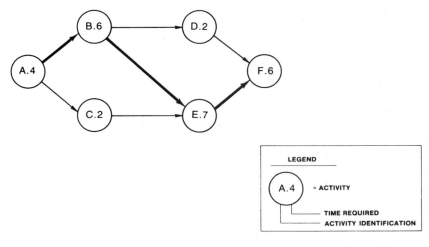

| | TIME REQUIRED, WEEKS | | COST $ | | CRASHING COST |
ACTIVITY	NORMAL	CRASH	NORMAL	CRASH	PER WEEK, $
A	4	2	10,000	14,000	2,000
B	6	5	30,000	42,500	12,500
C	2	1	8,000	9,500	1,500
D	2	1	12,000	18,000	6,000
E	7	5	40,000	52,000	6,000
F	6	3	20,000	29,000	3,000

Figure 12–12. CPM network.

developed), activities A, F, E, and B would be crashed in that order. The crashing cost would then be an increase of $37,500 from the base of $120,000 to $157,500. The corresponding time would then be reduced from 23 weeks to 15 weeks. This is shown in Figure 12–13 to illustrate how a trade-off between time and cost can be obtained. Also shown in Figure 12–13 is the increased cost of crashing elements not on the critical path. Crashing these elements would result in a cost increase of $7,500 without reducing the total project time. There is also the possibility that this figure will represent unrealistic conditions because sufficient resources are not, or cannot be, made available for the crashing period.

The purpose behind balancing time and cost is to avoid the useless waste of resources. If the direct and indirect costs can be accurately obtained, then a region of feasible budgets can be found, bounded by the early (crash) and late start (or normal) activities. This is shown in Figure 12–14.

Since the direct and indirect costs are not necessarily expressible as linear functions, time/cost trade-off relationships are made by searching for the low-

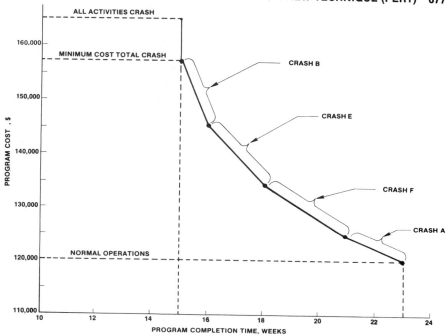

Figure 12-13. CPM crashing costs.

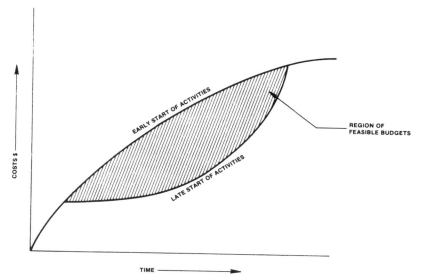

Figure 12-14. Region of feasible budgets.

est possible total cost (i.e., direct and indirect) that likewise satisfies the region of feasible budgets. This method is shown in Figure 12–15.

Like PERT, CPM also contains the concept of slack time, the maximum amount of time that a job may be delayed beyond its early start without delaying the project completion time. Figure 12–16 shows a typical representation of slack time using a CPM chart. In addition, the figure shows how target activity costs can be identified. Figure 12–16 can be modified to include normal and crash times as well as normal and crash costs. In this case, the cost box in the figure would contain two numbers: the first number would be the normal cost, and the second would be the crash cost. These numbers might also appear as running totals.

12.8 PERT/CPM PROBLEM AREAS

PERT/CPM models are not without their disadvantages and problems. Even the largest organizations with years of experience in using PERT and CPM have the same ongoing problems as the newer or smaller companies.

Many companies have a difficult time incorporating PERT systems because

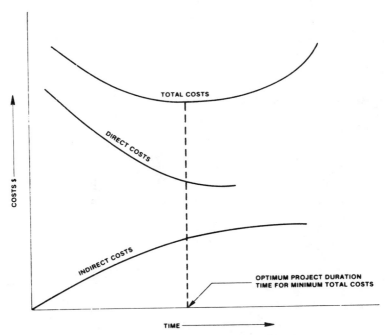

Figure 12–15. Determining project duration.

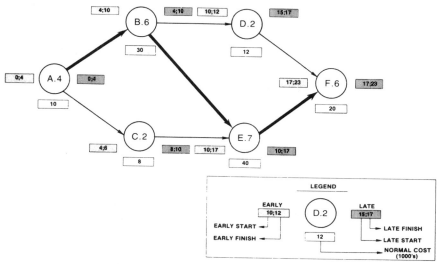

Figure 12–16. CPM network with slack.

PERT is end-item-oriented. Many upper-level managers feel that the adoption of PERT/CPM removes a good part of their power and ability to make decisions. This is particularly evident in companies that have been forced to accept PERT/CPM as part of contractual requirements.

There exists a distinct contrast in PERT systems between the planners and the doers. This human element must be accounted for in order to determine where the obligation actually lies. In most organizations PERT planning is performed by the program office and functional management. Yet once the network is constructed, the planners and managers become observers and rely on the doers to accomplish the job within time and cost limitations. Management must convince the doers that they have an obligation toward the successful completion of the established PERT/CPM plans.

Unless the project is repetitive, there usually exists a lack of historical information upon which to base the cost estimates of most optimistic, most pessimistic, and most likely times. Problems can also involve poor predictions for overhead costs, other indirect costs, material and labor escalation factors, and crash costs. It is also possible that each major functional division of the organization has its own method for estimating costs. Engineering, for example, may use historical data, whereas manufacturing operations may prefer learning curves. PERT works best if all organizations have the same method for predicting costs and performance.

PERT networks are based upon the assumption that all activities start as soon as possible. This assumes that qualified personnel and equipment are available. Regardless of how well we plan, there almost always exist differences in performance times from what would normally be acceptable for the model selected. For the selected model, time and cost should be well-considered estimates, not a spur-of-the-moment decision.

Cost control presents a problem in that the project cost and control system may not be compatible with company fiscal planning policies. Project-oriented costs may be meshed with non-PERT-controlled jobs in order to develop the annual budget. This becomes a difficult chore for cost reporting, especially when each project may have its own method for analyzing and controlling costs.

Many people have come to expect too much of PERT-type networks. Figure 12–17 illustrates a PERT/CPM network broken down by work packages with identification of the charge numbers for each activity. Large projects may contain hundreds of charge numbers. Subdividing work packages (which are supposedly the lowest element) even further by identifying all subactivities has the advantage that direct charge numbers can be easily identified, but the time and cost for this form of detail may be prohibitive. PERT/CPM networks are tools for program control, and managers must be careful that the original game plan of using networks to identify prime and supporting objectives is still met. Additional detail may mask this all-important purpose. Remember, networks are constructed as a means for understanding program reports. Management should not be required to read reports in order to understand PERT/CPM networks.

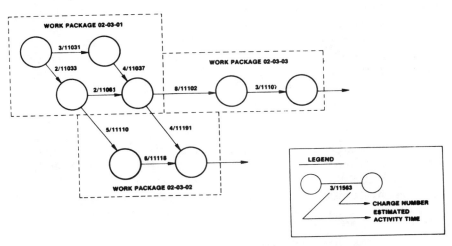

Figure 12–17. Using PERT for work package control.

12.9 ALTERNATIVE PERT/CPM MODELS

Because of the many advantages of PERT/time, numerous industries have found applications for this form of network. A partial list of these advantages includes capabilities for:

- Trade-off studies for resource control
- Providing contingency planning in the early stages of the project
- Visually tracking up-to-date performance
- Demonstrating integrated planning
- Providing visibility down through the lowest levels of the work breakdown structure
- Providing a regimented structure for control purposes to ensure compliance with the work breakdown structure and the statement of work
- Increasing functional members' ability to relate to the total program, thus providing participants with a sense of belonging

Even with these advantages, in many situations PERT/time has proved ineffective in controlling resources. In the beginning of this chapter we defined three parameters necessary for the control of resources: time, cost, and performance. With these factors in mind, companies began reconstructing PERT/time into PERT/cost and PERT/performance models.

PERT/cost is an extension of PERT/time and attempts to overcome the problems associated with the use of the most optimistic and most pessimistic time for estimating completion. PERT/cost can be regarded as a cost accounting network model based upon the work breakdown structure and capable of being subdivided down to the lowest elements, or work packages. The advantages of PERT/cost are that it:

- Contains all the features of PERT/time
- Permits cost control at any WBS level

The primary reason for the development of PERT/cost was so that project managers could identify critical schedule slippages and cost overruns in time for corrective action to be taken.

Many attempts have been made to develop effective PERT/schedule models. In almost all cases, the charts are constructed from left to right.[8] An example

---

8. Gary E. Whitehouse, "Project Management Techniques," *Industrial Engineering,* March 1973, pp. 24–29, for a description of the technique.

of such current attempts is the accomplishment/cost procedure (ACP). As described by Block:[9]

ACP reports cost based on schedule accomplishment, rather than on the passage of time. To determine how an uncompleted task is progressing with respect to cost, ACP compares (a) cost/progress relationship budgeting with (b) the cost/progress relationship expended for the task. It utilizes data accumulated from periodic reports and from the same data base generates the following:
- The relationship between cost and scheduled performance
- The accounting relationships between cost and fiscal accounting requirements
- The prediction of corporate cash flow needs

Unfortunately, the development of PERT/schedule techniques is still in its infancy. Although their applications have been identified, many companies feel locked in with their present method of control, whether it be PERT, CPM, or some other technique.

12.10 COMPUTERIZED PROJECT MANAGEMENT

Within the past few years there has been an explosion in project management software packages. Small packages may sell for a few thousand dollars, whereas the price for larger packages may be $70,000. Computerized project management can provide answers to such questions as:

- How will the project be impacted by limited resources?
- How will the project be impacted by a change in the requirements?
- What is the cash flow for the project (and for each WBS element)?
- What is the impact of overtime?
- What additional resources are needed to meet the constraints of the project?
- How will a change in the priority of a certain WBS element affect the total project?

The more sophisticated packages can provide answers to schedule and cost based upon:

- Adverse weather conditions
- Weekend activities

---

9. Ellery B. Block, "Accomplishment/Cost: Better Project Control," *Harvard Business Review,* May–June 1971, pp. 110–124. Copyright © 1971 by the President and Fellows of Harvard College; all rights reserved.

- Unleveled manpower requirements
- Variable crew size
- Splitting of activities
- Assignment of unused resources

Regardless of the sophistication of computer systems, printers and plotters prefer to draw straight lines rather than circles. Most software systems today use precedence networks, as shown in Figure 12–18, which attempt to show interrelationships on bar charts. In Figure 12–18, Task 1 and Task 2 are related because of the solid line between them. Task 3 and Task 4 can begin when Task 2 is half finished. (This cannot be shown easily on PERT without splitting activities.) The dotted lines indicate slack. The critical path can be identified either by putting an asterisk (*) beside the critical elements, by making the critical connections in a different-colored ink, or by making the critical path a bold-face type.

Precedence networks get very cumbersome to use if you have a great many tasks and complex interrelationships. To resolve this problem, computer plotters print out not only the precedence networks, but logic flows, as shown in Figure 12–19.

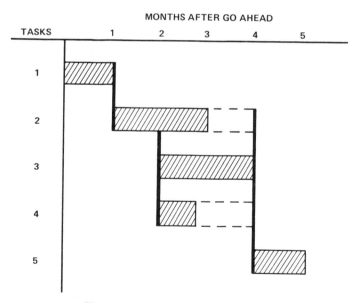

Figure 12–18. Precedence network.

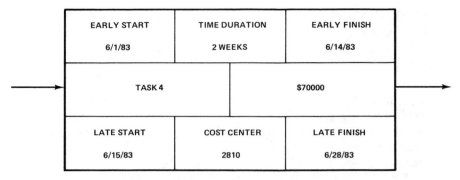

Figure 12–19. Computerized logic flow.

PROBLEMS

12–1 Should a PERT/CPM network become a means of understanding reports and schedules, or should it be vice versa?

12–2 Before PERT diagrams are prepared, should the person performing the work have a clear definition of the requirements and objectives, both prime and supporting? Is it an absolute necessity?

12–3 Who prepares the PERT diagrams? Who is responsible for their integration?

12–4 Should PERT networks follow the work breakdown structure?

12–5 How can a PERT network be used to increase functional ability to relate to the total program?

12–6 What problems are associated with applying PERT to small programs?

12–7 Should PERT network design be dependent upon the number of elements in the work breakdown structure?

12–8 Can bar charts and PERT diagrams be used to smooth out departmental manpower requirements?

12–9 Should key milestones be established at points where trade-offs are most likely to occur?

12–10 Would you agree or disagree that the cost of accelerating a project rises exponentially, especially as the project nears completion?

12–11 What are the major difficulties with PERT, and how can they be overcome?

12–12 Is PERT/cost designed to identify critical schedule slippages and cost overruns early enough such that corrective action can be taken?

12–13 Consider the following network for a small maintenance project: (all times are in days; network proceeds from node 1 to node 7).

| Job | Network NODE | | | Optimistic | Pessimistic | Most |
(Activity)	Initial	/	Final	Time	Time	Likely
A	1		2	1	3	2
B	1		4	4	6	5
C	1		3	4	6	5
D	2		6	2	4	3
E	2		4	1	3	2
F	3		4	2	4	3
G	3		5	7	15	9
H	4		6	4	6	5
I	4		7	6	14	10
J	4		5	1	3	2
K	5		7	2	4	3
L	6		7	6	14	10

a. Draw an arrow diagram representing the project.
b. What is the critical path and associated time?
c. What is the total slack time in the network?
d. What is the expected time for 68, 95, and 99 percent completion limits?
e. If activity G had an estimated time of 15 days, what impact would this have upon your answer to part b?

12–14 Consider the following network for a small MIS project (all times are in days; network proceeds from node 1 to node 10):

Job (Activity)	Network Initial /Final Node		Estimated Time
A	1	2	2
B	1	3	3
C	1	4	3
D	2	5	3
E	2	9	3
F	3	5	1
G	3	6	2
H	3	7	3
I	4	7	5
J	4	8	3
K	5	6	3
L	6	9	4
M	7	9	4
N	8	9	3
O	9	10	2

a. Identify the critical path.
b. Calculate the total network slack time.
c. Suppose that activities A, B, and C all utilize the same manpower base, and shortening any one of these three activities causes one of the other two to increase by the same amount. Can network replanning, only for these three activities, shorten the length of the critical path?
d. Repeat parts a, b, and c assuming that the estimated time for job C is 4.

12–15 On May 1, Arnie Watson sent a memo to his boss, the director of project management, stating that the MX project would require thirteen weeks for completion according to the figure shown below.

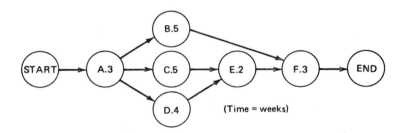

Arnie realized that the customer wanted the job completed in less time. After discussions with the functional managers, Arnie developed the table shown below:

Activity	NORMAL Time	NORMAL Cost	CRASH Time	CRASH Cost	Additional (Crash) Cost/Week
A	3	6,000	2	8,000	2,000
B	5	12,000	4	13,500	1,500
C	5	16,000	3	22,000	3,000
D	4	8,000	2	10,000	1,000
E	2	6,000	1	7,500	1,500
F	3	14,000	1	20,000	3,000
		$62,000			

a. According to the contract, there is a penalty payment of $5,000 per week for every week over six. What is the minimum amount of additional funding that Arnie should request?
b. Suppose your answer to part "a" gives you the same additional minimum cost for both an eight-week and a nine-week project. What factors would you consider before deciding whether to do it in eight or nine weeks?

12-16 On March 1, the project manager received three status reports indicating resource utilization to date. Shown below are the three reports as well as the PERT diagram.

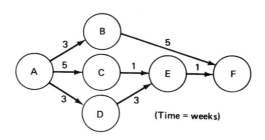

(Time = weeks)

PERCENT COMPLETION REPORT

Activity	Date Started	% Completed	Time to Complete
AB	2/1	100%	—
AC	2/1	60%	2
AD	2/1	100%	—
DE*	Not Started	—	3
BF	2/14	40%	3

*Note: Because of priorities, resources for activity DE will not be available until 3/14. Management estimates that this activity can be crashed from 3 weeks to 2 weeks at an additional cost of $3,000.

PROJECT PLANNING BUDGET: Weeks After Go-ahead

Activity	1	2	3	4	5	6	7	8	Total $
AB	2,000	2,000	2,000	—	—	—	—	—	6,000
AC	3,000	4,000	4,000	4,000	5,000	—	—	—	20,000
AD	2,000	3,000	2,500	—	—	—	—	—	7,500
BF	—	—	—	2,000	3,000	4,000	3,000	3,000	15,000
CE	—	—	—	—	—	2,500	—	—	2,500
DE	—	—	—	3,500	3,500	3,500	—	—	10,500
EF	—	—	—	—	—	—	3,000	—	3,000
Total	7,000	9,000	8,500	9,500	11,500	10,000	6,000	3,000	64,500

COST SUMMARY

Activity	Week Ending			Cumulative to Date		
	Budget Cost	Actual	(Over) Under	Budget Cost	Actual	(Over) Under
AB	—	—	—	6,000	6,200	(200)
AC	4,000	4,500	(500)	15,000	12,500	2,500
AD	—	2,400	(2,400)	7,500	7,400	100
BF	2,000	2,800	(800)	2,000	4,500	(2,500)
DE	3,500	—	3,500	3,500	—	3,500
Total	9,500	9,700	(200)	34,000	30,600	3,400

a. As of the end of Week 4, how much time is required to complete the project (i.e., time to complete)?
b. At the end of Week 4, are you over/under budget, and by how much, for the work (either partial or full) that has been completed to date? (This is *not* a cost to complete.)
c. At what point in time should the decision be made to crash activities?
d. Either construct a single table by which cost and performance data are more easily seen, or modify the above tables accordingly.

To solve this problem, you must make an assumption about the relationship between percent complete and time/cost. In the Project Planning Budget Table, assume that percent complete is *linear* with time and *nonlinear* with cost (i.e., cost must be read from table.).

12–17 Can PERT charts have more depth than the WBS?

12–18 Estimating activity time is not an easy task, especially if assumptions must be made. State whether each item identified below can be accounted for in the construction of a PERT/CPM network:

a. Consideration of weather conditions
b. Consideration of weekend activities
c. Unleveled manpower requirements
d. Checking of resource allocations
e. Variable crew size
f. Splitting (or interrupting) of activities
g. Assignment of unused resources
h. Accounting for project priorities

12–19 Scheduling departmental manpower for a project is a very difficult task, even if slack time is available. Many managers would prefer to supply manpower at a constant rate rather than continually shuffle people in and out of a project.

a. Using the information shown below, construct the PERT network, identify the critical path, and determine the slack time for each node.

ACTIVITY	WEEKS	PERSONNEL REQUIRED (FULL-TIME)
A–B	5	3
A–C	3	3
B–D	2	4
B–E	3	5
C–E	3	5
D–F	3	5
E–F	6	3

b. The network you have just created is a departmental PERT chart. Construct a weekly manpower plot assuming that all activities begin as early as possible. (Note: Overtime cannot be used to shorten the activity time.)

c. The department manager wishes to assign eight people full-time for the duration of the project. However, if an employee is no longer needed on the project, he can be assigned elsewhere. Using the base of eight people, identify the standby (or idle) time and the overtime periods.

d. Determine the standby and overtime costs, assuming that each employee is paid $300 per week and overtime is paid at time and one-half. During standby time the employee draws his full salary.

e. Repeat parts c and d and try to consider slack time in order to smooth out the manpower curve. (Hint: Some activities should begin as early as possible, while others begin as late as possible.) Identify the optimum manpower level so as to minimize the standby and overtime costs. Assume all employees must work fulltime.

f. Would your answer to parts d and e change if the employees must remain for the full duration of the project, even if they are no longer required?

12–20 How does a manager decide whether the work breakdown structure should be based upon a "tree" diagram or the PERT diagram?

12–21 Using Table A, draw the CPM chart for the project. In this case, make all identifications on the arrows (activities) rather than the events. Show that the critical path is 21 weeks.

Using Table B, draw the precedence chart for the project, showing interrelationships. Try to use a different color or shade for the critical path.

Calculate the *minimum* cash flow needed for the first four weeks of the project, assuming the following distribution.

Activity	Total Cost for Each Activity
A–H	16,960
I–P	5,160
Q–V	40,960
W	67,200
X	22,940

Furthermore, assume that *all* costs are linear with time and activity X cost must be spent in the first two weeks. Prove that the minimum cash flow is $92,000.

Table A. Data for Project CPM Chart.

ACTIVITY	PRECEDING ACTIVITY	NORMAL TIME (WEEKS)
A	—	4
B	A	6
C	B,U,V,N	3
D	C	2
E	C	2
F	C	7
G	C	7
H	D,E	4
I	—	2
J	I,R	1
K	J	1
L	K	2
M	L	1
N	M	1
O	N	2
P	O	1
Q	—	4
R	Q	1
S	—	1
T	—	1
U	S	2
V	T	2
W*	—	*
X	—	2

*Stands for total length of project. This is management support.

CASE STUDY: CROSBY MANUFACTURING CORPORATION

"I've called this meeting to resolve a major problem with our management cost and control system (MCCS)," remarked Wilfred Livingston, president. "We're having one hell of a time trying to meet competition with our antiquated MCCS reporting procedures. Last year we were considered nonresponsive to three large government contracts because we could not adhere to the customer's financial reporting requirements. The government has recently shown a renewed interest in Crosby Manufacturing Corporation. If we can computerize our project financial reporting procedure, we'll be in great shape to meet the competition head-on. The customer might even waive the financial reporting requirements if we show our immediate intent to convert."

Crosby Manufacturing was a $5 million a year electronics component manufacturing firm in 1975, at which time Wilfred "Willy" Livingston became president. His first major act was to reorganize the 700 employees into a modified matrix structure. This reorganization was the first step in Livingston's long-range plan to obtain large

Table B. Project Precedence Chart.*

Weeks

Activity	1	2	3	4	5	6	7	8	9	10	11	12	13	14	15	16	17	18	19	20	21
A																					
B																					
C																					
D																					
E																					
F																					
G																					
H																					
I																					
J																					
K																					
L																					
M																					
N																					
O																					
P																					
Q																					
R																					
S																					
T																					
U																					
V																					
W																					
X																					

*Draw the appropriate bar charts into the figure, assuming that such activity starts as early as possible. (Identify slack). Try to show the interrelationships as in a precedence network.

government contracts. The matrix provided the customer focal point policy that government agencies prefer. After three years, the matrix seemed to be working. Now we can begin the second phase, an improved MCCS policy.

On October 20, 1978, Livingston called a meeting with department managers from project management, cost accounting, MIS, data processing, and planning.

Livingston: "We have to replace our present computer with a more advanced model so as to update our MCCS reporting procedures. In order for us to grow, we'll have to develop capabilities for keeping two or even three different sets of books for our customers. Our present computer does not have this capability. We're talking about a sizable cash outlay, not necessarily to impress our customers, but to increase our business base and grow. We need weekly, or even daily, cost data so as to better control our projects."

MIS Manager: "I guess the first step in the design, development, and implementation process would be the feasibility study. I have prepared a list of the major topics which are normally included in a feasibility study of this sort. (See Exhibit 12–1.)"

Livingston: "What kind of costs are you considering in the feasibility study?"

MIS Manager: "The major cost items include input/output demands; processing; storage capacity; rental, purchase or lease of a system; nonrecurring expenditures; recurring expenditures; cost of supplies; facility requirements; and training requirements. We'll have to get a lot of this information from the EDP department."

EDP Manager: "You must remember that, for a short period of time, we'll end up with two computer systems in operation at the same time. This cannot be helped. However, I have prepared a typical (abbreviated) schedule of my own. (See Exhibit 12–2.) You'll notice from the right-hand column that I'm somewhat optimistic as to how long it should take us."

Livingston: "Have we prepared a checklist on how to evaluate a vendor?"

Exhibit 12–1. Feasibility Study

- Objectives of the study
- Costs
- Benefits
- Manual or computer-based solution?
- Objectives of the system
- Input requirements
- Output requirements
- Processing requirements
- Preliminary system description
- Evaluation of bids from the vendors
- Financial analysis
- Conclusions

Exhibit 12–2. Typical Schedule (in Months).

ACTIVITY	NORMAL TIME TO COMPLETE	CRASH TIME TO COMPLETE
Management go-ahead	0	0
Release of preliminary system specs.	6	2
Receipt of bids on specs.	2	1
Order hardware and systems software	2	1
Flow charts completed	2	2
Applications programs completed	3	6
Receipt of hardware and systems software	3	3
Testing and debugging done	2	2
Documentation, if required	2	2
Changeover completed	22	15*

*This assumes that some of the activities can be run in parallel, instead of series.

EDP Manager: "Besides the 'benchmark' test, I have prepared a list of topics that we must include in evaluation of any vendor. (See Exhibit 12–3.) We should plan to either call on or visit other installations that have purchased the same equipment and see the system in action. Unfortunately, we may have to commit real early and begin developing software packages. As a matter of fact, using the principle of concurrency, we should begin developing our software packages right now."

Livingston: "Because of the importance of this project, I'm going to violate our normal structure and appoint Tim Emary from our planning group as project leader. He's not as knowledgeable as you people are in regard to computers, but he does know how to lay out a schedule and get the job done. I'm sure your people will give him all the necessary support he needs. Remember, I'll be behind this project all the way. We're

Exhibit 12–3. Vendor Support Evaluation Factors.

- Availability of hardware and software packages
- Hardware performance, delivery and past track record
- Vendor proximity and service and support record
- Emergency backup procedure
- Availability of applications programs and their compatibility with our other systems
- Capacity for expansion
- Documentation
- Availability of consultants for systems programming and general training
- Who burdens training cost?
- Risk of obsolescence.
- Ease of use

going to convene again one week from today, at which time I expect to see a detailed schedule with all major milestones, team meetings, design review meetings, etc. . . . shown and identified. I'd like the project to be complete in 18 months, if possible. If there are risks in the schedule, identify them. Any questions?"

13
Project Graphics

13.0 INTRODUCTION

In Chapter 11, we defined the steps involved in establishing a formal program plan with detailed schedules such that the total program can be effectively managed. Once the need has arisen to commit the plan to paper via the master program plan, suitable notations must be adapted. Any plan, schedule, drawing, or specification that will be read by more than one person must be regarded as a vehicle for the communication of information. If effective communication is to be established and maintained in compliance with the requirements, this information must be expressed in a language that is understood by all recipients.

The ideal situation is to construct charts and schedules in suitable notation that can be used for both in-house control and out-of-house customer status reporting. Unfortunately, this is easier said than done. Whenever a project has to be accomplished according to a time or date deadline, then both the customer and contractor must have an accurate picture of the relations between the time allowed and the time needed. Both the customer and contractor are interested mainly in the three vital control parameters:

- Time
- Cost
- Performance

All schedules and charts should consider these three parameters and their relationship to corporate resources.

Information must be available such that proper project evaluation can be made. There are four methods for project evaluation:

- First-hand observation
- Oral and written reports
- Review and technical interchange meetings
- Graphical displays

First-hand observations are an excellent tool for obtaining nonfiltered information. Many times, functional managers get a deep sense of pride when they see key project personnel observing work, provided that these personnel are, in fact, observing and not providing direction. First-hand observation may not be possible on large projects.

Although oral and written reports are a way of life, they often contain either too much or not enough detail. Significant information may be disguised. Most organizations do not have standardized reporting procedures, which further complicates the situation.

Review and technical interchange meetings provide face-to-face communications between all concerned parties, a situation that can often result in immediate agreement on problem definitions or solutions, such as changing a schedule. The difficult problem is in the selection of attendees from the customer's and the contractor's organizations.

Graphical displays are the prime means for tracking cost, schedule, and performance. Good graphics usually makes the information easy to identify. Unfortunately, not all information can be displayed, and quite often any additional information requests require additional cost and effort. Proper graphical displays can result in:

- Cutting project costs and reducing the time scale
- Coordinating and expediting planning
- Eliminating idle time
- Obtaining better scheduling and control of subcontractor activities
- Developing better troubleshooting procedures
- Cutting time for routine decisions, but allowing more time for decision making

13.1 CUSTOMER REPORTING

There exist between thirty and forty different visual methods for the representation of activities. The exact method chosen should depend upon the intended audience. For example, upper-level management may be interested in costs and integration of activities, with very little detail. Summary-type charts normally suffice for this purpose. Daily practitioners, on the other hand, may require that as much detail as possible be included in activity schedules. If the schedule is to be presented to the customer, then the presentation should include cost and performance data.

The presentation of cost and performance data must be considered as both a science and an art. As a science, the figures and graphs should be describable in terms of symbols and expressions that are easily understandable. As an art, the diagram should rapidly bring across the intended message or objective. In many organizations, each department or division may have its own method of showing scheduling activities. Research and development organizations prefer to show the logic of activities rather than the integration of activities that would normally be representative of a manufacturing plant.

The ability to communicate is a definite prerequisite for successful management of a program. Program review meetings, technical interchange meetings, customer summary meetings, and in-house management control meetings all require different representative forms of current program performance status. The final form of the schedule may be bar charts, graphs, tables, bubble charts, or logic diagrams. In the sections that follow, a variety of charting techniques, together with the associated limitations, will be described for various types of a program. The reader should be able to realize the advantages and disadvantages of each chart in relation to his own program activities.

13.2 BAR (GANTT) CHART

The most common type of display is the bar or Gantt chart, named for Henry Gantt who first utilized this procedure in the early 1900s. The bar chart is a means of displaying simple activities or events plotted against time or dollars. An activity represents the amount of work required to proceed from one point in time to another. Events are described as either the starting or ending point for either one or several activities.

Bar charts are most commonly used for exhibiting program progress or defining specific work required to accomplish an objective. Bar charts often include such items as listings of activities, activity durations, schedule dates, and progress-to-date. Figure 13–1 shows nine activities required to start up a production line for a new product. Each bar in the figure represents a single activity. Figure 13–1 is a typical bar chart that would be developed by the program office at program inception.

Bar charts are advantageous in that they are simple to understand and easy to change. They are the simplest and least complex means of portraying progress (or the lack of it) and can easily be expanded to identify specific elements that may be either behind or ahead of schedule.

Bar charts provide only a vague description of how the entire program or project reacts as a system. There are three major discrepancies in the use of a bar chart. First, bar charts do not show the interdependencies of the activities, and therefore do not represent a "network" of activities. This relationship between activities is crucial for controlling program costs. Without this relationship, bar charts have little predictive value. For example, does the long-lead procurement activity in Figure 13–1 require that the contract be signed before procurement can begin? Can the manufacturing plans be written without the material specifications activity being completed? The second major dis-

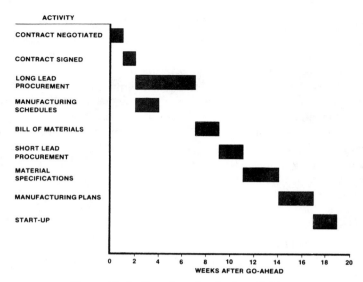

ACTIVITY

CONTRACT NEGOTIATED

CONTRACT SIGNED

LONG LEAD
PROCUREMENT

MANUFACTURING
SCHEDULES

BILL OF MATERIALS

SHORT LEAD
PROCUREMENT

MATERIAL
SPECIFICATIONS

MANUFACTURING PLANS

START-UP

0   2   4   6   8   10   12   14   16   18   20
WEEKS AFTER GO-AHEAD

Figure 13–1. Bar chart for single activities.

crepancy is that the bar chart cannot show the results of either an early or a late start in activities. How will a slippage of the manufacturing schedules activity in Figure 13–1 affect the completion date of the program? Can the manufacturing schedules activity begin two weeks later than shown and still serve as an input to the bill of materials activity? What will be the result of a crash program to complete activities in sixteen weeks after go-ahead instead of the originally planned nineteen weeks? Bar charts do not reflect true project status because elements behind schedule do not mean that the program or project is behind schedule. The third limitation is that the bar chart does not show the uncertainty involved in performing the activity and, therefore, does not readily admit itself to sensitivity analysis. For instance, what is the shortest time that an activity might take? What is the longest time? What is the average or expected time to activity completion?

Even with these limitations, bar charts do, in fact, serve as a useful tool for program analysis. Even the earliest form of bar chart, as developed by Henry Gantt, still has merit under certain circumstances. Figure 13–2 shows the conventional usage for work scheduled in a production facility for twelve days in January. On Thursday of the first week, the production facility was idle owing to lack of materials. By the end of the work day on Friday of the first week, only 280 out of the planned 300 units were produced. The production line was not available on either Saturday or Sunday, and operations resumed Monday. On Tuesday, the production line was down for repairs and did not resume oper-

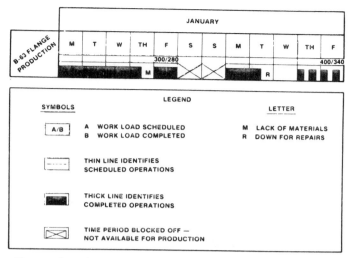

Figure 13-2. Manufacturing schedule for Model B-63 flanges.

ations until Thursday. Operations were sporadic on Thursday and Friday, and by the end of the day, only 340 out of a scheduled 400 units were completed. These types of applications are commonly used for equipment layout and usage, department loading, and progress tracking.[1]

Some of the limitations of bar charts can be overcome by combining single activities as shown in Figure 13-3. The weakness in this method is that the numbers representing each of the activities do not indicate whether or not this is the beginning or the end of the activity. Therefore, the numbers should represent events rather than activities, together with proper identification. As before, no distinction is made as to whether event 2 must be completed prior to the start of event 3 or event 4. The chart also fails to define clearly the relationship between the multiple activities on a single bar. For example, must event 3 be completed prior to event 5? Often, combined activity bar charts can be converted to milestone bar charts by placing small triangles at strategic locations in the bars to indicate completion of certain milestones within each activity or grouping of activities, as shown in Figure 13-4. The exact definition of a milestone differs from company to company, but usually implies some point where major activity either begins or ends, or cost data become critical.

Bar charts can be converted to partial interrelationship charts by indicating

1. A. C. Laufer, *Operations Management* (Cincinnati: Southwestern Publishing Co., 1975); see pp. 106–108 for examples of Gantt charts and nomenclature.

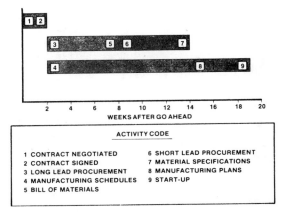

Figure 13–3. Bar chart for combined activities.

(with arrows) the order in which activities must be performed. Figure 13–5 represents the partial interrelationship of the activities shown in Figures 13–1 and 13–3. A full interrelationship schedule is included under the discussion of PERT networks in Chapter 12.

The most common method of presenting data to both in-house management and the customer is through the use of bar charts. Care must be taken not to make the figures overly complex so that more than one interpretation can exist. A great deal of information and color can be included in bar charts. Figure 13–6 shows a grouped bar chart for comparison of three projects performed during different years. Care must be taken when using different shading techniques that each area is easily definable and that no major contrast between shaded areas exists, except for possibly the current project. When grouped bars appear on one chart, nonshaded bars should be avoided. Each bar should have some sort of shading, whether it be cross-hatched or color-coded.

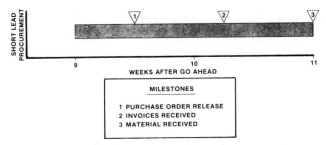

Figure 13–4. Bar/milestone chart.

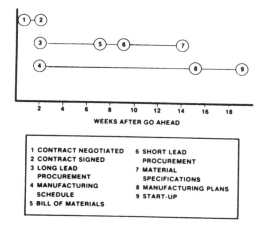

Figure 13–5. Partial interrelationship chart.

Contrasting shaded to nonshaded areas is normally used for comparing projected progress to actual progress as shown in Figure 13–7. The tracking date line indicates the time when the cost data/performance data was analyzed. Project 1 is behind schedule, project 2 is ahead of schedule, and project 3 is on target. Unfortunately, the upper portion of Figure 13–7 does not indicate the costs attributed to the status of the three projects. By plotting the total program

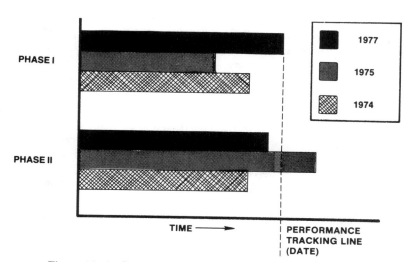

Figure 13–6. Grouped bar chart for performance comparison.

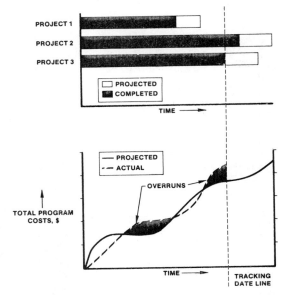

Figure 13–7. Cost and performance tracking schedule.

costs against the same time axis (as shown in Figure 13–7), a comparison between cost and performance can be made. From the upper section of Figure 13–7 it is impossible to tell the current program cost position. From the lower section, however, it becomes evident that the program is heading for a cost overrun, possibly due to project 1. It is generally acceptable to have the same shading technique represent different situations, provided that clear separation between the shaded regions appears, as in Figure 13–7.

Another common means for comparing activities or projects is through the use of step arrangement bar charts. Figure 13–8 shows a step arrangement bar chart for a cost percentage breakdown of the five projects included within a program. Figure 13–8 can also be used for tracking, by shading in certain portions of the steps that identify each project. This is not normally done, however, since this type of step arrangement tends to indicate that each step must be completed before the next step can begin.

Bar charts need not be represented horizontally. Figure 13–9 indicates the comparison between the 1975 and 1977 costs for the total program and raw materials. Again, care must be taken so as to make proper use of shading techniques. Three-dimensional vertical bar charts are often the most beautiful to behold. Figure 13–10 shows a typical three-dimensional bar chart for direct and indirect labor and material cost breakdowns.

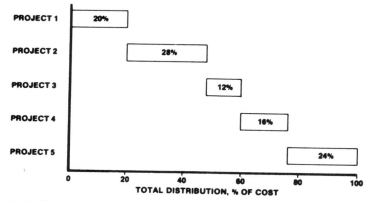

Figure 13–8. Step arrangement bar chart for total cost as a percentage of the five program projects.

Bar charts can be made quite colorful and appealing to the eye by combining them with other graphic techniques. Figure 13–11 shows a quantitative-pictorial bar chart for the distribution of total program costs. Figure 13–12 shows the same cost distribution in Figure 13–11, but represented with the commonly used pie technique. Figure 13–13 illustrates how two quantitative bar charts can be used side by side to create a quick comparison. The right-hand side shows the labor hour percentages. Figure 13–13 works best if the scale of each

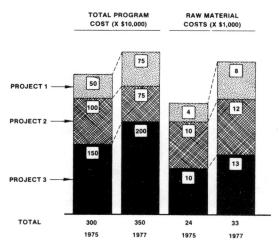

Figure 13–9. 1975 vs. 1977 cost comparison.

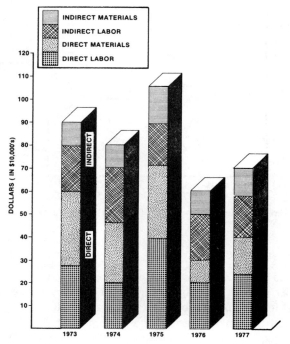

Figure 13–10. Direct and indirect material and labor costs breakdown for all programs per year.

axis is the same; otherwise the comparisons may appear distorted when, in fact, they are not.

The figures shown in this section have been previously used by the author for customer interchange meetings and do not, by any means, represent the only method of presented data in bar chart format. Several other methods exist, some of which will be shown in the sections that follow.

13.3 OTHER CONVENTIONAL PRESENTATION TECHNIQUES

Bar charts serve as a useful tool for presenting data at technical meetings. Unfortunately, programs must be won competitively or organized in-house before technical meeting presentations can be made. Competitive proposals or in-house project requests should contain descriptive figures and charts, not necessarily representing activities, but showing either planning, organizing, tracking, or technical procedures designed for the current program or used previously on other programs. Proposals generally contain figures that require either

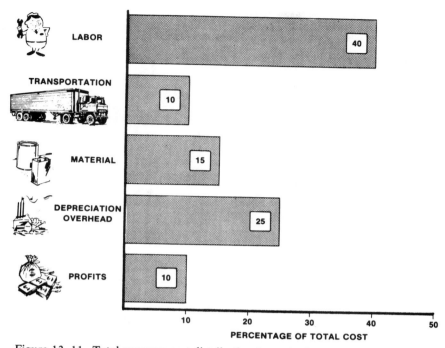

Figure 13–11. Total program cost distribution (quantitative-pictorial bar chart.)

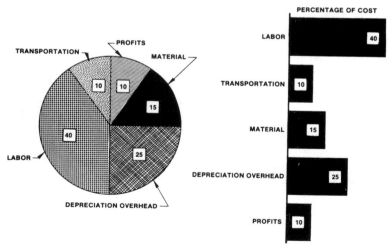

Figure 13–12. Distribution of the program dollar.

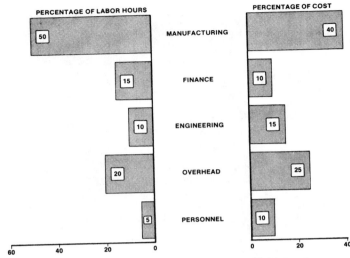

Figure 13-13. Divisional breakdown of costs and labor hours.

some interpolation or extrapolation. Figure 13-14 shows the breakdown of total program costs. Although this figure would also normally require interpretation, a monthly cost table accompanies it. If the table is not too extensive, then the table can be included with the figure. This is shown in Figure 13-15. During proposal activities, the actual and cumulative delivery columns, as well as the dotted line in Figure 13-15, would be omitted, but would be included after updating for use in technical interchange meetings. It is normally a good practice to use previous figures and tables whenever possible because management becomes accustomed to the manner in which data are presented.

Another commonly used technique is schematic models. Organizational charts are schematic models which depict the interrelationships between individuals, organizations or functions within an organization. One organizational chart normally cannot suffice for describing total program interrelationships. Figure 4-10 identified the Midas Program in relation to other programs within Dalton Corporation. The Midas Program is indicated by the bold lines. The program manager for the Midas Program was placed at the top of the column, even though his program may have the lowest priority. Each major unit of management for the Midas Program should be placed as close as possible to top-level management to indicate to the customer the "implied" relative importance of the program.

Another type of schematic representation is the work flow chart, synony-

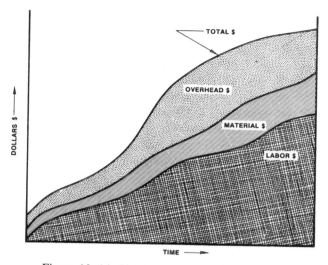

Figure 13–14. Total program cost breakdown.

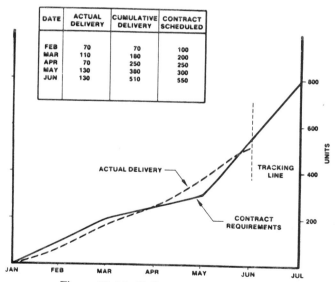

Figure 13–15. Delivery schedule tracking.

mous with the applications of flowcharting for computer programming. Flow charts are designed to describe, either symbolically or pictorially, the sequence of events required to complete an activity. Figure 13–16 shows the logic flow for production of molding VZ-3. The symbols shown in Figure 13–16 are universally accepted by several industries.

Pictorial representation, although often a costly procedure, can add color and quality to any proposal. Pictorial sketches provide the customer with a document easier to identify with than a logic or bubble chart. Customers may request tours during activities to relate to the pictorial figures. If at all possible, program management should avoid pictorial representation of activities which may be closed off to customer viewing, possibly due to security or safety.

Block diagrams can also be used to describe the flow of activities. Figures 4–10 and 4–11 are examples of block diagrams. Block diagrams can be used to show how information is distributed throughout an organization or how a process or activity is assembled. Figure 13–17 shows the testing matrix for

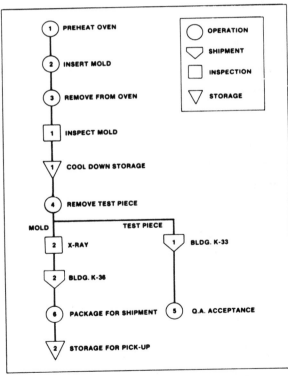

Figure 13–16. Logic flow for production of molding VZ-3.

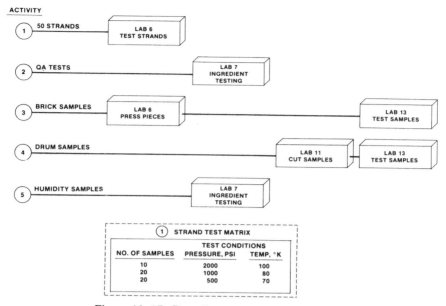

Figure 13–17. Propellant samples testing matrix.

propellant samples. Figures similar to this are developed when tours are scheduled during the production or testing phase of a program. Figure 13–17 shows the customer not only where the testing will take place, but what tests will be conducted.

Block diagrams, schematics, pictorials, and logic flows all fulfill a necessary need for describing the wide variety of activities within a company. The figures and charts are more than descriptive techniques. They can also provide management with the necessary tools for decision making.

13.4 LOGIC DIAGRAMS/NETWORKS

Probably the most difficult figure to construct is the logic diagram. Logic diagrams are developed to illustrate the inductive and deductive reasoning necessary to achieve some objective within a given time frame. The major difficulty in developing logic diagrams is the inability to answer such key questions as: What happens if something goes wrong? Can I quantify any part of the diagram's major elements?

Logic diagrams are constructed similar to bar charts on the supposition that nothing will go wrong, and are usually accompanied by detailed questions, possibly in a checklist format, which require answering. The following questions would be representative of those that might accompany a logic diagram for a research and development project:

- What documentation is released to start the described activity and possibly the elements within each activity?
- What information is required before this documentation can be released? (What prior activities must be completed, work designed, studies finalized, etc.?)
- What are the completion, or success, criteria for the activity?
- What are the alternatives for each phase of the program if success is not achieved?
- What other activities are directly dependent on the result of this activity?
- What other activities or inputs are required to perform this activity?
- What are the key decision points, if any, during the activity?
- What documentation signifies completion of the activity (i.e., report, drawing, etc.)?
- What management approval is required for final documentation?

These types of questions are applicable to many other forms of data presentation, not necessarily logic diagrams.

PROBLEMS

13-1 For each type of schedule defined in this chapter answer the following questions:
   a. Who prepares the schedule?
   b. Who updates the schedule?
   c. Who should present the data to the customers?

13-2 Should the customers have the right to dictate to the contractor how the schedule should be prepared and presented? What if this request is in contradiction to company policies and procedures?

13-3 Should a different set of schedules and charts be maintained for out-of-house as well as in-house reporting? Should separate schedules be made for each level of management? Is there a more effective way to ease these types of problems?

14
Pricing and Estimating

14.0 INTRODUCTION[1]

With the complexities involved, it is not surprising that many business managers consider pricing an art. Having the right intelligence information on customer cost budgets and competitive pricing would certainly help. However, the reality is that whatever information is available to one bidder is generally available to the others. Even more important, intelligence sources are often unreliable. The only thing worse than missing information is getting wrong or misleading information. When it comes to competitive pricing, the old saying still applies: "Those who talk don't know; and those who know don't talk!" It is true, partially, that pricing remains an art. However, a disciplined approach certainly helps one to develop all the input for a rational pricing recommendation. A side benefit of using a disciplined management process is that it leads to the documentation of the many factors and assumptions involved at a later point in time. These can be compared and analyzed, contributing to the learning experiences that make up the managerial skills needed for effective business decisions.

14.1 GLOBAL PRICING STRATEGIES

Specific pricing strategies must be developed for each individual situation. Frequently, however, one of two situations prevails when one is pursuing project acquisitions competitively. First, the new business opportunity may be a one-of-a-kind program with little or no follow-on potential, a situation classified as Type I acquisition. Second, the new business opportunity may be an entry point to a larger follow-on or repeat business, or may represent a planned penetration into a new market. This acquisition is classified as Type II.

Clearly, in each case, we have specific but different business objectives. The objective for Type I acquisition is to win the program and execute it profitably

---

1. Sections 14.0 and 14.1 have been adapted from H. Kerzner and H. J. Thamhain, *Project Management for the Small and Medium-Sized Business* (New York: Van Nostrand Reinhold, 1983), pp. 223–226.

and satisfactorily according to contractual agreements. The Type II objective is often to win the program and perform well, thereby gaining a foothold in a new market segment or a new customer community in place of making a profit. Accordingly, each acquisition type has its own, unique pricing strategy, as summarized in Table 14–1.

Comparing the two pricing strategies for the two global situations (as shown

Table 14–1. Two Global Pricing Strategies.

TYPE I ACQUISITION ONE-OF-A-KIND PROGRAM WITH LITTLE OR NO FOLLOW-ON BUSINESS	TYPE II ACQUISITION NEW PROGRAM WITH POTENTIAL FOR LARGE FOLLOW-ON BUSINESS OR REPRESENTING A DESIRED PENETRATION INTO NEW MARKETS
Pricing Strategy 1. Develop cost model and estimating guidelines; design proposed project/program baseline for minimum cost, to minimum customer requirements. 2. Estimate cost realistically for minimum requirements. 3. Scrub the baseline. Squeeze out unnecessary costs. Trade-offs, make-buy. 4. Determine realistic minimum cost. Obtain commitment from performing organizations. 5. Adjust cost estimate for risks. 6. Add desired margins. Determine the price. 7. Compare price to customer budget and competitive cost information. 8. Bid only if price is within competitive range.	*Pricing Strategy* 1. Design proposed project/program baseline compliant with customer requirements, with innovative features but minimum risks. 2. Estimate cost realistically. 3. Scrub baseline. Squeeze out unnecessary costs. 4. Determine realistic minimum cost. Obtain commitment from performing organizations. 5. Determine "should-cost" including risk adjustments. 6. Compare your final cost estimate to customer budget and the "most likely" winning price. 7. Determine the gross profit margin necessary for your winning proposal. This margin could be negative! 8. Decide whether the gross margin is acceptable according to the must-win desire. 9. Depending on the strength of your desire to win, bid the "most likely" winning price or lower. 10. If the bid price is below cost, it is often necessary to provide a detailed explanation to the customer of where the additional funding is coming from. The source could be company profits or sharing of related activities. In any case, a clear resource picture should be given to the customer to ensure cost credibility.

in Table 14–1) reveals a great deal of similarity for the first five points. The fundamental difference is that for a profitable new business acquisition the bid price is determined according to actual cost, whereas in a "must win" situation the price is determined by the market forces. It should be emphasized that one of the most crucial inputs in the pricing decision is the cost estimate of the proposed baseline. The design of this baseline to the minimum requirements should be started early, in accordance with well-defined ground rules, cost models, and established cost targets. Too often the baseline design is performed in parallel with the proposal development. At the proposal stage it is too late to review and fine-tune the baseline for minimum cost. Also, such a late start does not allow much of an option for a final bid decision. Even if the price appears outside the competitive range, it makes little sense to terminate the proposal development. As all the resources have been spent anyway, one might just as well submit a bid in spite of the remote chance of winning.

Clearly, effective pricing begins a long time before proposal development. It starts with preliminary customer requirements, well-understood subtasks, and a top-down estimate with should-cost targets. This allows the functional organization to design a baseline to meet the customer requirements and cost targets, and gives management the time to review and redirect the design before the proposal is submitted. Furthermore it gives management an early opportunity to assess the chances of winning during the acquisition cycle, at a point in time when additional resources can be allocated or the acquisition effort can be terminated before too many resources are committed to a hopeless effort.

The final pricing review session should be an integration and review of information already well-known in its basic context. The process and management tools outlined here should help to provide the framework and discipline for deriving pricing decisions in an orderly and effective way.

14.2 TYPES OF ESTIMATES

Projects can range from a feasibility study, through modification of existing facilities, to complete design, procurement, and construction of a large complex. Whatever the project may be, whether large or small, the estimate and type of information desired may differ radically.

The first type of estimate is an *order-of-magnitude* analysis, which is made without any detailed engineering data. The order-of-magnitude analysis may have an accuracy of $\pm 35\%$ within the scope of the project. This type of estimate may use past experience (not necessarily similar), scale factors, or capacity estimates (i.e., \$/# of product or \$/KW electricity).

Next, there is the *approximate estimate* (or top-down estimate), which is also made without detailed engineering data, and may be accurate to $\pm 15\%$. This type of estimate is prorated from previous projects that are similar in scope and capacity, and may be titled as estimating by analogy, rule of thumb, and indexed cost of similar activities adjusted for capacity and technology. In such a case, the estimator may say that this activity is 50 percent more difficult than a previous (i.e., reference) activity and requires 50 percent more time, man-hours, dollars, materials, etc.

The *definitive estimate* is prepared from well-defined engineering data including (as a minimum) vendor quotes, fairly complete plans, specifications, unit prices, and estimate to complete. The definitive estimate, also referred to as detailed estimating, has an accuracy of $\pm 5\%$.

Another method for estimating is the use of *learning curves*. Learning curves are graphical representations of repetitive functions in which continuous operations will lead to a reduction in time, resources, and money. The theory behind learning curves is usually applied to manufacturing operations.

Many companies try to standardize their estimating procedures by developing an *estimating manual*. The estimating manual is then used to price out the effort, perhaps as much as 90 percent. Estimating manuals usually give better estimates than industrial engineering standards because they include groups of tasks and take into consideration such items as down time, clean-up time, lunch, and breaks. Table 14–2 shows the table of contents for a construction estimating manual.

Table 14–2. Estimating Manual Table of Contents.

Introduction
  Purpose and types of estimates
Major Estimating Tools
  Cataloged equipment costs
  Automated investment data system
  Automated estimate system
  Computerized methods and procedures
Classes of Estimates
  Definitive estimate
  Capital cost estimate
  Appropriation estimate
  Feasibility estimate
  Order of magnitude
  Charts—estimate specifications quantity and pricing guidelines
Data Required
  Chart—comparing data required for preparation of classes of estimates
Presentation Specifications
  Estimate procedure—General
  Estimate procedure for definitive estimate
  Estimate procedure for capital cost estimate
  Estimate procedure for appropriation estimate
  Estimate procedure for feasibility estimate

Table 14–3. Classes of Estimates.

CLASS	TYPES	ACCURACY
I	Definitive	±5%
II	Capital cost	±10–15%
III	Appropriation (with some capital cost)	±15–20%
IV	Appropriation	±20–25%
V	Feasibility	±25–35%
VI	Order of magnitude	> ±35%

Estimating manuals, as the name implies, provide estimates. The question, of course, is, "How good are the estimates?" Most estimating manuals provide accuracy limitations by defining the type of estimates (shown in Table 14–2). Using Table 14–2, we can create Tables 14–3, 14–4, and 14–5, which illustrate the use of the estimating manual.

Not all companies can use estimating manuals. Estimating manuals work best for repetitive tasks or similar tasks that can use a previous estimate adjusted by a degree-of-difficulty factor. Activities such as R&D do not lend

Table 14–4. Checklist for Work Normally Required for the Various Classes of Estimate.

ITEM	CLASS I	II	III	IV	V	VI
1. Inquiry	X	X	X	X	X	X
2. Legibility	X	X	X			
3. Copies	X	X				
4. Schedule	X	X	X	X		
5. Vendor inquiries	X	X	X			
6. Subcontract packages	X	X				
7. Listing	X	X	X	X	X	
8. Site visit	X	X	X	X		
9. Estimate bulks	X	X	X	X	X	
10. Labor rates	X	X	X	X	X	
11. Equipment and subcontract selection	X	X	X	X	X	
12. Taxes, insurance, and royalties	X	X	X	X	X	
13. Home office costs	X	X	X	X	X	
14. Construction indirects	X	X	X	X	X	
15. Basis of estimate	X	X	X	X	X	X
16. Equipment list	X					
17. Summary sheet	X	X	X	X	X	
18. Management review	X	X	X	X	X	X
19. Final cost	X	X	X	X	X	X
20. Management approval	X	X	X	X	X	X
21. Computer estimate	X	X	X	X		

Table 14–5. Data Required for Preparation of Estimates.

	I	II	III	IV	V	VI
			CLASSES OF ESTIMATES			
General						
Product	X	X	X	X	X	X
Process description	X	X	X	X	X	X
Capacity	X	X	X	X	X	X
Location—general					X	X
Location-specific	X	X	X	X		
Basic design criteria	X	X	X	X		
General design specifications	X	X	X	X		
Process						
Process block flow diagram						X
Process flow diagram (with equipment size and material)				X	X	
Mechanical P&I's	X	X	X			
Equipment list	X	X	X	X	X	
Catalyst/chemical specifications	X	X	X	X	X	
Site						
Soil conditions	X	X	X	X		
Site clearance	X	X	X			
Geological and meteorlogical data	X	X	X			
Roads, paving, and landscaping	X	X	X			
Property protection	X	X	X			
Accessibility to site	X	X	X			
Shipping and delivery conditions	X	X	X			
Major cost is factored					X	X
Major Equipment						
Preliminary sizes and materials			X	X	X	
Finalized sizes, materials, and appurtenances	X	X				
Bulk Material Quantities						
Finalized design quantity take-off		X				
Preliminary design quantity take-off	X	X	X	X		
Engineering						
Plot plan and elevations	X	X	X	X		
Routing diagrams	X	X	X			
Piping line index	X	X				
Electrical single line	X	X	X	X		
Fire protection	X	X	X			
Sewer systems	X	X	X			
Pro-services—detailed estimate	X	X				
Pro-services—ratioed estimate			X	X	X	
Catalyst/chemicals quantities	X	X	X	X	X	
Construction						
Labor wage, F/B, travel rates	X	X	X	X	X	
Labor productivity and area practices	X	X				
Detailed construction execution plan	X	X				
Field indirects—detailed estimate	X	X				
Field indirects—ratioed estimate			X	X	X	

Table 14-5. Data Required for Preparation of Estimates.
(Continued)

	CLASSES OF ESTIMATES					
	I	II	III	IV	V	VI
Schedule						
Overall timing of execution				X	X	
Detailed schedule of execution	X	X	X			
Estimating preparation schedule	X	X	X			
Miscellaneous						
Transportation rates	X	X				
Start up	X	X	X			
Insurance and taxes	X	X	X	X	X	
Royalties	X	X	X	X	X	X
Import/export rates	X	X	X	X	X	
Financing data	X	X	X	X	X	
Escalation						
Escalation analysis	X	X	X	X	X	
Contingency						
Identifiable risk analysis	X	X				

themselves to the use of estimating manuals other than for benchmark, repetitive laboratory tests. Proposal managers must carefully consider whether or not the estimating manual is a viable approach. The literature abounds with examples of companies that have spent millions trying to develop estimating manuals for situations that just do not lend themselves to the approach.

During competitive bidding, it is important that the type of estimate be consistent with the customer's requirements. For in-house projects, the type of estimate can vary over the life cycle of a project:

- Conceptual stage: venture guidance or feasibility studies for the evaluation of future work. This estimating is often based upon minimum-scope information.
- Planning stage: estimating for authorization of partial or full funds. These estimates are based upon preliminary design and scope.
- Main stage: estimating for detailed work.
- Termination stage: reestimation for major scope changes or variances beyond the authorization range.

14.3 PRICING PROCESS

This activity schedules the development of the work breakdown structure and provides management with two of the three operational tools necessary for the control of a system or project. The development of these two tools is normally the responsibility of the program office with input from the functional units.

The integration of the functional unit into the project environment or system occurs through the pricing-out of the work breakdown structure. The total program costs obtained by pricing out the activities over the scheduled period of performance provide management with the third tool necessarry to successfully manage the project. During the pricing activities, the functional units have the option of consulting program management about possible changes in the activity schedules and work breakdown structure.

The work breakdown structure and activity schedules are priced out through the lowest pricing units of the company. It is the responsibility of these pricing units, whether they be sections, departments, or divisions, to provide accurate and meaningful cost data (based upon historical standards, if possible). All information is priced out at the lowest level of performance required, which, from the assumption of Chapter 11, will be the task level. Costing information is rolled up to the project level and then one step further to the total program level.

Under ideal conditions, the work required (i.e., man-hours) to complete a given task can be based upon historical standards. Unfortunately, for many industries projects and programs are so diversified that realistic comparison between previous activities may not be possible. The costing information obtained from each pricing unit, whether or not it is based upon historical standards, should be regarded only as an estimate. How can a company predict the salary structure three years from now? What will be the cost of raw materials two years from now? Will the business base (and therefore overhead rates) change over the duration of the program? The final response to these questions shows that costing data are explicitly related to an environment that cannot be predicted with any high degree of certainty. The systems approach to management, however, provides for a more rapid response to the environment than less structured approaches permit.

Once the cost data are assembled, they must be analyzed for their potential impact on the company resources of people, money, equipment, and facilities. It is only through a total program cost analysis that resource allocations can be analyzed. The resource allocation analysis is performed at all levels of management, ranging from the section supervisor to the vice-president and general manager. For most programs, the chief executive must approve final cost data and the allocation of resources.

Proper analysis of the total program costs can provide management (both program and corporate) with a strategic planning model for integration of the current program with other programs in order to obtain a total corporate strategy. Meaningful planning and pricing models include analyses for monthly manloading schedules per department, monthly costs per department, monthly and yearly total program costs, monthly material expenditures, and total program cash-flow and man-hour requirements per month.

Previously we identified several of the problems that occur at the nodes where the horizontal hierarchy of program management interfaces with the vertical hierarchy of functional management. The pricing-out of the work breakdown structure provides the basis for effective and open communication between functional and program management where both parties have one common goal. This is shown in Figure 14–1. After the pricing effort is completed, and the program is initiated, the work breakdown structure still forms the basis of a communications tool by documenting the performance agreed upon in the pricing effort, as well as establishing the criteria against which performance costs will be measured.

14.4 ORGANIZATIONAL INPUT REQUIREMENTS

Once the work breakdown structure and activity schedules are established, the program manager calls a meeting for all organizations that will be required to submit pricing information. It is imperative that all pricing or labor-costing representatives be present for the first meeting. During this "kickoff" meeting, the work breakdown structure is described in depth so that each pricing unit manager will know exactly what his responsibilities are during the program. The kickoff meeting also resolves the struggle-for-power positions of several functional managers whose responsibilities may be similar or overlap on certain activities. An example of this would be quality control activities. During the research and development phase of a program, research personnel may be per-

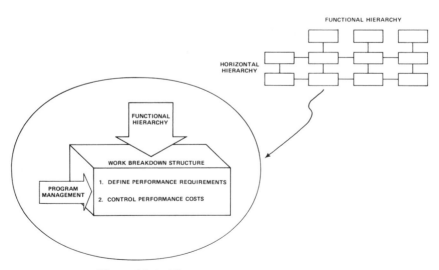

Figure 14–1. The vertical/horizontal interface.

mitted to perform their own quality control efforts, whereas during production activities the quality control department or division would have overall responsibility. Unfortunately, one meeting is not always sufficient to clarify all problems. Follow-up or status meetings are held, normally with only those parties concerned with the problems that have arisen. Some companies prefer to have all members attend the status meetings so that all personnel will be familiar with the total effort and the associated problems. The advantage of not having all program-related personnel attend is that time is of the essence when pricing out activities. Many functional divisions carry this policy one step further by having a divisional representative together with possibly key department managers or section supervisors as the only attendees at the kickoff meeting. The divisional representative then assumes all responsibility for assuring that all costing data are submitted on time. This arrangement may be beneficial in that the program office need contact only one individual in the division to learn of the activity status, but it may become a bottleneck if the representative fails to maintain proper communication between the functional units and the program office, or if the individual simply is unfamiliar with the pricing requirements of the work breakdown structure.

During proposal activities, time may be extremely important. There are many situations in which a request for proposal (RFP) requires that all responders submit their bids no later than a specific date, say within thirty days. Under a proposal environment, the activities of the program office, as well as those of the functional units, are under a schedule set forth by the proposal manager. The proposal manager's schedule has very little, if any, flexibility and is normally under tight time-constraints so that the proposal may be typed, edited, and published prior to the date of submittal. In this case, the RFP will indirectly define how much time the pricing units have to identify and justify labor costs.

The justification of the labor costs may take longer than the original cost estimates, especially if historical standards are not available. Many proposals often require that comprehensive labor justification be submitted. Other proposals, especially those that request an almost immediate response, may permit vendors to submit labor justification at a later date.

In the final analysis, it is the responsibility of the lowest pricing unit supervisor to maintain adequate standards, if possible, so that an almost immediate response can be given to a pricing request from a program office.

14.5 LABOR DISTRIBUTIONS

The functional units supply their input to the program office in the form of man-hours as shown in Figure 14–2. The input may be accompanied by labor justification, if required. The man-hours are submitted for each task, assuming

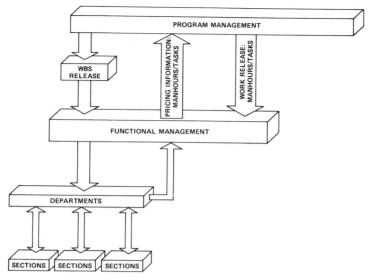

Figure 14–2. Functional pricing flow.

that the task is the lowest pricing element, and are time-phased per month. The man-hours per month per task are converted to dollars after multiplication by the appropriate labor rates. The labor rates are generally known with certainty over a twelve-month period, but from there on are only estimates. How can a company predict salary structures five years hence? If the company underestimates the salary structure, increased costs and decreased profits will occur. If the salary structure is overestimated, the company may not be competitive. If the project is government-funded, then the salary structure becomes an item under contract negotiations.

The development of the labor rates to be used in the projection is based upon historical costs in business base hours and dollars for the most recent month or quarter. Average hourly rates are determined for each labor unit by direct effort within the operations at the department level. The rates are only averages, and include both the highest-paid employees and lowest-paid employees, together with the department manager and the clerical support.* These base rates are then escalated as a percentage factor based upon past experience,

---

*Problems can occur if the salaries of the people assigned to the program exceed the department averages. Methods to alleviate this problem will be discussed later. Also, in many companies department managers are included in the overhead rate structure, not direct labor, and therefore their salaries are not included as part of the department average.

budget as approved by management, and the local outlook and similar industries. If the company has a predominant aerospace or defense industry business base, then these salaries are negotiated with local government agencies prior to submittal for proposals.

The labor hours submitted by the functional units are quite often overestimated for fear that management will "massage" and reduce the labor hours while attempting to maintain the same scope of effort. Many times management is forced to reduce man-hours either because of insufficient funding or just to remain competitive in the environment. The reduction of man-hours often causes heated discussions between the functional and program managers. Program managers tend to think in terms of the best interests of the program, whereas functional managers lean toward maintaining their present staff.

The most common solution to this conflict rests with the program manager. If the program manager selects members for the program team who are knowledgeable in man-hour standards for each of the departments, then an atmosphere of trust can develop between the program office and the functional department so that man-hours can be reduced in a manner that represents the best interests of the company. This is one of the reasons why program team members are often promoted from within the functional ranks.

The man-hours submitted by the functional units provide the basis for total program cost analysis and program cost control. To illustrate this process, consider Example 14–1 below.

Example 14–1. On May 15, Apex Manufacturing decided to enter into competitive bidding for the modification and updating of an assembly line program. A work breakdown structure was developed as shown below:

PROGRAM (01-00-00): Assembly Line Modification
    PROJECT 1 (01-01-00): Initial Planning
        Task 1 (01-01-01): Engineering Control
        Task 2 (01-01-02): Engineering Development
    PROJECT 2 (01-02-00): Assembly
        Task 1 (01-02-01): Modification
        Task 2 (01-02-02): Testing

On June 1, each pricing unit was given the work breakdown structure together with the schedule shown in Figure 14–3. According to the schedule developed by the proposal manager for this project, all labor data must be submitted to the program office for review no later than June 15. It should be noted here that, in many companies, labor hours are submitted directly to the pricing department for submittal into the base case computer run. In this case, the program office would "massage" the labor hours only after the base case figures are available. This procedure assumes that sufficient time exists for anal-

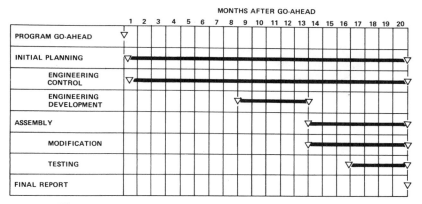

Figure 14–3. Activity schedule for assembly line updating.

ysis and modification of the base case. If the program office has sufficient personnel capable of critiquing the labor input prior to submittal to the base case, then valuable time can be saved, especially if two or three days are required to obtain computer output for the base case.

During proposal activities, the proposal manager, pricing manager, and program manager must all work together, although the program manager has the final say. The primary responsibility of the proposal manager is to integrate the proposal activities into the operational system so that the proposal will be submitted to the requestor on time. A typical schedule developed by the proposal manager is shown in Figure 14–4. The schedule includes all activities necessary to "get the proposal out of the house," with the first major step being the submittal of man-hours by the pricing organizations. Figure 14–4 also indicates the tracking of proposal costs. The proposal activity schedule is usually accompanied by a time schedule with detailed estimates checklist if the complexity of the proposal warrants one. The checklist generally provides detailed explanations for the proposal activity schedule.

After the planning and pricing charts are approved by program team members and program managers, they are entered into an electronic data processing (EDP) system as shown in Figure 14–5. The computer then prices the hours on the planning charts using the applicable department rates for preparation of the direct budget time plan and estimate-at-completion reports. The direct budget time plan reports, once established, remain the same for the life of the contract except for customer-directed or approved changes or when contractor management determines that a reduction in budget is advisable. However, if a budget is reduced by management, it cannot be increased without customer approval.

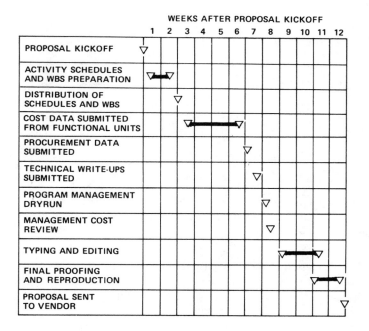

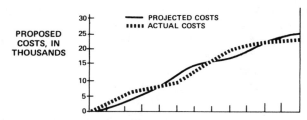

Figure 14–4. Proposal activity schedule.

The time plan is normally a monthly mechanical printout of all planned effort by work package and organizational element over the life of the contract, and serves as the data bank for preparing the status completion reports.

Initially, the estimate-at-completion report is identical to the budget report, but it changes throughout the life of a program to reflect degradation or improvement in performance or any other events that will change the program cost or schedule.

14.6 OVERHEAD RATES

The ability to control program costs involves more than tracking labor dollars and labor hours. Overhead dollars can be one of the biggest headaches in con-

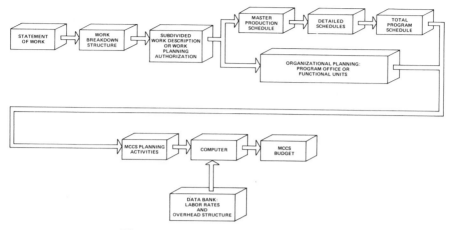

Figure 14–5. Labor planning flow chart.

trolling program costs and must be tracked along with labor hours and dollars. Although most programs have an assistant program manager for cost whose responsibilities include monthly overhead rate analysis, the program manager can drastically increase the success of his program by insisting that each program team member understand overhead rates. For example, if overhead rates apply only to the first forty hours of work, then, depending on the overhead rate, program dollars can be saved by performing work on overtime where the increased salary is at a lower burden. This can be seen in Example 14–2 below.

Example 14–2. Assume that Apex Manufacturing must write an interim report for Task 1 of Project 1 during regular shift or on overtime. The project will require 500 man-hours at $15.00 per hour. The overhead burden is 75 percent on regular shift but only 5 percent on overtime. Overtime, however, is paid at a rate of time and one-half. Assuming that the report can be written on either time, which is cost-effective—regular time or overtime?

- On regular time the total cost is:

(500 hours) × ($15.00/hour) × (100% + 75% burden) = $13,125

- On overtime, the total cost is:

(500 hours) × ($15.00/hour × 1.5 overtime) × (100% + 5% burden)
= $11,812.50

Therefore the company can save $1,312.50 by performing the work on overtime. Scheduling overtime can produce increased profits if the overtime overhead rate burden is much less than the regular time burden. This difference can be very large in manufacturing divisions, where overhead rates between 300 and 450 percent are common.

Regardless of whether one analyzes a project or a system, all costs must have associated overhead rates. Unfortunately, many program managers and systems managers consider overhead rates as a magic number pulled out of the air. The preparation and assignment of overheads to each of the functional divisions is a science. Although the *total dollar pool* for overhead rates is relatively constant, management retains the option of deciding how to distribute the overhead among the functional divisions. A company that supports its R&D staff through competitive bidding projects may wish to keep the R&D overhead rate as low as possible. Care must be taken, however, that other divisions do not absorb additional costs so that the company no longer remains competitive on those manufactured products that may be its bread and butter.

The development of the overhead rates is a function of three separate elements: direct labor rates, direct business base projections, and projection of overhead expenses. Direct labor rates have already been discussed. The direct business base projection involves the determination of the anticipated direct labor hours and dollars along with the necessary direct materials and other direct costs required to perform and complete the program efforts included in the business base. Those items utilized in the business base projection include all contracted programs as well as the proposed or anticipated efforts. The foundation for determination of the business base required for each program can be one or more of the following:

- Actual costs to date and estimates to completion
- Proposal data
- Marketing intelligence
- Management goals
- Past performance and trends

The projection of the overhead expenses is made by an analysis of each of the elements that constitute the overhead expense. A partial listing of those items that constitute overhead expenses is shown in Table 14–6. Projection of expenses within the individual elements is then made based upon one or more of the following:

- Historical direct/indirect labor ratios
- Regression and correlation analysis
- Manpower requirements and turnover rates
- Changes in public laws
- Anticipated changes in company benefits

Table 14-6. Elements of Overhead Rates.

Building maintenance	New business directors
Building rent	Office supplies
Cafeteria	Payroll taxes
Clerical	Personnel recruitment
Clubs/associations	Postage
Consulting services	Professional meetings
Corporate auditing expenses	Reproduction facilities
Corporate salaries	Retirement plans
Depreciation of equipment	Sick leave
Executive salaries	Supplies/hand tools
Fringe benefits	Supervision
General ledger expenses	Telephone/telegraph facilities
Group insurance	Transportation
Holiday	Utilities
Moving/storage expenses	Vacation

- Fixed costs in relation to capital asset requirements
- Changes in business base
- Bid and proposal (B&P) tri-service agreements
- IR&D tri-service agreements

For many industries, such as aerospace and defense, the federal government funds a large percentage of the B&P and IR&D activities. This federal funding is a necessity since many companies could not otherwise be competitive within the industry. The federal government employs this technique to stimulate research and competition. Therefore, B&P and IR&D are included in the above list.

The prime factor in the control of overhead costs is the annual budget. This budget, which is the result of goals and objectives established by the chief executive officer, is reviewed and approved at all levels of management. It is established at department level, and the department manager has direct responsibility for identifying and controlling costs against the approved plan.

The departmental budgets are summarized, in detail, for higher levels of management. This summarization permits management, at these higher organizational levels, to be aware of the authorized indirect budget in their area of responsibility.

Reports are published monthly indicating current month and year-to-date budget, actuals and variances. These reports are published for each level of management, and an analysis is made by the budget department through coordination and review with management. Each directorate's total organization is then reviewed with the budget analyst who is assigned the overhead cost responsibility. A joint meeting is held with the directors and the vice-president and general manager, at which time overhead performance is reviewed.

14.7 MATERIALS/SUPPORT COSTS

The salary structure, overhead structure, and labor hours fulfill three of four major pricing input requirements. The fourth major input is the cost for materials and support. Six subtopics are included under materials/support: materials, purchased parts, subcontracts, freight and travel, and other. Freight and travel can be handled in one of two ways, both normally dependent on the size of the program. For small-dollar-volume programs, estimates are made for travel and freight. For large-dollar-volume programs, travel is normally expressed as between 3 and 5 percent of the direct labor costs, and freight is likewise between 3 and 5 percent of all costs for material, purchased parts, and subcontracts. The category labeled "other support costs" may include such topics as computer hours or special consultants.

Determination of the material costs is very time-consuming, more so than cost determination for labor hours. Material costs are submitted via a bill of materials that includes all vendors from whom purchases will be made, projected costs throughout the program, scrap factors, and shelf lifetime for those products that may be perishable.

Upon release of the work statement, work breakdown structure, and subdivided work description, the end-item bill of materials and manufacturing plans are prepared as shown in Figure 14–6. End-item materials are those items identified as an integral part of the production end-item. Support materials consist of those materials required by engineering and operations to support the manufacture of end-items, and are identified on the manufacturing plan.

A procurement plan/purchase requisition is prepared as soon as possible after contract negotiations (using a methodology as shown in Figure 14–7). This plan is used to monitor material acquisitions, forecast inventory levels, and identify material price variances.

Manufacturing plans prepared upon release of the subdivided work descriptions are used to prepare tool lists for manufacturing, quality assurance, and engineering. From these plans a special tooling breakdown is prepared by tool engineering which defines those tools to be procured and the material requirements of tools to be fabricated in-house. These items are priced by cost element for input on the planning charts.

The materials/support costs are submitted by month for each month of the program. If long-lead funding of materials is anticipated, then they should be assigned to the first month of the program. In addition, an escalation factor for costs of materials/support items must be applied to all materials/support costs. Some vendors may provide fixed prices over time periods in excess of a twelve-

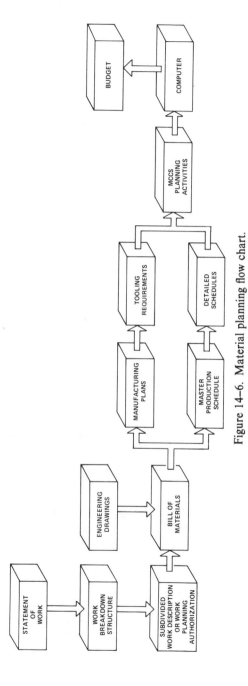

Figure 14-6. Material planning flow chart.

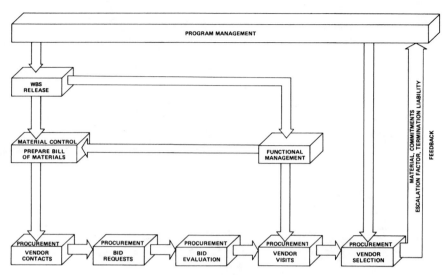

Figure 14–7. Procurement activity.

month period. As an example, Vendor Z may quote a firm-fixed price of $130.50 per unit for 650 units to be delivered over the next eighteen months if the order is placed within sixty days. There are additional factors that influence the cost of materials.

14.8 PRICING OUT THE WORK

Logical pricing techniques are available in order to obtain detailed estimates. The following thirteen steps provide a logical sequence in order to better control the company's limited resources. These steps may vary from company to company.

- Step 1: Provide a complete definition of the work requirements.
- Step 2: Establish a logic network with checkpoints.
- Step 3: Develop the work breakdown structure.
- Step 4: Price out the work breakdown structure.
- Step 5: Review WBS costs with each functional manager.
- Step 6: Decide upon the basic course of action.
- Step 7: Establish reasonable costs for each WBS element.
- Step 8: Review the base case costs with upper-level management.
- Step 9: Negotiate with functional managers for qualified personnel.

- Step 10: Develop the linear responsibility chart.
- Step 11: Develop the final detailed and PERT/CPM schedules.
- Step 12: Establish pricing cost summary reports.
- Step 13: Document the result in a program plan.

Although the pricing of a project is an iterative process, the project manager must still burden himself at each iteration point by developing cost summary reports so that key project decisions can be made during the planning. Detailed pricing summaries are needed at least twice: in preparation for the pricing review meeting with management and at pricing termination. At all other times it is possible that "simple cosmetic surgery" can be performed on previous cost summaries, such as perturbations in escalation factors and procurement cost of raw materials. The list identified below shows the typical pricing reports:

- A detailed cost breakdown for each WBS element. If the work is priced out at the task level, then there should be a cost summary sheet for each task, as well as rollup sheets for each project and the total program.
- A total program manpower curve for each department. These manpower curves show how each department has contracted with the project office to supply functional resources. If the departmental manpower curves contain several "peaks and valleys," then the project manager may have to alter some of his schedules to obtain some degree of manpower smoothing. Functional managers always prefer manpower-smoothed resource allocations.
- A monthly equivalent manpower cost summary. This table normally shows the fully burdened cost for the average departmental employee carried out over the entire period of project performance. If project costs have to be reduced, the project manager performs a parametric study between this table and the manpower curve tables.
- A yearly cost distribution table. This table is broken down by WBS element and shows the yearly (or quarterly) costs that will be required. This table, in essence, is a project cash flow summary per activity.
- A functional cost and hour summary. This table provides top management with an overall description of how many hours and dollars will be spent by each major functional unit, such as a division. Top management would use this as part of the forward planning process to make sure that there are sufficient resources available for all projects. This also includes indirect hours and dollars.
- A monthly labor hour and dollar expenditure forecast. This table can be combined with the yearly cost distribution, except that it is broken down

by month, not activity or department. In addition, this table normally includes manpower termination liability information for premature cancellation of the project by outside customers.

- A raw material and expenditure forecast. This shows the cash flow for raw materials based upon vendor lead times, payment schedules, commitments, and termination liability.
- Total program termination liability per month. This table shows the customer the monthly costs for the entire program. This is the customer's cash flow, not the contractor's. The difference is that each monthly cost contains the termination liability for man-hours and dollars, on labor and raw materials. This table is actually the monthly costs attributed to premature project termination.

These tables are used by both project managers and upper-level executives. The project managers utilize these tables as the basis for project cost control. Top-level management utilizes them for selecting, approving, and prioritizing projects.

14.9 SMOOTHING OUT DEPARTMENT MANHOURS

The dotted curve in Figure 14–8 indicates projected manpower requirements for a given department as a result of a typical program manloading schedule. Department managers, however, attempt to smooth out the manpower curve

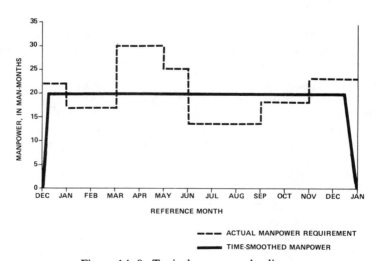

Figure 14–8. Typical manpower loading.

as shown by the solid line in Figure 14–8. Smoothing out the manpower requirements is always beneficial to the department managers by eliminating the necessity for scheduling fractional man-hours per day. The program manager must understand that if departments are permitted to eliminate peaks, valleys, and small step functions in manpower planning, small project and task man-hour (and cost) variances can occur, but should not, in general, affect the total program cost significantly.

One important question that needs to be asked by program management as well as by functional management is whether or not the department has sufficient personnel available to fulfill manpower requirements. Another important question that management must be concerned with is the rate at which the functional departments can staff the program. For example, project engineering requires approximately twenty-three people during January 1984. The function manager, however, may have only fifteen people available for immediate reassignment, with the remainder to be either transferred from other programs or hired from outside the company. The same situation occurs during activity termination. Will project engineering still require twenty-two people in August 1984, or can some of these people begin being phased to other programs, say, as early as June 1984? This question, specifically addressed to support and administrative tasks/projects, must be answered prior to contract negotiations. Figure 14–9 indicates the types of problems that can occur. Curve A shows the manpower requirements for a given department after time-

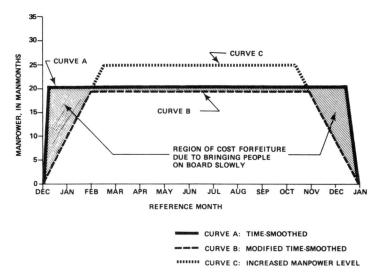

Figure 14–9. Linearly increased manpower loading.

smoothing. Curve B represents the modification to the time-phase curve to account for reasonable program manning and demanning rates. The difference between these two curves (i.e., the shaded area) therefore reflects the amount of money the contractor may have to forfeit owing to manning and demanning activities. This problem can be partially overcome by increasing the manpower levels after time-smoothing (see Curve C) such that the difference between Curves B and C equals the amount of money that would be forfeited from Curves A and B. Of course, program management would have to be able to justify this increase in average manpower requirements, especially if the adjustments are made in a period of higher salaries and overhead rates.

14.10 THE PRICING REVIEW PROCEDURE

The ability to project and analyze program costs so that a basis can be formed for program control requires coordination and control of all pricing information and obtaining agreement and cooperation between the functional units and upper-level management. A typical company policy for cost analysis and review is shown in Figure 14–10. Corporate management may be required to initiate or authorize activities, if corporate/company resources are or may be strained by the program, if capital expenditures are required for new facilities or equipment, or simply if corporate approval is required for all projects in excess of a certain dollar amount.

Upper-level management, upon approval by the chief executive officer of the company, approves and authorizes the initiation of the project or program. The actual performance activities, however, do not begin until the director of program management selects a program manager. The director of program management also authorizes, at this point, either the bid and proposal budget (if the program is competitive) or project planning funds.

The newly appointed program manager then selects his program team members. These team members, who are also members of the program office, may come from other programs, in which case the program manager may find it necessary to negotiate with other program managers, as well as with upper-level management, in order to obtain the individuals who he thinks are essential to the success of his program. The members of the program office are normally support-type individuals. In order to obtain team members representing the functional departments, the program manager must negotiate directly with the functional managers. Functional team members may not be selected or assigned to the program until the actual work is contracted for. Many proposals, however, require that all functional team members be identified, in which case selection must be made during the proposal stage of a program.

The first responsibility of the program office (not necessarily including functional team members) is the development of the activity schedules and the work

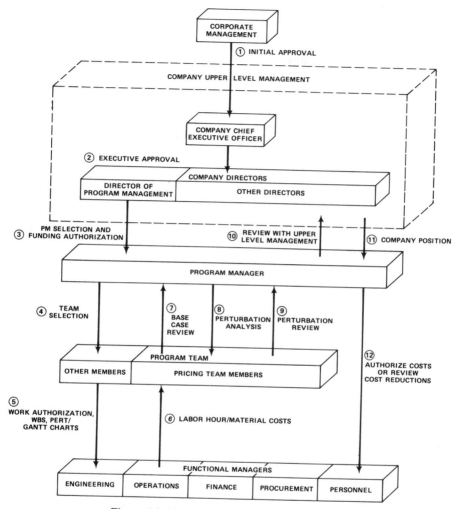

Figure 14–10. The pricing review procedure.

breakdown structure. The program office then provides work authorization for the functional units to price out the activities. The functional units then submit the labor hours, material costs, and justification, if required, to the pricing team member. The pricing team member is normally attached to the program office until the final costs are established. The pricing member also becomes part of the negotiating team if the project is competitive.

Once the base case is formulated, the pricing team member, together with the other program office team members, performs perturbation analyses in order to answer any questions that may come up during the final management review. The perturbation analysis is designed as a systems approach to problem solving where alternatives are developed in order to respond to any questions that management may wish to consider during the final review.

The base case, with the perturbation analysis costs, is then reviewed with upper-level management in order to formulate a company position for the program as well as to take a hard look at the allocation of resources required for the program. The company position may be to cut costs, authorize work, or submit a bid. If the program is competitive, corporate approval may be required if the company's chief executive officer has a ceiling on the dollar bids he can authorize to go out of house.

If labor costs must be cut, the program manager must negotiate with the functional managers as to the size and method for the cost reductions. Otherwise, this step would simply entail authorization for the functional managers to begin the activities.

Figure 14–10 represents the system approach toward determining total program costs. This procedure normally creates a synergistic environment, provides open channels of communication between all levels of management, and ensures agreement between all individuals as to program costs.

14.11 SYSTEMS PRICING

The basis of successful program management is the establishment of an accurate cost package from which all members of the organization can both project and track costs. The cost data must be represented in such a manner that maximum allocation of the corporate resources of people, money, and facilities can be achieved.

The systems approach to pricing out the activity schedules and the work breakdown structure provides a means for obtaining unity within the company. The flow of information readily admits the participation of all members of the organization in the program, even if on a part-time basis. Functional managers obtain a better understanding of how their labor fits into the total program and how their activities interface with those of other departments. For the first time, functional managers can accurately foresee how their activity can lead to corporate profits.

The project pricing model (sometimes called a strategic project planning model) acts as a management information system, forming the basis for the systems approach to resource control, as shown in Figure 14–11. The summary sheets from the computer output of the strategic pricing model provide man-

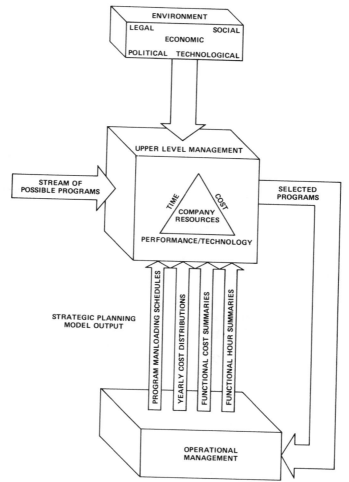

Figure 14–11. Systems approach to resource control.

agement with the necessary data from which the selection of possible programs can be made so that maximum utilization of resources will follow.

The strategic pricing model also provides management with an invaluable tool for performing perturbation analysis on the base case costs. This perturbation analysis provides management with sufficient opportunity for design and evaluation of contingency plans, should a deviation from the original plan be required.

14.12 DEVELOPING THE SUPPORTING/BACK-UP COSTS

Not all cost proposals require back-up support, but for those that do, the back-up support should be developed along with the pricing. Extreme caution must be exercised to make sure that the itemized prices are compatible with the supporting data. Government pricing requirements are a special case.

Most supporting data come from external (subcontractor or outside vendor) quotes. Internal data must be based upon historical data, and this historical data must be updated continually as each new project is completed. The supporting data should be traceable by itemized charge numbers.

Customers may wish to audit the cost proposal. In this case, the starting point might be with the supporting data. It is not uncommon on sole-source proposals to have the supporting data audited before the final cost proposal is submitted to the customer.

Not all cost proposals require supporting data; the determining factor is usually the type of contract. On a fixed-price effort, the customer may not have the right to audit your books. However, for a cost-reimbursable package, your costs are an open book, and the customer usually compares your exact costs to those of the back-up support.

Most companies usually have a choice of more than one estimate to be used for back-up support. In deciding which estimate to use, consideration must be given to the possibility of follow-on work:

- If your actual costs grossly exceed your back-up support estimates, you may lose credibility for follow-on work.
- If your actual costs are less than the back-up costs, you must use the new actual costs on follow-on efforts.

The moral here is that back-up support costs provide future credibility. If you have well-documented, "livable" cost estimates, then you may wish to include them in the cost proposal even if they are not required.

Since both direct and indirect costs may be negotiated separately as part of a contract, supporting data such as in Tables 14–7 through 14–10 and Figure 14–12 may be necessary to justify any costs that may differ from company (or customer-approved) standards.

14.13 THE LOW-BIDDER DILEMMA[2]

There is little argument about the importance of the price tag to the proposal. The question is, what price will win the job? Everyone has an answer to this

---

2. Adapted from H. Kerzner and H. J. Thamhain, *Project Management for the Small and Medium-Sized Business* (New York: Van Nostrand Reinhold, 1983), pp. 221–226

Table 14–7. Operations Skills Matrix.

FUNCTIONAL / AREAS OF EXPERTISE \ TECHNICAL STAFF	ABLE, J.	BAKER, P.	COOK, D.	DIRK, L.	EASLEY, P.	FRANKLIN, W.	GREEN, C.	HENRY, L.	IMHOFF, R.	JULES, C.	KLEIN, W.	LEDGER, D.	MAYER, Q.	NEWTON, A.	OLIVER, G.	PRATT, L.
Administrative management		a				a		a			a	a			a	
Control and communications	b	b	b	b	b		b	b		b	b	b		b	b	b
Environmental impact assessment	c	c	c						c		c		c			
Facilities management		d					d				d		d			
Financial management	e					e			e	e	e				e	e
Human resources management	f							f				f				
Industrial engineering	g				g					g						
Intelligence and security								h				h		h	h	h
Inventory control	i						i								i	i
Logistics			j		j			j				j				
OSHA	k									k			k			
Project management	l			l		l					l				l	
Quality control		m	m			m	m	m	m							
R&D			n	n			n				n		n			n
Wage and salary administration		o			o				o	o		o		o	o	

Table 14–8.   Contractor's Manpower Availability.

	NUMBER OF PERSONNEL			
	TOTAL CURRENT STAFF		AVAILABLE FOR THIS PROJECT AND OTHER NEW WORK 1/83	ANTICIPATED GROWTH BY 1/83
	PERMANENT EMPLOYEES	AGENCY PERSONNEL	PERMANENT + AGENCY	PERMANENT + AGENCY
Process engineers	93	—	70	4
Project Managers/engineers	79	—	51	4
Cost estimating	42	—	21	2
Cost control	73	—	20	2
Scheduling/scheduling control	14	—	8	1
Procurement/ purchasing	42	—	20	1
Inspection	40	—	20	2
Expediting	33	—	18	1
Home office construction Management	9	—	6	0
Piping	90	13	67	6
Electrical	31	—	14	2
Instrumentation	19	—	3	1
Vessels/exchangers	24	—	19	1
Civil/structural	30	—	23	2
Other	13	—	8	0

Table 14–9.   Staff Turnover Data.

	FOR TWELVE-MONTH PERIOD 1/1/82 TO 1/1/83	
	NUMBER TERMINATED	NUMBER HIRED
Process engineers	5	2
Project managers/engineers	1	1
Cost estimating	1	2
Cost control	12	16
Scheduling/scheduling control	2	5
Procurement/purchasing	13	7
Inspection	18	6
Expediting	4	5
Home office construction management	0	0
Design and drafting—total	37	29
Engineering specialists—total	26	45
Total	119	118

Table 14–10. Staff Experience Profile.

	NUMBER OF YEARS EMPLOYMENT WITH CONTRACTOR				
	0–1	1–2	2–3	3–5	5 OR MORE
Process engineers	2	4	15	11	18
Proj. managers/engineers	1	2	5	11	8
Cost estimating	0	4	1	5	7
Cost control	5	9	4	7	12
Scheduling and scheduling control	2	2	1	3	6
Procurement/purchasing	4	12	13	2	8
Inspection	1	2	6	14	8
Expediting	6	9	4	2	3
Piping	9	6	46	31	22
Electrical	17	6	18	12	17
Instrumentation	8	8	12	13	12
Mechanical	2	5	13	27	19
Civil/structural	4	8	19	23	16
Environmental control	0	1	1	3	7
Engineering specialists	3	3	3	16	21
Total	64	81	161	180	184

question. The decision process that leads to the final price of your proposal is highly complex with many uncertainties. Yet proposal managers, driven by the desire to win the job, may think that a very low-priced proposal will help. But, hopefully, winning is only the beginning. Companies have short- and long-range objectives on profit, market penetration, new product development, and so on. These objectives may be incompatible with or irrelevant to a low-price strategy per se; for example:

- A suspiciously low price, particularly on cost-plus type proposals, might be perceived by the customer as unrealistic, thus affecting the bidder's cost credibility or even the technical ability to perform.
- The bid price may be unnecessarily low, relative to the competition and customer budget, thus eroding profits.
- The price may be irrelevant to the bid objective, such as entering a new market. Therefore, the contractor has to sell the proposal in a credible way, e.g., using cost sharing.
- Low pricing without market information is meaningless. The price level is always relative to (1) the competitive prices, (2) the customer budget, and (3) the bidder's cost estimate.
- The bid proposal and its price may cover only part of the total program.

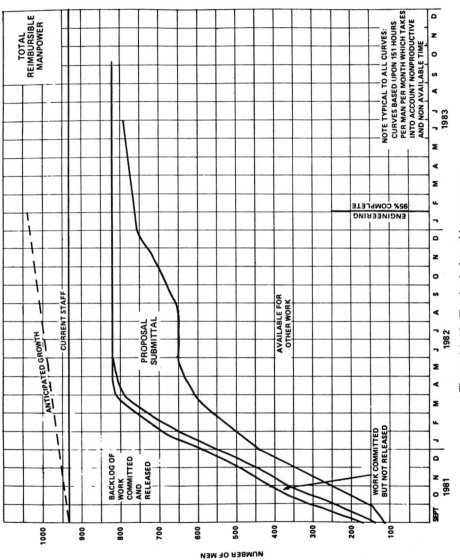

Figure 14–12. Total reimbursable manpower.

The ability to win Phase II or follow-on business depends on Phase I performance and Phase II price.
- The financial objectives of the customer may be more complex than just finding the lowest bidder. They may include cost objectives for total system life cycle cost (LCC), for design to unit production cost (DTUPC), or for specific logistic support items. Presenting sound approaches for attaining these system cost-performance parameters and targets may be just as important as, if not more important than, a low bid for its development.

Further, it is refreshing to note that in spite of customer pressures toward low cost and fixed-price, the lowest bidder is certainly not an automatic winner. Both commercial and governmental customers are increasingly concerned about cost realism and the ability to perform under contract. A compliant, sound, technical and management proposal, based on past experience with realistic, well-documented cost figures, is often chosen over the lowest bidder, who may project a risky image regarding technical performance, cost, or schedule.

14.14 SPECIAL PROBLEMS

There are always special problems that, although often overlooked, have a severe impact upon the pricing effort. As an example, pricing must include an understanding of cost control—specifically, how costs are billed back to the project. There are three possible situations:

- *Work is priced out at the department average, and all work performed is charged to the project at the department average salary, regardless of who accomplished the work.* This technique is obviously the easiest, but encourages project managers to fight for the highest salary resources, since only average wages are billed to the project.
- *Work is priced out at the department average, but all work performed is billed back to the project at the actual salary of those employees who perform the work.* This method can create a severe headache for the project manager if he tries to use only the best employees on his project. If these employees are earning substantially more money than the department average, then a cost overrun will occur unless the employees can perform the work in less time. Some companies are forced to use this method by government agencies and have estimating problems when the project that has to be priced out is of a short duration where only the higher-salaried employees can be used. In such a situation it is common to "inflate" the direct labor hours to compensate for the added costs.
- *The work is priced out at the actual salary of those employees who will*

perform the work, and the cost is billed back the same way. This method is the ideal situation as long as the people can be identified during the pricing effort.

Some companies use a combination of all three methods. In this case, the project office is priced out using the third method (because these people are identified early), whereas the functional employees are priced out using the first or second method.

14.15 ESTIMATING PITFALLS

Several pitfalls can impede the pricing function. Probably the most serious pitfall, and the one that is usually beyond the control of the project manager, is the "buy-in" decision, which is based upon the assumption that there will be "bail-out" changes or follow-on contracts later. These changes and/or contracts may be for spares, spare parts, maintenance, maintenance manuals, equipment surveillance, optional equipment, optional services, and scrap factors. Other types of estimating pitfalls include:

- Misinterpretation of the statement of work
- Omissions or improperly defined scope
- Poorly defined or overly optimistic schedule
- Inaccurate work breakdown structure
- Applying improper skill levels to tasks
- Failure to account for risks
- Failure to understand or account for cost escalation and inflation
- Failure to use the correct estimating technique
- Failure to use forward pricing rates for overhead, general and administrative, and indirect cost

Unfortunately, many of these pitfalls do not become evident until detected by the cost control system, well into the project.

14.16 ESTIMATING HIGH-RISK PROJECTS

The major difference between high-risk and low-risk projects depends upon the validity of the historical estimate. Construction companies have well-defined historical standards, which therefor makes their risk lower, whereas many R&D

The figures in Section 14.16 have been adapted from *Project Management Operating Guidelines,* by Harold Kerzner and Hans Thamhain, © 1986 by Van Nostrand Reinhold Co., Inc., New York, pp. 356–358.

Table 14–11. Low- Versus High-Risk Accuracies.

WBS		ACCURACY, PERCENT	
LEVEL	DESCRIPTION	LOW RISK PROJECTS	HIGH RISK PROJECTS
1	Program	35	75–100
2	Project	20	50–60
3	Task	10	20–30
4	Subtask	5	10–15
5	Work Package	2	5–10

and MIS projects are high-risk. Typical accuracies for each level of the WBS are shown below in Table 14–11:

One of the most common techniques used to estimate high-risk projects is the "rolling wave" or "moving window" approach. This is shown in Figure 14–13 for a high-risk R&D project. The project lasts for 12 months. The R&D effort to be accomplished for the first six months is well defined and can be estimated to level five of the WBS. However, the effort for the last six months is based upon the results of the first six months and can be estimated at level two only, thus incurring a high risk. Now consider Part (B) of Figure 14–13, which shows a six month moving window. At the end of the first month, in order to maintain a six month moving window (at level five of the WBS), the estimate for month seven must be improved from a level two to a level five estimate. Likewise, in Parts (C) and (D) of Figure 14–13, we see the effects of completing the second and third months.

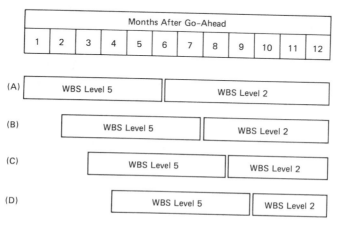

Figure 14–13. The moving window/rolling wave concept.

There are two key points to be considered in utilizing this technique. First, the length of the moving window can vary from project to project, and usually increases in length as you approach downstream life cycle phases. Second, this technique works best when upper-level management understands how the technique works. All too often senior management hears only one budget and schedule number during project approval and might not realize that at least half of the project might be time/cost accurate to only 50–60 percent. Simply stated, when using this technique, the word "rough" is not synonymous with the word "detailed."

Methodologies can be developed for assessing risk. Figures 14–14, 14–15, and Table 14–12 show such methodologies.

14.17 LIFE CYCLE COSTING (LCC)

For years, many R&D organizations have operated in a vacuum where technical decisions made during R&D were based entirely upon the R&D portion of the plan, with little regard for what happens after production begins. Today, industrial firms are adopting the life cycle costing approach that has been developed and used by military organizations. Simply stated, LCC requires that decisions made during the R&D process be evaluated against the total life cycle cost of the system. As an example, the R&D group has two possible design configurations for a new product. Both design configurations will require the same budget for R&D and the same costs for manufacturing. However, the maintenance and support costs may be substantially greater for one of the products. If these downstream costs are not considered in the R&D phase, large unanticipated expenses may result at a point where no alternatives exist.

Life cycle costs are the total cost to the organization for the ownership and acquisition of the product over its full life. This includes the cost of R&D, production, operation, support, and, where applicable, disposal. A typical breakdown description might include:

- *R&D costs:* The cost of feasibility studies; cost/benefit analyses; system analyses; detail design and development; fabrication, assembly, and test of engineering models; initial product evaluation; and associated documentation.
- *Production cost:* The cost of fabrication, assembly, and testing of production models; operation and maintenance of the production capability; and associated internal logistic support requirements, including test and support equipment development, spare/repair parts provisioning, technical data development, training, and entry of items into inventory.
- *Construction cost:* The cost of new manufacturing facilities or upgrading existing structures to accommodate production and operation of support requirements.

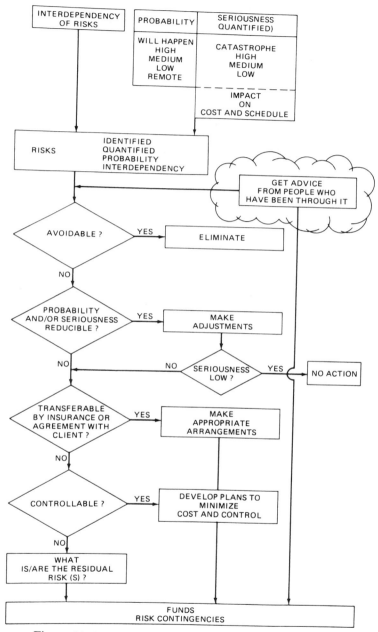

Figure 14–14. Decision elements for risk contingencies.

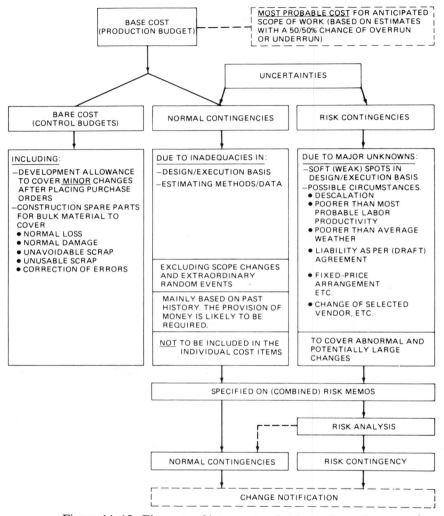

Figure 14–15. Elements of base cost and risk contingencies.

Table 14–12. Standard Form for Project Risk Analysis and Risk Contingencies.

PROJECT RISK ANALYSIS & RISK CONTINGENCY

REF.: PROCEDURE 0110E

RISK CONTINGENCY = 2 EXPECTED VALUES

Proposal/Order No.

Div./Dept.

Date

Issue No.

RISK — Expected Value

Transfer to:
- Normal Contingency
- Accept as Residual Risk
- Plan to Control
- Construction Spares
- Development Allowance
- Inclusion in Estimate
- Exclusion from Scope
- Subcontractor or Vendor
- Agreement
- Insurance
- Make Adjustments

Cat./High/Med./Low Seriousness

Interdependency of Risks

Possible Outcome — Amount

Probability

Maximum Risk — Amount

Description of Risk / Maximum Possible Change of Item Value in %

Risk: Yes/No

Value

Item

Sequence

- *Operation and maintenance cost:* The cost of sustaining operational personnel and maintenance support; spare/repair parts and related inventories; test and support equipment maintenance, transportation and handling, facilities, modifications, and technical data changes, and so on.
- *Product retirement and phaseout cost:* The cost of phasing the product out of inventory due to obsolescence or wearout, and subsequent equipment item recycling and reclamation as appropriate.

Life-cycle cost analysis is the systematic analytical process of evaluating various alternative courses of action early on in a project, with the objective of choosing the best way to employ scarce resources. Life cycle cost is employed in the evaluation of alternative design configurations, alternative manufacturing methods, alternative support schemes, and so on. This process includes:

- Defining the problem (what information is needed)
- Defining the requirements of the cost model being used
- Collecting historical data/cost relationships
- Developing estimate and test results

Successful application of LCC will:

- Provide downstream resource impact visibility
- Provide life cycle cost management
- Influence R&D decision-making
- Support downstream strategic budgeting

There are also several limitations to life cycle cost analyses. They include:

- The assumption that the product, as known, has a finite life cycle
- A high cost to perform, which may not be appropriate for low-cost/low-volume production
- A high sensitivity to changing requirements

Life cycle costing requires that early estimates be made. The estimating method selected is based upon the problem context (i.e., decisions to be made, required accuracy, complexity of the product, and the development status of the product) and the operational considerations (i.e., market introduction date, time available for analysis, and available resources).

The estimating methods available can be classified as follows:

- Informal Estimating Methods
  - Judgment based on experience

- Analogy
- SWAG method
- ROM method
- Rule of Thumb method
- Formal Estimating Methods
  - Detailed (from industrial engineering standards)
  - Parametric

Table 14–13 shows the advantages/disadvantages of each method.

Figure 14–16 shows the various life cycle phases for Department of Defense projects. At the end of the demonstration and validation phase (which is the completion of R&D) 85 percent of the decisions affecting the total life cycle cost will have been made, and the cost reduction opportunity is limited to a maximum of 22 percent (excluding the effects of learning curve experiences). Figure 14–17 shows that, at the end of the R&D phase, 95 percent of the cumulative life cycle cost is committed by the government. Figure 14–18 shows that, for every $12 that DOD puts into R&D, $28 are needed downstream for production and $60 for operation and support.

Life cycle cost analysis is an integral part of strategic planning since today's decisions will affect tomorrow's actions. Yet there are common errors made during life cycle cost analyses:

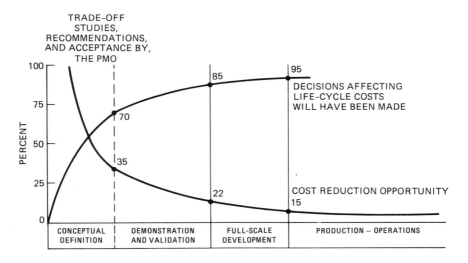

Figure 14–16. Department of Defense life-cycle phases.

Table 14–13. Estimating Methods.

ESTIMATING TECHNIQUE	APPLICATION	ADVANTAGES	DISADVANTAGES
Engineering Estimates Empirical	Reprocurement Production Development	• Most detailed technique • Best inherent accuracy • Provides best estimating base for future program change estimates	• Requires detailed program and product definition • Time consuming and may be expensive • Subject to engineering bias • May overlook system integration costs
Parametric estimates and scaling Statistical	Production Development	• Application is simple and low cost • Statistical data base can provide expected values and prediction intervals • Can be used for equipment or systems prior to detail design or program planning	• Requires parametric cost relationships to be established • Limited frequently to specific subsystems or functional hardware of systems • Depends on quantity and quality of the data base • Limited by data and number of independent variables
Equipment/ subsystem analogy estimates Comparative	Reprocurement Production development Program planning	• Relatively simple • Low cost • Emphasizes incremental program and product changes • Good accuracy for similar systems	• Require analogous product and program data • Limited to stable technology • Narrow range of electronic applications • May be limited to systems and equipment built by the same firm
Expert Opinion	All program phases	• Available when there are insufficient data, parametric cost relationships, or program/product definition	• Subject to bias • Increased product or program complexity can degrade estimates • Estimate substantiation is not quantifiable

- Loss or omission of data
- Lack of systematic structure
- Misinterpretation of data
- Wrong or misused techniques
- A concentration on insignificant facts
- Failure to assess uncertainty
- Failure to check work
- Estimating the wrong items

PROBLEMS

14-1   How does a project manager price out a job in which the specifications are not prepared until the job is half over?

14-2   Beta Corporation is in the process of completing a contract to produce 150 units for a given customer. The contract consisted of R&D, testing and qualification, and full production. The industrial engineering department had determined that the following number of hours were required to produce certain units:

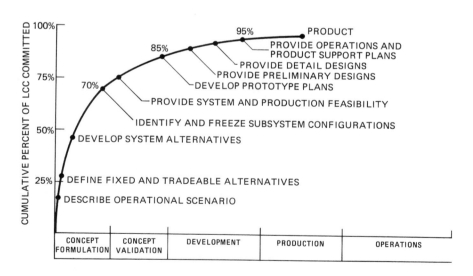

Figure 14–17. Actions affecting life cycle cost (LCC).

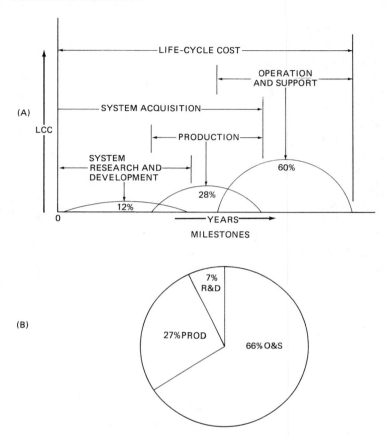

Figure 14–18. (A) Typical DOD system acquisition LCC profile; (B) Typical communication system acquisition LCC profile.

Unit	Hours required per unit
1	100
2	90
4	80
8	70
16	65
32	60
64	55
128	50

a. Plot the data points on regular graph paper with the Y-axis as hours and the X-axis as number of units produced.
b. Plot the data points on log–log paper and determine the slope of the line.
c. Compare Parts a and b. What are your conclusions?
d. How much time should it take to manufacture the 150th unit?
e. How much time should it take to manufacture the 1,000th unit? Explain your answer. Is it realistic? If not, why?
f. As you are producing the 150th unit, you receive an immediate follow-on contract for another 150 units. How many manufacturing hours should you estimate for the follow-on effort (using only the learning curves)?
g. Let's assume that industrial engineering determines that the optimum number of hours (for 100 percent efficiency) of manufacturing is forty-five. At what efficiency factor are you now performing at the completion of unit number 150? After how many units in the follow-on contract will you reach the optimum level?
h. At the end of the first follow-on contract, your team and personnel are still together and performing at a 100 percent efficiency position. (of Part g) You have been awarded a second follow-on contract, but the work will not begin until six months from now. Assuming that you can assemble the same team, how many man-hours/unit will you estimate for the next 150-unit follow-on?
i. Would your answer to Part h change if you could not assemble the same team? Explain your answer quantitatively.
j. You are now on the contract negotiation team for the second follow-on contract of 150 units (which is not scheduled to start for six months). Based upon the people available and the "loss of learning" between contracts, your industrial engineering department estimates that you will be performing at a 60 percent efficiency factor. The customer says that your efficiency factor should be at least 75 percent. If your company is burdened at $40/hour, how much money is involved between the 60 and 75 percent efficiency factors?
k. What considerations should be made in deciding where to compromise in the efficiency factor?

14–3 With reference to Figure 14-10, under what conditions could **each** of the following situations occur:

a. Program manager and program office determine labor hours by pricing out the Work Breakdown Structure without coordination with functional management.
b. Upper-level management determines the price of a bid without forming a program office or consulting functional management.
c. Perturbations on the base case are not performed.
d. The chief executive officer selects the program manager without consulting his directors.
e. Upper-level management does not wish to have a cost review meeting prior to submittal of a bid.

14–4 Can the figure below be used effectively to price out the cost of preparing reports?

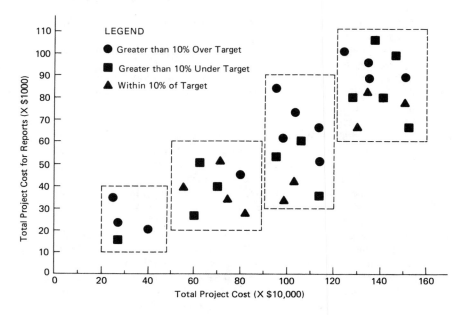

14-5 Answer the following questions with reference to Figure 14-10.

   a. The base case for a program is priced out at $22 million. The company's chief executive officer is required to obtain written permission from corporate to bid on programs in excess of $20 million. During the price review meeting the chief executive states that the bid will be submitted at $19.5 million. Should you, as program manager, question this?

   b. Would your answer to Part a. change if this program were a follow-on to an earlier program?

   c. Proposals normally consist of management, technical and cost volumes. Indicate in Figure 14-10 where these volumes can go to press, assuming each can be printed independently.

14-6 Under what kind of projects would each of the following parameters be selected:

   a. Salary escalation factor of 0 percent.
   b. Material termination liability of 0 percent or 100 percent.
   c. Material commitments for twenty months of a twenty-four-month program.
   d. Demanning ratio of 0 percent or 100 percent of following months labor.

14-7 How can upper-level management use the Functional Hour Summary Table to determine manpower planning for the entire company? How would you expect management to react if the Functional Hour Summary indicated a shortage or an abundance of trained personnel?

14-8   Which of the figures presented in this chapter should program management make available to the functional managers? Explain your answer.

14-9   The Jennings Construction Company has decided to bid on the construction for each of the two phases of a large project. The bidding requirements are that the costs for each phase be submitted separately together with a transition cost for turning over the first phase of the program to a second contractor should Jennings not receive both awards or perform unsatisfactorily on the first phase. The evaluation for the award of the second phase will not be made until the first phase is near completion. How can the transition costs be identified in the Strategic Planning Model?

14-10   Two contractors decide to enter into a joint venture on a project. What difficulties can occur if the contractors have decided on who does what work, but changes may take place if problems occur? What happens if one contractor has higher salary levels and overhead rates?

14-11   The Jones Manufacturing Company is competing for a production contract which requires that work begin in January, 1979. The cost package for the proposal must be submitted by July, 1978. The business base, and therefore the overhead rates, are uncertain because Jones has the possibility of winning another contract, to be announced in September, 1978. How can the impact of the announcement be included in the proposal? How would you handle a situation where another contract may not be renewed after January 1979, i.e., assume announcement would not be made until March?

14-12   Many competitive programs contain two phases: research and development, and production. Production profits far exceed R & D profits. The company which wins the R & D contract normally becomes a favorite for the production contract, as well as for any follow-on work. How can the dollar figures attached to follow-on work influence the cost package that you submit for the R & D phase? Would your answer change if the manhours submitted for the R & D phase become the basis for the production phase?

14-13   During initial pricing activities, one of the functional managers discovers that the Work Breakdown Structure requires costing data at a level which is not normally made, and will undoubtedly incur additional costs. How should you, as a program manager, respond to this situation? What are your alternatives?

14-14   Should the project manager give the final manpower loading curves to the functional managers? If so, at what point in time?

14-15   Estimating/pricing problem. You have been asked to price out a project for an outside customer. The project will run for eight months. Direct labor is $100,000 for each month and the overhead rate is fixed at 100 percent per month. Termination liability on the direct labor and overhead rate is 80 percent of the following month's expenses. Material expenses are as follows:

Material A: Cost is $100,000 payable 30 days net. Material is needed at the end of the fifth month. Lead time is four months with termination liability expenses as follows:

> 30 days: 25%
> 60 days: 75%
> 90 days: 100%

Material B: Cost is $200,000 payable on delivery. Material is needed at the end of the seventh month. Lead time is three months with termination liability as follows:

> 30 days: 50%
> 60 days: 100%

Complete the following table, neglecting profits:

	Month							
	1	2	3	4	5	6	7	8
Direct Labor								
Overhead								
Material								
Monthly Cash Flow								
Cumulative Cash Flow								
Monthly Termination Liability : Labor								
Cumulative Termination Liability : Labor								
Monthly Termination Liability : Material								
Cumulative Termination Liability : Material								
Total Project Termination Liability								

14–16 Should a project manager be appointed in the bidding stage of a project? If so, what authority should he have, and who is responsible for winning the contract?

14–17 Explain how useful each of the following can be during the estimating of project costs:

A. Contingency planning and estimating
B. Using historical data bases (See Figure 15–11)
C. Usefulness of computer estimating
D. Usefulness of performance factors to account for inefficiencies and uncertainties.

CASE STUDY: CONCRETE MASONRY CORPORATION[3]

Introduction

The Concrete Masonry Corporation (CMC), after being a leader in the industry for over twenty-five years, decided to get out of the prestressed concrete business. Although there had been a boom in residential construction in recent years, commercial work was on the decline. As a result, all the prestressed concrete manufacturers were going farther afield to big jobs. In order to survive, CMC was forced to bid on jobs previously thought to be out of their geographical area. Survival depended upon staying competitive.

In 1975, the average selling price of a cubic foot of concrete was $8.35, and in 1977, the average selling price had declined to $6.85. As CMC was producing at a rate of a million cubic feet a year, not much mathematics was needed to calculate they were receiving one-and-a-half million dollars per year less than they had received a short two years before for the same product.

Product management was used by CMC in a matrix organizational form. CMC's project manager had total responsibility from the design to the completion of the construction project. However, with the declining conditions of the market and the evolution that had drastically changed the character of the marketplace, CMC's previously successful approach was in question.

History

The Concrete Block Business

CMC started in the concrete block business in 1946. At the beginning, CMC became a leader in the marketplace for two reasons: (1) advanced technology of manufacturing, and (2) an innovative delivery system. With modern equipment, specifically the flat pallet block machine, CMC was able to make different shapes of block without having to make major changes in the machinery. This change, along with the pioneering of the self-unloading boom truck which made efficient, cost-saving delivery, contributed to the success of CMC's block business. Consequently, the block business success provided the capital needed for CMC to enter the prestressed concrete business.

---

3. Copyright © 1978 by Harold Kerzner.

The Prestressed Concrete Business

Prestressed concrete is made by casting concrete around steel cables that are stretched by hydraulic jacks. After the concrete hardens, the cables are released, thus compressing the concrete. Concrete is strongest when it is compressed. Steel is strongest when it is stretched, or in tension. In this way, CMC combined the two strongest qualities of the two materials. The effectiveness of the technique can be readily demonstrated by lifting a horizontal row of books by applying pressure at each end of the row at a point below the center of gravity.

Originally, the concrete block manufacturing business was a natural base from which to enter the prestressed concrete business because the very first prestressed concrete beams were made of a row of concrete block, prestressed by using high-tension strength wires through the cores of the block. The wire was pulled at a high tension, and the ends of the beams were grouted. After the grout held the wires or cables in place, the tension was released on the cables, with resultant compression on the bottom portion of the beams. Thus, the force on the bottom of the beam would tend to counteract the downward weight put on the top of the beam. By this process, these prestressed concrete beams could cover three to four times the spans possible with conventional reinforced concrete.

In 1951, after many trips to Washington, D.C., and an excellent selling job by CMC's founder T. L. Goudvis, CMC was able to land their first large-volume prestressed concrete project with the Corps of Engineers. The contract authorized the use of prestressed concrete beams, as described, with concrete block for the roofs of warehouses in the large Air Force Depot complex being built in Shelby, Ohio. The buildings were a success, and CMC immediately received prestige and notoriety as a leader in the prestressed concrete business.

Wet-cast beams were developed next. For wet-cast beams, instead of concrete block, the cables were placed in long forms and pulled to the desired tension, after which concrete was poured in the forms to make beams. As a result of wet-cast beams, prestressed concrete was no longer dependent on concrete block.

At first, prestressed concrete was primarily for floors and roofs, but, in the early sixties, precasters became involved in more complicated structures. CMC started designing and making not only beams, but columns and whatever other components it took to put together a whole structure. Parking garages became a natural application for prestressed concrete structures. Eventually an entire building could be precast out of prestressed concrete. (See Figure 14–19.)

Project Management

Constructing the entire building, as in the case of a parking garage, meant that jobs were becoming more complex with respect to interdependence of detailed task accomplishment. Accordingly, in 1967, project management was established at CMC. The functional departments did the work, but the project managers saw to it that the assigned projects were completed on schedule and within budget and specifications. A matrix organization, as illustrated in Figure 14–20, was adopted and used effectively by CMC. The concept of a matrix organization, as applied at CMC, entailed an orga-

Figure 14–19. Coliseum, Richfield, Ohio.

nizational system designed as a "web of relationships" rather than a line and staff relationship for work performance.

Each project manager was assigned a number of personnel with the required qualifications from the functional departments for the duration of the project. Thus, the project organization was composed of the project manager and functional personnel groups. Although the project manager had the responsibility and accountability for

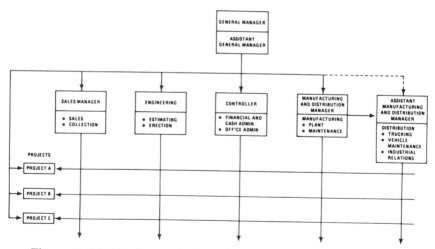

Figure 14–20. Matrix organization of Concrete Masonry Corporation.

the successful completion of the contract, he also had the delegated authority for work design, assignments of functional group personnel, and the determination of procedural relationships.

The most important functional area for the project manager was the engineering department, since prestressed concrete is a highly engineered product. A great deal of coordination and interaction was required between the project manager and the engineering department just to make certain that everything fit together and was structurally sound. A registered engineer did the design. The project manager's job was to see that the designing was done correctly and efficiently. Production schedules were made up by the project manager subject, of course, to minor modifications by the plant. The project manager was also required to do all the coordination with the customer, architect, general contractor, and his own erection force. The project manager was also required to have interaction with the distribution manager to be certain that the product designed could be shipped by trucks. Finally, there had to be interaction between the project manager and the sales department to determine that the product that he was making was what they had sold.

Estimating

Which Department?

At one time or another during CMC's history, the estimating function was assigned to nearly every functional area of the organization, including sales, engineering, manufacturing, and administration. Determining which functional area estimating was to be under was a real problem for CMC. There was a short time when estimating was on its own, reporting directly to the general manager.

Assignment of this function to any one department carried with it some inherent problems, not peculiar to CMC, but simply related to human nature. For example, when the estimating was supervised in the sales department, estimated costs would tend to be low. In sales, the estimator knows his boss wants to be the low bidder on the job and therefore believes he is right when he says, "It is not going to take us ten days to cast this thing; we could run three at a time."

When estimating was performed by production, the estimate would tend to be high. This was so because the estimator did not want his boss, the production manager, coming back to him and saying, "How come you estimated this thing at $5 a cubic foot and it's costing us $6? It's not the cost of production that's wrong, it's the estimate."

W. S. Lasch, general manager of CMC, had this comment about estimating in a project management situation: "It is very difficult to get accountability for estimating a project. When many of your projects are new ballgames, a lot of your information has to come from ... well, let's just say there is a lot of art to it as well as science. You never can say with 100 percent certainty that costs were high because you could have just as easily said the estimate was too low.

"So, as a compromise, most of the time we had our estimating made by engineering. While it solved some problems, it also created others. Engineers would tend to be more fair; they would call the shots as they saw them. However, one problem was that they still had to answer to sales as far as their work load was concerned. For example, an engineer is in the middle of estimating a parking garage, a task which might take several days. All of a sudden, the sales department wants him to stop and estimate another job. The sales department had to be the one to really make that decision because they are the ones that know what the priorities are on the bidding. So even though the estimator was working in engineering, he was really answering to the sales manager as far as his work load was concerned."

Costing

Estimating was accomplished through continual monitoring and comparison of actual vs. planned performance, as shown below.

The actual costing process was not a problem for CMC. In recent years, CMC eliminated as much as possible the actual dollars and cents from the estimator's control. A great deal of the "drudge work" was done on the computer. The estimator, for example, would predict how much the prestressed concrete must span, and how many cubic feet of concrete was needed. Once he had that information, he entered it in the computer. The computer would then come up with the cost. This became an effective method because the estimator would not be influenced by either sales or production personnel.

The Evolution of the Prestressed Concrete Marketplace

During the twenty or more years since prestressing achieved wide acceptance in the construction industry, an evolution has been taking place that has drastically changed the character of the marketplace and thus greatly modified the role of the prestresser.

Lasch had the following comments about these changes that occurred in the marketplace: "In the early days, designers of buildings looked to prestressers for the expertise required to successfully incorporate the techniques and available prestressed prod-

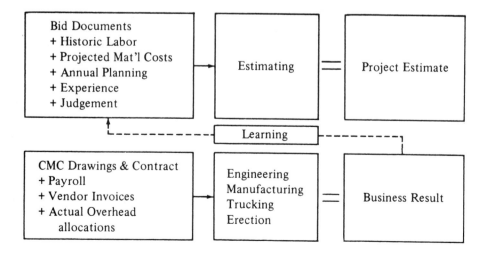

ucts into their structures. A major thrust of our business in those days was to introduce design professionals, architects and engineers to our fledgling industry and to assist them in making use of the many advantages which we could offer over other construction methods. These advantages included fire resistance, long spans, permanence, factory controlled quality, speed of erection, aesthetic desirability, virtual elimination of maintenance costs, and, last but of prime importance, the fact that we were equipped to provide the expertise and coordination necessary to successfully integrate our product into the building. Many of our early jobs were bid from sketches. It was then up to our in-house experts, working closely with the owner's engineer and architect, to develop an appropriate, efficient structure which satisfied the aesthetic and functional requirements and hopefully maximized production and erection efficiency, thereby providing maximum financial return to CMC. It should be noted that, although our contract was normally with the project's general contractor, most of our design coordination was through the owner's architect or engineer and, more often than not, it was our relationship with the owner and his design professional that determined our involvement in the project in the first place. It should be readily seen that, in such an environment, only organizations with a high degree of engineering background and a well-organized efficient team of professionals, could compete successfully. CMC was such an organization.

"There are however few, if any, proprietary secrets in the prestressing industry, and it was inevitable that this would in later years be largely responsible for a dramatic change in the marketplace. The widespread acceptance of the product which had been achieved through the success of companies like CMC carried with it a proliferation of the technical knowledge and production techniques for which design professionals had previously relied upon the producer to provide. In the later 1960s, some colleges and universities began to include prestressed concrete design as a part of their structural engineering programs. Organizations, such as the Portland Cement Association, offered seminars for architects and engineers to promote the prestressing concept. As a result, it is now common for architects and engineers to incorporate prestressed concrete products in bid drawings for their projects, detailing all connections, reinforcement, mix designs, etc. This, obviously, makes it possible for any organization capable of reading drawings and filling forms to bid on the project. We have found ourselves bidding against companies with a few molds in an open field and, in several cases, a broker with no equipment or organization at all! The result of all this, of course, is a market price so low as to prohibit the involvement of professional prestressing firms with the depth of organization described earlier."

Obtaining a Prestressed Concrete Job

The case writer believes the following example demonstrates the change in market conditions and best illustrates one of the reasons CMC decided not to remain in the prestressed concrete business. A large insurance company in Columbus, Ohio was planning a parking garage for 2,500 cars. CMC talked to the owner and owner's representative (a construction management firm) about using prestressed concrete in the design of their project rather than the poured-in-place concrete, steel, or whatever options they had. Just by doing this, CMC had to give away some knowledge. You just cannot walk in and say, "Hey, how about using prestressed concrete?" You have to tell them what is going to be saved and how, because the architect has to make the drawings. Once CMC felt there was an open door, and that the architect and owner would possibly incorporate their product, then sales would consult engineering to come up with a proposal. A proposal in the early stages was simply to identify what the costs were going to be, and to show the owner and architect photographs or sketches of previous jobs. As time went by, CMC had to go into more detail and provide more and more information, including detailed drawings of several proposed layouts. CMC illustrated connection details, reinforcing details, and even computer design of some of the pieces for the parking garage. Receiving all this engineering information, the owner and the construction management firm became convinced that using this product was the most inexpensive way for them to go. In fact, CMC demonstrated to the insurance company that they could save over one million dollars over any other product. At this point, CMC had spent thousands of dollars to come up with the solution for the problem of designing the parking garage.

Months and years passed until the contract manager chose to seek bids from other precasters, who, up to this time, had little or no investment in the project. CMC had made available an abundance of free information that could be used by the competition. The competition only had to put the information together, make a material take-off, calculate the cost, and put a price on it. Without the costly depth of organization required to support the extensive promotional program conducted by CMC, the competition could naturally bid the job lower.

Lasch felt that, as a result of present-day market conditions, there were only two ways that one survives in the prestressed concrete business: "Face the fact that you are going to be subservient to a general contractor and that you are going to sell not your expertise but your function as a 'job shop' manufacturer producing concrete products according to someone else's drawings and specifications. If you do that, then you no longer need, for example, an engineering department or a technically qualified sales organization. All you are going to do is look at drawings, have an estimator who can read the drawings, put a price tag on them, and give a bid. It is going to be a low bid because you have eliminated much of your overhead. We simply do not choose to be in business in this manner.

"The other way to be in the business is that you are not going to be subservient to a general contractor, or owner's architect or engineer. What you are going to do is to deal with owners or users. That way a general contractor may end up as a subcontractor to the prestresser. We might go out and build a parking garage or other structure and assume the role of developer or builder or even owner/leaser. In that way, we would control the whole job. After all, in most cases the precast contract on a garage represents more than half the total cost. It could be argued with great justification that the conventional approach (i.e., precaster working for general contractor) could be compared to the tail wagging the dog.

"With complete control of design, aesthetics, and construction schedule, it would be possible to achieve maximum efficiency of design, plant usage, and field coordination which, when combined, would allow us to achieve the most important requirement—that of providing the eventual user with maximum value for a minimum investment.

Unless this can be achieved, the venture would not be making a meaningful contribution to society, and there would be no justification for being in business."

CASE STUDY: CONSTRUCTION OF A GAS TESTING LAB IN IRAN

With the increase in the availability of natural gas, the country of Iran had decided to embark on an extensive development program to test and evaluate the gas-utilizing appliances and accessories that might be required to satisfy future demands. The Iranian government desired to have all such items tested prior to use. The responsibility for this testing was delegated to the National Iranian Gas Company (NIGC).

Testing requires a facility. NIGC employed the American Gas Association (AGA), a nonprofit organization. NIGC contracted AGA for engineering services, training, technical assistance, and special equipment fabrication work required for establishment of a testing lab. Testing for safety and performance would be in compliance with Iranian National Standards. Except for equipment installation and program startup, all work would be accomplished in the United States. The final assembly would be at the NIGC city gate station in Rey, Iran.

The project is a technical assistance contract to provide program planning, building design (but not construction), instruments purchasing, special equipment fabrication, operations personnel training, equipment installation and program startup aid.

The contractor will furnish general design specifications and lay-outs including mechanical and electrical drawings. Architectural details, building construction and site preparation are furnished by the customer.

The project consists of five phases with a total time frame of twenty-one months. The five phases are:

1. Program plan and building design
2. Equipment purchase
3. Equipment construction
4. Training
5. Plant startup

Work Breakdown Structure

The analysis of the cost associated with building the project begins with the separation of the program into its basic tasks. The tasks involved with the project are defined as engineering, procurement, and training. The costs associated with each of the basic tasks are broken out and allocated to specific cost centers.

PROJECT 1–1–00 PROGRAM PLAN AND BUILDING DESIGN

Project #1 consists of engineering and program management in the following areas:
Task 1–1–1 engineering
Engineering time required to design the testing building.
Task 1–1–2 program management
Management time allocated to project planning and building design.

PROJECT 1-2-00 EQUIPMENT PURCHASE

Project #2 included time required to specify and purchase the equipment for the testing laboratory as follows:

Task 1-2-1 program management
Time allocated for management of the purchasing function.
Task 1-2-2 engineering
Provides the basic specifications for the equipment to be purchased.
Task 1-2-3 testing and inspection
Ensures that all equipment meets the established specifications.
Task 1-2-4 shipping
Includes packing and storage for foreign shipment of the equipment.
Task 1-2-5 procurement
Purchase of all equipment and establishing dates that it will be shipped.

PROJECT 1-3-00 EQUIPMENT CONSTRUCTION

Project #3 is required to specify, purchase, and fabricate equipment that is not on the market.

Task 1-3-1 program management
Overall management of the special equipment function
Task 1-3-2 engineering
Developing the specifications for the special equipment
Task 1-3-3 procurement
The purchase and evaluation of special equipment, and the establishment of dates for shipment of the equipment
Task 1-3-4 shipping
The packing and shipment of the special equipment for foreign shipment.
Task 1-3-5 fabrication
Building and testing the equipment at selected vendors

PROJECT 1-4-00 TRAINING

Project #4 involves the preparation of material and equipment to train the testing laboratory personnel

Task 1-4-1 program management
Overall management of the training function
Task 1-4-2 engineering
Developing the materials used to train the laboratory personnel
Task 1-4-3 training
The actual time required to make the testing people proficient with their new equipment

PROJECT 1-5-00 PLANT STARTUP

Project #5 provides the time for field personnel to put the laboratory in operation.
Task 1-5-1 program management

Provides the overall coordination of the plant startup function
Task 1–5–2 field engineering
The time involved to provide the laboratory with startup personnel

OTHER COSTS ASSOCIATED WITH THE PROJECT

Purchased parts—Testing equipment
Freight—Shipping and packing
Travel—Procurement
Other—Purchased goods, freight, subcontracts, materials

Figure 14–21 contains the PERT chart for the program. Figure 14–22 shows the bar chart for the total program, together with monthly man-hours and initial salary structures.

Base Case Discussion

The parameters used in the strategic planning model are listed below:

1. Salary costs will increase 6 percent per year with the increase beginning January 1 of each year.
2. Raw material costs will increase 10 percent per year with the increase beginning January 1 of each year.
3. Demanning ratio is 10 percent of following month's labor and man-hour costs.
4. Termination liability on materials is 0 percent, and material commitments are based upon 6 months or less.
5. Indirect cost for each project is 14 percent of total cost of labor and materials.
6. Corporate cost for each project is 1 percent of total cost of labor and materials.
7. A profit of 12 percent is used for each project in the base case.
8. No delays or additional increased costs are assumed in the base case.
9. A separate overhead rate is included for each task (see Figure 14–21).

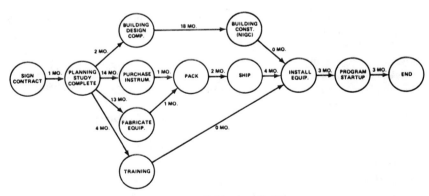

Figure 14–21. Critical path diagram.

Program Bar Chart

PROJECTS/TASKS	1977 JAN	FEB	MAR	APR	MAY	JUNE	JULY	AUG	SEPT	OCT	NOV	DEC	1978 JAN	FEB	MAR	APR	MAY	JUNE	JULY	AUG	SEPT
I. PROGRAM PLANS & BUILDING DESIGN																					
1. PROGRAM MANAGEMENT	102	50	48																		
2. ENGINEERING	20	174	283																		
II. EQUIPMENT PURCHASE																					
1. PROGRAM MANAGEMENT		52	40	40	30	30	30	30	30	30	20	20	20	20	20						
2. ENGINEERING		267	232	200	165	131	95	60	40												
3. TESTING & INSPECTION							154	154	154	266	266	266	154	112							
4. SHIPPING									154	154	154	154	308	308							
5. PROCUREMENT			154	154	154	154	154	77	77												
III. EQUIPMENT CONSTRUCTION																					
1. PROGRAM MANAGEMENT			20	20	30	30	30	30	30	30	20	20	20	20							
2. ENGINEERING			154	154	154	154	154	154	154	77	308	308	308	308							
3. PROCUREMENT										154	77	308	308	308							
4. SHIPPING						308	308	308	308	308	308	47	100	154							
5. FABRICATION			154	308	462	616	770	924	1078	1386	1848	1848	1848	1848							
IV. TRAINING																					
1. PROGRAM MANAGEMENT											20	20	20	20							
2. ENGINEERING											60	60	60	60							
3. TRAINING											154	154	154	154							
V. PLANT START-UP																					
1. PROGRAM MANAGEMENT													20	20	5	5	5	5	20		
2. FIELD ENGINEERING													154	154	154	308	154	154	154		

	RATE	OH
PROGRAM MANAGEMENT	11.00	120%
ENGINEERING	10.00	120%
TESTING	8.00	117%
PROCUREMENT	8.00	110%
SHIPPING	5.70	100%
FABRICATION	10.00	125%
TRAINING	10.50	120%
FIELD ENGINEERING	9.00	80%

(125%, 12%)

INDIRECT COSTS 14%
CORPORATE COSTS 1%
PROFIT: 12%

II. OTHER COSTS:
PURCHASED GOODS:	$121,981.
FREIGHT:	1,988.
OTHER:	3,049.
OVERSEAS PACKING:	6,242.
	$133,260.

III. OTHER COSTS:
PURCHASED MAT'LS:	39,527.
SUBCONTRACTS:	28,082.
OVERSEAS PACKING:	3,520.
FREIGHT:	2,598.
	$ 73,727.

IV. OTHER COSTS:
SUPPLIES:	$ 980.

RAW MATERIALS ESCALATION	10%
DEMANNING RATIO	10%
TERMINATION LIABILITY	0%
SALARY INCREASES	6%

NOTE: ONE MAN MONTH = 154 MAN HOURS

Figure 14-22. Program bar chart.

The output obtained from the model using the parameters established for the program are listed below:

1. The total cost of establishing a natural gas testing laboratory is $920,322 including a 12 percent profit, overhead rates, and corporate costs.
2. Cash flow for the first year, 1978, is $642,718 and $178,999 for the second year. Profit is not included in these figures.
3. The cost for each project and total program percentage is shown below.

Project 1	$ 17,649	2%
Project 2	$250,978	31%
Project 3	$496,005	60%
Project 4	$ 25,414	3%
Project 5	$ 31,671	4%

The two projects representing 91 percent of the total program are equipment purchasing and equipment construction. (Profit is not included.)

4. Total labor expenditure for the project is 23,830 hours, costing $583,410. This breaks down into 16,604 hours, costing $404,399 in 1978, and 7,226 hours, costing $179,011 in 1979.
5. Total material expenditure is $238,307 with the total commitment established in July of 1978.
6. A functional cost summary has the program divided into four major divisions, excluding material costs. The divisions and associated costs (including overhead) are as follows:

Engineering	$ 96,732	19%
Program mgt.	$ 26,349	5%
Finance	$ 14,654	3%
Operations	$368,953	73%

Problems

1. Construction of Special Equipment
   There is special test equipment required for the laboratory. Since many of the tests are unique to gas appliance testing under the American National Standards, the equipment cannot be purchased on the open market and must be constructed. The costs of construction are very difficult to estimate accurately, since many of these items are unique.

2. Building Construction
   The erection of the laboratory building is the critical path in the program. The construction is being supervised and contracted for in Iran by the overburdened engineering department of NIGC. Delay of building opening shifts the entire pro-

gram to the right (except for the planning stage), resulting in increased costs and scheduling problems as follows:

 a. Material costs
 b. Labor costs
 c. Scheduling problems
 d. Storage costs

3. Transportation of Equipment
The large amount of construction in Iran will result in long delays in unloading at Persian Gulf ports. On a similar program conducted previously, just before shipment of completed equipment and instruments, the contractor was made aware by the customer that there would be a delay of up to eighteen months. Alternate shipping plans were worked out by the customer (who was responsible for shipment from New York to the site in Tehran), involving shipment to Hamburg, Germany, and overland shipment by truck from Hamburg to Tehran. This shipping routing consumed about four months.

4. Language Difficulties
There was great uncertainty at the outset of the contract about accurate communication because of the language problem. All parties at the customer could speak English, but not well. This resulted in occasional misunderstandings.

5. Building Subcontractor
The building work was contracted out by NIGC to a local construction firm.

Results

The company's strategy for shipping the building materials was to fabricate components prior to shipping. The shipping schedule was of prime importance because a delay in shipping, for whatever cause, would immediately put the project behind. It was projected that any sizable delay would increase costs in the area of materials and labor.

Plans were initiated to commence with a screening of Iranian labor and for training of selected personnel in the event of a shipping delay. An analysis of costs was made based on an extension of the construction period over an additional twenty months; otherwise the training would take place at the completion of the construction. Iran had a shortage of labor and might be hard-pressed in finding an ample work force for this project.

Alternative plans were set up in the event of a delay in the construction schedule, problems involving scheduling personnel for transportation to the project, and storage of materials and supplies.

The following schedule is a comparative analysis of the two periods:

	18 mo.	38 mo.	Unfavorable Variance
Engineering	$ 96,731	$105,382	$ 8,651
Program management	26,349	28,424	2,075
Finance	14,654	15,980	1,326
Operations	368,953	406,567	37,614
Materials	206,987	216,749	9,762
Indirect costs	99,916	108,234	8,318
Corporate costs	8,127	8,806	679
Total Costs	$821,717	$890,142	$68,425

Plans were made to construct energy supply generators to combat the possibility of a power shortage, since there is a utility shortage in Iran.

A comparison of the base cost is estimated on an eighteen-month construction period extended to the thirty-eight months. The above analysis for the two periods does not reflect a profit factor. However, there is a 10 percent escalation factor for raw materials and a demanning ratio of 10 percent. The termination liability ratio is 0 percent, and salary increases are equal to 6 percent per year. Corporate costs and indirect costs are 1 percent and 14 percent, respectively.

CASE STUDY: POLYPRODUCTS INCORPORATED

Polyproducts Incorporated, a major producer of rubber components, employs 800 people and is organized with a matrix structure. Exhibit 14–1 shows the salary structure for the company, and Exhibit 14–2 identifies the overhead rate projections for the next two years.

Polyproducts has been very successful at maintaining its current business base with approximately 10 percent overtime. Both exempt and nonexempt employees are paid overtime at the rate of time and one-half. All overtime hours are burdened at an overhead rate of 30 percent.

On April 16, Polyproducts received a request for proposal from Capital Corporation (see Exhibit 14–3). Polyproducts had an established policy for competitive bidding. First, they would analyze the marketplace to see whether or not it would be advantageous for them to compete. This task was normally assigned to the marketing group (which operated on overhead). If the marketing group responded favorably, then Polyproducts would go through the necessary pricing procedures to determine a bid price.

On April 24, the marketing group displayed a prospectus on the four companies that would most likely be competing with Polyproducts for the Capital contract. This is shown in Exhibit 14–4.

At the same time, top management of Polyproducts made the following projections concerning the future business over the next eighteen months:

1. Salary increases would be given to all employees at the beginning of the thirteenth month.

Exhibit 14–1. Salary Structure.

	PAY SCALE	
	GRADE	HOURLY RATE
	1	8.00
	2	9.00
	3	11.00
	4	12.00
	5	14.00
	6	18.00
	7	21.00
	8	24.00
	9	28.00

Number of employees per grade

Department	1	2	3	4	5	6	7	8	9	TOTAL
R&D			5	40	20	10	12	8	5	100
Design		3	5	40	30	10	10	2		100
Project Engineering						30	15	10	5	60
Project Management							10	10	10	30
Cost Accounting				20	10	10	10	10		60
Contracts						3	4	2	1	10
Publications		3	5	3	3	3	3			20
Computers				2	3	3	1	1		10
Manufacturing Engineering				2	7	7	3	1		20
Industrial Engineering					4	3	2	1		10
Facilities					8	9	10	7	1	35
Quality Control				3	4	5	5	2	1	20
Production Line				55	50	50	30	10	5	200
Traffic				2	2	1				5
Procurement				2	2	2	2	1	1	10
Safety						2	2	1		5
Inventory Control	2	2	2	2	1	1				10

2. If the Capital contract was won, then the overhead rates would go down 0.5 percent each quarter (assuming no strike by employees).

3. There was a possibility that the union would go out on strike if the salary increases were not satisfactory. Based upon previous experience, the strike would last between one and two months. It was possible that, due to union demands, the overhead rates would increase by 1 percent per quarter for each quarter after the strike (due to increased fringe benefit packages).

4. With the current work force, the new project would probably have to be done on overtime. (At least 75 percent of all man-hours were estimated to be performed on overtime). The alternative would be to hire additional employees.

5. All materials could be obtained from one vendor. It can be assumed that raw

Exhibit 14–2. Overhead Structure.

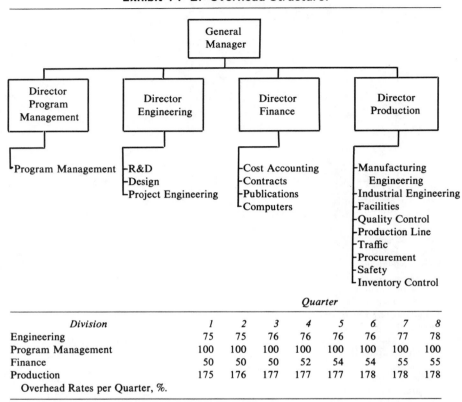

		Quarter							
Division	*1*	*2*	*3*	*4*	*5*	*6*	*7*	*8*	
Engineering	75	75	76	76	76	76	77	78	
Program Management	100	100	100	100	100	100	100	100	
Finance	50	50	50	52	54	54	55	55	
Production	175	176	177	177	177	178	178	178	

Overhead Rates per Quarter, %.

materials cost $200/unit (without scrap factors) and that these raw materials are new to Polyproducts.

On May 1, Roger Henning was selected by Jim Grimm, the director of project management, to head the project.

Grimm: "Roger, we've got a problem on this one. When you determine your final bid, see if you can account for the fact that we may lose our union. I'm not sure exactly how that will impact our bid. I'll leave that up to you. All I know is that a lot of our people are getting unhappy with the union. See what numbers you can generate."

Henning: "I've read the RFP and have a question about inventory control. Should I look at quantity discount buying for raw materials?"

Grimm: "Yes. But be careful about your assumptions. I want to know all of the assumptions you make."

Henning: "How stable is our business base over the next eighteen months?"

Grimm: "You had better consider both an increase and a decrease of 10 percent. Get me the costs for all cases. Incidentally, the grapevine says that there might be follow-on contracts if we perform well. You know what that means."

Henning: "Okay. I get the costs for each case and then we'll determine what our best bid will be."

Exhibit 14–3. Request for Proposal

Capital Corporation is seeking bids for 10,000 rubber components which must be manufactured according to specifications supplied by the customer. The contractor will be given sufficient flexibility for material selection and testing provided that all testing include latest developments in technology. All material selection and testing must be within specifications. All vendors selected by the contractor must be (1) certified as a vendor for continuous procurement (follow-on contracts will not be considered until program completion), and (2) operating with a quality control program that is acceptable to both the customer and contractor.

The following timetable must be adhered to:

Month after Go-ahead	Description
2	R & D completed and preliminary design meeting held
4	Qualification completed and final design review meeting held
5	Production set-up completed
9	Delivery of 3000 units
13	Delivery of 3500 units
17	Delivery of 3500 units
18	Final report and cost summary

The contract will be firm-fixed-price and the contractor can develop his own work breakdown structure upon final approval by the customer.

Exhibit 14–4. Prospectus.

COMPANY	BUSINESS BASE $ MILLION	GROWTH RATE LAST YEAR (%)	PROFIT %	R&D PERSONNEL	CONTRACTS IN HOUSE	NUMBER OF EMPLOYEES	OVERTIME (%)	PERSONNEL TURNOVER (%)
Alpha	10	10	5	Below Avg.	6	30	5	1.0
Beta	20	10	7	Above Avg.	15	250	30	0.25
Gamma	50	10	15	Avg.	4	550	20	0.50
Polyproducts	100	15	10	Avg.	30	800	10	1.0

On May 15, Roger Henning received a memo from the pricing department summing up the base case man-hour estimates. (This is shown in Exhibits 14–5 and 14–6.) Now Roger Henning wondered what people he could obtain from the functional departments and what would be a reasonable bid to make.

Exhibit 14–5.

To: **Roger Henning**
From: **Pricing Department**
Subject: **Rubber Components Production**

1. All manhours in the Exhibit (14–6) are based upon performance standards for a Grade 7 employee. For each grade below 7, add 10% of the Grade 7 standard and subtract 10% of the Grade standard for each employee above Grade 7. This applies to all departments as long as they are direct labor hours (i.e., not administrative support as in Project 1).
2. Time duration is fixed at 18 months.
3. Each production run normally requires four months. The company has enough raw materials on hand for R&D, but must allow 2 months lead time for purchases that would be needed for a production run. Unfortunately, the vendors cannot commit large purchases, but will commit to monthly deliveries up to a maximum of 1,000 units of raw materials per month. Furthermore, the vendors will guarantee a fixed cost of $200 per raw material unit during the first 12 months of the project only. Material escalation factors are expected at month 13 due to renegotiation of the United Rubber Workers contracts.
4. Use the following Work Breakdown Structure:

Program: Rubber Component Production
    Project 1: Support
        TASK 1: Project Office
        TASK 2: Functional Support
    Project 2: Preproduction
        TASK 1: R & D
        TASK 2: Qualification
    Project 3: Production
        TASK 1: Set-up
        TASK 2: Production

CASE STUDY: SMALL PROJECT COST ESTIMATING AT PERCY COMPANY

Paul graduated from college in June 1970 with a degree in industrial engineering. He accepted a job as a manufacturing engineer in the Manufacturing Division of Percy Company. His prime responsibility was performing estimates for the Manufacturing Division. Each estimate was then given to the appropriate project office for consideration. The estimation procedure history had shown the estimates to be valid.

In 1975, Paul was promoted to project engineer. His prime responsibility was the coordination of all estimates for work to be completed by all of the divisions. For one full year Paul went by the book and did not do any estimating except for project office personnel manpower. After all, he was now in the project management division which contained job descriptions including such words as "coordinating and integrating."

In 1976, Paul was transferred to small program project management. This was a new organization designed to perform low-cost projects. The problem was that these projects could not withstand the expenses needed for formal divisional cost estimates. For five projects, Paul's estimates were "right on the money." But the sixth project incurred a cost overrun of $20,000 in the Manufacturing Division.

In November 1977, a meeting was called to resolve the question of "Why did the overrun occur?" The attendees included the general manager, all division managers and directors, the project manager, and Paul. Paul now began to worry about what he should say in his defense.

CASE STUDY: CAPITAL INDUSTRIES

In the summer of 1976, Capital Industries undertook a material development program to see if a hard plastic bumper could be developed for medium-sized cars. By January 1977, Project Bumper (as it was called by management) had developed a material that endured all preliminary laboratory testing.

One more step was required before full-scale laboratory testing: a three-dimensional stress analysis on bumper impact collisions. The decision to perform the stress analysis was the result of a concern on the part of the technical community that the bumper might not perform correctly under certain conditions. The cost of the analysis would require corporate funding over and above the original estimates. Since the current costs were identical to what was budgeted, the additional funding was a necessity.

Frank Allen, the project engineer in the Bumper Project Office, was assigned control of the stress analysis. Frank met with the functional manager of the engineering analysis section to discuss the assignment of personnel to the task.

Functional Manager: "I'm going to assign Paul Troy to this project. He's a new man with a Ph.D. in structural analysis. I'm sure he'll do well."

Frank Allen: "This is a priority project. We need seasoned veterans, not new people, regardless of whether or not they have Ph.D.'s. Why not use some other project as a testing ground for your new employee?"

Functional Manager: "You project people must accept part of the responsibility for on-the-job training. I might agree with you if we were talking about blue collar workers on an assembly line. But this is a college graduate, coming to us with a good technical background."

Frank Allen: "He may have a good background, but he has no experience. He needs supervision. This is a one-man task. The responsibility will be yours if he fouls up."

Functional Manager: "I've already given him our book for cost estimates. I'm sure he'll do fine. I'll keep in close communication with him during the project."

Exhibit 14–6. Program: Rubber Component Production.

							MONTH			
PROJECT	TASK	DEPARTMENT	1	2	3	4	5	6	7	8	9
1	1	Prog. Mgt.	480	480	480	480	480	480	480	480	480
1	2	R & D	16	16	16	16	16	16	16	16	16
		Proj. Eng.	320	320	320	320	320	320	320	320	320
		Cost. Acct.	80	80	80	320	320	320	320	320	320
		Contracts	320	320	320	320	320	320	320	320	320
		Manu. Eng.	320	320	320	320	320	320	320	320	320
		Quality Cont.	160	160	160	160	160	160	160	160	160
		Production	160	160	160	160	160	160	160	160	160
		Procurement	80	80	80	80	80	80	80	80	80
		Publications	80	80	80	80	80	80	80	80	80
		Invent. Cont.	80	80	80	80	80	80	80	80	80
2	1	R & D	480	480							
		Proj. Eng.	160	160							
		Manu. Eng.	160	160							
2	2	R & D			80	80					
		Proj. Eng.			160	160					
		Manu. Eng.			160	160					
		Ind. Eng.			40	40					
		Facilities			20	20					
		Quality Cont.			160	160					
		Production			600	600					
		Safety			20	20					
3	1	Proj. Eng.					160				
		Manu. Eng.					160				
		Facilities					80				
		Quality Cont.					160				
		Production					320				
3	2	Proj. Eng.						160	160	160	160
		Manu. Eng.						320	320	320	320
		Quality Cont.						320	320	320	320
		Production						1600	1600	1600	1600
		Safety						20	20	20	20

Exhibit 14–6. Program: Rubber Component Production
(*Continued*)

10	11	12	13	14	15	16	17	18
480	480	480	480	480	480	480	480	480
16	16	16	16	16	16	16	16	16
320	320	320	320	320	320	320	320	320
320	320	320	320	320	320	320	320	320
320	320	320	320	320	320	320	320	320
320	320	320	320	320	320	320	320	320
160	160	160	160	160	160	160	160	160
160	160	160	160	160	160	160	160	160
80	80	80	80	40	40	40	40	40
80	80	80	80	80	80	80	80	600
80	80	80	80	80	80	40	40	40

160	160	160	160	160	160	160	160	160
320	320	320	320	320	320	320	320	320
320	320	320	320	320	320	320	320	320
1600	1600	1600	1600	1600	1600	1600	1600	1600
20	20	20	20	20	20	20	20	20

Frank Allen met with Paul Troy to get an estimate for the job.

Paul Troy: "I estimate that 800 hours will be required."

Frank Allen: "Your estimate seems low. Most three-dimensional analyses require at least 1,000 hours. Why is your number so low?"

Paul Troy: "Three-dimensional analysis? I thought that it would be a two-dimensional analysis. But no difference; the procedures are the same. I can handle it."

Frank Allen: "O.K. I'll give you 1,100 hours. But if you overrun it, we'll both be sorry."

Frank Allen followed the project closely. By the time the costs were 50 percent completed, performance was only 40 percent. A cost overrun seemed inevitable. The functional manager still asserted that he was tracking the job and that the difficulties were a result of the new material properties. His section had never worked with materials like these before.

Six months later Troy announced that the work would be completed in one week, two months later than planned. The two-month delay caused major problems in facility and equipment utilization. Project Bumper was still paying for employees who were "waiting" to begin full-scale testing.

On Monday mornings, the project office would receive the weekly labor monitor report for the previous week. This week the report indicated that the publications and graphics art department had spent over 200 man-hours (last week) in preparation of the final report. Frank Allen was furious. He called a meeting with Paul Troy and the functional manager.

Frank Allen: "Who told you to prepare a formal report? All we wanted was a go or no-go decision as to structural failure."

Paul Troy: "I don't turn in any work unless it's professional. This report will be documented as a masterpiece."

Frank Allen: "Your 50 percent cost overrun will also be a masterpiece. I guess your estimating was a little off!"

Paul Troy: "Well, this was the first time that I had performed a three-dimensional stress analysis. And what's the big deal? I got the job done, didn't I?"

CASE STUDY: PAYTON CORPORATION

Payton Corporation had decided to respond to a government RFP for the R&D phase on a new project. The statement of work specified that the project must be completed within ninety days after go-ahead, and that the contract would be at a fixed cost and fee.

The majority of the work would be accomplished by the development lab. According to government regulations, the estimated cost must be based upon the *average* cost of the entire department, which was $9.50 per hour (unburdened).

Payton won the contract for a total package (cost plus fee) of $102,000. After the first weekly labor report was analyzed, it became evident that the development lab was spending $13.75 per hour. The project manager decided to discuss the problem with the manager of the development lab.

Project Manager: "Obviously you know why I'm here. At the rate that you're spending money, we'll overrun our budget by fifty percent."

Lab Manager: "That's your problem, not mine. When I estimate the cost to do a job, I submit only the hours necessary based upon historical standards. The pricing department converts the hours to dollars based upon department averages."

Project Manager: "Well, why are we using the most expensive people? Obviously there must be lower-salaried people capable of performing the work."

Lab Manager: "Yes, I do have lower-salaried people, but none who can complete the job within the two months required by the contract. I have to use people high on the learning curve, and they're not cheap. You should have told the pricing department to increase the average cost for the department."

Project Manager: "I wish I could, but government regulations forbid this. If we were ever audited, or if this proposal were compared to other salary structures in other proposals, we would be in deep trouble. The only legal way to accomplish this would be to set up a new department for those higher-paid employees working on this project. Then the average department salary would be correct.

"Unfortunately the administrative costs of setting up a temporary unit for only two months is prohibitive. For long-duration projects, this technique is often employed.

"Why couldn't you have increased the hours to compensate for the increased dollars required?"

Lab Manager: "I have to submit labor justifications for all hours I estimate. If I were to get audited, my job would be on the line. Remember, we had to submit labor justification for all work as part of the proposal.

"Perhaps next time management might think twice before bidding on a short-duration project. You might try talking to the customer to get his opinion."

Project Manager: "His response would probably be the same regardless of whether I explained the situation to him before we submitted the proposal or now, after we have negotiated it. There's a good chance that I've just lost my Christmas bonus."

a. What is the basis for the problem?
b. Who is at fault?
c. How can the present situation be corrected?
d. Is there any way that this situation can be prevented from recurring?
e. How would you handle this situation on a longer-duration project, say one year, assuming that multiple departments are involved and that no new departments were established other than possibly the project office?
f. Should a customer be willing to accept monetary responsibility for this type of situation, possibly by permitting established standards to be deviated from? If so, then how many months should be considered as a short-duration project?

CASE STUDY: CORY ELECTRIC

"Frankly speaking, Jeff, I didn't think that we would stand a chance in winning this $20 million program. I was really surprised when they said that they'd like to accept our bid and begin contract negotiations. As chief contract administrator, you'll head up the negotiation team," remarked Gus Bell, vice-president and general manager of Cory Electric. "You have two weeks to prepare your data and line up your team. I want to see you when you're ready to go."

Jeff Stokes was chief contract negotiator for Cory Electric, a $250 million-a-year electrical components manufacturer serving virtually every major U.S. industry. Cory Electric had a well-established matrix structure that had withstood fifteen years of testing. Job casting standards were well established, but did include some "fat" upon the discretion of the functional manager.

Two weeks later, Jeff met with Gus Bell to discuss the negotiation process:

Gus Bell: "Have you selected an appropriate team? You had better make sure that you're covered on all sides."

Jeff: "There will be four, plus myself at the negotiating table; the program manager, the chief project engineer who developed the engineering labor package; the chief manufacturing engineer who developed the production labor package; and a pricing specialist who has been on the proposal since the kickoff meeting. We have a strong team and should be able to handle any questions."

Gus Bell: "Okay, I'll take your word for it. I have my own checklist for contract negotiations. I want you to come back with a guaranteed fee of $1.6 million for our stockholders. Have you worked out the possible situations based upon the negotiated costs?"

Jeff: "Yes! Our minimum position is $20 million plus an 8 percent profit. Of course, this profit percentage will vary depending upon the negotiated cost. We can bid the program at a $15 million cost; that's $5 million below our target, and still book a $1.6 million profit by overrunning the cost-plus-incentive-fee contract. Here is a list of the possible cases." (See Table 14–14.)

Gus Bell: "If we negotiate a cost overrun fee, make sure that cost accounting knows about it. I don't want the total fee to be booked as profit if we're going to need it later to cover the overrun. Can we justify our overhead rates, general and administrative costs, and our salary structure?"

Jeff: "That's a problem. You know that 20 percent of our business comes from Mitre Corporation. If they fail to renew our contract for another two-year follow-on effort, then our overhead rates will jump drastically. Which overhead rates should I use?"

Gus Bell: "Let's put in a renegotiation clause to protect us against a drastic change in our business base. Make sure that the customer understands that as part of the terms and conditions. Are there any unusual terms and conditions?"

Jeff: "I've read over all terms and conditions, and so have all of the project office personnel as well as the key functional managers. The only major item is that the

Table 14-14. Cost Positions.

NEGOTIATED COST	%	NEGOTIATED FEE			
		TARGET FEE	OVERRUN FEE	TOTAL FEE	TOTAL PACKAGE
15,000,000	14.00	1,600,000	500,000	2,100,000	17,100,000
16,000,000	12.50	1,600,000	400,000	2,000,000	18,000,000
17,000,000	11.18	1,600,000	300,000	1,900,000	18,900,000
18,000,000	10.00	1,600,000	200,000	1,800,000	19,800,000
19,000,000	8.95	1,600,000	100,000	1,700,000	20,700,000
20,000,000	8.00	1,600,000	0	1,600,000	21,600,000
21,000,000	7.14	1,600,000	−100,000	1,500,000	22,500,000
22,000,000	6.36	1,600,000	−200,000	1,400,000	23,400,000
23,000,000	5.65	1,600,000	−300,000	1,300,000	24,300,000
24,000,000	5.00	1,600,000	−400,000	1,200,000	25,200,000

Assume total cost will be spent:

NEGOTIATED COST	% FEE		
21,000,000	7.61		
22,000,000	7.27	Minimum position	= $20,000,000
23,000,000	6.96	Minimum fee	= 1,600,000 = 8% of minimum position
24,000,000	6.67	Sharing ratio	= 90/10%

customer wants us to qualify some new vendors as sources for raw material procurement. We have included in the package the cost of qualifying two new raw material suppliers."

Gus Bell: "Where are the weak points in our proposal? I'm sure we have some."

Jeff: "Last month, the customer sent in a fact-finding team to go over all of our labor justifications. The impression that I get from our people is that we're covered all the way around. The only major problem might be where we'll be performing on our learning curve. We put into the proposal a 45 percent learning curve efficiency. The customer has indicated that we should be up around 50 to 55 percent efficiency, based upon our previous contracts with him. Unfortunately, those contracts which the customer referred to, were four years ago. Several of the employees who worked on those programs have left the company. Others are assigned to ongoing projects here at Cory. I estimate that we could put together about 10 percent of the people we used previously. That learning curve percentage will be a big point for disagreements. We finished off the previous programs with the customer at a 35 percent learning curve position. I don't see how they can expect us to be smarter, given these circumstances."

Gus Bell: "If that's the only weakness, then we're in good shape. It sounds like we have a fool-proof audit trail. That's good! What's your negotiation sequence going to be?"

Jeff: "I'd like to negotiate the bottom line only, but that's a dream. We'll probably negotiate the raw materials, the man-hours and the learning curve, the overhead rate, and, finally, the profit percentage. Hopefully, we can do it in that order."

Gus Bell: "Do you think that we'll be able to negotiate a cost above our minimum position?"

Jeff: "Our proposal was for $22.2 million. I don't foresee any problem which will prevent us from coming out ahead of the minimum position. The five percent change in learning curve efficiency amounts to approximately $1 million. We should be well covered.

"The first move will be up to them. I expect that they'll come in with an offer of $18 to $19 million. Using the binary chop procedure, that'll give us our guaranteed minimum position.

Gus Bell: "Do you know the guys who you'll be negotiating with?"

Jeff: "Yes, I've dealt with them before. The last time, the negotiations took three days. I think we both got what we wanted. I expect this one to go just as smoothly."

Gus Bell: "Okay, Jeff. I'm convinced we're prepared for negotiations. Have a good trip."

The negotiations began at 9:00 A.M. on Monday morning. The customer countered the original proposal of $22.2 million with an offer of $15 million. After six solid hours of arguments, Jeff and his team adjourned. Jeff immediately called Gus Bell at Cory Electric:

Jeff: "Their counter-offer to our bid is absurd. They've asked us to make a counter-offer to their offer. We can't do that. The instant we give them a counter-offer, we are in fact giving credibility to their absurd bid. Now, they're claiming that, if we don't give them a counter-offer, then we're not bargaining in good faith. I think we're in trouble."

Gus Bell: "Has the customer done their homework to justify their bid?"

Jeff: "Yes. Very well. Tomorrow we're going to discuss every element of the proposal, task by task. Unless something drastically changes in their position within the next day or two, contract negotiations will probably take up to a month."

Gus Bell: "Perhaps this is one program that should be negotiated at the top levels of management. Find out if the person that you're negotiating with reports to a vice-president and general manager, as you do. If not, break off contract negotiations until the customer gives us someone at your level. We'll negotiate this at my level, if necessary."

CASE STUDY: CAMDEN CONSTRUCTION CORPORATION

"For five years I've heard nothing but flimsy excuses from you people as to why the competition was beating us out in the downtown industrial building construction business," remarked Joseph Camden, president. "Excuses, excuses, excuses; that's all I ever hear! Only 15 percent of our business over the past five years has been in this area, and virtually all of that was with our established customers. Our growth rate is terrible. Everyone seems to just barely outbid us. Maybe our bidding process leaves something to be desired. If you three vice-presidents don't come up with the answers then we'll have three positions to fill by midyear.

"We have a proposal request coming in next week, and I want to win it. Do you guys understand that?"

Background

Camden Construction Corporation matured from a $1 million to a $26 million construction company between 1969 and 1979. Camden's strength was in their ability to work well with the customer. Their reputation for quality work far exceeded the local competitors' reputation.

Most of Camden's contracts in the early seventies were with long-time customers who were willing to go sole-source procurement and pay the extra price for quality and service. With the recession of 1975, Camden found that, unless they penetrated the competitive bidding market, their business base would decline.

In 1976, Camden was "forced" to go union in order to bid government projects. Unionization drastically reduced Camden's profit margin, but offered a greater promise for increased business. Camden had avoided the major downtown industrial construction market. But with the availability of multi-million-dollar skyscraper projects, Camden wanted their share of the pot of gold that follows the rainbow.

Meeting of the Minds

On January 17, 1979, the three vice-presidents met to consider ways of improving Camden's bidding technique.

V.P. Finance: "You know fellas, I hate to say it, but we haven't done a good job in developing a bid. I don't think that we've been paying enough attention to the competition. Now's the time to begin."

V.P. Operations: "What we really need is a list of who our competitors have been on each project over the last five years. Perhaps we can find some bidding trends."

V.P. Engineering: "I think the big number we need is to find out the overhead rates of each of these companies. After all, union contracts specify the rate at which the employees will work. Therefore, except for the engineering design packages, all of the companies should be almost identical in direct labor man-hours and union labor wages for similar jobs."

V.P. Finance: "I think I can hunt down past bids by our competitors. Many of them are in public records. That'll get us started."

V.P. Operations: "What good will it do? The past is past. Why not just look toward the future?"

V.P. Finance: "What we want to do is to maximize our chances for success and maximize profits at the same time. Unfortunately, these two cannot be met at the same time. We must find a compromise."

V.P. Engineering: "Do you think that the competition looks at our past bids?"

V.P. Finance: "They're stupid if they don't. What we have to do is to determine their target profit and target cost. I know many of the competitors personally and have a good feel for what their target profits are. We'll have to assume that their target direct cost equals ours; otherwise we will have a difficult time making a comparison."

V.P. Engineering: "What can we do to help you?"

V.P. Finance: "You'll have to tell me how long it takes to develop the engineering design packages, and how our personnel in engineering design stack up against the competition's salary structure. See if you can make some contacts and find out how much money the competition put into some of their proposals for engineering design activities. That'll be a big help.

"We'll also need good estimates from engineering and operations for this new project we're suppose to bid. Let me pull my data together, and we'll meet again in two days, if that's all right with you two."

Reviewing the Data

The executives met two days later to review the data. The vice-president for finance presented the data on the three most likely competitors. (See Table 14–15.) These

Table 14–15. Proposal Data Summary (Cost in Tens of Thousands).

YEAR	ACME	AJAX	PIONEER	CAMDEN BID	CAMDEN COST
1970	270	244	260	283	260
1970	260	250	233	243	220
1970	355	340	280	355	300
1971	836	830	838	866	800
1971	300	288	286	281	240
1971	570	560	540	547	500
1972	240*	375	378	362	322
1972	100*	190	180	188	160
1972	880	874	883	866	800
1973	410	318	320	312	280
1973	220	170	182	175	151
1973	400	300	307	316	283
1974	408	300*	433	449	400
1975	338	330	342	333	300
1975	817	808	800	811	700
1975	886	884	880	904	800
1976	384	385	380	376	325
1976	140	148	158	153	130
1977	197	193	188	200	165
1977	750	763	760	744	640

*Buy-in contracts

companies were Ajax, Acme, and Pioneer. The vice-president for finance made the following comments:

1. In 1973, Acme was contract-rich and had a difficult time staffing all of their projects.
2. In 1970, Pioneer was in danger of bankruptcy. It was estimated that they needed to win one or two in order to hold their organization together.
3. Two of the 1972 contracts were probably a buy-in based upon the potential for follow-on work.
4. The 1974 contract was for an advanced state-of-the art project. It is estimated that Ajax bought in so that they could break into a new field.

The vice-president for engineering and operations presented data indicating that the total project cost (fully burdened) was approximately $5 million. "Well," thought the vice-president for finance, "I wonder what we should bid so that we will have at least a reasonable chance of winning the contract?"

15
Cost Control

15.0 INTRODUCTION

Cost control is equally important to all companies, regardless of size. Small companies generally have tighter monetary controls, mainly because of the risk with the failure of as little as one project, but with less sophisticated control techniques. Large companies may have the luxury to spread project losses over several projects, whereas the small company may have few projects.

Too many people have a poor definition of cost control, with the final result shown in Figure 15–1. Cost control is not only "monitoring" of costs and recording perhaps massive quantities of data, but also analyzing the data in order to take corrective action before it is too late. Cost control should be performed by all personnel who incur costs, not merely the project office.

Cost control implies good cost management, which must include:

- Cost estimating
- Cost accounting
- Project cash flow
- Company cash flow
- Direct labor costing
- Overhead rate costing
- Others, such as incentives, penalties, and profit-sharing

Cost control, is actually a subsystem of the management cost and control system (MCCS) rather than a complete system per se. This is shown in Figure 15–2, where the MCCS is represented as a two-cycle process: a planning cycle and an operating cycle. The operating cycle is what is commonly referred to as the cost control system. Failure of a cost control system to accurately describe the true status of a project does not necessarily imply that the cost control system is at fault. Any cost control system is only as good as the original plan against which performance will be measured. It is more common for the plan to be at fault than the control system. Therefore, the designing of a company's planning system must take into account the cost control system as well. For

Figure 15–1. Do you control costs, or do costs control you?

this reason, it is common for the planning cycle to be referred to as planning and control, whereas the operating cycle is referred to as cost and control.

The planning and control system selected must be able to satisfy management's needs and requirements in order that they can accurately project the status toward objective completion. The purpose of any management cost and control system is to establish policies, procedures, and techniques that can be used in the day-to-day management and control of projects and programs. The planning and control system must, therefore, provide information that:

- Gives a picture of true work progress
- Will relate cost and schedule performance
- Identifies potential problems with respect to their sources
- Provides information to project managers with a practical level of summarization
- Demonstrates that the milestones are valid, timely, and auditable

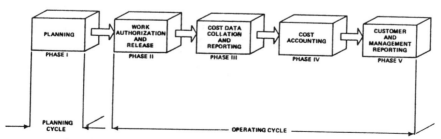

Figure 15–2. Phases of a management cost and control system.

The planning and control system, in addition to being a tool by which objectives can be defined (i.e., hierarchy of objectives and organization accountability), exists as a tool to develop planning, measure progress, and control change. As a tool for planning, the system must be able to be used to:

- Plan and schedule work
- Identify those indicators that will be used for measurement
- Establish direct labor budgets
- Establish overhead budgets
- Identify management reserve

The project budget that is the final result of the planning cycle of the MCCS must be reasonable, attainable, and based upon contractually negotiated costs and the statement of work. The basis for the budget is either historical cost, best estimates, or industrial engineering standards. The budget must identify planned manpower requirements, contract-allocated funds, and management reserve.

Establishing budgets requires that the planner fully understand the meaning of standards. There are two categories of standards. Performance results standards are quantitative measurements and include such items as quality of work, quantity of work, cost of work, and time-to-complete. Process standards are qualitative, including personnel, functional, and physical factors relationships. Standards are advantageous in that they provide a means for unity, a basis for effective control, and an incentive for others. The disadvantage of standards is that performance is often frozen, and employees are quite often unable to adjust to the differences.

As a tool for measuring progress and controlling change, the systems must be able to:

- Measure resources consumed
- Measure status and accomplishments
- Compare measurements to projections and standards
- Provide the basis for diagnosis and replanning

In using the MCCS, the following guidelines usually apply:

- The level of detail is specified by the project manager with approval by top management.
- Centralized authority and control over each project are the responsibility of the project management division.
- For large projects, the project manager may be supported by a project team for utilization of the MCCS.

Almost all project planning and control systems have identifiable design requirements. These include:

- A common framework from which to integrate time, cost, and technical performance
- Ability to track progress of significant parameters
- Quick response
- Capability for end-value prediction
- Accurate and appropriate data for decision making by each level of management
- Full exception reporting with problem analysis capability
- Immediate quantitative evaluation of alternative solutions

MCCS planning activities include:

- Contract receipt (if applicable)
- Work authorization for project planning
- Work breakdown structure
- Subdivided work description
- Schedules
- Planning charts
- Budgets

MCCS planning charts are worksheets used to create the budget. These charts include planned labor in hours and material dollars.

MCCS planning is accomplished in one of these ways:

- One level below the lowest level of the WBS
- At the lowest management level
- By cost element

Even with a fully developed planning and control system, there are numerous benefits and costs. The appropriate system must consider a cost/benefit analysis, and include such items as:

- Project Benefits
  - Planning and control techniques facilitate:
    - Derivation of output specifications (project objectives)
    - Delineation of required activities (work)
    - Coordination and communication between organizational units
    - Determination of type, amount, and timing of necessary resources
    - Recognition of high-risk elements and assessment of uncertainties

- Suggestions of alternative courses of action
- Realization of effect of resource level changes on schedule and output performance
- Measurement and reporting of genuine progress
- Identification of potential problems
- Basis for problem solving, decision making, and corrective action
- Assurance of coupling between planning and control
- Project Cost
  - Planning and control techniques require:
    - New forms (new systems) of information from additional sources and incremental processing (managerial time, computer expense, etc.)
    - Additional personnel or smaller span of control to free managerial time for planning and control tasks (increased overhead)
    - Training in use of techniques (time and materials)

A well-disciplined MCCS will produce the following results:

- Policies and procedures that will minimize the ability to distort reporting
- Strong management emphasis on meeting commitments
- Weekly team meetings with a formalized adgenda, action items, and minutes
- Top-management periodic review of the technical and financial status
- Simplified internal audit for checking compliance with procedures

In some industries, the MCCS must be used on all contracts of $2 million or more, including firm-fixed-price efforts. The fundamental test of whether or not to use the MCCS is to determine whether or not the contracts have established end-item deliverables, either hardware or computer software, that must be accomplished through measurable efforts.

Two new programs are currently being used by the government and industry in conjunction with the MCCS as an attempt to improve effectiveness in cost control. The zero-base budgeting program was established to provide better estimating techniques for the verification portion of control. The design-to-cost program assists the decision-making part of the control process by identifying a decision-making framework from which replanning can take place.

15.1 UNDERSTANDING CONTROL

Effective management of a program during the operating cycle requires that a well-organized cost and control system be designed, developed, and implemented so that immediate feedback can be obtained, whereby the up-to-date usage of resources can be compared to target objectives established during the planning cycle. The requirements for an effective control system (for both cost and schedule/performance) should include:[1]

- Thorough planning of the work to be performed to complete the project
- Good estimating of time, labor, and costs
- Clear communication of the scope of required tasks
- A disciplined budget and authorization of expenditures
- Timely accounting of physical progress and cost expenditures
- Periodic reestimation of time and cost to complete remaining work
- Frequent, periodic comparison of actual progress and expenditures to schedules and budgets, both at the time of comparison and at project completion

Management must compare the time, cost, and performance of the program to the budgeted time, cost, and performance, not independently but in an integrated manner. Being within one's budget at the proper time serves no useful purpose if performance is only 75 percent. Likewise, having a production line turn out exactly 200 items, when planned, loses its significance if a 50 percent cost overrun is incurred. All three resource parameters (time, cost, and performance) must be analyzed as a group, or else we might "win the battle but lose the war." The use of the expression "management cost and control system" is vague in that the implication is made that only costs are controlled. This is not true—an effective control system monitors schedule and performance as well as costs by setting budgets, measuring expenditures against budgets and identifying variances, assuring that the expenditures are proper, and taking corrective action when required.

Previously we defined the work breakdown structure as the element that acts as the source from which all costs and controls must emanate. The WBS is the total project broken down into successively lower levels until the desired control levels are established. The work breakdown structure therefore serves as the tool from which performance can be subdivided into objectives and subobjectives. As work progresses, the WBS provides the framework on which costs, time, and schedule/performance can be compared against the budget, for each level of the WBS.

The first purpose of control therefore becomes a verification process accomplished by the comparison of actual performance to date with the predetermined plans and standards set forth in the planning phase. The comparison serves to verify that:

---

1. Russell D. Archibald, *Managing High-Technology Programs and Projects* (New York: John Wiley, 1976), p. 191.

- The objectives have been successfully translated into performance standards.
- The performance standards are, in fact, a reliable representation of program activities and events.
- Meaningful budgets have been established such that actual vs. planned comparisons can be made.

In other words, the comparison verifies that the correct standards were selected, and that they are properly used.

The second purpose of control is that of decision making. Three useful reports are required by management in order to make effective and timely decisions:

- The project plan, schedule, and budget prepared during the planning phase.
- A detailed comparison between resources expended to date and those predetermined. This includes an estimate of the work remaining and the impact on activity completion
- A projection of resources to be expended through program completion.

These reports are then supplied to both the managers and the doers. Three useful results arise through the use of these three reports, generated during a thorough decision-making stage of control:

- Feedback to management, the planners, and the doers.
- Identification of any major deviations from the current program plan, schedule, or budget.
- The opportunity to initiate contingency planning early enough that cost, performance, and time requirements can undergo corrective action without loss of resources.

These reports, if properly prepared, provide management with the opportunity to minimize downstream changes by making proper corrections here and now. As shown in Figures 15–3 and 15–4, possible cost reductions are usually available more readily in the early project phases, but are reduced as we go further into the project life cycle phases.[2] Downstream the cost for changes could easily exceed the original cost of the project.

---

2. The source for Figure 15–4 is Max Wideman, "Managing Project Development for Better Results," *Project Management Quarterly,* September 1981, p. 16.

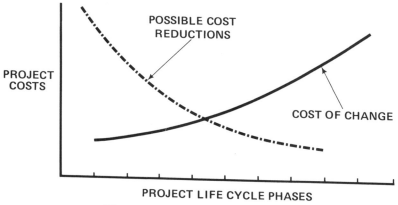

Figure 15–3. Cost reduction analysis.

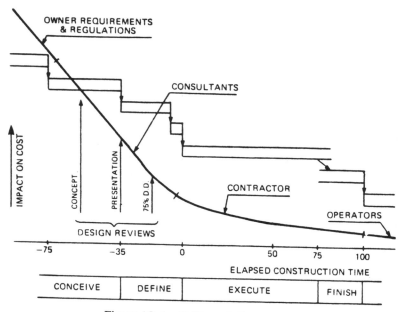

Figure 15–4. Ability to influence cost.

15.2 THE OPERATING CYCLE

The management cost and control system (MCCS) takes on paramount importance during the operating cycle of the project. The operating cycle is composed of four phases:

- Work authorization and release (Phase II)
- Cost data collection and reporting (Phase III)
- Cost analysis (Phase IV)
- Reporting: customer and management (Phase V)

These four phases, when combined with the planning cycle (Phase I), constitute a closed system network that forms the basis for the management cost and control system.

Phase II is considered as work release. After planning is completed and a contract is received, work is authorized via a work description document. The work description, or project work authorization form, is a contract that contains the narrative description, organization, and time frame for *each* WBS level. This multi-purpose form is used to release the contract, authorize planning, record detail description of the work outlined in the work breakdown structure, and release work to the functional departments.

Contract services may require a work description form to release the contract. The contractual work description form sets forth general contractual requirements and authorizes program management to proceed.

Program management may then issue a subdivided work description form to the functional units so that work can begin. The subdivided work description may also be issued through the combined efforts of the project team, and may be revised or amended when either the scope or time frame changes. The subdivided work description generally is not used for efforts longer than ninety days and must be "tracked" as if a project in itself. This subdivided work description form sets forth contractual requirements and planning guidelines for the applicable performing organizations. The subdivided work description package established during the proposal and updated after negotiations by the program team is incrementally released by program management to the work control centers in manufacturing, engineering, publications, and program management as the authority for release of work orders to the performing organizations. The subdivided work description specifies how contractual requirements are to be accomplished, the functional organizations involved, and their specific responsibilities, and authorizes the expenditure of resources within a particular time frame.

The work control center assigns a work order number to the subdivided work description form, if no additional instructions are required, and releases the document to the performing organizations. If additional instructions are required, the work control center can prepare a more detailed work-release document (shop traveler, tool order, work order release), assign the applicable work order number, and release it to the performing organization.

A work order number is required for all in-house direct and indirect charging. The work order number also serves as a cross-reference number for automatic assignment of the indentured work breakdown structure number to labor and material data records in the computer.

Small companies can avoid this additional paperwork cost by going directly from an awarded contract to a single work order, which may be the only work order needed for the entire contract.

15.3 COST ACCOUNT CODES

Since project managers control resources through the line managers rather than directly, project managers end up controlling direct labor costs by opening and closing work orders. To illustrate this, consider the cost account code breakdown shown in Figure 15–5 and the work authorization form shown in Figure 15–6. The work authorization form specifically identifies the cost cen-

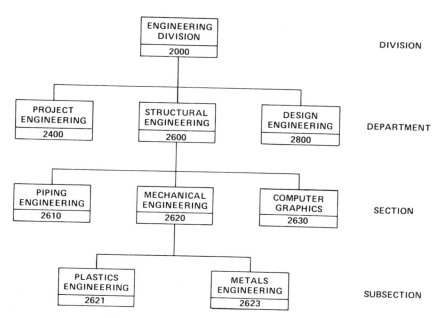

Figure 15–5. Cost account code breakdown.

```
┌──────────────────────────────────────────────────────────────────┐
│                    WORK AUTHORIZATION FORM                         │
│                                                                    │
│  WBS NO:   31-03-02              WORK ORDER NO:    D1385            │
│                                                                    │
│  DATE OF ORIGINAL RELEASE:          3 FEB 80                       │
│                                                                    │
│  DATE OF REVISION              :  18 MAR 80                        │
│                                                                    │
│  REVISION NUMBER               :    C                              │
└──────────────────────────────────────────────────────────────────┘
```

DESCRIPTION	COST CENTERS	HOURS	WORK BEGINS	WORK ENDS
TEST MATERIAL VB–2 IN ACCORDANCE WITH THE PROGRAM PLAN AND MIL STANDARD G1483-52. THIS TASK INCLUDES A WRITTEN REPORT.	2400 2610 2621 2623 5000*	150 160 140 46 600	1 AUG 80 ↓ ↓	15 SEPT. 80 ↓ ↓

PROJECT OFFICE AUTHORIZATION SIGNATURE _____

*NOTE: SOME COMPANIES DO NOT PERMIT DIVISION COST CENTERS TO CHARGE AT LEVEL 3 OF THE WBS

Figure 15–6. Work authorization form.

ters that are "open" for this charge number, the man-hours available for each cost center, and the operational time period for the charge number. Because the exact dates of operation are completely defined, the charge number can be assigned perhaps as much as a year in advance of the work-begin date. This can be shown pictorially, as in Figure 15–7.

If the man-hours are assigned to Cost Center 2400, then any 24xx cost center can use this charge number. If the work authorization form specifies Cost Center 2610, then any 261x cost center can use the charge number. However, if Cost Center 2623 is specified, then no lower cost accounts exist, and this is the only cost center that can use this work order charge number. In other words, if a charge number is opened up at the department level, then the department manager has the right to subdivide the assigned man-hours among the various sections and subsections. Company policy usually identifies the permissible cost center levels that can be assigned in the work authorization form. These permissible levels are related to the work breakdown structure level. For example, Cost Center 5000 (i.e., divisional) can be assigned at the project level of the work breakdown structure, but only department, sectional, or subsectional cost accounts can be assigned at the task level of the work breakdown structure.

If a cost center needs additional time or additional man-hours, then a cost

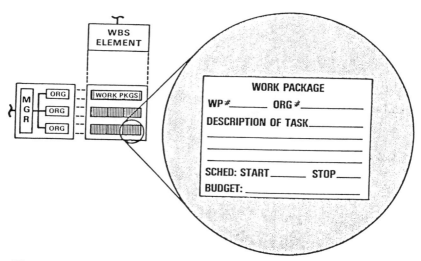

Figure 15–7. Planning and budgeting describe, plan, and schedule the work.

account change notice form must be initiated, usually by the requesting cost center, and approved by the project office. Figure 15–8 shows a typical cost account change notice form.

Large companies have computerized cost control and reporting systems. Small companies have manual or partially computerized systems. The major difficulty in using the cost account code breakdown and the work authorization form (Figures 15–5 and 15–6) is related to whether the employees fills out time cards, and the frequency with which the time cards are filled out. Project-driven organizations fill out time cards at least once a week, and the cards are inputted to a computerized system. Non-project-driven organizations fill out time cards on a monthly basis, with computerization depending on the size of the company.

Cost data collection and reporting constitute the second phase of the operating cycle of the MCCS. Actual cost (ACWP) and the budgeted cost for work performed (BCWP) for each contract or in-house project are accumulated in detailed cost accounts by cost center and cost element, and reported in accordance with the flow charts shown in Figure 15–9. These detailed elements, for both actual costs incurred and the budgeted cost for work performed, are usually printed out monthly for all levels of the work breakdown structure. In addition, weekly supplemental direct labor reports can be printed showing the actual labor charges incurred, and can be compared to the predicted efforts.

Table 15–1 shows a typical weekly labor report. The first column identifies

CACN No. _____   Revision to Cost Account No. _____   Date _____

DESCRIPTION OF CHANGE:

_____

_____

_____

_____

_____

_____

REASON FOR CHANGE:

_____

_____

_____

_____

_____

_____

	Requested Budget	Authorized Budget	
Labor Hours	_____	_____	Period of Performance:
Material $	_____	_____	From _____
Indirect $	_____	_____	To _____

BUDGET SOURCE:

    ☐ Funded Contract Change
    ☐ Management Reserve
    ☐ Undistributed Budget
    ☐ Other _____

INITIATED BY: _____

APPROVALS: Program Mgr. _____
Prog. Control _____

Figure 15-8. Cost account change notice (CACN).

the WBS number.[3] If more than one work order were assigned to this WBS element, then the work order number would appear under the WBS number. This procedure would be repeated for all work orders under the same WBS number. The second column contains the cost centers charging to this WBS element (and possibly work order numbers). Cost Center 41xx represents department 41 and is a roll up of Cost Centers 4110, 4115, and 4118. Cost Center 4xxx represents the entire division and is a roll up of all 4000-level departments. Cost Center xxxx represents the total for all divisions charging

---

3. Only three levels of cost reporting are assumed here. If work packages were used, then the WBS number would identify all five levels of control.

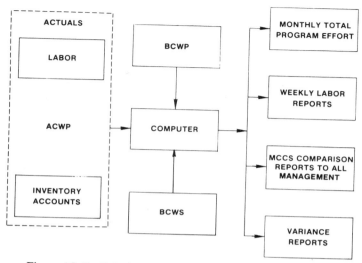

Figure 15–9. Cost data collection and reporting flow chart.

to this WBS element. The weekly labor reports must list all cost centers authorized to charge to this WBS element, whether or not they have incurred any costs over the last reporting period.

Most weekly labor reports provide current month subtotals and previous month totals. Although these also appear on the detailed monthly report, they are included in the weekly report for a quick-and-dirty comparison. Year-to-date totals are usually not on the weekly report unless the users request them for an immediate comparison to the estimate at completion (EAC) and the work order release.

Weekly labor output is a vital tool for members of the program office in that these reports can indicate trends in cost and performance in sufficient time for contingency plans to be established and implemented. If these reports are not available, then cost and labor overruns would not be apparent until the following month when the detailed monthly labor, cost, and materials output was obtained.

In Table 15–1, Cost Center 4110 has spent its entire budget. The work appears to be completed on schedule. The responsible program office team may wish to eliminate this cost center's authority to continue charging to this WBS element by issuing a new SWD or work order canceling this department's efforts. Cost Center 4115 appears to be only halfway through. If time is becoming short, then Cost Center 4115 must add resources in order to meet requirements. Cost Center 4443 appears to be heading for an overrun. This could also

Table 15–1. Weekly Labor Report.

WBS NO:	COST CENTER	H $	WEEKLY ACTUAL	CURRENT MONTH SUBTOTAL	PREVIOUS MONTH ACWP	PREVIOUS MONTH BCWP	YEAR TO DATE ACWP	YEAR TO DATE BCWP	YEAR TO DATE BCWS	TOTAL EAC	WORK ORDER RELEASE
01-03-06	4110	H	200	300	300	300	1000	1000	1000	1000	1000
		$	1000	1500	1500	1500	5000	5000	5000	5000	
	4115	H	200	300	300	300	1000	1000	1000	2000	2000
		$	1000	1500	1500	1500	5000	5000	5000	10000	
	4118	H	200	300	300	300	1000	1000	1000	2000	1800
		$	1000	1500	1500	1500	5000	5000	5000	10000	
	41XX	H	600	900	900	900	900	900	900	5000	4800
		$	3000	4500	4500	4500	4500	4500	4500	25000	
	4443	H	100	200	400	360	800	700	1400	2000	1800
		$	600	1200	2400	2260	4800	4200	8400	12000	
	4446	H	200	400	1000	1200	2000	2000	2300	3000	2500
		$	800	1600	4000	4800	8000	8000	9200	12000	
	4448	H	300	600	1000	1200	2000	2000	2300	3000	3000
		$	1500	3000	5000	6000	10000	10000	11500	15000	
	44XX	H	600	1200	2400	2760	4800	4700	6000	8000	7300
		$	2900	5800	11400	13060	22800	22200	29100	39000	
	4XXX	H	1200	2100	3300	3660	5700	5600	6900	13000	12100
		$	5900	10300	15900	17560	27300	26700	33600	64000	
	XXXX	H	8000	18000	20000	19000	50000	48000	47000	61000	58000
		$	56000	126000	140000	133000	350000	336000	329000	427000	

- Budget cost for work performed (BCWP) is the budgeted amount of cost for completed work, plus budgeted for level of effort or apportioned effort activity completed within a given time period. This is sometimes referred to as "earned value."
- Actual cost for work performed (ACWP) is the amount reported as actually expended in completing the work accomplished within a given time period.

These costs can then be applied to any level of the work breakdown structure (i.e., program, project, task, subtask, work package) for work that is completed, in-program, or anticipated. Using these definitions, the following variance definitions are obtained:

- Cost variance (CV) calculation:

$$CV = BCWP - ACWP$$

A negative variance indicates a cost-overrun condition.
- Schedule variance (SV) calculation:

$$SV = BCWP - BCWS$$

A negative variance indicates a behind-schedule condition.

In the analysis of both cost and schedule, costs are used as the lowest common denominator. In other words, the schedule variance is given as a function of cost. To alleviate this problem, the variances are usually converted to percentages:

- Cost variance % (CVP) $= \dfrac{CV}{BCWP}$
- Schedule variance % (SVP) $= \dfrac{SV}{BCWS}$

The schedule variance may be represented by hours, days, weeks, or even dollars.

As an example, consider a project that is scheduled to spend $100K for each of the first four weeks of the project. The actual expenditures at the end of week four are $325K. Therefore, BCWS = $400K and ACWP = $325K. From these two parameters alone, there are several possible explanations as to project status. However, if BCWP is now known, say $300K, then the project is behind schedule and overrunning costs.

Variances are almost always identified as critical items and are reported to all organizational levels. Critical variances are established for each level of the organization in accordance with management policies.

Not all companies have a uniform methodology for variance thresholds. Permitted variances may be dependent upon such factors as:

- Life cycle phase
- Length of life cycle phase
- Length of project
- Type of estimate
- Accuracy of estimate

Variance controls may be different from program to program. Table 15–2 identifies sample variance criteria for Program X.

For many programs and projects, variances are permitted to change over the duration of the program. For strict manufacturing programs (product management), variances may be fixed over the program time span using criteria as in Table 15–2. For programs that include research and development, larger deviations may be permitted during the earlier phases than during the later phases. Figure 15–10 shows time-phased cost variances for a program requiring research and development, qualification, and production phases. Since the risk should decrease as time goes on, the variance boundaries are reduced. Figure 15–11 shows that the variance envelope in such a case may be dependent on the type of estimate.

By using both cost and schedule variances, we can develop an integrated cost/schedule reporting system that provides the basis for variance analysis by measuring cost performance in relation to work accomplished. This system

Table 15–2. Variance Control for Program X.

ORGANIZATIONAL LEVEL	VARIANCE THRESHOLDS*
Section	Variances greater than $750 that exceed 25% of costs.
Section	Variances greater than $2500 that exceed 10% of costs.
Section	Variances greater than $20,000
Department	Variances greater than $2000 that exceed 25% of costs.
Department	Variances greater than $7500 that exceed 10% of costs.
Department	Variances greater than $40,000
Division	Variances greater than $10,000 that exceed 10% of costs

*Thresholds are usually tighter within company reporting system than required external to government.
Thresholds for external reporting are usually adjusted during various phases of program (% lower at end).

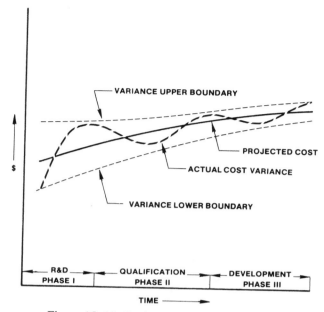

Figure 15-10. Project variance projections.

ensures that both cost budgeting and performance scheduling are constructed upon the same data base.

Figure 15-12 shows an integrated cost/schedule system. The figure identifies a performance slippage to date. This might not be a bad situation if the costs are proportionately underrun. However, from the upper portion of Figure 15-12, we find that costs are overrun (in comparison to budget costs), thus adding to the severity of the situation.

Also shown in Figure 15-12 is the management reserve. This is identified as the difference between the contracted cost for projected performance to date and the budgeted cost. Management reserves are the contingency funds established by the program manager to counteract unavoidable delays that can affect the project's critical path. It is a natural tendency for a functional man-

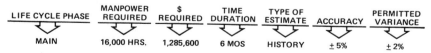

Figure 15-11. Methodology to determine variance.

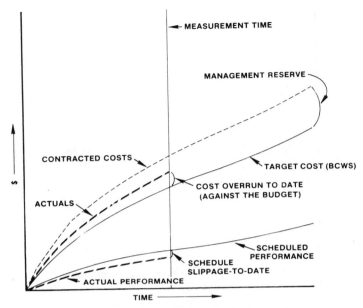

Figure 15–12. Integrated cost/schedule system.

ager (and some project managers) to substantially inflate estimates to protect the particular organization and provide a certain amount of cushion. Furthermore, if the inflated budget is approved, managers will undoubtedly use all of the allocated funds, including reserves. According to Parkinson:[5]

- The work at hand expands to fill the time available.
- Expenditures rise to meet budget.

Managers must identify all such reserves for contingency plans, in time, cost, and performance (i.e., PERT slack time).

The line indicated as actual cost in Figure 15–12 shows a cost overrun compared to the budget. However, costs are still within the contractual requirement if we consider the management reserve. Therefore, things may not be as bad as they seem.

Government subcontractors are required to have a government-approved

---

5. C. N. Parkinson, *Parkinson's Law* (Boston: Houghton Mifflin, 1957).

cost/schedule control system. The information requirements that must be demonstrated by such a system include:

- Budgeted cost for work scheduled (BCWS)
- Budgeted cost for work performed (BCWP)
- Actual cost for work performed (ACWP)
- Estimated cost at completion
- Budgeted cost at completion
- Cost and schedule variances/explanations
- Traceability

The last two items imply that standardized policies and procedures should exist for reporting and controlling variances.

When permitted variances are exceeded, cost account variance analysis reports as shown in Figure 15–13 are required. Signature approval of these reports may be required by:

- The functional employees responsible for the work
- The functional managers responsible for the work
- The cost accountant and/or the assistant project manager for cost control
- The project manager, work breakdown structure element manager, or someone with signature authority from the project office

For variance analysis, the goal of the cost account manager (whether project officer or functional employee) is to take action that will correct the problem within the original budget or justify a new estimate.

Five questions must be addressed during variance analysis:

- What is the problem causing the variance?
- What is the impact on time, cost, and performance?
- What is the impact on other efforts, if any?
- What corrective action is planned or under way?
- What are the expected results of the corrective action?

One of the key parameters used in variance analysis is the "earned value" concept, which is the same as BCWP. Earned value (or whatever other name might be used in the literature) is a forecasting variable used to predict whether the project will finish over or under the budget. As an example, on June 1, the budget showed that 800 hours should have been expended for a given task. However, only 600 hours appeared on the labor report. Therefore, the performance is (800/600) $\times$ 100, or 133 percent, and the task is under-

COST ACCOUNT NO/CAM						REPORTING LEVEL		
WBS/DESCRIPTION						AS OF		
COST PERF. DATA				VARIANCE		AT COMPLETION		
	BCWS	BCWP	ACWP	SCH	COST	BUDGET	EAC	VAR.
MONTH TO DATE ($)						//////	//////	//////
CONTRACT TO DATE ($K)								
PROBLEM CAUSE AND IMPACT								
CORRECTIVE ACTION (INCLUDE EXPECTED RECOVERY DATE)								

COST ACCOUNT MANAGER	DATE	COST CENTER MGR.	DATE	WBS ELEMENT MANAGER	DATE		DATE

Figure 15–13. Cost account variance analysis report.

running in performance. If the actual hours were 1,000, the performance would be 80 percent, and an overrun would be occurring.

The difficulty in performing variance analysis is in the calculation of BCWP because one must predict the percent complete. To eliminate this problem, many companies use standard dollar expenditures for the project, regardless of percent complete. For example, we could say that 10 percent of the costs are to be "booked" for each 10 percent of the time interval. Another technique, and perhaps the most common, is the 50/50 rule:

- Half of the budget for each element is recorded at the time that the work is scheduled to begin, and the other half at the time that the work is scheduled to be completed. For a project with a large number of elements, the amount of distortion from such a procedure is minimal. (Figures 15–14 and 15–15 illustrate this technique.)

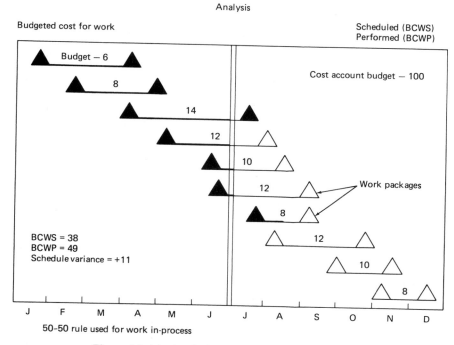

Figure 15–14. Analysis showing use of 50/50 rule.

One advantage of using the 50/50 rule is that it eliminates the necessity for the continuous determination of the percent complete. However, if percent complete can be determined, then percent complete can be plotted against time expended, as shown in Figure 15–16.

There are techniques available other than the 50/50 rule:

- 0/100—Usually limited to work packages (activities) of small duration (i.e., less than one month). No value is earned until the activity is complete.[6]
- Milestone—This is used for long work packages with associated interim milestones, or a functional group of activities with a milestone established at identified control points. Value is earned when the milestone is completed. In these cases, a budget is assigned to the milestone rather than the work packages.

---

6. These techniques, in addition to the 50/50 method for determining work in progress, are available in software packages. The reader might wish to contact AGS Management Systems, 880 First Avenue, King of Prussia, PA, 19406.

- Percent complete—Usually invoked for long duration work packages (i.e., three months or more) where milestones cannot be identified. The value earned would be the reported percent of the budget.
- Equivalent units—Used for multiple similar unit work packages, where earnings are on completed units, rather than labor.
- Cost formula (80/20)—A variation of percent complete for long duration work packages.
- Level of effort—This method is based on the passage of time. Often used for supervision and management work packages. The value earned is based on time expended over total scheduled time.
- Apportioned effort—A rarely used technique, for special related work packages. As an example, a production work package might have an apportioned inspection work package of 20 percent. There are only a few applications of this technique. Many people will try to use this for supervision, which is not a valid application.

Generally speaking, the concept of earned value may not be an effective control tool if used in the lower levels of the WBS. Task levels and above are normally worth the effort for the calculation of earned value. As an example, consider Figure 15–15, which shows the contractual cost data for task 3 of Project Z, and Table 15–3, which shows the cost data status at the end of the fourth month. The following is a brief summary of the cost data for each subtask in task 3 at the end of the fourth month:

- Subtask 1: All contractual funds were budgeted. Cost/performance was on time as indicated by the milestone position. Subtask is completed.
- Subtask 2: All contractual funds were budgeted. A cost overrun of $5,000 was incurred, and milestone was completed later than expected. Subtask is completed.
- Subtask 3: Subtask is completed. Costs were underrun by $10,000, probably because of early start.
- Subtask 4: Work is behind schedule. Actually, work has not yet begun.
- Subtask 5: Work is completed on schedule, but with a $50,000 cost overrun.
- Subtask 6: Work has not yet started. Effort is behind schedule.
- Subtask 7: Work has begun and appears to be 25 percent complete.
- Subtask 8: Work has not yet started.

The estimate at completion (EAC) is the best estimate of the total cost at the completion of the project. The EAC is a periodic evaluation of the project status, usually on a monthly basis or until a significant change has been identified. It is usually the responsibility of the performing organization to prepare the EAC.

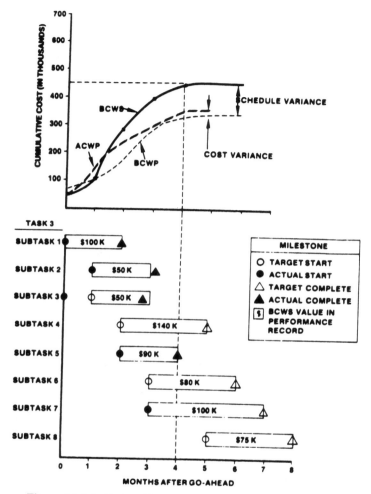

Figure 15–15. Project Z task 3 cost data (contractual).

The calculation of a new EAC and subsequent revision does not imply that corrective action has been taken. Consider a three-month task that is 99 percent complete and was budgeted to spend $400K (BCWS). The actual costs to date (ACWP) are $395K. Using the 50/50 rule, BCWP is $200K. The estimated cost-to-complete (EAC) ratio is $395K/$200K, which implies that we are heading for a 100 percent cost overrun. Obviously, this is not the case.

Using the data in Table 15–3, we can calculate the estimate at completion (EAC) by the expression

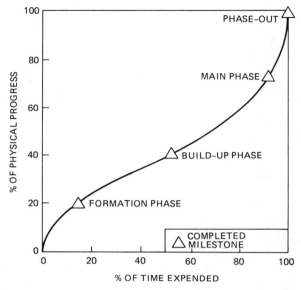

Figure 15–16. Physical progress vs. time expended.

$$EAC = (ACWP/BCWP) \times \text{Total budget}$$
$$= (360/340) \times 579,000$$
$$= \$613,059$$

This implies that we are overrunning our costs by 5.88 percent and the final cost will exceed the budget by \$34,059. However, we have not considered management reserve. The management reserve will reduce this overrun. The final

Table 15–3. Project Z Task 3 Cost Data Status at End of Fourth Month. (Cost in Thousands)

SUBTASKS	STATUS	BCWS	BCWP	ACWP
1	Completed	100	100	100
2	Completed	50	50	55
3	Completed	50	50	40
4	Not started	70	0	0
5	Completed	90	90	140
6	Not started	40	0	0
7	Started	50	50	25
8	Not started	—	—	—
TOTAL		450	340	360

(The data assume a 50/50 ratio for planned and earned values of budget.)

analysis is that the work is being accomplished almost on schedule, but costs are being overrun.

The question that remains to be answered is, "Where is the cost overrun occurring?" To answer this question, we must analyze the cost summary sheet for Project Z, task 3. Table 15-4 represents a hypothetical case for the cost elements of Project Z, task 3. From Table 15-4 we see that negative (overrun) variances exist for labor dollars, overhead dollars, and material costs. Because labor overhead is measured as a percentage of direct labor dollars, the problem appears to be in the direct labor dollars.

From the contractual column in Table 15-4 the project was estimated at $8.00 per hour direct labor (= $200,000/25,000 hours), but actuals to date are $131,000/14,000 hours, or $9.36 per hour. Therefore, more higher-salaried people than anticipated are being employed. This salary increase is partially offset by the fact that there exists a positive variance of 1,300 direct labor hours, indicating that these higher-salaried employees are performing at a more favorable position than expected on the learning curve. Since the milestones (from Figure 15-15) appear to be on target, work is progressing as planned, except for subtask 4.

The labor overhead rate has not changed. The contractual, BCWS, and BCWP overhead rates were estimated at 100 percent. The actuals, obtained from month-end reports, indicate that the true overhead rate is as predicted.

The following conclusions can be drawn:

- Work is being performed as planned (almost on schedule, although at a more favorable position on the learning curve), except for subtask 4 which is giving us a schedule delay.

Table 15-4. Project Z, Task 3 Cost Summary for Work Completed or in Progress. (Cost in Thousands)

	CONTRACTUAL	BCWS	BCWP	ACWP	COST VARIANCE	SCHEDULE VARIANCE
Direct labor hours	25,000	21,400	15,300	14,000	1,300	
Direct labor dollars	200	150	125	131	(6)	(25)
Labor overhead	200	150	125	131	(6)	(25)
Material dollars	70	66	26	30	(4)	(40)
Subtotal	470	366	276	292	(16)	(90)
G&A (10%)	47	36	28	29	(1)	(8)
Subtotal	517	402	304	321	(17)	(98)
Fee (12%)	62	48	36	39	(3)	(12)
TOTAL	579	450	340	360	(20)	(110)

Notes: 1. Direct labor hours are normally not shown in the cost package summaries but are included here for simplicity.
2. This page assumes a 50/50 ratio for planned and earned values of budget.

- Direct labor costs are increasing through the use of higher-salaried employees.
- Overhead rates are as anticipated.
- Direct labor hours must be reduced even further to compensate for increased costs, or else profits will be drastically reduced.

This type of analysis could have been carried out to one more level by identifying exactly which departments were using the more expensive employees. This step should probably be completed anyway to see if lower-paid employees are available and can work at the required position on the learning curve. Had the labor costs been a result of increased labor hours, this step would have definitely been necessary to identify the reason for the overrun in-house. Perhaps poor estimating was the cause.

In Table 15–4, there also appears a positive variance in materials. This likewise should undergo further analysis. The cause may be the result of improperly identified hardware, material escalation costs increasing beyond what was planned, increased scrap factors, or a change in subcontractors.

It should be obvious from the above analysis that a detailed investigation into the cause of variances appears to be the best method for identifying causes. The concept of earned value, although a crude estimate, identifies trends concerning the status of specific WBS elements. Using this concept, the budgeted cost for work scheduled (BCWS) may be called planned earned value (PEV), and the budgeted cost for work performed (BCWP) may be referred to as actual earned value (AEV). Earned values are used to determine whether costs are being incurred faster or slower than planned. However, cost overruns do not necessarily mean that there will be an eventual overrun, because the work may be getting done faster than planned.

There exist thirteen cases for comparing planned vs. actual performance. These thirteen cases are shown in Table 15–5. Each case is described below using the relationships:

- Cost variance = Planned earned value − Actuals
- Schedule/performance variances = Actual earned value − Planned earned value

Case 1: This is the ideal planning situation where everything goes according to schedule.

Case 2: Costs are behind schedule, and the program appears to be underrunning. Work is being accomplished at less than 100 percent, since actuals exceed AEV (or BCWP). This indicates that a cost overrun

Table 15-5. Variance Analysis Case Studies.

CASE	PLANNED EARNED VALUE (BCWS)	ACTUALS (ACWP)	ACTUAL EARNED VALUE (BCWP)
1	800	800	800
2	800	600	400
3	800	400	600
4	800	600	600
5	800	800	600
6	800	800	1,000
7	800	1,000	1,000
8	800	600	800
9	800	1,000	800
10	800	1,000	600
11	800	600	1,000
12	800	1,200	1,000
13	800	1,000	1,200

can be anticipated. This situation grows even worse when we see that we are 50 percent behind schedule also. This is one of the worst possible cases.

Case 3: In this case there exists good news and bad news. The good news is that we are performing the work efficiently (efficiency exceeds 100 percent). The bad news is that we are behind schedule.

Case 4: The work is not being accomplished according to schedule (i.e., is behind schedule), but the costs are being maintained for what has been accomplished.

Case 5: The costs are on target with the schedule, but the work is 25 percent behind schedule because the work is being performed at 75 percent efficiency.

Case 6: Because we are operating at 125 percent efficiency, work is ahead of schedule by 25 percent but within scheduled costs. We are performing at a more favorable position on the learning curve.

Case 7: We are operating at a 100 percent efficiency and work is being accomplished ahead of schedule. Costs are being maintained according to budget.

Case 8: Work is being accomplished properly, and costs are being underrun.

Case 9: Work is being accomplished properly, but costs are being overrun.

Case 10: Costs are being overrun while underaccomplishing the plan. Work is being accomplished inefficiently. This situation is very bad.

Case 11: Performance is ahead of schedule, and the costs are lower than planned. This situation results in a big Christmas bonus.

Case 12: Work is being done inefficiently, and a possible cost overrun can

Case 13: occur. However, performance is ahead of schedule. The overall result may be either an overrun in cost or an underrun in schedule. Although costs are greater than those budgeted, performance is ahead of schedule, and work is being accomplished very efficiently. This is also a good situation.

In each of these cases, the concept of earned value was used to predict trends in cost and variance analysis. This method has its pros and cons. According to Martin:[7]

The usefulness of earned value measurements in project management is controversial. The most enthusiastic managers regard it as the best way to prevent surprises and as a most workable tool. Others consider the information helpful in managing the project but not worth the cost of obtaining it. Still others say the information becomes available too late or there are better ways to obtain it. The most critical managers view it as a complete waste of time.

Each of the critical variances (or earned values) identified usually require a formal analysis to determine the cause of the variance, the corrective action to be taken, and the effect on the estimate to completion. These analyses are performed by the organizations that were assigned the budget (BCWS) at the level of accumulation directed by program management.

Organization Level Analysis

Each critical variance identified on the organizational MCCS reports may require the completion of MCCS variance analysis procedures by the supervisor of the cost center involved. Analyzing both the work breakdown and organizational structure, the supervisor systematically concentrates his efforts on cost and schedule problems appearing within his organization.

Analysis begins at the lowest organizational level by the supervisor involved. Critical variances are noted at the cost account on the MCCS report. If a schedule variance is involved and the subtask consists of a number of work packages, the supervisor may refer to a separate report that breaks down each cost account into the various work packages that are ahead or behind schedule. The supervisor can then analyze the variance on the basis of the work package involved and determine with the aid of supporting organizations the cause of the variance, the corrective action that can be taken, or the possible effect on associated or future planned effort.

---

7. Charles C. Martin, *Project Management: How to Make it Work* (New York: AMACOM, a Division of American Management Associations, 1976), p. 203.

Cost variances involving labor are analyzed by the supervisor on the basis of the performance of his organization in accomplishing the work assigned, within the budgeted man-hours and planned labor rate. The cause of any variance to this performance is determined, and corrective action is then implemented.

Cost variances on nonlabor effort are analyzed by the supervisor with the aid of the program team member and other supporting organizations.

All material variance analyses are normally initiated by cost accounting as a service to the using organization. These variance analyses are completed, including cause and corrective action, to the extent that can be explained by cost accounting. They are then sent to the using organization, which reviews the analyses and completes those resulting from schedule performance or usage. If a variance is recognized as a change in the material acquisition price, this information is supplied by cost accounting to the responsible organization and a change to the estimate-to-complete is initiated by the using organization.

The supervisor should forward copies of each completed MCCS variance analysis/EAC change form to his higher level manager and the program team member.

Program Team Analysis

The program team member may receive a team critical variance report that lists variances in his organization at the lowest level of the work breakdown structure at the division cost center level by cost element. Upon request of the program manager, analyses of variances contributing to the variances on the team critical variance report are summarized by the responsible program team member and reviewed with the program manager.

The program manager uses this information to review the program status with upper-level management. This review is normally on a monthly basis. In addition, the results of these analyses are used to explain variances in the contractually required reports to the customer.

After the analyses of the variances have been made, reports must be developed for both the customer and in-house (upper-level) management. Customer reporting procedures and specifications can be more detailed than in-house reporting and are often governed by the contract. Contractual requirements specify the reports required, the frequency of submission and distribution, and the customer regulation that specifies the preparation instructions for the report.

The types of reports required by the customer and management depend upon the size of the program and the magnitude of the variance. Most reports usually contain the tracking of the vital technical parameters. These might include:

- The major milestones necessary for project success
- Comparison to specifications
- Types or conditions of testing
- Correlation of technical performance to the activity network and the work breakdown structure

One final note need be mentioned concerning reports. To facilitate time and money savings, each of these reports might be no more than one or two pages. In many cases, the reports are merely fill-in-the-blank types. When necessary, explanations can be provided by additional pages.

15.6 STATUS REPORTING

One of the best ways of reducing or even eliminating executive meddling on projects is to provide executives with frequent, meaningful status reports so that they can accurately realize the true status of the project. Figure 15–17 shows a relatively simple status report based upon data accumulation in the form of Figures 15–18 and 15–19. These types of status reports should be short and concise, containing pertinent information only.

Reporting procedures for variance analysis should be as brief as possible. The reason for this is simple: the shorter and more concise the report is, the faster it is that feedback can be generated and responses developed. The time parameter becomes critical if rescheduling must be accomplished with limited resources. The two most common situations providing constraints on resource rescheduling are that:

- The end-date is fixed.
- The resources available are constant (or limited).

With a fixed end-date, program rescheduling generally requires that additional resources be supplied. In the second situation, program slippage may be the only alternative unless a constant sum of resources can be redistributed so as to shorten the length of the critical path.

Once the variance analysis is completed, both project and functional management must diagnose the problem and search for corrective actions. This includes:

- Finding the cure for the problem
- Developing a plan to recover the position

This by no means implies that all variances require corrective action. There are four major responses to a variance report:

June 1, 1982

1. *VARIANCE ANALYSIS* (Cost in Thousands)

SUBTASK	MILESTONE STATUS	BUDGETED COST WORK SCHEDULE	BUDGETED COST WORK PERFORMED	ACTUAL COST	VARIANCE, % SCHEDULE	VARIANCE, % COST
1	Completed	100	100	100	0	0
2	Completed	50	50	55	0	−10
3	Completed	50	50	40	0	20
4	Not Started	70	0	0	−100	—
5	Completed	90	90	140	0	−55.5
6	Not Started	40	0	0	−100	—
7	Started	50	50	25	0	50
8	Not Started	0	0	0	—	—
Total		450	340	360	−24.4	−5.9

2. *ESTIMATE AT COMPLETION (EAC)*
$$EAC = (360/340) \times \$579,000 = \$613,059$$
$$Overrun = 613,059 - 579,000 = \$34,059$$

3. *COST SUMMARY*
Costs are running approximately 5.9% over budget because of higher-salaried labor.

4. *SCHEDULE SUMMARY*
The 24.4% behind-schedule condition is due to subtasks 4 and 6 which have not yet begun owing to lack of raw materials and the 50/50 method for booking costs. Overtime will get us back on schedule but at an additional cost of 2.5% of direct labor costs.

5. *MILESTONE REPORT*

MILESTONE/SUBTASK	SCHEDULED COMPLETION	PROJECTED COMPLETION	ACTUAL COMPLETION
1	4/1/82		4/1/82
2	5/1/82		5/8/82
3	5/1/82		4/23/82
4	7/1/82	7/1/82	
5	6/1/82		6/1/82
6	8/1/82	8/1/82	
7	9/1/82	9/1/82	
8	10/1/82	10/1/82	

Figure 15–17. Blue Spider Project, monthly project report #4.

6. *EVENT REPORT*

CURRENT PROBLEM	POTENTIAL IMPACT	CORRECTIVE ACTION
(a) Lack of raw materials.	Cost overrun and behind schedule condition.	Overtime is scheduled. We will try to use lower-salaried people. Raw materials are expected to be on dock next week.
(b) Customer unhappy with test results, and wants additional work.	May need additional planning.	Customer will provide us with revised statement of work on 6/15/82.

Gary Anderson, Project Manager

Figure 15–17. (*Continued*).

- Ignoring it
- Functional modification
- Replanning
- System redesign

Permissible variances exist for all levels of the organization. If the variance is within these permitted deviations, then there will be no response, and the variance may be ignored. In some situations where the variance is marginal (or even within limits), corrective action may be required. This would normally occur at the functional level and might simply involve using another test procedure or possibly considering some alternative not delineated in the program plan.

If major variances occur, then either replanning or system redesign must take place. The replanning process requires the redefining and reestablishing of project goals as work progresses, but always within system specifications. This might include making trade-offs in time, cost, and performance or defining new project activities and methods of pursuing the project, such as new PERT networks. If resources are limited, then a proper redistribution or reallocation must be made. If resources are not limited, then additional personnel, financing, equipment, facilities, or information may be required.

If replanning cannot be accomplished without system redesign, then system specifications may have to be changed.[8] This is the worst possible case because

---

8. Here we are discussing system specifications. Functional modification responses can also require specification changes, but not on the system level. Examples of functional modifications might be changes in tolerances for testing or for purchasing raw materials.

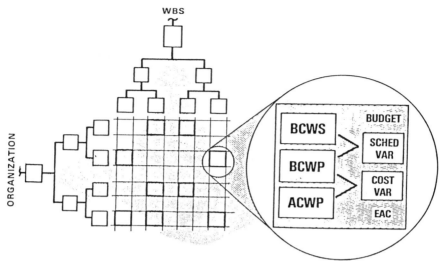

Figure 15-18. Data accumulation.

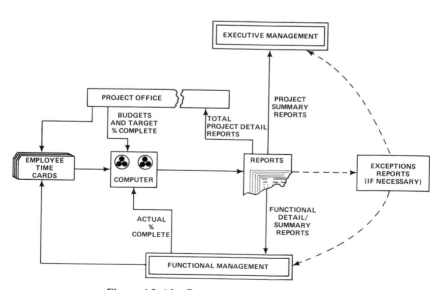

Figure 15-19. Cost control and report flow.

performance may have to be sacrificed to satisfy the constraints of time and money.

Whenever companies operate on a matrix structure, job descriptions, responsibilities, and management directives must be carefully prepared and distributed to all key individuals in the organization. This is an absolute necessity when a multitude of people must interact to control company resources. Management policies must establish the decision-making policies associated with management cost and control systems. Otherwise, dual standards can occur within the same organization, and the decision-making process becomes a tedious flow of red tape. The following might be a management policy guide for a program or project manager:

- Approving all estimates, and negotiating all estimates and the definition of work requirements with the respective organizations.
- Approving the budget, and directing distribution and budgeting of available funds to all organizational levels by program element.
- Defining the work required and the schedule.
- Authorizing work release. He may not, however, authorize work beyond the scope of the contract.
- Approving the program bill-of-materials, detailed plans, and program schedules for need and compliance with program requirements.
- Approving the procuring work statement, the schedules, the source selection, the negotiated price, and the type of contract on major procurement.
- Monitoring the functional organization's performance against released budgets, schedules, and program requirements.
- When cost performance is unacceptable, taking appropriate action with the affected organization to modify the work requirements or to stimulate corrective action within the functional organization so as to reduce cost without changing the contracted scope of work.
- Being responsible for all communications and policy matters on contracted programs so that no communicative directive shall be issued without the signature or concurrence of the program manager.

Describing the responsibilities of a manager is only a portion of the management policy or management guideline package. Because the program manager must cross over functional boundaries to accomplish all of the above, it is also necessary to describe the role and responsibility of the functional manager as well as the relationship between functional and program management for major program activities. Table 15–6 defines the responsibilities for the program manager and the functional manager and their relationship (i.e., interraction) for development and implementation of a management cost and control system. Similar tables can be developed for planning and scheduling, communications, customer relations, and contract administration.

15.7 COST CONTROL PROBLEMS

No matter how good the cost and control system is, problems can occur, as shown in Figure 15–20. Below are common causes of cost problems:

- Poor estimating techniques and/or standards, resulting in unrealistic budgets
- Out-of-sequence starting and completion of activities and events
- Inadequate work breakdown structure
- No management policy on reporting and control practices
- Poor work definition at the lower levels of the organization
- Management reducing budgets or bids to be competitive or to eliminate "fat"
- Inadequate formal planning that results in unnoticed, or often uncontrolled, increases in scope of effort
- Poor comparison of actual and planned costs
- Comparison of actual and planned costs at the wrong level of management
- Unforeseen technical problems
- Schedule delays that require overtime or idle time costing
- Material escalation factors that are unrealistic

Cost overruns can occur in any phase of project development. Below are the most common causes for cost overruns:

- Proposal phase:
  - Failure to understand customer requirements
  - Unrealistic appraisal of in-house capabilities
  - Underestimating time requirements
- Planning phase:
  - Omissions
  - Inaccuracy of the work breakdown structure
  - Misinterpretation of information
  - Use of wrong estimating techniques
  - Failure to identify and concentrate on major cost elements
  - Failure to assess and provide for risks
- Negotiation phase:
  - Forcing a speedy compromise
  - Procurement ceiling costs
  - Negotiation team that must "win this one"
- Contractual phase:
  - Contractual discrepancies
  - SOW different from RFP requirements
  - Proposal team different from project team

Table 15-6. Program Controls Interrelationships.

PROGRAM MANAGER	FUNCTIONAL MANAGER	RELATIONSHIP
Program Controls Makes or approves all decisions that affect the contractually committed target time, cost, and performance requirements or objectives of the program.	*Program Controls* Assembles and furnishes the information needed to assist the program manager in making decisions. Submits to the program manager all proposed changes that affect program cost, schedule targets, and technical requirements and objectives through the program team member.	*Program Controls* Management controls, contract administration, budgeting, estimating, and financial controls are a functional specialty. The program manager utilizes the services of the specialist organizations. The specialists retain their own channels to the general manager but must keep the program manager informed through the program team member.
Approves all engineering change control decisions that affect the contractually committed target time, cost, and performance requirements or objectives of the program.	Implements engineering change decisions approved by the program manager. Advises him of any resulting programming impasses and negotiates adjustments through the program team member.	
Establishes program budgets in conjunction with the cognizant program team members; monitors and negotiates changes.		In all matters pertaining to budget and cost control, the program manager utilizes the services of the program team member representing the cognizant financial control organization.
Authorizes release of the budget and work authorization for the performance of approved work, and negotiates any intradirectorate reallocation above section level with the affected functional organizations through the program team members.	Within the allocated budget, provides manpower skills, facilities, and other resources pertaining to his functional specialty to the degree and level necessary to meet program schedule, cost, and technical performance requirements of the contract.	

Requests the assignment of program team members to the program, and approves the release of the team member from the program.	Coordinates with the program manager in the selection and assignment of a program team member to the program or release of the program team member from the program.	Program manager does not hire or fire functional personnel. Program team members should not be removed from the program without the concurrence of the program manager.
Establishes report requirements and controls necessary for evaluation of all phases of program performance consistent with effective policies and procedures.	Works in concert with other functional organizations to ensure that he and they are proceeding satisfactorily in the completion of mutually interdependent program tasks and events.	Insofar as possible, program controls must be satisfied from existing data and controls as defined by division policies and procedures.
Measures and evaluates performance of tasks against the established plan. Identifies current and potential problems. Decides upon and authorizes corrective action.	Follows-up all activities of his organization to ensure satisfactory performance to program requirements. Detects actual or potential problems. Takes timely corrective action in his organization, and when such problems involve interface with other functional organizations, notifies them and coordinates the initiation of mutually satisfactory remedial action. Keeps the program manager advised (through the program team member) of conditions affecting the program, existing, or expected problems, problems solved, and corrective action required or performed.	The program manager directs or redirects activities of functional organizations only through the cognizant program team member. Functional managers are responsible for the performance of their organizations. Functional managers do not implement decisions involving increased total program costs, changes in schedule, or changes in technical performance without prior approval of the program team members and the program manager.
Apprises the program team members and/or functional organizations of program changes affecting their function.		
Assures the establishment, coordination, and execution of support programs to the extent required or permitted by the contract.		This includes such programs as value engineering, data management, and configuration management.

Figure 15–20. Was there a reason for the cost overrun?

- Design phase:
  - Accepting customer requests without management approval
  - Problems in customer communications channels and data items
  - Problems in design review meetings
- Production phase:
  - Excessive material costs
  - Specifications that are not acceptable
  - Manufacturing and engineering disagreement

PROBLEMS

15–1   Do cost overruns just happen, or are they caused?

15–2   Cemeteries are filled with projects that went out of control. Below are several causes that can easily develop into out-of-control conditions. In which phase of a project should each of these conditions be detected and, if possible, remedied?

- a. Customer's requirements not understood
- b. Project team formed after bid was prepared
- c. Accepting unusual terms and conditions
- d. Permitting a grace period for changing specifications
- e. Lack of time to research specifications
- f. Overestimation of company's capabilities

15–3   Below are several factors that can result in project delays and cost overruns. Explain how these problems can be overcome.

a. Poorly defined milestones
b. Poor estimating techniques
c. A missing PERT/CPM chart
d. Functional managers not having a clear understanding of what has to be done
e. Poor programming procedures and techniques
f. Changes constantly being made deep in the project's life cycle

15–4 Under what conditions would each of the figures in Chapter 13 be applicable for customer reporting? In-house reporting? Reporting to top-level management?

15–5 What impact would there be on BCWS, BCWP, ACWP, and cost and schedule variances as a result of the:

a. Early start of an activity on a PERT chart?
b. Late start of an activity on a PERT chart?

15–6 Alpha Company has implemented a plan whereby functional managers will be held totally responsible for all cost overruns against their (the functional managers') original estimates. Furthermore, all cost overruns must come out of the functional managers' budgets, whether they be overhead or otherwise, not the project budget. What are the advantages and disadvantages of this approach?

15–7 Karl has decided to retain a management reserve on a $400,000 project that includes a $60,000 profit. At the completion of the project, Karl finds that management reserve fund contains $40,000. Should Karl book the management reserve as excess profits (i.e., $100,000), or should he just book the target profit of $60,000 and let the functional managers "sandbag" on the slush fund until it is depleted?

15–8 ABC Corporation has recently given out a nine-month contract to a construction subcontractor. At the end of the first month, it becomes obvious that the subcontractor is not reporting costs according to an appropriate WBS level. ABC Corporation asks the subcontractor to change its cost reporting procedures. The subcontractor states that this cannot be done without additional funding. This problem has occurred with other subcontractors as well. What can ABC Corporation do about this?

15–9 What would be the result if all project managers decided to withhold a management reserve? What criteria should be used for determining when a management reserve is necessary?

15–10 Alpha Company, a project-driven organization, pays its department managers a quarterly bonus that is dependent upon two factors: the departmental overhead rate and direct labor dollars. The exact value of the bonus is proportional to how much these two factors are underrun.

Department man-hours are priced out against the department average, which does not include the department manager's salary. His salary is included under his departmental overhead rate, but he does have the option of charging his own time as direct labor to the projects for which he must supply resources.

What do you think of this method? Is it adequate inducement for a functional manager to control resources more effectively? How would you feel, as a project manager, knowing that the functional managers got quarterly bonuses and you got none?

15-11 Many executives are reluctant to let project managers have complete control of project costs because then the project managers must know the exact salaries of almost all project personnel. Can this situation be prevented if the contract requires reporting costs as actuals?

15-12 How can a country's inflation rate influence the contractual payment policy?

15-13 Consider a situation in which several tasks may be for one to two years rather than the 200 hours normally used in the work-package level of the WBS.

a. How will this impact cost control?
b. Can we still use the 50/50 rule?
c. How frequently should costs be updated?

15-14 By now you should be familiar with the various tools that can be used for planning, controlling, scheduling, and directing project activities. Table 15-7 contains a partial list of such tools and how they relate to specific project management functions. Complete the table (using the legend at the bottom) to indicate which are very useful and which are somewhat useful.

Table 15-7. Project Planning, Controlling, and Directing.

	USEFUL FOR			
TOOL	PLANNING	CONTROLLING	DIRECTING	INTERFACE RELATIONSHIPS
Project organizational charts				
Work breakdown structure				
Task descriptions				
Work packages				
Project budget				
Project plan				
Charts/schedules				
Progress reports				
Review meetings				

o somewhat useful
● very useful

Obviously there will be some question about what is very useful and what is somewhat useful. Be able to defend your answers.

15-15 Complete the table below and plot the EAC as a function of time. What are your conclusions?

	CUMULATIVE COST, IN THOUSANDS			VARIANCE $		
WEEK	BCWS	BCWP	ACWP	SCHEDULE	COST	EAC
1	50	50	25			
2	70	60	40			
3	90	80	67			
4	120	105	90			
5	130	120	115			
6	140	135	130			
7	165	150	155			
8	200	175	190			
9	250	220	230			
10	270	260	270			
11	300	295	305			
12	350	340	340			
13	380	360	370			
14	420	395	400			
15	460	460	450			

15–16 Using the information in Chapter 12, problem 12–16, complete the following table:

CASE STUDY: THE BATHTUB PERIOD

The award of the Scott contract on January 3, 1977 left Park Industries elated. The Scott Project, if managed correctly, offered tremendous opportunities for follow-on work over the next several years. Park's management considered the Scott Project as strategic in nature.

The Scott Project was a ten-month endeavor to develop a new product for Scott Corporation. Scott informed Park Industries that sole-source production contracts would follow, for at least five years, assuming that the initial R&D effort proved satisfactory. All follow-on contracts were to be negotiated on a year-to-year basis.

Jerry Dunlap was selected as project manager. Although he was young and eager, he understood the importance of the effort for future growth of the company. Dunlap was given some of the best employees to fill out his project office as part of Park's matrix organization. The Scott Project maintained a project office of seven full-time people, including Dunlap, throughout the duration of the project. In addition, eight people from the functional department were selected for representation as functional project team members, four full-time and four half-time.

Although the work load fluctuated, the manpower level for the project office and team members was constant for the duration of the project at 2,080 hours per month. The company assumed that each hour worked incurred a cost of $20.00 per person, fully burdened.

At the end of June, with four months remaining on the project, Scott Corporation

Columns

1	2	3	4	5	6	7
Activity	Percent complete	Budgeted cost for work scheduled	Budgeted cost for work performed	Actual cost for work performed	Cost variance = 4 − 5	Schedule variance = 4 − 3
Total						

Cost variance ($) = Column 4 − Column 5 = ___

Schedule variance ($) = Column 4 − Column 3 = ___

Schedule variance (weeks) = $\dfrac{\text{Schedule variance (\$)}}{\text{Average weekly budgeted \$}} = \dfrac{\text{Column 3} \div 4 \text{ weeks}}{} =$ ___

Time-to-complete = ___

Cost-at-completion = rate of spending × Total budget = $\dfrac{\text{Column 5}}{\text{Column 4}} \times ($ ___ $) =$ ___

Cost-to-complete = (Cost-at-completion) − ACWP = ___

informed Park Industries that, owing to a projected cash flow problem, follow-on work would not be awarded until the first week in March (1978). This posed a tremendous problem for Jerry Dunlap because he did not wish to break up the project office. If he permitted his key people to be assigned to other projects, there would be no guarantee that he could get them back at the beginning of the follow-on work. Good project office personnel are always in demand.

Jerry estimated that he needed $40,000 per month during the "bathtub" period to support and maintain his key people. Fortunately, the bathtub period fell over Christmas and New Year's, a time when the plant would be shut down for seventeen days. Between the vacation days that his key employees would be taking, and the small special projects that his people could be temporarily assigned to on other programs, Jerry revised his estimate to $125,000 for the entire bathtub period.

At the weekly team meeting, Jerry told the program team members that they would have to "tighten their belts" in order to establish a management reserve of $125,000. The project team understood the necessity for this action and began rescheduling and replanning until a management reserve of this size could be realized. Because the contract was firm-fixed-price, all schedules for administrative support (i.e., project office and project team members) were extended through February 28 on the supposition that this additional time was needed for final cost data accountability and program report documentation.

Jerry informed his boss, Frank Howard, the division head for project management, as to the problems with the bathtub period. Frank was the intermediary between Jerry and the general manager. Frank agreed with Jerry's approach to the problem and requested to be kept informed.

On September 15, Frank told Jerry that he wanted to "book" the management reserve of $125,000 as excess profit since it would influence his (Frank's) Christmas bonus. Frank and Jerry argued for a while, with Frank constantly saying, "Don't worry! You'll get your key people back. I'll see to that. But I want those uncommitted funds recorded as profit and the program closed out by November 1."

Jerry was furious with Frank's lack of interest in maintaining the current organizational membership.

a. Should Jerry go to the general manager?
b. Should the key people be supported on overhead?
c. If this were a cost-plus program, would you consider approaching the customer with your problem in hopes of relief?
d. If you were the customer of this cost-plus program, what would your response be for additional funds for the bathtub period, assuming cost overrun?
e. Would your previous answer change if the program had the money available as a result of an underrun?
f. How do you prevent this situation from recurring on all yearly follow-on contracts?

16
Trade-off Analysis in a Project Environment

"When we try to pick out anything by itself, we find it hitched to everything else in the universe."—Muir's Law

16.0 INTRODUCTION

Successful project management is both an art and a science and attempts to control corporate resources within the constraints of time, cost, and performance. Most projects are unique, one-of-a-kind activities for which there may not have been reasonable standards for forward planning. As a result, the project manager may find it extremely difficult to stay within the time–cost–performance triangle of Figure 16–1.

The time, cost, and performance triangle is the "magic combination" that is continuously pursued by the project manager throughout the life cycle of the project. If the project were to flow smoothly, according to plan, there might not be a need for trade-off analysis. Unfortunately, most projects eventually find crises where this delicate balance necessary to attain the desired performance within time and cost is no longer possible.

This is shown in Figure 16–2, where the Δ's represent deviations from the original estimates. The time and cost deviations are normally overruns, whereas the performance error will be an underrun. No two projects are ever exactly alike, and trade-off analysis would appear to be an ongoing effort throughout the life of the project, continuously influenced by both the internal and the external environment. Experienced project managers may have predetermined trade-offs in reserve as appropriate crises arise, recognizing that trade-offs are part of a continuous thought process, as shown in Figure 16–3. Inexperienced project managers may consider trade-off analysis as shown in Figure 16–4.

Trade-offs are always based upon the constraints of the project. Table 16–1 illustrates the types of constraints commonly imposed. Situations A and B are the typical trade-offs encountered in project management. For example, situation A-3 portrays most research and development projects. The performance

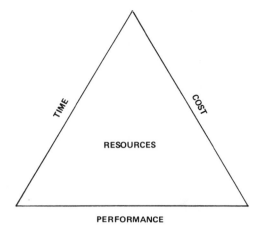

Figure 16–1. Overview of project management.

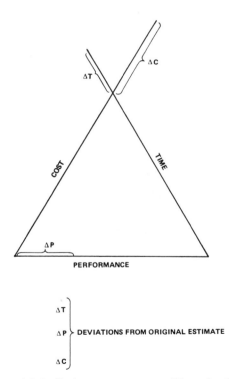

Figure 16–2. Project management with trade-offs.

Figure 16–3. Trade-off analysis.

Figure 16–4. Is this how you solve project problems?

Table 16–1. Categories of Constraints.

	A. ONE ELEMENT FIXED AT A TIME		
	TIME	COST	PERFORMANCE
A-1	Fixed	Variable	Variable
A-2	Variable	Fixed	Variable
A-3	Variable	Variable	Fixed

	B TWO ELEMENTS FIXED AT A TIME		
	TIME	COST	PERFORMANCE
B-1	Fixed	Fixed	Variable
B-2	Fixed	Variable	Fixed
B-3	Variable	Fixed	Fixed

	C. THREE ELEMENTS FIXED OR VARIABLE		
	TIME	COST	PERFORMANCE
C-1	Fixed	Fixed	Fixed
C-2	Variable	Variable	Variable

of an R&D project is usually well defined, and it is cost and time that may be allowed to go beyond budget and schedule. The determination of what to sacrifice is based on the available alternatives. If there are no alternatives to the product being developed and the potential usage is great, then cost and time are the trade-offs.

Most capital equipment projects would fall into situation A-1 or B-2, where time is of the essence. The sooner the piece of equipment gets into production, the sooner the return of investment can be realized. Often there exist performance constraints that determine the profit potential of the project. If the project potential is determined to be great after all alternatives have been established, cost will be the slippage factor, as in situation B-2.

Non-process-type equipment, such as air pollution control equipment, usually develops a scenario around situation B-3. Performance is fixed by the Environmental Protection Agency. The deadline for compliance can be delayed through litigation, but if the lawsuits fail, most firms then try to comply with the least expensive equipment that will meet the minimum requirements.

The professional consulting firm operates primarily under situation B-1. In situation C, the trade-off analysis will be completed based on the selection criteria and constraints. If everything is fixed (C-1), there is no room for any outcome other than total success, and if everything is variable (C-2), there are no constraints and thus no trade-off.

Many factors go into the decision to sacrifice either time, cost, or perfor-

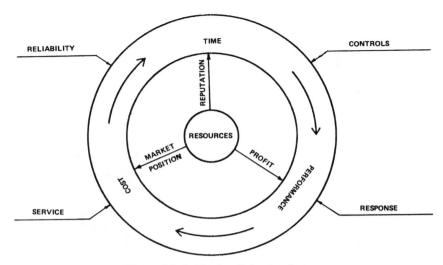

Figure 16–5. Trade-off forcing factors.

mance. It should be noted, however, that it is not always possible to sacrifice one of these items without affecting the others. For example, reducing the time could have a serious impact on performance and cost (especially if overtime is required).

There are several factors, such as those shown in Figure 16–5, that tend to "force" trade-offs. Poorly written documents (e.g., statements of work, contracts, and specifications) are almost always inward forces for conflict in which the project manager tends to look for performance relief. In many projects, the initial sale and negotiation, as well as the specification writing, are done by highly technical people who are driven to create a monument rather than meet the operational needs of the customer, the operator of the system. When the operating forces dominate outward from the project to the customer, project managers may tend to seek cost relief.

16.1 METHODOLOGY FOR TRADE-OFF ANALYSIS

Any process for managing time, cost, and performance trade-offs should emphasize the systems approach to management by recognizing that even the smallest change in a project or system could easily affect all of the organization's systems. A typical systems model is shown in Figure 16-6. Because of this, it is often better to develop a process for decision-making/trade-off analysis rather than to maintain hard and fast rules on trade-offs. The following

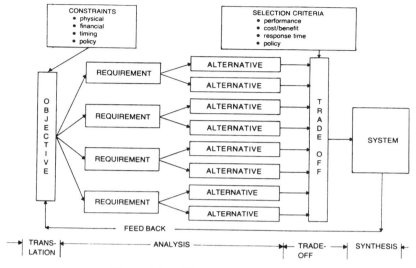

Figure 16–6. The systems approach.

six steps might be a representative method for managing project time, cost, and performance trade-offs:

- Recognizing and understanding the basis for project conflicts
- Reviewing the project objectives
- Analyzing the project environment and status
- Identifying the alternative courses of action
- Analyzing and selecting the best alternative
- Revising the project plan

The first step in any decision-making process must be recognition and understanding of the conflict. Most projects have management cost and control systems that compare actual vs. planned results, scrutinize the results through variance analyses, and provide status reports so that corrective action can be taken to resolve the problems. Project managers must carefully evaluate project problems because information concerning a potential problem may not always be what it appears to be. The source of the early warning and the validity of the intelligence data should first be tested. Management control of a project team organization is usually quite sensitive to both the accuracy and timeliness of data communications. Typical questions that should be asked at this point might be:

- Is the information pertinent?
- Is the information current?

- Are the data complete?
- Who has determined that this situation exists?
- How does he/she know this information to be correct?
- If this information is true, what are the implications for the project?

The major reason for this first step is to understand the potential cause for the conflict, and thus for trade-offs. Most causes can be categorized as human errors or failures, uncertain problems, and totally unexpected problems. This is shown below:

- Human Errors/Failures
  - Impossible schedule commitments
  - Poor control of design changes
  - Poor project cost accounting
  - Machine failures
  - Test failures
  - Failure to receive a critical input
  - Failure to receive anticipated approvals
- Uncertain Problems
  - Too many concurrent projects
  - Labor contract expiration
  - Change in project leadership
  - Possibility of project cancellation
- Unexpected Problems
  - Overcommitted company resources
  - Conflicting project priorities
  - Cash flow problems
  - Labor contract disputes
  - Delay in material shipment
  - "Fast-track" people having been promoted off the project
  - "Temporary" employees having to be returned to their home base
  - Inaccurate original forecast
  - Change in market conditions
  - New standards having been developed

The second step in the decision-making process is a complete review of the project objectives. This review must include an analysis of these objectives as seen by the various participants in the project, ranging from top management to project team members. These objectives and/or priorities were originally set with many environmental factors being considered. These factors must be reviewed because they may have changed over the lifetime of the project.

The nature of these objectives will usually determine the degree of rigidity that has been established between time, cost, and performance. This may very well require review of all project documentation, including:

- Project objectives
- Project integration into sponsor's objectives and strategic plan
- Statement of work
- Schedules, cost, and performance specifications
- Resources consumed and projected

The third step in the methodology is the analysis of the project environment and status. This step includes a detailed measurement of the actual time, cost, and performance results with the original or revised project plan. This step should not turn into a "witch hunt" but instead should focus upon project results, problems, and roadblocks. Factors such as financial risk, potential follow-up contracts, the status of other projects, and relative competitive positions are just a few of the environmental factors that should be reviewed. Some companies have established policies toward trade-off analysis, such as "never compromise performance." Even these policies, however, have been known to change when environmental factors add to the financial risk of the company. The following topics may be applicable under step 3:

- Discuss the project with the project management office to:
  - Determine relative priorities for time, cost, and performance
  - Determine impact on firm's profitability and strategic plan
  - Get a management assessment (even a hunch as to what the problems are)
- If the project is a contract with an outside customer, meet with the customer's project manager to assess his/her views relative to project status and assess the customer's priorities for time, cost, and performance.
- Meet with the functional managers to determine their views on the problem and to gain an insight regarding their commitment to a successful project. Where does this project sit in their priority list?
- Review in detail the status of each project work package. Obtain a clear and detailed appraisal by the responsible project office personnel as to:
  - Time to complete
  - Cost to complete
  - Work to complete
- Review past data to assess credibility of cost and schedule information in the previous step.

The project manager may have sufficient background to assess quickly the significance of a particular variance and the probable impact of that variance on project team performance. Knowledge of the project requirements (possibly with the assistance of the project sponsor) will usually help a project manager determine whether corrective action must be taken at all, or whether the project should simply be permitted to continue as originally conceived.

Whether or not immediate action is required, a quick analysis of why a potential problem has developed is in order. Obviously, it will not help to "cure the symptoms" if the "disease" itself is not remedied. The project manager must remain objective in such problem identification, since he himself is a key member of the project team and may be personally responsible for problems that are occurring. Suspect areas typically include:

- Inadequate planning. Either planning was not done in sufficient detail or controls were not established to determine that the project is proceeding according to the approved plan.
- Scope changes. Cost and schedule overruns are the normal result of scope changes that are permitted without formal incorporation in the project plan or increase in the resources authorized for the project.
- Poor performance. Because of the high level of interdependencies that exist within any project team structure, unacceptable performance by one individual may quickly undermine the performance of the entire team.
- Excess performance. Frequently an overzealous team member will unintentionally distort the planned balance between cost, schedule, and performance on the project.
- Environmental restraints—particularly on projects involving "third party approvals" or dependent upon outside resources. Changes, delays, or nonperformance by parties outside the project team may adversely impact the team performance.

Some projects appear to be out of tolerance when, in fact, they are not. For example, some construction projects are so front-loaded with costs that there appears to be a major discrepancy when one actually does not exist. The front-end loading of cost was planned for.

The fourth step in the project trade-off process is to list alternative courses of action. This step usually means brainstorming the possible methods of completing the project by compromising some combination of time, cost, or performance. Hopefully, this step will refine these possible alternatives into the three or four most likely scenarios for project completion. At this point, some intuitive decision-making may be required to keep the list of alternatives at a manageable level.

In order fully to identify the alternatives, the project manager must have specific answers to key questions involving time, cost, and performance:

- Time
  - Is a time delay acceptable to the customer?

- Will the time delay change the completion date for other projects and other customers?
- What is the cause for the time delay?
- Can resources be recommitted to meet the new schedule?
- What will be the cost for the new schedule?
- Will the increased time give us added improvement?
- Will an extension of this project cause delays on other projects in the customer's house?
- What will the customer's response be?
- Will the increased time change our learning curve?
- Will this hurt our company's ability to procure future contracts?
- Cost
  - What is causing the cost overrun?
  - What can be done to reduce the remaining costs?
  - Will the customer accept an additional charge?
  - Should we absorb the extra cost?
  - Can we renegotiate the time or performance standards to stay within cost?
  - Are the budgeted costs for the remainder of the project accurate?
  - Will there be any net value gains for the increased funding?
  - Is this the only way to satisfy performance?
  - Will this hurt our company's ability to procure future contracts?
  - Is this the only way to maintain the schedule?
- Performance
  - Can the original specifications be met?
  - If not, at what cost can we guarantee compliance?
  - Are the specifications negotiable?
  - What are the advantages to the company and customer for specification changes?
  - What are the disadvantages to the company and customer for performance changes?
  - Are we increasing or decreasing performance?
  - Will the customer accept a change?
  - Will there be a product or employee liability incurred?
  - Will the change in specifications cause a redistribution of project resources?
  - Will this change hurt our company's ability to procure future contracts?

Once the answers to the above questions are obtained, it is often best to plot the results graphically. Graphical methods have been used during the past two decades to determine "crashing" costs for shortening the length of a project.

To use the graphical techniques, we must decide upon which of the three parameters to hold fixed.

Situation 1: Performance Is Held Constant (to Specifications)

With performance fixed, cost can be expressed as a function of time. Sample curves appear in Figures 16–7 and 16–8. In Figure 16–7, the circled X indicates the target cost and target time. Unfortunately, the cost to complete the project at the target time is higher than the budgeted cost. It may be possible to add resources and work overtime so that the time target can be met. Depending upon the way that overtime is burdened, it may be possible to find a minimum point in the curve where further delays will cause the total cost to escalate.

Curve A in Figure 16–8 shows the case where "time is money," and any additional time will increase the cost to complete. Factors such as management support time will always increase the cost to complete. There are, however, some situations where the increased costs occur in plateaus. This is shown in Curve B of Figure 16–8. This could result from having to wait for temperature conditioning of a component before additional work can be completed, or simply waiting for nonscheduled resources to be available. In the latter case, the trade-off decision points may be at the end of each plateau.

With performance fixed, there are four methods available for constructing and analyzing the time/cost curves:

- Additional resources may be required. This will usually drive up the cost very fast. Assuming that the resources are available, cost control problems can occur as a result of adding resources after initial project budgeting.
- The scope of work may be redefined and some work deleted without changing the project performance requirements. Performance standards may have been set too high, or the probability of success demanded of the project team may have been simply unrealistic. Reductions in cost and improvements in schedules would typically result from relaxing performance specifications, provided that the lower quality level will still meet the requirements of the customer.
- Available resources may be shifted in order to balance project costs or to speed up activities that are on the "critical" path work element that is trailing. This process of replanning shifts elements from noncritical to critical activities.
- Given a schedule problem, a change in the logic diagram may be needed to move from the current position to the desired position. Such a change could easily result in the replanning and reallocation of resources. An example of this would be to convert from "serial" to "parallel" work efforts. This often requires that a large risk be incurred.

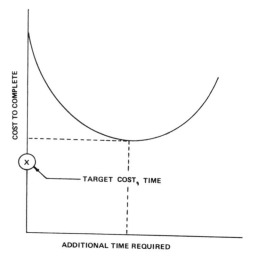

Figure 16–7. Trade-offs with fixed performance.

Trade-offs with fixed performance levels must take into account the dependence of the firm on the customer, priority of the project within the firm, and potential for future business. A basic assumption here is that the firm may never sacrifice its reputation by delivering a product that performs to less than the specifications called for. The exception might be a recommended engineer-

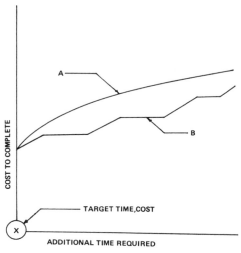

Figure 16–8. Trade-offs with fixed performance.

ing change that would enhance performance capability to such a degree that the scope change would allow the contractor to pull the project back on schedule. This is always worth investigating before entering into time/cost tradeoffs.

Time and cost are interrelated in a labor-intensive project. As delivery slips, cost growth usually occurs. Slipping delivery schedules and minimizing cost growth through the use of overtime usually constitute the recommended alternative for projects in which the dependence of the firm on the customer, the priority of the project within the firm's stream of projects, and the future business potential in terms of sales represent a low- to medium-risk area. Even in some high-risk situations, the contractor may have to absorb the additional cost himself. This decision is often based upon estimating the future projects from this customer so that the loss is amortized against future business. Not all projects are financial successes.

A company's reputation for excellence is often hard to establish and can be extremely fragile. It is probably a contractor's greatest asset. This is particularly true in high-liability contracts, where the consequences of failure are extremely serious. There are companies that have been very successful in aerospace and advanced technology contracting but have seldom been the low bidder. Where the government is the contractor, performance is rated far above cost. An example here would be contracting for the U.S. Navy's nuclear reactor components. The costs incurred in the Navy's work could not be tolerated in commercial nuclear reactor components. (This has been true, but after the Three Mile Island incident, commercial nuclear energy interests may have to adopt the higher standards of quality and reliability—and cost—that characterize the Navy's nuclear energy programs.)

The consequences of a commercial aircraft crash are of such magnitude that cost and time are relatively insignificant compared with precision manufacturing and extremely high reliability. As fuel costs rise, demands become even more stringent, with efficiency assuming greater importance along with the already extremely high reliability requirements.

Sometimes projects may have fixed time and costs, leaving only the performance variable for trade-offs. However, as shown in the following scenario, the eventual outcome may be to modify the "fixed" cost constraint.

The hypothetical situation involves a government hardware subcontract, fixed-price, with delivery to the major government contractor. The major contractor had a very tight schedule, and the hardware being supplied had only a one-week "window" in which to be delivered, or the major contractor would suffer a major delay. Any delay at this point would place the general contractor in serious trouble. Both the government contracting officer and the purchasing manager of the general contractor had "emphasized" the importance of making the delivery schedule. There was no financial penalty for being late, but the contracting officer had stated in writing that any follow-on contracts, which were heavily counted upon by the company top management, would be placed with other vendors if delivery was not made on time.

Quality (performance) was critical but had never been a serious problem. In fact, performance had exceeded the contractual requirements because it had been company policy to be the "best" in the industry. This policy had, at times, caused cost problems, but it had ensured follow-on orders.

This project was in trouble at the halfway point, three months into the six-month schedule. The latest progress report indicated that the delivery would be delayed by three weeks. Costs were on target to date, but the shipping delay was expected to result in extra costs that would amount to 20 percent of the planned profit.

The project got off schedule when the flow of raw materials from a major vendor was interrupted for three weeks by a quality problem that was not discovered until the material was placed in production. Since the manufacturing time was process-controlled, it was very difficult to make up lost time.

The first decision was that everything possible would be done to make delivery within one week of the original schedule. The potential lost revenue from future orders was so great that delivery must be made "at all costs," to quote the company president.

The quality system was then thoroughly investigated. It appeared that by eliminating two redundant inspection operations, one week could be saved in the total schedule. These two time-consuming inspection operations had been added when a quality problem developed on a former contract. The problem had been solved, and with present controls there was no reason to believe the inspections were still necessary. They would be eliminated with no determinable risk in performance.

Another two weeks were made up by working three production people seven days a week for the remainder of the project. This would permit delivery on the specified date of the contract, and would allow one week for other unforeseen problems so there would be a high probability of delivery within the required "window."

The cost of the seven-day-per-week work had the net effect of reducing the projected profit by 40 percent. Eliminating the two inspection operations saved 10 percent of the profit.

The plan outlined above met the time and performance specifications with increased cost that eventually reduced profit by an estimated 30 percent. The key to this situation was that only the labor, material, and overhead costs of the project were fixed, and the contractor was willing to accept a reduced profit.

Situation 2: Cost Is Fixed

With cost fixed, performance will vary as a function of time, as shown in Figure 16-9. The decision of whether or not to adhere to the target schedule data is

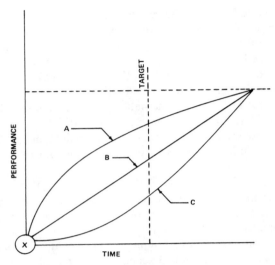

Figure 16–9. Trade-offs with fixed cost.

usually determined by the level of performance. In Curve A, performance may increase rapidly to the 90 percent level at the beginning of the project. A 10 percent increase in time may give a 20 percent increase in performance. After a certain point, a 10 percent increase in time may give only a 1 percent increase in performance. The company may not wish to risk the additional time necessary to attain the 100 percent performance level if it is possible to do so. In Curve C, the additional time must be sacrificed because it is unlikely that the customer will be happy with a 30 to 40 percent performance level. Curve B is the most difficult curve to analyze unless the customer has specified exactly which level of performance will be acceptable.

If cost is fixed, then it is imperative that the project have a carefully worded and understood contract with clear specifications as to the required level of performance and very clear statements of inclusion and exclusion. Careful attention to costs incurred because of customer changes or additional requirements can help reduce the possibility of a cost overrun. Experience in contracting ensures that costs that may be overlooked by the inexperienced project manager are included. Careful and skillful negotiations going in are essential to have all costs included in the contract and hopefully minimize the need for such trade-offs downstream. Common items that are often overlooked and can drive up costs include:

- Excessive detailed reporting
- Unnecessary documentation

- Excessive tracking documentation for time, cost, and performance
- Detailed specification development for equipment that could be purchased externally for less cost
- Wrong type of contract for this type of project

Often with a fixed-cost constraint, the first item that is sacrificed to meet that constraint is performance. But such an approach to trade-offs can contain hidden disasters over the life of a project if those performance specifications that were given up prove to have been essential to meeting some unspecified requirement such as long-term maintenance. In the long run, a degraded performance can actually increase costs rather than decrease them. Therefore, the project manager and his assistants should be sure they have a good analysis and understanding of the real costs associated with any trade-offs in performance.

Situation 3: Time Is Fixed

Figure 16–10 identifies the situation in which time is fixed and cost varies with performance. Figure 16–10 is similar to Figure 16–9 in that the rate of change of performance with cost is the controlling factor. If performance is at the 90

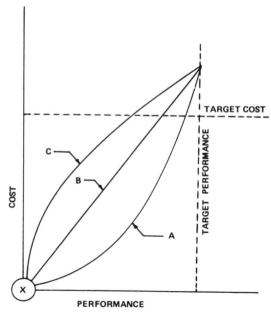

Figure 16–10. Trade-offs with fixed time.

percent level with the target cost, then the contractor may request performance relief. This is shown in Curve A. However, if the actual situation reflects Curve B or C, additional costs must be incurred with the same considerations of Situation 1—namely, how important is the customer and what emphasis should be placed upon his follow-on business?

Completing the project on schedule can be extremely important in certain cases. For example, if an aircraft pump is not delivered when the engine is ready for shipment, it can hold up the engine manufacturer, the airframe manufacturer, and ultimately the customer. All three can incur substantial losses due to the delay of a single component. Moreover, customers who are unable to perform and who incur large unanticipated costs tend to have long memories. An irate vice-president at a high level in the customer's shop can kill further contracts out of all proportion to the real failure to deliver on time.

Sometimes, even though time is supposedly fixed, there may be latitude without inconvenience to the customer. This could come about because the entire program (of which your project is just one subcontract) is behind schedule, and the customer is not ready for your particular project.

Another aspect of the time factor is that "early warning" of a time overrun can often mitigate the damage to the customer and greatly increase his favorable response. Careful planning and tracking, close coordination with all functions involved, and realistic dealing with time schedules before and during the project can ensure early notification to the customer and the possible negotiation of a trade-off of time and dollars or even technical performance. The last thing that a customer ever wants is to have a favorable progress report right up to the end of scheduled time and then to be surprised with a serious schedule overrun.

When time is fixed, the customer may find that he has some flexibility in determining how to arrive at the desired performance level. As shown in Figure 16–11, the contractor may be willing to accept additional costs to maximize employee safety.

Situation 4: No Constraints Are Fixed

Another common situation is that in which neither time, cost, nor performance is fixed. The best method for graphically showing the trade-off relationships is to develop parametric curves as in Figure 16–12. Cost and time trade-offs can now be analyzed for various levels of performance. The curves can also be redrawn for various cost levels (i.e., 100, 120, 150 percent of target cost) and schedule levels.

Another method for showing a family of curves is illustrated in Figure 16–13. Here, the contractor may have several different cost paths for achieving the desired time and performance constraints. The final path selected depends upon the size of the risk that the contractor wishes to take.

Figure 16–11. Performance vs. cost.

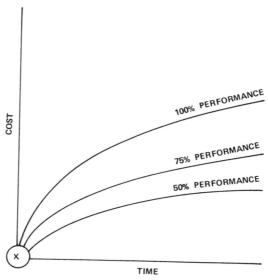

Figure 16–12. Trade-off analysis with family of curves.

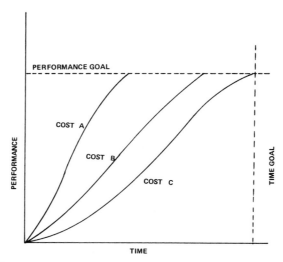

Figure 16–13. Cost/time/performance family of curves.

There have been several attempts to display the three-dimensional trade-off problem graphically. Unfortunately, such a procedure is quite complex and difficult to follow. A more common approach is to use some sort of computer model and handle the trade-off as though it were a linear programming or dynamic programming problem. This too is often difficult to perform and manage.

Trade-offs can also be necessary at any point in time during the life cycle of a project. It is quite possible, and probable, for the criteria for the trade-offs to change over the life cycle of the project. Figure 16–14 identifies how the relative importance of the constraints of time, cost, and performance can change over the life cycle of the project. At project initiation, costs may not have accrued to a point where they are important. On the other hand, project performance may very well be overstressed until it becomes even more important than the schedule. At this point, additional performance can be "bought." As the project nears termination, the relative importance of the cost constraint may increase drastically, especially if project profits are the company's major source of revenue. Likewise, it is probable that the impact of performance and schedule will be lower.

Once the alternative courses of action are determined, Step 5 in the methodology is employed in order to analyze and select the feasible alternatives. Analyzing the alternatives should include the preparation of the revised project objectives for cost, performance, and time, along with an analysis of the required resources, general schedules, and revised project plans necessary to support each scenario. It is then the function of top management in conjunction

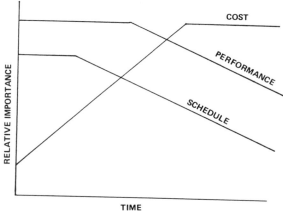

Figure 16–14. Life-cycle trade-offs. (Schedule not necessarily typical.)

with the project and functional managers to choose the solution that minimizes the overall impact to the company. This impact need not be measured just in short-term financial results, but should also include long-term strategic and market considerations.

The following tasks can be included in this step:

- Prepare a formal project update report including alternative work scopes, schedules, and costs to achieve:
  - Minimum cost overrun
  - Conformance to project objectives
  - Minimum schedule overrun
- Construct a decision tree including costs, work objectives, and schedules, and an estimate of the probability of success for each condition leading to the decision point.
- Present to internal and external project management the several alternatives along with an estimate of success probability.
- With management's agreement, select the appropriate completion strategy, and begin implementation. This assumes that management does not insist on an impossible task.

The last item requires further clarification. Many companies use a checklist to establish the criteria for alternative evaluation as well as for assessment of potential future problems. The following questions may be part of such a checklist:

- Will other projects be affected?
- Will rework be required in previous tasks?

- Are repair and/or maintenance made more difficult?
- Will additional tasks be required in the future?
- How will project personnel react?
- What is the effect on the project life cycle?
- Will project flexibility be reduced?
- What is the effect on key employees?
- What is the effect on the customer(s)?

The probability of occurrence and severity should be assessed for all potential future problems. If there is a high probability that the problem will recur and a high probability that the severity will be critical, a plan should be developed to reduce the probability of recurrence and severity. Internal restrictions such as manpower, materials, machines, money, management, time, policies, quality, and changing requirements can cause problems throughout the life cycle of a project. External restrictions of capital, completion dates, and liability also limit project flexibility.

One of the best methods for comparing the alternatives is to list them and then rank them in order of perceived importance relative to certain factors such as customer, potential follow-on business, cost deficit, and loss of good will. This is shown in Table 16–2. In the table each of the objectives is weighted according to some method established by management. The percentages represent the degree of satisfactory completion for each alternative. This type of analysis, often referred to as decision making under risk, is commonly taught in operations research and management science coursework. Weighing factors are often used to assist in the decision-making process. Unfortunately, this can add mass confusion to the already confused process.

Table 16–3 shows that some companies perform trade-off analysis by equat-

Table 16–2. Weighing the Alternatives.

OBJECTIVES / WEIGHTS	INCREASE FUTURE BUSINESS	READY ON TIME	MEET CURRENT COST	MEET CURRENT SPECS	MAXIMIZE PROFITS
ALTERNATIVES	0.4	0.25	0.10	0.20	.05
Add resources	100%	90%	30%	90%	10%
Reduce scope of work	60%	90%	90%	30%	95%
Request specification change	90%	80%	95%	5%	80%
Complete project late	80%	0%	20%	95%	0%
Bill customer for added cost	30%	85%	0%	60%	95%

Table 16-3. Trade-off Analysis for Improving Project Performance Capability.

ASSUMPTION	DESCRIPTION	CAPITAL EXPENDITURE $	TIME TO COMPLETE, MOS.	PROJECT PROFIT, $	RANKING IN PROFIT $
1	No change	0	6	100,000	5
2	Hire higher-salaried people	0	5	105,000	3
3	Refurbish equipment	10,000	7	110,000	2
4	Purchase new equipment	85,000	9	94,000	6
5	Change specifications	0	6	125,000	1
6	Subcontract	0	6	103,000	4

ing all alternatives to a lowest common denominator, dollars. Although this conversion can be very difficult, it does ensure that we are comparing "apples with apples." All resources such as capital equipment can be expressed in terms of dollars. Difficulties arise in assigning dollar values to such items as environmental pollution, safety standards, or the possible loss of life.

There are often several types of corrective action that can be utilized. Below are several examples:

- Overtime
- Double shifts
- Expediting
- Additional manpower
- More money
- Change of vendors
- Change of specifications
- Shift of project resources
- Waiving equipment inspections
- Change in statement of work
- Change in work breakdown structure
- Substitution of equipment
- Substitution of materials
- Use of outside contractors
- Providing bonus payments to contractors

- Single-sourcing
- Waiving drawing approvals

The corrective actions defined above can be used for time, cost, and performance. However, there are specific alternatives for each area. Assuming that a PERT/CPM analysis was done initially to schedule the project, then the following options are available for schedule manipulation:

- Prioritize all tasks and see the effect on the critical path of eliminating low-priority efforts.
- Use resource leveling.
- Carry the work breakdown structure to one more level, and reassess the time estimates for each task.

Performance trade-offs can be obtained as follows:

- Excessive or tight specifications that are not critical to the project may be eased. (Many times standard specifications such as mil-specs are used without regard for their necessity.)
- Requirements for testing can be altered to accommodate automation (such as accelerated life testing) to minimize costs.
- Set an absolute minimum acceptable performance requirement below which you will not pursue the project. This gives a bound at the low end of performance that can't be crossed in choosing between trade-off alternatives.
- Only give up those performance requirements that have little or no bearing on the overall project goals (including implied goals) and their achievement. This may require the project manager to itemize and prioritize major and minor objectives.
- Consider absorbing tasks with dedicated project office personnel. This is a resource trade-off that can be effective when the tasks to be performed require in-depth knowledge of the project. An example would be the use of dedicated project personnel to perform information gathering on rehabilitation-type projects. The improved performance of these people in the design and testing phases due to their strong background can save considerable time and effort.

The most promising areas for cost analysis include:

- Incremental costing (using sensitivity analysis)
- Reallocation of resources

- Material substitution where lower-cost materials are utilized without changing project specifications

Depending upon the magnitude of the problem, the timeliness of its identification, and the potential impact on the project results, it may be that no actions exist that will bring the project in on time, within budget, and at an acceptable level of performance. The following viable alternatives usually remain:

- A renegotiation of project performance criteria could be attempted with the project sponsor. Such action would be based upon a pragmatic view of the acceptability of the probable outcome. Personal convenience of the project manager is not a factor. Professional and legal liability for the project manager, project team, or parent organization may be very real concerns.
- If renegotiation is not considered a viable alternative, or if it is rejected, the only remaining option is to "stop loss" in completing the project. Such planning should involve both line and project management, since the parent organization is at this point seeking to defend itself. Options include:
  - Completing the project on schedule, to the minimum quality level required by the project sponsor. This results in cost overruns (financial loss) but should produce a reasonably satisfied project sponsor. (Project sponsors are not really comfortable when they know a project team is operating in a "stop loss" mode!)
  - Controlling costs and performance, but permitting the schedule to slide. The degree of unhappiness this generates with the project sponsor will be determined by the specific situation. Risks include loss of future work or consequential damages.
  - Maintaining schedule and cost performance by allowing quality to slip. This high-risk approach has a low probability of achieving total success and a high probability of achieving total failure. Quality work done on the project will be lost if the final results are below minimum standards.
  - Seeking to achieve desired costs, schedule, and performance results in the light of impossible circumstances. This approach "hopes" that the inevitable won't happen, and offers the opportunity to fail simultaneously in all areas. Criminal liability could become an issue.
  - Project cancellation, in an effort to limit exposure beyond that already encountered. This approach might terminate the career of a project manager but could enhance the career of the staff counsel!

The sixth and final step in the methodology in the management of project trade-offs is to obtain management approval and replan the project. The project manager usually identifies the alternatives and prepares his recommendation. He then submits his recommendation to top management for approval. Top-management involvement is necessary because the project manager may try to make corrective action in a vacuum. Top management normally makes decisions based upon the following:

- The firm's policies on quality, integrity, and image
- The ability to develop a long-term client relationship
- Type of project (R&D, modernization, new product)
- Size and complexity of the project
- Other projects under way or planned
- Company's cash flow
- Bottom line—ROI
- Competitive risks
- Technical risks
- Impact on affiliated organizations

After choosing a new course of action from the list of alternatives, management and especially the project team must focus upon achieving the revised objectives. This may require a detailed replanning of the project, including new schedules, PERT Charts, work breakdown structures, and other key benchmarks. The entire management team (i.e., top management, functional managers, and project managers) must all be committed to achieving the revised project plan.

16.2 CONTRACTS: THEIR INFLUENCE ON PROJECTS

The final decision on whether to trade-off cost, time, or performance can vary depending upon the type of contract. Table 16–4 identifies seven common types of contracts and the order in which trade-offs will be made.

The Firm-Fixed-Price Contract. Time, cost, and performance are all specified within the contract, and all are the contractor's responsibility. Because all constraints are equally important with respect to this type of contract, the sequence of resources sacrificed is the same as for the project-driven organization shown previously in Table 16–1.

The Fixed-Price-Incentive-Fee Contract. Cost is measured to determine the incentive fee, and thus is the last constraint to be considered for trade-off. Because performance is usually more important than schedule for project completion, time is considered the first constraint for trade-off, and performance is the second.

The Cost-Plus-Incentive-Fee Contract. The costs are reimbursed and measured for determination of the incentive fee. Thus, cost is the last constraint to

Table 16–4. Sequence of Resources Sacrificed Based upon Type of Contract.

	FIRM-FIXED PRICE (FFP)	FIXED-PRICE INCENTIVE FEE (FPIF)	COST CONTRACT	COST SHARING	COST PLUS INCENTIVE FEE (CPIF)	COST PLUS AWARD FEE (CPAF)	COST PLUS FIXED FEE (CPFF)
TIME	2	1	2	2	1	2	2
COST	1	3	3	3	3	1	1
PERFORMANCE	3	2	1	1	2	3	3

1 = first to be sacrificed.
2 = second to be sacrificed.
3 = third to be sacrificed.

be considered for trade-off. As with the FPIF contract, performance is usually more important than schedule for project completion, and so the sequence is the same as for the FPIF contract.

The Cost-Plus-Award-Fee Contract. The costs are reimbursed to the contractor, but the award fee is based on performance by the contractor. Thus, cost would be the first constraint to be considered for trade-off, and performance would be the last constraint to be considered.

The Cost-Plus-Fixed-Fee Contract. Cost are reimbursed to the contractor. Thus, cost would be the first constraint to be considered for trade-off. Although there are no incentives for efficiency in time or performance, there may be penalties for bad performance. Thus, time is the second constraint to be considered for trade-off, and performance is the third.

16.3 INDUSTRY TRADE-OFF PREFERENCES

Table 16–5 identifies twenty-one industries that were surveyed on their preferential process for trade-offs. Obviously, there are external variables that affect each decision. The data in the table reflect the interviewees' general responses, neglecting external considerations. External variables probably would alter the order of preference. For example, plastics manufacturing rated performance the first choice for trade-offs. This assumes that a low-liability item is being manufactured. Utilities rated cost as the last item for trade-off, whereas prior to 1970, performance would have been the last item, with cost ranking second.

Table 16–6 shows the relative grouping of Table 16–5 into four categories; project-driven, non-project-driven, nonprofit, and banks.

In all projects in the banking industry, whether regulated or nonregulated,

Table 16–5. Industry General Preference for Trade-offs.

INDUSTRY	TIME	COST	PERFORMANCE
Construction	1*	3	2
Chemical	2	1	3
Electronics	2	3	1
Automotive manu.	2	1	3
Data processing	2	1	3
Government	2	1	3
Health (nonprofit)	2	3	1
Medicine (profit)	1	3	2
Nuclear	2	1	3
Manu. (plastics)	2	3	1
Manu. (metals)	1	2	3
Consulting (mgt.)	2	1	3
Consulting (eng.)	3	1	2
Office products	2	1	3
Machine tool	2	1	3
Oil	2	1	3
Primary batteries	1	3	2
Utilities	1	3	2
Aerospace	2	1	3
Retailing	3	2	1
Banking	2	1	3

*1 indicates parameter to be sacrificed first.

Table 16–6. Special Cases.

	TYPE OF ORGANIZATION					
	PROJECT-DRIVEN ORGANIZATIONS				BANKS	
	EARLY LIFE-CYCLE PHASES	LATE LIFE-CYCLE PHASES	NON-PROJECT-DRIVEN ORGANIZATIONS	NONPROFIT ORGANIZATIONS	LEADER	FOLLOWER
TIME	2	1	1	2	3	2
COST	1	3	3	3	1	1
PERFORMANCE	3	2	2	1	2	3

cost is the first resource to be sacrificed. The major reason for this trade-off is that banks in general do not have a quantitative estimation of what actual costs they incur in providing a given service. One example of this phenomenon is that a number of commercial banks heavily emphasize the use of *Functional Cost Analysis,* a publication of the Federal Reserve, for pricing their services. This publication is a summary of data received from member banks, of which the user is one. This results in questionable output because of inaccuracies of the input.

In cases where federal regulations prescribe time constraints, cost is the only resource of consideration, since performance standards are also delineated by regulatory bodies.

In nonregulated banking projects the next resource to be sacrificed depends upon the competitive environment. When other competitors have developed a new service or product that a particular bank does not yet offer, then the resource of time will be less critical than the performance criteria. A specific case in point is the development of the automatic teller machine (ATM). After the initial introduction of the system by some banks (leaders), the remainder of the competitors (followers) chose to provide a more advanced ATM with little consideration for the time involved for procurement and installation. On the other hand, with the introduction of negotiable order of withdrawal (NOW) accounts, the January 1, 1981 change in federal regulations allowed banks and savings and loans to offer interest-bearing checking accounts. The ensuing scramble to offer the service by that date led to varying performance levels, especially on the part of savings and loans. In this instance the competitors sacrificed performance in order to provide a timely service.

In some banking projects, the time factor is extremely important. A number of projects depend on federal laws. The date that a specific law goes into effect sets the deadline for the project.

Generally, in a nonprofit organization, performance is the first resource that will be compromised. The United Way, free clinics, March of Dimes, American Cancer Society, and Goodwill are among the many nonprofit agencies that serve community needs. They derive their income from donations and/or federal grants, and this funding mechanism places a major constraint on their operations. Cost overruns are prohibited by the very nature of the organization.

For example, the services offered by a free clinic are dependent upon the quality and expertise of the physicians it can attract. Usually two major types of doctors will work at such a clinic. The first group includes young, inexperienced doctors who are using the clinic as a vehicle for gaining needed practical experience and exposure in the community, whereas the second group includes established physicians who feel morally obligated to render services to the needy. Because of inexperience and time constraints, the two groups provide services that often fall short of the quality obtainable from private medical practices. Additionally, much of the medical equipment bought or received by the clinic is inferior to what can be found in medical centers.

The time resource is compromised again in the area of customer service. The free clinic will require its clerical and medical staff to work longer hours to obtain a performance level that could be achieved in a shorter period of time in a private medical facility. The inexperience of the staff and lack of funds necessitate the time trade-off.

The non-project-driven organization is structured along the lines of the traditional vertical hierarchy. Functional managers in areas such as marketing, engineering, accounting, and sales are involved in planning, organizing, staffing, and controlling their functional areas. Many projects that materialize, specifically in a manufacturing concern, are a result of a need to improve a product or process and can be initiated by customer request, competitive climate, or internal operations.

The first resource to be sacrificed in the non-project-driven organization is time, followed by performance and cost, respectively. The Battery Products Division of a major corporation is a non-project-driven organization that in 1980 became involved in a plant expansion program. In response to the economic downturn which affected market conditions, the facility expansion was delayed.

In most manufacturing concerns, budgetary constraints outweigh performance criteria. The proposed expansion described above now specifies less floor space and less sophisticated machinery, resulting in decreased production capacity (decreased performance).

In a non-project-driven organization, new projects will take a back seat to the day-to-day operations of the functional departments. The organizational funds are allocated to individual departments rather than to the project itself. When functional managers are required to maintain a certain productivity level in addition to supporting projects, their main emphasis will be on operations at the expense of project development. When it becomes necessary for the firm to curtail costs, special projects will be deleted in order to maintain corporate profit margins.

Resource trade-offs in a project-driven organization depend upon the life-cycle phase of a given project. During the conceptual, definition, and production phases and into the operational phase of the project, the trade-off priorities are cost first, then time, and finally performance. In these early planning phases the project is being designed to meet certain performance and time standards. At this point the cost estimates are based on the figures supplied to the project manager by the functional managers.

During the operational phase the cost factor increases in importance over time and performance, both of which begin to decrease. In this phase the organization attempts to recover its investment in the project and therefore emphasizes cost control. The performance standards may have been compromised, and the project may be behind schedule, but management will analyze the cost figures to judge the success of the project.

The project-driven organization is unique in that the resource trade-offs may vary in priority, depending upon the specific project. Research and development projects may have a fixed performance level, whereas construction projects normally are constrained by a date of completion.

16.4 CONCLUSION

It is obvious from the above discussion that a project manager does have options to control a project during its execution. Project managers must be willing to control minor trade-offs as well as major ones. However, the availability of specific options is a function of the particular project environment.

Probably the greatest contribution a project manager makes to a project team organization is through the stability he can impart as adverse conditions are encountered. Interpersonal relationships have a great deal to do with the alternatives available and their probability of success. Normally, solution of a potential performance problem requires a team solution, since it is team performance that is demanded. Through a combination of management skill and sensitivity, project managers can make the trade-offs, encourage the team members, and reassure the project sponsor in order to produce a satisfactory project.

17
Project Management Software[1]

17.0 INTRODUCTION

Efficient project management requires more than good planning, it requires that relevant information be obtained, analyzed, and reviewed in a timely manner. This can provide early warning of pending problems and impact assessments on other activities, which can lead to alternate plans and management actions. Today, project managers have a large array of software available to help in the difficult task of tracking and controlling projects. While it is clear that even the most sophisticated software package is not substitute for competent project leadership—and by itself does not identify or correct any task-related problems—it can be a terrific aid to the project manager in tracking the many interrelated variables and tasks that come into play with a modern project. Specific examples of these capabilities are given below:

- Project data summary: expenditure, timing, and activity data
- Project management and business graphics capabilities
- Data management and reporting capabilities
- Critical path analysis
- Customized, as well as standard, reporting formats
- Multiproject tracking
- Subnetworking
- Impact analysis (what if . . .)
- Early warning systems
- On-line analysis of recovering alternatives
- Graphical presentation of cost, time, and activity data
- Resource planning and analysis
- Cost analysis, variance analysis

---

1. Sections 17.0 through 17.2 have been adapted from *Project Management Operating Guidelines: Policies, Procedures and Forms* by Harold Kerzner and Hans Thamhain. Copyright 1986 by Van Nostrand Reinhold Co., Inc., New York, 1986 pp. 475–483.

- Multiple calendars
- Resource leveling

Further, many of the more sophisticated software packages that, until the mid-1980s, needed mainframe computer support, are now available for personal computers. This offers many advantages ranging from true user interaction, to ready access and availability, to simpler and more user-friendly interfaces, to often considerably lower software cost. Yet the biggest impact might be to smaller businesses and projects that in the past could not afford the luxury of mainframe computers, but now have access to computer-aided project management systems.

17.1 SOFTWARE FEATURES OFFERED

Project management software capabilities and features vary a great deal among the many products available. However, the variation is more in the depth and sophistication of the feature, such as its storage, display, analysis, interoperability, and user friendliness, rather than in the type of features offered, which are very similar for most software programs. Specifically, the following features are being offered by most project management software packages:

1. Planning, Tracking and Monitoring.   These most common features provide for planning and tracking of the projects's tasks, resources, and costs. The data format for describing the project to the computer is usually based on standard network typologies such as the Critical Path Method (CPM), Program Evaluation and Review Technique (PERT), or Activity-on-Error Method (AEM). Task elements, with their estimated start and finish times, their assigned resources, and actual cost data can be entered and updated as the project progresses. The software provides an analysis of the data and documents the technical and financial status of the project against its schedule and original plan. Usually, the software also provides impact assessments of plan deviations and resource and schedule projections. Many systems also provide resource leveling, a feature that averages out available resources to determine task duration and generates a leveled schedule for comparison. The specific analysis reports are described next.
2. Reports.   Project reporting is usually achieved via a menu-driven report writer system which allows the user to request several standard reports in a standard format. The user can also modify these reports or create new ones. Depending on the sophistication of the system and its peripheral hardware, these reports are supported by a full range of Gantt charts, network diagrams, tabular summaries, and business graphics. A sample of reporting capabilities available today includes:

- Budgeted Cost for Work Scheduled (BCWS) Report
- Budgeted Cost for Work Performed (BCWP) Report
- Actual versus planned Expenditure Report
- Earned Value Analysis
- Cost and Schedule Performance Indices
- Cash-Flow Reports
- Critical Path Analysis
- Change Order Reports
- Standard Government Reports (DOD, DOE, NASA), formatted for the Performance Monitoring System (PMS)

In addition, many software packages feature a user-oriented, free format report writer for styled project reporting.

3. Project Calendar.   This feature allows the user to establish workweeks based on actual workdays. Hence, the user can specify nonwork periods such as weekends, holidays, and vacation. The project calendar can be printed out in detail or in a summary format and is automatically the basis for all computer-assisted resource scheduling.

4. What-If Analysis.   Some software is designed to make what-if analyses easy. A separate, duplicate project data base is established and the desired changes are entered. Then the software performs a comparative analysis and displays the new against the old project plan in tabular or graphical form for fast and easy management review and analysis.

5. Multi-Project Analysis.   Some of the more sophisticated software packages feature a single, comprehensive data base which facilitates cross-project analysis and reporting. Cost and schedule modules share common files which allow integration among projects and minimize problems of data inconsistencies and redundancies.

17.2 SOFTWARE CLASSIFICATION

For purposes of easy classification, project management software products have been divided into three catagories based on the type of functions and features they provide.[2]

Level I Software.   Designed for single project planning, these software packages are simple, easy to use, and their outputs are easy to understand. They do provide, however, only a limited analysis of the data. They do not provide automatic rescheduling based on specific changes. Therefore, deviations from

---

2. Some standards were initially set by PC Magazine, "Project Management with the PC," Volume 3, No. 24, December 11, 1984.

the original project plan require complete replanning of the project and a complete new data input to the computer.

Level II Software. Designed for single project management, these software packages aid project leaders in the planning, tracking, and reporting of projects. They provide a comprehensive analysis of the project, progress reports, and plan revisions, based on actual performance. This type of software is designed for managing projects beyond the planning stage, and for providing semiautomatic project control.

Level III Software. These packages feature multiproject planning, monitoring, and control by utilizing a common data base and sophisticated cross-project monitoring and reporting software.

Most software packages at level II and III have the following extensive capabilities for project monitoring and control:

1. System Capacity. The number of activities and/or number of sub-networks that may be used.
2. Network Schemes. The network schemes are activity diagram (AD) and/or precedence relationship (PRE).
3. Calendar Dates. An internal calendar is available to schedule the projects's activities. The variations and options of the different calendar algorithms are numerous.
4. Gantt or Bar Charts. A graphic display of the output on a time scale is available if desired.
5. Flexible Report Generator. The user can specify within defined guidelines the format of the output.
6. Updating. The program will accept revised time estimates and completion dates and recompute the revised schedule.
7. Cost Control. The program accepts budgeted cost figures for each activity and then the actual cost incurred, and summarizes the budgeted and actual figures on each updating run. The primary objective is to help management produce a realistic cost plan before the project is started and to assist in the control of the project expenditures as the work progresses.
8. Scheduled Dates. A date is specified for the completion of any of the activities for purposes of planning and control. The calculations are performed with these dates as constraints.
9. Sorting. The program lists the activities in a sequence specified by the user.
10. Resource Allocation. The program attempts to allocate resources optimally using one of many heuristic algorithms.
11. Plotter Availability. A plotter is available to plot the network diagram.
12. Machine Requirements. This is the minimum hardware memory requirement for the program (in units of bytes).

13. Cost. Indicates whether the program is sold and/or leased and the purchase price and/or lease price (where available).

For a detailed, up-to-date evaluation of project management software, the best available report appears to be the *Revision 1988 of Project Management Software Packages* by Francis M. Webster, Jr., Ph.D., distributed by the Project Management Institute, P.O. Box 43, Drexel Hill, PA, 19026 (215-622-1796).

17.3 PROJECT SOFTWARE EVALUATION

With perhaps more than 150 different software packages available for project management, software evaluation and selection can become a tedious process. Project-driven organizations seem to prefer the mainframe packages, whereas nonproject-driven organizations look for the smaller packages. Mainframe packages (with earned value modules) can cost $75,000–$130,000, whereas smaller packages can range from $300 to $3,000.

Table 17–1 identifies several of the critical factors for software evaluation. The item in Table 17–1 which the author considers as the most critical is visiting other buyers that have used the software package for at least six months or longer. This way, the limitations and benefits are readily apparent, and can accelerate the selection process.

Table 17–1. Software Evaluation Factors.

- Documentation
  - Is the software package well documented?
  - Are the instructions easy to learn and follow?
  - Is the overall package user-friendly?
- Vendor support
  - Will the vendor supply us with support if custom-designed features are necessary?
  - Will the vendor assist in package installation?
  - Will the vendor provide us with a list of other users in our area? Can we visit their sites and see the system in action?
  - Does the vendor have periodic user group meetings?
  - Does the vendor provide contact with users after sale of the software package?
  - Does the vendor update the software package? If so, how frequently and what is our cost for the upgraded package?
- Flexibility
  - Can the package handle multiple projects?
  - Does it have limitations on size, number of nodes or calendar dates?
  - Does it provide accurate tracking of progress?
  - Does the software require special hardware?

17.4 IMPLEMENTATION PROBLEMS

Generally speaking, mainframe software packages are more difficult to implement than smaller packages, because everyone is requested to use the same package, perhaps even the same way. The following are common difficulties during implementation:

- *Upper-level management may not like the reality of the output.*
  The output usually shows top management that more time and resources are needed than originally anticipated. This can also be a positive note for the project manager, who is forced to deal with severe resource constraints.
- *Upper-level management may not use the packages for planning, budgeting, and decision-making.*
  Upper-level personnel generally prefer the more traditional methods, or simply refuse to look at reality because of politics. As a result, the plans they submit to the board are based upon an eye-pleasing approach for quick acceptance, rather than reality.
- *Day-to-day project planners may not use the packages for their own projects.*
  Project managers often rely upon other planning methods and tools from previous assignments. They rely heavily upon instinct and trial and error.
- *Upper-level management may not demonstrate support and commitment to training.*
  On-going customized training is mandatory for successful implementation, even though each project may vary.
- *Use of mainframe software requires strong internal communications lines for support.*
  Managers who share resources must talk to one another continuously.
- *Clear, concise reports are lacking.*
  Large mainframe packages can generate volumes of data, even if the package has a report writer package.
- *Mainframe packages do not always provide for immediate turnabout of information.*
  This is often the result of not understanding how to utilize the new systems.
- *The business entity may not have any project management standards in place prior to implementation.*
  This relates to a lack of WBS numbering schemes, no life-cycle phases, and a poor understanding of task dependencies.
- *Implementation may highlight middle-management's inexperience in project planning and organizational skills.*
  Fear of its use is a key factor in not obtaining proper support.

- *The business environment and organizational structure may not be appropriate to meet project management/planning needs.*
  If extensive sharing of resources exists, then the organizational structure should be a formal or informal matrix. If the organization is deeply entrenched in a traditional structure, then organizational mismatch exists and the software system may not be accepted.
- *Sufficient/extensive resources (staff, equipment, etc.) are required.*
  Large mainframe packages consume a significant amount of resources in the implementation phase.
- *The business entity must determine the extent of, and appropriate use of, the systems within the organization.*
  Should it be used by all organizations? Should it be used only on high-priority projects?
- *The system may be viewed as a substitute for the extensive interpersonal skills required by the project manager.*
  Software systems do not replace the need for project managers with strong communications and negotiation skills.
- *Software implementation is less likely to succeed if the organization does not have sufficient training in project management principles.*
  This barrier is perhaps the underlying problem for all of the other barriers.

17.5 MIS REQUIREMENTS

The basic requirements for a project management information system are:

- Each project leader updates his project on a monthly basis utilizing standardized project management forms or software entry.
- The project leader manually derives the information needed to measure the progress of the project from the computerized reporting systems.
- The project leader then reviews his project plans and predicts the required dollars by week or month to complete the project.
- The project leader analyzes the reasons in the exception report.
- The exception reports are then printed for distribution.

One can argue that the forms shown in Figures 17–1 through 17–3 satisfy the above basic requirements, although most of these forms are labor-intensive. These forms are manually generated, but are restricted mainly to non-project-driven organizations. Most project-driven organizations have a strong need for computerized, rather than manual, project management information systems. Today, minicomputers and PCs have allowed companies to overcome such present system shortcomings as:

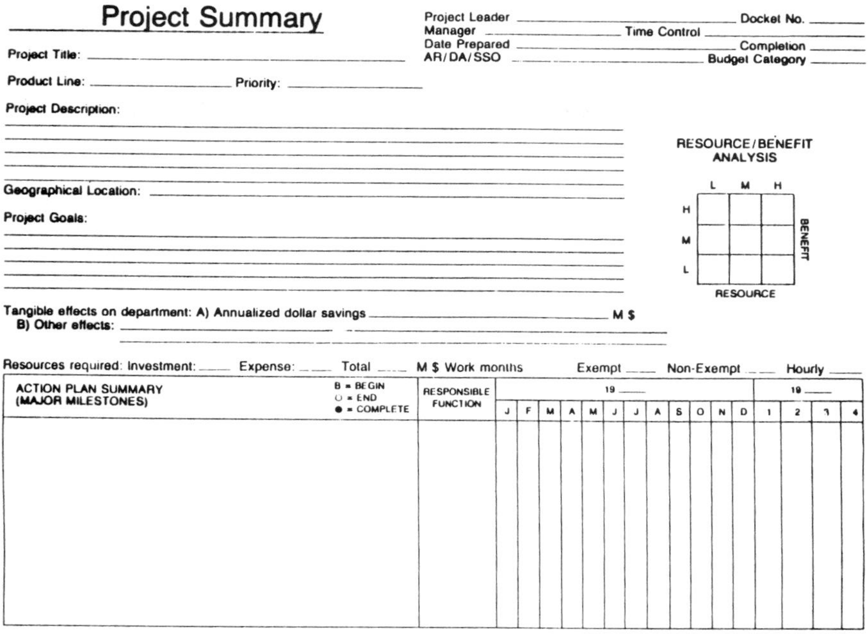

Project Summary

Project Leader ______ Docket No. ______
Manager ______ Time Control ______
Date Prepared ______ Completion ______
AR/DA/SSO ______ Budget Category ______

Project Title: ______

Product Line: ______ Priority: ______

Project Description: ______

Geographical Location: ______

Project Goals: ______

RESOURCE/BENEFIT ANALYSIS

	L	M	H
H			
M			
L			

BENEFIT

RESOURCE

Tangible effects on department: A) Annualized dollar savings ______ M $
B) Other effects: ______

Resources required: Investment: ____ Expense: ____ Total ____ M $ Work months Exempt ____ Non-Exempt ____ Hourly ____

ACTION PLAN SUMMARY (MAJOR MILESTONES) B = BEGIN ○ = END ● = COMPLETE	RESPONSIBLE FUNCTION	19 ____												19 ____			
		J	F	M	A	M	J	J	A	S	O	N	D	1	2	3	4

Figure 17–1. Project summary.

- Not being up-to-date
- Labor-intensiveness
- Inconsistent information
- All pertinent information not being exchanged
- Lack of commitment by user groups and executives

Applications software, which formerly was restricted by cost considerations to megacorporations, has been scaled down to the smaller computer systems and is now more readily available to small organizations. Thus, it is possible for small companies today to achieve objectives (through computerization) that may not have been possible just a few years ago. Such new system objectives (which are obviously impacted by computer technology) might include:

- More uniform procedures for orderly completion of projects
- Communication to all involved of their role and project status
- Better upper-management direction for setting realistic and challenging priorities

Detail Plan

Project Leader _____ Page ____ of ____
Date Prepared _____ Docket No. ____
Project Title: _____   AR/DA/SSO _____ Time Control ____

			RESOURCE AGREEMENT																				
FUNCTIONAL TASKS:	B – BEGIN U – END	X – CHANGE ● – COMPLETED	PERSON	DAYS REQ'D	MGR INIT	_19_												_19_			
						J	F	M	A	M	J	J	A	S	O	N	D	1	2	3	4

Figure 17–2. Detail plan.

- Better middle-management resource allocation
- More efficient project management
- Ability to streamline the current performance appraisal system
- Reduced project cost overruns and schedule misses
- Simplification of the numbering system
- Ability to secure better commitments from line managers for the allocation of human resources

The optimum project management information system may be described as follows:

- Existing information systems
  - Human resources
  - Financial resources
  - Material resources
- Direct entry of data is via terminals with CRTs.
- Individual reports may be generated for other than project management needs.

Project Analysis

Project Title:			

PROJECT LEADER _____ DOCUMENT NO. ____
MANAGER _____ TIME CONTROL ____
*DATE THIS REPORT _____ AR/DA/SSO ____

ACTION PLAN SUMMARY (MAJOR MILESTONES)	B - BEGIN X - CHANGED ⊔ - END ● - COMPLETED	RESPONSIBLE FUNCTION	J	F	M	A	M	J	J	A	S	O	N	D	1	2	3	4

PLANT & EQUIPMENT EXPENDITURES: TOTALS M$ _____ M$ _____   INVESTMENT / EXPENSES

Planned Completion Date _____ Revised _____   Revised _____ Revised _____

RESOURCE TRACKING: EXCEPTION REPORT

ACTUAL % OF TOTAL PLANNED*

Planned	10 20 30 40 50 60 70 80 90 100 110 120
Exempt Hrs.	
N. Exempt Hrs.	
Hourly Hrs.	
M$ Investment	
M$ Expense	
M$ Material	

Figure 17–3. Project analysis.

- Information is formulated along with estimates supplied by the project leader to display a current summary, plan, and analysis on the CRT and/or as a hard copy (i.e., with computer graphics, possibly color-coded).
- The program administrator or management can request updated information for decision making and subsequent reporting at any time and have a CRT display and/or a hard copy. (Information will be current to within the past twenty-four hours.)
- Additional reports could be generated from this information, such as facilities scheduling, design services scheduling, or manufacturing engineering work planning.
- Project plans can be transferred by project leaders to line managers via a CRT to get their commitment for human resources.
- The system will have the capability to access pertinent central files.
- The system will have the capability for data correction at the original source, thus reducing the labor required.

17–1 Would you be willing to attack or defend the following two statements:

A. In today's society, computers plan and control projects, rather than the project manager and his staff.

B. Too many young project managers believe that their role is one of sitting in front of a small screen in which the entire project effort can be seen and evaluated in support of their decision-making responsibilities.

CASE STUDY: MARGO COMPANY

"I've called this meeting, gentlemen, because that paper factory we call a computer organization is driving up our overhead rates," snorted Richard Margo, president, as he looked around the table at the vice-presidents of project management, engineering, manufacturing, marketing, administration, and information systems. "We seem to be developing reports faster than we can update our computer facility. Just one year ago, we updated our computer and now we're operating three shifts a day, seven days a week. Where do we go from here?"

V.P. Information: "As you all know, Richard asked me, about two months ago, to investigate this gigantic increase in the flow of paperwork. There's no question that we're getting too many reports. The question is, are we paying too much money for the information that we get? I've surveyed all of our departments and their key personnel. Most of the survey questionnaires indicate that we're getting too much information. Only a small percentage of each report appears to be necessary. In addition, many of the reports arrive too late. I'm talking about scheduled reports, not planning, demand, or exception reports."

V.P. Project Management: "Every report my people receive is necessary for us to effectively make decisions with regard to planning, organizing, and controlling each project. My people are the biggest users and we can't live with less reports."

V.P. Information: "Can your people live with less information in each report? Can some of the reports be received less frequently?"

V.P. Project Management: "Some of our reports have too much information in them. But we need them at the frequency we have now."

V.P. Engineering: "My people utilize about 20 percent of the information in most of our reports. Once our people find the information they want, the report is discarded. That's because we know that each project manager will retain a copy. Also, only the department managers and section supervisors read the reports."

V.P. Information: "Can engineering and manufacturing get the information they need from other sources, such as the project office?"

V.P. Project Management: "Wait a minute! My people don't have time to act as paper pushers for each department manager. We all know that the departments can't function without these reports. Why should we assume the burden?"

V.P. Information: "All I'm trying to say is that many of our reports can be combined into smaller ones and possibly made more concise. Most of our reports are flexible enough to meet changes in our operating business. We have two sets of reports: one for the customer and one for us. If the customer wants the report in a specific fashion, he pays for it. Why can't we act as our own customer and try to make a reporting system that we can all use?"

V.P. Engineering: "Many of the reports obviously don't justify the cost. Can we generate the minimum number of reports and pass it on to someone higher or lower in the organization?"

V.P. Project Management: "We need weekly reports, and we need them on Monday mornings. I know our computer people don't like to work on Sunday evenings, but we have no choice. If we don't have those reports on Monday mornings, we can't control time, cost, and performance."

V.P. Information: "There are no reports generated from the pertinent data in our original computer runs. This looks to me like every report is a one-shot deal. There has to be room for improvement.

"I have prepared a checklist for each of you with four major questions. Do you want summary or detailed information? How do you want the output to look? How many copies do you need? How often do you need these reports?"

Richard Margo: "In project organizational forms, the project exists as a separate entity except for administrative purposes. These reports are part of that administrative purpose. Combining this with the high cost of administration in our project structure, we'll never remain competitive unless we lower our overhead. I'm going to leave it up to you guys. Try to reduce the number of reports, but don't sacrifice the necessary information you need to control the projects and your resources."

18
Procedural Documents[1]

18.0 INTRODUCTION

People communicate in many ways. Often communications get filtered and somewhat distorted. For many reasons, agreements in a project environment must be in writing. Project management believes in the philosophy that only what is on paper is really important.

Another important facet of any project management system is to provide the people in the organization with procedureal guidelines for how to conduct project-oriented activities and how to communicate in such a multidimensional environment. The project management policies, procedures, forms, and guidelines can provide some of these tools for delineating the process, as well as a format for collecting, processing, and communicating project-related data in an orderly, standardized format. Project planning and tracking, however, involves more than just the generation of paperwork. It requires the participation of the entire project team, including support departments, subcontractors, and top management. It is this involvement of the entire team that fosters a unifying team environment oriented toward the project goals, and ultimately to the personal commitment of the team members to the various tasks within time and budget constraints. The specific benefits of procedural documents, including forms and checklists, are that they help to:

- Provide guidelines and uniformity
- Encourage documentation
- Communicate clearly and effectively
- Standardize data formats
- Unify project teams
- Provide a basis for analysis
- Document agreements for future reference
- Refuel commitments

---

1. Adapted from Harold Kerzner and Hans J. Thamhain, *Project Management Operating Guidelines,* Van Nostrand Reinhold Co., New York, 1986, pp. 3–6.

- Minimize paperwork
- Minimize conflict and confusion
- Delineate work packages
- Bring new team members on board
- Build an experience track and method for future projects.

Done properly, the process of project planning must involve both the performing and the customer organizations. This involvement creates new insight into the intricacies of a project and its management methods. It also leads to the visibility of the project at various organizational levels, management involvement, and support. It is this involvement at all organizational levels that stimulates interest in the project and the desire for success, and fosters a pervasive reach for excellence that unifies the project team. It leads to commitment toward establishing and reaching the desired project objectives and to a self-forcing management system where people want to work toward these established objectives.

Few companies have introduced project management procedures with ease. Most have experienced problems ranging from skepticism to sabotage of the procedural system. Realistically, however, program managers do not have much of a choice, especially for the larger, more complex programs. Every project manager who believes in project management has his or her own success story. It is interesting to note, however, that many use incremental approaches to develop and implement their project management system.

Developing and implementing such a system incrementally is a multifaceted challenge to management. The problem is seldom to understand the techniques involved, such as budgeting and scheduling, but to involve the project team in the process, to get their input, support, and commitment, and to establish a supportive environment. Furthermore, project personnel must have the feeling that the policies and procedures of the project management system facilitate communication, are flexible and adaptive to a changing environment, and provide an early warning system through which project personnel obtain assistance rather than punishment in case of a contingency.

The procedural guidelines and forms of an established project management system can be especially useful during the project planning/definition phase. Not only does it help to delineate and communicate the four major sets of variables for organizing and managing the project—(1) tasks, (2) timing, (3) resources, and (4) responsibilities—it also helps to define measurable milestones, as well as report and review requirements. This provides the ability to measure project status and performance, and supplies crucial inputs for controlling the project toward the desired results.

However, none of these systems will really control project performance or rectify a problem unless the project plan has received approval and commitment from the people behind it. Such a self-forcing project control system[2] is based on the following six key components:

1. *Objectives* and *Measurability*. Existence of a sound system of standards and tools for planning and tracking the project effort, such as procedures and forms.
2. *Involvement* of all key personnel during project planning.
3. *Agreement* and *commitment* by all key personnel to the project plan and its specific results and performance measures.
4. *Senior management commitment* and continuous *involvement*.
5. *Availability* of *quality personnel*.
6. *Proper project direction* and *leadership*.

Some of the strongest drives toward high project performance are derived from an interesting and professionally stimulating work environment. For example, Thamhain and Wilemon found, in various field studies,[3] that project success is directly associated with personal commitment, involvement, and top management support. These factors are the strongest in a professional stimulating work environment, characterized by interesting, challenging work, visibility and recognition for achievements, growth potential and good project leadership. Furthermore, the same conditions are associated with other criteria for project success. Specifically, the more professionally stimulating and interesting the work environment is perceived to be by the project team, the more involved and committed are the people, and the more innovative, creative, and change-oriented are they being perceived by top management.

In summary, developing an effective project management system takes more than just a set of policies and procedures. It also requires the integration of these guidelines and standards into the culture and value system of the organization. Management must lead the overall efforts and foster an environment conducive to teamwork. The greater the team spirit, trust, commitment, and quality of information exchange among team members, the more likely the team will develop effective decision-making processes, make individual and group commitments, focus on problem solving and operate in a self-forcing, self-correcting control mode. These are the characteristics which will support and pervade the

2. The concept of self-enforcing project control was first discussed in detail by Leonard R. Sayles and Margaret K. Chandler in *Managing Large Systems,* Harper & Row, 1971.

3. For more detail see articles by Hans J. Thamhain and David L. Wilemon, "Managing engineers effectively," IEEE Transactions on Engineering Management, August 1983, "Team building in project management," Project Management Quarterly, June 1983, and "Anatomy of a high performing new product team," Proceedings of the Annual Symposium of the Project Management Institute, 1984.

formal project management system and make it work for you. When understood and accepted by the team members, such a system provides the formal standards, guidelines, and measures needed to direct a project toward specific results within the given time and resource constraints.

18.1 ESTABLISHED PRACTICES

Although project managers have the right to establish their own policies and procedures, many companies have taken the route of designing project control forms which can be used uniformly on all projects to assist in the communications process. Project control forms serve two vital purposes by establishing a common framework from which: (1) The project manager will communicate with executives, functional employees, and clients; and (2) Executives and the project manager can make meaningful decisions concerning the allocation of resources

Success or failure of a project depends upon the ability of key personnel to have sufficient data for decision making. Project management is often considered to be both an art and a science. It is an art because of the strong need for interpersonal skills, and the project planning and control forms attempt to convert part of the "art" into a science.

Many companies tend not to realize until too late the necessity of good planning and control forms. Today, some of the larger companies with mature project management structures maintain a separate functional unit for forms control. This is quite common in the aerospace and defense industries, and is also becoming common practice in other industries. Yet some executives believe that forms are needed only when the company grows to a point where a continuous stream of unique projects necessitates some sort of uniform control mechanism.

In some small or non-project-driven organizations, each project can have its own forms. But for most other organizations, uniformity is a must. Quite often, the actual design and selection of the forms is made by individuals other than the users. The remainder of this section provides several forms for control.

RESEARCH AND TECHNOLOGY OBJECTIVES AND PLANS

1. DATE PREPARED	2. (RESERVED)	3. RELEVANCE CODE	4. CURRENT NUMBER/CODE

5. TITLE

6. FORMER RTOP NO. (IF APPLICABLE)	10. RESPONSIBLE ORGANIZATION
	NAME
7. RELATED RTOPS (IF APPLICABLE)	
	ADDRESS
8. CONSOLIDATION OF RTOP NO'S.	RESPONSIBLE INDIVIDUAL
	NAME
9. SCIENTIFIC AND TECHNICAL AREAS	TELEPHONE

11. STATUS OF THIS RTOP   FY _____
- ☐ NEW RTOP   ☐ CONTINUING RTOP (___ NO CHANGE; ___CHANGE IN SCOPE)
- ☐ TERMINATING   ☐ RTOP COMPLETED THIS FISCAL YEAR
    ACTIVITY

11.a. PROPRIETARY INFORMATION CONTAINED IN RTOP   ☐YES   ☐NO

12. BRIEF TECHNICAL SUMMARY (OBJECTIVES AND APPROACH)

13. KEYWORDS

INSTALLATION CONCURRENCE			HQ CONCURRENCE		
PROG. MGR.	DATE	DIVISION MGT.	DATE	SIGNATURE	DATE

APPROVALS				
INSTALLATION (SIGNATURE AND TITLE) ASSISTANT LABORATORY DIRECTOR	DATE	HQ (SIGNATURE AND TITLE)		DATE

Figure 18–1. Project initiation form (research/technology).

RESEARCH AND DEVELOPMENT OBJECTIVE

R & D OBJECTIVE

OBJECTIVE NO. _____
SUPERVISOR _____
SUBMITTED BY _____

FUNCTION NO. _____
LOCATION NO. _____
W.O. NO. ASSIGNED _____

STATEMENT OF OBJECTIVE

REASON FOR OBJECTIVE:

OUTLINE OF STEPS TO ACHIEVE OBJECTIVE	RESPONSIBLE PERSON	STEP COMPLETION DATE	MAN-DAYS	EQUIPMENT AND MATERIALS REQUIRED TO COMPLETE STEP.	FUNCTION COST	PLANT COST

COMPLETION DATE _____FUNCTION COSTS _____PLANT COSTS _____SAVINGS _____

MAN-DAYS REQUIRED FOR COMPLETION:
STAFF _____DIVISION _____DISTRICT _____OTHER _____

Figure 18–2. Project initiation form (R & D).

```
┌──────────────────────────────────────────────────────────────┐
│ TO: _____                                            │
│ ENGINEER: _____                       T.P. NO. _____  │
│ JOB NO. _____          TASK PLAN                         │
│ DATE _____                                             │
│                      TASK _____                    │
│                                                                │
│ PURPOSE: _____ │
│ _____ │
│ _____ │
│ _____ │
│ _____ │
│                                                                │
│ TASK PLAN: _____ │
│ _____ │
│ _____ │
│ _____ │
│ _____ │
│ _____ │
│ _____ │
│ _____ │
│ _____ │
│ _____ │
│ _____ │
│ _____ │
│ _____ │
│ _____ │
│ _____ │
│ _____ │
│ _____ │
│ _____ │
│ _____ │
│                                                                │
│                               PAGE _____OF _____           │
└──────────────────────────────────────────────────────────────┘
```

Figure 18–3. Project summary form.

PROGRAM NAME:

CUSTOMER _____
USER _____
TYPE OF CONTRACT _____

BUSINESS AREA:

PROP MGR.:
MKTG. MGR.:

RFP DATE _____

PROPOSAL DUE _____ AWARD _____

DATE:
REVISION NO.:

INITIAL CONTRACT VALUE: _____
TOTAL CONTRACT VALUE: _____
CUSTOMER BUDGET: _____
COST ESTIMATE: _____
B&P, B&P ADMIN. COST EST.: _____

SCOPE OF WORK:

PERSPECTIVE

WHY SHOULD WE BID (OUR ROLE/STRATEGIC VALUE):

FUTURE VALUE:

ALTERNATIVES:

RISKS:

POSITION SUMMARY

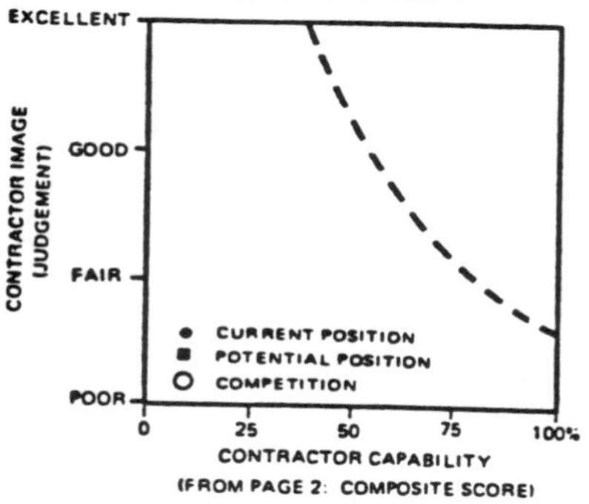

EXCELLENT

CONTRACTOR IMAGE (JUDGEMENT)

GOOD

FAIR

POOR

● CURRENT POSITION
■ POTENTIAL POSITION
○ COMPETITION

0   25   50   75   100%
CONTRACTOR CAPABILITY
(FROM PAGE 2: COMPOSITE SCORE)

PROBLEMS/SOLUTIONS:

TEAMING CONSIDERATION:

Figure 18–4. Strategic assessment of new business opportunity form.

		MERIT POINTS (0 - 100)						
	CAPABILITY	US			COMPETITION				
		CURRENT	POTENTIAL	CORRECTIVE ACTION	I	II	III	IV	V
1.	CUSTOMER RELATIONS								
2.	UNDERSTANDING OF PROBLEM								
3.	COMPLIANCE								
4.	DESIGN								
5.	FABRICATION								
6.	PRODUCTION								
7.	TEST								
8.	LOGISTICS								
9.	MANAGEMENT								
10.	RESOURCES								
11.	RELATED EXPERIENCE								
12.	PAST PERFORMANCE								
13.	PRICE/COST								
14.									
	COMPOSITE CAPABILITY			SCORE AVERAGES →|				

COMPETITIVE SUMMARY

US:	MAJOR STRENGTH	MAJOR WEAKNESS

COMPETITION:		

Figure 18-5. Competitive assessment form.

BASED ON STRATEGIC ASSESSMENT (FORM ESG-ED 2583)

| PROGRAM NAME: | BUSINESS AREA: | DATE |
| | | REVISION |

CUSTOMER _____   RESPONSIBLE INDIVIDUAL _____

_____ DAYS TO RFP   _____ DAYS RESPONSE TIME   AWARD DATE _____

A. **ASSESSMENT OF OPPORTUNITY:**

B. **WIN STRATEGY:**

C. **MILESTONE (KEY EVENTS & REVIEWS)**   SUMMARY OF MASTER SCHEDULE

MILESTONES	TIMING (MONTH)

Figure 18–6. Capture plan form.

D. KEY ROLES AND RESPONSIBILITIES

ROLE/SUPPORT	RESPONSIBLE INDIVIDUAL(S)	%APPLIED TIME
BUSINESS AREA MANAGER		
PROPOSAL MANAGER		
PROPOSAL SPECIALIST		
MARKETING		
MARKETING COMMUNICATION		
ENGINEERING		
OPERATIONS		
PRODUCT ASSURANCE		
CONTRACTS		
COST ESTIMATING		
OTHER		

E. ACTION PLAN

ACTIVITY	ACTION	COMPLE-TION DATE	FUNDING $	RESPONSIBLE INDIVIDUAL
CUSTOMER RELATIONS & MKTG COMM				
TECHNICAL READINESS				
PROPOSAL				
POST SUBMISSION				
OTHER				

F. ACQUISITION BUDGET

B&P $	PRE-RFP PERIOD $
	PROPOSAL PREPARATION $
	POST PROPOSAL PERIOD $
B&P ADMIN $	TOTAL ACQUISITION $

Figure 18–6. Capture plan form. (continued)

						NO.	

PROGRAM NAME

CUSTOMER _____

USER _____

BUSINESS AREA

PRO MGR.:

DATE:

REVISION NO.:

INITIAL CONTRACT VALUE: _____

TASK NAME:			AUTHORITY			
WBS NUMBER		ORDER NOTICE NO				
TYPE OF CONTRACT:			APPROVALS			
CONTRACT NO:		PROGRAM OFFICE-DATE	LINE ORG. DATE		FINANCIAL CONT. -DATE	
PROG/PROJ MANAGER:						
RESP. TASK MANAGER:						
RESP. ORGANIZATION:						

1. SCHEDULE	TASK DESCRIPTION	RESPONSIBLE INDIVIDUAL	COMPLETION DATE	COST ACCOUNT	$ BUDGET

2. BUDGET   DOLLARS & MANHOURS

3. WORK STATEMENT (INCLUDING APPLICABLE REFERENCE DOCUMENTS)

Figure 18–7. Task authorization form.

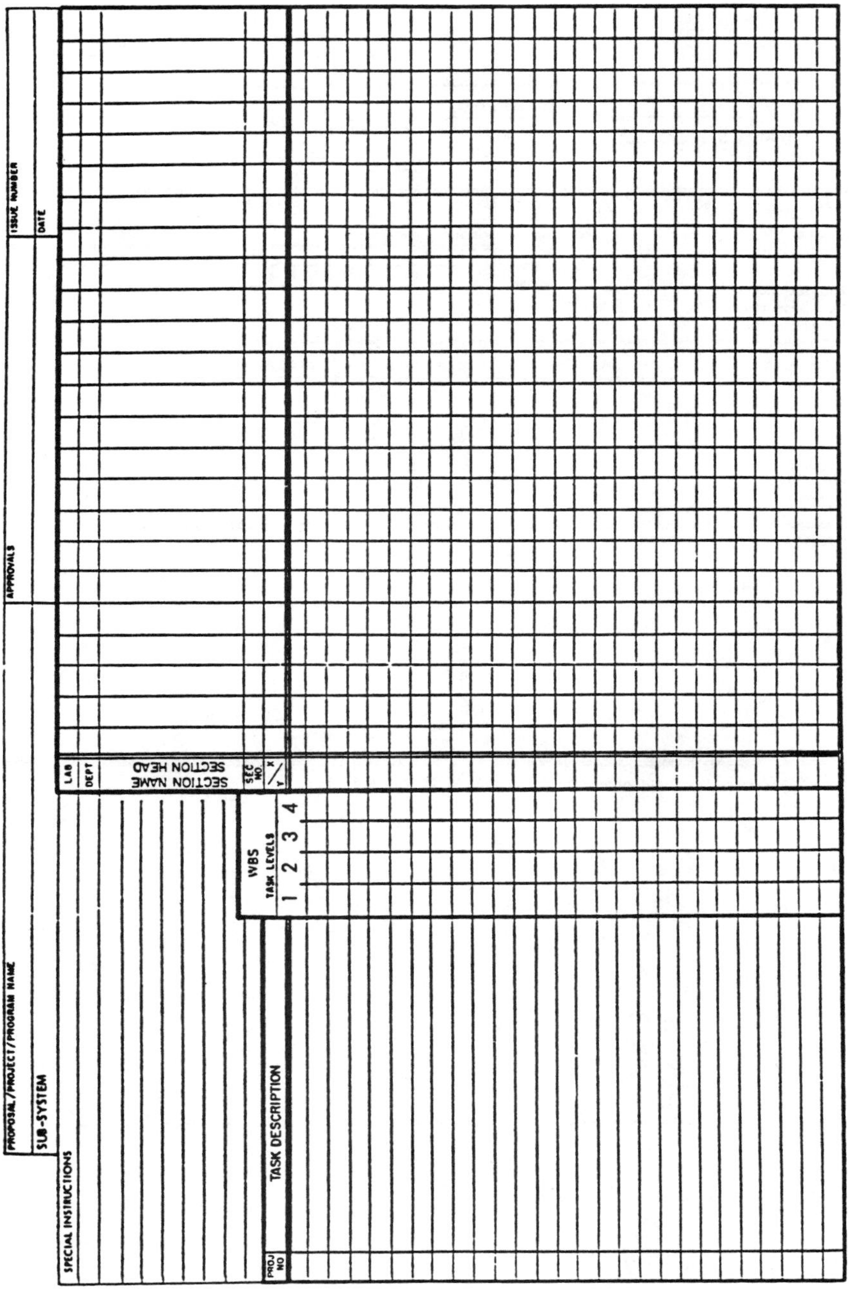

Figure 18–8. Task matrix form.

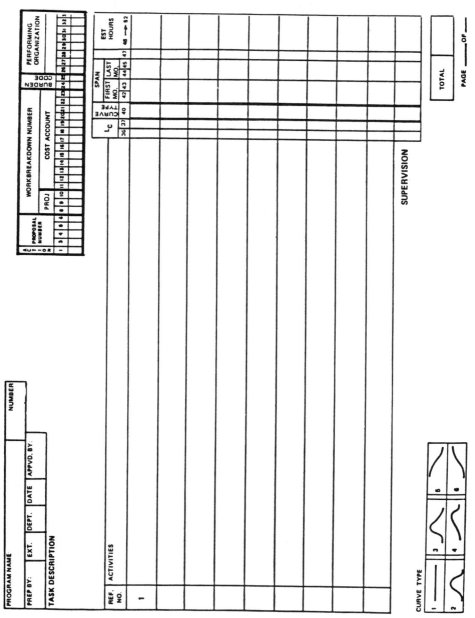

Figure 18–9. Manpower estimate form.

EXPERIMENT ______________________ NO. ________

PREPARED BY ______________ PHONE ______________ DATE ______________

PHASE NO.	DESCRIPTION	DATES		ESTIMATED COSTS			
		START	END	EQUIPMENT	MATERIALS	LABOR	TOTAL

Figure 18–10. Cost estimate (equipment, material, labor) form.

doing, instead of going to the executive board room, I went to the junior board room with the English engineer. We dined on the same food and had a little bit more interesting conversation, but I was never invited back to the executive board room to have lunch.

19.1 HOW DO FOREIGN CLIENTS REALLY SEE AMERICAN PROJECT MANAGERS?[1]

Introduction

Do I really know how my foreign labor force views me? Many American project managers have returned home to the United States without ever answering this question. Since the project manager's impact on a work group ultimately influences their productivity, this is a vital question. It is difficult enough to interpret the behavior of a work group, and from those actions gain understanding of the group's morale and motivation. When the work force has a national and cultural origin that is different from that of the manager, it becomes a monumental task. This is perfectly understandable, since we, as American project managers, view a foreign work force through the cultural filters of the American experience. This section will discuss some of the views that foreign managers and workers have of American project managers. These views will be addressed in regard to their implications for work force productivity. The section will conclude with suggestions for a transcultural management training program for deploying American project managers.

Method. In conducting this study, it was felt that there is only one intelligent way to determine how foreign workers really see American project managers: ask them! The population that was interviewed included professors, students, managers, and workers from other nations, all of whom had worked with American project managers. One hundred and three people were interviewed. The composition of the group included fourteen nations; Nigeria, Kenya, Ethiopia, Brazil, Venezuela, Mexico, India, Iran, Pakistan, Saudi Arabia, Taiwan, Thailand, the Philippines, and Japan. The interviews were tape-recorded and the respondents were asked to do two things:

1. Think of at least one situation in which you felt that an American project manager had a negative impact on you.
2. Tell why the manager had a negative impact.

---

1. Philip B. Arms and Elmer Lucas, "How Do Foreign Clients Really See American Project Managers?," *Proceedings of the 1978 Annual Seminar/Symposium on Project Management,* pp. II-K-1 through II-K-7; reproduced by permission of the Project Management Institute.

How Do They Really See Us?

In analyzing the interview data, no attempt was made to determine how valid the respondent's perceptions were. Rather, they form a mosaic of opinions which can serve as food for thought for those American project managers who are working abroad. Since attitudes and behaviors are based upon each individual's unique view of the world, the views shared by the respondents become important feedback for American project managers.

American Project Managers Have Any Resource. Many host national managers and workers often initially see American project managers as a cornucopia of money, knowledge, expertise, and equipment. Thus, when the American project manager faces a seemingly insolvable problem, the host national managerial staff is perplexed when the American is unable to reach into his bag of tools and produce startling new knowledge to reach a solution. The implications of this host national perception are far-reaching. The host nationals may view the American project manager's inability to reach a solution not as an inability, but rather, as an act of withholding. If this is the case, they may feel that the act of withholding is a result of a dislike of host nationals. On the other hand, if they see the inability to solve the problem as resulting from poor skills, they may figure that they have the only inept manager in America, or at least one of the few inept ones. In either case, the host national work force may develop a low sense of trust and decreased productivity. What might be the cause of this opinion? If the host nation is technologically underdeveloped, it could be a result of a growing anxiousness to acquire technology. This is something over which the project manager has no control. But, more important, the opinion could be a result of bragging or overinflated behavior by the American project manager. It is difficult to avoid the trap of continually praising one's company, country, and self. If one strategy can be recommended which will help a deploying project manager avoid this situation, it would be: "establish the limits of your resources and ability early in the project and avoid bragging or overstating your ability." Although this is a simple prescription, it is one cure that many of us find difficult to take.

American Project Managers Just Don't Understand Us. To some Americans, it may seem absurd to be concerned if the boss doesn't understand us. As long as we are paid properly and the work is interesting, we are usually content to plod along in our task. Of course there are exceptions to this, even among the American work force. Some Americans place a high premium on respect and understanding from their superiors. But in those cases where it is not forthcoming, the worker will usually do a good job in order to continue to receive his pay and get the job done. This is not always the case in other cultures. In many countries, the host nationals place an extremely high value on visitors understanding their culture. As one Japanese businessman put it: "Unless the American with whom I am dealing gets to know me, how does he know whether I mean what I say? For that matter," he added after a moment, "unless I know him rather well, how do I know whether to say what I mean?"[2]

An act by an American project manager may be construed by the host national as an insult because the culture of his country was not taken into consideration. Besides the obvious effect on relations between the project manager and the work force, a reluctance to attempt understanding of the host culture can also result in production losses and project inertia. In one case, the American government and private business interests were attempting to set up a trade school in Ethiopia and were meeting with little success. All of the students wished to be electricians and very few wished to study the trades of plumbing, bricklaying, and other manual labor trades. The school failed. If the American advisors would have understood the host culture, the expense and time could have been saved. There is an Ethiopian folk belief that manual laborers in general, and metal workers in particular, can turn into hyenas at night.[3]

If an American manager finds himself in the Middle East, he may be terribly surprised and upset when his work force does not meet production goals set for them. In planning his quarterly production schedule he may not consider the religious holidays in the host nation. This is not a problem in the United States where these type holidays are relatively few in number. In addition, the American worker can often be lured into working on this type of holiday with the consideration of overtime or holiday pay rates. In many areas of the Middle East, there are over fifty religious holidays each year, and they are staunchly observed. Thus, if the project manager finds himself very short of his project deadline with a high absence rate, he may have forgotten to consider this most basic issue. The view of Americans as insensitive can be caused by two primary factors: a genuine insensitivity by the manager, or insensitivity by the host nationals and an unwillingness to accept the fact that Americans are different from them. In either case, the work force may develop the attitude that "if the project manager doesn't care enough to try and understand us, then we don't care enough to help him finish his project."

It is simply not realistic to expect the host national work force to change their cultural outlook to reach agreement with the American project manager.

---

2. H. Cleveland, G. J. Managone, and J. C. Adams, *The Overseas American* (New York: McGraw-Hill Book Company, Inc., 1960).
3. E. Lord, *Cultural Patterns in Ethiopia* (Washington, D.C.: U.S. Agency for International Development, 1963).

In this situation, the old adage, "the customer is always right," holds true again. The project manager must make an effort to look at the worker's world as they view it, and not as an American world. This in itself does not mean the overadaption syndrome of "going native." In this approach the American project loses his cultural identity and may even give up traits or behaviors which lead the client to seek American technology. How can an American project manager learn to be Iranian when the Iranian people have spent an entire lifetime learning to do just this? Rather it calls for a common sense approach which takes cultural differences into consideration when planning and running the project and attempts to avoid behavior which will affront the host nationals.

Americans Are Impatient.   How many times in our adult lives have we heard the words: "Don't sit there! Do something!" This is a perfect acceptable statement in our society, since we consider time a valuable resource. But this is not true in a variety of other nations. In Latin American countries, time has a different perspective. Thus, when a Latin American businessman shows up for a meeting thirty minutes late by American standards, he will be on time by local standards. Or a more accurate statement might be that the American showed up thirty minutes early. It really depends upon from which perspective you are viewing it. The fact that Americans have a great preoccupation with time can be easily seen by looking at the many proverbs or clichés in the language which deal with time: "a stitch in time saves nine," "early to bed early to rise, makes a man healthy, wealthy, and wise," and "the early bird gets the worm." Is it any wonder that we are impatient with those whom we feel are not responding quickly enough? There is nothing wrong with a "let's get on with it attitude" as long as it is congruent with that of the local perspective on time and efficiency.

In many oriental countries, the ultimate goal is much more important than how long it takes to get there. This is understandable if one looks at the history of many of these nations. Their histories are filled with natural disasters, wars, and famines that have molded into their citizens a fatalistic view of life. This leads them to look at problems and missed target dates as just small problems that will either take care of themselves or be solved in time.

Fortunately, there are realistic ways which the manager can address this problem. First and foremost, the American project manager should determine the local perspective of time. This should be accomplished as quickly as possible after arrival in the country. Secondly, he should set schedules and completion dates with this information in mind. Last of all, he should be continually conscious of demands which he places on the work force so that he will not become impatient with them. The last step is probably the most important and yet the most difficult to accomplish. One thing to remember is that "the tortoise was slower than the hare, but he still won the race."

Americans Know Everything about Technology and Nothing about People. Before Americans go into cardiac arrest over this statement, all should rest assured that this statement is an opinion, and not necessarily based in fact. It would appear with only cursory examination that the ability and desire to care for and respect people is pretty much equally distributed throughout all parts of the world. It can be stated that American technology and engineering research and skill is slightly ahead of the social sciences, but this is due to an earlier start and not a lack of desire, motivation, or skill among social scientists.

In almost every instance where the respondent made this statement, it could be traced back to a lack of understanding by the American project manager of local social and cultural norms. More accurately, it could be said that Americans know little about people of other nations where they are deployed. Those who labor solely in the engineering and project management areas often forget that people are the one thing which can foul up the smoothest-operating project management system. People are complex and unpredictable. No one can really say that he has a guaranteed method for analyzing human behavior. The best that one can do is to understand the cultural framework of a particular nation. If a project manager is aware of the general rules by which people operate in a particular country, then at least he has a starting point from which he can increase his overall understanding of the host national.

When the American project manager addressed his Saudi Arabian project engineer, the Saudi Arabian shows respect by lowering his voice. The American unconsciously raises his voice level in the tried-and-true American method in order to signal the engineer to speak up. The Saudi Arabian reads this as a signal that he is not being polite enough and he lowers his voice even more. This continues until the American is screaming and the Saudi Arabian is whispering or mumbling.[4] At this point the American may lose control and angrily storm away. The Saudi Arabian stands puzzled and amazed at the American's inability to understand people. After all, he was polite in the Arab fashion, and the American got angry. It's not that the American knows little about people. It's just that he knows little about Saudi Arabians, and even less about their rules of speech etiquette.

Americans Are Insensitive to Needs and Problems. In this issue, as in all others addressed in this section, the perceived insensitivity is usually not actual but rather is a result of what Sapir, the noted anthropologist/linguist, would call a difference in "world view" between the American project manager and

---

4. E. T. Hall, and W. F. Whyte, "Intercultural Communications: A Guide to Men of Action," *Human Organizations,* Volume 19, No. 1, December 1960, pp. 5–12.

the host national client. Thus, each of them looks at the world from a frame of reference, which is a collective total of each individual's unique life experience. An example noted by one of the respondents explains this problem in a graphic manner. In order to fully grasp the implications of this case, it is necessary to look briefly at Maslow's hierarchy of needs theory. According to Maslow, man's needs or desires drive his actions or behavior. He further postulated that these needs or desires are in the form of a pecking order or hierarchy in which man does not pursue one particular need until he has satisfied the one which is just below it on the hierarchy. Figure 19-1 illustrates this theory. At the lowest level is man's basic or physiological needs which include thirst, hunger, and desire for warmth. Once these are satisfied, man looks for safety or security. Feeling safe and secure, he then seeks love or a sense of belonging. Having found this, he expresses his need for responsibility, the respect of others, and self-respect through the pursuit of ego needs. At the top of the hierarchy is man's need to self-actualize or reach his full potential as he sees fit.

Consider the American project manager, Mr. X, who deploys to country Y, an underdeveloped nation. Mr. Z, is a host national job site foreman who works for Mr. X. Mr. Z has seven children and has it very rough economically. Mr. X needs extra production and faster work from Mr. Z in order to meet the project deadline. Since most workers in American industry are striving for greater challenge and responsibility or better social relationships at work, Mr. X automatically sees Mr. Z from this frame of reference. He takes the crew out to dinner. The next day, he gives Mr. Z more authority and responsibility. Mr. Z does not pick up his pace or work any harder. Mr. X thinks that Mr. Z is lazy and stupid. On the other hand, Mr. Z, like most of his co-workers, would do anything for more pay to feed his family and provide economic security. What he wants is a raise because he is operating on the basic needs level of the needs hierarchy. He feels Mr. X is insensitive to his needs. After all, Mr. X wants him to work harder and faster, but he does nothing to help Mr. Z get a raise. It is apparent that the American just does not care. The entire misunderstanding is a group of perceptions caused by a difference in how two people view the world around them. Since the old adage, "the client is always right,"

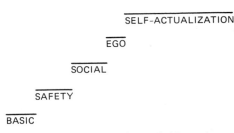

SELF-ACTUALIZATION

EGO

SOCIAL

SAFETY

BASIC

Figure 19–1. Maslow's needs hierarchy.

will probably remain a truism, it is foolish to ask the host national to change his view of the world. Rather, the American project manager is faced with two alternatives: remove the American filters through which he sees the world and/ or put on a pair from the host nation.

Americans Are Too Concerned with Efficiency and Effectiveness. In order to examine the basis for this perception, it is first necessary to develop an operational definition of "efficiency and effectiveness" from an American perspective. The terms are complementary in nature and meaning. To be "effective" is to get desired results with your efforts or to perform to a standard. To be "efficient" is to get those results with the minimum expenditure of money, time, materials, and manpower. It is obvious that the operational definition of "effectiveness" is probably much the same throughout the world. The difference lies is the definition of "efficiency." In the American definition, minimum expenditure of resources is the key factor. In a nation with an overabundance of people, the blend of money, time, materials, and manpower might not be the same. It is precisely this difference in the definition of "efficiency" which causes many host nationals to view American project managers as overly concerned with efficiency and effectiveness. Conversely, it also causes the host national to appear as noncommitted to the American.

Let's Look at the Client Differently. In the traditional sense of the meaning, the client is the person who pays the bills and signs the checks. In meeting project specifications and deadlines, it is reasonable and wise to follow the orders of the person or persons who pull the purse strings. But for the actual management of the project, this definition must be expanded to include all of the work force on the project. This is particularly true in a cross-cultural management situation.

In managing the project, we always take into consideration all possible worst case situations with materials, money, time, and equipment. On a really large project, this calls for a true systems approach in which the interaction of all of these variables is considered in great depth. Usually manpower is considered in a simple manner, in which only two factors are analyzed: availability and skill level. In fact, the manpower question is much more difficult than this to answer.

Figure 19–2 illustrates the complicated nature of the productivity issue. Thus, a sure supply of skilled manpower doesn't necessarily guarantee high productivity and project quality. Attitudes can either aid or hinder productivity, depending upon whether they are positive or negative. If a person has a strong positive attitude toward the job, it can make up for a shortage of skills. A negative attitude can cause a highly skilled worker to drag his feet or perform in a sloppy manner.

The worker's attitude towards the job can be the result of a variety of factors.

WORKER'S PERCEPTIONS OF MANAGER   MANAGER'S PERCEPTION OF WORK FORCE

SKILL LEVEL   TOOLS AND EQUIPMENT

MOTIVES   MANAGERIAL TREATMENT

CULTURAL NORMS   TRAINING

WORK EXPERIENCE

ATTITUDE   WORKER PRODUCTIVITY   NATURE OF TASK

FEELINGS   NATURE OF MOTIVATION

SOCIAL NORMS   FATIGUE

NEEDS

PERCEPTIONS OF TASK   PERFORMANCE FEEDBACK

Figure 19–2. Factors affecting productivity.

Work experience is one factor which can affect attitude. If the worker has experienced negative treatment on the job before, he will be apt to react to his present task in a negative manner. If he has a negative experience with his manager, this will carry over to his next task with that project manager, or possibly other project managers. The worker's cultural background may negatively or positively influence the worker's productivity, depending upon whether the task, or any portion of it, is in conflict with his cultural norms.

Since there are so many factors affecting the worker's productivity, it becomes apparent that the manager must strive to prevent any behavior which might negatively influence the worker. First and most important, the project manager must learn to look at the entire work force as his client, not just the people at the top of the organization who furnish and control project guidelines and specifications. The work force, including managers in the host national work force, are even more important in a way than those at the top because they are the ones who actually do the work. If they do not cooperate, or work at full capacity, the project will become more difficult. Thus, the effective project manager must learn to keep top management happy and be sensitive to the needs of the subordinate managers, engineers, and work force.

Summary. Analyzing the interview data, it became apparent that to many host national workers, the problem of the American project manager/host national interface is a vital one. The reasons expressed for the negative impact of American project managers are as follows:

1. Actions by American project managers which are in violation of worker cultural and social norms
2. American project managers following American cultural and social norms in managing the host national work force

to work in other academic disciplines. As career Navy personnel they have been exposed to a significant variety of management styles (and the relative effectiveness of those styles) and management situations. The concept of project management is used extensively in the Navy, and its techniques are applicable in many management areas not specifically identified as "project management." From these perspectives conclusions have been drawn which can best be summarized in a message.

The message is a simple one which American firms should listen to closely. The multinational nature of projects is now a reality. The successful firm of the future will be the one which has managers who are successful in a cross-cultural environment. The only way that this is possible is for companies to accept the fact that problems can arise in a cross-cultural management setting which do not normally occur in other environments, and to translate this acceptance into a financial commitment which will provide the training needed to make the American project manager as skilled in cross-cultural management as he is in the traditional skills of logical hard-nosed project management.

19.2 GUIDELINES FOR SUCCESSFUL MANAGEMENT OF PROJECTS IN THE MIDDLE EAST: THE CLIENT POINT OF VIEW[5]

Introduction

Two factors have made the Middle East important as an area whose attitudes and outlook may have a decisive influence on the rest of the world. One is the fact that the Middle East occupies a strategic position between the East and the West. Second is that, in an age when industrial production is dependent on petroleum, the countries of the Middle East possess more than half of the world's petroleum reserves.

This position has enabled some of the Middle East countries to forge ahead with economic development at a rate which was undreamed of only ten years ago. At the same time, businessmen of the Western world have turned beyond their traditional boundaries. In the second half of this century, we have seen the emergence of an interdependent world economy. For example, we are now witnessing a struggle for markets, especially in the developing Middle East.

Doing business in the Middle East, however, has not been easy, and only a handful of American companies have reached the profits which they expected.

---

5. Hamed K. Eldin and Ivar Avots, "Guidelines for Successful Management of Projects in the Middle East: The Client Point of View," *Proceedings of the 1978 Annual Seminar/Symposium on Project Management*, pp. II-M-1 through II-M-5; reproduced by permission of the Project Management Institute.

One of the principal reasons for the failures has been unfamiliarity with the local customs, laws, and conditions, and the inability to communicate with the client and deal with him effectively.

This section suggests guidelines for the successful management of projects in the Middle East. These guidelines are addressed to two types of persons:

- Corporation executives dealing with project planning and initiation
- Project managers responsible for project development and implementation

Project Management Environment in the Middle East

In an attempt to understand the constraints under which Middle East projects are managed, one must briefly examine the political economic environment.

Political Climate. Although the Middle East appears to the casual observer as a homogeneous area, there is a deep ideological gap between the "socialist" and "capitalist" camps. Iraq, with its wide-ranging state capitalism, stands near one end of the spectrum, while the ultraconservative Saudi Arabia stands at the other.

Economic Development. The economics of the Middle Eastern countries are very different. Iraq, Kuwait, Saudi Arabia, Libya, and the United Arab Emirates have some of the most profitable oil fields in the world. Iraq, Syria, and Sudan have a rich agricultural potential. Egypt is not so fortunate, and besides, it has a serious overpopulation problem.

Private enterprise is as important an impetus to industrialization in the Arab world as it is in the West. When it comes to large-scale projects, however, both the "socialist" and "capitalist," governments play a key role. This is only because the governments in these countries command the financial and other resources such projects require.

Middle Eastern governments speak of development plans and targets for takeoff into self-sustained growth. The rich countries have budgets for financing sound projects, while the poor ones have been successful in securing loans and credit when they have been able to justify the economic feasibility of their projects. These loans and credits are provided by rich Arab states, the World Bank, or governmental agencies such as USAID (United States Agency for International Development).

Both the rich and the poor Middle East countries share many economic and managerial problems with developing countries throughout the world. Of particular interest to us are the following:

- In poor countries, like Egypt and Sudan, production has not kept pace with the relentless population pressure which has resulted in a steadily sinking standard of living for the masses. These countries, however, share the same aspirations of a raised standard of living through rapid economic development.

- Most of these countries have geared their economics to agriculture. In many instances, the development in this sector of the economy has not been significant.
- Industrialization has been generally regarded as the fastest way to achieve a balance between production and population. Industry in these countries has so far been very limited and has largely been the result of efforts exerted by a few ambitious individuals.
- The main problem facing rich countries, such as Saudi Arabia, is the underdevelopment of human resources. If a country is unable to develop its human resources, it cannot develop much else. As a prerequisite for sustained economic growth, a number of problems must be resolved.
- Educational deficiencies which hold back the development of human resources.
- Governmental inefficiencies which hamper management, despite the fact that government may be the only source of managerial experience. Until the role of entrepreneur is restored to where it belongs in the private enterprise, the problems of modernizing the public administration deserves high priority.
- National pride which can lead to unrealistic attitudes. For example, local management personnel are often allowed to take over from foreign management teams prematurely.

Project Environment. Recently, Middle Eastern countries have become increasingly aware of the need for a systematic approach to the management of development projects. This demand arises from the complexity of such projects and the need for coordination and cooperation between many different government agencies and various other bodies. Figure 19–3 shows the typical project environment. This organization must relate to all appropriate agencies of the government as well as to the internal relationships common to conventional project management. These external and internal relationships define the organizational project environment.

In this environment, as a project moves from initiation to implementation, the principal responsibility for management and decision making changes. For example, the state council of planning may do the preliminary project analysis, the state planning board may make the evaluation and selection, and an implementation agency may manage the design and engineering. Since the quality of the work in each of these steps affects later phases of the project, the interfacing at the points where responsibility shifts becomes very important. The situation is reflected in the responsibility matrix in Figure 19–4.

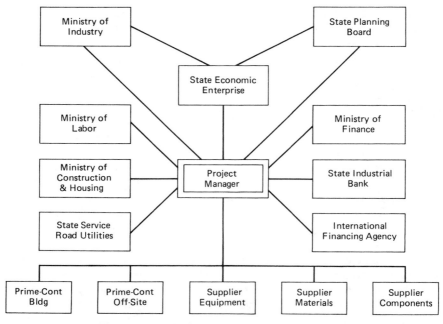

Figure 19–3. Project management environment.

Guidelines for Successful Project Management

To be successful in project management in the Middle East, the foreign executive must understand the work environment of the host country and be able to cope with it. The specific factors that must be considered include social and cultural, governmental and political, economic, technical, and operational.

Social and Cultural Considerations.   It is important to recognize that the cultures of the people in the developing countries have not yet reached the degree of sophistication existing in the West. As a result, not every people is ready for the introduction of formalized and structured management techniques into their work habits. Life in such countries is still informal and has no rigid structure. The application of modern management techniques will mean that peoples' life styles will become more formal. As a result, such techniques might meet with great resistance.

There is nothing more important to the host country than the foreign manager's respect for its social and cultural values. Before the foreigner can apply modern management techniques, he must understand the deeply rooted social and cultural values of the country. The built-in assumptions in modern technology may clash with these values. Commonly accepted goals of management techniques, such as "optimizing cost" and "maximizing profit" may be unacceptable, and could be replaced by status, stability, consensus, etc.

Governmental and Political Considerations.   Since the governments in the Middle East play a major role in project development, it is always important for the foreign executive to learn to communicate and deal with these governments.

- Develop a long-range plan for dealing with the host country. Study its development plan and define priorities over the planning horizon. Due to lack of experience, situations arise where government authorities arrive at a decision and are later discouraged when implementation does not achieve the established objectives. For example, there are many situations where political decisions were taken without sufficient consideration of availability of technical and planning information. Sometimes there is a

	STAGES OF INDUSTRIAL DEVELOPMENT PROJECT	DECISION MAKING BODIES							
		HIGHER AUTHORITIES COUNCIL FOR PLANNING[1]	STATE PLANNING BOARD	PROJECT IMPLE-MENTATION AGENCY	PROJECT MANAGER[2]	ASSISTANT PROJECT MANAGER	CONTRAC-TORS[3]	SUBCON-TRACTORS	SUPPLIERS
1	IDENTIFICATION OF PROJECT IDEA (PRELIMINARY ANALYSIS)	a	b	c					
2	PRELIMINARY SELECTION	b	a	b	c				
3	FEASILILITY (FORMULATION)	c	b/c	a	b				
4	POST FEASILILITY EVALUATION AND DECISION	a	a	b	b				
5	DETAILED PROJECT DESIGN AND ENGINEERING; AND INITIAL PROJECT IMPLEMENTATION, SCHEDULING		c	a	b	b	b/c	c	c
6	CONTRACTING AND PURCHASE			a/b	a	b	b	b	c
7	CONSTRUCTION AND PRE-OPERATIONS (SYSTEM IMPLEMENTATION, START-UP)			b	a	b	b	b	b
	INVOLVEMENT:	a ULTIMATE RESPONSIBILITY b ASSIGNED TO PROJECT c PERIPHERAL ACTIVITIES		[1]DEVELOPMENT STRATEGY AND POLICY, TARGET APPROVAL [2]OR, PRIME CONTRACTOR [3]OR, PROJECT CO-ORDINATOR					

Figure 19–4. Types of decision-making bodies involved with project management.

tendency of human nature to subscribe to political optimism to make over-commitments which are not feasible.

- Study the specific project justification and its feasibility from the technical, economic, and operational point of view. Lack of sufficient and accurate information is one of the most important areas that should be considered. The governmental central planning agency may be helpful in providing such information. Other agencies that provide accurate but not necessarily up-to-date information are the United Nations, The World Bank, and USAID.

Economic Considerations. Many development plans and programs are not supported by well-studied and well-conceived projects. Also, there are many projects which require common and limited resources. The use of such resources may not have been coordinated between government bodies with different responsibilities.

If a company is entering the Middle East for the first time, it is important to start with a project which is economically sound and contributes to the development of the host country. Understanding of the contracting procedures is also important, since these differ considerably, depending on the circumstances and conditions set by the agency supporting the project. For example, requirements will change if the project is financed by foreign aid, or if investment in a joint-venture arrangement is involved.

Operational Considerations. The foreign executive in the Middle East must know how to communicate with the client and how to deal with counterparts effectively. This requires an understanding of the Middle East managers who are bound by strict traditions of social and cultural background. Many of these differences have a direct effect on the operations of the project and must be considered by the manager. Some of the examples are:

- The Middle Eastern manager tends to remain with the same company or at least within the same industry all his productive life. That is why he is skeptical of the notion that management is a separate branch of knowledge that can be learned in a business school or management institute. Also, he is less mobile than the American manager. One of the theories of sociology states that when a person remains in one geographic locality throughout his life, he tends to be more individualistic and to have less conformity.
- The Middle Eastern manager tends to rely upon personal decision-making rather than the use of committees and shared decision-making as practiced by a typical American manager. That is why more centralization of

managerial authority and a more autocratic approach is used in dealing with subordinates.

- There is a greater separation between the business life and personal life of the individual in the Middle East. For example, it is rare for a businessman to introduce his family to his fellow businessmen. When he entertains, he entertains at a restaurant or some other public place. Also, rarely does he discuss business problems at a social function.
- There is a greater interest in governmental affairs on the part of the Middle Eastern manager than in his American counterpart. The government owns and controls business activities to a considerable degree in the Middle East.
- In most of the Middle Eastern countries, the managers have fewer problems with unions than in the United States. This is partly because governments require the business to provide social services to their workers.

Technical Considerations. Examples of the technically oriented problem areas are:

- Failures of the technologist and the project planning community to adapt their planning approach to the political/environmental/strategic situation.
- Lack of common language between scientists, technologists, economists, and politicians and failure of the technologist to present his information in an understandable form.
- Insufficient and unsystematic project organization.
- Too much concentration on individual planning techniques instead of integrating all relevant techniques and methods into a comprehensive project planning concept.
- Inertia of planning system and inability to handle the dynamic characteristics of projects.
- Lag in the development and state-of-the-art of project management methods and techniques compared to science and technology.
- Unsuitability of existing administration structures and practices for efficient project work.
- Inefficient and complicated administrative and management decision-making and planning procedures.
- Emphasis on science and technology rather than on management, resulting in a lack of appreciation for systematic project planning and implementation.
- Difficulty in obtaining agreement and cooperation from many diverse public and private organizations which are needed for project implementation.

Recommendations for Improvement.

- Successful utilization of project management requires personnel who are well-trained in the techniques, as well as well-trained decision-makers. The most important consideration to assure success of the implementation is to ensure top management support. Seminars or round-table discussions can be instrumental in acquainting them with the concepts of project management. Detailed training programs may follow for the project management level and the task or operational level.
- There is a need for a scientific approach in handling project management. This can be facilitated by providing meaningful information about institutions and courses available for instruction in project management. In addition, information should be provided on recent literature and applications in this subject.
- The reporting system for project implementation should meet at least a minimum set of standards permitting effective corrective actions. Specific formats should be designed to suit the reporting needs of different levels of management.
- The executing organization or contractor should be encouraged to use network planning techniques. Manual network analysis should be emphasized at the early stage of the project or where the size of the project is not so large as to require computerized processing.
- The main functions of project management, namely, planning, scheduling, budgeting and control, should be understood, and the related responsibilities should be clearly assigned. The following are some specific recommendations in this respect:
  - Management should clearly assign the responsibility and authority for project implementation. A task team should be established whose leader reports to the program manager. This team should be responsible for developing implementation plans which are approved and monitored by management. One of the most important top-management responsibilities is to assure the integration of the planning of the project with related projects.
  - Time estimating for project tasks should be assigned to personnel who are familiar with the work to be performed. Work breakdown structures should be used as a basis for network development and budgeting. The work packages should be well-defined and should be related to the internal organization and responsibilities. All organizations involved in performing a work package should understand and agree to its scope and time, i.e., identifying the precise start and completion events or milestones for each work package.
  - Release of funds to work packages should be through work control bud-

gets which are established at the time when work is defined in detail and which are used to control physical as well as cost progress.

- Project control information should be designed with the management level of the user in mind. Bulky reports should be avoided. At the management level, emphasis should be on trends, variance analysis, and identification of specific problem areas. Display techniques should be used which permit evaluation of the effects of critical items on the total project.

Conclusions

The following recommendations should lead to more successful management of projects in the Middle East.

Guidelines for Foreign Executives Involved in Initiation and Planning of Projects.

- Be aware of the environment of the host country.
- Study the host country's developing plans and develop a long-range plan for future cooperation.
- Survey the financial institutions involved in the project and study the investment laws if applicable.
- Before undertaking a project, study its feasibility from the technical, economic, and operational point of view. Also, study the contribution of the project to the development of the host country.
- Develop relationships with governmental and business leaders and develop special relationship with the project's local "godfather."
- Choose the right project manager for managing and implementing the project, and assign him to the project at an early stage.

Guidelines for Foreign Project Managers Involved in Project Development and Implementation.

- Be aware of the new environment: social and cultural; political and economic.
- Communicate with the client and learn how to deal with the counterpart effectively.
- Study the different phases and stages of the project: preparation and initiation; implementation; and operation.
- Study the decision-making process and the different organizations responsible for project implementation and operation.

A foreign manager in the Middle East has to work in a potpourri of social, cultural, religious, and political values which may be quite alien to him. He requires a keen awareness and an uncommon capability in dealing with the overlapping forces which constitute the overall environment. Therefore, he should not hesitate to question any so-called basic assumptions which have been established beforehand but may not reflect the real world. He should have a subtleness to point out the areas requiring change, though he should neither be rudely firm nor firmly rude. In brief, he should be empathetic, not apathetic.

Following these recommendations, the foreign project manager should be better able to understand his client's point of view and deal more effectively with his counterparts in the host country. Through this mutual understanding, project management in the Middle East could be both exciting and rewarding.

PROBLEM

19–1 The successful implepentation of project management requires overcoming several difficulties and problems. For each of the items listed below, state whether overcoming the obstacles would be easier for U.S. corporations, or developing countries, assuming both are interested in implementing project management:

a. Good forward-planning capability
b. Understanding the importance of project management
c. Availability of coputers
d. Understanding of project management principles by remote-site personnel and subcontractors
e. Ability to update status as events are completed
f. Understanding the reasons for the need of trade-offs
g. Centralization of decision-making
h. Short-term resource control
i. Ability to assimilate large amounts of data
j. Variety and frequency of political changes
k. Variety and frequency of economic changes
l. Governmental supporting-policy measures
m. Inadequacies of subcontractors
n. Lack of accurate information

20
Project Management in the Year 2000

20.0 INTRODUCTION

What will project management be like in the year 2000? This simple question raises the broader issues of "What will business in general be like?" and "What will our future lifestyle be?" While it is impossible to predict with certainty even fifteen or so short years ahead, certain trends (below) can be identified, and additional speculations may be helpful:

- Engineering/technology appears to be doubling every five years or less.
- Computer technology is doubling every two years.
- Product life cycles are becoming shorter.
- There is a greater demand for new-product introduction, with shorter product-development time.
- Manager and executives are requiring more information and at a faster rate for strategic decision-making.
- More and more managers are becoming people- rather than task-oriented.
- Executives have come to realize that they cannot manage a $50MM/year corporation with a $10MM/year system.

The following paragraphs seek to explore possible changes in our future way of doing business and then suggest some of the implications for tomorrow's project managers.

20.1 ORGANIZATIONAL CONSIDERATIONS

Even a conservative view of the future requires a great deal of imagination. Our business views appear to be changing, with an extremely strong emphasis being placed on middle managers to be evaluated solely on ROA or profit contributions. Since most horizontal lines are profit centers, project management appears to be an excellent method for training future managers and executives to be cost-conscious as well as profit-oriented.

Our basic business principles need serious revision in the near future because of this short-term approach and long-term implications. Business and government seem to have opposing views, and these additional complications are all combining to reduce efficiency. Technology is making the world smaller and making obsolete more of the operational tasks, while at the same time business is finding it more difficult to operate profitably.

If growth continues as it has in the past twenty years, we can expect to see major changes through technological developments. Project management will be widely implemented and accepted only when it clearly proves that increased profits may be realized.

If change is slow and automation is resisted, the more centralized traditional organizations will still be used throughout the remainder of the twentieth century. If so, improved productivity can be gained only through internal resource sharing and horizontal work flow, the basic ingredients of project management. Therefore, since project management organizational forms seem to be more adaptable than the traditional ones, they will most likely become almost universally accepted over the next twenty years. Functional specialist positions would most likely remain as an organizational line element. All or most staff organizations presently servicing internal operations are likely to become smaller in number and will generally be aligned in a matrix to serve all functional disciplines.

As the project management structure and the position of the project manager become more mature, emphasis will be placed upon reducing the overhead rate by eliminating several layers of supervisory positions that exist between the project managers and upper-level management. The secret, of course, will rest in the ability and confidence that the executives impart to the project managers. This should not pose much of a problem—the majority of the executive management positions probably will be filled from the project management ranks, since the project managers may conceivably be the only individuals who will understand the operations of the total company, not merely one line organization.

20.2 PROJECT VS. PRODUCT MANAGEMENT

Without some insight into or understanding of project management, organizations of the future will find it more difficult to manage during periods of growth without creating some degree of havoc with operating procedures. In order to cope with such problems, organizations have slowly increased the indirect population of the traditional structure with the rationale that "If we throw enough people at these problems, they must eventually figure out a way to handle them." This technique usually fails because of poor communications, mistrust, and duplication of efforts.

The necessity for quick resolution to these problems will prompt management to think that "permanent" task forces or project teams will result in improved productivity and effectiveness. Yet even with continued success at task force management, executives will struggle with this concept of full-time project management until either the next step becomes obvious or new entrants in top management force us into full-time project management. Companies may experience disastrous results by going piecemeal into project management.

By the year 2000, product lines that cannot justify continuous full-time utilization of resources will be controlled by product managers using project management. The terms "project management" and "product management" may even become synonymous. Companies of the future will be structured by market segment, with each market segment run by a product manager. These product managers will constitute a project team one level below the functional vice-presidents. The project team will be responsible for the complete operation of existing products, and will also be part of the planning function project, which will also include vice-presidents and the CEO. Product managers will report to the vice-president of operations, whereas full-time project managers will report to the vice-president of marketing.

Since products and applications are becoming more and more technically oriented, future project managers generally will be twenty-five to thirty-five years old. They will have production, design, processing, or laboratory training. Individuals who demonstrate effective interpersonal skills and an ability to get the job done will be promoted to project management positions. As project managers, they will coordinate and manage all projects established by the executive level and both screened and prioritized by the executive project team, composed of the CEO, the functional vice-president, and the product managers.

20.3 ROLE OF THE COMPUTER

As data processing managers come up through the ranks, project management will be a way of life. It could even be said that computer technology in the seventies and eighties has hastened the development of project management. This is so primarily because of the cross-functional involvement of complex and systematized computer systems.

If computer systems are to be successfully installed for individual projects by the year 2000, functional departments must cooperate and trade information to one another so that the desired results are obtainable. Data processing project management will become a strong driving force by the year 2000 because the overlap of computerization will force functional organizations within a company to become more integrated. With the computer as a catalyst, by the year 2000 there will be much more matrix management than currently exists. Project management will evolve into a way of life.

Large, complex projects will have to include major social programs, energy-related programs, and continuing defense programs. Financial, human, and raw material resources will have become more limited by the year 2000. This will mean increased controls, especially in setting priorities, more sophisticated methods of trade-off analysis, and improved overall project control. Computers will become more extensively used in all areas of control.

There seems to be sufficient evidence that even a more revolutionary growth era could be forthcoming. With technological breakthroughs and reduced costs, microprocessors and "smart terminals" will provide mechanisms for this growth. Software project planning models will become more evident in the offices of the future. It is also conceivable that more and more project managers will work out of their homes. If the current trend continues and accelerates, by the year 2000 the (two-dimensional) traditional and matrix organizations as we know them may not physically exist at all. Individuals or groups of individuals functioning from their homes would rely totally on a telecommunications center as a communications vehicle. However, the strategic decision center and organizational centers will still remain within the parent organization. Hosts of computers could control large conglomerate projects, all linked together by a massive interdependent system.

The computer itself will become increasingly important and eventually may take the place of many middle managers, operational employees, and clerks. The CEO, computer hardware, and systems personnel are likely to be centralized within the executive decision-making group. If so, this group will ultimately function as the manager of project managers and will dictate work flow plans based upon project plans and master production schedules.

"Smart terminals" will play an ever-increasing role in project control. Terminal screens will be color-coded to provide an up-to-the-minute accounting for all assigned resources as well as for cost control. Corrective action and trade-off analysis can be taken instantaneously from these terminals. Inventory control problems will become a thing of the past. Project managers will have a complete picture of their own projects as well as other projects that are sharing common resources.

20.4 IMPACT ON BUSINESS ORGANIZATIONS

Assuming continuation of a partially regulated capitalistic structure, future business organizations will compete less on the basis of marketing or production capability and more on the basis of management ability and technological sophistication. This assumption is based on the idea that operational planning, production, production control, administration, and even marketing, will be automated and optimized to the extent that no "competitive edge" can long endure. Successful firms will be differentiated by their ability to do strategic planning, to develop optimal products, to mitigate governmental intervention, and to respond correctly to environmental change.

Functional middle managers are likely to become an "endangered species" by the year 2000. They can and will be replaced by highly skilled technicians who operate the complex organization to achieve specific results ordered by a computerized control system. People will become unnecessary, even detrimental, in the optimization of operational programming, planning, and budgeting. Administrative functions, even including performance appraisal, will not require human intervention, except for review.

Top management will be more directly involved and more completely in control of the total business operations. Company software will be available to translate strategic goals and short-range objectives into action plans, and will faithfully report the results achieved directly to the top.

If this is true, these changes will give rise to a different type of middle manager—the project manager—to plan and execute those unique efforts that have not been placed under computer control.

20.5 ROLE OF THE PROJECT MANAGER

Within the speculative framework outlined above, the extreme flexibility of a matrix organization and the adaptive ability of the project manager to deal with the changing array of projects may justify his continued existence. It is presupposed that automation and computerized optimization techniques will make recurring operations as efficient and effective as is technologically possible. However, the "one of a kind" project (R&D, capital facility development, acquisition or divestment of a product line, etc.) will require project manager leadership. The following project management skills will likely be important in the future:

- Producing an "end result" within the constraints of available resources and performance requirements. This will require a "global view" of the project objectives and accurate planning of how success will be achieved.
- Leadership aspects of directing the project team effort. However, reporting of results and control feedback will be highly automated, and will require relatively less attention.
- Decision making, which although based on the use of all pertinent data, typically will still involve uncertainty within an uncontrolled environment.
- Negotiations for needed resources and resolution of conflicting demands on those resources. In fact, the interface requirement will take on the larger proportions of the conflict between computer control and human

initiative. Resolution across that man–machine interface will be particularly demanding.

The anticipated role of the future project manager is largely related to operational planning for unique projects. While the computer can make real contributions in all program development, it probably will not be capable of identifying all relevant alternatives, testing them against the broader environment, and charting an operational plan to achieve the unique objectives of a "one-shot" project. The project manager's "systems view" of the world will permit evaluation of the true alternatives and "coaching" of the project team to execute the selected action plan.

20.6 PROJECT MANAGER SELECTION AND TRAINING

Assuming an increasingly responsible role for future project managers, their selection, training, evaluation, and retention will also become increasingly important. It is logical to anticipate that optimization techniques will be applied to personnel selection as well as to other aspects of business management. All available sources of information, including personal history, academic achievement, performance appraisals, psychological testing, and career development counseling, will be used to select future project managers.

It seems likely that formal education will be interspersed throughout the future project managers' work life, so they may continue to cope with a rapidly changing world. Future project managers will likely come from a particular discipline, but their specialization may shift over time, and a career development plan will concentrate on broadening their experience base through both formal education and job rotation. In addition to disciplinary skills, future project managers will require communications and general business skills, knowledge of the man–machine interface with computers, knowledge of governmental restraints and a feeling for how public policy decisions are made, a global view of business economics, and a general understanding of human behavior.

At various points in their career development, project managers should interface directly with top management to understand the development of strategic goals, how those goals are translated into project objectives, and how project results impact the overall organization. This will also permit the development of managerial competence through increasingly responsible assignments and through "mentor" relationships with top managers.

Throughout the process, the organization must provide compensation, status, growth, and achievement recognition needed to motivate and retain competent project managers. This must be accomplished, however, without creating an "elitist group" that could not obtain project team cooperation and support in the matrix structure.

20.7 PERFORMANCE MEASUREMENT

Through powerful information systems and development of optimal control, feedback, and reporting schemes, the appraisal of managerial performance will become highly objective. To be accurate, however, such performance appraisal must be based upon stated objectives and performance against those objectives in the context of environmental conditions encountered. Today, most management appraisal systems focus on how well actual performance compares with stated performance objectives. Present systems either ignore environmental changes that should affect the appraisal, or else sanctify environmental change or external restraint as the justification for neglecting performance standards. Expanded use of the information system data base will permit more accurate analysis and better evaluation of project manager results.

Based on full information and powerful computer support (approaching "artificial intelligence"), the real evaluation of managerial performance will shift from "What happens if we depart from our operational plan?" to the more penetrating question of "What happens if we achieve our intended plan?" The quality of strategic goals selected by top management will determine whether a proper project objective was conceived. And, the quality of the operational planning function performed by future project managers will largely determine project success.

20.8 GOVERNMENT

A futuristic analysis of the role of the project manager cannot be made without analyzing the environment in which he will be operating. It is probable that the impact of government on the lives of individual citizens will continue to increase, with environmental regulations increasing sharply. The government may well become heavily involved in the enforced recycling of nonrenewable resources wherever this is possible. Internationally, it is likely that democracy will continue to decline in the world and the remaining democracies (including the United States) will become increasingly socialized. Much has been said about pollution of air and water, but these are relatively easy to clean up compared to the pollution of the land that has taken place. It is entirely likely that vast project teams will be necessary to clean up (if this is possible) the damage that has been done to the land, and that these project teams will involve the resources of business and government jointly. Very sophisticated project management techniques will be necessary for this activity.

20.9 SOCIAL CHANGE

With the increasing automation of production and the demand of the work force that tedium be removed from the work place, it is likely that the working week will be reduced, there will be considerably more leisure than is currently possible, and education will increase to such a degree that work and education will become difficult to separate. The rate of change of knowledge will mean that it will be impossible for people to focus on a life's career, but rather they must focus on several careers sequentially in a given lifetime. It is also likely that the flex-hours concept will find increasing acceptance, with the result that all of these changes will have profound effects on how project managers will have to function. Also, the work force will be considerably more mobile—not geographically, but vocationally. Thus key and entrusted project team members will become less and less available because of reeducation, flex-hours, increased leisure time, and so on.

20.10 DEMOGRAPHICS

There are huge demograhic changes taking place in the United States. There are strong trends toward smaller families, single-parent families, dual or multiple-career families, and migratory changes in the United States. Again, these changes will increase the *uncertainty of availability* of trained personnel to project teams, thus making the project manager's job more difficult and complex.

20.11 PHYSICAL RESOURCES

OPEC is a Third World cartel that controls much of the world's crude oil resources. The use of crude oil is expected to continue to increase, and to peak in the year 2000. The vast majority of crude oil is used as fuel and thus is nonrecoverable, with only about 5 percent being converted into chemicals. Increasingly, fuel, in the form of crude oil, will be difficult to acquire and projects that in the past could afford to regard fuel as a factor of low importance will now have to consider the impact of very high prices on project activity. Again, project management will be made all the more complex because of the need to plan for adequate fuel availability for the project.

If the availability of organic resources (crude oil, natural gas, and their derivatives) in the future is not encouraging, then the potential for inorganics is downright disastrous. The United States has largely depleted its reserves of key inorganics, such as zinc, copper, molybdenum, chromium, and nickel, and already there are moves by those countries that possess the resources to cartelize and form their own "OPEC." Project managers, as part of their project, may well have to consider alternatives to these key resources, with government-mandated recycling becoming a part of the total project.

20.12 THE MARKETS

The marketplace that project management will have to respond to will become increasingly complex and changeable. Project management will have to be constantly aware of changing techniques and regulatory rules in responding to rapid market shifts. It is very likely that the goals and objectives of a given project team will change during its lifetime even though the original plan was for a relatively short-lived project. Contingency planning in this environment will become an absolute necessity, and it is possible that new courses in this discipline will emerge at specific universities.

Colleges and universities will begin teaching graduate and undergraduate interdisciplinary courses in project management. There may also exist massive continuing education programs in the areas of project and product management.

Companies will become not just international, but supranational. Concurrent with the emergence and growth of the new supranational company, there will be a blurring of the distinction between government and business. One manifestation of this lack of distinction is the profit-oriented, nationalized company (of which there are many successful examples around the world). Within the supranational company, the project manager's task will become increasingly complex and difficult as he tries to coordinate the activities of many people, of many languages, in several countries, with different skill levels in what will become increasingly international projects.

20.13 LIFE STYLES

Life generally, in the United States and elsewhere, will become more complex with faster change, necessitating a change away from a single-career lifetime to a multiple-career lifetime. The project manager will probably have an even more difficult job because the number of tasks that have to be done will continue to increase, with a high probability that there will be very large numbers of jobs in existence in the year 2000 that do not exist now and cannot even be forecast. In all probability, the emerging tendency will be for a project manager to be assigned a project management task, upon completion of which he is returned to a mundane non-project-management task as recuperation. This will evolve into the need to retrain the project manager in some new skill or discipline upon the completion of each project. The rate of change of technology and science will not merely necessitate this but will demand it. Large, long-term projects may eventually burn out good project managers.

20.14 CONCLUSION

Project management and the "systems approach" to human enterprise today constitute an extremely flexible and highly effective approach to multidisciplinary program management. This approach is likely to be even more important in the future, as less flexible or less creative methods are executed by computers or robots.

Successful future enterprises will be differentiated by the quality of management planning and decision making. By virtue of broad experience, flexible approach, and a "people-oriented" leadership style, tomorrow's project managers should be able to cope in the year 2000.

Appendix A
Project Management
Final Exam (A)

For each question, there is one, and only one satisfactory answer.

1. Which of the following is not characteristic of a project?
   a. A finite lifetime
   b. Must have both a formal and informal reporting system
   c. Designed to accomplish a single objective
   d. Designed usually for unique, one-of-a-kind activities

2. The best definition for an ongoing project would be
   a. A project
   b. A program
   c. A system
   d. A continuous stream of unrelated tasks

3. Another name for aggregate projects would be
   a. Individual
   b. Line/staff
   c. Special
   d. Matrix

4. John has been assigned a project which requires communications between two departments within the same division. Which of the following forms would be the *least* appropriate?
   a. Individual
   b. Line/staff
   c. Special
   d. Matrix

5. The conflict resolution procedure works best if the project manager and resource managers report to the same person.
   a. True
   b. False

6. An employee refuses to dress appropriately when interfacing with the customer. The responsibility rests with the

   a. Project manager
   b. Functional manager

7. The inability for functional members to keep current in their respective disciplines is characteristic of which organizational form?

   a. Line/staff
   b. Product
   c. Matrix
   d. none of the above

8. The time required to change over from a traditional structure to a matrix structure can be expected to take (for large companies)

   a. six months or less
   b. six months to one year
   c. two years
   d. three years

9. Who determines which member of a functional department will present technical data to the customer? (Assume that more than one functional team member is assigned to this project.)

   a. The project manager
   b. The functional manager
   c. The Director of Project Management
   d. The Director of Engineering

10. The highest ranking individual in the company, who would have as his/her responsibility the resolution of project conflicts, would be the

    a. Vice-President and General Manager
    b. Functional manager
    c. Project manager
    d. Director of Project Management

11. In general, which of the following would not pertain to the functions of a project manager

    a. Planning
    b. Staffing
    c. Controlling
    d. Directing

12. Master production schedules are prepared by the

    a. Functional managers or functional team members
    b. Project manager
    c. Project office team members

13. Departmental PERT Charts are prepared by the project office team members for the functional departments to follow.
   a. True
   b. False

14. Adhering to the milestones established by the customer is the responsibility of
   a. The project manager
   b. The functional manager
   c. Both the project and functional manager

15. The project plan is a document designed to tell _____ exactly what should be happening in a given period of time.
   a. Anyone associated with the project
   b. The project manager
   c. The functional manager

16. Adhering to contractual requirements is the responsibility of
   a. The project manager
   b. The functional manager
   c. The Director of Project Management
   d. The contracts team member

17. The decision to increase resources on the project is the responsibility of the
   a. The functional manager
   b. The project manager
   c. The Director of Project Management
   d. The customer

18. Which of the following is *not* considered as a role for top management?
   a. Setting the selection criteria for projects
   b. Selecting functional team members for project assignments
   c. Establishing priorities among projects

19. A functional manager would most likely consider project management as a
   a. Threat to establish authority
   b. Challenge
   c. Research area
   d. Means to an end

   Answer Questions 20-23 using the choices given below:
   a. Conceptual Phase
   b. Definition Phase
   c. Production Phase
   d. Operational Phase
   e. Divestment Phase

20. In which phase do we identify human and non-human resources?

21. In which phase do we perform a feasibility study?

22. In which phase do we examine alternative ways of accomplishing the objectives?

23. In which phase do we transfer resources to other systems?

24. Which of the following is not a characteristic of a dynamic system?
    a. Subsystem integration
    b. System effectiveness
    c. System efficiency
    d. System life cycles
    e. None of the above

25. One of the major causes for the failure of the line/staff form of project management was that upper-level management was reluctant to relinquish any of their power and authority to project managers.
    a. True
    b. False

26. Which of the following are characteristics of a project manager?
    a. Honesty and integrity
    b. Decision-making ability
    c. Understanding of personnel problems
    d. Versatility
    e. All of the above

27. A project manager is far more likely to succeed if it is obvious that general management has appointed him.
    a. True
    b. False

28. Which of the following is not a prime responsibility of a project manager?
    a. In-house communications
    b. Evaluating interface employee for promotion
    c. Customer communications
    d. Negotiation with functional management

29. Insuring that all work performed is both authorized and funded by contractual documentation is the responsibility of the
    a. Functional manager
    b. Project manager
    c. Director of Project Management

30. Which of the following factors would have the least effect on project office membership?

   a. Customer support requirements
   b. Project size
   c. Employee pay grade and level
   d. Type of project
   e. Level of technical competency required

31. The project manager may have the authority to make commitments in which of the following areas?

   a. Salary
   b. Grade
   c. Bonus and overtime pay
   d. An individual's assignment after project termination
   e. None of the above

32. In many project organizational forms, project office team members worry more about setbacks in their careers than do functional personnel.

   a. True
   b. False

33. Planning is

   a. Selecting policies and procedures in order to achieve objectives
   b. Decision making
   c. A means for monitoring and controlling work
   d. All of the above

34. Which of the following is *not* one of the major reasons why plans fail?

   a. Plan requires too much in too little time
   b. Planning performed by a planning group
   c. Management assumes that all activities will not be completed on schedule
   d. Poor financial estimates
   e. None of the above

35. The project manager must be given sufficient authority to organize activities across functional lines.

   a. True
   b. False

36. Which of the following is *not* a major result of poor authority relations being established?

   a. Poor communications channels
   b. Misleading information
   c. Good employee working relations
   d. Surprises for the customer

37. Which individual or group would normally not be shown on a linear responsibility chart?
    a. Functional members
    b. Functional managers
    c. Directors
    d. Vice-presidents and general managers
    e. They can all be shown on an LRC

    Answer Questions 38–40 using the alternatives shown below:
    a. Formal authority
    b. Reward power
    c. Penalty power
    d. Expert power
    e. Referent power

38. Which interpersonal influence results from having a project manager reporting to someone high in the organization?

39. Which interpersonal influence would be most common if a functional manager were promoted to project manager for a high-technology effort?

40. Which interpersonal influence would be impacted by the relationships that exist in the informal organization?

41. The relative influence in decision making that a functional manager possesses depends upon the organization form of project management.
    a. True
    b. False

42. Which of the following is the responsibility of functional manager?
    a. What is to be done?
    b. When will the task be done?
    c. Where will the task be done?
    d. Why will the task be done?
    e. How much money is available to do it?

43. In the inevitable conflict between project and functional managers, the project manager blames cost overruns on the functional manager with the argument that there were too many changes.
    a. True
    b. False

44. Which of the following reasons for project management failure is the one most often overlooked?
    a. The wrong man as project manager
    b. Poorly defined tasks
    c. Project termination not planned
    d. Company management unsupportive
    e. Management techniques misused

45. The major obstacle in using MBO in project management is

    a. Evaluating how people spend their time
    b. Giving employees clearly defined objectives
    c. Letting employees have a part in setting their own objectives

46. A resource manager would best be defined as a

    a. Department manager
    b. Project manager
    c. Division manager
    d. Director

47. If a project office has a diversity of disciplinary expertise, then

    a. The project will be a success
    b. There will be no overlap of activities
    c. Conflicts will probably occur
    d. All of the above

    Answer Questions 48-52 using the following alternatives

    a. Withdrawal
    b. Smoothing
    c. Compromising
    d. Forcing
    e. Confrontation

48. Most project managers would prefer to resolve conflicts by _____.

49. Hierarchical referral is suggestive of which mode for handling conflicts? (Two answers are possible.)

50. Which mode gives a win or lose position?

51. Which mode usually ends up with a give and take position?

52. Which mode does the least to resolve a conflict?

53. If project management is to be successful, functional employees must be willing to be treated as both theory X and theory Y.

    a. True
    b. False

54. Communications can best be defined as

    a. Providing written or oral directions
    b. An exchange of information
    c. Eliminating the filters and barriers that stand between people
    d. None of the above

55. Which of the following cannot be tracked using the Work Breakdown Structure?
    a. Time
    b. Cost
    c. Performance
    d. None of the above

56. The fourth level in the Work Breakdown Structure is the
    a. Project
    b. Subtask
    c. Level of effort
    d. Work package
    e. Task

57. For effective project management to exist, there should be flexibility built into the Work Breakdown Structure.
    a. True
    b. False

58. Which is considered to be a part of the planning cycle?
    a. Work authorization
    b. Data collection
    c. Variance analysis
    d. Cost accounting
    e. Information reporting
    f. None of the above

59. Most organizations prepare multiple schedules in order to satisfy
    a. Upper-level reporting
    b. Customer reporting
    c. Functional reporting
    d. All of the above

60. Reviewing schedules with the customer during the planning cycle shows him that you welcome his help and input.
    a. True
    b. False

61. The program plan can be used to eliminate conflict between functional managers.
    a. True
    b. False

62. Which of the following is not one of the primary needs for good charting and scheduling?
    a. Cutting costs and reducing time
    b. Increase the time required for routine decisions
    c. Eliminating idle time
    d. Develop better troubleshooting procedures

Answer Questions 63-68 based upon the PERT network shown below:

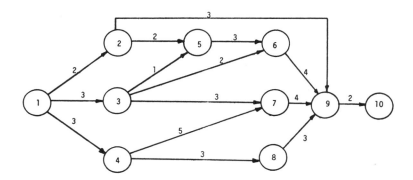

63. The critical path contains events
    a. 1-2-9-10
    b. 1-2-5-6-9-10
    c. 1-3-5-6-9-10
    d. 1-3-6-9-10
    e. 1-4-8-9-10
    f. 1-4-7-9-10

64. For Event 8, the early time will be
    a. 3 days
    b. 4 days
    c. 6 days
    d. 8 days
    e. 9 days
    f. 12 days
    g. none of the above

65. For Event 8, the late time will be
    a. 3 days
    b. 6 days
    c. 9 days
    d. 12 days
    e. 15 days
    f. none of the above

66. The total slack time for event 8 is
    a. 2 days
    b. 3 days
    c. 5 days
    d. 6 days
    e. 9 days
    f. none of the above

67. If activities 1-2, 1-3, and 1-4 use the same manpower, and if a one day decrease in one activity causes a one day increase in one of the other two activities, then replanning will reduce the length of the critical path by
    a. 0 days
    b. 1 day
    c. 2 days
    d. 3 days
    e. none of the above

68. If the most likely time for activity 4-7 is the same as the estimated time, and if the pessimistic time is 8 days, then the optimistic time is
    a. 0 days
    b. 2 days
    c. 3 days
    d. 4 days
    e. none of the above

69. The environmental factors (legal, social, political, technological, and economical):
    a. Are always monitored by the project manager, especially during project execution.
    b. Are the responsibility of the functional manager
    c. Are the responsibility of top-level management
    d. None of the above

70. If material expenditures are $1000 per month, commitments are six months and termination liability is 80%, what is the termination liability for the second month?
    a. $4800
    b. $6000
    c. $5600
    d. $7000
    e. none of the above

71. The time necessary to complete a project is referred to as
    a. Implementation time
    b. Life cycle
    c. Operations cycle
    d. none of the above

72. The most important paperwork to help a project manager control the project is the
    a. Work Breakdown Structure
    b. Specifications
    c. Statement of Work
    d. Schedule

73. The successful project managers spend most of their time
    a. Planning with top management
    b. Planning with their personnel
    c. Studying project results
    d. Talking with personnel

74. The term interface refers to
    a. The relationship between various parts of a project
    b. How a project looks to the outsiders
    c. How a project looks to its personnel
    d. The beginning and end of a project

75. Good project managers:
    a. Have at least one heart attack a year
    b. Drive people into the ground until success is at hand
    c. Love power and title
    d. Make X-rated movies in their spare time
    e. All of the above
    f. none of the above

Appendix B
Project Management
Final Exam (B)*

PROJECT MANAGEMENT EXAM (B)*

1. The primary responsibility of the Project Management Department is:

   A. to maintain the necessary good working relationships with functional departments to complete the project.
   B. to ensure the functional groups conform to the cost, schedule, and technical requirements of the project.
   C. the development and implementation of plans for assigned projects.
   D. conformance to project cost and schedule constraints.

2. Projects assigned to Project Management:

   A. encompass the planning, design, construction, start-up, and associated activities required for the completion and operation of any new effort.
   B. include any task assigned by management.
   C. include responsibility for new projects and planning.
   D. A and C but not B.

3. The Project Management Department is dependent upon the functional departments to provide qualified personnel for assignment to projects and:

   A. to perform project supporting work.
   B. to prepare analysis of project variance reports for the functional area.
   C. to maintain a commitment system for the functional area.
   D. to communicate decisions regarding the project to upper management in a timely manner.

*Adapted from *Project Management Workshop,* developed by Project Control Services Department, Florida Power & Light Company. Reproduced by permission of Florida Power & Light Company.

4. For some project decisions, Project Management and other departments act in concurrence. This is:

   A. because when it is mutually agreed, the decision is the best one for the project.
   B. not relevant since concurrence is a term used in Mission Statements.
   C. part of a "checks and balance" system.
   D. what happens when upper management makes the decision.

5. Which of the following is *not* an objective of the Project Management Department:

   A. timely, good quality planning for assigned projects with realistic schedules and accurate cost forecasts.
   B. timely, decisive response to project needs based upon objective analysis of available information.
   C. completion of original projects within approved budget and schedule constraints and in compliance with technical specifications, regulations and agreements made with outside agencies or organizations.
   D. to provide project information identifying deviations and trends from approved plans, schedules, cash flows or budgets.

6. "Success" targets for the Project General Manager (PGM) are:

   A. cost, schedule, and technical performance objectives and other specifications of the project defined by the approved project plan.
   B. cost, schedule, and technical performance objectives and other specifications of the project set when the PGM was assigned.
   C. under-budget and ahead of schedule targets.
   D. There are no "success" targets. Response to a dynamic environment precludes meeting fixed targets.

7. In order to successfully develop and implement an approved plan for a project, the PGM:

   A. must be technically competent in all disciplines.
   B. must be able to select the functional personnel.
   C. has the responsibility for managing, directing and controlling project activities.
   D. has the authority to override functional department heads.

8. The basic performance indices for the Project General Manager are:

   A. actual milestone dates met vs. planned milestone dates met.
   B. actual project costs vs. planned project costs.
   C. actual plant reliability vs. planned plant reliability.
   D. actual performance vs. planned performance to targets in approved project plan.

9. Using a football team as an analogy, the PGM performs the role of:

    A. Coach
    B. Quarterback
    C. Owner
    D. Trainer

10. Project Management:

    A. is not needed if all functional managers would carry out their assigned responsibilities.
    B. is needed because the functional organization and its methods of planning and control cannot otherwise assure that complex projects will be completed on schedule and within budget.
    C. is not needed unless the project is in serious trouble.
    D. is needed only on projects which have high visibility.

11. Project Management uses a matrix organization because:

    A. with functional organizations, the burden of managing projects falls on upper management.
    B. project needs overlap functional boundaries.
    C. it prevents problems within functional departments.
    D. A and B but not C.

12. The key concepts of Project Management are:

    A. appointment of a Project General Manager with total authority and responsibility for the project, and with direct control of all contributing specialists.
    B. formation of a separate division or other self-supporting organization specifically for the project, with the Project General Manager in charge.
    C. identification of a single point of integrative responsibility for the project in addition to existing responsibilities of contributing functional managers, and establishment of integrated planning and control of all aspects of the project.
    D. establishment of integrated planning and control of all phases of and all functional contributions to the project, and appointment of a Project Engineer for its technical aspects.

13. The Project General Manager assignment should ideally be rotated during each project.

    A. True, because it is the best way to fill the Project General Manager role, since the assigned person in each phase is very knowledgeable of that phase.
    B. False, because it breaks the continuity of responsibility and allows unsolved problems to be swept forward to the end of the project.
    C. True, because it is the only practical approach, since no one person will have the required expertise to manage the project in all its phases.
    D. False, because it combines functional and project management responsibilities, thereby creating organizational conflicts.

14. The task of providing necessary expertise to solve project related technical problems is:

   A. a role of the functional departments.
   B. a role of the Project General Manager.
   C. a task of the consultants hired by the project team.
   D. the role of upper-level management.

15. The Project General Manager's basic responsibility is:

   A. to provide the functional departments with budget and to schedule constraints for completing the project.
   B. to act as the interface with top management.
   C. to complete the project within established budget, schedule and project specifications.
   D. to act as the central collection point for budget and schedule information.

16. The Project General Manager is designated a line manager

   A. and has decision making authority on all project matters.
   B. and has decision making authority on all project matters, but his decisions may be disputed by functional department heads with PGM having the last word.
   C. and has decision making authority on all project matters, but his decisions may be disputed by functional department heads with mutual agreement necessary prior to implementation.
   D. and has decision making authority on all project matters, but his decision may be disputed by functional department heads with conflict being resolved by a common boss.

17. In dealing with functional managers and their functional project leaders, the Project General Manager should:

   A. maintain a formal and official relationship with each, in order to ensure respect and acceptance of his authority.
   B. avoid too much personal contact, which tends to generate unnecessary interpersonal conflict, and rely mainly on the formal organization communications structure.
   C. develop a personal rapport with each manager through frequent face-to-face contact, and provide each with pertinent available information on the project.
   D. restrict information to what a manager absolutely has to know about his part of the project.

18. The Project General Manager should use an organization development (team-building) program. Organization Development is:

    A. a process by which the overall effectiveness of the project team is maximized in achieving its objectives.
    B. a process by which the functional departments are reorganized to more effectively support project management.
    C. a process by which the Project General Manager can make the project team as large as he believes necessary to support the project.
    D. a process by which project correspondence can be classified to improve team communications.

19. The Project General Manager should seek speedy resolution of conflict between the project and functional departments primarily because

    A. conflict impedes the decision-making necessary to stay within schedule and budget constraints.
    B. conflict represents a challenge to authority.
    C. conflict indicates that the Project Management concept is not well understood.
    D. None of the above. The resolution of conflict is a problem to be resolved by the Director of Projects.

20. Project General Managers:

    A. must approve all project expenditures.
    B. may delegate the approval of expenditures to Team Members in an amount selected by the PGM.
    C. have corporate defined limits of approval and delegation of approval.
    D. can approve only customer-specified expenditures.

21. Timely decisions directly and dramatically affect the ability of the project team to meet commitments to cost and schedule constraints. Therefore:

    A. the project team must be able to make decisions or obtain decisions from upper management.
    B. functional departments should make their decisions as quickly as possible.
    C. upper management should communicate decisions to the project team at least weekly.
    D. since consensus decision making is time consuming, provisions have been made for budget and schedule revisions.

22. Project Team Members:

    A. are in a "line" reporting relationship to the PGM and are extensions of his authority.
    B. have relatively little authority and responsibility and usually can only recommend courses of action.
    C. primary allegiance should be to their functional department.
    D. receive technical and administrative direction from the PGM.

23. Careful and early planning for a project provides an integrated, comprehensive approach to successfully meeting project schedule and budgetary constraints. Such planning means:

   A. that a comprehensive approach to project objectives (including alternative approaches) is developed early, when the ability to influence costs is greatest.
   B. development of achievable schedules to control design, procurement, and construction activities.
   C. development of sound cost estimates, budget items, and cash flow estimates.
   D. sound and comprehensive plans, supported by schedules, yield control points, or definitive decision points for the project.
   E. All of the above

24. The project plan is developed by:

   A. the PGM
   B. the Director of Projects
   C. the Project Team
   D. top management

25. For the comprehensively planned project, the schedule is:

   A. the agenda for carrying out the plan or a portion of it.
   B. not important, as each team member acts according to plan.
   C. used to generate a time table of major commitments for the project.
   D. provides opportunities for upper-management to significantly alter the course of the project.

26. The primary objective of Project Control Services is to identify deviations and trends from approved plans and to:

   A. request the functional managers to take steps to correct the deviations.
   B. evaluate the impact of suggested, forced or actual deviations from the approved plan.
   C. monitor project cash flow.
   D. prepare budget items and revisions for projects.

27. For projects assigned to Project Management, Project Control Services is responsible for:

   A. revising project plans and schedules when deviations occur.
   B. obtaining Budget Committee approval for project budget revisions.
   C. collecting, analyzing and reporting the cost, budget and schedule data.
   D. the team members compliance to budget and schedule constraints.

28. Planning and Scheduling are:

   A. separate and distinct tasks and have little relationship with each other.
   B. distinct but inseparable aspects of the successful project.
   C. the only means for assuring project success.

29. The control of Project Cost is through the Project Schedule.

   A. True
   B. False

30. Projected cost tied to schedule equals cash flow.

   A. True
   B. False

31. Cash flow is monitored by relating project cost to physical progress.

   A. True
   B. False

32. Earned value versus actual cost ties cost to progress.

   A. True
   B. False

33. Ordinarily the analyst seeks to correct identified deviations from planned targets by:

   A. making recommendations to the PGM or appropriate Team Member.
   B. working with counterparts in other organizations to adjust targets.
   C. reporting the deviation so that the appropriate persons know action is required.
   D. working with the Supervisor of the Planning, Scheduling and Cost Group to effect correction to the deviation.

34. The purpose of project reporting is to:

   A. keep company management informed and to check progress by reporting pertinent facts.
   B. allow for communication of plans, performance, and problems to the proper decision making level of management.
   C. apprise company management of project status.
   D. All of the above.

35. The primary purpose of the reporting system is:

   A. to inform the PGM of project progress.
   B. to apprise management of the status of each project.
   C. to apprise management of costs and cost trends of each project.
   D. provide management with the information necessary to make project decisions.

36. You start developing the logic diagram from:

   A. The beginning.
   B. The middle.
   C. The tail end.
   D. Any place.

37. The next step after development of the logic is:

    A. Make a "forward pass."
    B. Develop the duration of each activity.
    C. Make a "backward pass."
    D. Determine the critical path.

38. The critical path is calculated by:

    A. Making a forward pass.
    B. Making a backward pass.
    C. Making a forward and a backward pass.
    D. Adding up the durations of all the important activities.

39. The range of time (i.e., the time between early finish and late finish date) to complete an activity is called:

    A. Expected time.
    B. Float (or slack).
    C. Planned start date.
    D. Allowable time.

40. Five weeks negative float for an activity means the activity is scheduled to start, or did start, five weeks after the late start date.

    A. True
    B. False

41. A man-loaded schedule means that:

    A. Manpower requirements, by craft, are assigned to each activity.
    B. Extra men are required to "load" the schedule in to the computer.
    C. We have loaded more men into the schedule than required.
    D. Manpower availability was superimposed on the schedule.

42. Resource (manpower) allocation is a process whereby activities are scheduled within the constraints imposed by labor availability or self-set limits of desired or affordable manpower.

    A. True
    B. False

43. Manpower levels can be constrained to less than the amount required but this will:

    A. Require more manpower in the long run.
    B. Push out the end date.
    C. Reduce total manpower costs for the project.
    D. Have no effect on the schedule.

44. A report listing only those activities with four weeks negative float cannot be obtained.

    A. True
    B. False

45. A report listing only those activities scheduled to start next month can be produced.

    A. True
    B. False

46. Why do we need good estimates?

    A. to correct poor estimating history.
    B. to give management confidence in estimates.
    C. to determine budget costs.
    D. to provide work for good estimators.

47. What are estimating objectives? (Answer one or more.)

    A. to determine the time sequence of expenditures.
    B. to keep project costs from increasing.
    C. to provide input to the scheduling process.
    D. to give management confidence in estimates.

48. What does the estimate control?

    A. costs
    B. schedule
    C. productivity
    D. quantities
    E. all of the above
    F. none of the above

49. What are the functions of the Project Estimating Group? (Answer one or more.)

    A. to do all estimating.
    B. to review and analyze contractor estimates.
    C. to provide technical direction and coordination of estimating activities.
    D. to provide estimating support to all departments, as required.

50. What are Project Estimating prerequisites for doing a detailed project estimate?

    A. contractual requirements to do the estimate.
    B. detailed written scope document agreed to by top management.
    C. milestone summary schedule.
    D. availability of estimating personnel.
    E. all of the above.

51. Which of the following items must be evaluated in developing an estimate work plan with the contractor? (Answer one or more.)

    A. in-house requirements for information
    B. results of quantity take-offs
    C. scope of estimate
    D. productivity assumptions

52. Which portions of an estimate are usually developed internally rather than by the contractor? (Answer one or more.)

    A. major equipment pricing
    B. builders risk insurance
    C. cost of money
    D. temporary construction facilities
    E. labor costs

53. Management considers the most important output of an estimate to be:

    A. total cost.
    B. bid comparison estimates.
    C. defined scope base.
    D. control base for field.

54. Which of the following are characteristics of Estimated Value of Uncertainty?

    A. the magnitude and timing of costs are unknown.
    B. the overall risk is low.
    C. sufficient scope definition is available.
    D. occurrence is probable.
    E. all of the above.

55. What is required to determine the Estimated Value of Uncertainty?

    A. crystal ball
    B. knowledge
    C. experience
    D. judgement
    E. details of estimate

56. In general, why does any management lack confidence in estimates?

    A. lack of good estimators
    B. lack of understanding
    C. bad estimates by contractors

57. Which of the following are types of estimates that Project Estimating will be involved in?

    A. definitive estimates
    B. conceptual estimates
    C. budget estimates
    D. order of magnitude estimates
    E. A, B and D, but not C

58. Key factors that govern *how* an estimate will be prepared are:

    A. end use of the estimate.
    B. tools available.
    C. time available.
    D. information available.
    E. all of the above.

59. What is contingency?

    A. money to cover costs which, based on past experience, are likely to be encountered but difficult or impossible to qualify at the time the estimate is prepared.
    B. money to cover uncertainties in the estimate within the defined scope and schedule.
    C. money to cover changes in scope.
    D. the Project Manager's fund.

60. Which of the following are elements of cost control?

    A. estimates, commitments, and corrective action.
    B. budgets, performance analysis, and corrective action.
    C. forecasts, performance analysis, and follow-up.
    D. performance analysis, corrective action, and follow-up.

61. Which of the following are *not* major judgement areas in a contractor's estimate? (Answer one or more.)

    A. quantities
    B. productivity
    C. escalation
    D. contingency
    E. none of the above

62. Which of the following are essential to a successful estimating department?

    A. the availability of computer estimating systems
    B. detail definition of project scope
    C. management recognition/support
    D. all of the above

63. "Work Sampling" is a technique that provides estimators with the following information: (Answer one or more.)

    A. a measure of actual productivity.
    B. a measure of labor effectiveness.
    C. a measure of schedule performance.
    D. a measure of time spent working vs. time spent not working.
    E. a measure of actual work vs. planned work.

64. Although "time lapse photograph" is primarily intended as a tool for management to view job progress, it also has several specific applications in regard to estimates. (Answer one or more.)

    A. it can show actual productivity for specific tasks.
    B. it can be used to evaluate material handling effectiveness.
    C. it can be used to evaluate schedule performance.
    D. it can show safety hazards.
    E. it can be used to identify poor supervision.

65. Unit rates for work performed on past jobs are commonly:

   A. averaged and used as a basis for current estimates.
   B. not useful since they contain all the errors of the previous work.
   C. disregarded since each job is different.
   D. adjusted by specific factors for use on current estimates.
   E. none of the above.

66. A power plant project is estimated to cost one billion dollars and take twelve million labor man-hours to construct. Ten percent allowance for contingency has been included in the estimate of cost. *Total* project man-hours are likely to be:

   A. less than twelve million
   B. between twelve and fifteen million
   C. between fifteen and twenty million
   D. over twenty million

67. Three 800 MW power plants in different parts of the country went into service in December, 1976. Plant A cost $200 million, Plant B cost $400 million and Plant C cost $600 million. What are the most likely reasons for the differences.

   A. labor productivity, wages, and supervision.
   B. quantities, schedule, and wages.
   C. scope, schedule, and labor productivity.
   D. owner imposed requirements, management, and equipment cost.

Appendix C
Solutions to the
Project Management
Conflict Exercise

PART ONE: FACING THE CONFLICT

After reading the answers which follow, record your score on line 1 of the worksheet.

A. Although many project managers and functional managers negotiate by "returning" favors, this custom is not highly recommended. The department manager might feel some degree of indebtedness at first, but will surely become defensive in follow-on projects in which you are involved, and might even get the idea that this will be the only way that he will be able to deal with you in the future. If this was your choice, allow one point on line 1.

B. Threats can only lead to disaster. This is a sure-fire way of ending a potentially good arrangement before it starts. Allow no points if you selected this as your solution.

C. If you say nothing, then you accept full responsibility and accountability for the schedule delay and increased costs. You have done nothing to open communications with the department manager. This could lead into additional conflicts on future projects. Enter two points on line 1 if this was your choice.

D. Requesting upper-level management to step in at this point can only complicate the situation. Executives prefer to step in only as a last resort. Upper-level management will probably ask to talk to the department manager first. Allow two points on line 1 if this was your choice.

E. Although he might become defensive upon receiving your memo, it will become difficult for him to avoid your request for help. The question, of course, is when he will give you this help. Allow eight points on line 1 if you made this choice.

F. Trying to force your solution upon the department manager will severely threaten him and provide the basis for additional conflict. Good project managers will always try to predict emotional reactions to whatever decisions they might be forced to make. For this choice, allow two points on line 1 of the worksheet.

G.   Making an appointment for a later point in time will give both parties a chance to cool off and think out the situation further.   He will probably find it difficult to refuse your request for help and will be forced to think about it between now and the appointment. Allow ten points for this choice.

H.   An immediate discussion will tend to open communications or keep communication open. This will be advantageous. However, it can also be a disadvantage if emotions are running high and sufficient time has not been given to the selection of alternatives. Allow six points on line 1 if this was your choice.

I.   Forcing the solution your way will obviously alienate the department manager. The fact that you do intend to honor his request at a later time might give him some relief especially if he understands your problem and the potential impact of his decision upon other departments. Allow three points on line 1 for this choice.

PART TWO: UNDERSTANDING EMOTIONS

Using the scoring table shown below, determine your total score. Record your total in the appropriate box on line 2 of the worksheet. There are no "absolutely" correct answers to this problem, merely what appears to be the "most" right.

PART THREE: ESTABLISHING COMMUNICATIONS

A.   Although your explanations may be acceptable and accountability for excess costs may be blamed upon the department manager, you have not made any attempt to open communications with the department manager. Further conflicts appear inevitable. If this was your choice, allow a score of zero on line 3 of the worksheet.

B.   You are offering the department manager no choice but to elevate the conflict.   He probably has not had any time to think about changing his requirements and it is extremely doubtful that he will give in to you since you have now backed him into a corner. Allow zero points on line 3 of the worksheet.

C.   Threatening him may get him to change his mind, but will certainly create deteriorating working relationships both on this project as well as any others which will require that you interface with his department. Allow no points if this was your choice.

D.   Sending him a memo requesting a meeting at a later date will give him and you a chance to cool down but might not improve your bargaining position. The department manager might now have plenty of time to reassure himself that he was right because you probably aren't under such a terrible time constraint as you led him to believe if you can wait several days to

	REACTION	PERSONAL OR GROUP SCORE
A. I've given you my answer. See the general manager if you're not happy.	Hostile or Withdrawing	4
B. I understand your problem. Let's do it your way.	Accepting	4
C. I understand your problem, but I'm doing what is best for my department.	Defensive or Hostile	4
D. Let's discuss the problem. Perhaps there are alternatives.	Cooperative	4
E. Let me explain to you why we need the new requirements.	Cooperating or Defensive	4
F. See my section supervisors. It was their recommendation.	Withdrawing	4
G. New Managers are supposed to come up with new and better ways, aren't they?	Hostile or Defensive	4
	TOTAL: PERSONAL	
	TOTAL: GROUP	

see him again. Allow four points on line 3 of the worksheet if this was your choice.

E. You're heading in the right direction trying to open communications. Unfortunately, you may further aggravate him by telling him that he lost his cool and should have apologized to you when all along you may have been the one that lost your cool. Expressing regret as part of your opening remarks would benefit the situation. Allow six points on line 3 of the worksheet.

F. Postponing the problem cannot help you. The department manager might consider the problem resolved because he hasn't heard from you. The confrontation should not be postponed. Your choice has merit in that you are attempting to open up a channel for communications. Allow four points on line 3 if this was your choice.

G. Expressing regret and seeking immediate resolution is the best approach. Hopefully, the department manager will now understand the importance of this conflict and the need for urgency. Allow ten points on line 3 of the worksheet.

PART FOUR: CONFLICT RESOLUTION

Use the table shown below to determine your total points. Enter this total on line 4 of the worksheet.

PART FIVE: UNDERSTANDING YOUR CHOICES

A. Although you may have "legal" justification to force the solution your way, you should consider the emotional impact on the organization as a result of alienating the department manager. Allow two points on line 5 of the worksheet.

B. Accepting the new requirements would be an easy way out if you are willing to explain the increased costs and schedule delays to the other participants. This would certainly please the department manager and might even give him the impression that he has a power position and can always resolve problems in this fashion. Allow four points on line 5 of the worksheet.

C. If this situation cannot be resolved at your level, you have no choice but to request upper-level management to step in. At this point you must be pretty sure that a compromise is all but impossible and are willing to accept

	MODE	PERSONAL OR GROUP SCORE
A. The requirements are my decision and we're doing it my way.	Forcing	4
B. I've thought about it and you're right. We'll do it your way.	Withdrawal or Smoothing	4
C. Let's discuss the problem. Perhaps there are alternatives.	Compromise or Confrontation	4
D. Let me explain why we need the new requirements.	Smoothing, Confrontation, or forcing	4
E. See my section supervisors; they're handling it now.	Withdrawal	4
F. I've looked over the problem and I might be able to ease up on some of the requirements.	Smoothing or Compromise	4
	TOTAL: PERSONAL	
	TOTAL: GROUP	

a go-for-broke position. Enter ten points on line 5 of the worksheet if this was your choice.

    D. Asking other managers to plead your case for you is not a good situation. Hopefully upper-level management will solicit their opinions when deciding upon how to resolve the conflict. Enter six points on line 5 if this was your choice, and hope that the functional managers do not threaten him by ganging up on him.

PART SIX: INTERPERSONAL INFLUENCES

    A. Threatening the employees with penalty power will probably have no effect at all because your conflict is with the department manager who at this time probably could care less about your evaluation of his people. Allow zero points on line 6 of the worksheet if you selected this choice.

    B. Offering rewards will probably induce people toward your way of thinking provided that they feel that you can keep your promises. Promotions and increased responsibilities are functional responsibilities, not those of a project manager. Performance evaluation might be effective if the department manager values your judgement. In this situation it is doubtful that he will. Allow no points for this answer and record the results on line 6 of the worksheet.

    C. Expert power, once established, is an effective means of obtaining functional respect provided that it is used for a relatively short period of time. For long-term efforts, expert power can easily create conflicts between project and functional managers. In this situation, although relatively short-term, the department manager probably will not consider you as an expert, and this might carry on down to his functional subordinates. Allow six points on line 6 of the worksheet if this was your choice.

    D. Work challenge is the best means of obtaining support and in many situations can overcome personality clashes and disagreements. Unfortunately, the problem occurred because of complaints by the functional personnel and it is therefore unlikely that work challenge would be effective here. Allow eight points on line 6 of the worksheet if this was your choice.

    E. People who work in a project environment should respect the project manager because of the authority delegated to him from the upper levels of management. But this does not mean that they will follow his directions. When in doubt, employees tend to follow the direction of the person that signs their evaluation form, namely the department manager. However, the project manager has the formal authority to "force" the line manager to adhere to the original project plan. This should be done only as a last resort and here, it looks as though it may be the only alternative. Allow ten points if this was your answer and record the result on line 6 of the worksheet.

    F. Referent power cannot be achieved overnight. Furthermore, if the department manager feels that you are trying to compete with him for the friendship of his subordinates, additional conflicts can result. Allow two points on line 6 of the worksheet if this was your choice.

Appendix D
Solution to
Leadership Exercise

SITUATION 1

A. This technique may work if you have proven leadership credentials. Since three of these people have not worked for you before, some action is necessary.

B. The team should already be somewhat motivated and reinforcement will help. Team building must begin by showing employees how they will benefit. This is usually the best approach on long-term projects. (5 points)

C. This is the best approach if the employees already understand the project. In this case, however, you may be expecting too much out of the employees this soon. (3 points)

D. This approach is too strong at this time, since emphasis should be on team-building. On long-term projects, people should be given the opportunity to know one another first. (2 points)

SITUATION 2

A. Do nothing. Don't overreact. this may improve productivity without damaging morale. See the impact on the team first. If the other members accept Tom as the informal leader, because he has worked for you previously, the results can be very favorable. (5 points)

B. This may cause the team to believe that a problem exists when, in fact, it does not.

C. This is duplication of effort and may reflect upon your ability as a leader. Productivity may be impaired. (2 points)

D. This is a hasty decision and may cause Tom to overreact and become less productive. (3 points)

SITUATION 3

A. You may be burdening the team by allowing them to struggle. Motivation may be impacted and frustration will result. (1 point)

B. Team members expect the project manager to be supportive and to have ideas. This will reinforce your relationship with the team. (5 points)

C. This approach is reasonable as long as your involvement is minimum. You must allow the team to evolve without expecting continuous guidance. (4 points)
D. This action is premature and can prevent future creativity. The team may allow you to do it all.

SITUATION 4

A. If, in fact, the problem does exist, action must be taken. These types of problems do not go away by themselves.
B. This will escalate the problem and may make it worse. It could demonstrate your support for good relations with your team, but could also backfire. (1 point)
C. Private meetings should allow you to reassess the situation and strengthen employee relations on a one-on-one basis. You should be able to assess the magnitude of the problem. (5 points)
D. This is a hasty decision. Changing the team's schedules may worsen the morale problem. This situation requires replanning, not a strong hand. (2 points)

SITUATION 5

A. Crisis management does not work in project management. Why delay until a crisis occurs and then waste time having to replan?
B. This situation may require your immediate attention. Sympathizing with your team may not help if they are looking towards you for leadership. (2 points)
C. This is the proper balance: participative management and contingency planning. This balance is crucial for these situations. (5 points)
D. This may seriously escalate the problem unless you have evidence that performance is substandard. (1 point)

SITUATION 6

A. Problems should be uncovered and brought to the surface for solution. It is true that this problem may go away, or that Bob simply does not recognize that his performance as substandard.
B. Immediate feedback is best. Bob must know your assessment of his performance. This shows your interest in helping him improve. (5 points)
C. This is not a team problem. Why ask the team to do your work? Direct contact is best.
D. As above, this is your problem, not that of the team. You may wish to ask for their input, but do not ask them to perform your job.

SITUATION 7

A. George must be hurting to finish the other project. George probably needs a little more time to develop a quality report. Let him do it. (5 points)

B. Threatening George may not be the best situation because he already understands the problem. Motivation by threatening is normally not good. (3 points)

C. The other team members should not be burdened with this unless it is a team report.

D. As above, this burden should not be placed upon other team members unless, of course, they volunteer.

SITUATION 8

A. Doing nothing in time of crisis is the worst decision that can be made. This may frustrate the team to a point where everything that you have built up may be destroyed.

B. The problem is the schedule slippage, not morale. In this case, it is unlikely that they are related.

C. Group decision-making can work but may be difficult under tight time constraints. Productivity may not be related to the schedule slippage. 3 points)

D. This is the time when the team looks to you for strong leadership. No matter how good the team is, they may not be able to solve all of the problems. (5 points)

SITUATION 9

A. A pat on the back will not hurt. People need to know when they are doing well.

B. Positive reinforcement is a good idea, but perhaps not through monetary rewards. (3 points)

C. You have given the team positive reinforcement and have returned authority/responsibility to them for Phase III. (5 points)

D. Your team has demonstrated the ability to handle authority and responsibility except for this crisis. Dominant leadership is not necessary on a continuous basis.

SITUATION 10

A. The best approach. All is well. (5 points)

B. Why disturb a good working relationship and a healthy working environment? Your efforts may be counterproductive.

C. If the team has done their job, they have already looked for contingencies.

Why make them feel that you still want to be in control? However, if they have not reviewed the Phase III schedule, this step may be necessary. (3 points)
D. Why disturb the team? You may convince them that something is wrong or about to happen.

SITUATION 11

A. You cannot assume a passive role when the customer identifies a problem. You must be prepared to help. The customer's problems usually end up being your problems. (3 points)
B. The customer is not coming into your company to discuss productivity.
C. This places a tremendous burden on the team, especially since it is the first meeting. They need guidance.
D. Customer information exchange meetings are *your* responsibility and should not be delegated. You are the focal point of information. This requires strong leadership, especially during a crisis. (5 points)

SITUATION 12

A. A passive role by you may leave the team with the impression that there is no urgency.
B. The team is motivated and has control of the project. They should be able to handle this by themselves. Positive reinforcement will help. (5 points)
C. This approach might work but could be counterproductive if employees feel that you question their abilities. (4 points)
D. Do not exert strong leadership when the team has already shown their ability to make good group decisions.

SITUATION 13

A. This is the worst approach and may cause the loss of both the existing and follow-on work.
B. This may result in overconfidence and could be disastrous if a follow-on effort does not occur.
C. This could be very demoralizing for the team, because they may view the existing program as about to be cancelled. (3 points)
D. This should be entirely the responsibility of the project manager. There are situations where information may have to be withheld, at least temporarily. (5 points)

SITUATION 14

A. This is an ideal way to destroy the project/functional interface.
B. This consumes a lot of time, since each team member may have a different opinion. (3 points)

C. This is the best approach, since the team may know the functional personnel better than you do. (5 points)

D. It is highly unlikely that you can accomplish this.

SITUATION 15

A. This is the easiest solution, but the most dangerous if it burdens the rest of the team with extra work. (3 points)

B. The decision should be yours, not your team's. You are avoiding your responsibility.

C. Consulting with the team will gain support for your decision. It is highly likely that the team will want Carol to have this chance. (5 points)

D. This could cause a demoralizing environment on the project. If Carol becomes irritable, so could other team members.

SITUATION 16

A. This is the best choice. You are at the mercy of the line manager. He may ease up some if not disturbed. (5 points)

B. This is fruitless. They have obviously tried this already and were unsuccessful. Asking them to do it again could be frustrating. Remember, the brick wall has been there for two years already. (3 points)

C. This will probably be a wasted meeting. Brick walls are generally not permeable.

D. This will thicken the brick wall and may cause your team's relationship with the line manager to deteriorate. This should be used as a last resort *only* if status information cannot be found any other way. (2 points)

SITUATION 17

A. This is a poor assumption. Carol may not have talked to him or may simply have given him her side of the project.

B. The new man is still isolated from the other team members. You may be creating two project teams. (3 points)

C. This may make the new man uncomfortable and feel that the project is regimented through meetings. (2 points)

D. New members feel more confortable one-on-one, rather than having a team gang up on them. Briefings should be made by the team, since project termination and phaseout will be a team effort. (5 points)

SITUATION 18

A. This demonstrates your lack of concern for the growth of your employees. This is a poor choice.

B. This is a personal decision between you and the employee. As long as his performance will not be impacted, he should be allowed to attend. (5 points)

C. This is not necessarily a problem open for discussion. You may wish to informally seek the team's opinion. (2 points)

    D.   This approach is reasonable but may cause other team members to feel that you are showing favoritism and simply want their concensus.

SITUATION 19

    A.   This is the best choice. Your employees are in total control. Do nothing. You must assume that the employees have already received feedback. (5 points)

    B.   The employees have probably been counseled already by your team and their own functional manager. Your efforts can only alienate them. (1 point)

    C.   Your team already has the situation under control. Asking them for contingency plans at this point may have a detrimental effect. They may have already developed contingency plans. (2 points)

    D.   A strong leadership role now may alienate your team.

SITUATION 20

    A.   A poor choice. You, the project manager, are totally accountable for all information provided to the customer.

    B.   Positive reinforcement may be beneficial, but does nothing to guarantee the quality of the report. Your people may get over-creative and provide superfluous information.

    C.   Soliciting their input has some merit, but the responsibility here is actually yours. (3 points)

    D.   Some degree of leadership is needed for all reports. Project teams tend to become diffused during report writing unless guided. (5 points)

A Project Management /
Systems Management
Bibliography

1. Abt Associates Inc. *Applications of Systems Analysis Models: A Survey.* Washington, D.C.: Technology Utilization Division, Office of Technology Utilization, National Aeronautics and Space Administration, 1968.
2. Ackoff, Russell Lincoln, and Emery, Fred E. *On Purposeful Systems.* Chicago: Aldine/Atherton, 1972.
3. Ackoff, Russell Lincoln, *Redesigning the Future: A Systems Approach to Societal Problems.* New York: John Wiley, 1974.
4. Alderfer, Clayton P. *Change Processes in Organizations.* New Haven, Connecticut, Department of Administrative Sciences, Yale University, 1971.
5. Allen, Louis A., *The Professional Manager's Guide,* (USA: Louis A. Allen Associates, 1969).
6. Anthony, Robert N. Planning and Control Systems: *A Framework for Analysis.* Boston: Division of Research, Graduate School of Business Administration, Harvard University, 1965.
7. Archibald, Russell D. *Managing High-Technology Programs and Projects.* New York: John Wiley, 1976. pp. 55, 82, 176, 191.
8. Argyris, Chris, "How Tomorrow's Executives Will Make Decisions," *Think,* vol. 33: (November-December 1967), pp. 18-23.
9. Argyris, Chris, "Resistance to Rational Management Systems," *Innovation,* issue 10: (1969), pp. 28-42.
10. Argyris, Chris, "Today's Problems with Tomorrow's Organizations," *Journal of Management Studies* 4: (February 1967), pp. 31-55.
11. ARINC Research Corporation. *Guidebook for Systems Analysis/Cost Effectiveness.* Washington, D.C.: U.S. Department of Commerce, National Bureau of Standards; distributed by Clearinghouse for Federal Scientific and Technical Information, 1969.
12. Association for Systems Management. *An Annotated Bibliography for the Systems Professional.* 2nd ed. Cleveland: Association for Systems Management, 1970.
13. Avots, Ivars. "Why Does Project Management Fail?" *California Management Review* 12 (Fall 1969), pp. 77-82.
14. Avots, Ivars, "Making Project Management Work: The Right Tools For The Wrong Project Manager," *S.A.M. Advanced Management Journal,* vol. 40: (Autumn, 1975), pp. 20-26.

15. Bachman, J., et al., "Bases of Supervisory Power: A Comparative Study in Five Organizational Settings," in *Control in Organizations*, A. Tannenbaum, Ed. New York: McGraw-Hill, 1968, pp. 229–238.
16. Baker, Frank, ed. *Organizational Systems; General Systems Approaches to Complex Organizations* Homewood, Illinois: R.D. Irwin Series in Management and the Behavioral Sciences, 1973.
17. Barnes, Lewis B. "Project Management and the Use of Authority: A Study of Structure, Role, and Influence Relationships in Public and Private Organizations." Ph.D. Dissertation, University of Southern California, 1971.
18. Baumgartner, John Stanley. *Project Management.* Homewood, Illinois: R.D. Irwin series, 1963.
19. Beckett, John A. *Management Dynamics: The New Synthesis.* New York: McGraw-Hill, 1971.
20. Benne, K.D. and Birnbaum, M., "Principles of Changing" in Bennis, W.G., et al., *The Planning of Change,* New York: Holt, Rinehart, and Winston, 1969.
21. Bennigson, Lawrence. "The Team Approach to Project Management." *Management Review* 61: (January 1972):pp. 48–52.
22. Bennigson, Lawrence, *Project Management.* McGraw-Hill, 1970.
23. Bennis Warren G. "The Coming Death of Bureaucracy." *Think* 32: (November–December 1966):pp. 30–35.
24. Benton, John Breen. *Managing the Organizational Decision Process.* Lexington, Mass.: Lexington Books, 1973.
25. Berlinski, David J. "On Systems Analysis: An Essay Concerning the Limitations of some Mathematical Methods in the Social, Political, and Biological Sciences." Cambridge, Mass.: M.I.T. Press, 1976.
26. Berrien, F. Kenneth. *General and Social Systems.* New Brunswick, N.J.: Rutgers University Press, 1968.
27. Bertalanffy, Ludwig von. *General Systems Theory; Foundations, Development, Applications.* New York: G. Braziller, 1972.
28. ——. *General Systems Theory.* New York: G. Braziller, 1968.
29. Bingham, John E., and Davies, G.W.P. *A Handbook of Systems Analysis.* London: Macmillan, © 1972, 1974. Distributed in North America by Halsted Press, a division of John Wiley, New York and Toronto.
30. Blake, R.R. and Mouton, J.S., *The Managerial Grid,* Houston: Gulf Publishing, 1964.
31. Blankstein, Charles Sidney. *The Base Level Development Assistance Project: A Managerial Perspective.* M.I.T., ms., 1972. Cambridge, Mass. Thesis, M.S.
32. Block, Ellery B. "Accomplishment/Cost: Better Project Control." *Harvard Business Review* 49: (May 1971), pp. 110–24.
33. Bobrowski, T.M., "A Basic Philosophy of Project Management," *Journal of Systems Management,* May–June 1974.
34. Boulding, Kenneth. "General Systems Theory—The Skeleton of Science," *Management Science,* (April 1956), pp. 197–208.
35. Bowman, R.R., "An Analysis of Project Management Concepts in the Missile/Space Industry," MBA Thesis, Utah State University, 1967.
36. Boyatzis, R.E., "Building Efficacy: An Effective Use of Managerial Power," *Industrial Management Review,* vol. 11, no. 1 (Fall 1969) pp. 65–75.
37. ——, "Leadership: The Effective Use of Power", *Management of Personnel Quarterly,* Graduate School of Business Administration, University of Michigan (Fall, 1971), pp. 21–25. Reprinted in Richards, Max D., and William A. Nielander, *Readings in Management,* fourth edition, (Cincinnati: Southwestern Publishing Co., 1974), pp. 623–629.

38. Brandon, Dick H., and Gray, Max. *Project Control Standards*. Princeton: Brandon/Systems Press, 1970.
39. Burke, R.J., "Methods of Resolving Interpersonal Conflict," *Personnel Administration*, July–August, 1969, pp. 48–55.
40. ——, "Methods of Managing Superior-Subordinate Conflict," *Canadian Journal of Behavioral Science*, 2, 2: 1970, pp. 124–135.
41. Burke, W.W. and Hornstein, H.A., *The Social Technology of Organization Development*. Fairfax, Virginia, NTL Learning Resources Corporation, 1972.
42. Burt, David N., "Getting the Right Price With the Right Contract," *Management Review* (May 1976), pp. 24–34.
43. Butler, Arthur G., Jr., "Project Management: A Study in Organizational Conflict," *Academy of Management Journal* 16 (March 1973), pp. 84–101.
44. ——, "Behavioral Implications for Professional Employees of Structural Conflict Associated with Project Management in Functional Organizations." Ph.D. Dissertation, University of Florida, 1969.
45. Butler, D., and Miller, N. "Power to Reward and Punish in Social Interaction," *Journal of Experimental Social Psychology*, vol. 1, no. 4: (1965), pp. 311–322.
46. Cicero, John P., and Wilemon, David L. "Project Authority: A Multidimensional View." *IEEE Transactions on Engineering Management*, EM-17: (May 1970), pp. 52–57.
47. Chapman, Richard L. *Project Management in NASA; the System and the Men*. Washington: Scientific and Technical Information Office, National Aeronautics and Space Administration; for sale by the Superintendent of Documents, U.S. Government Printing Office, 1973.
48. Chen, Gordon K., and Kaczka, Eugene E. *Operations and Systems Analysis; A Simulation Approach*. Boston: Allyn and Bacon, 1974.
49. Churchman, Charles West. *The Systems Approach*. New York: Dell Publishing Company, 1968.
50. Cleland, David I. "Organizational Dynamics of Project Management." *IEEE Transactions on Engineering Management*. EM-13:(December 1966), 201–5.
51. ——, "The Deliberate Conflict," *Business Horizon*, vol. 11, no. 1:(1968), pp. 78–80.
52. ——, "Project Management in Industry: An Assessment," *Project Management Quarterly*, vol. 5, no. 2 and 3:(1974), pp. 19–21.
53. ——, "Defining A Project Management System," *Project Management Qaurterly*, vol. 8, no. 4:(1977), pp. 37–40.
54. ——. "Why Project Management?" *Business Horizons*, 7:(Winter 1964), pp. 81–88.
55. Cleland, David I., and King, William R. *Management: A Systems Approach*. New York: McGraw-Hill, 1972.
56. ——, *Systems Analysis and Project Management*. New York: McGraw-Hill, 1968.
57. ——. *Systems Analysis and Project Management*. New York, McGraw-Hill, 1975. pp. 271, 371–380.
58. ——. *Systems, Organizations, Analysis, Management; A Book of Readings*. New York: McGraw-Hill, 1969.
59. Couger, J. Daniel, ed. and Knapp, Robert W., Ed. *System Analysis Techniques*. New York: John Wiley, 1974.
60. Crowston, Wallace B. "Models for Project Management." *Sloan Management Review*, 12:(Spring 1971), pp. 25–42.
61. Cullingford, G. and Prideaux, J.D.C.A. "A Variational Study of Optimal Resource Profiles," *Management Science* 19:(May 1973), pp. 1067–81.
62. Dahl, R., "The Concept of Power," *Behavioral Science*, vol. 2:(July 1957), pp. 201–215.

63. Datz, Marvin A. and Wilby, L.R., "What Is Good Project Management?" *Project Management Quarterly,* vol. 8, no. 1:(March 1977).
64. Davis, Keith, "The Role of Project Management in Scientific Manufacturing," *Arizona Business Bulletin* 9:(May 1962), pp. 1-8.
65. ——, "The Role of Project Management in Scientific Manufacturing." *IRE Transactions on Engineering Management,* vol. 9, no. 3, (1962).
66. Davis, S., "An Organic Problem-Solving Method of Organizational Change," *Journal of Applied Behavioral Science,* (January 1967), pp. 3-21.
67. Davis, Stanley, "Two Models of Organization: Unity of Command Versus Balance of Power," *Sloan Management Review,* (Fall 1974), pp. 29-40.
68. Davis, S.M., and Lawrence, P.R., *Matrix,* Reading, Mass.: Addison-Wesley, 1977.
69. De Greene, Kenyon Brenton. *Sociotechnical Systems: Factors in Analysis, Design, and Management.* Englewood Cliffs, N.J.: Prentice-Hall, 1973.
70. ——, Ed. *Systems Psychology.* New York: McGraw-Hill, 1970.
71. Delbecq, André L.; Schull, Fremont A.; Filley, Alan C.; and Grimes, Andrew J. Matrix Organization: *A Conceptual Guide to Organizational Variation.* Wisconsin Business Papers no. 2. Madison: University of Wisconsin, Bureau of Business Research and Service, 1969.
72. Delbecq, André L., and Filley, Alan C. *Program and Project Management in a Matrix Organization: A Case Study.* Madison: University of Wisconsin, Bureau of Business Research and Service, 1974.
73. Dibble, E.T. and Suojanen, Waino, "Project Management in a Crisis Economy," *Infosystems-Spectrum,* vol. 23:(January 1976), pp. 44-46.
74. Doering, Robert D. "An Approach Toward Improving the Creative Output of Scientific Task Teams," *IEEE Transactions on Engineering Management,* EM-20:(February 1973), pp. 29-31.
75. Earle, V.H. "Once Upon a Matrix: A Hindsight on Participation." *Optimum* 4, no. 2:1973), pp. 28-36.
76. Eirich, Peter Lee. "An Information System Design Analysis for a Research Organization." Cambridge, Mass., M.S. Thesis, M.I.T., 1974.
77. Emery, F.E. *Systems Thinking: Selected Readings.* New York: Penguin Education, 1974.
78. Emery, J.C. *Organizational Planning and Control Systems.* New York: Macmillan, 1969.
79. Emshoff, James R. *Analysis of Behavioral Systems.* New York: Macmillan, 1971.
80. European Conference on the Management of Large Space Programs, Paris, 1970. London, New York: Gordon and Breach Science Publishers, 1971.
81. Evan, W.M., "Conflict and Performance in R & D Organization," *Industrial Management Review,* vol. 7:(1965), pp. 37-45.
82. Evan, W.M., "Superior-Subordinate Conflict in Research Organizations," *Administrative Science Qaurterly,* (July 1965), pp. 52-64.
83. Exton, William. *The Age of Systems: The Human Dilemma.* New York: American Management Association, 1972.
84. Fiore, Michael V. "Out of the Frying Pan into the Matrix," *Personnel Administration* 33, no. 3:(1970), pp. 4-7.
85. Fisher, Gene Harvey. *Cost Considerations in Systems Analysis.* New York: American Elsevier, 1971.
86. FitzGerald, John M. and Ardra F. *Fundamentals of Systems Analysis.* New York: Wiley, 1973.
87. Flaks, Marvin, and Archibald, Russell D. "The EE's Guide to Project Management."

Electronic Engineer 27:(April 1968), pp. 28+; (May), pp. 20+; (June), pp. 27–32; (July), pp. 33–34+; (August), pp. 33+.

88. Forrester, Jay W. "A New Corporate Design," *Industrial Management Review* 7 (Fall 1965), pp. 5–17.

89. Frankwicz, Michael J. "A Study of Project Management Techniques," *Journal of Systems Management* 24:(October 1973), pp. 18–22.

90. French, J.R., Jr., and Raven, B. "The Bases of Social Power," in *Studies in Social Power,* D. Cartwright, Ed., Ann Arbor, Mich.: Research Center for Group Dynamics, 1959, pp. 150–165.

91. Fried, Louis. "Don't Smother Your Project in People," *Management Advisor* 9: (March 1972), pp. 46–49.

92. Friend, Fred L., "Be A More Effective Program Manager," *Journal of Systems Management,* vol. 27:(February 1976), pp. 6–9.

93. Fuller, R. Buckminster, *Synergetics: Explorations in the Geometry of Thinking.* New York: Macmillan, 1975.

94. Gaddis, P.O. "The Project Manager." *Harvard Business Review,* May–June 1959, pp. 89–97.

95. Galbraith, Jay R. "Matrix Organization Designs—How to Combine Functional and Project Forms," *Business Horizons,* February 1971.

96. Geisler, M.A. "How to Plan for Management in New Systems." *Harvard Business Review,* September–October 1962.

97. Gemmill, G., "Managerial Role Mapping," *The Management Personnel Quarterly,* vol. 8, no. 3:(Fall 1969), pp. 13–19.

98. Gemmill, G., and H. Thamhain, "The Power Styles of Project Managers: Some Efficiency Correlates," *20th Annual JEMC, Managing for Improved Engineering Effectiveness* (Atlanta, Ga., Oct. 30–31, 1972), pp. 89–96.

99. Gemmill, G.R. and Thamhain, H.J., "Project Performance as a Function of the Leadership Styles of Project Managers: Results of a Field Study," *Convention Digest, 4th Annual Meeting of the Project Management Institute,* Philadelphia, October 18–21, 1972.

100. ——, and ——, "Influence Styles of Project Managers: Some Project Performance Correlates," *Academy of Management Journal,* vol. 17, no. 2:(June 1974), pp. 216–224.

101. Gemmill, Gary, and Thamhain, Hans J. "The Effectiveness of Different Power Styles of Project Managers in Gaining Project Support." *IEEE Transactions on Engineering Management* EM-20 (May 1973), pp. 38–44.

102. ——, "Interpersonal Power in Temporary Management Systems," *Journal of Management Studies,* (October 1971).

103. ——, and Wilemon, David L. "The Power Spectrum in Project Management," *Sloan Management Review* 12:(Fall 1970), pp. 15–25.

104. Gemmill, Gary and David Wilemon, "The Product Manager as an Influence Agent," *Journal of Marketing,* vol. 36:(January 1972), pp. 26–31.

105. Gibson, James L., ed. *Readings in Organizations: Structure, Processes, Behavior.* Dallas: Business Publication, 1973.

106. Gildersleeve, Thomas R., *Data Processing Project Management,* New York: Van Nostrand Reinhold, 1974.

107. Gill, P.G. *Systems Management Techniques for Builders and Contractors.* New York: McGraw-Hill, 1968.

108. Goggin, William C., "How the Multidimensional Structure Works at Dow Corning," *Harvard Business Review,* (January–February 1974), pp. 54–65.

109. Goodman, Richard A. "Ambiguous Authority Definitions in Project Management," *Academy of Management Journal* 10:(December 1967), 395–408.

110. Goodman, Richard A., "Organizational Preference in Research and Development," *Human Relations* 23:1970 pp. 279-298.

111. Goodman, R., "Ambiguous Authority Definition in Project Management," *Academy of Management Journal*, vol. 10 (1967), pp. 395-407.

112. Grinnell, S.K., and Apple, H.P., "When Two Bosses are Better than One," *Machine Design*, 9:(January 1975), pp. 84-87.

113. Grimes, A., S. Klein, and F. Shull, "Matrix Model: A Selective Empirical Test," *Academy of Management Journal*, vol. 15, no. 1:(March 1972), pp. 9-31.

114. Gross, Paul F. *Systems Analysis and Design for Management.* New York: Dun-Donnelley, 1976.

115. Gullet, C. Ray. "Personnel Management in the Project Organization," *Personnel Administration and Public Personnel Review.* 1 (November 1972), pp. 17-22.

116. Hall, D.M. *Management of Human Systems.* Cleveland, Ohio: Association for Systems Management, 1971.

117. Hall, H. Lawrence. "Management: A Continuum of Styles," *S.A.M. Advanced Management Journal* 33:(January 1968), pp. 68-74.

118. Hansen, J.J. "The Case of the Precarious Program," *Harvard Business Review,* (January-February 1968).

119. Health Research, Center for. "Health Research: The Systems Approach." New York: Springer, 1976.

120. Hellriegel, Don and John W. Slocum, Jr., "Organizational Design: A Contingency Approach," *Business Horizons,* vol. 16, no. 2:(April 1 1973), pp. 59-68. Reprinted in Richards, Max. D., and William A. Nielander, *Readings in Management,* fourth edition, (Cincinnati: Southwestern, 1974), pp. 516-527.

121. Hersey, Paul, and Blanchard, K.H. "The Management of Change," *Training and Development Journal,* vol. 26, no. 1:(January 1972); vol. 26, no. 2:(February 1972); and vol. 26, no. 3:(March 1972).

122. Hlavacik, James D., and Thompson, Victor A. "Bureaucracy and New Product Innovation," *Academy of Management Journal* 16:(September 1973), pp. 361-72.

123. Hodgetts, Richard M. "An Interindustry Analysis of Certain Aspects of Project Management." Ph.D. Dissertation, University of Oklahoma, 1968.

124. ———. "Leadership Techniques in the Project Organization." *Academy of Management Journal* 11:(June 1968), pp. 211-19.

125. Hoge, R.R. "Research and Development Project Management: Techniques for Guiding Technical Programmes Towards Corporate Objectives," *Radio and Electronic Engineer* 39:(January 1970), pp. 33-48.

126. Holland, Ted. "What Makes a Project Manager?" *Engineering* 207 (February 14 1969), p. 262.

127. Hoos, Ida Russakoff. *Systems Analysis in Public Policy; A Critique.* Berkeley: University of California Press, 1972.

128. Hopeman, Richard J. *Systems Analysis and Operations Management.* Columbus, Ohio: Merrill, 1969.

129. Hopeman, R.J. and D.L. Wilemon, *Project Management/Systems Management-Concepts and Applications.* Syracuse: Syracuse University/NASA, 1973.

130. Horowitz, J. *Critical Path Scheduling-Management Control Through CPM and PERT.* New York: Roland Press, 1967.

131. Houre, Henry Ronald. *Project Management Using Network Analysis.* New York: McGraw-Hill, 1973.

132. Hynes, Cecil V., "Taking a Look at the Request For Proposal," *Defense Management Journal,* (October 1977), pp. 26-31.

133. International Congress for Project Planning by Network Analysis. *Project Planning by Network Analysis*. Amsterdam: North-Holland Publishing Company, 1969.
134. Ivancevich, J., and J. Donnelly. "Leader Influence and Performance," *Personal Psychology*, vol. 23:(1970), pp. 539-549.
135. Jacobs, Richard A., "Project Management—A New Style For Success," *S.A.M. Advanced Management Journal*, vol. 41:(Autumn 1976), pp. 4-14.
136. ——. "Putting Management Into Project Management," Paper presented at A.S.M. Workshops in Detroit, Tulsa, Oakland and Las Vegas (1976).
137. Janger, Allen R. "Anatomy of the Project Organization," *Business Management Record* (November 1963), pp. 12-18.
138. Jantsh. Erich. *Design for Evolution; Self-Organization and Planning in the Life of Human Systems*. New York: G. Braziller, 1975.
139. Jenett, E., "Guidelines for Successful Project Management," *Chemical Engineering*, (July 9 1973), pp. 70-82.
140. Johnson, James R., "Advanced Project Control," *Journal of Systems Management*, (May 1977), pp. 24-27.
141. Johnson, Marvin M., ed. *Simulation Systems for Manufacturing Industries*. La Jolla, California: The Society for Simulation, Simulation Councils Inc., t.p. 1973.
142. Johnson, Richard Arvid; Newell, William T.; and Vergin, Roger C. *Operations Management; A Systems Concept*. Boston: Houghton-Mifflin, 1972.
143. Johnson, R.A.; Kast, F.E.; and Rosenzweig, J.E. *The Theory and Management of Systems*, New York: McGraw-Hill, 1973.
144. Jonason, Per, "Project Management, Swedish Style," *Harvard Business Review*, (Nov/Dec, 1971), pp. 104-109.
145. Kahn, R.L.; Wolfe, D.M.; Quinn, R.P.; Snock, J.D.; and Rosenthal, R.A. *Organizational Stress: Studies in Role Conflict and Ambiguity*, New York: John Wiley, 1964.
146. Kast, Fremont E., and Rosenzweig, James E. "Organization and management of Space Programs," in *On Advances in Space Science and Technology*. edited by Frederick I. Ordway III. New York: Academic Press 1965.
147. ——. *Organization and Management; A Systems Approach*. 2nd ed. New York: McGraw-Hill, 1974.
148. Kast, F.E. and Rosenzweig, J.E. *Contingency Views of Organization and Management*, Science Research Associates, 1973.
149. Kast, D. "The motivational basis of organizational behavior," *Behavioral Science*, vol. 9, no. 2:(1964), pp. 131-143.
150. Kelleher, Grace J. *The Challenge to Systems Analysis: Public Policy and Change*. New York:
151. Kelley, William F. *Management Through Systems and Procedures: A Systems Concept*. New York: 1969.
152. Kerzner, Harold, "Systems Management and the Engineer," *Journal of Systems Management*, (October, 1977), pp. 18-21.
153. Killian, William P., "Project Management—Future Organizational Concepts," *Marquette Business Review* 2:(1971), pp. 90-107.
154. Kindred, Alton R. *Data Systems and Management: An Introduction to Systems Analysis and Design*. Englewood Cliffs, N.J.: Prentice-Hall, 1973.
155. Kingdon, Donald R. "The Management of Complexity in a Matrix Organization: A Socio-Technical Approach to Changing Organizational Behavior." Los Angeles: University of California, M.S. Thesis, 1969.
156. ——. *Matrix Organization: Managing Information Technologies*. London: Tavistock Publications, 1973.

157. Kirchner, Englebert. "The Project Manager." *Space Aeronautics,* 43:(February 1965), pp. 56–64.
158. Klir, George J. *Trends in General Systems Theory.* New York: John Wiley, 1972.
159. Koplow, Richard A., "From Engineer to Manager–And Back Again," *IEEE Transactions on Engineering Management* vol. EM-14:(June 1967), pp. 88–92.
160. Larsen, Niels Ove. "An Evaluation of Managerial Strategies for Dealing with Work Pressure in a Project Oriented Environment." Ph.D. dissertation, M.I.T., Alfred P. Sloan School of Management, 1969.
161. Laszlo, Ervin. *A Strategy for the Future: The Systems Approach to World Order.* New York: G. Braziller, 1974.
162. Lawrence, Paul R. and Lorsch, Jay W., "New Management Job: The Integrator," *Harvard Business Review,* (November/December 1967), p. 142.
163. Lawrence, P.R. and Lorsch, J.W., *Organization and Environment.* Boston: Division of Research, Harvard Business School, 1967.
164. Lazer R. G., and A.G. Kellner, "Personnel and organizational development in an R and D Matrix-Overlay operation," *IEEE Trans. Eng. Manag.* vol. EM-11:(June 1964), pp. 78–82.
165. Ler, Alec M. *Systems Analysis Frameworks.* New York: John Wiley, 1970.
166. Lewin, K., "Frontiers in Group Dynamics," *Human Relations,* vol. 1. no. 1, (1947).
167. Lewin, K., "Group Decision and Social Change," in Maccoby, E.E., et al., *Readings in Social Psychology,* New York: Holt, Rinehart, and Winston, 1958, pp. 197–211.
168. Livingstone, G.S. "Weapon System Contracting." *Harvard Business Review,* (July-August 1959).
169. Lock, D. *Project Management.* London: Gower Press, 1969.
170. Logistics Management Institute. *Introduction to Military Program Management.* Washington, D.C.: Superintendant of Documents, U.S. Government Printing Office, 1971.
171. London, Keith R. *The People Side of Systems: The Human Aspects of Computer Systems.* New York: McGraw-Hill, 1976.
172. Ludwig, Ernest E. *Applied Project Management for the Process Industries.* Houston, Texas: Gulf Publishing Company, 1974.
173. Lutes, Gerald Scott. "Project Selection and Scheduling in the Massachusetts Department of Public Works." M.S. Thesis M.I.T. Alfred P. Sloan School of Management, 1974.
174. McGregor, D., *The Professional Manager.* New York: McGraw-Hill, 1967.
175. McMillan, Claude, and Gonzalez, Richard F. *Systems Analysis: A Computer Approach to Decision Models.* Irwin, Homewood, Ill., 1973.
176. Maieli, Vincent. "Management by Hindsight: Diary of a Project Manager," *Management Review* 60:(June 1971), pp. 4–14.
177. ———. "Sowing the Seeds of Project Cost Overruns," *Management Review* 61:(August 1972), pp. 7–14.
178. Maier, N.R., and Hoffman, L.R., "Acceptance and Quality of Solutions as Related to Leader's Attitudes Toward Disagreement in Group Problem Solving," *Journal of Applied Behaviorial Science,* (1965), pp. 373–386.
179. Marquis, D.G., and Straight, Jr., D.M., "Organizational Factors in Project Performance," Working Paper No: pp. 133–65, Cambridge, M.I.T., School of Management, 1965.
180. Martin, Charles C. *Project Management: How to Make It Work.* New York: Amacom, 1976, pp. 41, 137.
181. Martin, James Thomas. *Systems Analysis for Data Transmission.* Englewood Cliffs: Prentice-Hall, 1972.

182. Martino, R.L. *Project Management.* Wayne, Pa.: MDI Publications, Management Development Institute, 1968.
183. ———. *Resources Management.* Wayne, Pa.: MDI Publications, Management Development Institute, 1968.
184. Matthies, Leslie H. *The Management System: Systems are People.* New York: John Wiley, 1976.
185. Mechanic, D., "Sources of Power of Lower Participants in Complex Organizations," *Administrative Science Quarterly,* vol. 7:(December 1962), pp. 349–364.
186. Mee, John F. "Project Management." *Business Horizons* 6:(Fall 1963), pp. 53–55.
187. ———., "Matrix Organization," *Business Horizons* (Summer, 1964), p. 70.
188. Melchner, Arlyn J., ed. *General Systems and Organization Theory: Methodological Aspects.* Kent, Ohio: Kent University Press, 1975.
189. Melchner, Arlyn J., and Kayser, Thomas A. "Leadership without Formal Authority: The Project Department." *California Management Review.* Vol. 13, no. 2:(1970), pp. 57–64.
190. Meinhart, W.A., and Delionback, Leon M. "Project Management: An Incentive Contracting Decision Model," *Academy of Management Journal,* vol. 11:(December 1968), pp. 427–34.
191. Metz, William W. "Identification and Analysis of Research and Development Project Management Problems Based on Nonnuclear Munitions Development in the Air Force." Ph.D. dissertation. George Washington University, 1970.
192. Middleton, C.J. "How to Set Up a Project Organization." *Harvard Business Review* 45:(March-April 1967), pp. 73–82.
193. Miller, E.J. *Systems of Organization.* New York: Barnes and Noble Book Company, 1967.
194. Moder, Joseph J., and Phillips, Cecil R. *Project Management with CPM and PERT.* 2nd ed., New York: Van Nostrand Reinhold, 1970.
195. Mordlea, Irwin. "A Comparison of a Research and Development Laboratory's Organization Structures." *IEEE Transactions on Engineering Management* EM-14 (December 1967), pp. 170–76.
196. Morgan, John. "Coping with Resistance to Change." *Ideas for Management.* Cleveland, Ohio: Association for Systems Management, 1971.
197. Morton, D.H., "The Project Manager, Catalyst to Constant Change: A Behaviorial Analysis," *Project Management Quarterly,* vol. 6, no. 1:(1975), pp. 22–3.
198. Mungo, B.B. "Management Studies in the Field of Aeronautics: Management of Projects." *Journal of the Royal Aeronautical Society* vol. 71 (May 1967), pp. 334–36, 336–38 (discussion).
199. Myers, S.M., Conditions for Manager Motivation, *Harvard Business Review,* (Jan–Feb. 1966), pp. 58–71.
200. NATO Institute on Decomposition as a Tool for Solving Large-Scale Problems, Cambridge, England. *Decomposition of Large-Scale Problems.* Amsterdam, North-Holland Publishing Company, 1973.
201. Neuschel, Richard F. *Management Systems for Profit and Growth.* New York: McGraw-Hill, 1976.
202. O'Brien, James B. "The Project Manager: Not Just a Firefighter," *S.A.M. Advanced Management Journal* 39:(January 1974), pp. 52–56.
203. Optner, Stanford L. *Systems Analysis for Business and Industrial Problem Solving.* Englewood Cliffs, N.J.: Prentice-Hall, 1965.
204. ———. *Systems Analysis for Business Management.* Englewood Cliffs, N.J.: Prentice-Hall, 1968.

205. ——. *Systems Analysis for Business Management.* Englewood Cliffs, N.J.: Prentice-Hall, 1975.
206. ——. "Organizational Preference in Research and Development," *Human Relations,* 23:(August 1970), pp. 279-98.
207. Oyer, David William. "The Use of Automated Project Management Systems to Improve Information Systems Development, Cambridge, Mass.: M.S. Thesis, Alfred P. Sloan School of Management, M.I.T. 1975.
208. Pastore, Joseph M. "Organizational Metamorphosis: A Dynamic Model," *Marquette Business Review* 15:(Spring 1971), pp. 17-31.
209. Patchen, M., *Some Questionnaire Measures of Employee Motivation and Morale: A Report on their Reliability and Validity,* Ann Arbor, Michigan: Institute for Social Research, 1965.
210. Paul, W.J., K. Robertson, and F. Herzberg "Job Enrichment Pays Off," *Harvard Business Review,* vol. 47, no. 2:(1969), pp. 61-78.
211. Peart, Alan Thomas. *Design of Project Management Systems and Records.* London: Gower Press, 1971.
212. ——. *Design of Project Management Systems and Records.* Boston: Cahners Books, 1971.
213. Pegels, C. Carl. *Systems Analysis for Production Operations.* New York: Gordon and Science Publishers, 1976.
214. Pondy, L.R., "Organizational Conflict: Concepts and Models," *Administrative Science Quarterly,* September 1967, pp. 298-307.
215. Potter, William J. "Management in the Ad-hocracy," *S.A.M. Advanced Management Journal,* 39:(July 1974), pp. 19-23.
216. Reeser, Clayton. "Some Potential Human Problems of the Project Form of Organization." *Academy of Management Journal* 12:(December 1969), pp. 459-68.
217. Rogers, L.A. "Guidelines for Project Management Teams," *Industrial Engineering,* (December 1974), p. 12.
218. Rudwick, Bernard H. *Systems Analysis for Effective Planning: Principles and Cases.* New York: John Wiley, 1969.
219. Rubin, Irwin M., and Seilig, Wychlam. "Experience as a Factor in the Selection and Performance of Project Managers." *IEEE Transactions on Engineering Management* vol. EM-(September 1967), pp. 131-35.
220. Sadler, Philip. "Designing an Organization Structure." *Management International Review,* vol. 11, No. 6, 1971, pp. 19-33.
221. Sapolsky, Harvey M. *The Polaris System Development: Bureaucratic and Programmatic Success in Government.* Cambridge, Mass.: Harvard University Press, 1972.
222. Sayels, Leonard R., and Chandler, Margaret K. *Managing Large Systems: Organizations for the Future.* New York: Harper and Row, 1971.
223. Schaller, L.E., *The Change Agent,* New York: Abington Press, 1972.
224. Schoderbek, Peter P.; Kefalas, A.G.; and Schoderbek, Charles G. *Management Systems: Conceptual Considerations.* Dallas: Business Publications, 1975.
225. Schmidt, Joseph William. *Mathematical Foundations for Management Science and Systems Analysis.* New York: Academic Press, 1974.
226. Schroder, Harold J. "Making Project Management Work." *Management Review,* vol. 54:(December 1970), pp. 24-28.
227. ——, "Project Management: Controlling Uncertainty," *Journal of Systems Management,* vol. 24:(February 1975), pp. 28-29.
228. Seiler, J.A., "Diagnosing Interdepartmental Conflict," *Harvard Business Review,* (September-October 1963), pp. 121-132.
229. Shah, Ramesh P. "Project Management: Cross Your Bridges Before You Come to Them," *Management Review* 60 (December 1971), pp. 21-27.

230. Sharad, D., "About Delays, Overruns and Corrective Actions," *Project Management Quarterly*, December 1976, pp. 21-25.
231. Shannon, Robert E. "Matrix Management Structures." *Industrial Engineering* 4 (March 1972), pp. 26-29.
232. Sheriff, M., "Superordinate Goals in the Reduction of Intergroup Conflict," *American Journal of Sociology*, no. 63:(1958), pp. 349-358.
233. Shrode, William A., and Voich, Jr., Dan. *Organization and Management: Basic Systems Concepts*, Homewood, Illinois: R.D. Irwin, 1974.
234. Shull, Fremont, and Judd, R.J. "Matrix Organizations and Control Systems." *Management International Review* 11, no. 6:(1971), pp. 65-72.
235. Shull, Fremont A. *Matrix Structure and Project Authority for Optimizing Organizational Capacity.* Business Science Monograph No. 1. Carbondale: Business Research Bureau, Southern Illinois University, 1965.
236. Simmons, John R. *Management of Change: The Role of Information:* based on a research project sponsored by the Institute of Office Management. London: Gee & Company, 1970.
237. Sivazlian, B.D., and Stanfeld, L.E. *Analysis of Systems in Operations Research.* Englewood Cliffs, N.J.: Prentice-Hall, 1973.
238. Smith, G.A. "Program Management—Art or Science?" *Mechanical Engineering* vol. 96 (September 1974), pp. 18-22.
239. Smith, Michael Gary. *PCS: A Project Control System.* Thesis, M.I.T., Cambridge, Mass., 1973.
240. Smith, William N. "Problem-Solving and Bargaining as Modes of Constructive Conflict Resolution in Aerospace Matrix Organizations." Ph.D. dissertation, University of California, Los Angeles, 1972.
241. Smyster, Craig H., "A Comparison of the Needs of Program and Functional Management": Unpublished Masters Thesis, School of Engineering, Wright-Patterson Air Force Base, Air Force Institute of Technology, 1965.
242. Starr, Martin Keneneth. *Production Management: Systems and Synthesis.* 2nd ed. Englewood, N.J.: Prentice-Hall, 1972.
243. Stasch, Stanley F. *Systems Analysis for Marketing Planning and Control.* Glenview, Illinois: Scott, Foresman, 1972.
244. Steger, W.A. "How to Plan for Management in New Systems," *Harvard Business Review*, September–October 1962.
245. Steiner, George A., "Project Managers' Problems with the Development of High Performance Aerospace Systems," *Astronautics and Aeronautics* (June 1966), pp. 75-76.
246. ——, and Ryan, William G. *Industrial Project Management.* New York: Macmillan, 1968, p. 24.
247. Stewart, John M. "Making Project Management Work." *Business Horizons* 8:(Fall 1965), pp. 54-68.
248. Stopher, Peter R., and Meyburg, Arnim H. *Transportation Systems Evaluation.* Lexington, Massachusetts: Lexington Books, 1976.
249. Tannenbaum, Robert and Warren H. Schmidt, "How to Choose a Leadership Pattern," *HBR Classic,* (May-June 1973), pp. 162-180.
250. Taylor, W.J., and Watling, T.F. *Successful Project Management.* London: Business Books, 1970, p. 32-; 1972.
251. ——. "Teamwork Through Conflict," *Business Week* (March 20 1971), pp. 44-45.
252. Thamhain, Hans J., and Wilemon, David L. "Diagnosing Conflict Determinants in Project Management." *IEEE Transactions on Engineering Management,* vol. EM-22 (February 1975), pp. 35-44.

253. ——, and Gemmill, Gary R. "Influence Styles of Project Managers: Some Project Performance Correlates," *Academy of Management Journal* vol. 17 (June 1974), pp. 216–24.

254. Thamhain, H.J., and Wilemon, D.L., "Conflict Management in Project-Oriented Work Environments," *Proceedings of the Sixth International Meeting of the Project Management Institute,* Washington, D.C., September 18–21, 1974.

255. ——, "Conflict Management in Project Life Cycles," *Sloan Management Review,* (Summer 1975), pp. 31–50.

256. ——, "The Effective Management of Conflict in Project-Oriented Work Environments," *Defense Management Journal* vol. 11, no. 3, July 1972, p. 975.

257. Thompson, J.D. *Organization in Action.* New York: McGraw-Hill, 1967.

258. Thompson, Victor A. "Bureaucracy and Innovation," *Administrative Science Quarterly* vol. 10:(June 1965), pp. 1–20.

259. Toellner, John, "Project Estimating," *Journal of Systems Management,* (May 1977), pp. 6–9.

260. Trower, Michael H., "Fast Track to Project Delivery: Systems Approach to Project Management," *Management Review* vol. 62 (April 1973), pp. 19–23.

261. Tsai, Martin Chia-Ping. "Contingent Conditions for the Creation of Temporary Management Organizations." M.S. Thesis, Alfred P. Sloan School of Management, M.I.T. Cambridge, Mass., 1976.

262. Vaughn, Dennis Henry. "Key Variables of a Management Information System for a Department of Defense Project Manager." M.S. Thesis, Alfred P. Sloan School of Management, M.I.T. Cambridge, Mass., 1976.

263. ——. "Understanding Project Management," *Manage* vol. 19, no. 9: (1967), pp. 52–58.

264. Wadsworth, M. *EDP Project Management Controls.* Englewood Cliffs, N.J.: Prentice-Hall, 1972.

265. Walton, R.E., and Dutton, J.M., "The Management of Interdepartmental Conflict: A Model and Review," *Administrative Science Quarterly,* vol. 14, no. 1:(March 1969), pp. 73–84.

266. Walton, R.E.; Dutton, J.M.; and Cafferty, T.P., "Organizational Contest and Interdepartmental Conflict," *Administrative Science Quarterly,* vol. 14, no. 4:(December 1969), pp. 522–542.

267. Webb, James E. "NASA as an Adaptive Organization," in *On Technological Change and Management,* ed. by David W. Ewing. Cambridge, Massachusetts: Harvard University Press, 1970.

268. Weinberg, Gerald M. *An Introduction to General Systems Thinking.* New York: John Wiley, 1975.

269. Wetzel, John Jay. "Project Control at the Managerial Level in the Automotive Engineering Environment," M.S. Thesis, Alfred P. Sloan School of Management, M.I.T. Cambridge, Mass., 1973.

270. Whitehouse, Gary E., "Project Management Techniques," *Industrial Engineering* vol. 5:(March 1973), pp. 24–29.

271. ——. *Systems Analysis and Design Using Network Techniques.* Englewood Cliffs, N.J.: Prentice-Hall, 1973.

272. Whiting, Richard J., "In Defense of Functional Organization," *Management Review,* vol. 58, no. 7:(July 1969), pp. 49–52.

273. Wilemon, David L., "Managing Conflict in Temporary Management Systems," *Journal of Management Studies* vol. 10 (October 1973): pp. 282–96.

274. Wilemon, D.L., "Project Management Conflict: A View from Apollo," *Third Annual Symposium of the Project Management Institute,* Houston, Texas, October, 1971.

275. ——, "Managing Conflict on Project Teams," *Management Journal,* (Summer 1974), pp. 28–34.
276. Wilemon, D.L., "Project Management and its Conflicts: A View from Apollo," *Chemical Technology,* vol. 2, no. 9:(September 1972), pp. 527–534.
277. ——, and Gary R. Gemmill, "Interpersonal Power in Temporary Management Systems." *Journal of Management Studies,* 8 (October 1971): pp. 315–28.
278. ——, and Cicero, John P. "The Project Manager: Anomalies and Ambiguities." *Academy of Management Journal* vol. 13:(September 1970), pp. 269–82.
279. Willoughby, Theodore C. *Business Systems.* Cleveland: Association for Systems Management, 1975.
280. ——, and Senn, J.A. *Business Systems.* Cleveland: The Association for Systems Management, 1975.
281. Wilson, Ira Gaulbert. *Management Innovation and System Design.* Princeton: Auerbach, 1971.
282. Woodgate, Harry Samuel. *Planning by Network: Project Planning and Control Using Network Techniques.* London: Business Publications, 1967.
283. Wooldridge, Susan. *Project Management in Data Processing.* 1st ed. New York: Petrocelli/Charter, 1976.
284. Wrong, D., "Some Problems in Defining Social Power," *American Journal of Sociology,* vol. 73, no. 6:(May 1968), pp. 673–681.

Competitive Bidding
Bibliography

1. Anderson, R.M., "Handling Risk in Defense Contracting," *Harvard Business Review* (1969), pp. 90–98.
2. Arps, J.J., "A Strategy for Sealed Bidding," *Journal Petroleum Technology* (September 1965), p. 1033.
3. Baumgarten, R.M., "Discussion for Opbid-Competitive Bidding Strategy Model" by Morin and Clough, *Journal of the Construction Division of ASCE 96,* (1970) p. 88.
4. Benjamin, N.B.H., "Competitive Bidding for Building Construction Contracts," Technical Report No. 106, Department of Civil Engineering, Stanford University, June 1969.
5. Bell, L.B., "A System for Competitive Bidding," *Journal of Systems Management 20,* (1969), pp. 26–29.
6. Bristor, J.D., "Discussion for Bidding Strategies and Probabilities, by Gates" (March 1967), *Proceedings of the American Society of Civil Engineers Journal,* Construction Division 94, (1968), p. 109.
7. Bristor, J.D., "Discussion for 'Bidding-Work Loading Game' by Torgersen, et al." (Oct 1968), *Proceedings of the American Society of Civil Engineers Journal,* Construction Division 95, (1969) pp. 139–140.
8. Broemser, G.M., "Competitive Bidding in the Construction Industry," Ph.D. Dissertation, Stanford University, Ca. 1968.
9. Brown, K.C., "A Theoretical and Statistical Study of Decision-Making under Uncertainty—Competitive Bidding for Leases on Offshore Petroleum Lands," Ph.D. Dissertation, Southern Methodist University, Dallas, Texas, 1966.
10. Casey, B.J. and L.R. Shaffer, "An Evaluation of Some Competitive Bid Strategy Models for Contractors," Report No. 4 Department of Civil Engineering, University of Illinois, Urbana, Illinois.
11. Christenson, C., *Strategic Aspects of Competive Bidding for Corporate Securities,* Boston, Mass.: Division of Research, Harvard, University School of Business.
12. Clough, R.H., *Construction Contracting,* Appendix L, 2nd Ed., New York: John Wiley, 1969.
13. Cook, Paul W., Jr., "Fact and Fancy on Identical Bids," *Harvard Business Review, 41,* pp. 67–72 (January–February, 1963).
14. Crawford, P.B., "Pattern of Offshore Bidding," Society of Petroleum Engineers of AIME, Paper No. 2613, Dallas, Texas: 1969.
15. Crosby, A.R., "The Client/Contractor Syndrome," *Chemical Engineering Program 61,* no. 11, (1965) pp. 44–48.

16. Edelman, F., "Art and Science of Competitive Bidding," *Harvard Business Review 43*, (July–August, 1965), pp. 53–66.
17. Emerick, R.H., "How to Find the Unforeseen in Competitive Bidding," *Power Engineering 69*, August 1965, pp. 45–46.
18. Flueck, J.A., "A Statistical Decision Theory Approach to a Seller's Bid Pricing Problem under Uncertainty," Ph.D. Thesis, University of Chicago, School of Business, 1967.
19. Frey, J.B., "Competitive Bidding on General Construction Contracts," Thesis, University of Delaware, 1962.
20. Friedman, L., "A Competitive Bidding Strategy," *Operations Research 4*, pp. 104–112 (1956).
21. Gates, M., "Aspects on Competitive Bidding," Connecticut Society of Civil Engineers, 1959.
22. Gates, M., "Statistical and Economic Analysis of a Bidding Trend," *Journal of the Construction Division*, ASCE, Paper 2651, pp. 13–35 (November 1960).
23. Gates, M., "Bidding Strategies and Probabilities," *Journal of the Construction Division*, ASCE, Paper 5159, *93*, (1967) pp. 75–107; see subsequent closure, p. *96*, (1970) 77–78 and 93.
24. Green, P., "Bayesian Decision Theory in Pricing Strategy," *Journal of Marketing 27*, (1963) pp. 5–14.
25. Griesmer, J.H. and M. Shubik, "The Theory of Bidding," IBM Research Report, RC-629, IBM Research Center, Yorktown Heights, N.Y., March 1, 1962.
26. Griesmer, J.H. and M. Shubik, "The Theory of Bidding II," IBM Research Report, RC-688, IBM Research Center, Yorktown Heights, N.Y., May 25, 1962.
27. Griesmer, J.H. and M. Shubik, "The Theory of Bidding III," IBM Research Report, RC-874, IBM Research Center, Yorktown Heights, N.Y., January 29, 1963.
28. Griesmer, J.H., R.E. Levitan, and M. Shubik, "Towards a Study of Bidding Processes, Part Four, Unknown Competitive Costs–," IBM Research Paper RC-1532, IBM Research Center, Yorktown Heights, N.Y., January 1966.
29. Hanssman, F. and Rivett, B.H.P., "Competitive Bidding," *Operations Research, Quarterly 10*, pp. 49–55 (1959).
30. Harsanyi, J.C., "Games with Incomplete Information Played by Bayesian Players, Parts I–III," *Management Science 14*, (1967–68) pp. 159–182, 320–334, 486–502.
31. Hugo, G.R., "How to Prepare Bids for Crown Lease Sales," *Oil Week 16*, (1965) pp. 56–60.
32. Lavalle, I.H., "A Bayesian Approach to an Individual Player's Choice of Bid in Competitive Sealed Auctions," *Management Science 13*, A584–597 (1967).
33. Moriguti, S. and S. Suganami, "Notes on Auction Bidding," *J. Opns, Res. Soc. (Japan)*, 2, (1959) pp. 43–59.
34. Morin, T.L., and R. H. Clough, "Opbid–Competitive Bidding Strategy Model," *Journal of Construction Division*, ASCE, Paper 6690; (June, 1970) see subsequent discussion, pp. *96*, 88–97.
35. Ortega-Reichert, A., "Models for Competitive Bidding under Uncertainty," Technical Report No. 103, Department of Operations Research, Stanford University, Stanford, CA., January 1968.
36. Park, W.R., "How Low to Bid to Get Both Job and Profit," *Engineering News-Record 168*, (April 19 1962), pp. 38–40.
37. Park, W.R., "Less Bidding for Bigger Profits," *Engineering News-Record 170*, 41 (February 14 1963).
38. Park, W.R., "Bidders and Job Size Determine Your Optimum Markup, *Engineering News-Record 170*, (June 13 1963), pp. 122–123.

39. Park, W.R., "Bidding: When to Raise and When to Fold," *The Modern Builder*, Kansas City, Mo., (July 1963).
40. Park, W.R., "The Problem of Breaking Even," *The Modern Builder*, Kansas City, Mo. (September 1963).
41. Park, W.R., "The Strategy of Bidding for Profit," *The Modern Builder*, Kansas City, Mo. (Sept. 1963).
42. Park, W.R., "Better Bidding Will Beget Bigger Profits," *The Modern Builder*, Kansas City, Mo. (October 1963).
43. Park, W.R., "How Much to Make to Cover Costs," *Engineering News-Record 171*, pp. 168–170 (December 19 1963).
44. Park, W.R., "It Takes a Profit to Make a Profit," *Mid-West Contractor*, Kansas City, Mo. (March 11, 1964).
45. Park, W.R., "Profit Optimization Through Strategic Bidding," *AACE Bulletin, 6*, No. 5 (December 1964).
46. Park, W.R. *The Strategy of Contracting for Profit.* Englewood Cliffs, N.J.: Prentice-Hall, 1966.
47. Rothkopf, M.H., "A Model of Rational Competitive Bidding," *Management Science 15*, (1969) pp. 362–373.
48. Sakaguchi, M. "Mathematical Solutions to Some Problems of Competitive Bidding," *Proceedings of the Third International Conference on Operational Res.* (Oslo, 1963), 1964, pp. 179–191, Dunod (Paris) and English University Press (London).
49. Schlaifer, R. *Probability and Statistics for Business Decisions.* New York: McGraw-Hill, 1959.
50. Simmonds, K., "Adjusting Bias in Cost Estimates," *Opnal. Res. Quart., 19*, (1968) pp. 325–327.
51. Simmonds, K., "Competitive Bidding—Deciding the Best Combination of Non-Price Features," *Operational Research Quarterly 19* (1968) pp. 5–15.
52. Stark, Robert M., "Competitive Bidding: A Comprehensive Bibliography," *Opns. Res. 19*, (1971) pp. 484–490.
53. Symonds, G.H., "A Study of Management Behavior by Use of Competitive Business Games," *Management Science 11*, (1964) pp. 135–153.
54. Vickrey, W., "Counterspeculation, Auctions, and Competitive Sealed Tenders," *Journal of Finance 16*, (1961) pp. 8–37.
55. Wasson, C.R., *Understanding Qualitative Analysis*, New York: Appleton-Century-Crofts, 1969.
56. Wilson, R.B., "Competitive Bidding with Disparate Information," Working Paper No. 114, Graduate School of Business, Stanford University, October 1966.
57. Wilson, R.B., "Competitive Bidding with Asymmetrical Information," *Management Science 13*, (1967) A816–820.
58. Wilson, R.B., "Competitive Bidding with Disparate Options," *Management Science 15*, (1969) pp. 46–48.

Author Index

Subject Index